MW01134830

The First

The
Fred W.
Morrison
Series in
Southern
Studies

The
University
of North
Carolina
Press

Chapel Hill
& London

American Frontier

TRANSITION TO CAPITALISM IN

SOUTHERN APPALACHIA, 1700–1860

Wilma A. Dunaway

© 1996 The University of North Carolina Press

Manufactured in the United States of America

The paper in this book meets the guidelines for permanence and durability of the Committee on Production Guidelines for Book Longevity of the Council on Library Resources.

Library of Congress Cataloging-in-Publication Data

Dunaway, Wilma A.

The first American frontier: transition to capitalism in southern Appalachia, 1700–1860 / Wilma A. Dunaway.

 p. cm.

Includes bibliographical references and index.

ISBN 0-8078-2236-1 (cloth).

ISBN 0-8078-4540-X (pbk.)

1. Capitalism—Appalachian Region—History.

2. Capitalism—Southern States—History.

3. Appalachian Region—Economic conditions.

4. Southern States—Economic conditions. I. Title.

HC107.A127D86 1996   95-2790

330.974—dc20   CIP

00 99 98 97 96 5 4 3 2 1

Publication of this book has been supported by a generous grant from the L. J. Skaggs and Mary C. Skaggs Foundation.

To Donald Armour Clelland
professor extraordinaire

It is no small thing to have given
your life to liberation of the world
through the vehicle of teaching and
inspiring those who go forth.

CONTENTS

Maps

Figures

ACKNOWLEDGMENTS

Without two rounds of funding from the Woodrow Wilson National Fellowship Foundation, I could never have aggregated the research materials or
traveled to the distant sites of so many manuscript collections. In addition, the
Appalachian Studies Fellowship Program at Berea College invested start-up
funds in my research when some regional scholars considered my work to be
too radical a departure from the conventional wisdom. Having had my journal
articles disappear for four to six months into the "black hole" of peer review, I
was deeply gratified when Stanley L. Engerman and Immanuel Wallerstein
completed their readings of my manuscript and returned their comments to
the Press within six weeks. I must also thank Immanuel Wallerstein for granting me permission to reprint portions of Chapter 1 that appeared previously
in *Review of the Fernand Braudel Center*. Lewis Bateman demystified for me
the publication process and made this a "smooth sailing." Sian Hunter White
and Pam Upton have charted the course through the editorial process, and
they have kept us all smiling through the maze.

   I received the inspiration to undertake this research when I collected the
oral histories of three elderly Appalachian women who were born in the early
1900s into sharecropping families on plantations. Real-life experiences like
theirs are absent from the usual scholarly analyses, so their anomalies spurred
me to dig further. When I did so, I discovered that there were several such
categories of Southern Appalachians "without history." I enjoyed the rare
privilege of discussing my research questions and of sharing sections of my
writing with one of these special women. She told me when my inquiries were
headed in the wrong directions, and she reacted with joy when she found
some glimmer of her own history in my theoretical explanations. I may have
learned more from those exchanges than from all the usual academic inputs
about methodology. Indeed this "poorly educated" woman taught me to ask
questions that were a closer reflection of everyday life; she showed me the
ignored factors when I assumed easy explanations; and she chastised me
when I overlooked the unexpected linkages between people at different economic levels. All three of these beautiful women have died since I interviewed
them, so I feel especially grateful for the knowledge they imparted to me.

   During my research, I traveled throughout Southern Appalachia and utilized so many local historical societies and college libraries that I cannot enumerate every kindness I received from archival staff. When I arrived unexpect-
edly on their doorsteps, I received an Appalachian welcome and enthusiastic

interest from those I inconvenienced. One hot summer day, for example, I wove my way to Pippa Passes, Kentucky, to find the Alice Lloyd College Library in the midst of construction and reorganization. The staff dropped their own work to clear space for me to peruse their oral history collection. When I had found those kernels of information I needed, the clerical staff in another department photocopied numerous transcripts. Such generosity was replicated at most of the smaller archives and museums I visited.

I particularly appreciate the time and camaraderie of several volunteers who operate the Family History Center of the Church of Jesus Christ of the Latter Day Saints at Knoxville. Without their assistance, I could never have procured and utilized more than one hundred reels of microfilm that contained antebellum public records not available from any archives outside Salt Lake City. By suggesting a starter list of manuscripts, Kate Black helped me to glean efficiently the University of Kentucky collections; no other archivist was willing to give me that much extra work. Finally, I must express my amazement at the efficiency and cordiality with which the interlibrary loan staff at the University of Tennessee helped me locate and borrow hundreds of reels of microfilm and numerous obscure primary sources.

A project as wide in scope as this one cannot be done in an intellectual vacuum, and I have had the advantage of a scholarly exchange with more sociologists, economic historians, world-systems analysts, local historians, and Appalachian specialists than I can enumerate individually. Each of those encounters contributed small, but significant, pieces to the research puzzle. However, there are some people who have gone beyond the call of duty in their support of this book's completion. From its conception, John Gaventa has consistently demonstrated his belief in the "cutting-edge" importance of this regional history. John has never flinched in his support, not even during the first year when some regional writers hurtled verbal assaults at us both. John even offered himself as the "willing scapegoat" against whom I should level my criticism of the unwitting reliance by Appalachian researchers upon untested generalizations about the region's exceptionalism. Despite his workload at Highlander Center, John read every chapter as I wrote it, and he did so with candor and enthusiasm.

During the formative stages, several sociologists helped me to sharpen concepts, to ask unusual research questions, and to measure the right linkages. Early on, world-systems critic Tom Hall chided me to look at social change from the perspective of the impacted people and not to overlook Native Americans. Statistical input collected by Chuck Cleland from several agricultural economists at the University of Tennessee proved crucial to my revisions of cliometric measurements. Dwight Billings, Gary Gereffi, and Phil McMichael shared their own fine-tuning of concepts like subsistence, commodity chains, and the relationship between land tenure and labor formation. Indeed I have borrowed extensively from the unfolding work of many world-systems specialists, especially that of Immanuel Wallerstein; and I have bene-fited from the suggestions of many members of the World-Systems Section of the American Sociological Association.

In addition, many participants in the Appalachian Studies Association have given my work their critical attention and have fostered an unsolicited oral history about its promise. I have not even discussed my research with some of you; but I have heard by the grapevine of your interest and support. People like John Inscoe, Loyal Jones, Gordon McKinney, Mary Beth Pudup, Paul Salstrom, Marie Tedesco, Altina Waller, David Whisnant, and John Alex-ander Williams have generously made room for my dissidence. Some of us have disagreed about my theoretical arguments, but none of you has ever dis-missed my empirical findings or cautioned me to do the conventional thing.

Finally, I must thank Don Clelland, under whose tutelage I learned de-velopment and world-systems theory. Like several generations of his graduate students, I have benefited from four gifts from this extraordinary master of ideas. First, because he is a gentle soul, he has sheltered his students from academic attacks upon their dissidence. Second, he devoted his energies to teaching, even though the system would have rewarded him more for using that time to publish. Third, he gave priority to exposing us to that part of the world inhabited by forgotten peoples in distress. Finally, he has encouraged us all to test the professional limits and not to be afraid to tread on the cutting edge. On behalf of all those students whose variance from the convention you have encouraged, I thank you. Without your intellectual nurturing, this breaching of the accepted canon could never have been risked.

1

THE TRANSITION TO CAPITALISM

ON AMERICAN FRONTIERS:

TOWARD A PARADIGM SHIFT

Appalachia and the Agrarian Myth

Outsiders have had a long-running love affair with Southern Appalachia. Setting forth at the Gulf of Mexico, the Spaniards undertook three sixteenth-century expeditions into the inland mountains to search for silver and the "fountain of youth" among the vast indigenous chiefdoms of northern Georgia, western North Carolina, and East Tennessee. Because they believed these ranges to be mineral rich and inhabited by exotic kingdoms, the French and the British were also lured into the southern backcountry, labeling it on their early maps the "Montes Appalatci." Numerous pre-Revolutionary explorations were made into the rugged terrain, and early travel diaries called attention to the region's primeval splendor and geological significance.[1]

Euro-American settlers on the Atlantic Coast were just as infatuated with this region. The Allegheny-Appalachian mountain systems lay at the back doors of seven of the original colonies, separating the seaboard from the Ohio and Mississippi Valleys (see Map 1.1). Southern Appalachia is the land of the Cumberland Gap, the first western frontier of the United States, and the Watauga Association—all glorified in popular culture as symbols of the American dream of freedom and equality. Imposing mountain sites like Hawk's Nest, the Cyclopean Towers, the Natural Bridge, and the Tallulah Gorge rejuvenated the spirits of antebellum adventurers. Those escaping the summer epidemics of the plantation South sought serenity and "exclusive company" at 134 mineral springs sprinkled throughout the mountains. The persistence of the region's tourist appeal is evidenced by contemporary public funding of forests and recreational areas, like Shenandoah National Park, the Blue Ridge Parkway, and the Great Smoky Mountains. In fact, federal and

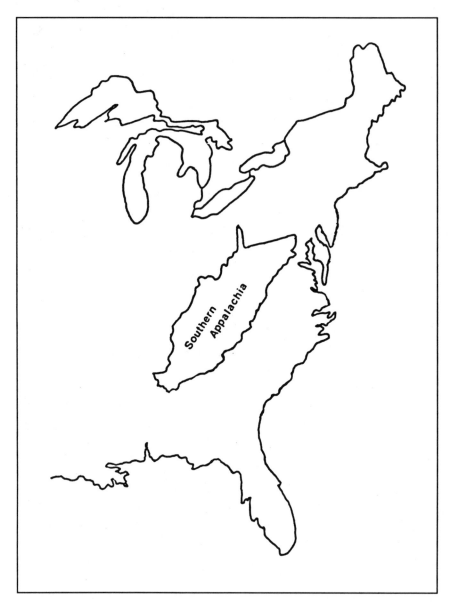

Map 1.1. Southern Appalachia

state governments have confiscated about one-fifth of Southern Appalachia's land area for these purposes.[2]

Americans have kept alive their romance with Appalachia in another way. Thomas Jefferson and other eighteenth-century writers fashioned for the emergent nation an agrarian myth that celebrated a new folk hero. The yeoman farmer was idealized "not for his capacity to exploit opportunities and make money" but for "his honest industry, his independence, his frank spirit of equality, and his ability to produce and enjoy a simple abundance." Moreover, the Jeffersonians "made the agrarian myth the basis of a strategy of continental development. Many of them expected that the great empty inland regions would guarantee the preponderance of the yeoman—and therefore the dominance of Jeffersonianism and the health of the state—for an unlimited future."[3]

Despite its origins among the country's wealthiest planters, the "myth of the happy yeoman" was well entrenched by the early nineteenth century, and the southern mountains have been idealized in the contemporary period as one of the strongest bastions of such self-sufficient farmers. Many historians glorified the recreation of this simpler way of life on the advancing frontiers. In the late nineteenth century, Frederick Jackson Turner argued that American development had exhibited not merely progress along a single line of social evolution "but a return to primitive conditions on a continually advancing frontier line, and a new development for that area." Soon after Turner's thesis was advanced, scholars declared Southern Appalachia to be "a retarded frontier" comprised of a large land-locked collection of people caught "in a Rip Van Winkle sleep."[4]

Outsiders proclaimed that early-twentieth-century Southern Appalachians had "worked out their individual existence far removed from the forward march of progress." From the late nineteenth century until the 1970s, this area was nostalgically described as the last place in the country where "time stood still," preserving the vanishing American frontier life. Presuming that the region had not undergone the "normal" linear advance toward modernity, journalists and intellectuals contended that isolation froze Appalachians into "a folk world of small, isolated, homogeneous societies" shaped by the traditions of early settlers. Fascinated with the imagery of a "strange land" and a "peculiar folk," Americans still view Southern Appalachia as one of the most distinct subregions left in the United States.[5]

On the other hand, this region is the quintessence of rural America, described by many as the avatar of what is best about country life and family farms. Much of what has been heralded as peculiar about Southern Appalachia is also characteristic of other agricultural areas. Thus, analysis of this region can be instructive about problems surrounding the generation of "sustainable development" in other agrarian societies. Rural America, including Appalachia, has been romantically envisioned as the living representation of the nation's egalitarian goals. The most widely held explanations focus on the linear evolution from the rural stage to industrialization, arguing that simpler agrarian communities are disrupted by the changes wrought by capitalist modernity. This rural-industrial continuum is grounded in generalizations that the preindustrial United States was characterized by fiercely egalitarian subsistence economies that offered widespread opportunities for upward economic mobility.[6]

In this view, the availability of inexhaustible open wilderness "made owner-ship of a relatively large amount of land possible for the common person," and "this abundant land was distributed in a relatively equal manner" among "small freeholders." Supposedly, preindustrial Americans enjoyed equal ac-cess to family life rooted in land ownership, and the vast majority were self-employed on their own farms. Scholars present a similar picture of a prein-dustrial Appalachian economy characterized by five central features: a wide and equitable distribution of land ownership; subsistence agriculture; reliance on local barter networks rather than upon commercial markets; utilization of family labor; and autonomy from external trade.[7]

Despite the nostalgia associated with its land and its family farms, Southern Appalachia is a national tragedy. This region is one of the most impoverished and most ecologically damaged sections of the country. How have scholars explained the prevalence of such economic crisis in the midst of the agrarian utopia they have portrayed? According to the conventional wisdom, the re-gion developed very slowly prior to the postbellum intrusion of corporate industry. The region remained undeveloped, in this scenario, because there had been "little in Appalachia to attract capitalist development" and because the area lacked the infrastructure and investment capital needed to effect an economic takeoff. Rugged terrain, the lack of roads, and Appalachian opposi-tion to slavery and plantations, these scholars insist, deterred the expansion of trade; prevented the growth of an export economy; and slowed the develop-ment of capitalistic enterprises.[8]

According to the conventional wisdom, isolation "permitted an independent economy to persist in the Appalachian mountains long after it had vanished elsewhere in the United States." Rather than being integrated into national networks, Appalachia became increasingly isolated because of competitive changes in eighteenth- and nineteenth-century international trade. The dis-ruption of overseas markets during and after the Revolutionary War triggered a reorientation of farms away from "production for external markets in favor of production for local subsistence." Supposedly, the center of the Appalachian barter economy was the local merchant who extended credit and exchanged retail commodities for surplus agricultural products. This form of commerce "reinforced the autonomy of the local market system and provided mountain communities with considerable freedom from the fluctuations of the national cash economy."[9]

According to most scholars, Appalachia's late transition to capitalism was particularly destructive because it represented a massive upheaval of "a par-ticular culture quite different from that of the industrial society developing around it." Shut off from forces that shaped the modern world, "Appalachia on the eve of industrialization was a land of scattered, loosely integrated, and self-sufficient island communities" that rarely interacted with the rest of the nation. Thus, cultural resistance is advanced as an additional component of Appalachia's slow transition to capitalism.[10]

In the received model, the transition to capitalism began in the late nineteenth century. During that transformation, the subsistence and petty commodity producers of Appalachia clashed with a new class of postbellum capitalists who sought to expand the market economy. In contrast to other regions that experienced gradual transition along with the national economy, "Appalachia experienced the sudden penetration of mature, corporate capitalist institutions rather than the slow evolution of work relations." On the one hand, precapitalist farmers were belatedly and frailly integrated into the market economy only after new railroads and boom towns were financed by external sources of capital. On the other hand, the ascendancy in rural Appalachia of coal and extractive industry set off four socioeconomic changes. As the region was linked into the national economy, agriculture declined dramatically, and urban populations escalated. Perhaps the most significant restructuring, however, was the corporate transformation of small, independent commodity producers into wage laborers. Modern industrialization "created a working class by separating Appalachians from the land."[11]

In the predominant view, Appalachia's transition to capitalism was peculiar and unique. It was late and it involved little agrarian transformation toward market production. Unlike other regions of the country, it is thought, Appalachia was "a colonial appendage of the industrial East and Middle West." As such, the transition to capitalism brought to Appalachia a one-industry export economy operated by "particularly exploitative and brutal" capitalists who disrupted rural communities with new company towns.[12]

Toward a Paradigm Shift

What is offered in this study is a radical and purposeful departure from that conventional wisdom about the first western frontier of the United States. The world-systems paradigm is proposed as a more promising explanatory framework than any of the existing approaches for exploring the transition to rural capitalism in the United States. Using new empirical research, this study places regional agrarian change within the global context of the systematic contradictions that accompany the growth of a capitalist economy. The development of rural communities has not occurred in a vacuum, outside the ebbing and flowing of changes in market demand within the world metropolis. Agrarian economies have not "failed to develop." Rather, that development—however inequitable, haphazard, or uneven—has derived from the cyclical expansions and contractions of the capitalist world economy. It is necessary, then, to turn the popular modernization theoretic on its ear. We need to reconceptualize preindustrial communities in more dynamic terms that will permit recognition of internal diversity while searching for complex external linkages.

The Debate about the Rural Transition to Capitalism

Three counterarguments have emerged to explain the transition to capitalism in the rural United States. The traditional view has been that the country's eighteenth- and nineteenth-century farmers were low-yield, subsistence producers who were culturally and geographically isolated from markets. In these agrarian societies the transition to capitalism is equated with the sudden, disruptive, and destructive changes wrought by the Industrial Revolution at the end of the nineteenth century, as we have seen with the most popular suppositions about Appalachian development. According to the radical variant of this perspective, the logic of subsistence governed agricultural production before the Civil War, retarding the expansion of capitalism by robbing industry of its needed investment capital and labor supply.[13]

Skeptical of the argument that market economics did not come to rural America until after the Civil War, a second school of thought focuses on the beginnings of transition during the early 1800s. Arguing that the colonial economy was structured around a "household mode of production," more recent scholars contend that a majority of pre-Revolutionary Americans "lived in a distinctive subsistence culture remote from river navigation and the market world." What energized the American transition to capitalism was a far-reaching *market revolution* between 1815 and 1848, during which capitalist forms of industry, agriculture, and labor were established in the North and a slave-based order was entrenched in the South. Thus, the post-Revolutionary transition to domestic capitalism was a product of several historical developments: (1) European demand for agricultural products; (2) rapid American population growth; (3) the structuring of political systems that became increasingly responsive to the interests of capitalists; (4) the increased mobility of capital effected through new credit, currency, and investment opportunities; (5) and technological and transportation advances. Increasing involvement in the market fueled a gradual accretion toward capitalism, culminating in two significant transformations in American rural society: a shift from local self-sufficiency toward increased dependence on outside markets and the replacement of household manufacturing by centralized workshops and factories.[14]

Taking still another position in the "transition" debate, a third group of scholars contends that "some though not all marks of capital formation were apparent in early America from 1607." Challenging the "agrarian myth," these writers insist that American farmers participated in global trade networks as early as the eighteenth century. In this view, the intention of farmers "was to make money, not subsistence, from the land," and rural Americans have always been "closely tied to the market as both producers and consumers." In the eighteenth century, the United States was linked into the world economy in two different structural arrangements. New England and the Middle Atlantic regions were dominated by trading and nascent manufacturing while the South maintained a staple export economy.[15]

All three of these approaches have in common a powerful Anglo-centricity; history is written as though white outsiders "discovered" and civilized an empty wilderness. Almost all of these writers ignore the presence of Native American civilizations and neglect the displacement of indigenous populations by advancing settler frontiers. In addition, these explanations share an insular focus on internal barriers and stimuli to development. These approaches have relied on small community studies—overwhelmingly focused on the Northeast and New England—from which broad-sweeping generalizations have been derived about the transition to capitalism throughout the entire United States. Moreover, rural history is conceptualized as an integral element of the rise of *national* urban-industrial complexes, with insufficient attention directed to the larger global setting within which this single country developed.[16]

Inherent in two of the arguments is a shaky dichotomizing of *subsistence* and *market* as antagonistic ideal types on a continuum of social transition. Neither term is satisfactorily conceptualized, and the communities categorized under each term are too often described as though they are static and homogeneous. The term "subsistence" is probably the most misused, for it has been applied to a wide range of farms producing disparate levels of surpluses and participating in market exchanges to varied degrees. As a result, authors underestimate preindustrial commercial exchange, labeling as "subsistence" or "household" modes what were actually local communities increasingly becoming imbedded in market linkages and forms of wage labor.

Furthermore, reliance on loose generalizations about "cultural resistance to capitalism" is a highly dubious form of scholarship. The popular rural-industrial continuum erroneously portrays Appalachia as a region that has been homogeneous in economic pursuits, in culture, in ethnic composition, and in distribution of wealth. As a result, internal diversity has been denied, leaving too many Appalachians "without history." Because the intellectual discourse upon the Appalachian region has emanated from the dominant culture, much of the resultant research is steeped in an erroneous image of the region as a deviant subculture. Many of our contemporary perceptions about this region were largely shaped by works written at the turn of the twentieth century. Concomitant with the postbellum industrial boom, altruistic outsiders and yellow journalists redefined what they saw in the region, often labeling as "peculiarly Appalachian" folkways that have been present in practically every rural section of the United States.[17]

This tendency toward cultural stereotyping has developed out of two limitations. On the one hand, there has been a provincial reticence to test the so-called peculiarity of Appalachia against comparisons with trends in other areas. On the other hand, much of the accumulated knowledge about Appalachia has been generated out of "history written backwards." Regional scholarship has been grounded in small community ethnographies completed after the turn of the twentieth century, and their authors have staged their discussions of social change against a backdrop of untested assumptions about antebellum Appalachia. Thus, they draw broad generalizations about preindustrial Appalachia, but they have failed to examine historical evidence about the region's pre-twentieth-century political economy. Consequently, successive generations of academics have faithfully re-legitimated, without accumulating any empirical evidence, the colorful exaggerations of early-twentieth-century novelists and journalists.

Advantages of World-Systems Analysis

There are empirical indices associated with the rural transition to capitalism which are neither predicted nor analyzed by these existing models. The expansion of the United States from the Atlantic Coast westward was not the single event that these explanations imply. In reality, different frontiers were absorbed at different periods in history. Neither was the unfolding of every one of those frontiers a predictable linear evolution from a primitive stage to modern industrialization. Instead, those frontiers differed in the degree to which they expanded or declined and in the extent to which they exhibited cyclical ups and downs. Nothing is offered in either of the transition arguments to explain why regions like Appalachia never quite follow the predicted linear path from rural to full-blown industrial or market economies. Moreover, the rural inequalities identified by this present study vary so widely from the conventional logic that they cry out for a different conceptual framework. A world-systems inquiry offers several key opportunities for advancing our understanding of American rural history.

In contrast to any of the other three explanations for the transition to capitalism in the United States, world-systems analysis offers the advantage of providing an amplified and refined theoretical paradigm from which to draw. In its repudiation of nineteenth-century social science, world-systems analysis "necessarily rejects its reigning faith, the belief in inevitable progress." Grounded in new scientific notions that there is an "unbroken wholeness of the totality of existence" and that complex systems achieve "order through chaos," the world-systems approach poses an alternative model of social change. Contrary to the model of a rural-industrial continuum of modernization, Wallerstein argues that "nonlinear processes . . . eventually reach bifurcation points, whereupon slight fluctuations have large consequences." In this perspective, "the key variable becomes time, reconceptualizing reality as involving stochastic and irreversible processes, within which deterministic, reversible processes constitute a limited, special case." In short, the world-systems framework permits us to examine frontiers in terms of "structures that reproduce themselves while they constantly change and consequently never reproduce themselves" in the clonelike fashion predicted by the other theories about the transition to rural capitalism in the United States.[18]

Moreover, the conventional arguments script social change as though modern society somehow causes its forerunner to disappear; there seem to be no forces internal to the rural communities that were shaping agents for the transition to capitalism. In contrast, world-systems analysis posits the origins of capitalism in agricultural societies. Wallerstein locates the beginnings of capitalism between 1450 and 1640 in several major transformations of the western European agrarian system—including expansion of commodity production for regional markets, a steady increase in the size of average landholdings, a rise in the number of city-dwelling absentee landlords, and growth of a large class of landless farmers.[19]

Perhaps the most troublesome weakness of the other three transition arguments is the narrow way in which "capitalism" is conceptualized. One argument equates capitalism with international commerce and with the presence of exchange mechanisms; but it is possible for localities to engage in long-distance trade without becoming capitalist. The other two approaches, including the most popular explanation for the transition in Appalachia, designate capitalism to be that "set of social relations in which labor is commonly divorced from the ownership of the land, tools, or materials that form the means of production" so that "there exists in society a significant number of people whose principal means of livelihood is the wage work that they can obtain." This narrow framing of capitalism ignores several antebellum forms of wage labor that emerged outside industry and excludes from consideration the large groups of landless agrarians who sold their labor power. Moreover, capitalism is equated with factory manufacturing; thus, it is not possible for the capitalist mode of production to emerge where the economy remains reliant on agriculture. World-systems theory offers a more inclusive definition of capitalism since economic transformation away from subsistence is conceptualized around the interrelated alterations of the relations of production, of governance structures, of land tenure arrangements, and of labor mechanisms.[20]

The *longue durée* approach of world-systems analysis permits a longitudinal examination of those preindustrial eras that have been neglected by Appalachian specialists. Consequently, this research closes wide gaps in the frontier and agricultural history of Southern Appalachia. Utilization of world-systems analysis permits a tracing of the region's economic development all the way back to the transition to capitalism that occurred in the region's Native American societies. To avoid the "quantum leap" methodology of making regional generalizations from a single rural community or from a narrow sample and short time frame, this study draws on a large statistical and archival database from 215 counties in nine states from 1700 to 1860. Thereby, the diversity of the region and internal causative forces can be assessed against the backdrop of broader national and international trends.

World-systems theory also offers two advances in the examination of frontier expansion of rural areas. The traditional approach has been to romanticize American frontiers as rural areas characterized by unique histories and by a return to primitive economic mechanisms. However, there has been an overestimation of the duration of a primarily subsistent agriculture. Seldom were early American frontiers "reduced to a raw state of economic evolution distinguished by geographical isolation, complete self-sufficiency, and marginal living standards. Such conditions were, at most, a temporary feature of the first year or two of initial permanent settlement." We should, then, analyze the successive opening of new territories as having been propelled "by the search for and exploitation of goods in demand on world markets" and by the search for areas to supply cheap laborers.[21]

Moreover, American frontiers have been conceptualized as the capture of land areas by settlers; there has been too little focus upon the collision between cultures. A world-systems approach permits examination of frontier expansion in terms of the politico-economic struggle between civilizations. In this way, we can more adequately frame a "frontier" as "a territory or zone of interpenetration between two previously distinct societies. Usually, one of the societies is indigenous to the region, or at least has occupied it for many generations; the other is intrusive." We can say that incorporation into the capitalist world economy has begun "when the first representatives of the intrusive society arrive." We then view the transition to capitalism as having been accomplished when the intruding "political authority has established hegemony over the zone."[22]

Southern Appalachia as a Frontier of the World System

How, then, does this frontier expansion unfold? There are processes internal to the capitalist world economy that push it recurrently to expand its outer boundaries. Simply put, we may view "incorporation" as the global process by which capitalism pushes beyond its economic and political perimeters to absorb zones "outside" its limits. The drive of capitalism for "ceaseless accumulation" explains its longevity. Capitalism expands into new frontiers because core nations rival for hegemonic status in the world system. Because "acute competition among capitalists has always been one of the *differentia specifica* of historical capitalism," it is the normal routine for those countries in the core to fight against a declining economic position; for those nations in the semiperiphery to seek to join the core; and for peripheral zones to seek to become semiperipheral in role.[23]

As a result of this international rivalry for hegemonic status, the capitalist world system has been characterized by intermittent cycles of contraction and expansion that greatly alter the fate of different areas of the world economy. On the one hand, core countries face the danger of losing hegemonic status during downswings. On the other hand, semiperipheries often have seized opportunities during such crises to rise to the core. During the expansion cycle of 1672–1700, the *semiperipheries* of the world economy included Spain, Portugal, Germany, Italy, Sweden, Russia, Prussia, Denmark, Austria, and the northern and middle colonies of North America. During this same period, the *peripheries* of the world economy included eastern Europe, southern Europe, Hispanic America, and the extended Caribbean, which stretched from northeast Brazil to Maryland. During this global expansion, Southern Appalachia was incorporated as a *peripheral fringe* of the European colonies located along the southeastern coasts of North America.[24]

Capitalism survives, grows, and combats crises through the operation of five recuperative mechanisms that trigger the capture of new frontiers: (1) alteration of production strategies, (2) redistribution of the world surplus, (3) the international search for cheaper labor, (4) industrial transfer to the semiperiphery, and (5) expansion into new geographical zones. Consequently, the conquest and opening up of the periphery occurred as a result of the inherent tendency of capitalism to expand markets and to export capital. By 1700, when the incorporation of Southern Appalachia had been initiated, twenty-eight separate settler colonies had been established in the Western Hemisphere; these peripheral economies were dominated by and dependent upon the European core.[25]

Politically, 1689–1763 was an era of "unbroken Anglo-French rivalry" for the position of hegemonic power in the western European core; and this struggle was acted out in the peripheries and semiperipheries of the world economy.[26] As Wallerstein notes, "The continual commercial conflict of Britain and France in the Americas 'merged almost imperceptibly, but none the less certainly,' into the culminating struggle that was the Seven Years' War. The Dutch tried to remain neutral but were constrained by British force to limit their trade with France. The Spanish were tempted into joining France as a way to abolish British privileges at last, but it did France no good. The Treaty of Paris of 1763 marked Britain's definitive achievement of superiority in the 100 years struggle with France."[27] In fact, this international rivalry was the impetus for the incorporation of Southern Appalachia when Britain, Spain, and France all sought political alliances and trade agreements with the region's indigenous peoples.

By the eighteenth century, European nations were competing for American settler colonies for three crucial reasons. First, colonies provided the monetary wealth, particularly gold and silver bullion, needed to bolster the hegemonic rivalry among the European core and semiperipheral nations. It was the global search for gold and silver, for example, that would spur the Spanish, the British, and the French to make inland explorations into the southern mountains beginning as early as 1540. The outcome of the uneven and imbalanced hierarchy of the world system is an unequal exchange process in which the periphery is continually weakened by economic expansion of the core and the semiperiphery. The surplus value extracted from the periphery is transferred to the core, thereby polarizing the zones of the world system. Because of the increasingly uneven development in different zones, the core and the periphery are far apart in levels of well-being, social structure, labor specialization, and wealth.[28]

The eighteenth-century core also sought to expand into new territories for a second reason. Because historical capitalism has involved the widespread commodification of production, marketing, distribution, and investment processes, the three tiers of the world economy are linked through vast *commodity chains* that operate as the mechanisms of exchange between the distant corners of the world market. By the expansion era of 1672–1700, western European capitalism had consolidated along five significant lines: improvement in agricultural techniques; development of an expansive shipbuilding industry; emergence of proto-industrialization, particularly in textiles; and advancement of trade linkages with Asia, eastern Europe, and the Atlantic arena.[29]

Between 1650 and 1750, Great Britain utilized global mercantilism to rise to hegemonic power in the world economy. The British government had destroyed Ireland's woolen manufacturing and held monopolistic control over Irish corn, devices used to control world prices and markets. British industrial exports spiraled due to their high productivity from activities in mining, quarrying, ironworks, lime kilns, textiles, and light manufactures. As the core country with the greatest stake in the Atlantic, English ships were monopolizing trade with most Western Hemisphere colonies. Not only were settler colonies a source of slaves and tropical produce (sugar, cotton, tobacco, naval stores), but also they provided a market for European exports. Because of increased English consumption of raw commodities from its colonies, two new economic classes emerged in the peripheries. *Commission merchants* marketed in Europe the agricultural crops that had been produced by *coerced laborers* in the peripheral zones of the world economy. Slavery, tenantry, and cash-cropping were instituted as the basic relations of production in the peripheries. During this historical phase, Southern Appalachia's indigenous people were incorporated into the commodity chains of the world economy to supply slaves, to produce raw materials for Europe's emerging leather manufacturing, and to absorb surplus manufactured goods.[30]

Third, colonies were important to the European core because they provided geographical areas to absorb the surplus population from the overcrowded European cities and countryside. Because the world system is characterized by a tendency toward centralization of wealth and a wide gap between economic classes, the European core needed to search out new land areas to drain off its impoverished urban and rural masses. Land concentration into large estates had become typical of European agriculture, and Scotland had become a commercial farming region totally dependent on Great Britain. Because a sizeable class of tenants and share-farmers provided the labor for the large commercial estates, the European peasantry was landless and pauperized. By 1775 there was no place left in Europe for the traditional peasantry, and there was a social reaction against the rural vagabonds that roamed the countryside. As a direct result of the international movements of people during "the second era of great expansion of the capitalist world-economy," several Third World zones and the inland regions of the United States were resettled. As on other American frontiers, lands were confiscated from Southern Appalachia's Native Americans and concentrated into the hands of absentee speculators. Subsequently, the region was repopulated by Euro-American settlers in three historical phases that stretched from the early 1700s through 1840.[31]

On the eve of the American Revolution, the northern and middle colonies formed a semiperiphery in the world economy. In less than a century after their founding, the northeastern colonies came to occupy a position in the expanding world capitalist system "as a submetropolis of Western Europe." As such, the Northeast shared in "the exploitation of the South, the West Indies, and indeed Africa, and indirectly the mining regions and the Orient. This privileged position, not shared by others in the New World, must be considered as a crucial factor in the economic development of the northeast during colonial times." By 1700 when the incorporation of Southern Appalachia had been initiated, New England and the Middle Atlantic colonies were making great strides as shipbuilders and as commercial middlemen. Nearly one-third of all British ships were built in the northern colonies. In addition, the middle colonies (New York, New Jersey, Delaware, and Pennsylvania) supplied a large portion of the grains required to feed the cities of western and southern Europe and the coerced laborers of the West Indies.[32]

Because of the relative scarcity of labor and capital, because of the limited size of the market in the colonies, and because of British restrictions, North American industry remained small in scale, and most manufactures were imported from Britain. Colonial manufacturing was confined to limited production of iron, lumber milling, and raw-material processing—especially rum distilling, homespun textiles, brick making, and timbering. As a market for European goods, the North American colonies were consuming, by 1766, nearly a quarter of all British exports; and more than one-third of all colonial exports were marketed to England.[33]

The great bulk of North America's accumulated wealth was derived either directly or indirectly from commerce. During the 1700s worldwide trade expanded fivefold; the explanation for this dramatic increase lay in the "triangular trade" system, in which North American ships and plantations played a crucial role.[34] Eric Williams has explained that

> in this triangular trade England—France and Colonial America equally— supplied the exports and the ships; Africa the human merchandise; the plantations the colonial raw materials. The slave ships sailed from the home country with a cargo of manufactured goods. These were exchanged at a profit on the coast of Africa for Negroes, who were traded on the plantations, at another profit, in exchange for a cargo of colonial produce to be taken back to the home country. As the volume of trade increased, the triangular trade was supplemented, but never supplanted, by a direct trade between the home country and the West Indies, exchanging home manufactures directly for colonial produce.[35]

Southern Appalachia was linked into the commodity chains of the triangular trade through the exchange by colonial merchants of Cherokee deerskins for slaves and European manufactured goods.

While the northern colonies developed around shipbuilding, fishing, and foreign trade, the southern colonies specialized in agrarian capitalism. To the northeast of Southern Appalachia, Virginia and Maryland were the major commercial agricultural exporters in colonial America. Southern tobacco "constituted almost half of the total value of commodity exports from the mainland British colonies in 1750 and remained the dominant export throughout the colonial period." To the southeast of Southern Appalachia, Georgia and the Carolinas exported deerskins, rice, indigo, and naval stores to western Europe. Organized around plantation agriculture and economically dependent on the Northeast and on England, the southern colonies remained a periphery of the world system.[36] As Chase-Dunn observes:

> The peripheralized colonial Southern economy based on tobacco, rice, and indigo seemed to have reached its zenith before the turn of the [eighteenth] century. . . . The growth of the new core-periphery division of labour between the South and England also had its effects on the maritime and commercial interests of the North. . . . New York merchants established factors in the port cities of the South that enabled them to ship directly. But they maintained financial control of most of the trade between the South and England. Credit facilities by which American merchants could purchase English goods with drafts on London banks were established by specialized [Northeastern] merchant-banker firms.[37]

Deerskins, a high proportion produced by the Southern Appalachian peripheral fringe, were the most stable economic product of the southern colonies before the Revolutionary War, and the Indian trade was the chief instrument of southern economic expansion during the early colonial period.

Even if they were slightly more egalitarian than their European predecessors, the North American colonies exhibited wide inequities in wealth and land distribution by 1760. One-third of all adult males were landless, and coerced labor mechanisms (slavery, tenancy, and crop-sharing) were entrenched throughout the northern, middle, and southern colonies. Moreover, wealth was concentrated into the hands of a small group of elites, a landed gentry in the South and the merchant class in the Northeast. Henretta informs us that "within a few decades of settlement the wealth structure of the frontier states was nearly indistinguishable from that in the agricultural areas of the more densely settled east." In short, the pattern of inequity that typified the expansion of capitalism throughout the world system was replicated on each American frontier, and Southern Appalachia did not escape this historical process.[38]

Organization of the Study

It is against this backdrop of unfolding historical events that we must analyze the beginnings of the transition to capitalism on the first western frontier of the North American continent. As eighteenth-century capitalism expanded its global reach, inland areas of Southern Appalachia were explored and claimed by European powers. Initially, Southern Appalachia was incorporated as a "marginal periphery" over which the Europeans exercised dominance through *preemptive colonization*.[39]

Theoretical Argument: Regional Transition to Capitalism

When economic contractions threatened British hegemony in the world economy, the Euro-American colonists intensified their rivalry for control over the Southern Appalachian land area, fur trade, and Cherokee allies. In the subsequent international rivalry for the hegemonic position in the world system, England, Spain, and France competed for political alliances and trade linkages with the Cherokees, whose territory served as a buffer zone between the empires of the three powers in the southeastern sector of the North American continent. As a result of slave trading, warfare, and the core-controlled fur trade, Cherokee society was restructured as a putting-out economy. Subsequently, eighteenth-century Southern Appalachia quickly became an export-oriented *region of refuge* that was racially segregated from, but dependent upon, adjacent settler-capitalist zones.[40]

Southern Appalachia was, in fact, one of the major frontier arenas in which England, France, and Spain played out their hegemonic imperialism for core status in the capitalist world economy.

The colonial-commercial competition between Britain and France gave rise to a series of four wars. The first three wars [between 1689 and 1738] were not decisive in North America. The French enjoyed the support of most of the native inhabitants, partly because their missionaries were more active than the British and partly because the steady advance of British settlement beyond the Appalachian Mountains was a much greater threat than the scattered French outposts. With their Indian allies, the French constantly undermined British expansion. . . . The fall of Montreal in 1760 [during the French and Indian War] spelled the doom of the French colonial empire in North America. In the peace of Paris in 1763 Britain received from France the whole of the St. Lawrence Valley and all the territory east of the Mississippi.[41]

Subsequently, the British utilized the Treaty of Paris to try to centralize their American colonists along the controllable seacoasts and to monopolize fur trading with the Native Americans located in Northern and Southern Appalachia. After 1763 settlers were forbidden west of a "proclamation line" drawn down the crest of the Appalachian-Allegheny mountain belt. Despite official edicts, several large companies and syndicates initiated vigorous speculation in the prohibited inland Appalachian areas between 1750 and the Revolutionary War.[42]

After the American Revolution, Southern Appalachia was further incorporated, through a second historical wave, as part of the first frontier-periphery located within the United States when it was a new nation holding semiperipheral status in the capitalist world system. Control over the people, the land, and the natural resources of the southern mountains was of economic and political significance to the fledgling new nation. The lands of Southern Appalachia were considered to be strategic "prizes" in the westward expansion of settlers from the Atlantic seaboard. When the eighteenth-century Northeast ascended into semiperipheral status (catapulted by the fur trade and mercantilism), the peripheral southern colonies (Virginia, South Carolina, and Georgia) competed for their share of global profits by encroaching steadily into the Southern Appalachians in search of mineral wealth, new trading markets, and fresh plantation soils.

Because Appalachia's new settlers emigrated from zones that had been incorporated into the modern, capitalist system before the region was repopulated, it is historically and theoretically inappropriate to categorize the region's inhabitants as precapitalist. The region's settlers were not peasants, as many scholars claim. Settler Appalachia was *born capitalist*, for the region was repopulated by "the children and grandchildren of eighteenth century colonists . . . from an agricultural and mercantile capitalist country about to enter into the industrial revolution." Over the *longue durée*, the incorporation of Southern Appalachia into the capitalist world system entailed nearly 150 years of societal, politico-economic, and cultural change. Incorporation took the form, over two long historical waves, of creating a peripheral zone that is situated in modern times within the geographical boundaries of one of the core countries of the world system.[43]

Exploring Articulation with the World System

The incorporation of Southern Appalachia's local economies into the capitalist world system involved every level of society. To demonstrate the complexity and the uneven diversity of this historical process, this research investigates five levels of articulation with the world system, as illustrated in Figure 1.1. By doing so, I have added two elements of the social change process that are often overlooked in world-systems analyses: the disruption of cultures and the exploitation of the environment. In the chapters that follow, I examine these different levels of articulation in Appalachian communities.

In simplest terms, we can think of "articulation" as all those complex restructurings that must occur when a newly absorbed arena is integrated with the other zones of the capitalist world system. At its most abstract level, "incorporation" involves three concurrent macroscopic social changes: transformation of the sphere of economic production; restructuring of mechanisms for local governance; and dramatic alteration of dominant cultural values and institutions. Three major mechanisms have enabled this world system to persist: the concentration of military strength in the hands of dominant forces; the pervasiveness of an ideological commitment to the system as a whole; and the division of the majority into a larger lower stratum and a smaller middle stratum. As a result, the modern world system operates as a *trimodal structure* consisting of core, semiperipheral, and peripheral zones that are interdependent—that is, each level of the world economy vies for a position in the global division of labor. Most typically, external zones are incorporated as peripheries of the world economy, and the affected peoples quite often trade economic and political autonomy for dependence on a worldwide network of production. "Once masters of their own history, they become via incorporation bound into a world network . . . in a subordinate position."[44]

"Effective incorporation" is said to have begun when exogenous catalysts stimulate restructuring of the economy. As the frontier is developed, the traditional activities of the external arena are "modified in some fundamental way and integrated in a wider, world network dominated by capitalist relations of production." The zone undergoes institutional shifting until it can successfully interact with other sectors of the world market. Local economies are integrated with production, investment, and distribution processes in other zones until they are interdependent with other areas of the world economy.[45]

Comprised of interacting subsystems that are held together by conflicting forces and long-term historical processes, capitalism has been able to flourish precisely because the world economy has had within its bounds a multiplicity

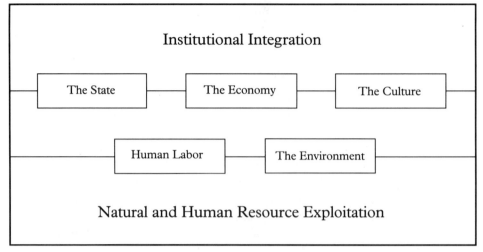

Figure 1.1. Theoretical Model of Local Incorporation into the Capitalist World System

of nation-states. The absence of a single political authority makes it impossible for one state to curtail the capitalist mode of production. In addition, "the existence of state machineries makes it possible for the capitalist sellers to organize the frequently necessary artificial restraints on the operation of the market." The intrusion of the world economy into an external arena "entails the creation of political structures that can assure the participation of the area within the global division of labor."[46]

One of the central incentives behind this global process is the capitalist world system's defensive reaction toward conflicting economic systems. Consequently, cultures are transformed—even obliterated—when global capitalism captures new zones. "In as much as capitalist commerce thrives upon systematization and efficiency, it abhors the nontechnical, irrational economic traits of precapitalist peoples, who must consequently be brought under the influence of the market and made to conform to its rules." Because capitalist transformation is "unthinkable without society's active complicity," the incorporation process disrupts and reshapes local economies, social orders, political structures, and even entire civilizations. Consequently, the cultures of peoples who had formerly been outside the world system are dramatically altered or destroyed.[47]

In addition to institutional restructuring, the articulation of a frontier with the world system triggers the exploitation of natural and human resources. Agglomerating an available, dispensable, and disciplined workforce is the most crucial requirement for the continued expansion and survival of capitalism. Accordingly, integration with the world economy demands a realignment of labor mechanisms and of the family units that reproduce workers. A society undergoing incorporation would, consequently, experience a realignment of labor around three major objectives: export production, subsistence production, and biological reproduction of the labor force.[48]

However, people are not the only local resources that are transformed. The world system is attracted to arenas out of its "craving for supplies of scarce commodities and for new sources of wealth." When the world system advances into new frontiers, "capitalism takes over land and effectively subjects it to its own rules, completely reshaping its organization." Four major alterations occur to effect the capture of territory through the commodification of land. First, indigenous people are displaced so that property rights can be redefined to permit the sale and transfer of ownership in the marketplace. Second, public commons are eliminated through various forms of private enclosure, thereby increasing landlessness among a sizeable segment of the population. Third, land tenure arrangements are modified to encourage the agglomeration of large landholdings. Finally, as a result of the commodification of land, the environment of the frontier is also articulated with the world economy. Natural resources and land are exploited to generate exports for global markets, thereby shifting previous ecological balances and relationships.[49]

Overview

World-systems analysis is a protest against the kind of social scientific inquiry that has characterized much of the scholarly research on preindustrial American societies. Because they have grounded their research in several faulty politico-historical myths, too many analysts of the American frontier have operated out of a priori assumptions that have "the effect of closing off rather than opening up many of the most important questions." Methodologically, world-systems analysis compels questions that stimulate the "unthinking" of a litany of revered tenets about what so-called "preindustrial" America was like. By returning to Southern Appalachia's historical roots in hundreds of obscure primary sources, this research seeks to appraise with critical skepticism many of the cultural stereotypes, agrarian myths, and romanticized generalizations that have permeated traditional explanations for the transition to rural capitalism in the United States. In the chapters that follow, no underlying premise is treated as sacred or as a given; thus, cultural caricatures and long-standing political stereotypes are debunked.[50]

Chapter 2 investigates the first wave of the incorporation of Southern Appalachia by documenting the Cherokee slave-fur trade with the European world market. Careful attention is paid to the political, economic, cultural, and environmental disruptions of the region's Native American societies. Chapter 3 examines the commodification of land that accompanied the transition to capitalism. By constructing from manuscript records a regionwide database on more than 22,000 Appalachian households, this investigation advances knowledge about landholding patterns in Southern Appalachia at the beginning and the end of the antebellum period. Land ownership patterns and absentee speculation are traced over the period from 1790 to 1860 by using county tax lists and census enumerator manuscripts. Land speculation, tenancy, and intergenerational landlessness are examined in statistical records, archival sources, obscure published materials, and oral histories. Significant new conclusions are drawn about the level of absentee control over land and about the extent of conventionally denied Appalachian tenancy.

Chapter 4 examines the emergence of Southern Appalachia's landless agrarian labor force, which was structured around several free and unfree labor mechanisms. Contrary to the myth of family farm laborers producing only their survival needs, Southern Appalachian farm owners produced market surpluses by relying heavily upon coerced and wage laborers. Antebellum tenancy, cropping, and slavery are documented. In addition, several types of agricultural wage laborers and semicoerced workers are described. In all, twelve structural categories of agricultural laborers are fleshed out through the use of census manuscripts, archival family collections, slave narratives, and Civil War veteran questionnaires.

By providing a cliometric analysis of the agricultural production of farm owners, Chapter 5 debunks the agrarian myth of the "subsistent home-steader." In order to distinguish surplus producers, cliometric techniques are applied to isolate those farm households that consumed most of their food crops or that allocated most of their labor time toward the production of their own survival needs. Contrary to long-standing stereotypes, there were few subsistent producers in Southern Appalachia. Rather, the region's farms exported grains, livestock, tobacco, and cotton to adjacent coastal entrepôts of the lower South and the Northeast. Dominant in their local economies, the region's agrarian capitalists invested in manufacturing enterprises that were complementary to those agricultural activities stimulated by integration into the world market. Thus, the region's manufacturing remained closely linked to the processing of raw agricultural commodities for export.

To attack the myth of a postbellum "industrial discovery" of Southern Appalachia, Chapter 6 catalogues the emergence of antebellum industry, focusing on the concentration of investment capital into export-oriented mining and timbering. By specifying the extent and nature of the region's external trade linkages, Chapters 7 and 8 call into question the historical myths of geographical isolation and economic autonomy. Southern Appalachia was articulated with the world economy as a support zone for New World plantation economies and for the industrial centers of the American Northeast and western Europe. The region's export systems were spatially organized through heavy reliance upon turnpikes, waterways, and local middlemen. Regional "bulking centers" linked Appalachian communities to intermediate inland trade centers and to seacoast entrepôts. In addition, the region was heavily dependent upon travel capitalism that catered to the itinerant livestock trade and to national and international tourist elites. In reality, the reach of global commodity chains into antebellum Southern Appalachia was so pervasive that few households remained outside capitalist relations.

Chapter 9 focuses on the noneconomic articulation of local Appalachian economies with the capitalist world system. Four structural and institutional elements of the incorporation process are examined by applying the model diagrammed in Figure 1.1. Finally, Chapter 10 analyzes the deepening economic crises of antebellum Southern Appalachia. After its integration into the capitalist world system, the region paralleled, in many ways, the development patterns that were occurring in other peripheral zones of the nineteenth-century world system. By 1860, this agrarian region was being handicapped by downswings in its trade position in the national and global economies, by environmental degradation, and by the economic policies implemented by the region's wealth and resource monopolizers. As a result, the economic and social gap was widening between Southern Appalachia and the rest of the United States. On the eve of the Civil War, Appalachians were much more likely than other Americans to be impoverished, illiterate, and landless.

2

SLAVES, SKINS, AND WAMPUM:

DESTRUCTION OF SOUTHERN APPALACHIA'S

PRECAPITALIST MODE OF PRODUCTION,

1540–1763

Southern Appalachia as External Arena

"To enter the interior, seek alliance with the natives, spread the Gospel among the heathen and open a borderland trail" all the way from the coast of Florida to Mexico—these were the official objectives of the three sixteenth-century Spanish explorations into the indigenous Appalachian settlements of North Carolina, Tennessee, Georgia, and Alabama. Just as significant was their visionary search for a Northwest Passage that would link Spanish traders to the Orient. The Spanish also tramped into the mountains to kidnap slaves and "to trade for hides and pieces of guanin," an alloy of copper and gold that they believed popular among the Indians. Just as they had in other parts of the New World, the Spanish sought precious metals, filling their expedition journals with reports that "this land is very good and . . . there are metals of gold and silver." In similar fashion, the French were attracted by reports of mineral wealth; so their 1560s exploratory maps labeled this copper-bearing region the "Montes Appalatci."[1]

For more than a century after these earlier regional penetrations, there was little or no contact between the Southern Appalachian indigenes and the Europeans. Yet there was a constant flow of European goods into Southern Appalachia through the aboriginal trade networks from coastal areas. These early exchanges introduced into the southern mountains several European manufactured commodities, including glass and crystal beads, brass bells, iron axes and knives, and looking glasses.[2]

Until after the 1670 founding of Charleston, South Carolina, however, Southern Appalachia remained an *external arena* of the world system, and European trade goods were fairly rare among the Cherokees. Still, the sixteenth-century explorations of the region set in motion a series of historical transformations that dramatically altered Cherokee culture between the late sixteenth and early eighteenth centuries. Prior to European contact, Southern Appalachia was inhabited by several strong chiefdoms organized around capitol-centered leaders with ultimate religious and political power. For example, there were such Mississippian Period settlement clusters at Garden Creek, North Carolina; Hiwassee Island and Citico in Tennessee; and Etowah, Georgia.[3]

Within a forty-year period after Spanish infiltration, these chiefly organizations began to erode. In the face of European-transmitted epidemics of smallpox, measles, and influenza, there emerged a "progressive lack of faith in the traditional beliefs and explanations" provided by their chiefs. Consequently, the powerful chief was replaced by a looser decision-making council, and the construction of mounds and large public edifices ceased. Because the chiefdom societies of the Southeast were all interlinked, changes in those that came under early European control reverberated throughout the region's networks of trade, war, and tribute, upsetting the delicate balances between them all.[4]

Political Articulation with the Capitalist World System

The period from 1600 to 1750 was dominated by the efforts of England and France first to destroy Dutch hegemony in the world system and then to succeed to the top position. As part of that hegemonic struggle, twenty-eight new colonized zones were established in the Western Hemisphere: three Dutch, eight French, and seventeen English. During the long global economic contraction from 1600 to 1750, another large colonized zone was absorbed into the capitalist world economy. This new peripheral region was the *extended Caribbean,* stretching from northeast Brazil to Maryland. The establishment of European colonies in Virginia, Carolina, and Georgia and the subsequent incorporation of the Southern Appalachian hinterland ensued as part of the creation of this large new peripheral region. When the European powers turned their attention to competition for the Ohio Valley and for the southeastern territories of North America, they sought to "checkmate" one another by establishing alliances with the inland peoples. Segments of several indigenous peoples settled intermittently within the boundaries of eighteenth-century Southern Appalachia, including the Tuscarora, the Susquehannas, the Delawares, the Senedos, the Toteros, the Sioux, the Shawnees, the Chickasaws, and the Creeks. However, the only group of Native Americans whose entire nation was situated within the region were the Cherokees, who claimed almost all the region's land area.[5]

As Map 2.1 demonstrates, control of the inland mountains was crucial to all three European powers. By the early 1700s, Southern Appalachia formed a buffer zone between British settlements along the Atlantic seaboard and the French in the Ohio and Mississippi Valleys. From their vantage points in present-day Alabama, Louisiana, and the American Northwest, the French carried on trade and diplomatic relations with all the southeastern Indians and with the northern Iroquois Confederacy. Entrenched to the south in Florida, the Spanish might have captured the entire Southeast away from the other two powers if they could have engineered alliances with the Cherokees and Creeks. "Which side held the upper hand depended largely on which side had the most loyal and most numerous Indian allies." Of the four great nations in the Southeast, "the Choctaw generally sided with France, while the Chickasaw and Cherokee favored England; the Creek sought to play off the two powers to their best advantage though they were most often aligned with the English."[6]

Each of the colonizers sought to take hold of the Southern Appalachians out of fear that one of the other powers would capture those crucial mountains. In a sense, their strategy was one of preemptive retention. For this vast region formed a geographical barrier between the coast and the rich inland valleys of the Ohio and Mississippi Rivers. All three colonizing powers knew that "whoever [was] master of the Cherrockee Nation" might hold the key to further advancement into the continent, for their ancestral lands stretched from Blue Ridge and Shenandoah Valley in Virginia and East Kentucky to northern Alabama and northern Georgia. The Cherokees occupied sixty towns dispersed among three geographical centers: the Lower Towns on the Savannah River, the Middle Towns in western North Carolina and northern Georgia, and the Overhill Towns mainly in East Tennessee.[7]

The Southern Appalachians were important to the colonizers for four reasons. First, the geographical location situated the Cherokees at a focal point for movement of northern Indians into the Southeast, and those Indians were allied with the French. In the military estimation of the Europeans, Southern Appalachia was "a most important Country by its nature and Situation, lying in a very extraordinary and remarkable manner among the Mountains in the midst of the Heads of several large Rivers, that ha[d] Communication with different and remote parts on all sides." Consequently, "the Cherokee country [was] the best formed by nature for dominion of the Inland Indian nations on this side of the Mississippi and the [Great] Lakes."[8]

Second, Southern Appalachia was crucial to the colonizers because Cherokee and Creek alliances provided the only frontier defense available to the coastal settlements of the British. Since "the design of the French" was to

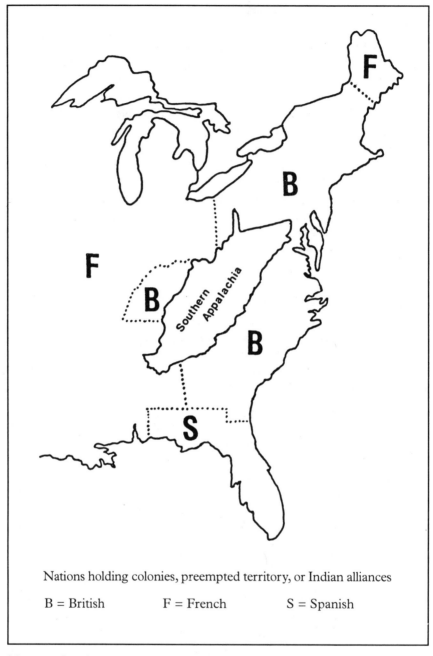

Nations holding colonies, preempted territory, or Indian alliances

B = British   F = French   S = Spanish

Map 2.1. Southern Appalachia's Significance to the International Rivalry for North American Territory, Early 1700s "establish themselves, settle their Indians, and build [inland] forts just on the back of [British] settlements," English colonists understood that the "the Cheapest and strongest Barrier for the Protection of [their] Settlements" was formed by the Cherokee towns. "South Carolina is a weak frontier colony," assessed the governor, "and in case of an invasion by the French, would be their first object of attack." The colonists believed that they did not have "much to fear" while they "retain[ed] the affection of the Indians" around them. "Should we forfeit that by any mismanagement on our part, or by the superior address of the French," the governor recognized, "we are in a miserable situation. The Cherokees alone, have several thousand gunmen, all well acquainted with every inch of this province—their country is the key of Carolina."[9]

The entire militia force of Georgia and South Carolina numbered less than 3,500 because the two colonies were "utterly incapable of finding funds sufficient for the defence of this wide frontier, and so destitute of white men, that even money itself cannot here raise a sufficient body of them." Thus, the Cherokees were of political significance to the British and Spanish in a third way. Indians were also "a Bullwork" at the backs of the coastal settlers because they served as deterrents to runaway slaves and to slave insurrections. "In our quarrels with the Indians," one mid-1700s journalist surmised, "it can never be our interest to extirpate them, or to force them from their lands; their ground would be seen taken up by runaway Negroes from our settlements, whose numbers would daily increase, and quickly become more formidable enemies than Indians can ever be."[10]

Finally, commerce with the Indians was designed to have the greatest political impact. Trade was essential to the diplomatic process with the Appalachian indigenes, and no alliances could be secured without the exchange of economic commodities. One 1730 journal reports, for instance, that Creek messengers were sent to the Cherokees "desiring them to come over to the French Interest, who promised to send them back, loaded with Presents." The Europeans utilized gifts to bolster the standing of favorite chiefs or warriors, to negotiate peace between Indian groups, to facilitate treaties or land cessions, and to discourage alliances with enemy Indians or colonizing powers. The Southeastern Indians effected a diplomatic process in which they held the British "in one hand and the French in the other . . . as if they meant to play between [them], in order to trade with and get presents from both, and if forced out of this state of neutrality to side with the strongest."[11]

The French might have gained the alliance of all the Indians between the Gulf of St. Lawrence and the Gulf of Mexico had it not been for the fact that the English were consistently able to furnish the Indians with better trade goods at cheaper prices. The French recognized that "they Effect [the Indians] most who sell best cheap." In the early 1700s, one Louisiana official lamented that "All the Indians like the French much better than they do the

English and if we could give them the same prices as the latter when we pay them for the skins that they offer in trade, we should attract them all."[12]

The cornerstone, then, of British political leverage with the Cherokees was trade. "Being supplyed with European goods is to the Indians the first essential interest of their politicks: Is the sole and actual object of their alliance with us, and the only real and permanent motive of their attachment to us," concluded one eighteenth-century strategist. "The first and fundamental object of the English measures should be to provide for these in a regular and sufficient manner, the being able to do this is our peculiar advantage and superiority over the French." The British were careful not to "disgust the Cherokees by stopping all Trade to that Nation, for they [would] certainly throw themselves into the Arms of the French." In fact, Cherokee chiefs courted the Spanish or the French when the British threatened to cut off the supply of trade goods to their towns. As a diplomatic strategy, the British treated their Cherokee allies as though they had *favored nation* status. South Carolinian traders charged higher prices to the Creeks, who were less stable political allies to the British.[13]

Even in the face of low profits by the mid-1700s, the British nurtured their political alliances with the Cherokees by sustaining trade. Even though exchanges with the Creeks and the Chickasaws were much more profitable, South Carolinians continually reinforced their trade agreements with the poorer Cherokees. Virginia even devised a scheme during the 1760s to exchange manufactured goods at cost for pelts in order to keep the Cherokees friendly to the British cause. After 1763, Charleston's skin industry was confined to the Cherokees even though their trade was not very lucrative. South Carolina's governor thought they commanded attention more upon political than commercial considerations "as they formed a barrier against the incursions of the powerful Indians of the Ohio and Illinois tribes and a counterbalance against the Creeks in case of war."[14]

European Instigation of Indian Wars

Articulation of the Cherokees with the European world system was accompanied by repeated warfare among the southeastern Indian groups. The promotion of Indian strife was a significant strategy followed by the colonies to protect their own settlements. "It is always the maxim of our Government," reported the South Carolina governor in the 1730s, "to promote war between Indians of different Nations . . . for in that consists our safety, being at War with one another prevents their uniting against us." In addition, the three colonizing powers promoted warfare among those Indians allied with their competitors.[15]

Thus, the hostilities between the southeastern Indians were no longer the traditional revenge disputes among these Native American populations but were an Appalachian manifestation of the global conflict between France, Spain, and England, and the European rivals recklessly played Indians off against one another. When the French began to feel the disadvantage from these frequent wars, they outlawed slave raids to deter intertribal strife and to protect their Indian alliances. "It is not an evil that the Indian nations should be at war with each other," wrote a Louisiana official. However, he recognized that the English "profit[ed] by their quarrels to penetrate into the nations that are most attached to us, which cannot be prevented except by keeping as we do all the nations in peace among themselves, making them understand that the English are seeking to have them destroyed among themselves in order to be masters of their country." In short, the French believed that "when they see that we do not wish any slaves and that we forbid the trade in them they will be easily persuaded that we are better friends of theirs than the other European nations."[16]

Agreements to fight the enemies of their diplomatic ally were typical requirements of trade treaties between the Indians and the European nations. As a result of their affiliation with the British, the Cherokees were engaged in chronic warfare with their Indian neighbors throughout the eighteenth century. The British planned numerous schemes in which the Creeks and Cherokees would attack and destroy the French-allied Choctaws, Chickasaws, or Yazoos, thereby permitting the establishment of new forts from which they could attract the Indian trade of the Mississippi Valley and weaken Spanish Florida. In turn, the French tried to exterminate the British-allied Chickasaws by inciting the Choctaws, and they prodded the northern Shawnees to make raiding parties into Cherokee territory. The Spanish repeatedly tried to inflame the Creeks and Cherokees against the other two powers.[17]

By engaging in an eighteenth-century arms race in which they supplied guns and ammunition to both sides, the Europeans incited the Creeks and the Cherokees toward mutual destruction. When the Lower Creeks aligned themselves with the French, the British aroused the Cherokees against them, instructing their traders to use their "utmost endeavors to set the Cheerokees out against the Lower Creeks, & in as many parties as possible you can." If the traders found them "backward in going out," they were to "bribe some of the young fellows to head parties out, cost what it will." After selling guns to the Creeks in 1718, the British denied to the Cherokees their role in agitating intertribal warfare. We are surprised, the Trade Commissioners declared, "that the Charikees should suspect our Men of joyning with their Enemies against them; and if it be true that there was white Men with the Creeks . . . they were certainly French or Spaniards, for it is not our Way to deal so perfidiously; and . . . if we had such a Design, we should not supply them with Ammunition to oppose us."[18]

Changes in Cherokee Governance during the Colonial Era
As a result of such international intrigues in Southern Appalachia, Cherokee governance was restructured to effect articulation of the region with the interstate network that comprised the capitalist world system. During the colonial

era, the British were most instrumental in pressuring the loosely knit Cherokee towns toward *secularization* and *centralization* of their nonstate political mechanisms. Because early Cherokee law was grounded in spiritual traditions and executed by a priestly complex, eighteenth-century British observers erroneously believed that "there [was] no law or subjection among them."[19]

In reality, each Cherokee town was structured around a bifurcate political organization comprised of complementary hierarchies. The Red or White organizations were never in operation at the same time since they alternately exerted control during times of war or peace respectively. The White organization was headed by an older "beloved man," whom colonial officials equated with their European notion of king. The White Chief convened and presided over council meetings and served as the overseer in important communal activities. The Red organization assumed town leadership only in times of military emergency. Headed by the "Raven" (the greatest warrior elected to this office), the Red organization functioned during three significant dilemmas faced by the town: external warfare, diplomatic liaisons with foreign powers, and the establishment of trade agreements with outsiders. In cases of conflict in authority, the White group controlled the younger Reds.[20]

Before European contact, then, the Cherokees were an agglomeration of independent villages, without any unifying structure to facilitate coordination of all the dispersed settlements. When diplomatic matters were to be negotiated, the colonial governments summoned, as in 1721, "A Head man out of each Town." In addition, the British specified a leadership pattern in treaties or "commissioned" certain Cherokee warriors to control their settlements. By 1725, the British colonies behaved politically as though there were four prominent Cherokee leaders in control of all the settlements—two from the combined Overhills and Middle Towns and two from the Lower Towns. In addition, the British set one scale of prices on trade goods for all the Cherokee towns and required the Cherokees to use a centralized pass system when traveling to British settlements. The British also pressured the Cherokees toward centralization by establishing regional storehouses that were to be utilized by several towns. Moreover, it became advantageous for the Cherokees to relocate their towns closer together in order to organize a more rapid and concerted defense in times of war.[21]

By 1730, a new Cherokee *priest-state* had emerged in response to crises that grew out of articulation of Cherokee towns with the European trade and war complex. Ultimately, the British coerced the Cherokees to "elect" a puppet government derived from the war hierarchy rather than from a coalition of the traditional bifurcated village organizations. In his 1730 journal, Sir Alexander Cuming reported the significant structural reorganization of the Cherokees under a single hand-picked emperor who controlled key town elites who were easily co-opted by the British. The whole Cherokee "nation" was governed, he reported, by seven mother Towns, each of these Towns chuse a King to preside over them and their Dependants. . . . There are several Towns that have Princes. . . . Besides these, every Town has a Head Warrior, who is in great Esteem among them, and whose Authority seems to be greater than their Kings. . . . Their Conjurers are the Persons consulted in every Affair of Importance, and seem to have the Direction of every Thing. . . . [Cuming required] all the head Warriors to acknowledge themselves dutiful Subjects and Sons to King George. . . . Sir Alexander order'd that the head Warriors should answer for the Conduct of their People to Moytoy, whom he appointed their [Emperor], by unanimous Consent of the whole People.[22]

With the emergence of this "tribal half-government," traditional shared leadership by the Red and White Councils was destroyed. In the face of their incapacity to cure epidemics, the White chiefs were further overshadowed. Subsequently, the White organization no longer shared leadership over villages, as had been customary.[23]

Articulation with the world system necessitated a political structure that permitted the European powers to negotiate with the Cherokees as a single corporate entity. It was more *rational* and more *efficient* to collect trade debts, make treaties, engineer war alliances, and seek reparations from one leader who was the "Mouth of the Nation" and who could enter into agreements that "should be binding upon him and all the Nation." Every Cherokee village was held responsible by the British for the behavior of each of its residents. Moreover, "the loosely tied villages as a group were strictly accountable for the dereliction of any one," and treaties made with one town or even one individual were frequently considered as binding upon all.[24]

The priest-state was the first joint attempt by the several Cherokee villages to prevent any individual from acting in a way that would bring reprisals against the entire group. Now the Cherokees were forced to abandon their ultrademocratic methods to support, instead, a single tribewide sentiment and to legitimate that decision with universally applied sanctions against violators. Structurally, "the priest-state was the traditional village structure for general councils of the capitol village plus a system of representation from all other villages." Because of the distance between settlements, selected spokesmen acted at the capitol on behalf of their villages, establishing a system by which the Europeans could easily co-opt a small number of elites.[25]

Economic and Labor Articulation with the World System

Prior to European incorporation, Cherokee settlements engaged in a communal-subsistence mode of production, organized around mixed hunting, fishing, gathering, and agricultural functions. Before guns were introduced, hunting and gathering were secondary to agriculture; and communal hunts were conducted only during the winter season. Articulation of the Cherokees with the European world system triggered far-reaching transformations in that traditional economy.

Emergence of a Capitalist Export Economy

Within a few decades, Cherokee village activities were restructured into an export economy in which hunting for slaves and deerskins and gathering marketable herbs assumed primacy.[26] English merchants shipped Cherokee ginseng and other native herbs from Charleston to China and to Europe, where it was marketed as an aphrodisiac and to combat venereal disease. In 1767, six tons of Cherokee clay were transported by pack horse to Charleston and then exported to Europe for the manufacture of Wedgewood porcelain. The Euro-Americans also traded with the Indians for livestock (particularly horses) and for food for their forts. Indians represented about 10 percent of the total slave population in South Carolina in the early 1700s. By 1710, perhaps as many as 12,000 Indians had been exported from South Carolina to the northern colonies and the Caribbean. The most coveted Cherokee commodities, however, were their deerskins. In the early 1700s, Charleston merchants exported as many as 121,355 skins annually, and that number rose steadily to 255,000 skins by 1730.[27]

Because of the demands for labor in the West Indies and in the emergent North American colonies, Indian slaves were the first profitable commodity to attract the interest of the world economy in Southern Appalachia. By 1681, the capture and selling of Cherokee slaves had begun; the Cherokees' first diplomatic mission to Charleston in 1693 was aimed at seeking relief from slavery raids. By 1700 guns had been introduced so that the Cherokees could protect themselves against the slave raids of neighboring Indians, and by 1703 the Cherokees were marketing Indian slaves themselves.[28]

Slavery raids were an organized extension of European instigation of warfare among the Native Americans. Indian enslavement was not just profitable business; it also offered military advantages. A 1680 commentator observed that "The good prices The English Traders give them for slaves Encourage [the Indians] to this trade Extreamly and some men think it both serves to lessen their number before the French can arm them and it is a more Effectuall way of Civilising and Instructing." The Europeans traded their manufactured goods for war prisoners, so this commodification stimulated the Indians to further conflict. The British even organized slave raids in which white traders led warriors to attack the settlements of Indians allied with their European rivals. As the result of such forays, for instance, the population of 25,000 Indians in Spanish Florida was annihilated.[29]

As international transfer of African slaves expanded, Appalachian deerskins became much more essential to the core than Indian laborers. In contrast to their northern counterparts, the Cherokees did not produce luxury furs; rather the southern Indians provided to the world market the raw commodities needed to fuel the European leather manufacturing industry. By the fifteenth century, there was a shortage of fur-bearing animals in Europe, so American deerskins were cheaper than other hides to use in the production of shoes, gloves, jackets, artisans' aprons, book covers, box and trunk coverings, and a wide array of products in demand for daily use. In addition, deerskins were in demand for production of military uniforms and equipment used by troops in European wars.[30]

Deerskins were important enough to core manufacturing that England placed them on the list of "enumerated" items requiring its colonies to ship them only to British ports. Consequently, deerskins were the most stable economic product of the southern colonies before the Revolutionary War. Deerskin exports to England were so crucial to the development of the southern colonies that Virginia, South Carolina, and Georgia competed intensely for monopolistic control over the Indian trade. In South Carolina and Georgia, the Indian trade was the chief instrument of economic expansion during the early colonial period. "The profits of the Indian trade supplied capital for agricultural development and sustained the infant colonial establishment until agriculture could gain a foothold." Charleston was the most important center for the southeastern Indian trade, "overshadowing the French Mobile and the Spanish St. Augustine; superior in strength and importance to Montreal and comparable only to Albany, the great fur mart of the northern colonies."[31]

Until rice and naval stores were produced in quantity after the beginning of the eighteenth century, deerskins to England were the most important export from Charleston; two-thirds of those pelts came from the Cherokees. Even after 1730, the deerskin trade remained South Carolina's second most lucrative economic activity. In fact, when world markets for naval stores and rice were depressed in the late 1720s, Charleston's export of deerskins tripled. By 1765, Charleston had widened its markets so that its 300 topsails transported deerskins and leather manufactures principally to Holland, the Mediterranean, and Portugal. In similar fashion, deerskins were second only to tobacco as the most profitable 1674 commodity exported by Virginia. Savannah, Georgia, had emerged by the mid-1700s as a commercial rival to Charleston because that new port was able to supply the world market with hides from half a million deer between 1764 and 1773.[32]

Deerskins were essential to the European core in five ways. First, trading for these commodities was utilized to reinforce political alliances with the Indians located in areas adjacent to European colonies on the North American continent. Second, these hides provided essential raw materials for the development of its burgeoning leather manufacture. Third, the deerskin trade provided a highly profitable peripheral outlet for European manufactured goods, particularly irons and woolens. Fourth, duties on deerskins were the biggest revenue producers for the provincial governments, thereby relieving the colonizers of the financial burden of funding the infrastructure of these new peripheral areas. Finally, deerskins helped the European powers to maintain their balances of trade with other world-market participants through an elaborate chain of commodity exchanges that circled the globe.[33]

Through articulation with extensive commodity chains, Southern Appalachia was inexorably hooked "into the orbit of the world-economy in such a way that it virtually [could] no longer escape." The Cherokees marketed slaves and deerskins to Charleston for re-export to the West Indies and to the northern colonies. Cherokee deerskins were exported via Charleston, Virginia, and Georgia primarily to England, with about 5 percent going to the northern colonies. In return, Charleston received sugar and tobacco from the West Indies and rum from the northern colonies. The rum traded to Charleston merchants, a large part of which ended up in Cherokee villages, had its origins in West Indian molasses, for which the northern colonies swapped lumber and provisions. In exchange for the deerskins exported to England, Charleston received manufactured goods—including woolens, clothing, guns, and iron tools that were bartered to the Indians for slaves and deerskins. In return for the leather goods it manufactured from Cherokee deerskins, England received raw materials, luxury goods, and meat provisions from all over the globe.[34]

Colonial Restructuring of the Cherokee Economy

The English fur trade in America was controlled by one group of politicians in England. "Hudson Bay, New York, and the southern colonies of Virginia and Carolina were three fields of exploitation by which the fur business of the world was made to revolve about London." The southeastern deerskin trade was dominated by a narrow field of mercantile interests that secured Crown charters to explore and exploit resources. Except for short periods when special acts created governmental monopolies, the southeastern Indian trade was carried on by speculative companies that were licensed and regulated by the colonies. These publicly subsidized enterprises explored the inland mountains, establishing linkages that connected Virginia, the Carolinas, and Georgia via trading paths through Cherokee settlements.[35]

By 1750 the deerskin commerce at Augusta, Georgia, was "nearly monopolized by a company of seven, who ha[d] a general store at Augusta, and each one license[d] for different towns in the Indian nation." Similarly, the earliest Virginia trade was controlled by a handful of planters, like Abraham Wood and William Byrd, who imported "Goods proper for such a trade from England and then either venture[d] them out at their own Risk to the Indian Towns or Credit[ed] some Traders with them . . . to be paid in Skins at a certain Price agreed betwixt them." Byrd operated from his James River plantation near the great trading path that led southward to the Catawbas and the

Cherokees. His trading caravans consisted of fifteen or more hired traders utilizing more than a hundred pack horses to transport European goods to exchange for light furs and skins.[36]

By 1721, however, Virginia's commerce with the Cherokees had been eclipsed by that of Charleston. A 1725 journalist reported that "the Virginia traders . . . cannot do any prejudice to [South Carolina] in the way of Trade, there not being above 2 or 3 of them and their goods noways sortable or Comparable to ours." In South Carolina, there were at least thirty-one Charleston firms engaged in the Cherokee trade, and there were more than 150 traders and pack horsemen in the Appalachian settlements by the mid-1700s. The trade was regulated by the Commons House of Assembly, which appointed commissioners and an agent who was responsible for licensing all traders. The Indian Trade Commission was comprised of five Charleston merchants who received a 2.5 percent commission on the sale of skins and a 2.5 percent commission on the purchase of goods for the Indian business. The Trade Commissioners used public funds to supply the Indians with British manufactures "at a cheap and easy rate to prevent their seduction by the French and Spanish." In addition, the Trade Commissioners sold at Charleston auctions the deerskins brought from Cherokee country and fixed the rate of exchange at which goods were to be sold to the Indians.[37]

Trading on the world market bore a high cost for Southern Appalachia's indigenous people. The Cherokee economy was transformed into a *putting-out* system that destroyed traditional economic activities, generated dependency upon European trade goods, and stimulated debt peonage. As had been the case with the development of protoindustrialization in Europe, the Cherokee deerskin trade was dependent upon merchant capital from foreign entrepreneurs. The century from 1660 to 1760 was an era dominated by global mercantilism; thus, the American Midland and Southeast were dependent on the great trading houses of London for the handling of their goods and for credit.[38]

Three distinct levels of speculators were engaged in the deerskin trade. London importers and commission houses made advances to the exporting companies located in the North American colonies, which "received supplies from their British correspondents on credit or in partnership and fitted out traders." Coastal planters and merchants hired their own Indian hunters, invested capital, and lobbied in the legislative bodies that regulated the trade. "Much of the profit was siphoned off by the middlemen, the Charleston merchants, who benefitted from their connections with the English mercantile houses across the ocean and the risk-taking Indian traders on the frontier." Factors in London and Bristol maintained the strongest links to Charleston merchants, and those two British ports received over 90 percent of all deerskins shipped.[39]

South Carolina established its "fur factory" system in 1716, dividing the

Cherokee territory into five trading districts, each with a "trading house" located at a fort. After 1721, British "factories" operated directly out of Cherokee villages, and every indigenous settlement had its own permanent European traders. By 1750, the deerskin trade had expanded so much that Cherokee settlements were marked off by the British into thirteen hunting districts with 200 warriors to each district. Charleston merchants extended credit or financed the lower-level trading companies that were licensed to operate in specific Indian towns. These smaller traders established direct linkages with the Indians, often residing in the distant settlements nine months of the year.[40]

As the last link in the commodity chain, these village-situated traders extended commodity advances to the Cherokee producers. Local traders advanced goods, including rum, on credit to the Cherokees to provision the settlements between hunts. Traders supervised processing of the skins so that hooves and snouts were removed and the pelts were dried properly to prevent molding. Then deerskins were graded into three sizes and priced according to weight and quality. Finally, the skins were branded with a legally prescribed code for each different Cherokee town to designate them as commodities to be exported from Charleston.[41]

The average trading company received a 500 to 600 percent profit on the goods advanced in exchange for skins, yet the Cherokees became "perennial debtors to the traders who staked them in their winter hunts. The Cherokees roamed the forests almost as employees of a trading system built around the faraway demands of European society." In 1711, the Cherokees owed British debts amounting to 100,000 deerskins. In one settlement, for instance, the warriors could not be collected to attend a diplomatic meeting because "they being all out a hunting about sixty miles from hence & being so much indebted to the Stores."[42]

The European traders implemented several techniques to keep the indigenous settlements in debt peonage. Because Cherokee demand for manufactured goods was relatively inelastic, British traders identified a commodity that would be in constant demand. Introduced to the Cherokees by 1700, rum became the trade good that spurred abandonment of subsistence production and intensified dependency upon deerskin exporting. In addition to its addictive quality, rum was advantageous because traders could follow the Cherokee "black drink" custom and offer alcohol to initiate each exchange. According to the British Indian Commissioner's report for 1755:

Many Traders licensed and unlicensed . . . have made a constant Practice of carrying very little Goods, but chiefly . . . Rum from Augusta; from whence as soon as the Indian Hunters are expected in from their Hunts, they set out. . . . Then some of those Rum Traders place themselves near the Towns, in the way of the Hunters returning home with their deer skins. The poor

Indians in a manner fascinated, are unable to resist the Bait; and when Drunk are easily cheated. After parting with the fruit of 3 or 4 Months Toil, they find themselves at home, without the means of buying the necessary Clothing for themselves or their Families.[43]

Price gouging, stealing, and watered rum were also utilized to cheat the Cherokees out of their raw commodities. Like their northern counterparts, Cherokee traders utilized "overplus" tactics, cutting yard sticks short or tampering with weighing mechanisms to permit them to grade skins into cheaper price categories.[44]

More significantly, the British utilized the puppet priest-state to treat each Cherokee settlement as a corporate entity. The unpaid debts of any single member of the town became the obligation of the entire village. If one or a few Cherokees stole from a trader, for example, the Charleston Commissioners would threaten to withdraw all trading until the settlement paid the debt. In addition, traders seized skins or horses from the clan members who were kin to a deceased debtor.[45]

Increasingly, the deerskin trade and the European impetus to war became the central economic and political foci. The resultant new division of labor disrupted traditional production of survival essentials and intensified Cherokee dependency upon expensive core-manufactured commodities. When hunting and warfare were transformed into year-round activities, there emerged a growing sexual bifurcation of tasks. Emphasis upon hunting and the trading-diplomacy process siphoned Cherokee males away from the seasonal rhythm of economic production. In addition to commercial hunting, the male labor force was proletarianized as burdeners, canoers, or pack horsemen for traders—to help build forts, to engage in slave raids, and to fight wars. The new emphasis upon hunting and warfare also necessitated greater male labor time for the production of weapons and canoes. Moreover, the labor of young males especially was lost due to the consumption of rum.[46]

Prior to European incorporation, males were involved in agricultural production, leaving only the lighter field maintenance to the women, children, and the elderly. Before the priest-state entrenched the Red organization as the village leadership, all members of the town "were periodically summoned by the leaders of the White organization to work together in clearing, planting and harvesting crops," and part of their communally raised crops was stored in a public granary for emergencies. Sexual and economic bifurcation weakened these *gadugi* traditions by which the entire village engaged in communal production because Cherokees were now drawn away from subsistence into those activities that sustained the export economy. By the mid-1700s, British observers reported that the Cherokee "women alone do all the laborious tasks of agriculture," freeing the men to hunt or go to war and "leave their women to hoe their corn." Export production even drained away a large segment of the labor time of the women who assisted with annual forest burning and the dressing of deerskins to meet British trading guidelines.[47]

"Disarticulation" between subsistence activities and the export sector of the Cherokee economy brought serious repercussions for the Cherokee villages. As commercial hunting expanded, the Cherokees became less sufficient in agriculture. Public granaries were deemphasized since the villages could now depend upon the British trading process to meet emergency needs. By the early 1700s, the British were supplying corn, pork, and beef to Cherokee settlements that encountered shortages. When trade was cut off by the British in the mid-1700s, some Cherokee towns broke up and combined with other villages because they could no longer survive the scarcity of food, guns, and ammunition.[48]

As traditional artisan crafts were devalued for the consumption of imported European guns, axes, tomahawks, hatchets, knives, beads, pipes, pottery, fur-stretching equipment, clothing, and cooking utensils, Cherokee villages were "deindustrialized." Even specialized copper work, body paint preparation, and salt manufacturing were displaced by European commodities. By the mid-1700s, the British could report that "The Indians, by reason of our supplying them so cheap with every sort of goods, have forgotten the chief part of their ancient mechanical skill, so as not to be well able now, at least for some years, to live independent of us."[49]

Only twenty-five years after organized trading had begun, a new generation of young Cherokees had, according to the head warrior of Tunissee at a 1725 Upper Towns ceremonial gathering, "been brougt up after another Manner then their forefathers," and their head warriors taught them that "they could not live without the English." Commercial hunting, population declines, and frequent warfare resulted in lowered production in those agricultural and craft functions that were essential to the survival of the villages. Cherokee craftsmen further disrupted traditional economic activities by concentrating on the production of items that could be traded to other Indians for deerskins to be exported. Those who were not good hunters "dress[ed] skins, ma[d]e bowls, dishes, spoons, tobacco-pipes, with other domestick implements." These indigenous manufactures were "usually transported to some remote nations" where the Cherokees "barter[ed] these commodities for their raw hides with the hair on, which [we]re brought home and dressed" for export to the British.[50]

Such trade-induced acculturation provided the leverage needed by the British to manipulate the Cherokees into land cessions and war alliances. In agreeing to the 1730 treaty, for instance, the Cherokees accepted several provisions that had nothing to do with trading, as Chief Ketagustah indicates in his reply to the treaty:

We are come hither from a dark mountainous Place, where nothing but Darkness is to be found; but are now in a Place where there is Light. . . . In War we shall always be as one with you, the Great King George's Enemies shall be our Enemies, his People and ours shall be always one, and shall die together. We came hither naked and poor as the Worm of the Earth; but you have every Thing, and we that have Nothing must love you, and can never break the Chain of Friendship which is between us. . . . If we catch your Slaves, we shall bind them as well as we can, and deliver them to our Friends again, and have no Pay for it. . . . Your White People may very safely build Houses near us, we shall hurt Nothing that belongs to them.[51]

Little more than half a century after trade had been initiated with the Europeans, the Cherokees recognized that they could not "live independent of the English." By 1751, Cherokee Chief Skiagonota would lament that "the clothes we wear we cannot make ourselves. They are made for us. We use their ammunition with which to kill deer. We cannot make our guns. Every necessity of life we have from the white people." The greater their export of deerskins, the more deepened was their dependency upon British commodities. "Once a demand for merchandise not manufactured by the Indians was created or the native Indian industries had fallen into disuse, a threat to cut off the trade was sufficient to bring a recalcitrant tribe to terms." For example, when the Cherokees permitted French-allied Indians among them, South Carolina ceased the flow of commodities to bring the rebellious villages to terms. At the end of subsequent 1751 treaty negotiations with the South Carolinians, the Raven celebrated the promise of reopened trade. "We are a poor people and can make nothing ourselves, nor have we anything but what we get from the white people," he stated. "We know we cannot be supplied with anything but what comes over the Great Water, from the Great King George," he continued. "We own we came here naked and now we go away well cloathed." By 1765, European commodities were necessities of survival for Cherokee villages, where so much social change had occurred that any young warrior "would [have] handle[d] a flint ax or any other rude utensil used by his ancestors very awkwardly."[52]

Cultural Articulation with the World System

The historical development of global capitalism among the Cherokees involved a societal thrust toward the commodification of everything. "In as much as capitalist commerce thrives upon systematization and efficiency, it abhors the nontechnical, irrational economic traits of precapitalist peoples, who must consequently be brought under the influence of the market and made to conform to its rules." Political and economic realignment around warfare and commercial hunting triggered a "falling-dominoes" effect within their cultural traditions.

The Commodification of Everything

Prior to white contact, the Cherokees had engaged in limited intertribal warfare, and hostilities had primarily erupted as short-term clan revenge by small numbers from a particular village. By the early 1700s, the Cherokees had taken on the European style of fighting, with emphasis upon fortified settlements, territorial expansion, mass annihilation, and the taking of prisoners to be sold as commodities on the world market. Small war parties and sudden raids gave way to political alliances with the British that necessitated the permanent restructuring of village governance around its warriors and around the use of guns. By the mid-eighteenth century, Cherokee warriors earned their status by retrieving runaway slaves or by collecting scalps of the enemies of the British. "A certain Number of Scalps [we]re required from the Hands of a young Indian before he c[ould] be honoured with the first military Title, which is a Slave-Catcher; and a certain Number more for the next higher Title, which is a Raven."[53]

The commercialization of hunting, "blood revenge," and slavery accompanied the commodification of war. Communal seasonal hunting was expanded into year-round production of deerskins for export, thereby disrupting the traditional rhythm of other economic activities and of village spiritual ceremonies. The tradition of clan revenge upon enemies who had harmed a clan member was displaced by the paying of a certain value of goods or deerskins. Beginning with the 1730 treaty, the Cherokees relinquished revenge customs to permit the British to punish both Cherokees and whites for crimes in their villages. By 1767, the British were settling Cherokee complaints about whites by making compensation of "500 wt. of half-dressed Deer Skins, or the value in goods for the death of a Relation," and this practice had been adopted by the Cherokees when dealing among themselves. Prior to European contact, the Cherokees had a sacred "town of refuge" where any violator could seek sanctuary. "Even a willful murderer who might succeed in making his escape to that town was safe so long as he remained there." After trade agreements were cemented, however, those seeking to escape the wrath of the British found no safety there. As soon as the offender got in view of the town, "the inhabitants discovered him by the close pursuit of the shrill war whoops; and for fear of irritating the English, they instantly answered the war cry, ran to arms, intercepted, and drove him off into Tennessee River."[54]

Until extensive contact with Europeans and the development of a market for war captives, slaves remained only a by-product of conflicts waged primarily for vengeance. Cherokee clans frequently adopted prisoners of war to replace kinsmen who had died, or captives could be ransomed by the enemies from whom they had been captured. In contrast to the Europeans, the Cherokees considered children of slave parents to be free and equal with other members of the clan. "Until the traders began exchanging goods for war captives, sufficient revenge appeased and pacified the warriors, but the value of the captives as saleable items meant that the frequency and extent of warfare increased." Once slavery was commercialized, the Cherokees engaged in war, "not in reprisal but to obtain slaves to exchange for the European goods without which they could no longer manage." One early-eighteenth-century clergyman reported that there was "no other necessity for those [Indian] Nations to Warr against their Neighbors but that of making slaves to pay for goods the traders sell them."[55]

Just as far-reaching in impact as the cultural redefinitions of warfare, slavery, and hunting was the commodification of trade. Prior to European linkages, the Cherokees engaged in only two types of trading: localized redistribution and long-distance exchange of rare products. Southeastern Indians were interconnected through itinerant traders who transported goods throughout the region. Because these Indian traders never engaged in warfare, they could move freely to transact exchanges. Precontact trade items significant to the Cherokees included corn, salt, copper, and decorative items. With its emphasis on exchanges of presents and little reliance on pricing, the precontact trading process was communal in nature. Upon a blanket spread for that purpose, the trader placed the item to be exchanged. Individual Indians came forward and placed whatever they could contribute until the trader accepted the communal total. During this process, women handled exchanges of food, clothing, and decorative items.[56]

After European linkages, trading developed as an individualized relationship rather than the communal activity it had once been. Because European trade was linked to political alliances, Cherokee hunters were also the warriors among the villages, and women were almost totally excluded from the fur-trading process. The development of trade relations with the Europeans restructured hunting from a part-time subsistence function into an endeavor for profit that became the central focus of most villages. Like hunting, agricultural production was also commodified. Beginning in the early 1700s, Cherokee women marketed agricultural surpluses to the British forts and to the traders. By 1750, Cherokee agriculture had been modified to reflect European patterns: larger parcels, intensive cultivation, abandonment of communal effort for individual farming, and the production of surplus livestock in the forests.[57]

Practically every aspect of Cherokee life was impacted by European trade. Spiritual customs gave way to expediency and efficiency. For example, the sacred wampum belts were now made of manufactured glass beads and came to represent money, in the eyes of the Europeans, rather than the archival records for which the Indians had made them. Cherokee tobacco was replaced with West Indian trade tobacco, and the ceremonial "black drink" of the Cherokees was rapidly displaced by trade rum. Conjurers, myth tellers, and musicians—who once received presents as tokens of respect—were paid for their services after European trading began.[58]

Burial practices also changed in the face of new European contacts. During epidemics, the dead were left unburied from fear of smallpox, a violation of ancient religious traditions. In the early years after trading linkages had been established, the Cherokees substituted European commodities for the traditional items left with the body after death. "All the . . . common people ha[d] vast quantities of all sorts of goods buried with them which [wa]s a great advantage to the merchants of South Carolina and especially to the Indian traders that trade[d] amongst them. . . . [The Cherokees were] of the opinion that the Soul [would] stay with the riches till it [wa]s consumed." This tradition of burying property with corpses ultimately gave way to inheritance practices, European fashion.[59]

Even traditional dress gave way to European fashions and fads. By the mid-1700s, most Cherokees were purchasing clothing and jewelry from the British traders. Deerskin coverings were replaced by manufactured woolens, ruffled shirts, calico, and broadcloth. "They that [could] afford it [wore] a collar of wampum . . . , a silver breast-plate, and bracelets on their arms and wrists of the same metal . . . a shirt of the English make . . . a large mantle or matchcoat." Similarly, Cherokee women's dress had "become very much like the European; and, indeed, that of the men [wa]s greatly altered."[60]

Ideological Dominance and Resistance to Cultural Hegemony

Significantly, the Europeans assumed that the process of getting the Cherokees to accommodate themselves to new cultural traditions would be much easier than in fact it was. In attempts to remain autonomous, the Cherokees played the three European powers off against one another; their towns sometimes capitalized upon the intense competition between South Carolina, Virginia, and Georgia. Cherokee emissaries frequently promised conciliatory actions, then purposely failed to comply. Despite the professed self-derision evident in British records of diplomatic meetings with them, the Cherokees were resistant to European infringement upon many of their traditions. When told in the 1720s of the benefits of Christianity over their spiritualism, a Cherokee priest responded sarcastically that "these white men that live amongst us a trading are more debauched and more wicked than the beatest of our young fellows. Is it not a shame for them that has such good priests and such knowledge as they have to be worse than the Indians that are in a manner but like wolves?"[61]

Relations with the Europeans fomented internal dissension among the Cherokees, with some factions almost always resistant to trade, war alliances, or land cessions. Disillusioned by the inability of recognized elites to resolve the crises that came in the wake of contact with the whites, some Cherokees reverted to traditionalism. "Dependence on the very agents who were also undermining their chances of survival produced among the [Cherokees] strong currents of ideological resistance," especially among the Overhill settlements. Between 1751 and 1761, a nativist movement centered at Tellico tried to return the Cherokees to their communal economy. Similarly, Chota's Little Carpenter warned that the European way of life was "a tree that may fall and bury [us] under it." Hard-core anti-British sentiment was reflected in the alignment of three Outtowns on the Tuckasegee River with the French-allied northern Indians. Dissidents attacked British forts, killed white traders, "broke open the Stores and divided the Goods," exacted blood revenge from white murderers, and harassed white squatters. Upon cession of present-day Kentucky lands about which the towns disagreed, dissident Dragging Canoe warned whites: "You have bought a fair land, but there is a cloud hanging over it. You will find its settlement dark and bloody."[62]

There were two main motives behind these enforced cultural changes: economic efficiency and political security for the Europeans. "If given persons were expected to perform in given ways in the economic arenas, it was efficient both to teach them the requisite cultural norms and to eradicate competing cultural norms." In short, it was believed that "if the so-called elites of peripheral areas were 'westernized', they would be separated from their 'masses', and hence less likely to revolt." Despite elements of antisystemic resistance among the Cherokees, the Europeans were successful at sustaining their ideological dominance. By dealing only with established elites, the British discredited and refused to receive other representatives. As the most influential class, the priest-elites served as the primary negotiators with the colonial governments. "Any hope that reaction against the new economic life might produce a revival of the ancient religion was undermined by the close identification of the ancient priestly class with the new commercialism." Commissions, medals, liquor, guns, and clothing were bestowed upon co-opted tribal leaders while "upstart" Cherokees who "did not know their place" were punished by being excluded or by seeing trade to their towns terminated. At 1721 treaty negotiations with the British, for example, little more than half the towns were represented when the British designated the first Cherokee supreme head, mandated trading methods, and fixed the boundary between the Cherokees and the colonists.[63]

For the Cherokees, trade was transformed from a friendly relationship among equals into an economic exchange in which the Indians were acculturated to idealize the British as having everything and to denigrate themselves as less favored by the Great Spirit. British paternalism cast the Cherokees into the role of "children of the King," who were reminded, during treaty negotiations, of the grim conditions of their civilization before contact with the Europeans. In 1751, for example, the South Carolina governor chastised recalcitrant warriors who were too young to remember existence before English trade. Consult your old men, he said, what was the Condition of your country at that Time, and compare it with your Circumstances now. Instead of the admirable Fire Arms that you are now plentifully supplied with, your best arms were bad Bows, and wretched Arrows headed with Bills of Birds, Bones of Fishes, or at best with sharp Stones. Instead of being decently or comfortably dressed in English Cloaths, you were forced to cover yourselves with the Skins of wild Beasts. Your knives were split Canes, and your Hatchets were of Stone, so that you spent more Days in felling a Tree, than you now do in minutes.[64]

British control over the Cherokees demanded "nothing short of the destruction of their culture and religion and their replacement by European civilization and Christianity."[65]

Environmental Articulation with the World System

Articulation with the European world economy also stimulated the depopulation of the Cherokees from epidemics, from slavery, from warfare, from famines, and from alcoholism. Between 1513 and 1672, southeastern Indians were devastated by European epidemics of malaria, measles, typhoid, Bubonic plague, typhus, mumps, influenza, and syphilis. When the Spanish made their first sixteenth-century expedition among the Cherokees, Coosa was a strong chiefdom stretching two hundred miles from present-day Knoxville into north-central Alabama; only twenty years after that first European contact, Coosa had disintegrated into a thinly populated province of poor Indians.[66]

Because they were concentrated in towns along the trails and waterways that became major trading routes, the Cherokees were highly susceptible to European diseases. Consequently, smallpox, influenza, and venereal diseases were the major causes of Cherokee population declines during the 1700s. As a result of the first smallpox epidemic in 1698, the Cherokee population had declined by two-thirds by 1700. A British historian reported in the early 1700s that "the Small-Pox and Rum have made such a Destruction amongst them that, on good grounds, I do believe, there is not the sixth Savage living within 200 Miles of all our Settlements, as there was Fifty Years ago."[67]

During the 1700s, a total of 93 epidemics spread among the southeastern Indians from the coastal European settlements, and a devastating disease was transmitted to the Indian towns about every four years. Because of their increased exposure to infectious illnesses to which they had no natural immunity and due to the greater frequency of warfare, the Cherokees enjoyed a life expectancy in the eighteenth century of only twenty-one years. In 1738 and 1740, for instance, two epidemics of smallpox were brought to Charleston by slave traders and subsequently conveyed to the Cherokees in trade goods.

More than half their population was decimated by the 1738 epidemic, and another one-fifth of the people were lost in 1740.[68]

During the French and Indian War, the Cherokees lost 5,000 people and one-half of their warriors; by 1765, two-thirds of the Cherokee warriors had died from epidemics or warfare. Reporting that he could "never remember to see any sickness" like the 1766 influenza epidemic, one diarist described how the illness raced through the settlements, killing greater numbers. In the mornings, he wrote, he "could hear nothing but the cries of women and children for the loss of their relations, in the evenings there are nothing to be seen but smoak and houses on fire, the dwellings of the deceased." Consequently, the Cherokee population declined by 90 percent during the eighteenth century, primarily from European-induced causes.[69]

Articulation with the capitalist world system also produced radical changes in Cherokee settlement patterns. Initially, the Cherokees were forced inland and southward into Southern Appalachia by the coastal settlements of the British in Charleston and Virginia. Prior to European contact, Southern Appalachia's residents were sedentary urban dwellers concentrated in palisaded villages. After European trade began, the Cherokees moved their settlements more often, becoming more nomadic due to the pressures to follow the abundant game, to escape diseases, and to deter attacks by other tribes.[70]

Wars, disease, colonial reprisals, encroachments, and the emergence of trade centers triggered the relocation of Cherokee towns. Population declines necessitated realignments and coalescing of populations into a smaller number of towns. Because of deaths from the 1738 epidemic, for instance, the Cherokees subsequently abandoned their northern Georgia settlements. The Cherokees also moved some towns to improve trade linkages and to be closer to British forts. "A gradual shift in the nature of Cherokee settlements began to occur soon after European contacts, as the geographic focal point for trade and communication with the colonists shifted from one division [of towns— i.e., Upper, Middle, or Overhills] to another."[71]

As the direct result of such disruptive forces, Cherokee settlements diminished in number from sixty towns in 1715 to thirty-nine towns in 1755. Not only did the pattern of Cherokee settlements alter after European contact, but also the nature of the structures forming them changed. After European contact, nucleated towns located along rivers were restructured into loosely grouped houses arranged in linear patterns. As the Cherokee populations became more and more dispersed in their land usage, towns diminished in size and complexity.[72]

Environmental Degradation

Just as disruptive as depopulation and resettlement was the environmental degradation that accompanied articulation of Cherokee society with the European world economy. Prior to their dependency upon European trading, the Cherokees exploited natural resources with great care and reverence. "The Cherokees had to kill deer for food, but they were careful to utter the appropriate prayers, and to kill only for necessity." Economic restructuring around commercial hunting meant the deterioration of that balanced relationship to the natural world, a dramatic shift that effected massive disruption of spiritual traditions. Before colonization, the Cherokees "made no use of the Skins of deer, and other beasts, than to cloath themselves, [consuming] their carcasses for Food, probably them being as much Value to them as the Skins." After the Indian trade was established, the use of guns allowed them to slaughter a much greater number of animals. "This destruction of deer and other animals being chiefly for the sake of their skins, a small part of the venison they kill[ed] suffice[d] them; the remainder [wa]s left to rot."[73]

As the result of such reckless slaughtering, buffalo were depleted in Southern Appalachia by the end of the first decade of the 1700s; deer were in short supply by the mid-1750s. While traveling in the Southern Appalachian backcountry in the late 1700s, Bartram found "the wild country now almost depopulated," except for "heaps of white gnawed bones of ancient buffalo, elk, and deer." Moreover, many Appalachian forests were burned annually to "alure the Deer upon the new Grass" and to support commercial agriculture. In similar fashion, the region's ginseng was depleted for trading on the world market. By the late 1700s, "ginseng ha[d] been so much sought by the Cherokee Indians for trade, that at th[at] time it [was] by no means so plenty as it used to be."[74]

Commodification of Land

Nevertheless, the most dooming articulation between Cherokee environment and European world system was the commodification of land that accompanied dependency upon capitalistic trading. Prior to European influences, the Cherokees did not have any conception of private ownership. Land was controlled by towns, and "ownership" was essentially a matter of occupancy. According to indigenous Cherokee traditions, "ownership" of hunting grounds was communal while "ownership" of house lots and planting fields was individual. Land within settlements passed through matrilinear lineage to the same families, and it was customary to rebuild houses and facilities on the same lots within the community. These tenure customs and Cherokee misunderstanding of treaty cessions facilitated British commodification of land. In their transactions with the Europeans, the Indians believed that they would always retain the privilege of free passage over the ceded land. Moreover, they thought land transfers would terminate with the death of the individual purchaser with whom they had negotiated.[75]

Because they valued their political alliance and export commodities more, at first the British regulated against white settlement on Indian lands. However, once colonists were established on the frontiers and forts were needed, Cherokee land became just as essential to the British as were their slaves and skins. Within little more than fifty years, the British extinguished Cherokee title to 57 percent (a total of 43,872,000 acres) of their ancestral lands through four land-grabbing tactics: (1) illegal squatting and speculating behind the treaty line between the colonists and the Indians; (2) repeated redrawing of the boundaries between the Cherokees and colonists; (3) threatening the Cherokees with the cessation of trade if land were not relinquished for the establishment of forts, stores, or white settlers; and (4) confiscation of lands in payment of trade debts.[76]

The British made early exploratory trips into the mountains in search of mineral wealth, and this 1689 letter indicates their early concern over an emerging international rivalry for control of this region: "I made a journey . . . over the Apalathean Mountains and took up seven sorts of ore or mineral stones. . . . On the same journey I was informed that the Spaniards had been at work within 20 miles of me. The natives described to me their bellows and furnaces and said they killed the Spaniards for fear they should make slaves of them to work in the mines as they had other Indians. . . . Reflecting upon the weakness of our colony and the report of a silver mine among us would incite the French in America, if not in Europe, to invade us."[77] The British were convinced that the Cherokees' "mountains contain[ed] very rich mines of gold, silver, lead, and copper . . . and many salt springs." Such official claims attracted farsighted speculators into Southern Appalachia. As early as 1735, white itinerant hunters had entrenched themselves on Cherokee lands throughout present-day Alabama, Georgia, the Carolinas, Tennessee, and Virginia. By 1750, colonists' farms and large plantations were multiplying rapidly on Cherokee hunting grounds. As a result, the boundary lines were renegotiated five times, culminating in the cession of 34,138,240 acres of Appalachian land to the British.[78]

It was the trading paths that opened the way for white hunter and settler encroachments on Southern Appalachian lands. In the treaties of 1721 and 1755, the Cherokees surrendered 7,205,120 acres to permit the building of trade factories and to cement trade agreements with the British. The Creeks even ceded land in exchange for lower trade prices. Once the Cherokees welcomed the British traders, hundreds of encroachers followed to situate farms and livestock on their trading paths. In a 1764 grievance to the governor of Virginia, a Cherokee chief complained that "encroachments were daily made upon them, notwithstanding the [1763] proclamation issued by the King to the contrary; that their hunting grounds, their only support, would be soon entirely ruined by the English; that frequent complaints had been made to the Governors to no purpose."[79]

Cherokee dependency upon British commodities necessitated other land cessions. On one such occasion, Chief Oconostota explained: "We considered the state of our debts justly due to our traders; & out of consideration of their forwardness to supply us with our necessary goods . . . as we were not able to pay them of all at once, and the Deer growing scarcer every year . . . we have therefore unanimously agreed with the consent of our young men to give our traders a tract of land to be enabled to support us further with our necessarys." Traders were interested in acquiring Appalachian lands for resale to settlers, as was the case in the British treaty of 1773 to which Oconostota refers. In their memorial to the Crown, the lucky traders argued that this Cherokee tract "would contain upwards of 3,000,000 acres of wonderful land, especially good for the culture of tobacco" that would be in demand by colonists from Virginia and North Carolina. Between 1765 and 1777, the Cherokees lost 2,528,640 acres (at the rate of the value of one matchcoat per 100 acres) for trading debts to Virginia, Georgia, and South Carolina.[80]

Summary

The period from 1600 to 1750 was dominated by the efforts of England and France first to destroy Dutch hegemony in the world system and then to succeed to the top position. During the long global economic contraction from 1600 to 1750, a major new peripheral region was absorbed into the capitalist world economy. This new periphery was the extended Caribbean, stretching from northeast Brazil to Maryland. Establishment of European settlements in Virginia, Carolina, and Georgia and the subsequent preemptive colonization of the Southern Appalachian hinterland ensued as part of the incorporation of this large external arena. After 1690, the incorporation of Southern Appalachia as a peripheral fringe of the British coastal colonies entailed three historical transformations: establishing political control over the indigenous people and their territory; securing initial Appalachian markets for British commodities; and exporting a European white settler class into Southern Appalachia to supervise the region's first "cash crop" production.[81]

When the European powers turned their attention to competition for the Ohio Valley and for the southeastern territories of North America, they sought to "checkmate" one another by establishing alliances with the inland peoples. By the early 1700s, Southern Appalachia formed a buffer zone between British settlements in Virginia and the French in the Ohio Valley and between British Carolina and Georgia, Spanish Florida, and the French entrenched in present-day Alabama and in the Mississippi Valley. Seeking to minimize contraction of their economic activities, England, France, and Spain competed intensely, partly by seeking preemptive control over the Indians of the American Southeast. The three European powers colonized the North American coastal areas and sought to keep each other from colonizing strategic inland areas like the Southern Appalachians. Because it was too expensive to seize the territory outright, the three powers instigated intertribal warfare in an attempt to weaken their rivals.[82]

In the sixteenth and seventeenth centuries, the core powers established contact and political domination over Southern Appalachia as an *external arena* of the European world system. During this contact period, production processes were not structurally altered, and little direct trade with the capitalist core occurred. Still, the Appalachian indigenes were depopulated by European epidemics, and their culture was inexorably disrupted. Subsequent deterioration of the region's strong chiefdoms laid the groundwork for easier future absorption of that zone into the capitalist world system. The European powers sought to hold "preemptive" control over this external arena for two key reasons. First, each of the colonial powers needed to effect political alliances with the Cherokees to prevent inland expansion or attack by the others. Second, the region was pinpointed in the sixteenth century as a potential source of the silver, gold, and other mineral wealth demanded to support further European imperialism.

Effective incorporation of the southern mountains did not begin until about twenty years after the founding of Charleston. Initially, the historical process was propelled by the capitalistic search for cheaper labor. Thus, Indian slaves were the first Southern Appalachian commodities to be marketed. When African slaves replaced Indian labor on the world market, Southern Appalachia provided raw materials to support core manufacturing and British re-export to the Orient. Once deerskins became essential to core leather manufacturing, the Cherokee economy underwent massive alteration of its relations of production to become restructured around export activity that was "part of the commodity chains of the capitalist world-economy." Moreover, the region became enmeshed via Charleston in the "triangular trade" that linked Europe, the West Indies, Africa, and the North American colonies.[83]

Incorporation necessitated a reorientation of preexisting subsistence patterns and the creation of new economic activities geared toward commodity production, market exchanges, and the creation of surplus. In the wake of this global process, Southern Appalachia's communal mode of production was displaced by the deerskin trade, a putting-out system financed by foreign merchant-entrepreneurs. Once external trade goods displaced subsistence activities, traditional crafts were "deindustrialized," cementing their economic subordination. To finance their importation of European commodities, the Cherokees increased their deerskin production, thereby intensifying their debt peonage. Relentlessly, the Cherokees were locked into an "unequal exchange" that drained Appalachian surpluses away to benefit the expanding core. Within less than fifty years, the Cherokees lost economic and political autonomy and became dependent upon the worldwide network of production.[84]

During the eighteenth century, a prime response by Cherokee villages to the need to meet debt obligations for survival commodities was to increase deerskin output for market disposal. Establishment and continuation of this type of relationship with the capitalist market entailed far more than simply increasing surpluses. Economic articulation with the world system brought about dramatic political and cultural transformations in Cherokee society. As export production was entrenched, there emerged new hunting and warfare techniques and an altered division of labor within the household and within the village. Despite resistance movements, the British were ideologically dominant, and few Cherokee cultural traditions were left unchanged. The British coerced the indigenous society toward secular and national governance, eventuating in the "tribal half-government" that permitted the Europeans to treat the Cherokees as a unified corporate entity. As Cherokee households were reshaped around export activities, communal labor arrangements were replaced by a new sexual bifurcation of tasks. Cherokee males were primarily engaged in export activities while the women were left responsible for subsistence production.[85]

Articulation with the European world system also generated a dramatic impact upon the Cherokee environment. Due to warfare and epidemics, the Cherokee population declined by 90 percent during the 1700s. Moreover, the numerous Cherokee urban settlements had degenerated into dispersed, isolated farmsteads by the beginning of the nineteenth century. Wildlife was decimated by export activities, and forests were destroyed as part of the hunting process. Most significant, however, was the alteration of land tenure arrangements to guarantee individual property rights to white settlers. By 1780, the Cherokees had lost nearly three-fifths of their ancestral lands to cement trade agreements, to pay trader debts, and to settle boundary disputes with the British.

3

SETTLERS, SPECULATORS, AND SQUATTERS:

COMPETITION FOR APPALACHIAN LAND

RESOURCES, 1790–1860

Prerequisites for Capitalist Incorporation

Capitalist expansion does not proceed equitably or peacefully, for people are often culturally and spiritually anchored on the land in ways they are not attached to any other element of the production process (including their own labor). Initially, the commodification of land requires severing the powerful connections between indigenous peoples and their ancestral homes, followed by public policies that circumvent their "legal rights" to compete with new settlers for use of the soil. Dramatic changes in land tenure necessitate bloody displacements of peoples who had previously been producing their livelihoods on the frontiers of the world economy. In Southern Appalachia, settler capitalism could not advance until several Native American groups had been displaced.

Displacement of Native Americans

The British Proclamation Line of 1763 marked the watershed of the Appalachian Mountains as the limits for white resettlement. Areas west of the line were reserved as Indian hunting grounds, and families who had "inadvertently seated themselves upon any lands . . . reserved to the Indians" were ordered "to remove themselves from such settlements." Because Tidewater elites speculated in lands beyond this line as early as the 1740s, permanent settlements had already been established too far west along the Virginia frontier. However, these engrossers were not deterred by such bureaucratic constraints. For example, George Washington surmised that the proclamation was nothing more than "a temporary expedient to quiet the minds of the Indians." He admonished his peers that "any person, therefore, who neglects the present opportunity of hunting out good lands, and in some measure marking and distinguishing them for his own (in order to keep others from settling them), will never regain them."[1]

Virginia, North Carolina, and Georgia titled Indian lands to speculators and to war veterans long before cessions had been negotiated. Land companies engaged in their own treaty meetings and made illegal acquisition agreements. In the face of royal edicts against private claims of Indian lands, the Transylvania Company arranged the lease-purchase of 20,000,000 acres of Cherokee lands located in present-day Kentucky, Tennessee, and North Carolina. After the heads of the Loyal and Greenbrier companies were appointed as boundary commissioners at the 1770 treaty of Lochaber, the new line was run far enough west to clear 800,000 company acres in West Virginia for resale and resettlement. The Ohio Company of Virginia even attempted to weaken Cherokee control over their lands by extending "them Credit for [goods] in the Companies Store." Between 1763 and 1773, settlers engrossed 4,545,908 acres from the indigenous peoples. By the end of the eighteenth century, Cherokee territory had been diminished by nearly 60 percent.[2]

Restructuring Feudalistic Land Tenure

In addition to the extermination of indigenous peoples, capitalist incorporation hinges upon the contractualization of land tenure into forms that permit individual wealth accumulation and demographic growth. Settler capitalism could not expand into Southern Appalachia until the remnants of feudalistic European landholding institutions had been transformed to permit market trading. Under the colonial headright and quitrent systems, land was not patented to individuals in fee simple ownership but was burdened with escheat, alienation fines and perpetual annual rents. Tenancies for three lives were common; and, in European fashion, the sheriffs collected rents for a 10 percent commission. Large grants were made only to persons of British or Irish descent, and settlements of non-Anglican ethnic groups were closely regulated. Moreover, land claimants were required to be owners of five servants or slaves.[3]

When it proved too costly to induce repopulation on land granted for importing settlers (headright), the proprietaries began to sell large holdings. Subsequently, the land disposal process was increasingly controlled by Virginia and Maryland Legislative Councils, and the land companies became "united in a sort of gigantic, loose, yet interlocking corporation" of speculators.[4]

Land engrossment had been deterred by the earlier headright requirement that grantees resettle hundreds of people; thus, transformation of land tenure made possible new profits and wealth accumulation. Because short-term tenancy and direct ownership were more appealing to poorer emigrants, abatements from quitrents attracted new customers for the land companies. The market was further enlarged once the land syndicates were successful in eliminating restrictions upon nonslaveholders, religious groups, and eastern Europeans. In 1753, the Ohio Company of Virginia advertised for German settlers, affirming that "A large Accession of foreign Protestants will not only be advantageous to this Colony but the most effectual method of promoting a speedy Settlement on the Ohio." As to their civil rights, the company guaranteed that they would "be entitled to Naturalization which will be attended with all the Priviledges and Advantages of English natural born Subjects." Moreover, they promised that "all foreign protestants coming to Settle West of our Great Mountains" would be exempted "from paying Levies of all kinds for the term of ten Years from their Settlement." In these ways, the land syndicates hastened the incorporation of Southern Appalachia into the world economy. As their visions of geographic empires broadened, planter-capitalists lobbied for restructuring of public control over land tenure to stimulate "an increase of population, extension of the market, and exploration of new and latent resources."[5]

Land Speculation on the Southern Appalachian Frontier

Southern Appalachia was never a unified frontier; in reality, the region was resettled in the four major historical stages depicted in Map 3.1. Before the 1763 Proclamation Line was mandated, repopulation was underway in the Blue Ridge and Shenandoah Virginia, the eastern and Ohio River fringes of West Virginia, northwestern South Carolina, and western Maryland. In a second phase, upper East Tennessee, the northwestern tip of North Carolina, and the area around Madison County, Kentucky, were repeopled between 1770 and 1789. In the flurry of post-Revolutionary expansion, emigrants flowed into East Kentucky, the Cumberland Plateau of middle Tennessee, the middle sector of western North Carolina, and the western side of West Virginia. Additional areas opened for resettlement after the 1819 cession of Cherokee lands in southwestern North Carolina, southeastern Tennessee, and northern Alabama. The final era of resettlement did not occur until the later 1830s—after the forced removal from Southern Appalachia of the remaining Native Americans.[6]

No Public Domain in Southern Appalachia

Except for the remaining small enclave of Cherokee settlements, Southern Appalachia's lands were privatized before the public domain and federal land policy had been formulated. Virginia, Georgia, and the Carolinas had refused to ratify the Articles of Confederation until they were assured their inland holdings would not become part of the new country's public domain. As Map 3.2 illustrates, westward movement into the Appalachian frontiers involved

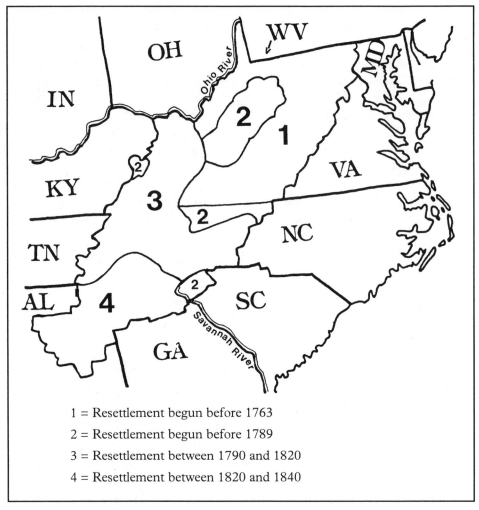

Map 3.1. The Repeopling of Southern Appalachia, 1740–1840

1 = Resettlement begun before 1763
2 = Resettlement begun before 1789
3 = Resettlement between 1790 and 1820
4 = Resettlement between 1820 and 1840

military bounties, grants, and sales to individuals by those four states. More-over, the federal laws designed to establish the rights of small homesteaders and squatters came too late to benefit Appalachia's poorer landless emigrants; the Midwest was the first frontier to be impacted by nationally regulated land policies. Before 1820 the regulations for the sale of public lands affected only about one-fourth of the people who were engaged in the westward movement. Of the settlers west of the Appalachians in 1820, "fully one half had taken up lands in regions which had never come under the federal land system."[7]

By the mid-1700s, a few of the wealthiest Tidewater planters and British court favorites had expropriated much of the Valley of Virginia and western Maryland. By the 1730s, Blue Ridge Virginia and much of present-day West

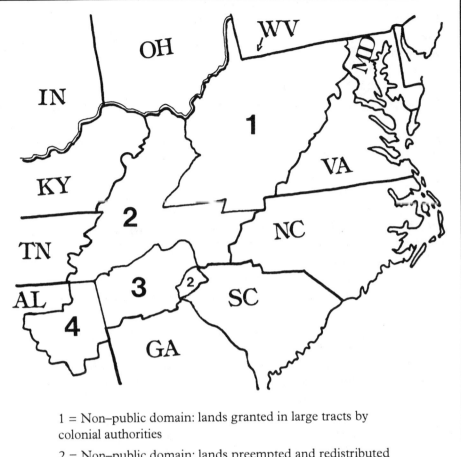

1 = Non–public domain: lands granted in large tracts by colonial authorities

2 = Non–public domain: lands preempted and redistributed through post-Revolutionary grants or sales by Virginia and the Carolinas

3 = Non–public domain: Indian lands redistributed by Tennessee, North Carolina, and Georgia

4 = Public domain: lands sold through federal Huntsville Land Office after 1819

Map 3.2. Disposal of the Lands of Southern Appalachia

Virginia had been carved into large estates. The Ohio Company absorbed a large slice of the remaining frontier by negotiating a Crown grant for 500,000 West Virginia acres. The Greenbrier Company and the Loyal Company engrossed more than 300,000 acres in eastern West Virginia and southwestern Virginia. During the 1740s, Tidewater merchants and planters gained control of more than three-quarters of the surveyed lands in western Maryland. Practically every Maryland Tidewater elite speculated in that state's Appalachian lands. In western North Carolina, a few Virginia Tidewater planter families, the Loyal Company, and the Henderson Company engrossed much of the northern sector.[8]

Absentee Engrossment on the Southern Appalachian Frontier

By 1800, absentee landholders owned three-quarters of the total acreage reported in county tax lists (see Table 3.1). In Virginia and West Virginia, little acreage was left for residents. After 1790, distant speculators gobbled up more than 90 percent of the lands when the Virginia Assembly began to sell its frontier areas at very cheap prices. In 1793, the Virginia Treasury was peddling Appalachian lands for an average of two cents per acre. The effect of selling at below-market valuations was to stimulate distant brokerage-house trading in Virginia Treasury warrants. Even in the 1780s, James Madison had queried "Why did not the Assembly stop the sale of land warrants?" Such government activity was dangerous, he warned because "They bring no profit to the public Treasury, are a source of constant speculation on the ignorant, and will finally arm numbers of Citizens of other States & even foreigners with claims and clamors against the faith of Virginia." He was particularly disturbed that "Immense quantities ha[d] from time to time been vended . . . at immense profit" in Philadelphia and Boston.[9]

After Virginia opened its western lands for sale in 1792, the state sold 2,590,059 acres to just fourteen speculators. In 1794, the state Treasury disposed of 8,000,000 Appalachian acres, and the state Land Office received an average of 620 new surveys per week. Within less than five years, Virginia's flooding of northeastern markets with these cheap warrants had thrown its Appalachian lands "into the hands of a few individuals."[10]

By examining land grants made in this era, it is possible to assess the extent to which the Virginia frontier was falling into the hands of settlers. The absentee landholders in three West Virginia counties were predominantly speculators from other states who were seeking to amass mineral holdings. The greatest level of distant speculation and the largest grants occurred in mountainous Randolph County, where nine-tenths of the lands were reallocated to absentees who averaged 21,980 acres each. Only slightly less distant trading was directed toward the other two counties. In the ridge-valley county of Hampshire, more than three-quarters of the land area was engrossed by absentee owners. Similarly, seven-tenths of hilly Monongalia County was monopolized by nonresidents, more than half the land area being controlled by out-of-state speculators.[11]

Because the region's most intense speculation occurred in the frontiers that had been shaped by the land policies of Virginia, East Kentucky also experienced high levels of engrossment. It is likely that absentee ownership of East Kentucky lands was even higher than the 56 percent reflected in Table 3.1, for

Table 3.1. Absentee Engrossment of Southern Appalachian Lands, 1790–1810

Appalachian Counties of	Acres Owned			
	Residents		Absentees	
	No. acres	%	No. acres	%
Kentucky	56,855.5	43.8	72,961.0	56.2
Maryland	169,795.9	67.1	83,410.0	32.9
North Carolina	237,914.5	57.1	178,676.0	42.9
South Carolina	48,824.5	48.0	52,852.0	52.0
Tennessee	120,368.3	31.1	266,201.0	68.9
Virginia	328,994.5	10.7	2,757,465.3	89.3
West Virginia	324,388.5	6.7	4,525,153.0	93.3
Region	12,526,649.8	24.1	39,451,150.2	75.9

Source: Derived from analysis of county tax lists; see Table A.1 for sampling details.

local courthouse officials often colluded with distant speculators to have their tax records "disappear." One gubernatorial assessment points out that the major weakness of the state's nineteenth-century tax system was that "much land of non-residents [was] not listed." By the end of the 1700s, one-quarter of the entire area of Kentucky had been claimed by twenty-one land barons. Northeastern land mongers were pouring into East Kentucky to buy discounted Virginia military and treasury warrants for resale at distant brokerage houses. Since nearly 80 percent of East Kentucky's land claims were made by absentee speculators, three-quarters or more of East Kentucky's frontier lands were probably held by absentees.[12]

In 1783, North Carolina threw open its own western sector and the lands of Tennessee for purchase at very cheap prices. Shortly, land jobbers began a speculative rampage that resulted in the disposal of 4,000,000 acres within seven months. In Tennessee, absentee merchant-investors, land companies, and distant planters amassed nearly seven-tenths of the Appalachian lands (see Table 3.1). Territorial Governor William Blount and his family had expectations of financial windfalls on the expanding frontiers. One Blount brother, an eastern Carolina planter and shipping magnate, effected a virtual monopoly in the acquisition of North Carolina and Tennessee state warrants; he subsequently resold 1,184,460 Appalachian acres in the Northeast and in Europe. By 1795, the Blounts owned large sections of upper East Tennessee.[13]

Soon after the Revolutionary War, a few absentee speculators monopolized all the available lands in western North Carolina. Kept by a northern land speculator during his travels through western North Carolina, John Brown's 1795 business journal provides unique insights into the techniques utilized by absentee investors to engross the southern mountains. The "spirit of spec-ewlation" was pandemic in North Carolina's small towns and courthouses, and the Philadelphia capitalist engaged in land trades with nearly every social or political acquaintance, with each "Confab on the Business" pointing him to additional contacts. In less than three wintry weeks, John Brown "Procured near five hundred thousand Acrs" in Buncombe, Burke, and Wilkes Counties. State assemblymen and county surveyors were bribed to manage paper-work favorably and to delay fees, but "keep it secret." The State Treasurer even forewarned him to hasten his filings in order to circumvent stricter regulations to be enacted by an impending new law. When other tactics did not produce quick results, Brown even tried to convince a Buncombe County official to "sell his place as surveyor" to a more cooperative crony.[14]

The earliest grants in 1787 were to North Carolina planter-officials for all the best agricultural lands in Buncombe, Burke, and Rutherford Counties. In the early 1790s, the Blounts acquired half the land area of Madison, Yancey, and Buncombe Counties. Forty absentee speculators engrossed the entire land area of present-day McDowell County. Eastern mineral speculators William Cathcart and George Latimer agglomerated all of Mitchell and Avery Counties and most of Jackson County while several Philadelphia merchant-investors accumulated thousands of acres east and west of the Blue Ridge. In addition, North Carolina planter families and state officials invested their own money and that of eastern backers in huge tracts, embracing much of present-day Haywood, Jackson, Swain, and Macon Counties.[15]

These engrossers paid only fifty shillings to one pound per 100 acres for western North Carolina holdings. Subsequently, they resurveyed their plats into smaller parcels, advertised in eastern cities, and sold farms at consider-able profit. Due to the insider monopolizing techniques of such capitalists, it is likely that much more than the 43 percent of western North Carolina territory reflected in Table 3.1 remained in the hands of absentee holders in the early 1800s. Nonstate investors are probably underrepresented in these early tax lists due to their evasive and illegal tactics. In order to sidestep North Carolina's residency laws, speculative claims were registered in the names of local agents. For example, Philadelphia capitalist John Brown paid several locals to make entries in their own names for more than 1,133,000 acres.[16]

Because of its Tugaloo River access to the Savannah River and the coast, the northwestern tip of South Carolina also attracted external interest. There absentee speculators amassed more than half the Appalachian acreage (see Table 3.1). By analyzing 374 early deeds of this area, it is possible to specify more closely how frontier land transfers were transacted. Less than one-half (174) of the 1789–1792 deeds were made between resident buyers and sellers; however, 200 (53.5 percent) of the deeds were made to absentees. In nearly one-third of the transactions, residents made deeds to absentees; another one-fifth of the land sales were paper trading between distant buyers and sellers.

Only 4 of the deeds represented estate settlements, and all of these transferred the land to nonresidents, not to local family heirs; 2 of the deeds resulted from public auctions of land to settle unpaid debts or taxes, a favored technique by which frontier speculators amassed holdings cheaply. In sharp contrast, only 22 (5.9 percent) were transactions in which absentee sellers passed lands to actual settlers. Clearly, speculators controlled such hinterland markets; acreage was filtering down very slowly to resident farmers; and there was little evidence that local family members were inheriting land.[17]

Speculation in Antebellum Towns

In addition to their engrossment of large tracts, absentee speculators and local elites also incited a furor of investment in boom towns. Contrary to contemporary stereotypes, roads and towns came first on the Appalachian frontiers, and they were patterned after European market villages with a grid layout around public buildings. Even from the early frontier years, every county of the region had one to five small villages or towns, and these were the hubs from which the adjacent rural hinterlands were gradually populated by streams of resettlers. In fact, the region's earliest towns were created out of the entrepreneurial imaginations of capitalists in search of profits. Much of the speculative fervor of the early 1800s was directed to the organization of joint-stock town companies. One regional newspaper observed that "There is an astonishing rage at the present day for the establishment of new towns. Does a man possess a tract of land convenient to river navigation, if he be a man of enterprise, he starts the plan of a town—lays off his land into lots, and expects to make his fortune by selling out. . . . It is in this way that towns are springing up in every thriving section of the country; some of them generated by the spirit of improvement, but others, it is to be apprehended, by that of speculation." In effect, these early towns were public monopolies, authorized by legislative enabling acts but operated for the benefit of the speculators.[18]

Southern Appalachian towns were laid out for one of several profit-making ventures. On the frontiers, village forts were established to secure the safety of settlers and to serve as travel termini. Towns were also laid out to spur repopulation of certain geographical areas. Asheville, Canton, and Waynesville were created when North Carolina granted 200-acre town tracts to individual speculators and their "heirs and assigns forever." In fact, most of the early towns in Southern Appalachia were laid out to attract new settlers and to speed up the sale of adjacent agricultural lands. In addition, towns like Strasburg, Virginia, or Shepherdstown, West Virginia, were established to attract specific ethnic groups—like the Germans—to settle in the region.[19]

A township might also be laid out to initiate a local government center, a market, a store, or a transportation terminus. Most county seats were also the central markets, slave-auction blocks, and post offices for their hinterlands. In all nine Southern Appalachian states, county seats were the focal points for mandated agricultural markets and annual fairs. This legislation provided the basis for land speculators to accumulate wealth, not only from their investment in lots, but also from fees associated with commerce. For instance, land engrosser Daniel Dulaney laid out a western Maryland town in 1745 to recruit artisans and professionals. Three years later, the speculator lobbied the formation of a new county with its courthouse at his town. In addition to perpetual rents on 340 rectangular lots, Dulaney collected road tolls and stallage fees at weekly markets "for buying & Selling all sorts of Cattle & other Provisions of every kind."[20]

To capitalize on geographical locations at or near navigable streams, early legislation authorized the creation of many Appalachian towns, like Harpers Ferry, West Virginia, or Cumberland, Maryland, as multipurpose defense, transportation, and commercial centers. Similarly, an 1816 speculator "Laid out a Town" in Allegany County, Maryland, "Just on the Bank of the River & directly on the Turnpike road which he calls Smythfield and is now disposing of Lots some of them he says sells at $250 which is one quarter of an Acre & fronting on the road." The land jobber exclaimed to his clients, "Baltimoreans Looke, Land Selling in the Middle of the Allegany Mountains @ $1000 pr Acre!"[21]

Finally, some towns boomed as part of commercial or industrial promotions. Hagerstown, Maryland, and Staunton, Virginia, were developed around the milling industry. Crowsville, Virginia, was initially laid out as a warehouse for the reception and inspection of tobacco for export. In Frederick County, Virginia, four towns were spaced by speculators to form a commercial belt; as a result, Winchester, Kernstown, Stephensburg, and Middle Town became nuclei for the sale of goods and services associated with the export of wheat. The towns of Florence and Rocky Mount in Virginia were developed around iron works while Saltville and Big Lick (Roanoke) in Virginia and Charleston in West Virginia were founded to capitalize on salt manufacturing. Dahlonega, Georgia, was laid out as a gold-mining district; and Sewanee, Tennessee, emerged as an antebellum coal-mining village. Some towns were developed as resorts for wealthy planters, such as Lexington, Virginia; Warm Springs, North Carolina; Clarkesville, Georgia; Berkeley, West Virginia; and Winchester, Tennessee.[22]

The economic centrality of these frontier towns is reflected in the level of absentee speculation. In the early nineteenth century, nearly one-half of the town lots of each Appalachian zone were owned by nonresidents; the rest were overwhelmingly concentrated into the hands of resident elites. Thus, Appalachian town lots were a source of steady rental income for their owners. Typical of this pattern were two northern Georgia towns. In Clarkesville, Georgia, more than two-fifths of the lots were purchased by absentees when the town was laid out in 1823. In 1832, Etowah, Georgia, was established as an iron-manufacturing village; less than two decades later, the entire town was sold for $450,000. As a result of such intense speculation, the prices of town lots increased at a much faster rate than the cost of nearby agricultural lands.[23]

Who Were the Appalachian Speculators?

Obviously, land exchanges did not take place apart from competitive markets. Who, then, were the speculators? Map 3.3 provides a summary map of the regional speculator activity by northeastern merchant-investors, land syndicates, and southern planters. Extensive absentee speculation occurred in every geographical zone of the region, and ten national land syndicates engrossed large tracts in every sector except the Appalachian counties of Georgia, Maryland, and South Carolina. In addition, Tidewater elites accumulated large holdings in the Appalachian counties of Maryland, Virginia, North Carolina, Tennessee, Georgia, South Carolina, and Alabama. Thus, Appalachian acreage was overwhelmingly concentrated in the hands of out-of-state investors.

To pinpoint more closely the types of profiteers who invested in the westward expansion of Southern Appalachia, I made a genealogical search to categorize the absentee landholders identified in the frontier tax lists (see Table 3.2). Even though heirs to small holdings made up the greater number of absentee holders, they owned less than one-tenth of the total land area held by nonresidents. Instead, distant merchants, planters, and investors in large holdings monopolized more than nine-tenths of the absentee acreage. Southern Appalachian lands were owned by some of the country's wealthiest land barons, including Henry Banks, Francis and William Deakins, Jonathan De-Witt, Standish Ford, Michael Gratz, Robert Morris, Wilson Nicholas, James Swann, William Tilton, and Alexander Walcott. Since northeastern speculators were particularly oriented toward mineral tracts near river access, they controlled nearly three-fourths of the total absentee acreage of Virginia, West Virginia, and Tennessee. Regionally based merchants and planters were particularly active in East Kentucky and western Maryland; however, northeastern capitalists engrossed more Appalachian acreage than any other absentee group.[24]

Why, then, were these distant investors so eager to accumulate Appalachian frontier acreage? Since they believed these areas would be the crossroads for commerce, eighteenth-century investors like George Washington and Albert Gallatin believed that property values along the Ohio River and in Kentucky would escalate rapidly after the Revolutionary War. Thus, elites in adjacent counties accumulated sizeable holdings for speculative trading in rental properties and to operate absentee-owned plantations. In sharp contrast to the conventional view that there was "little in Appalachia to attract capitalist development," the country's 1810 iron manufacturing and salt production were concentrated in Southern Appalachia. Moreover, the country's first gold rush fed the national Treasury from the hills of Georgia, North Carolina,

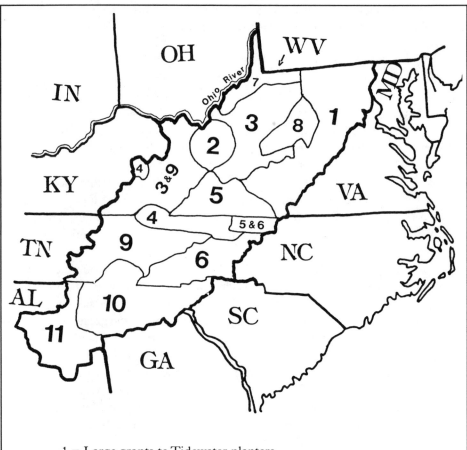

1 = Large grants to Tidewater planters

2 = Large grants to British Louisa Company

3 = Ohio Company, North American Land Company

4 = Transylvania Company, Henderson and Associates

5 = Loyal Company and Ohio Company

6 = North Carolina elites and eastern capitalists

7 = Vandalia Company

8 = Greenbrier Company

9 = Tidewater Virginia and North Carolina planters and eastern capitalists

10 = Georgia and South Carolina planter speculation

11 = Yazoo and North American Land Companies

Map 3.3. Speculative Land Syndicates in Southern Appalachia, 1750–1840

Table 3.2. Who Speculated in Southern Appalachian Lands?:
Analysis of Absentee Landholdings, 1790–1810

Appalachian Counties of	Average Absentee Holding (Acres)	Investment Capitalists[a]		Distant Planter Capitalists[b]	
		Acres	%	Acres	%
Kentucky	1,463	17,031.0	23.6	5,934.0	8.2
Maryland	153	23,444.0	28.1	6,971.0	8.3
North Carolina	730	42,553.5	23.8	96,294.3	53.9
South Carolina	359	18,545.5	35.1	13,129.2	24.8
Tennessee	1,626	187,594.0	70.5	30,800.0	11.6
Virginia	3,237	2,211,000.5	80.2	33,095.0	1.2
West Virginia	5,485	3,087,025.0	68.2	1,187,626.5	26.2

Appalachian Counties of	Adjacent Area Merchants and Planters[c]		Small Investors and Heirs[d]		Total Absentee Acres
	Acres	%	Acres	%	
Kentucky	42,828.0	59.3	6,396.0	8.9	72,189
Maryland	47,351.0	56.8	5,644.0	6.8	83,410
North Carolina	38,340.0	21.5	1,488.3	0.8	178,676
South Carolina	21,177.3	40.1	000.0	0.0	52,852
Tennessee	29,770.0	11.2	18,037.0	6.7	266,201
Virginia	508,531.2	18.4	4,838.3	0.2	2,757,465
West Virginia	206,250.0	4.6	44,251.5	1.0	4,525,153

Source: Derived from analysis of county tax lists; see Table A.1 for sampling details. Sixty-one local history sources and genealogical lists were utilized to identify and categorize absentee owners.
[a]Includes northeastern capitalists and land companies.
[b]Planters residing in other states.
[c]Planters and merchants residing in non-Appalachian counties of the states where their landholdings were located.
[d]Nonresident heirs of properties previously held by residents and nonresident holders of single parcels of small size.

Virginia, and Tennessee. The nation's only supply of manganese was mined in Appalachian Virginia, and coal, lead, and copper were being exported from the mountain South by 1820. By 1860, some of the country's most heavily capitalized extractive industries were situated in Southern Appalachia where company towns averaged 30,000 acres and hundreds of laborers.[25]

In addition to the pursuit of mineral lands, absentee investors quickly recognized the profitability of summer mountain resorts. By 1800, several well-known Appalachian mineral springs had become summer meccas for planter elites, European tourists, and northeastern city dwellers. By 1830, Southern Appalachia's wealthiest commercial enterprises were 134 mineral spas sprinkled all over the region. Moreover, hundreds of boom towns attracted a frenzy of absentee speculation. For example, William Blount proposed the joint development with a New York capitalist of a 150-mile-square city adjoining Knoxville; lots for the new city of Palmyra were to be sold only in Europe.[26]

Early-nineteenth-century trading in Southern Appalachian lands evolved into an interlocking, systematic network in which distant speculators utilized several levels of international, national, and regional marketing strategies. Distant exchanges were facilitated by brokerage houses in Richmond, Philadelphia, Washington, D.C., New York, and Boston. For resale and margin trading, these firms bought *at discount* state land grants, military warrants, and land company stock. Several eastern capitalists, like Robert Morris of the North American Land Company, engaged in the practice of dodging, by which lands were sold in Europe before acreage was actually acquired on Appalachian frontiers.[27]

To manage their far-flung investments, financiers engaged several layers of petty capitalists. Hired on commission, land jobbers—like Daniel Boone or Uria Brown—set out to the frontiers "on the business of speculating on military land warrants." In local newspapers they advertised to buy "a few thousand acres of military land warrants, for which the highest price will be given." In addition to evaluating, optioning, and selling land, jobbers supervised surveys, contested squatter claims, paid taxes, bribed courthouse officials, and managed annual tenancy agreements.[28]

In dealing with the adverse claims of small West Virginia homesteaders in the early 1800s, Brown demonstrated the crucial role played by antebellum real estate middlemen. Land jobbers protected the interests of distant engrossers against settlers and squatters who lacked political connections and legal sophistication. In order to safeguard his clients' West Virginia holdings, Brown determined to "Appear solid & firm & presist in Establishing the rights of Lands that my friend Jn Trimble [a Baltimore capitalist] claims; as the Tuffest skin shall hold out the Longest; & surveys on surveys is there nee Deep and deeper."[29]

Three types of resident professionals were also crucial to the land speculation process. Local attorneys often contracted with parties holding military warrants to "carry the claim into grant," the legal fee being one-half the land. In addition, lawyers settled adverse claims and managed the lands of absentee heirs. Some frontier lawyers, like David Goff or Lewis Maxwell of West Virginia, amassed their own estates by utilizing "insider" information about absentee claims. For example, Maxwell allowed the taxes on a client's lands to become delinquent; then he bought them at public auction. He responded to subsequent complaints by countering, "I cannot act as agent for you to pay taxes on the land you claim. The same land was sold to me . . . and I have a deed for it. I have paid the taxes thereon and have tenants now in possession of the land."[30]

Surveyors, like George Washington and William Calk, reconnoitered newly opened frontiers to identify investments for absentee financiers. To make Appalachian holdings more profitable, they laid off large tracts into farm parcels that combined cultivable acreage with sections that ran "to the top of them mountains." Seeing no conflict with their public duties, county surveyors routinely offered their services to large landholders. For instance, the public surveyor for Lewis County, West Virginia, advertised his services to one absentee land baron, assuring him that he made "a business of hunting up land and surveying it on commission for men liveing at a distance."[31]

Courthouse officials sought to make their own fortunes by engaging in land ventures. Local "discoverers" were employed to select, procure at discount, and survey military warrants. In this manner, John May amassed a vast empire in East Kentucky lands while serving as court clerk of Jefferson County. When land jobber Uria Brown complained about the large bill for delinquent taxes on an absentee parcel of 50,000 acres, the court clerk of Harrison County, West Virginia, offered "for $150.00 . . . to get a Law passed by the Legislature of Virginia to strike off all the taxes." In the case of Alexander Quarrier, public corruption was even more aggressively proffered. While Kanawha County tax assessor, Quarrier served absentee engrossers by arranging for their delinquent taxes to "disappear" from public records. For example, he wrote to land baron Eugene Levassor that "the Sheriff is always in my debt . . . but recollect his list of delinquent lands are every year returned to me, and it is my duty to certify copies of these delinquents to the auditors at Richmond; of course your lands are not on this list. And the best evidence that the taxes are paid is that they are not returned delinquent. And I beg you to be assured that so long as I live your interests here shall suffer in nothing that I can avert."[32]

Land barons, like Eugene Levassor, followed the practice of selecting "an agent in each county where the land lies." For one-third commission and expenses, local merchants and planters handled sales and collected rents. Even wage laborers engaged in land speculation. Tenants were employed to move to the frontier to "seat" large holdings and prepare the land for occupancy by a subsequent purchaser. Without settling on the land, outlyers made the legally required improvements on the speculator's holdings. To enlarge the boundaries of their newly surveyed claims, jobbers even hired local people to "destroy the Corners of Unseated Lands."[33]

Land Ownership Patterns in
Southern Appalachia, 1790–1810

Through their land-engrossing strategies, distant merchant-investors, absentee planters, and local elites choreographed—rather clumsily—the advancing resettlement of Southern Appalachia. Exacerbated by official collusion with absentee engrossers, the morass of overlapping titles slowed repopulation of Southern Appalachian frontiers. In an 1816 report, Kentucky's auditor lamented that Kentucky's land titling was dangerously haphazard. Nonresidents had sold and resold lands to settlers without transferring deeds, then the state confiscated such resident-held lands when the absentee sellers failed to pay taxes. One early-nineteenth-century land jobber predicted the two-century-long litigation that would ensue from hastily drawn boundaries and multiple titling. Uria Brown prophesied correctly that "titles in Kentucky would be Disputed for a Centry to Come yet, when it was an old Settled Country."[34]

How Land Engrossment Deterred Settlement

Absentee speculators systematically engaged in profit-oriented tactics that bypassed small homesteaders or kept prices out of their reach. In 1810, the population density was lowest in those geographical zones where absentee speculators controlled the greatest proportion of the land area. Consequently, the repopulation of Virginia-controlled frontier areas lagged behind that of the rest of the region. Even though emigration began there fifty years later, the Appalachian counties of North Carolina, Tennessee, and South Carolina were repopulated at a faster pace than were East Kentucky or West Virginia, where there were such high levels of absentee engrossment. Even though there was little topographical difference between the two areas and even though emigration into Maryland began a decade later, West Virginia was reinhabited much more slowly than western Maryland, where less than one-third of the land area was held by nonresidents.[35]

The principal reason that West Virginia had not been more fully resettled by the 1780s was that "the greater part if not all the good Lands, on the main river, [we]re in the hands of persons who d[id] not incline to reside thereon themselves, and possibly h[e]ld them too high for others." By 1810, Appalachian Maryland had a population density that was nearly three times the total national average. In contrast, Appalachian Virginia had a population density less than half that of western Maryland. In 1810, Frederick County, Maryland (founded 1748), had a population density that was five times the national average. On the other hand, Frederick County, Virginia (founded 1743), had a population density of only 10.9 persons per square mile—less than a quarter of that of the neighboring Maryland county.[36]

Despite its higher land prices and taxes, western Maryland attracted many more settlers than the Virginia frontiers. In comparison with the other sections of Southern Appalachia, much less distant trading occurred in western Maryland where out-of-state speculation was deterred by legislation (see Table 3.1). Several key public policies set Maryland apart from all the other Southern Appalachian states. Because of residency requirements, state dwellers squeezed absentee speculators out of the market. In contrast to Virginia and North Carolina, where wealthier officers could appropriate a military bounty of up to 10,000 acres, Maryland awarded its officers only one hundred acres. Significantly, Maryland had passed eighteenth-century legislation to reserve lands to parties who would cultivate it—a land policy that *was not duplicated by any of the other state governments* where Appalachian counties were located. Beginning in 1671, land registration and tax collection were decentralized into the Appalachian counties in order to deter absentee tax delinquency. As early as 1718, Maryland legislated positions for nine public surveyors for each county, a precedental maneuver that averted the quagmire of disputed claims that plagued the rest of the region. "The conflicting surveys and the resulting sale to several persons of the same property [we]re monstrosities which happen[ed] every day in Virginia, Kentucky, the two Carolinas, and Georgia."[37]

Always waiting for prices to rise, speculators held off the market large tracts of Appalachian land for as long as thirty years. George Washington's tactics were typical. To one inquiry about his Kanawha County holdings, he replied, "When you asked me if I was disposed to sell these Lands, I answered and truly that I had never had it in contemplation because I well knew they would rise more in value than the purchase money at the present time would accumulate by interest. . . . I am not inclined to part with any of these Lands, as an inducement to settle the rest. My mind is so well satisfied of the superior value of them to most others, that there remains no doubt on it of my obtaining my own terms, as the country populates and the situation and local advantages of them unfold."[38]

When land was marketed, it was often too expensive for average Appalachians. As a result, most of the region's best agricultural lands were inaccessible to small farmers. Furthermore, the region was repeopled more slowly than Ohio, "where lands [could] be bought in small tracts for farms, by real settlers, at a reasonable rate, whereas the Virginia lands [i.e., in Virginia, West Virginia, and Kentucky] belonging mostly to wealthy and great landholders [were] held at four or five times the Ohio price."[39]

The State of Kentucky did very poorly in distributing "the Promised land" to people who lived on and cultivated the soil. Rather than legislate the transfer of acreage to small homesteaders in the early 1800s, Kentucky's early-nineteenth-century policymakers favored land grants to "monopolizing capitalists" for "the purpose of speculation" and to promote industry. As a result, less than one-third of Kentucky's frontier titles were held by inhabitants.

Among the early grants made in Floyd, Laurel, Pulaski, and Whitley Counties, there were no settlement entries. In 1782, Kentucky smallholders petitioned the Virginia Assembly to change the land policies that were causing "very unequal distribution of land" by "giving enormous Quantities to those who could advance most money." Without further compulsory acts, the settlers argued, "the Engrosser will neither settle himself, nor dispose of [land] to those who will." Despite subsequent legislation restricting Green River claims to families that had already resided there one year, Kentucky even sold more than three-fourths of that land to absentee speculators.[40]

Frontier Land Ownership Patterns

Capitalistic speculation not only deterred resettlement of Southern Appalachia but also stimulated the further concentration of land into the control of settler-elites. In the face of two layers of land engrossment, poorer Appalachians stood little chance of competing for farms or town lots. Resident planters, professionals, and merchants—like Thomas Jefferson (Albermarle, Virginia), Peyton Skipwith (Mason, Kentucky), Albert Gallatin (Monongalia, West Virginia), John Calhoun (Pickens, South Carolina), John Sevier (Knox, Tennessee), and William Lenoir (Caldwell, North Carolina)—amassed sizeable speculator holdings.[41]

Southern Appalachia's frontier lands were very inequitably distributed. The commodification of land was so extensive that the soil was monopolized by the privileged local elites as the basis for sustaining their social and economic status within a highly polarized economic structure. The wealthiest decile of households engrossed more than three-fifths of the region's resident-held acres. Moreover, "the engrossing of the better lands by the great planters . . . had a part in pushing the poore and less efficient producers back from the rivers onto the ridges and westward away from navigable rivers." In East Tennessee, one-sixth of the people held more than one-half of all acres titled to residents. In Appalachian South Carolina, the top 15 percent owned all the resident acreage. In Frederick County, Virginia, for instance, the largest plantations and towns were situated in the eastern Shenandoah Valley; smaller holdings were more often located in the western part of the county, toward the mountains and foothills.[42]

By the end of the 1790s, most of the emigrants flowing into the region were poor, but there was no free land available to them. One 1795 report estimated that three-quarters of the settlers of Mason County, Kentucky, were landless. In the Valley of Virginia, landlessness increased steadily from the 1750s until 1800. By 1782, almost all the small farmers of Loudon County, Virginia, were tenants. These unpropertied families were highly mobile, moving from year to year, ever westward to new frontiers, in search of affordable land. A 1797 journal describes the living conditions and the prospects for such frontier families:

I cannot ommitt Noticeing the many Distressd families I passd in the Wilderness [Road] nor can any thing be more distressing to a man of feeling than to see woman and Children in the month of Decembr. Travelling a Wilderness Through Ice and Snow passing large rivers and Creeks without Shoe or Stocking, and barely as maney raggs as covers their Nakedness, with out money or provisions except what the Wilderness affords. . . . to say they are poor is but faintly express'g there Situation. . . . Ask these Pilgrims what they expect when they git to Kentuckey the Answer is Land. have you any. No, but I expect I can git it. have you any thing to pay for land, No. did you Ever see the Country. No but Every Body says its good land. . . . and when arrivd at this Heaven in Idea what do they find? a goodly land I will allow but to them forbidden Land. exhausted and worn down with distress and disappointment they are at last Obligd to become hewers of wood and Drawers of water.[43]

Once they reached the frontier, what lay in store for such itinerants? Landless families were crucial to the resettlement of Southern Appalachia. As a direct result of speculative activity, tenancy was entrenched on every Southern Appalachian frontier. During the late 1700s, absentee investors preferred to lease their holdings "for 21, 99, or 100 years, renewable forever, on encreasing rents." George Washington, for example, repeatedly surveyed his West Virginia tracts into smaller parcels to "rent them for as much as [he could] get." Speculators preferred to utilize tenants to open new lands for two reasons. The first "was to accommodate weak handed [i.e., poorer] people who were not able to purchase, thereby inviting and encouraging a number of useful Husbandmen and Mechanicks to settle. . . . The other, that [speculators] might have [their lands] restored to [them] at the expiration of the term for wch. they were granted, in good order and well improved."[44]

In western Maryland, large estates were established by hiring German tenants to clear immense forests and to set up plantations for distant landlords. In East Kentucky and frontier Virginia, absentee owners hired landless families to seat their holdings, to clear and improve parcels, and to prevent the development of "claims by adverse possession" of squatters. Tenants also provided defense against Indian incursions, served as a stimulus for new inhabitants, and provided one-third of their harvest to enrich their landlords.[45]

Once tenants had cleared fields, planted orchards, cut roads, and erected buildings, absentee owners could sell to wealthier emigrants at higher profits. An early-nineteenth-century traveler described this practice on the East Tennessee frontier: "The second year after [the arrival of a tenant] the price of two hundred acres of land . . . increases nearly thirty percent; and this [improved] estate is purchased in preference by a new emigrant." None of the Appalachian land laws conceded rights to "trespassers having no color

Table 3.3. Land Ownership in Southern Appalachia, 1790–1810

Appalachian Counties of	% All Households	
	Landless	Land-owning
Kentucky	56.9	43.1
Maryland	42.3	57.7
North Carolina	35.8	64.2
South Carolina	86.0	14.0
Tennessee	55.3	44.7
Virginia	62.9	37.1
West Virginia	62.7	37.3
Region	57.2	42.8

Source: Derived from analysis of county tax lists; see Table A.1 for sampling details. Landless households are undercounted since the slave and Cherokee populations are not included in these estimates. In order to avoid an overcount of landless households, care was taken to distinguish the landless kin of property holders from other landless families; see Appendix.

of title" (i.e., squatters). Consequently, there was little prospect for a poor family to acquire land in Southern Appalachia. If it cost $1,000 to set up a forty-acre farm on the midwestern frontier, Appalachian settlers would have needed even more capital to initiate small homesteads, for Appalachian acreage sold at higher prices than public lands further west. In addition, many early squatters were pushed off their improved land by those acquiring grants or military warrants. Settlers were even charged for acreage to which they had been granted "preemption" rights, and squatters were liable for damages to absentee holdings, under legislation like Kentucky's Occupying Claimant's Law. Even poor relief carried a price tag. For example, North Carolina and Virginia empowered surveyors to lay off tracts of wasteland for destitute residents. Still, payment was due from the poor within two and a half years.[46]

Beneath two layers of monopolizers, *the bottom half* of the region's free households—those most likely to become subsistence producers—owned *less than one percent* of the land. Even when care is taken to control for the landless kin of property holders, nearly three-fifths of all frontier Appalachian households were unpropertied (see Table 3.3). Such rural frontier populations "paid a disproportionate price for access to the productive system because bankers, speculators and merchants were able to use their political and economic power to set the terms of exchange in order to gain a greater share of the growing wealth of the society than was warranted by their entrepreneurial contribution."[47]

Landholding in the Middle Nineteenth Century

After 1810, two additional Appalachian frontiers opened for resettlement after indigenous populations were displaced from their ancestral lands. In the early 1800s, the Cherokees and Creeks ceded an additional 3,000,000 acres of their Appalachian claims, so in 1819 the region's only federal lands opened in northern Alabama. By 1820, only a small enclave of indigenous villages remained in southeastern Tennessee, western North Carolina, and northern Georgia. Encroachers encamped illegally, waiting like vultures for the inevitable demise of the Cherokee Nation. In southeastern Tennessee, settlers "owned herds of cattle which they kept in the range on the Indian side" of the Tennessee River. Even when federal troops removed trespassers near Cherokee settlements, the intruders "returned as thick as crows that are scattered from their food by a person passing on the road, but as soon as he is passed they return again."[48] Planter pressures for fresh cotton lands and the discovery of gold in Indian territory culminated in federal legitimation of state control over local Indians. After the forced removals of the Cherokees and Creeks, the region's last frontier opened in the late 1830s.

Speculation in the Public Domain

The availability of added resources in the public domain of northern Alabama still did not facilitate the access of poorer buyers to the market, for public transactions were just as embedded in commodity markets as private speculation had been. The Huntsville Land Office was overtly corrupt under the supervision of John Coffee, a Nashville commission merchant and slave trader with a wide range of land, commercial, and manufacturing interests from Tennessee and Mississippi to Illinois. Coffee's official clique advertised their willingness to "give any information to people wishing to purchase to an advantage, for a liberal per centum, we would also do business on commission, and receive in pay either a part of the land purchased; or money. . . . those persons wishing to purchase to a great advantage and who have not a good knowledge of the country, would do well to give us a call."[49]

As a result, a sizeable proportion of the speculators in northern Alabama were wealthy planters "flocking from every quarter of the adjacent territories." One middle Tennessean observed that "A large quantity of the travellers are from old Virginia some of them having a hundred slaves. . . . The emigration to the southern country with the wealth they are carrying along with them will of itself make the country overflow with wealth." In addition to activity by national syndicates, numerous small combines of public officials, southern planters, and eastern backers engrossed the public domain. Using insider information from Coffee's clerks, syndicates organized to eliminate competition at public sales. By sending scouts out along the roads into Huntsville, these companies pressured new emigrants to join their ranks or risk acquiring no land at all. At subsequent auctions, the companies operated as cartels to control prices and to monopolize the best river tracts.[50]

Moreover, the combines solicited "hush money" from squatters who had already made improvements on acreage, promising that company speculators would not bid against them when their tracts were auctioned. Because there was keen rivalry for river and valley tracts, poorer settlers were pushed off such lands. Using insider information and bribes to the combines, planters and company-employed shills bid prices up above the level squatters could afford. Planters were so successful in monopolizing the best agricultural tracts that poorer settlers were driven into the least cultivatable sections of northern Alabama. Once squatters were pushed off improved valley holdings, they sought out and resettled tracts not desired by the speculators. Most of the public land entries lay along creeks or streams where the population density was twelve to thirteen people per square mile. Consequently, the poorer squatters resorted to the hillier and more mountainous lands where there were only two persons per square mile in 1820.[51]

Subsequently, the rush for northern Alabama lands generated an intense class struggle as squatters organized their own schemes to resist the speculators. Teams of settlers rode through the countryside, marking prices on sections that had already been improved. "Those marks they took care to have considerably above the real value of the land. The company purchasers and other men of capital who went to explore the country previous to these sales finding such immense value set upon lands as they supposed, returned home and did not attend the sales." As a consequence of monopolistic tactics and official fraud, northern Alabama lands were overwhelmingly engrossed by absentee speculators and wealthy settler elites. Because public lands were redistributed in 160-acre parcels at $2.00 per acre, two-thirds of the northern Alabama settler households were priced out of the market and remained landless.[52]

Land Speculation on the Last Indian Frontiers

After the 1838 Cherokee removal, land redistribution by North Carolina, Tennessee, and Georgia was even more inequitable than had been late-eighteenth-century land dispersion. In Tennessee, newly acquired Cherokee lands were sold in parcels of 160 to 640 acres, at $2.00 to $7.00 per acre. North Carolina surveyed only those lands worth more than fifty cents per acre, auctioning acreage mostly in 640-acre tracts that ranged in price from fifty cents to $4.00 per acre.[53]

By structuring parcel requirements and prices so that only inferior acreage was within the reach of poorer settlers, state land policies favored large speculators. In addition, absentee buyers circumvented residency requirements by hiring local agents. Typical of the subsequent engrossment was the agglomeration of thousands of acres through ninety-six grants to two New Orleans and New York City capitalists. Neither North Carolina nor Tennessee granted preemption rights to poorer settlers. Not until after 1823 did Tennessee acknowledge squatters' needs by allowing them to purchase for a six-month period their occupied parcels at $1.50 per acre—a higher price than the twelve and a half cents per acre paid by later nonresidents. Not until forty years later did North Carolina legislate preemption rights. Beginning in 1850, the state made available to such families previously unsurveyed areas that "were not considered worth twenty cents per acre."[54]

It is enlightening to examine the redistribution of Cherokee lands in Georgia, the only Appalachian state to operate a "land lottery." Because Georgia declared squatters on Indian lands ineligible for the lottery, Georgia was not very successful at redistributing these lands to actual settlers. Despite state requirements that grantees live on the awarded parcels for at least five years, nearly half the land was held by absentees two years after the lottery. In spite of Georgia's "free" acreage policy, a small elite among the households held all the land while eight-tenths of the frontier families remained landless.[55]

Southern Appalachian Land Ownership Patterns, 1860

What distinguished Southern Appalachia from other American frontiers was the manner in which absentee investors disposed of large parcels. In the Midwest, for example, a majority of the best farm lands had been transferred into the hands of resident owners by the end of the first decade of settlement. In contrast, absentee speculators hoarded large Appalachian tracts believed to be rich in minerals, thereby preventing settlement of vast segments of the land area. International investors, like Eugene Levassor, were just beginning to sell their Kentucky and West Virginia holdings in the 1820s. New York land baron John Grieg did not dispose of 23,108 acres of prime Monongalia County farms until three decades after the start of resettlement. James Swan and Albert Gallatin retained control over their West Virginia holdings into the 1830s. Because long-term investors held onto lots obtained when the frontiers opened, many Appalachian towns were heavily engrossed by absentee speculators well into the twentieth century.[56]

In addition, local elites bought up mineral tracts for distant capitalists—a practice that agglomerated the lands exploited in the postbellum mineral and timber boom. To attract mineral developers, every Appalachian state funded geological surveys beginning in the 1820s. By 1860, Kentucky had completed three such surveys, and Tennessee had funded eight. Moreover, national syndicates employed geologists and engineers to locate and map major mineral fields. Consequently, planters invested part of their profits in adjacent Appalachian holdings. Many regional lawyers and politicians represented Philadelphia, New York, and European interests who were accumulating mineral, timber, and railroad tracts throughout the southern mountains. Lively competitive speculation continued until the Civil War, and additional large tracts were withdrawn from the pool of resident farmland every time geologic surveys discovered new pockets of mineral wealth.[57]

Until the early twentieth century, Appalachian elites leased acreage, accumulated mineral holdings, or marketed timber for absentee landholders. For instance, William McCoy and John Rogers managed rental properties in nine West Virginia counties for distant investors. Facing the threat of passage of the Homestead Act in the 1850s, local land agents advised engrossers to move quickly to dispose of their Appalachian holdings before emigrants were attracted to cheaper opportunities in the Far West. Lewis Maxwell warned several of his clients, "The homestead bill has not passed Congress but will likely do so in a year or two, if so such land must fall in value. I believe that lands in this section of Country will sell higher the pre-sent and next year than at any time thereafter for the next ten years."[58]

Even more significantly, absentee speculators initiated schemes to get publicly funded internal improvements located where their holdings would appreciate in value. Utilizing Virginia Senate connections to manipulate routing of a new West Virginia railroad, Lewis Maxwell reported to his Baltimore and Philadelphia clients that he had "failed at obtaining money to construct a branch rail road" to their West Virginia holdings. Another legislator representing absentees "came in with his scheme for a Railroad from Clarksburg to Big Sandy—that alarmed the Central Railroad men." When four alternate proposals ensued, "there had been such demonstration that a jealousy was excited and my scheme looked upon as a mere lever [of] power to git through to Big Sandy."[59]

Midwestern and northwestern frontiers were characterized by low costs and "active local markets." In sharp contrast, speculators kept prices high and bypassed landless Appalachian families to "sell profitably" in European markets. In 1845, for example, Cincinnati merchant Louis Chitti advertised in Europe 200,000 acres of Levassor's holdings in Lewis, Doddridge, and Gilmer Counties. His two new "colonies in Western Virginia" consisted of "9,377 acres subdivided into 83 lots of different sizes, from between 82 to 214 acres, at the rate of $ 2.00 an acre." According to the prospectus, "the boundaries of the first Village ha[d] been laid out," but only "About 100 acres of land" were "already cleared and include[d] several log cabins." Once twenty families settled there, the owner promised to "build at his own expense a temporary church."[60]

With so many large tracts concentrated into the hands of absentee speculators and local elites, international land speculation reached even into the backways of Southern Appalachia. As a direct result of such long-term investment strategies, land was out of the reach of the bottom segments of Southern Appalachia's settler families and their descendants. From the perspective of the region's poor, acreage was never cheap or easily acquired. Consequently, resources did not filter down to ordinary Appalachians any better during later

Table 3.4. Land Ownership in Southern Appalachia, 1860

A. By State Subregions

Appalachian Counties of	% All Households	
	Landless	Land-owning
Alabama	44.9	55.1
Georgia and South Carolina	39.6	60.4
Kentucky	35.7	64.3
Maryland	42.9	57.1
North Carolina	46.1	53.9
Tennessee	45.6	54.4
Virginia	51.3	48.7
West Virginia	48.7	51.3
Region	45.8	54.2

B. By Terrain Type

Appalachian Counties of	% All Households	
	Landless	Land-owning
Mountains	44.6	55.4
Hills-Plateaus	44.0	56.0
Ridges-Valleys	49.0	51.0
Region	45.8	54.2

Source: Derived from analysis of household sample ($N = 3,056$) drawn from the 1860 Census of Population enumerator manuscripts; see Table A.2 for sampling detail. Care was taken to distinguish the landless kin of property holders from other landless families; see Appendix.

eras than they had during the frontier years. Even in 1860, nearly half the region's households remained landless, and there was a large propertyless population in every Appalachian geographical zone (see Table 3.4). Southern Appalachians could not even alleviate their landless condition by escaping to the region's most isolated hollows and coves. In fact, families who resided in counties with the most rugged mountains and ridges were slightly more likely to experience landlessness than were their counterparts in the counties with more cultivatable acreage. For it was just such less tillable (described as "valueless" by many contemporary scholars) lands that peaked the attention of nineteenth-century mineral and tourism speculators.

Historical Pressures toward Wage Labor

A number of sweeping social changes occur when global capitalism reaches out to bring in an external zone. Transforming economic production usually involves "upsetting or adapting land tenure arrangements, relocating labor forces, changing the relations of production, altering balances of social power." Agriculture in the peripheral zones of the capitalist world economy is structured around the inequitable distribution of the means of production. Absentee speculators and settler elites systematically acquire control over most of the land, forcing indigenous peoples off their ancestral territories. Subsequently, poorer settler families are either unable to acquire farmland or are restricted to the least productive areas.[61]

The Scarcity of Appalachian Farmland

In Southern Appalachia, such land engrossment generated local communities in which the bottom half of the households had no access—either as owners or as tenants—to farm acreage upon which they could produce either their own subsistence or commodities for market. In 1860 three-fifths of the region's households either resided off farms or were legally restricted (i.e., as Appalachian slaves and Cherokees) from acquiring land (see Table 3.5). Rather than being the idyllic haven in which everyone could easily become a cultivator of the soil, Southern Appalachia was a region in which a minority of the families actually held direct control over most of the agricultural land. In western Maryland, less than one-quarter of the households lived on farms. Only about one-third of the families of the Appalachian counties of Georgia, South Carolina, and Virginia had access to farmland. Appalachians fared little better in Alabama, North Carolina, Tennessee, or West Virginia, where slightly less than half of the households resided on farms. Only in eastern Kentucky did the proportion having access to farmland slightly exceed one-half of the resident households. If, as most scholars claim, the family farm was the backbone of the antebellum economy, nearly three-fifths of the region's families had no access to the most important factor of production, the soil needed for cultivation. Between 1810 and 1860, these nonfarm Appalachians were increasingly centralized into the region's towns, villages, and hamlets. By 1860, about one-quarter of Southern Appalachians resided in a few towns (averaging 4,040 population) and in many villages (averaging 350 population).[62]

By 1860, more than three-quarters of Southern Appalachia's free households were employed in agriculture (see Table 3.6). However, those households that operated farms comprised only three-fifths of the region's entire free agricultural labor force. Two-fifths of the region's free agricultural households worked as wage laborers who had no access to farmland. In addition, unfree laborers—black slaves and Cherokee squatters—comprised an important segment of the region's agricultural households. When all the region's free and unfree laborers are acknowledged, a picture emerges that is very different from the romantic stereotype of a region predominated by the small family farm.

Table 3.5. Access to Farm Land by Southern Appalachian Households, 1860

Appalachian Counties of	Total Households Having No Access to Farm Land[a]		Free Households Living on Farms[b]		Total Households[c]
	No.	%	No.	%	No.
Alabama	14,652	51.9	13,552	48.1	28,204
Georgia	18,952	63.0	11,145	37.0	30,097
Kentucky	15,235	46.3	17,631	53.7	32,866
Maryland	14,560	75.8	4,659	24.2	19,219
North Carolina	13,781	53.0	12,232	47.0	26,013
South Carolina	2,455	65.4	1,301	34.6	3,756
Tennessee	38,276	57.7	28,026	42.3	66,302
Virginia	55,832	67.3	27,139	32.7	82,971
West Virginia	37,253	56.7	28,430	43.3	65,683
Region	210,996	59.4	144,115	40.6	355,111

Sources: Aggregated data from published 1860 censuses.

[a]Aggregated sum of free households residing off farms, plus slave households and Cherokee households (estimated using published counts). The number of free households residing off farms was calculated by subtracting the number of farm households from the total number of households reported for each county in the published Census of Population. Slave households averaged 5.2 persons per house, according to 1860 census counts of slave houses; see Fogel and Engerman, *Time on the Cross*, p. 115. The aggregated count of slaves in the published Census of Population was divided by this average. Cherokee households were estimated by using population counts from 1848 and 1884 censuses since Indians were not counted in the regular 1860 census; see *Report of Indian Commissioners*, 1848, p. 399; *Report of Indian Commissioners*, 1884, pp. li–lii.

[b]Aggregated from county data in published Census of Agriculture; includes all owners and tenants.

[c]Aggregated sum of free households, estimated slave households, and estimated Cherokee households.

Table 3.7 provides an overview of Southern Appalachia's combined free and unfree agricultural labor force in 1860. With very little statistical variation from one state subregion to another, fewer than two-fifths of Southern Appalachia's 1860 agricultural households owned farmland. The largest category consisted of those agricultural households that had no access to farmland. Roughly half of Southern Appalachia's 1860 agricultural labor force was comprised of free white and black wage laborers and unfree slave and Cherokee workers who had no access to farmland. In reality, more than three-fifths of the region's agricultural households were landless laborers.[63]

Table 3.6. Free Households Engaged in Agriculture, 1860

Appalachian Counties of[a]	Proportion of All Free Households with Members Employed in Agriculture[b]	Total Number of Free Households Engaged in Agriculture[c]	Number of Households That Operated Farms[d]	Agricultural Households without Access to Farm Land[e]	
				No.	%
Alabama (N = 25,264)	.827	20,893	13,552	7,341	35.1
Georgia and South Carolina (N = 27,787)	.732	20,345	12,446	7,899	28.4
Kentucky (N = 30,514)	.934	28,500	17,631	10,869	38.1
Maryland (N = 18,318)	.610	11,174	4,659	6,515	58.3
North Carolina (N = 22,749)	.886	20,156	12,232	7,924	39.3
Tennessee (N = 59,570)	.909	54,149	28,026	26,123	48.2
Virginia (N = 62,395)	.692	43,177	27,139	16,038	37.2
West Virginia (N = 62,530)	.641	40,082	28,430	11,652	29.1
Region (N = 309,127)	.772	238,476	144,115	94,361	39.6

Sources: Aggregated data from published 1860 censuses.

[a]N = aggregate total of free households derived from county data in the published Census of Population. For sampling purposes, the one South Carolina county was grouped with the Georgia counties.

[b]Proportion derived from analysis of household sample (N = 3,056) drawn from the 1860 Census of Population enumerator manuscripts; see Table A.2 for sampling details.

[c]Proportion in first column multiplied by aggregated number of free households reported for each county in the published Census of Population.

[d]Aggregated from published 1860 Census of Agriculture.

[e]Second column minus aggregated total number of farms.

Table 3.7. Landlessness among All Free and Unfree Agricultural Households, 1860

A. Landless Agricultural Laborers

| | Free Landless Farm Operators[a] | | Laborers with No Access to Land | | | |
| | | | Free Laborers[b] | | Unfree Laborers[c] | |
Appalachian Counties of	No.	Proportion	No.	Proportion	No.	Proportion
Alabama	3,875	.165	7,341	.312	2,606	.111
Georgia and South Carolina	4,087	.159	7,899	.309	5,233	.205
Kentucky	4,619	.156	10,869	.367	1,121	.038
Maryland	588	.049	6,515	.546	759	.064
North Carolina	2,874	.124	7,924	.343	2,968	.128
Tennessee	7,861	.131	26,123	.436	5,835	.097
Virginia	4,772	.078	16,038	.261	18,136	.296
West Virginia	8,927	.209	11,652	.272	2,706	.063
Region	37,603	.135	94,361	.340	39,364	.142

B. Summary of Landless and Owner Households

| | Total Laborer Households | | Farm Owner and Cash Renter Households[a] | | Total Agricultural Households |
Appalachian Counties of	No.	Proportion	No.	Proportion	
Alabama	13,822	.588	9,677	.412	23,499
Georgia and South Carolina	17,219	.673	8,359	.327	25,578
Kentucky	16,609	.561	13,012	.439	29,621
Maryland	7,862	.659	4,071	.341	11,933
North Carolina	13,766	.595	9,358	.405	23,124
Tennessee	39,819	.664	20,165	.336	59,984
Virginia	38,946	.635	22,367	.365	61,313
West Virginia	23,285	.544	19,503	.456	42,788
Region	171,328	.617	106,512	.383	277,840

Sources: Aggregated from manuscript samples and published censuses.

[a]Proportions of farm operators derived from analysis of farm sample ($N = 3,447$); see Table A.3 for sampling details. Those proportions were then multiplied by the total number of farm households reflected in Table 3.5. Since they typically owned wealth, slaves, and means of production other than land, cash renters have been counted with farm owners to distinguish them from laborers.

[b]Derived from analysis of sample of households drawn from the Census of Population enumerator manuscripts. These proportions were then multiplied by the total number of households (Table 3.5).

[c]The proportion of farms holding slaves was determined by cross-matching the sample of farms with the manuscript slave schedules; these proportions were then multiplied by the total number of slave households. For methods of estimating slave and Cherokee households, see Table 3.5.

The chances of a nineteenth-century Southern Appalachian rising from the bottom of the social ladder were empirically delimited by three harsh realities. First, land was heavily concentrated, and in antebellum America economic wealth did not trickle down to those households on the bottom rungs. In those sections of the country where a large agricultural proletariat emerged in the early 1840s, monthly wage rates stagnated or fell. Moreover, inheritance practices had grown increasingly inegalitarian between 1800 and 1840.[64]

Second, there were few employment and entrepreneurial opportunities in the region, and wages for agricultural labor were seasonal and low. In contrast to the egalitarian view of Appalachians who had acquired land and wealth, nearly nine-tenths of the impoverished Appalachian veterans were convinced that "the poor man had no chanc[e]" to accumulate enough wealth to buy land. Averaging 23.4 years of age at the beginning of the Civil War, these young men at the bottom of the Appalachian social scale had few jobs available to them, except unstable agricultural labor at wages averaging $6.00 per month. For these households, "money was mighty scarce . . . money jobs were hard to be had."[65]

In some counties, one-quarter or more of laboring men were "out of honest work." For instance, Marion County, Tennessee, was described as "full of pore men" who "had to wourk hard on farming to raise their family." A Hall County, Georgia, veteran reported that landless young men like himself "could not get a job." Such households moved about frequently in search of work, like this itinerant northern Georgia family who owned only "a cart but no horse. The man had a belt over his shoulders and he drew in the shafts— the son worked by traces tied to the ends of the shafts and assisted his father to draw the cart: the son's wife rode in the cart, and the old woman was walking, carrying a rifle and driving a cow."[66]

While food prices rose across the country, agricultural wage rates stayed at the same levels or fell. Between 1840 and 1855, the wage differential between unskilled agricultural workers and skilled industrial laborers widened dramatically. By the mid-1800s, great numbers of Southern Appalachia's landless families were emigrating further westward in search of affordable land. One Civil War veteran recalled that "most of [the] emigrants to [the] northwest were of [the] lower classes. North Carolina and E. Tenn. supplied thousands of these. 'Twas a standing saying that poor whites moving in covered wagons from North Carolina or E. Tenn. [when] asked 'whence and where to' always replied 'Come fun Nawth Caliner; gwyne ter the Ielinoy.'" At best, the antebellum economy promised the laborer a living, but little more. Thus, poorer households barely earned enough to meet subsistence needs, so there were no assets left over to accumulate toward the future.[67]

Because "it took all that a family could make to live," the surveyed Appalachian Civil War veterans with limited antebellum means experienced work histories in which there was little possibility of acquiring land. In their estimation, it took considerable "time and toil for a young man to save enough to buy a farm for some of them had to take trade for their labor." Thus, very few of the poorer veterans ever "saved enough to buy a farm." In some counties, even the opportunities to become a tenant farmer were seriously limited because the largest slaveholders would rather "allow their lands to grow up in sprouts" than rent parcels to poor whites. Consequently, the region's nineteenth-century farm laborers were sharply differentiated from the landholders who employed them. The typical farm-owning household had accumulated twenty-six times more wealth than free agricultural laborers who averaged little more than $250 in household assets, livestock, or tools.[68]

Finally, those antebellum workers who improved their lot were those who acquired a professional or specialized skill to supplement their agricultural pursuits. In Southern Appalachia, however, education was accessible only to those who could afford to pay subscription fees or send their children to distant academies. In Appalachian Tennessee, for example, the school term ran only four months; but fewer than a quarter of the school-age children were enrolled. As a result, more than one-quarter of the whites older than twenty were illiterate. In 1853, North Carolina's superintendent of schools reported that even in "the most enlightened" Appalachian counties, "the leading heads of families could not succeed oftener than once in two years in getting up a subscription school for the three winter months." In short, antebellum Southern Appalachia mirrored the economic conditions of the global economy in that a large number of laborers were trapped permanently at the bottom and led economically precarious lives. Even though free Appalachian agricultural laborers comprised more than two-fifths of the region's households (see Table 3.5), they controlled less than 2 percent of the total wealth and resources.[69]

Intergenerational Landlessness

One of the most popular theses about the unfolding of rural capitalism in the United States is the notion that acquisition of farmland has been relatively easy and equitable. Since the early 1900s, many scholars have argued that "passage from a propertyless to a propertied condition was almost certain in its possibilities of accomplishment by any able-bodied, industrious individual." The central assumption of this agricultural ladder hypothesis is that, over their life cycles, agricultural households are upwardly mobile. Typically, advancement to farmland ownership has been viewed as a series of short-term occupational stages in which working as a wage earner, as a tenant, and as an owner-farmer are successive rungs on a ladder of progress.[70]

If the agricultural ladder thesis is accurate and most Appalachians owned their own land by the turn of the twentieth century, we should see significant accretions between 1810 and 1860 in the proportion of Southern Appalachian households that owned land. However, land ownership did not expand in Southern Appalachia as dramatically as the conventional wisdom would lead us to predict. Inheritance was not a mechanism that insured land ownership to Appalachians. Rather, in the antebellum period only a little more than one-tenth of the nation's farm owners acquired their land from family estates. Similarly, only 10.9 percent of the surveyed Appalachian Civil War veterans inherited acreage from families who owned land. More importantly, this sort of optimistic conceptualization is flawed and naive. First, the notion of wide-spread inheritance fails to take into account the frequency with which ante-bellum estate settlements absorbed the land to resolve parental debts. Second, antebellum estate settlements divided larger farms into smaller land parcels distributed among several heirs, thereby diminishing their profitability and increasing the likelihood of loss of family farms. More significantly, the land-less son of an antebellum farm owner would have waited until the age of fifty or later to inherit the land upon the death of both parents, thereby losing the most productive years of his life as an unpropertied laborer. Why, then, should such a person not be considered the equivalent of other landless laborers who lacked control over the most essential factor of production?[71]

On every American frontier, agrarian capitalism was accompanied by patterns of speculation and land concentration. For antebellum families of limited means, there was no easy or quick avenue to land ownership. In the peripheral regions of the United States, therefore, agricultural land remained historically concentrated in the control of an elite minority; thus, the proportion of landless households either expanded or remained static across succeeding generations. Claims of an easy rise from landlessness have been vastly exaggerated with respect to Southern Appalachia. Among the 10,405 sampled households, land ownership showed only very marginal increases between 1810 and 1860. During this period, the ratio of landed to landless households improved only slightly in the Appalachian counties of Tennessee, Virginia, and West Virginia; but the ratio of landed to landless actually worsened in the Appalachian counties of Maryland and North Carolina. In East Kentucky, where the largest accretion occurred, the proportion of landed households rose by about one-fifth, a change due in large part to that state's mid-century grants of small wasteland parcels to residents. This time period is short enough to encompass households that were counted in 1810 as young, landless families. So, in line with the agricultural ladder thesis, we should expect to see sizeable declines in the proportion of landless as these heads of households aged. Contrary to agricultural ladder notions, however, the ratio of landless to landed households remained relatively static over this fifty-year period, with only a small minority of propertyless households moving into the ranks of the landholders.[72]

Typical of this pattern of long-term landlessness are the work histories of fifty-nine laborers on the Lenoir plantations of western North Carolina. Several of these agricultural households initiated sharecropping arrangements before the 1820s; yet none of them experienced this form of land tenure as a transitory step toward ownership. In fact, it was not unusual for the Lenoir tenants to renew their annual contracts for twenty to thirty years or longer. Josiah Anderson, for example, leased from 1828 until 1858. Daniel Henson, who began sharecropping in 1820, saw two of his sons become tenants in 1826 and 1833; in 1837 all three were still landless Lenoir laborers.[73]

In contrast to the agricultural ladder thesis that landless households fell only among the young, there was little age difference between Southern Appalachian owners and tenants. In 1860, landholders averaged 46 years of age while landless heads of household averaged 39.3 years. Moreover, more than half of the unpropertied heads were older than 35, with nearly one-fifth of them older than 55. This regional pattern is certainly not consistent with the "life cycle pattern of occupational mobility" predicted by the agricultural ladder thesis, for more than a third of the Southern Appalachian households remained landless most of their productive years. Typical of this pattern was Isaac Brown of Rhea and Meigs Counties, Tennessee, who reported at the age of 80 that he had farmed all his life "mostly on rented land."[74]

At least one-quarter of Southern Appalachia's agricultural families experienced intergenerational landlessness. A long-term analysis of landholding in Blount County, Tennessee, offers enlightening insight into the longevity of this pattern. Randomly selected for analysis by computer, Blount contains part of the present-day Great Smoky Mountains National Park and has been stereotyped as an Appalachian county characterized by the presence of landholding families who have remained there since original settlement. Contrary to the agricultural ladder thesis that tenants gradually improve their situations to become owners, less than one-quarter of the Appalachian surname groups that were landless in 1801 had acquired land by 1860. More than three-quarters of surname groups that were landless in 1801 were either still unpropertied in 1860 or gone from the county. In addition, 16 percent of the 1801 land-owning surname groups had lost their holdings by 1860.

What, then, of the popular notion that young landless Appalachians inherited land over time? To allow for this optimistic eventuality, I tracked what happened over the fifty-year period to 142 landless households that had the same surnames as 1801 landholders. An examination of the 1860 Census of Population reveals that 48.6 percent of these landless households were no longer in the county at the end of the era. More than one-third of these propertyless kin of landholders remained landless over the entire fifty-year period. Only a small minority of them could have inherited property, for less than 15 percent of them acquired acreage between 1801 and 1860. In short, we cannot explain away the presence of landless Appalachians with the oversimplified belief that they were just waiting to take over the family farms when their parents died.[75]

A similar pattern occurred in Greene and Johnson Counties, Tennessee, where three-fifths of the landless households tracked over a twenty-year period failed to acquire land, and 15 percent of the landowners lost their property. Intergenerational landlessness recurred throughout Southern Appalachia, in a pattern parallel to the life history of one elderly East Tennessee woman whose ancestors settled first in Pennsylvania, where they "cropped on shares there before the Revolutionary War." Her great-grandfather "moved to Kentucky where he worked for a store owner." Subsequently, "he lost what little he had saved to buy a farm. So he took up sharecropping for a family who owned about 500 acres someplace in southeastern Kentucky." Then about 1830 her grandparents moved to East Tennessee, where they took up sharecropping. After the Civil War, two other generations of this agricultural family "never owned their own farmland."[76]

Summary

The extension of agrarian settler capitalism into Southern Appalachia coincided with three significant economic conjunctures in the world system. First, the initial phase of capitalist penetration into Southern Appalachia from the 1730s to 1763 correlated with an era of renewed economic expansion of the capitalist world economy, characterized by a struggle between England, France, and Spain for control of North America and culminating in Britain's victory over France for hegemony.[77]

The global expansion of capitalism was accompanied in the North American colonies by exploration of inland frontiers, by massive disruption of Native American cultures, by an increase in concentration of wealth, and by chronic poverty among at least one-fifth of the seaboard households. During this era, wealthy Tidewater planters and northeastern merchant-investors utilized their accumulated wealth to invest in lands and towns on the western frontiers of Maryland and Virginia, gambling that the growing populations on the coast would continue to thrust inland and that virgin zones of minerals would be discovered.[78] During this era, Native Americans "relinquished" their claims to lands in Maryland and Virginia. Thus, the repopulation of western Maryland, the Valley of Virginia, the eastern edge of West Virginia, and the northern fringe of western North Carolina was well underway before the 1763 Proclamation Line was established.

Second, two global wars to effect the decolonization of North America from the European powers were played out within the period of 1775–1819.[79] In opposition to the British Proclamation Line of 1763, American speculators and settlers began to acquire lands and to repeople parts of Southern Appalachia before the United States came into being as a new nation. After the Revolutionary War, emigrants flowed into the first American frontier in three waves of resettlement, displacing most of the indigenous populations. The final phase of expansion into Southern Appalachia from 1833 to 1840 coincided with the emergence of the United States as a world trade power; rising international demand for American wheat, cotton, and tobacco; and increased national requirements for gold.[80] After a decade of political lobbying by southern planters and after the discovery of gold in the Cherokee Nation, the remaining Native Americans were forcibly removed from their small Appalachian enclaves.

Throughout the historical period from 1790 to 1860, speculative expansions swelled or ebbed in response to conditions in the national and world economies. When international prices for northern manufactures, tobacco, cotton, grains, or slaves increased, speculation in frontier lands intensified. Southern Appalachia was articulated with the capitalist world economy through a multilevel market structure in which absentee foreign, national, and regional investors and local engrossers monopolized the region's natural resources. An interlocking network of distant brokerage houses, planters, merchants, corrupt local officials, and resident petty capitalists choreographed the slow redistribution of land on the Appalachian frontiers. By 1810, three-quarters of the region's acreage was absentee-owned, and distant speculators laid out towns, sold or leased farms to settlers, and engrossed areas believed to offer wealth in minerals or resort attractions.[81]

Because the region was incorporated as a peripheral fringe of the emerging national economy, the engrossment of Southern Appalachian lands provided the basis for wealth accumulation that distant capitalists utilized to develop other regions. Expropriation of surplus value from the marketing of Appalachian lands augmented the capital used to finance the distant commerce and early industrial advances of the Northeast. In addition, eastern capitalists engaged in long-term investments in Southern Appalachian lands that would provide the mineral and timber resources needed to fuel the Industrial Revolution. In similar fashion, southern planters utilized their land-trading ventures to accumulate wealth that was poured into slaves, reinvested on other western frontiers, or used to finance expansion of the export economy.

Southern Appalachia's local societies were microcosms of the region's polarized position within the world economy. Land was heavily concentrated into the hands of a few local elites who accumulated wealth by leasing or selling tracts to settlers, by acting as land agents for absentee engrossers, or by holding natural features that were attractive as resorts. These local elites utilized their landed estates to profit from legally mandated towns, toll roads, ferries, railroads, canals, mills, and iron foundries that operated as publicly subsidized monopolies. On the one hand, land was the basis for the capital accumulation required for the development of local industry and commerce. On the other hand, local elites exported most of the region's monetary surpluses to purchase luxury imports and slaves or to invest in economic ventures in the Northeast, the Southwest, and the Midwest.

Land provided the economic basis for the structuring of a polarized Appalachian society in which the wealthy landed gentry amassed a majority of the acreage while more than half the settler households remained landless. Because of the concentration of resources into the hands of a few absentee speculators and local elites, resettlement of the region was slowed. There was no such thing as "free" land or "squatters'" rights on the Southern Appalachian frontiers, and a majority of the emigrants to the region after the Revolutionary War were too poor to afford the prices set by speculators. Consequently, farm acreage was heavily concentrated in the hands of the top decile of farm operators, leaving little more than one-seventh of the land resources to the poorer bottom half of the region's farmers. Because of the heavy concentration of resources, three-fifths of the region's families resided off farms, and only two-fifths of all the agricultural households owned farms. Consequently, the scarcity of farmland, social immobility, and intergenerational landlessness operated as significant historical pressures toward the formation of an agrarian labor force.

THE POOR MAN HAD NO CHANCE:

FORMATION OF A LANDLESS AGRARIAN

SEMIPROLETARIAT

Emergence of a Capitalistic Agrarian Labor Force

Before an area can be incorporated into the network of world-capitalist processes, one of the major stumbling blocks that must be overcome is the lack of
available labor. Following the expansion of capitalism into peripheral areas,
scarce productive resources are monopolized by local elites and absentee
capitalists. Subsequently, land serves as the critical mechanism for *anchoring
labor relations* between landholders and propertyless families. Because control
over land, the primary factor of production, is denied to them, a sizeable
segment of the rural population is transformed into a surplus of landless
laborers. Never fully integrated into the local economy as independent producers and never completely proletarianized into wage occupations, much of
the rural population is economically "marginalized." These rural workers
neither own the means of production nor are they remunerated for their labor
on a reliable or equitable basis. "They are at once more desperate and more
mobile than the permanently employed, however much the latter are exploited." Such semiproletarians "are indeed the 'wretched of the earth.' "[1]

Nineteenth-century capitalist agriculture created demands for laborers
from several types of farm owners. Workers were recruited by middling households for whom farming was secondary to other occupations; by wealthy
"gentleman farmers" who spent their time in commerce or their professions;
by middling and large commercial farmers producing surpluses for the market; by women farmers who could afford to hire workers; and by families for
whom wage labor was a substitute for family labor until children were old
enough to work in the fields. Except for the rare subsistence producer, nearly
every farmer required short-term day laborers for planting and harvesting.

Southern Appalachia's farm owners attempted to protect themselves against labor shortages by utilizing three mechanisms: *long-term contracting* with workers who fulfilled a range of duties over at least a year; *public regulation* of labor mobility; and *short-term labor arrangements* structured around completion of specific tasks. In this array of mechanisms, money was not the only form of remuneration; still, all these agricultural workers were paid wages. "Even if [they] received so much of [their] pay in kind that [they] practically never had two coins to rub together at the end of the year, [they] had grown accustomed to reckoning in money terms."[2]

Central to our understanding of the capitalist world economy should be the recognition that its processes generate a variety of forms of labor relations. Far from causing nonwage work to disappear, capitalism seizes its means of production, including labor, "from all levels of civilisation and from all forms of society." Thus, capitalism is characterized by a structural tendency to transform the labor force into wage workers in a sporadic and uneven fashion. Capitalists combine wage labor and commercialized land with many forms of nonwage labor and land tenure. The labor force of peripheral zones takes a variety of forms that are not parallel "to the completed proletarianisation process" in core regions where wage earners predominate. In the peripheries of the world economy, agrarian capitalists coordinate both free and unfree workers, both owners and nonowners of land.[3]

Labor Mechanisms Utilized on Appalachian Farms

One of the most long-standing stereotypes about preindustrial Appalachian agriculture is the notion that the region's farmers cultivated their land by relying solely on the labor provided by their own families. In reality, no more than two of every five of the region's farm owners could have relied exclusively upon the labor of family members (see Table 4.1); furthermore, this count is an overestimation since there is no way to ascertain how many of that number actually utilized short-term wage laborers or pooled labor during harvest with their neighbors. While the minority of poorer subsistence farmers may have had access only to the labor of household members to produce crops on small holdings, the region's predominant segment of middling and larger farmers relied on a mix of several sources for labor.[4]

Across the region, there was a great deal of disparity in the agricultural labor mechanisms. Family members seem to have supplied the dominant labor source in only one geographical zone—i.e., East Kentucky, where little more than half of the farm owners reported no other labor source. About two-fifths of the farm owners in the Appalachian counties of Alabama, Georgia, North Carolina, Tennessee, and West Virginia and about one-third of those in western Maryland depended solely upon family members. At the other end of the spectrum, Appalachian Virginia's farm owners were more likely to utilize

Table 4.1. Labor Mechanisms Utilized by Farm Owners and Cash Renters, 1860

A. Farms Utilizing Family and Wage Laborers

	% of Farms Using Labor Mechanism		
Appalachian Counties of	Family Labor Only	Family and Paid Labor	Total
Alabama	40.6	5.4	46.0
Georgia and South Carolina	38.4	6.1	44.5
Kentucky	52.9	8.1	61.0
Maryland	31.6	14.0	45.6
North Carolina	40.0	1.2	41.2
Tennessee	44.9	8.9	53.8
Virginia	17.6	10.7	28.3
West Virginia	44.1	13.0	57.1
Region	38.3	9.0	47.3

B. Farms Utilizing Coerced Laborers

	% of Farms Using Labor Mechanism			
		Slaveholders		
Appalachian Counties of	Nonslaveholders Using Tenants	Slave Labor	Slaves and Tenants	Total
Alabama	14.8	26.6	12.6	54.0
Georgia and South Carolina	14.0	27.3	14.2	55.5
Kentucky	25.0	4.4	9.6	39.0
Maryland	15.8	17.8	20.8	54.4
North Carolina	17.1	19.3	22.4	58.8
Tennessee	13.3	20.4	12.5	46.2
Virginia	14.3	29.1	28.3	71.7
West Virginia	29.4	10.3	10.2	42.9
Region	17.0	20.6	15.1	52.7

Source: Derived from analysis of all farm owners and cash renters included in the sample of farms ($N = 3,447$) drawn from the 1860 Census of Agriculture; see Table A.3 for sampling details.

workers pooled from outside kinship ties. In fact, less than one in five of those agricultural producers reported total reliance on family labor.

Less than half of the region's farm owners drew their labor exclusively from their families or from paid resident laborers (see Table 4.1). Farm owners of East Kentucky and West Virginia exhibited the greatest reliance upon family and wage labor, and slightly more than half the farm owners of Appalachian Tennessee relied solely on such labor mechanisms. However, nearly three-fifths of the farm owners in the Appalachian counties of Alabama, Georgia, Maryland, North Carolina, and South Carolina were more likely to employ slaves and tenants, often in combination with free laborers. At the far end of the spectrum, seven-tenths of Appalachian Virginia's farm owners depended upon slaves and tenants, with less than one-fifth of the farmers in that zone utilizing family workers only.[5]

Surprisingly, more than half of the antebellum farm owners of Southern Appalachia depended upon *coerced workers* as their predominant source of labor. Farm owners of East Kentucky used fewer tenants, croppers, and slaves than any other zone of the region, followed by West Virginia and Appalachian Tennessee. The Appalachian counties of Alabama, Georgia, Maryland, North Carolina, and South Carolina exceeded regional averages in farm utilization of coerced laborers; however, nearly three-fourths of the farm owners of Appalachian Virginia depended primarily upon landless farm operators and slaves to cultivate the soil.[6]

The transition to rural capitalism triggers the historical evolution of a landless semiproletariat. These workers are "only marginally or partially proletarianized as, over the life cycle, they derive the bulk of the means of subsistence for their families from outside the wage economy." Over their work lives, agricultural laborers in peripheral areas accrue part of their income from subsistence farming, part from direct wages (in cash or in kind), part from sales of commodities or services on the market, and part from public subsidies or family gifts.[7]

By 1860, nearly two-thirds of Southern Appalachia's agricultural households were *semiproletarianized* into coerced labor arrangements or into unstable wage employment (see Table 3.7). Such work lives left them impoverished and seasonally unemployed for three to five months per year. These incompletely integrated households offered two key advantages to agrarian capitalists. "First, these households constitute a flexible labor reserve that is 'on call' to meet the requirements for seasonal labor. . . . Second, the semiproletarian status of the majority of wage-workers cheapens the cost of labor power to capital because a portion of their subsistence is generated out of [household] production. Therefore, they are able to work for lower wages than can full proletarians." As in other peripheral areas of the world economy, the transition to capitalism in antebellum Southern Appalachia triggered a restructuring of labor mechanisms and of the household units that reproduced workers. A hallmark of households in peripheral societies is their capacity to weave together a variety of labor forms so that "subsistence and reproduction costs are provided by a combination of resources other than just the wage."[8]

By the late eighteenth century, two key definitions had been legitimated by public labor law. As early as 1769, absentee owners of Southern Appalachian lands differentiated between "laboring Hands" who contracted to receive wages and "such hands as are Generally allowed and acknowledged . . . to be full sharers in a crop." Moreover, the region's eighteenth- and nineteenth-century farm owners contractually distinguished between those agricultural laborers who would "find themselves" provisions and those to whom the employer made advances of subsistence against future wages or crop shares. For example, an Albermarle, Virginia, planter contracted in 1858 with M. M. Darnell. "I am to give hime one dollar a day," the employer noted in his journal, "and charge no rent for but house whilst he works for me—He finds himself—Full deduction to be made for absence."[9]

By 1860, Southern Appalachian agricultural labor contracts varied around five key elements: the proportion of the factors of production allocated by the landlord; the degree to which the landlord controlled the labor time of the worker; the extent to which the landlord advanced subsistence needs to the laborer household; the nature of the remuneration to be paid the laborer; and the degree to which the laborer engaged in independent cultivation of farmland. In order to survive, Southern Appalachia's antebellum landless agrarians structured their households as income-pooling units around a number of *exploitative labor contracts*, including sharecropping, tenant farming, cottage tenantry, squatting, unstable "wage" labor, indenturement, and slavery. In the sections that follow, each of these labor mechanisms is discussed in greater detail.[10]

Southern Appalachia's Landless Farm Operators

By 1860, nearly two-fifths of the farms in Southern Appalachia were cultivated by operators who did not own the land (see Table 4.2). Surprisingly, the region's *terrain disparity* offers no historical explanation for the presence or absence of farmland ownership. Instead, antebellum tenancy was geographically pervasive, and there was very little comparative difference in the extent to which farms were operated by nonowners in the mountainous, the hill-plateau, or the ridge-valley sectors of the region. In reality, tenant farming in the United States has become established first in those regions where the average acreage per farm has been large but where methods of cultivation have remained relatively simple—two conditions that have occurred frequently in areas like Southern Appalachia that are interspersed with rugged terrain.[11]

Farm tenancy permeated every economic level because it was a cheap mechanism for overcoming labor and currency shortages. Any small farmer who needed to clear "new grounds" out of surplus acres could become a landlord. As we have previously seen, only about one-tenth of the landless kin of antebellum property holders acquired farmland over time through inheritance. By controlling for intrafamily tenancy, I was able to examine the degree to which landless relatives were providing labor on family farms. Antebellum census takers collected household data from each residence; thus, each separate dwelling on a farm was enumerated as a distinct household. By utilizing

Table 4.2. Land Ownership by Southern Appalachian Farm Operators, 1860
A. By State Subregion

	Proportion of Households Operating Farms			
	Method 1		Method 2	
Appalachian Counties of	All Landless Operators Counted		With Adjustment for Kin of Farm Owners[a]	
	Owner	Landless	Owner	Landless
Alabama	.619	.381	.699	.301
Georgia	.575	.425	.648	.352
Kentucky	.622	.378	.738	.262
Maryland	.735	.265	.781	.219
North Carolina	.666	.334	.765	.235
South Carolina	.560	.440	.652	.348
Tennessee	.588	.412	.700	.300
Virginia	.698	.302	.774	.236
West Virginia	.686	.314	.788	.212
Region	.632	.368	.732	.268
B. By Terrain Type				
Mountains	.633	.367	.731	.269
Hills-Plateaus	.652	.348	.737	.263
Ridge-Valleys	.628	.372	.721	.279
Region	.632	.368	.732	.268

Source: Derived from analysis of farm sample ($N = 3,447$); see Table A.3 for sampling details. Here "landless" farm operators include cash renters.

[a]By examining the census enumeration order in the manuscripts, I identified landless farm operators who appear to have been living as part of an extended family on family-owned land. The census enumerators used identifying notations like "son of John," making it easy to link kin who lived immediately adjacent to one another.

the enumeration order of the manuscripts, I isolated landless farm operators who appear to have been living as part of extended families on land owned by relatives. The enumerators used identifying notations like "son of John," making it relatively easy to link kin who lived immediately adjacent to one another. Relatives of farm owners who were residing at a geographical distance from their kin were selling their labor services as tenants on land owned by nonrelatives. As Table 4.2 demonstrates, fewer than one-tenth of the region's landless farm operators appear to have been utilizing family-held acreage. In short, it is empirically unsound to explain away such landless farm operators with the notion that they are simply waiting to inherit land from their families.[12]

Furthermore, being kin to their landlords did not necessarily protect landless farm operators from being controlled by exploitative land tenure arrangements. Instead of relatives being allowed to use family land on an equitable basis, written contracts were often drawn to monetarize the values of land, labor time, and crops. Even *kinship was contractualized* so that landholders could profit from the labor of relatives. In 1838–1839, for example, the Ferry Hill Plantation owner of western Maryland rented farms to his son and to two of his wife's poorer relatives for shares of their crops and for specified labor allocations—a pattern typical of the region's farm owners. An 1857 tenancy contract between a Cherokee, North Carolina, smallholder and his son exemplifies the treatment of landless sons by farm-owning parents. In the articles of agreement, the son was "to have the land for seven years, to pay one-third, and to tend the land in a good farmer-like manner in corn and small grain. . . . Corn to be delivered at [the father's] crib and the small grain at [the father's] stock yard. . . . If [the son] chooses to take the [father's] land at $1,500 he is to have the refusal." The son was also required to care for his father and mother, excepting their food and clothing. Some Appalachian kinship contracts were much more exploitative. In 1848 upcountry South Carolina, for example, tenant farmer John Floyd was evicted by his middling landlord-uncle just after spring planting—an action forbidden by state law. When the tenant refused to move, his uncle plowed up all his crops, replanted the land in cotton, and seized a part of his nephew's livestock.[13]

No wonder then that tenancy and share-farming arrangements provide the cheapest supply of agricultural labor in the peripheral areas of the world economy. Since the land allotment operates as "wages in kind," the farm owner offers ancillary rights to land use as a means of subsidizing very low wages and long hours. "With the labor-tenancy system, capitalist farmers provided their labor-tenants with 'wages' (whether in cash or kind) and with certain privileges (i.e., grazing, cultivation, and residential 'rights') in exchange for capital's command over the expenditure of concrete labor in a determinate labor process. In effect, labor-tenant households received a 'guaranteed subsistence' in return for providing 'labor services.' "[14]

Only a small minority of the region's landless farm operators were independent *cash renters* who entered into land tenure contracts specifying payment of fixed rates of money or produce (see Table 4.3). Nineteenth-century legal custom recognized this landlord-tenant relationship as one in which "the owner of land grants to another simply the right to possess and enjoy the use of such land," with the renter maintaining legal ownership over crops produced. Had they chosen to do so, Appalachian cash renters held enough assets to purchase farmland. They typically owned the means of production other than farmland: slaves, other real estate, commercial property, or considerable assets. Thus, cash renters were not forced to market their personal labor services in exchange for land access, and they had "possession of the premises, exclusive of the landlord."[15]

Table 4.3. Labor Contracts of Southern Appalachia's Landless Farm Operators, 1860

Appalachian Counties of	Proportion with Crop-Sharing Contracts			Proportion with No Crop-Sharing Contracts	
	Sharecroppers	Farm Managers	Tenant Farmers	Cottage Tenants	Squatters
Alabama	.419	.062	.320	.129	.020
Georgia	.519	.049	.236	.130	—
Kentucky	.400	.022	.289	.289	—
Maryland	.318	.043	.442	.098	—
North Carolina	.474	.055	.310	.119	.042
South Carolina	.412	.019	.407	.162	—
Tennessee	.457	.030	.253	.194	.001
Virginia	.390	.077	.298	.123	—
West Virginia	.487	.011	.315	.131	—
Region	.459	.041	.318	.125	.007

Source: Derived from analysis of farm sample ($N = 3,447$); see Table A.3 for sampling details. I utilized several types of information from the farm census manuscripts to categorize landless farm operators, including (a) ownership of work stock; (b) ownership of farm tools; (c) size of parcel; (d) household wealth; (e) identifying labels or comments made by the enumerators; (f) nature and level of crops and livestock produced; (g) the degree to which the household was food-deficient in its crop production. I counted farm operators as "farm managers" or as "squatters" only when they were so labeled by the enumerators. Squatters are undercounted since Cherokee farmers were not enumerated in the 1860 census. Moreover, squatters had every legal reason to hide from census enumerators or to conceal lack of a land tenure contract. The following proportions of landless operators were cash renters: Alabama, .050; Georgia, .066; Kentucky, —; Maryland, .099; North Carolina, —; South Carolina, —; Tennessee, .065; Virginia, .112; West Virginia, .056; Region, .050. Nonagricultural cropping arrangements are not accurately reflected in this statistical analysis.

Cash renting occurred a little more often in western Maryland or Appalachian Virginia, where plantations and slaves could be leased by semisedentary farmers who kept moving westward when staple-crop lands were exhausted. However, cash renters were rare in the rest of Southern Appalachia, where the vast majority of the landless farm operators were impoverished. By 1860, agrarian capitalism in Southern Appalachia had become dependent upon labor power secured through five distinct land tenure arrangements (see Table 4.3). Nine-tenths of the region's landless farm operators indentured their labor time to pay for land access, household subsistence, and a share of the crops—either as tenant farmers, sharecroppers, farm managers, cottage tenants, squatters, or nonagricultural croppers.[16]

Independent tenant farming emerged historically on the Appalachian frontier as a technique by which absentee investors cleared trees, opened new roads, and improved land for resale. By 1770, Robert Carter of Nomini Hall had nineteen tenants improving his Shenandoah Valley lands. Soon after, George Washington had placed thirty-seven tenants on his isolated West Virginia holdings. In the early 1800s, it was customary for absentee owners to market western Maryland, Appalachian Virginia, and West Virginia tenant leases just like land. In 1803 and 1805, for instance, William McCoy rented "all his land & tenements" on a Pendleton County plantation. In these early contracts, it was "very common to set lands for one-third of the produce"—that is, two-thirds of the crop production (minus indebtedness to the owner) was retained by the tenant farmer.[17]

Absentee owners utilized local county agents to monitor their far-flung tenant farming contracts. At the turn of the nineteenth century, an agent for absentee owners of Appalachian Virginia properties found thirty-two tenant farmers on a 4,600-acre tract in Fauquier County; twelve tenant farmers on 1,200 acres toward the Potomac River; forty-two tenant farmers on tracts along the Shenandoah River; and twenty-one tenant farmers at Powell's Fork —all improving the land and cropping on shares. By the early 1800s, large sections of Frederick County, Virginia, were being cultivated by many "tenants upon short leases" whose production of grain was "apparently inferior" to adjacent farm owners. Uria Brown, agent for Baltimore investors, also visited numerous tenant farms in western Maryland and northern West Virginia. Similar early-nineteenth-century tenancy contracts were located for practically every section of Southern Appalachia, including areas like the Big Sandy Valley of East Kentucky, the Cumberland Plateau of Tennessee, and the mountainous counties of western North Carolina.[18]

Well into the mid-nineteenth-century, absentee owners were still following the frontier custom of subdividing their undeveloped lands into parcels that were rented to several tenants who were monitored by local county agents. Battaile Muse of Berkeley County, West Virginia, and William G. Dickson of Burke County, North Carolina, were typical of Appalachian elites who accumulated part of their wealth by collecting rents and managing tenant parcels for absentee investors. In West Virginia, state politicians and local elites— like William Ewin, Samuel Tolbert, George W. Smith, James Wilson, and William McCoy—managed leases for out-of-state clients. Attorney-politician Lewis Maxwell managed his distant West Virginia investments through an agent who repeatedly rented Ritchie County tenant farms on shares from the 1840s until after the turn of the twentieth century. From his home farm in Wood County, Cabell Tavenner operated many tenant farms in Harrison and Monongalia Counties.[19]

Planters residing in adjacent non-Appalachian counties sometimes maintained *long-term investments* in rental properties located in the hills and mountains. For example, Robert Wickliffe, one of Kentucky's wealthiest Bluegrass slaveholders, leased multiple holdings to tenant farmers from 1815 to 1859 in Lee and Estill Counties. Similarly, Walter Alves of Orange County, North Carolina, arranged numerous tenant farm agreements to exploit his extensive landholdings in the Clinch and Powell River areas of East Tennessee.[20]

To expand their control over the labor of the tenant farmers, many Appalachian landlords partitioned their farms with leased parcels adjacent to their own fields. As early as 1797, one East Kentucky planter marketed 10,000 bushels corn and 3,000 bushels wheat yearly by utilizing a few slaves and forty tenant farms.[21] On the East Tennessee frontier, tenant farmers were obligated to clear land, build fences, construct log houses, and pay a share of the crops to their landlords. One traveler reported in 1801 that

> Among the emigrants that arrive annually from the eastern country at Tennessea there are always some who have not the means of purchasing estates; still there is no difficulty in procuring them at a certain rent; for the speculators who possess many thousand acres are very happy to get tenants for their land, as it induces others to come and settle in the environs; since the speculation of estates in Kentucky and Tennessea is so profitable to the owners, who reside upon the spot, and who, on the arrival of the emigrants, know how to give directions in cultivation.[22]

By 1815, the five thousand acres of Jefferson's Monticello were "divided into numerous leased farms that [were] well taken care of." In western North Carolina, one planter maintained his thousand-acre farm with two tenant parcels adjacent to his own fields: one "with a house upon it, rented for one-third the produce, and another smaller farm, similarly rented." Other "gentleman-farmers" engaged overseers to manage slaves; then much of the remainder of their acreage was split into multiple tenant farms to collect crop shares from several "renters."[23]

By the mid-1800s in Southern Appalachia, "about the only way a landless young man could get along was to rent a farm." The pervasiveness of tenant farming is evidenced by the customary dialect of the Civil War veterans. I. F. Fisher "made a one-horse crop 2 years" in Knox County, Tennessee, while William Allen "had a 4 horse crop rented on the Tennessee River bottoms" in Jackson County, Alabama. These expressions indicate that the tenants supplied their own work stock to cultivate a ten-acre parcel and a forty-acre parcel, paying one-fourth to one-third of their crops to their landlords.[24]

Because they perceived land to be plentiful but labor scarce, Appalachian landlords contracted much less frequently with tenant farmers than they did with other types of landless farm laborers. By 1860, therefore, only about one-third of Southern Appalachia's landless farm operators were tenant farmers who contracted to pay a share of crop production in exchange for land use (see Table 4.3). Five key characteristics distinguished tenants from the other landless farm operators. They owned (1) the work animals and (2) farm utensils essential to cultivate crops, and they held (3) more accumulated assets than the other landless farmers (except cash renters). In addition, tenant farmers contracted for land parcels ranging from twenty to 200 acres in order to cultivate small farms that were (4) more independent of day-to-day owner supervision. Thus, tenant farmers (5) produced their own subsistence and additional surpluses, including livestock.[25]

The landlord's crop share was financially linked to the monetary value placed on the specific parcels of land. On the Lenoir Plantation in Haywood County, North Carolina, the owner charged one-third crop share for "new grounds" and one-quarter share for old land. In the 1840s in East Tennessee, it was "customary for the Proprietor to receive one-third the crop from the Uplands, and some of the River Bottom Lands; but on very superior River Bottom Lands, from one-third to one-half." Moreover, the landlord's crop share increased as the degree of investment of factors of production expanded. If seed or work stock were advanced by the Lenoirs, for example, their portion of the crop was contracted at one-half share.[26]

In contrast to the other landless farm operators, the tenant contracted for a situation that promised less daily landlord control over labor time. Typically, the tenant invested more labor in improvement of the rented land with fewer actual work hours spent in the landlord's fields. When the tenant farmer was expected to work for the owner, the tasks were specified in the contract; the tenant farmer was not obligated to furnish general labor at the command of the landlord. For example, Peter Hamlet leased Lenoir land for a one-third share plus his promise to haul manure from the stables and to clear, ditch, and fence certain areas. A West Virginia tenant agreed "to repair the fence around [his landlord's] lott in the town of Franklin." Tenant farmers usually contracted "to keep the fences and enclosures . . . in good repair" on the parcels they leased.[27]

In most tenant agreements, landlords sought to keep closer control over use and maintenance of the land, with less attention to commanding labor contributions toward the owner's cash crops. Thomas Jefferson carefully itemized in his "Farm Book" the land-use regulations that were stipulated in each of his tenant contracts. He specified the order of crop rotation, prescribed road access and maintenance, stipulated the number and type of livestock, and required fencing. In addition, Jefferson prohibited timber cutting and subleasing. These particular covenants must have become the custom, for similar requirements are found in most nineteenth-century tenant agreements.[28]

Typically, Appalachian landlords instructed tenants to "use no timber except dead and fallen timber without permission," prohibited tenants from allowing their livestock "to range at large on the farm," and specified that tenants "cultivate the upland in horizontal drills to prevent washing." To minimize overcropping and erosion, landlords often designated the types of crops to be planted; many leases even dictated grain and pasture crops for specific fields. In the southern hills and mountains, share renting on the "thirds and fourths system" was common. Owners stipulated how parcels were to be cultivated, and the tenants paid to the landlord one-third of the grain and one-fourth of the tobacco or cotton.[29]

An unusual type of tenancy developed in some of the most mountainous sections of Southern Appalachia. Valley planters and large farmers engaged tenant farmers to tend their cattle on small upland parcels. On an isolated mountain farm, for instance, a West Virginia tenant contracted on a one-third share basis with a large livestock dealer to "take your land and pay you fair rent in corn and will be glad to take your stock of hogs and pay you in pork." The tenant was also willing to share-crop cattle with the landlord "on such terms as are fair and just."[30]

In order to expand their cattle production, Virginia lowland farmers purchased mountain pastures that were used by cowboy-tenant farmers to graze great herds. One Charleston, West Virginia, real estate agent advertised rent collection services; "grazing lands a specialty," his calling card claimed. From the early 1800s through the Civil War, for instance, Billy Bradshaw managed as a year-round livestock complex the Blue Ridge Meadows, owned by the wealthy Penlands. Bradshaw, in turn, hired several tenant farmers to tend livestock and raise corn on a share basis. Near Deep Gap, North Carolina, a tenant farmer tended sheep and cattle for Colonel Jim Horton, a prosperous gentleman-farmer of Lenoir. Other tenant farmers drove cattle to the mountains only in the summer months to pasture herds until the fall.[31]

Antebellum Sharecropping Arrangements

Historically, tenant farming and sharecropping appeared simultaneously in the United States. Even though tenancy was crucial to the settlement of Southern Appalachia's frontiers, *sharecropping* emerged and proliferated at an even faster pace. To maximize their undeveloped, isolated, or mountainous land holdings, capitalists entrenched tenant farming throughout the region. Sharecropping, on the other hand, emerged as a contractual mechanism favored by resident farmers who needed to capture cheap labor. By the early 1700s, it was customary for American farm owners to offer crop shares in lieu of wages. In the South, croppers commonly received one-third of tobacco production when the landlord provided minimal subsistence provisions. Plantation overseers, on the other hand, were paid only one-tenth to one-fifth shares of the agricultural surplus remaining after expenses.[32]

Eighteenth- and nineteenth-century public laws in most southern states drew sharp distinctions between "renters" and "croppers." Declaring that "the case of the cropper is rather a mode of paying wages than a tenancy," antebellum laws clearly specified that payment for labor could take the form of shares of the goods produced. Southern legal custom recognized an implication of cropping whenever the arrangement was on shares and the landlord furnished provisions, as in the case of an 1837 North Carolina Supreme Court ruling that "if a man engages another person to come and labour on his farm, as overseer or cropper, and stipulates with him that he will have a share of the crop for his labour and attention, the property in the entire crop is in the employer until the share of the overseer, or cropper is separated from the general mass. . . . Before separation it could not be levied on to satisfy the labourer's debts." Consequently, the cropper was considered to be an employee of the landlord, with no property rights in the crop.[33]

An 1847 North Carolina contract demonstrates the extent to which landlords could restrict the crop distribution. The laborer contracted "to do a faithful year's work" for a landlord who was to furnish fields, horses, and tools as the factors of production. In addition to cultivating assigned cash crops, the laborer agreed "to tend his employer's truck patches" and "to make up the time" should he be sick. A major portion of the laborer's household subsistence was to be advanced by the landlord, including a house, a garden lot, one barrel of corn, two bushels of wheat, 100 pounds of pork, five gallons of whiskey, and ten pounds of coffee. The landlord's legal control over the cropper's labor and possessions was complete, for the contract stipulated that "it is distinctly understood that the [landlord] is to keep the [laborer's] part of the crop or so much thereof as will Satisfy him for what he may be out for articles for the Support of [the laborer's] family."[34]

By the mid-1700s, such labor management strategies were common in Southern Appalachia. When recruiting laborers to open his undeveloped lands in West Virginia, George Washington touted the advantages for capitalists of share agreements when he wrote, "to give standing wages: for what then . . . do you think a sober, industrious & knowing Farmer might be had?" A waged laborer "who is compleatly fit for my purposes, would be above my price." As early as 1798, Appalachian Thomas Jefferson was managing part of his massive Albermarle County, Virginia, acreage through sharecropping arrangements in which he partitioned two small plantations into twelve fields of forty acres each. To his croppers, Jefferson advanced work animals, farm utensils, and provisions. A one-third share was commonly provided to croppers who "Belted fields" on Jefferson's Lego Plantation or who produced swine for his slave population. Methods like those of Jefferson were popular well into the mid-1800s, for many other Appalachian large landholders split their extensive multiple-county holdings into smaller plots farmed on a sharecropping basis, with livestock, seed, and food advances to laborers.[35]

By 1819, the influx of itinerant laborers had become such a nuisance in the Cherokee Nation that the governing council "passed a law that no Cherokee shall employ white persons as farmers or croppers." In spite of that prohibition, trespassers so proliferated that, by 1828, there were more than 200 white croppers in the Cherokee Nation. In 1844, the South Carolina State Agricultural Society distributed questionnaires in the upcountry that included this query: "What effect is produced on the agriculture of the district by the practice of leasing land upon shares?" Subsequently, the society reported that sharecropping had driven upcountry rents to extremely high levels that fell most heavily on the "poor people who can neither buy [land] nor move away."[36]

Croppers on the Appalachian frontier "was vary pore men" who moved almost yearly, like an 1849 northern Georgia family that was escaping from one exploitative contract into another county "in search of a new location." Their meager material goods were packed into "a very small covered wagon . . . which was laden with corn husks, a few bedclothes, and several rude cooking utensils. Behind this team marched a man and his wife, five boys, & eight girls, and in their rear the skeleton of a cow and 4 hungry-looking dogs."[37]

By 1860, nearly one-half of Southern Appalachia's landless farm operators were sharecroppers (see Table 4.3). The popularity of this mechanism is evidenced by the frequency with which antebellum census enumerators entered as occupational categories for Southern Appalachians the terms "cropper," "cropping on shares," "share renter," or "sharecropper." For example, Samuel Lowman of Botetourt County, Virginia, was identified in the 1860 census manuscripts as a "Cropper" who headed a household comprised of three adults and four children under fifteen. The family's total accumulated assets were household furnishings and livestock worth about $80. The manuscript farm schedule reveals that Lowman was an agricultural laborer who owned neither the work animals nor the farm utensils required to cultivate a farm. Yet the family's total agricultural production consisted of 1,500 pounds of tobacco, 200 bushels of corn, one milk cow, and five hogs. In short, the Lowmans were a poor household that was allocating its labor time toward the production of cash crops, even though it was not producing enough foodstuffs for its members to survive.[38]

Thus, sharecropper households emerged as part of the labor force of Southern Appalachian farmers who produced cash crops for market. Typically, sharecroppers were able to contract three to twenty-acre tracts of "new ground" on which they cultivated cash crops specified by the landlord. For instance, the landless farm households of Hannah Snody (Surry, North Carolina), John Phillips (Calhoun, Alabama), John Tray (Floyd, Georgia), Marian Fellers (Greene, Tennessee), Levy Brannum (Amherst, Virginia), and John Boggs (Coffee, Tennessee) reported high production of tobacco or cotton but little or no cultivation of foodstuffs.[39]

Since none of the sharecroppers owned work stock, landlords typically supplied seed, mules, and farm tools. In return, the cropper gave the owner "first call" on all production, agreed to clear land and build fences, and indentured personal assets and labor time for the entire year as collateral against any indebtedness. As remuneration, the sharecropper was entitled to receive a fixed share of the crop production (ranging from one-tenth to one-third), minus indebtedness to the landlord.[40]

What set the antebellum sharecropper apart from other landless farm operators was the extent to which subsistence provisions were advanced by the landlord. Antebellum farm account books from all over the region show clear evidence of landlords advancing provisions and housing to croppers. At annual settling up, the cropper's proceeds from the landlord's sale of the crop share was credited against the laborer's accumulated indebtedness. Typically, the cropper signed a note for any outstanding debts to the landlord.[41]

In fact, more than three-quarters of the Appalachian cropper households were food-deficient; that is, they failed to produce enough food crops to supply their household consumption needs. To maintain greatest control over labor time, landlords characteristically agreed to "find provisions" for the laborer households, including a garden lot, food, housing, and often cash advances. An 1841 West Virginia contract is typical. Negotiating use of thirty acres and the advancement of subsistence needs, the cropper wrote to his landlord: "Perhaps it would be best for you to take the whole matter on my own account and pay me in front in whatever I wished to purchase at the beginning of next year to commence cropping. . . . I only want hogs enough for Pork for the next year." A diary entry for Cherokee County, Georgia, depicts a laborer under even greater control of the landlord. In 1840, the German farmer father of Nathaniel Reinhardt "rented out the most of his corn land; one tenant was taken in, boarded and everything found him, and he paid two-thirds as rent."[42]

About 5 in every 100 landless farm operators was a *farm manager* who contracted to open undeveloped areas from among the owner's sizeable holdings. Farm managers typically contracted their labor for one- to three-year periods; if they were opening new plantation territory, they sometimes supervised slaves. For example, Glover Moore managed three farms covering one square mile of land for a slaveholder of the "leisure class" in Calhoun County, Alabama. As their hired farm manager, Glover's social status was only slightly above that of a tenant farmer. Like other Appalachian overseers, Glover walked or rode through the fields to "push [the] work" of the slaves. As was the case with most other farm managers who supervised the landowner's slaves, Glover worked on nightly patrols "to regulate the comings and going of the Negroes" and to make sudden raids "on suspected Negro quarters to catch persistent offenders and runaways."[43]

Absentee farming was a common practice in Southern Appalachia, and it was not unusual for such holdings to be operated as intergenerational investments within the same families. For example, John Norton subdivided his eighteenth-century Fauquier, Virginia, holdings into three overseer-managed plantations that were later inherited by his sons. One of the Fauquier farm managers negotiated an additional sharecropping arrangement for his sons. "Sir, I should be willing to serve you another year," he wrote, "if you would rent me the place belonging to you that you have formerly rented to Smith for to put my stock at and boys." However, he specified, it would be essential for the landlord to advance provisions to the new sharecroppers. "As I have a large family," he continued, "I should wish for them to be agiting something as well as I for their maintenance." In similar fashion, Benjamin Yancey of South Carolina utilized overseers to manage absentee plantations in Cherokee County, Alabama, and in Floyd County, Georgia. Wealthy Milledgeville and Savannah planters Farish Carter and John Berrien operated summer estates in Appalachian Georgia by relying on the services of farm managers who worked for crop shares.[44]

In another form of "absentee farming," owners of multiple estates within the same geographical vicinity employed several overseers to manage their far-flung holdings. Thomas Jefferson paid crop shares to farm managers that ranged from sixteen barrels of corn (for management of a small farm) to one-fifth of the tobacco (for management of a middling plantation with slaves). James McDowell of Rockbridge County, Virginia, and Edmund Jones of Wilkes County, North Carolina, "absentee farmed" holdings in several adjacent counties by relying on farm managers who were paid crop shares. In order to "engage on any terms not involving the payment of money," Appalachian Tennessee and Virginia planters hired sons of poor farmers "to work with the [slaves] for a term of a year for good wages or a share of crops and stock grown on the farm." A Haywood, North Carolina, overseer contracted for one-seventh of the grains, a share of blacksmithing receipts, all the butter churned, all goose feathers plucked, and one-tenth of the wool.[45]

Southern Appalachian landholders often engaged farm managers to produce livestock on their most rugged surplus lands, particularly the more mountainous sections. In order to cultivate small amounts of corn and tobacco in 1860, Abraham Chandler had improved only 10 acres of the 135-acre Lawrence County, Kentucky, farm he managed. Chandler's landlord placed greater priority on utilizing the unimproved woodlands to graze twenty-four sheep, thirty-six cattle, and forty-nine swine. In similar fashion, James Ogle managed a 525-acre farm in mountainous Fannin County, Georgia. Using a slave, eleven horses and mules, and farm implements supplied by his landlord, Ogle produced 1,700 bushels corn, nineteen cattle, and 120 swine—reflecting no doubt his landlord's interest in marketing pork to the burgeoning company towns at nearby copper mines.[46]

Usually, the landlord supplied work stock, farm implements, seed, and early provisions—part of which was charged against the manager's annual wages at "settling up" time. A typical agreement allowed the landless farmer to "take a support for himself and family out of what the farm grows. But whatever else he needs he is to pay for. . . . [The owner] has full right and privilege to take a proportion of all things of which the said [manager] shall charge [others] for." The farm manager agreed to keep no personal livestock and retained no right to any share of the production beyond his annual wages and subsistence. Determination of this subsistence level was at the discretion of the owner, who charged extra provisions against the household's preset annual wage. In most instances, the farm manager agreed to purchase all food items, "foreign articles," and even furniture from the landlord. Lost work time was also debited against the manager's annual wage, as in one East Kentucky contract that deducted "$1 a day for personal time attending [church] meeting or handling family affairs."[47]

A slightly different type of cropper household emerged as a mechanism used by owners who simultaneously engaged in farming and nonagricultural pursuits. In order to market artisan services to neighboring farmers, Southern Appalachia's large farm owners leased flour mills, sawmills, blacksmith shops, and grist mills on a share basis. In addition, they contracted timber and firewood to be cut on shares. At Monticello in Albermarle County, Virginia, coopers earned one barrel out of every twenty-four produced; blacksmiths earned half the annual receipts; and the nailery manager earned "one-eighth of the price of all the nails made, deducting the cost of the iron." One "mountaineer capitalist" in western North Carolina "owned a grist mill, which he rented to a miller for half the tolls." Sometimes cropper households simultaneously engaged in share-farming and craft-sharing with their landlords. In the Lemmons household of mountainous Marion County, Tennessee, for example, an elderly father, the daughter-in-law, and four children sharecropped a small parcel to produce 150 bushels of corn and twenty pounds of tobacco. Simultaneously, the head of the household worked on shares as a millwright in the landlord's grist mill.[48]

In addition to share contracts with artisans, farm owners employed sharecroppers to engage in nonagricultural pursuits on sections of their surplus lands. While the women and children produced subsistence crops on a garden plot, the adult males were engaged by the owner to cut, haul, and market timber; chop and store ice; provide rafting or ferry operations; or distill liquors. In Virginia, West Virginia, East Kentucky, East Tennessee, and northern Alabama, Appalachian farm owners also engaged in antebellum mining on a sharecropping basis. A northern Alabama smallholder provided an old cabin and small garden lot to a family that had not been able to find work and were "powerful poor." One laborer "was picking in a vein, having excavated a short adit; the other man picked looser ore exterior to the vein. The woman and children shoveled out the ore and piled it on kilns of timber, where they roasted it to make it crumble. It was then carted to a forge, where they were paid for it by the load."[49]

Appalachian land owners in Virginia, North Carolina, and Georgia also utilized sharecroppers to mine for gold on their farms. For example, one South Carolina uplands planter initiated a three-year contract permitting the cropper "to mine, bore, and explore for Gold and other minerals" in return for "one-sixth of the gross proceeds of all Gold, Minerals, and other substances yielded by the mining operations." In all these nonagricultural contracts, typically no more than a third of the production went to the landless household (minus, of course, any indebtedness to the owner). These families resided in the most rugged, least cultivatable areas of the hills and mountains, probably the most geographically isolated of Southern Appalachia's landless farm laborers.[50]

Cottage Tenants

In addition to these first three forms of land tenure, one of every eight of Southern Appalachia's landless farm operators was a *cottage tenant*. Unlike the farm managers, croppers, or tenant farmers, they did not share in the crop production. Instead, they furnished work time in return for the use of a small garden plot and housing.[51] For instance, a small slaveholder of Kanawha County, West Virginia, cultivated his four hundred acres by "hir[ing] men the year round from seven to twelve dollars a month. Day's work was thirty-seven cents for most jobs, fifty cents for clearing land or rolling logs, and one dollar for pulling flax. The men who lived in the log tenant houses on the farm paid house rent at the rate of a dollar or a dollar and a half a month. They had their noon meal at our family table. He paid them largely with supplies of meat, cornmeal, etc. or gave them orders on the stores in town. They were allowed to have cows and chickens and large gardens."[52]

It was not unusual for cottage tenants to be engaged to provide support services to the landlord. On the Ferry Hill Plantation in western Maryland, the owner retained two widow households to function as midwife and seamstress for the slaves. Other members of these cottager households worked for wages in the planter's fields or chopped wood. An East Kentucky cottager, for instance, contracted for the use of the upper end of one field at the rate of $20 per year, to be paid to the owner "at the rate of $1 per 100 rails" to be installed on fencing. Similarly, Mrs. J. M. Beasley of mountainous McMinn County, Tennessee, was engaged as a washwoman while her son hired himself out as a farm laborer for the landlord. In the 1840s, a colony of European settlers was established by New York owners of more than 35,000 acres in the Sylco Mountains of southeastern Tennessee. By 1852, six cottage-tenant families were engaged from Germany, Italy, and France to produce wine for export. Each tenant was assigned specific duties for the proprietorship while being allowed to produce subsistence crops on a small parcel.[53]

Typically, the owner made no agreement to supply specified amounts of subsistence, and it was not unusual for cottage tenants to eat noon and evening meals with the landlord's household. Since provision advances were charged against wages in several regional farm account books, it must have been necessary for the cottager to negotiate repeatedly with the landlord. One midwife-cottager on the Ferry Hill Plantation approached the planter frequently for small food and cash advances, and an 1840 East Kentucky cottager offered to exchange mowing, butter, and lambs for "2 or 3 barrel of potatoes."[54]

These households retained very limited crop production rights. Two-thirds of the 1860 Southern Appalachian cottage tenants were typified by William Childress of Surry, North Carolina, John Pinsley of Marshall, Alabama, and Eliza Scritchfield of Claiborne, Tennessee, who raised only one to four hogs or one to two cattle to supplement their garden vegetables. Little more than one-sixth of the cottagers—like Wilkerson Crain of Habersham, Georgia, or Job Hampton of Jefferson, Tennessee—reported no production at all except their garden patches. The remaining minority of cottage tenants—like Jacob Hosey of Webster, West Virginia, Azariah Hemberton of Alleghany, Maryland, and Henry Taylor of Ashe, North Carolina—must have had access to larger land allotments. In contrast to the majority of the region's cottagers, these fortunate few produced an average of ten to forty bushels of corn, four to twelve hogs, and a few head of cattle or sheep, in addition to their garden vegetables.[55]

There was at least one type of cottager whose families remained on the same land over several generations. Such cottagers grazed livestock in the Blue Ridge Mountains, the Great Smokies, or in the ridges adjacent to the Shenandoah Valley. For example, Blue Ridge cottagers tended hogs and cattle for their landlords in the Humpback Rocks, on Licklog Ridge, and at Potato Field Gap, famous for the cottager custom of tending summer gardens.[56] To monitor their free-ranging herds on Tanners Ridge in Shenandoah Virginia, numerous valley farmer-graziers retained cottagers who neither paid rent nor received a share of the production. Such families would " 'salt the cattle.' . . . If the fence was down anywhere, they'd make emergency repairs. . . . They grew vegetables, often with separate patches for potatoes and corn, and orchard fruit. It was customary . . . for the tenant family to make small gifts of wild nuts or berries . . . to the owner family, perhaps also to feed and lodge them occasionally. . . . Both tenant family and owner family might have been parts of the scene from generations back. . . . If the land was sold, the new owner customarily acquired the tenants along with the land."[57]

Appalachian Squatters

During frontier years, many early settlers were cast into the role of squatters in court disputes over landholdings, as is evidenced by this 1792 ad in a frontier newspaper reminding "people who have settled within [my land] claims that unless they forewith make acknowledgements of tenancy to me . . . suits will be commenced against them." Frontier squatters in western North Carolina were scattered throughout the countryside, living on "Beaking & Greens." One squatter household included "a Woman and Six Children who lived in a small shack." Squatters along the Kanawha and Big Sandy Rivers lived in miserable structures or in makeshift houseboats or flatboats. Numerous trespassers, like one who "cultivated 3 acres of indifferent highland," hid in the mountainous parts of Virginia that were claimed by absentee speculators.[58]

Without benefit of any legal agreement, squatter households set down on out-of-the-way tracts. Squatters in northern Alabama were luckier than their counterparts throughout the rest of Southern Appalachia, for in that subregion there was much more abandoned absentee or public land that no one monitored. For instance, Jane Duncan's household of five adults and one child squatted on the Marshall, Alabama, land of "an absentee owner in Texas." Without any mules and very little in the way of farming utensils, the Duncans managed somehow to produce 150 bushels of corn, 15 bushels of wheat, two bales of cotton, four swine, and one cow. Similarly, Noah Jennings squatted on sixteen acres of Calhoun, Alabama, public land where he grew 100 bushels of corn, six hogs, and two cattle.[59]

However, the typical Southern Appalachian squatters had minimal access to cultivatable land. Clinging to tiny fields, to boats along rivers, or to temporary dwellings on the farms of owners who employed them erratically, most squatters wandered the countryside ceaselessly, trying to avoid arrest for violation of state vagrancy laws. To avoid public scrutiny, squatters selected abandoned tracts in some of the most rugged terrain, like "a great many on the mountain" in Jackson County, Alabama, or three squatters on 1,000 acres of mountainous wasteland in Habersham County, Georgia, or squatter Hammett on a small, out-of-the way ridge in Fauquier County, Virginia. The 1860 census enumerator parenthetically described in the manuscript borders a Greene County, Tennessee, squatter family that would have been typical of the living conditions of such farmers. "These Morgans live on the side of the Allegheny Mountain in a very savage state," he wrote. "They raise a little corn by digging up the ground with a hoe. Sometimes some of them come down into the county and work by the day and bring corn to sell."[60]

Free Agricultural Wage Laborers

Even though tenant farming and sharecropping were generalized throughout antebellum Southern Appalachia, these landless farm operators supplied only a little more than one-tenth of the region's total agricultural labor force (see Table 3.7). Instead, more than one-third of the labor supply derived from wage workers, most of whom *resided off farms*—often in adjacent towns. Only about one in every eight of the region's agricultural laborer households were landless farm operators, yet wage laborers accounted for more than one out of every two of these Appalachian families.

Most of these free wage laborers were engaged to complete specific short-term tasks or to assist with planting and harvest. *Day laborers* were hired by all economic levels of farm operators, and their "wages" often amounted to no more than subsistence. The Civil War veterans indicated that it was not unusual for day laborers to be paid "in trade" rather than in "money wages." The Ferry Hill Plantation sometimes hired thirty or more such laborers at a time, some exchanging their work for firewood or for housing in the planter's town properties. East Tennessean John Sevier remunerated his farm laborers with such provisions as "an order to Millers store for half bushel salt." A larger West Virginia farmer paid day laborers on a weekly basis in meat; for instance, one worker "had worked four days and a quarter got a shoulder fifteen pound." Only the wealthiest farmers paid money wages, leaving housing and meals to the workers. On the Barbour Plantation, for instance, typical day laborer agreements required that the worker was "to have one dollar a day also finding himself." South Carolina's governor estimated in 1850 that at least one-quarter of these day laborers could "not gain a decent living."[61] The nineteenth-century observations of an Appalachian farmer provide a telling synopsis of the economic circumstances of Southern Appalachia's day laborers who remained unemployed five to six months of the year:

> Laborers wages [in western North Carolina] were from 50 cents to one dollar a day or eight dollars a month. . . . ain't general for people to hire here only for harvest time; fact is, a man couldn't earn his board, let alone his wages, for six months in the year.
> But what do these men who hire out during harvest time do during the rest of the year; do they have to earn enough in those two to three months to live on for the other eight or nine?
> Well they gets jobs sometimes, and they goes from one place to another.
> But in winter time, when you say there's not work enough to pay their board?
> Well, they keeps a goin' round from one place to another, and gets their living somehow.[62]

In addition to those wage laborers who lived in nonfarm housing, about one-tenth of the region's middling to larger farm owners and cash renters employed annual *contract laborers* who boarded with their employers. Laborers who resided on farms, but who did not have dwellings separate from the owners, were enumerated by 1860 census-takers as though they were part of the households of their employers. Therefore, these live-in hands are not counted in the earlier summary of the agricultural labor force (Table 3.7). Using the proportion of 1860 farm owners who reported such resident laborers, I estimate that there must have been at least 20,571 contract workers living on farms. Many of these long-term laborers were unmarried males, typically the sons of adjacent farm operators. However, part of them were hired as family units, like one of Thomas Jefferson's resident laborers who "received 176 lb pork nett. he is to have for him & his wife's year allowance 600 lb. I am indebted to him 20 barrels of corn for the year 1781. . . . to find them corn and meat." In contrast to the cottage tenants and croppers, however, these laborers had no access to farmland, so they did not engage in any subsistence agricultural production.[63]

Contrary to stereotype, family members on larger farms did not engage in manual field labor. The Civil War veterans estimated that 5 to 10 percent of the farm owners "had other men to do their work," including "merchants, lawyers, doctors, the majority of slaveholders, preachers, school teachers, and livestock traders." The largest plantations—like Monticello and Aldie in Virginia, Ferry Hill in western Maryland, the Lenoir plantations in western North Carolina, or Ellerslie in East Kentucky—employed great numbers of such workers using a great variety of contractual agreements about the provision of worker subsistence and often paying wages "in kind." In some instances, the employer agreed "to find [the laborer] Diet & Lodging" while another worker would be required to "find himself Diet, Lodging, Hawling &c." In short, the largest segment of the region's agricultural labor force—contract and day laborer households—had no access to farmland or to subsistence garden plots, and they remained unemployed one-third to one-half of the year.[64]

Pooling a Coerced Labor Force

In the peripheries of the world economy, "non-free labor market mechanisms assume unusual importance in the early stages of proletarianization." Antebellum agrarian capitalism in Southern Appalachia was grounded in "the systematic reproduction of non-wage forms of labor." In addition to the application of "extra-economic coercion" toward the free landless agricultural households described in the previous chapter, Southern Appalachian farm owners and cash renters exacted significant labor contributions from three groups of legally unfree workers who comprised more than one-fifth of the region's total antebellum agricultural labor force: the Cherokee squatters, black slaves, and indentured persons.[65]

Cherokee and Slave Laborers

In 1860, only three-fifths of the eastern Cherokee households had "uneasy" access to farms as land users with no legal standing to own property. The remaining Indian families struggled to survive as migratory laborers, squatting temporarily on hillier sections of "friendly" white farmers.[66] The living conditions of one Blount County, Tennessee, squatter household is typical of the circumstances of these itinerant Cherokees during the period from 1838 to 1860. After sharecropping for a number of different landlords, the family moved to a farm where they tended the grist mill.

Table 4.4. Slaveholding by Appalachian Farm Owners and Cash Renters, 1860

Appalachian Counties of	% of Farm Households Owning Slaves
Alabama	39.2
Georgia	41.5
Kentucky	14.0
Maryland	18.9
North Carolina	21.5
South Carolina	52.0
Tennessee	32.9
Virginia	57.4
West Virginia	9.3
Region	31.1

Source: Derived from cross-matching the manuscript sample of farm owners and cash renters with the manuscript slave schedules.

[M]y grand pa used to sleep in a cave up on the hill above the mill. . . . I would climb mountains hunting cows and would bring them home for the folks [we worked for]. . . . grand ma would make baskets and go peddlen. . . . And my grand pa made some chairs and he would take his chairs too to sell [at a nearby town]. . . . [Another farmer's wife] hired grandma to wash for her and we use to go there often to work—one day she asked grandma to split shucks for to put in bed ticks. . . . she would pay grand ma in something to eat meat or flour.[67]

Southern Appalachia's largest group of unfree laborers were 257,729 black slaves. More than one-third of the region's farm owners and cash renters held slaves (see Table 4.4). The greatest dependence on these unfree laborers occurred in Appalachian Virginia, where almost three out of every five farm owners or cash renters were slaveholders. In Appalachian Alabama, Georgia, and South Carolina, where tobacco and cotton cultivation were entrenched, nearly two of every five farm owners or cash renters held slaves. About three in every ten east and middle Tennessee farm owners or cash renters owned slaves. Fewer than one of every five farm owners in the Appalachian counties of Maryland and North Carolina held slaves. However, reliance on slave labor was least characteristic of West Virginia and East Kentucky, where fewer than one in every seven farm owners or cash renters held slaves.[68]

Tenancy occurred in East Kentucky four times more often than slavery, but this pattern was an anomaly in Southern Appalachia. Farm owners and cash renters in Appalachian Alabama, North Carolina, Tennessee, and West Vir-

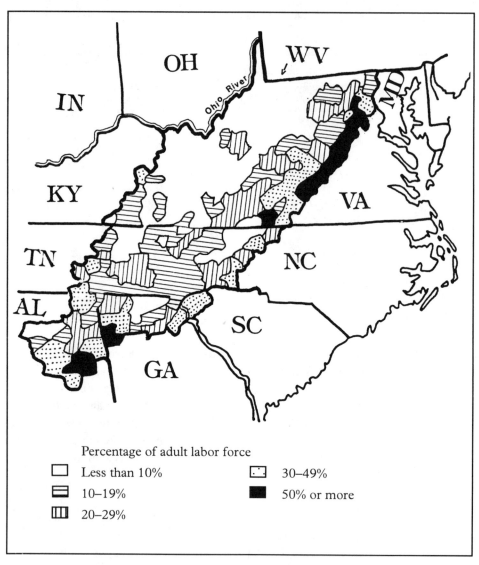

Map 4.1. Slaves in the Appalachian Labor Force, 1860
Source: Aggregated data from U.S. Census Office, *Population of the United States in 1860* (Washington, D.C.: Government Printing Office, 1864).

ginia utilized slaves and tenants at roughly equivalent rates. However, some subsections exhibited much greater exploitation of slave labor. In Appalachian Maryland, Georgia, and South Carolina, there were nearly two slaves to every tenant or cropper. In Appalachian Virginia, however, the incidence of black slavery was six times that of white tenancy. In the region as a whole, farm owners and cash renters relied to a greater extent upon slavery as a long-term labor mechanism than upon tenancy and cropping. In fact, one of every five Appalachian agricultural laborer households was enslaved, indentured, or an unfree Cherokee while only about one out of every eight laborer households was a landless farm operator (Table 3.7).

Thus, slavery was entrenched across Southern Appalachia in an uneven pattern that reflected crop specializations, degree of industrialization, and commercial expansion. Nearly three of every ten adults (fifteen to fifty-nine years of age) in the region's labor force were enslaved. The lowest incidence of slavery occurred in the mountainous Appalachian counties, where one of every 6.4 laborers was enslaved. At the other end of the spectrum, the ridge-valley counties reported the greatest reliance on slavery, with unfree laborers utilized more than twice as often (one of every 2.8 laborers enslaved) as they were used in the zones of the most rugged terrain (Table 3.7).[69]

Map 4.1 illustrates the diverse levels at which Appalachian farms depended upon slave labor. In 1860, slaves comprised less than one-fifth of the adult labor force in two-thirds (138) of the region's counties. In another 64 counties, slaves accounted for 20 to 49 percent of the adult labor force. However, the greatest incidence of slavery occurred in 13 counties of Alabama, Georgia, and Virginia, where one-half to two-thirds of the adult labor force were slaves. In short, slaves comprised more than one-fifth of the adult labor force in one-third of the Southern Appalachian counties.

Indentured Laborers

In addition to Cherokees and slaves, there was another group of coerced Appalachian laborers. By the mid-nineteenth century, Southern poor relief programs had been shaped by public hostility toward the growing population of vagrants. According to the philosophy of the times, unconditional assistance to the poor failed to check their demoralization and encouraged "habitual indolence." The laboring poor were characterized in the press as "virtually a different, permanently degraded species of mankind." It was believed that nothing should be done to mitigate the near-starvation of the "vagrants and offals of society," for only those who were responsive to hunger—the most elemental of labor incentives—could be induced "to fulfil the most servile, the most sordid, the most ignoble offices in the community."[70]

Consequently, compulsory labor by paupers was touted as the only effective act of public benevolence; poor relief—particularly in the South—became structured around temporary sustenance for the elderly or disabled destitute and the location of work situations for the healthy. By 1860, about two-thirds of the Southern Appalachian counties operated poorhouses; but the only inmates residing in these facilities on a long-term basis were elderly, physically or mentally handicapped, or insane persons. Able-bodied adults and children were institutionalized only temporarily until placed in the community.[71]

Archival records reflect six "placement" strategies that were followed by

Risking indenturement in Chattanooga, Tennessee. Appalachian towns dealt with the problem of "wayward youth," like these street peddlers, by declaring them orphans so they could be sold into indenturement by local poorhouses. (From *Harper's Monthly*, August 1858)

Appalachian poorhouses to "solve the pauper problem" in their local communities. First, vagrancy laws authorized poorhouses to "auction off" to community employers adults with no visible means of support. Some counties merely sold the pauper to the person with the highest bid for a work contract; other counties offered the pauper to the lowest bidder, the employer who was willing to accept the least public subsidy toward the new worker's subsistence costs. Second, the county sheriff could arrest and auction off the labor and possessions of persons against whom the courts had made legal judgment for unpaid debts. Third, able-bodied paupers were contracted to work for a local farmer or merchant in exchange for their subsistence.

As a fourth strategy, trouble-making or illegitimate children, the offspring of adults assigned to poorhouses, and orphans were apprenticed to farmers or artisans in every Southern Appalachian state until they reached the age of eighteen or twenty-one. For instance, the West Virginia Humane Society "placed" homeless children through such long-term labor contracts. Similarly, in 1828 and 1846, the Winchester, Virginia, Poor House apprenticed orphans for fourteen years to a local shoemaker. Homeless street children were indentured for as long as fourteen years by the western Maryland Orphans Courts. Similarly, indigent or illegitimate children of the Carolinas were never permitted to become paupers dependent upon the public; rather, they were apprenticed until the age of twenty-one. From 1831 to 1835, the Poor Wardens of Rutherford County, North Carolina, indentured more than one hundred orphans annually. Children in western North Carolina were even bound out by the sheriff when the mother was caught "abusing & beating her children in a barbarous & inhuman manner."[72]

A fifth type of placement strategy was invoked when the pauper was a free black. Local courts sometimes ordered the poorhouses to auction, to apprentice, or to place at compulsory labor some indigent, unemployed, "troublesome," or unwanted free black who had already been warned to "stay out of the county." Any free resident black found spending time "in idleness and dissipation, or having no regular or honest employment" was typically arrested and bound out for three to ten years. After 1826, the southern states placed severe restrictions upon migration by free blacks. In Tennessee and North Carolina, Appalachian counties led the political push for severe restrictions on migration by free blacks, a prohibition that was quickly adopted by most of the southern legislatures. In their petition for the new law, Buncombe County residents complained that "Anterior to 1823–24 we had enough of this unfortunate & trouble-some portion of our species to feel them a public nuisance. . . . there has been a constant influx of free negroes of every character and description into the western part of the state." Subsequently, any nonresident black who remained longer than twenty days in North Carolina was subject to arrest and long-term indenturement. In addition, abandoned or impoverished children of free blacks were taken from their parents and assigned to the poorhouse "to be bound out."[73]

Finally, southern ordinances mandated special public treatment for a "socially embarrassing" category that encompassed a sizeable segment of the region's African-Americans. "Free issue" slaves were descendants of their masters while some free blacks were the children of poor white women. State laws prescribed the manner in which such offspring were to be handled by public officials. In all the Appalachian states, they were assigned to the poorhouses for apprenticeship until their manumission at the age of twenty-one.

For example, the courts of Augusta County and Staunton, Virginia, registered 701 free blacks (as required by state law) between 1801 and 1864. Of this group, 123 were ordered by public officials to be "bound out by the Overseers of the Poor." The Monroe County, West Virginia, courts disposed of nearly two-thirds of its registered free blacks in this manner.[74]

As a result of these public policies, Southern Appalachian farm owners and cash renters could, by the mid-nineteenth century, exploit a third group of unfree workers. About 15 percent of the agricultural laborers residing on the region's farms were adults and children who had been indentured out of county poorhouses. For example, one Calhoun, Alabama, planter reported among his workforce three poorhouse inmates who had been "bound out as farm laborers." In Wayne and Magoffin Counties, Kentucky, farmers worked eight-year-old and twelve-year-old children who had been "bound out by the poor house to work." In Rockbridge County, Virginia, one planter enumerated twenty-one free black workers on his farm, ten of them having been "auctioned off by the Poor house."[75]

Poorhouses were not, however, the only suppliers of the region's indentured laborers. One of the laws of the Cherokee Nation empowered the superintendent of the missionary stations "to take out of their schools such scholars as they deem proper . . . and bind them out to learn such mechanical trades as may be attached to their respective establishments." Well into the 1900s, immigrants bound themselves out to farmers who agreed to pay their transportation costs and provide them jobs. In South Carolina, for example, Scottish and Irish immigrants to the Appalachian country indentured themselves "to serve, for a year or two" those farmers "who paid . . . for their passage." Yet there is one other method of indenturement that is not reflected in public records. Locked into an economically marginal position, poor Appalachian households were often forced into a most extreme form of the *contractualization of kinship*. As a last-ditch mechanism for sustaining the household unit, impoverished parents bound out their own offspring or kin. Unmarried women with several children often apprenticed their sons for seven years or longer to learn a trade from some artisan or farmer. As early as the 1820s, upcountry South Carolina parents indentured their children to work on annual contracts in the cotton mills. Because of severely limited economic opportunities, free blacks also indentured their own children. For example, two Appalachian free blacks were bound out by their grandmother to work for their "vittils and clothes and schoolin'." Several Civil War veterans also reported that they were indentured on annual contracts as farm laborers. For example, one McMinn County, Tennessee, son of a tenant farmer was bound out "from the time [he] was nine yeares of age every year until the [Civil] war as a hired hand on other men's farmes." A Coffee County, Tennessee, veteran reported that, from the age of eight, he "plowed every day" because his unmarried mother bound him out "for two dollars a month."[76]

Labor Maximization Strategies

It is clear, then, that Southern Appalachia's antebellum farm owners pooled labor from many sources. Even the small farms that appear so dependent upon family members pooled labor with neighbors to capture tenants, slaves, or other laborers whom they did not control. "In crop gathering the man who owned slaves would send his slaves to help take care of his [neighbor's] crop" in exchange for the labor of the neighbor's resources in his own harvest. The labor of tenants and croppers was monitored and supervised as closely as that of the slaves. In practice, the tenant or cropper "swapped his labor for the right to use a little of the owner's farm land." On larger antebellum farms, "the tenant's or cropper's share" amounted to no more than what the laborer's family could produce on an assigned field, a crop that could be confiscated for indebtedness to the landlord. In practice on nonslaveholding and slaveholding farms, all the landlord's tenants and croppers worked together, under the supervision of the owner or overseer, in the same field each day. In return for their labor, the farm owner "set aside a large field [for the tenant or cropper]. After [the tenant] worked for 'the man' he could work his [parcel], and they'd loan him the horses to work with. . . . That corn was [the tenant's] to put in his crib."[77]

Rural Labor Pooling

Community activities like log rollings, corn shuckings, and barn raisings were important labor-pooling strategies that were carefully structured to centralize labor in ways that were time and cost effective. At such gatherings, the contribution of slaves was significant. Once a year, cooperating farm owners "come fust to one place, den to de udder, 'til dey makes dr 'roun's." In this way, nonslaveholders and small slaveholders could generate a large centralized labor force. More than a social affair, such activities were closely structured to effect task completion, as one slave narrative illustrates. In middle Tennessee, they would "call up the crowd and line the men up and give them a drink. I was a corn general—would stand out high above everybody, giving out corn songs and throwing down corn to them. There would be two sides of them, one side trying to outshuck the other. . . . The ladies would wait on us and give us cakes and pies and all kind of good things to eat." Sevier County, Tennessee, farm owners also pooled free and unfree labor for flax pullings. Neighboring farmers "would meet at some house or plantation and pull flax until they had finished, then give a big party. There'd be the same thing at the next plantation and so on until they'd all in that neighborhood got their crops gathered."[78]

In order to centralize the large labor forces they needed, East Tennesseans, western Maryland farmers, and Appalachian Virginians also harvested wheat in this manner. The oral history of a white East Tennessee tenant wife makes clear that such labor pooling was neither informal nor fully egalitarian, for it was the farms of land owners that benefited from this process. In East Tennessee, antebellum tenant farmers and croppers rarely cultivated wheat. The pooling arrangements often reached beyond small communities to permit farm owners at a geographical distance to pool their laborers. During wheat harvest

all the farm owners helped each other and that way Dad [a sharecropper] had money coming in against his yearly account because [his landlord] would pay him to go help other land owners. Then when they came to [the landlord's] farm, they'd bring a whole crew to work on the farm. All the owners up and down Hardin Valley, they'd check the wheat fields. Whichever one was ripest that's the one they'd start. They'd go from one farm to the other. The tenant wives along with the owners' wives would gather at the "big house" of the land owner and cook the midday meal for the work hands. There would be an enormous crowd of men—at least forty, two eating tables of twenty each. Sometimes it would take several days to get the crop of one farm in. Then they'd move to another until they got all the crops of wheat in. . . . They came in later after wheat harvest with the same big crews and baled the straw left behind by the wheat thresher.

They began work at sunup and worked from "can see" till dark. If they went outside the community, they had to stay overnight; and all the workers would be boarded at the farm where they were harvesting.[79]

When there was more than one large farm in a community, the slaveholders pooled their slaves among themselves to handle wheat harvests, hog killing, corn husking, quiltings for the slave quarters, tobacco harvests, or cotton picking. "Wid plenty to eat and good liquor to drink on hand," the slaves were organized to "shuck corn or pick cotton all night." All day before the "corn-shuckin' dey hauled corn and put it in great piles. . . . [The slaves were given] coffee and whiskey all night." Under the supervision of a female driver, the slave women also gathered to produce bedding. "It warn't nothing for 'omans to quilt three quilts in one night. Dem quilts had to be finished 'fore dey stopped t'eat a bit of de quiltin' feast." Cotton pickings were also held in a similar fashion, the masters giving "a day off" to those who picked the most cotton.[80]

Labor was rewarded with the social gathering, whiskey, and small prizes. However, these gatherings were neither haphazard nor informal; the work was highly organized and production-oriented, as this slave recollection from western North Carolina indicates:

The man designated to act as the general would stick a peacock tail feather in his hat and call all the men together and give his orders. He would stand in the center of the corn pile, start the singing, and keep things lively for them. Now and then he would pass around the jug. . . . Great excitement was expressed whenever a man found a red ear of corn, for that counted 20 points, a speckled ear was 10 points and a blue ear 5 points, toward a special extra big swig of liquor whenever a person had as many as 100 points. After the work was finished they had a big feast spread on long tables in the yard, and dram flowed plentiful.[81]

It is evident, then, that the conventional historical stereotype of "the prevalence of small-scale agriculture" in which mountaineers cultivated their land only "with the manpower provided by their families" is empirically incorrect. An accurate portrayal of Southern Appalachia's antebellum farms must acknowledge the diverse sources of labor employed by a majority of the region's farm owners. It is essential to put aside the nostalgic tendency to look back and see only a simpler and happier time in which everything seemed to fall into place in a rather informal and relaxed manner. Like their southern counterparts, Appalachian farm owners considered reliable labor to be a scarce and precious commodity. In an era when cash flow was also often limited, it was crucial for them to maximize labor output in return for the expense they had incurred to secure workers.

Extraeconomic Coercion of Appalachian Farm Women

As it incorporates new zones of the globe, capitalism embraces two antithetical labor recruitment mechanisms: (1) a historical proletarianizing of males into wage laborers who produce commodities for the market and (2) a simultaneous historical generalization of nonwage labor that is overwhelmingly conducted by women in arenas that are never fully integrated into the cash economy. Fueled by the ideological "mystification that women are basically housewives," a society undergoing the transition to capitalism experiences a realignment of labor so that *subsistence production* for survival of the household and *biological reproduction* of the labor force are devalued. Thus, women are transformed into "the last link in a chain of exploitation, permitting by their unpaid labour the reproduction" of the workforce at lower cost to the employers.[82]

In the peripheries of the world system, poorer farm women must move back and forth continually between household subsistence work, activities to generate a few market commodities, and semiwage labor arrangements in an attempt to agglomerate the survival needs of their households. Despite their complex interlinkages across several economic arenas, however, such women are less likely than the male members of their households to receive "wage" remuneration for their labor. Essentially, "women's work" is socially invisible because "much of it is unpaid or paid for only indirectly through male intermediaries as heads of households; and there is a tendency to view it as a form of domestic labour without economic value."[83]

Unlike their more well-to-do counterparts who had access to servants, poor Appalachian farm wives carried the burden alone for reproduction, child rearing, household maintenance, and the care of ill or elderly relatives. In addition, these women were responsible for tending the family garden plot, poultry, and livestock. To finance the family's medical care, the wife usually raised an extra head of beef or a hog to be used in barter with the physician. If her household were to survive, however, the poorer woman was required to overextend herself so that she also committed time and energy to several other economic activities. Virtually every poor Appalachian wife whose husband worked in close proximity to the home was expected to contribute labor in the fields. In this regard, poor farm women "went and helped the men folkes in the field," quite often to plant and "layby" crops, cut firewood, make hay, or even to plow. Yet the women's portion of the labor was seldom remunerated with separate wages. Instead their work was an invisible element of the husbands' enterprises.[84]

Though her labor contribution remained hidden behind that of her husband, the typical landless Appalachian farm wife was intricately controlled by the land tenure contract. She was expected—along with her children—to become an "unpaid employee of her husband" in the cultivation of the landlord's cash-crop fields or in the completion of other assigned tasks. When local farmers were short-handed at harvest or spring planting, "all worked alike." Thus, the husbands might sell more of their wives' labor time to neighbors, then collect the wages for their work. One northern Alabama wife maintained a ramshackle cabin, tended the family garden, cared for the children, and did housework—after working all day to increase the husband's share of production from a farmer's coal pit. "They were all clothed very meanly and scantily. The woman worked, as far as I could see, as hard as the men. The children, too, even to the youngest—a boy of eight or ten—were carrying large lumps of ore, and heaving them into the kilh."[85]

In farm manager households, wives endured even greater "extra-economic coercion" from husbands who contractualized their kinship and who negotiated in "the marketplace as the 'possessors' of their wives' labor." It was not unusual for the husband to obligate his wife to complete cash-crop tasks for the landlord. In an 1828 East Kentucky agreement, one husband contracted his wife's time "for her care and attention to the dairy and smokehouse" and to spin clothes for the owner's slaves. In an 1840 letter, one farm manager resisted his landlord's continued demands on his wife's labor. "She has not been inside a meeting house since I have been under employment," he protested. "She has been confined down and have exposed herself in attending to the dairy and the sick [slaves], cutting and making of your clothing until she has lost her health and has become so much reduced in strength."[86]

In other instances, the landlord brought pressure to bear directly on the landless wife so that she contracted out additional labor for tasks like sewing clothes for the owner's household, providing midwifery or medical services to the slaves, "weaving jeans and cotton goods," manufacturing tobacco twists, making rag rugs, or weaving cloth. Landlords were also able to expropriate unpaid labor from the landless wives by requiring them to undertake additional tasks in exchange for food allocations. Rather than charging provisions against the husband's future crop production, the landlord could mandate a "pay-as-you-go" arrangement in which the woman traded "piecework labor" for rations. In one East Kentucky contract, for example, the farm manager agreed "to purchase all the family's produce and provisions and furniture for their personal use through [the landlord], . . . [the landlord expecting the wife's] spinning and milk in exchange for the wheat."[87]

Summary

Before Southern Appalachia could be incorporated into the network of world-capitalist processes, one of the major stumbling blocks that had to be overcome was the lack of available labor. Following the expansion of settler capitalism into the region, scarce productive resources were monopolized by local elites and absentee capitalists. Subsequently, land served as the critical mechanism for anchoring labor relations between landholders and propertyless families. Emanating out of competition over the region's scarce land resources, three historical pressures hastened and reinforced the commodification of labor. First, absentee speculators and settler elites systematically acquired control over three-fifths of the region's agricultural acreage. Contrary to historical mythology, fewer than one-third of the region's total agricultural labor force owned farmland. Instead, land engrossment generated local communities in which the bottom three-fifths of all the households had no access, either as owners or tenants, to farm acreage.

The second historical impetus to labor commodification was the low likelihood of social mobility in the region. Nearly nine-tenths of the Appalachian veterans were convinced that "the poor man had no chanc" to accumulate enough assets to buy land or to initiate a business in the antebellum period.[88] Facing erratic wages, few chances to locate rental farms, and limited educational opportunities, a sizeable segment of the Southern Appalachian population led economically precarious lives and was trapped permanently at the bottom. In local economies that did not permit wealth accumulation for the bottom majority of the population, only a small minority of propertyless Appalachian households became landholders between 1810 and 1860. Consequently, intergenerational landlessness was a third impelling force toward labor commodification. Rather than being a transitory step toward land ownership, tenancy proved to be an agricultural "dead end" for many Southern Appalachians; thus, one-quarter or more of the region's households remained landless on an intergenerational basis.

Peripheral capitalism unfolded in Southern Appalachia as a mode of production that combined proletarian labor and commercialized land with several forms of nonwage labor and land tenure. By 1860, one-quarter to one-third of the region's farms were cultivated by operators who did not own the land, and nine-tenths of these landless farm operators were impoverished. Agrarian capitalism was structured in antebellum Southern Appalachia as a form of economic relations in which direct producers sold their labor power to capitalists as part of five distinct land tenure arrangements. Tenant farmers, sharecroppers, farm managers, cottage tenants, and squatters comprised an important segment of the agricultural labor force. Even kinship was contractualized by relatives who captured the labor of family members to maximize the profitability of their land investments.

Because control over land, the primary factor of production, was denied to them, the unpropertied majority of the Appalachian population was transformed into an agricultural proletariat. The most important regional supply of farm workers derived from short-term day laborers who resided off farms and from longer-term contract laborers who lived in farm-owner households. Because they had no access whatsoever to agricultural land and since they were unemployed three to five months of each year, these workers probably led even more precarious existences than any of the other categories of Appalachian laborers.

However, articulation with the world economy did not trigger only the appearance of free wage labor; capitalist dynamics in antebellum Southern Appalachia also generated a variety of unfree labor mechanisms. "The process of incorporation . . . involved the subordination of the labor force to the dictates of export-oriented commodity production, and thus occasioned increased coercion of the labor force as commodity production became generalized."[89] In sharp contrast to the notion that Southern Appalachian farms relied solely on family laborers, the region's producers agglomerated an ethnically and sexually diverse labor force that creatively combined free laborers from the ranks of the landless tenants, croppers, poor women, and wage laborers with unfree workers from four sources. Legally restricted from free movement in the marketplace, the region's free blacks, Cherokee households, and indentured paupers contributed coerced labor to the region's farms. However, Southern Appalachia's largest group of unfree laborers were slaves who supplied long-term labor to one of every three farm owners and who accounted for one of every five agricultural laborer households.

The capitalist incorporation of antebellum Southern Appalachia initiated the evolution of an agricultural semiproletariat whose members were able to obtain only a portion of their subsistence needs from wage income. Over their work lives, agricultural laborers in antebellum Southern Appalachia were forced to subsidize low and unreliable wages with subsistence farming, with sales of commodities or services on the market, with part-time nonagricultural employment, and with exchanges in the informal sector.

Peripheral capitalism, as it developed in antebellum Southern Appalachia, was characterized by two contradictory historical trends. On the one hand, labor was increasingly commodified between 1800 and 1860, with the largest segment of the agricultural labor force working for wages (either in cash or crop share). On the other hand, the incorporation process stimulated in the region a structural tendency to slow that transition to free wage labor and to deter the complete proletarianization of the entire labor force. Never fully integrated into the local economy as independent producers and never completely proletarianized into wage occupations, much of the antebellum Southern Appalachian population was economically "marginalized"—that is, they neither owned the means of production nor were they remunerated for their labor on a reliable or equitable basis.

5

MAKIN' DO OR CHASING PROFITS?

THE AGRARIAN CAPITALISM OF

SOUTHERN APPALACHIA

Debunking the Subsistent Homesteader Myth

The preindustrial Appalachian economy has primarily been conceptualized as a "folk world of small, isolated, homogeneous societies with a simple and almost self-sufficient economy" that consisted predominantly of small homesteads operated by precapitalist farm owners. Left as they stand in the current literature, simplistic generalizations about "self-sufficiency" or "subsistence" enlighten us very little about antebellum modes of economic production. Stereotypical applications of these concepts have generated several widely held misconceptions. The broad ascription of these terms to almost all American antebellum rural families masks wide disparities in land ownership, occupational status, and wealth. Some writers would have us believe that none of the country's eighteenth- and nineteenth-century farmers were producing commodities for the market or utilizing wage laborers. Moreover, the romantic vulgarization of these concepts prevents our recognition that there were agricultural households who lacked access to land or other means of production and who were forced to sell their labor to wealthier farmers.[1]

It is necessary, then, to recast these notions into more theoretical terms. Since it is not possible for households to survive without any interdependence with others, we should begin by disposing of the term "self-sufficiency." For some time, economic historians have questioned the notion that American antebellum farmers were either "self-sufficient" or "subsistent." As part of the political ideology associated with the egalitarian "family farm," they argue, the concept "self-sufficiency" does not provide the analytic precision necessary to uncover the complexity and the disparities of rural social structure. The concept *subsistence* offers more utility since it has been more closely conceptualized by social scientists.[2]

Conceptual Clarification of Subsistence

We can initially delimit the notion of subsistence by specifying some instances that are *not* encompassed by the concept. First, the agrarian economy as a whole should not be conceived as a homogeneous subsistent entity, thereby masking internal diversity. Second, it is conceptually inappropriate to assume that the presence of a *barter* system of exchange is evidence of subsistence production. Barter is simply a nonmoney form of trade; profits and wealth accumulation can accrue from barter. Third, it is conceptually inaccurate to think of any agricultural household as subsistent when its production processes incorporate the labor of slaves, indentured servants, tenant farmers, sharecroppers, or nonfamily wage earners. The presence of such workers indicates the presence of surplus wealth and the intent of the employers to produce surplus crops.[3]

Instead, subsistence should be viewed as the human work and natural resources required to produce the items that are "physically indispensable" to human maintenance from day to day and to family reproduction from generation to generation. Subsistence production, then, must be narrowed to those activities that are geared to produce survival needs "that are the result of transformation activities conducted by the household," utilizing materials they own. This definition focuses our attention upon two points of clarification: (1) an emphasis upon production by household pooling units and (2) the centrality of household consumption. In short, *producer* and *consumer* are the same entity. Since commodities are generated for their immediate "use value," truly subsistent households produce no surplus commodities that can be used to earn money.[4]

However, subsistence producers cannot be delineated solely in terms of their *consumption* of major food crops, for such a faulty technique would place many plantations under the rubric of nonmarket cultivators. Analyzing consumption as the only indicator of subsistence production ignores (1) cultivation of cash staple crops; (2) types of nonfamily labor utilized; (3) nonfarm sources of cash income; and (4) the availability of surplus land or slaves as marketable commodities. In line with the popular stereotype that Appalachian farmers produced everything they needed from the land, this study defines a true subsistence producer as a *farm owner* who held fewer than 100 acres; owned less than $100 in assets; relied solely on family labor; cultivated no cash staple crops (i.e., tobacco or cotton); had no second source of cash income or wealth; and consumed 80 percent or more of the farm's total grain, swine, and cattle production. In contrast, a farm family that consumed most of its food production was a *capitalist* enterprise when the household held surplus land, hired laborers, owned slaves, utilized tenants or croppers, or held more than minimal wealth.[5]

One final clarification is crucial. Although few scholars have done so, it is conceptually important to draw a distinction between true farm household subsistence and the application of food crops to generate market surpluses. Any farm which cultivates more than its family survival needs in order to support paid or coerced laborers or to feed surplus livestock is *not subsistent*, even if that farm consumes all its major food crops. In reality, such a farm is producing surplus grains and meat that are needed to maximize the yield of profitable commodities for the market. It was not unusual, for instance, for Southern Appalachia's small slaveholders to consume most of their food crops in order to feed tenants, slaves, or surplus livestock on farms producing livestock and staples for export. In reality, farm owners *reinvested* a portion of their food crops in order to generate additional surpluses. In Southern Appalachia, one-tenth to two-fifths (depending on the geographical zone) of the total grain and livestock production was absorbed to provide food for paid laborers and slaves, to fatten surplus livestock, and to store seed reservations for the next year's surplus grains. These reinvestments cannot be considered a part of subsistence allowances and were isolated in this research.[6]

Southern Appalachia's Subsistent Farmers

Contrary to popular stereotypes, subsistence farming was *not* characteristic of antebellum Southern Appalachia. Instead, little more than one-tenth of the region's farm owners were either subsistence or near-subsistence producers (see Table 5.1). Fewer than one of every fifty farm owners was a subsistent producer who held few resources beyond survival needs and who had no access to any other source of livelihood. Indeed, farm owners like Agnes Coon of Roane County, West Virginia, were a *rarity* in the 1860 Census of Agriculture manuscripts. A true subsistence producer, Coon supported two adults and seven children on forty-eight acres where she cultivated one hundred bushels of wheat, one hundred bushels of corn, one cow, eleven sheep, and one hog. Although the family consumed everything it grew (and a little besides), they still sold $25 worth of market produce. However, they had no land surplus, reported no wages, and grew no tobacco—unlike many of their neighbors.[7]

Still, the extent of subsistence farming varied slightly from one geographical sector to another. The stereotypical "subsistent homesteaders" were absent from the census manuscripts for the Appalachian counties of Alabama, Georgia, Maryland, and South Carolina, and they made a very scant appearance in the Appalachian counties of North Carolina, Tennessee, and Virginia. West Virginians operated farms at the subsistence level more often than did residents of other Appalachian zones. There one of every seventeen

Table 5.1. Subsistence and Surplus Agricultural Producers, 1860

A. Subsistence and Near-Subsistence Producers

| | % of All Farm Owners and Cash Renters | | | |
Appalachian Counties of	Subsistence Producers	Subsistence Producers with Wages	Marginal Surplus Producers	Total
Alabama	—	8.1	0.9	9.0
Georgia and South Carolina	—	6.1	1.0	7.1
Kentucky	2.2	8.8	2.9	13.9
Maryland	—	17.5	3.5	21.0
North Carolina	1.0	18.1	—	19.1
Tennessee	0.4	2.7	—	3.1
Virginia	0.8	4.1	—	4.9
West Virginia	6.3	13.0	0.4	19.7
Region	1.9	8.5	0.7	11.1

B. Surplus Producers

| | % of All Farm Owners and Cash Renters | | | |
Appalachian Counties of	Nonslaveholders	Small to Medium Slaveholders	Plantations	Total
Alabama	51.8	29.6	9.6	91.0
Georgia and South Carolina	51.4	31.6	9.9	92.9
Kentucky	72.1	11.9	2.1	86.1
Maryland	50.5	26.2	2.3	79.0
North Carolina	58.5	18.3	4.1	80.9
Tennessee	64.0	28.0	4.9	96.9
Virginia	37.7	43.2	14.2	95.1
West Virginia	66.8	11.8	1.7	80.3
Region	52.8	28.6	7.5	88.9

Source: Derived from analysis of all farm owners and cash renters included in the sample of farms ($N = 3,447$) drawn from the 1860 Census of Agriculture enumerator manuscripts.

owners eked out a narrow survival, with less than one-fifth of crop production remaining after household consumption. Women were overrepresented among the region's subsistent farmers. Even though they accounted for less than one-tenth of the region's farm owners, females headed more than one-fifth of the truly subsistent farm households.[8]

In reality, it would be very difficult to identify any western society that practiced a "pure subsistence lifeway," even as far back as two thousand years. Almost every agricultural system includes elements of subsistence production, alongside market exchanges of labor and commodities. Thus, so-called "subsistent" Appalachians were not precapitalist, and they did not exist totally outside market connections or trade exchanges. In fact, more than half of the "truly subsistent" households produced grain and livestock surpluses that were probably exchanged, and three-fourths of them reported to census enumerators that they had sold market produce and home manufactures.[9]

In addition, nearly half the "truly subsistent" households reported food crops that met only one-third to one-half of their total annual food needs. These households must have traded for food, engaged in unreported commodity sales, or sold unreported part-time labor. Many of these subsistent households were enmeshed in capitalist activities as *semiproletarians* who combined irregular wage income with limited farming. Thus, subsistence production does not mean that families exist totally outside market connections or trade exchanges. Furthermore, consumption in subsistent households came to include the routine use of imported foodstuffs (e.g., salt, sugar, tea, coffee) and the purchase of commodities to meet needs previously satisfied by home manufactures (e.g., shoes). Even if their market linkages and surplus profits were minimized, there was still a low level of exchange that pulled even the subsistent household into capitalistic commodity chains and permitted them to consume exotic imports from distant reaches of the global economy.[10]

The extent of these invisible market linkages becomes clear when we examine those farm owners who were subsistent wage earners or marginal surplus producers (Table 5.1). Because they combined wages with small agricultural operations, a majority of the nearly subsistent farm owners were enmeshed in capitalist activities as semiproletarians who survived by supplementing irregular wage income with subsistence agriculture. Typical of such households was the family of Joshua Dixon of Frederick County, Maryland; Dixon occupied himself with full-time farming while two of the other six adults earned nonagricultural wages. On their twenty acres, the Dixons produced one hundred bushels of wheat, two hundred bushels of corn, five cattle, and six hogs; still the household remained food-deficient. In western Maryland and western North Carolina, nearly one-fifth of the farm-owner households were supplementing their agricultural production with cash earnings, followed closely by West Virginia, where thirteen of every one hundred farm owners was a wage-earning subsistence producer. Similarly, six to eight of every one hundred owner households in northern Georgia, northern South Carolina, northern Alabama, and East Kentucky had household members who were nonagricultural wage laborers or artisans.

In addition to subsistent wage earners, a small sector of "marginal surplus producers" made crop choices that clearly indicate their orientation to the market. Even in the face of household food deficits, these farm owners cultivated small cash crops. Consider, for example, the Jasper Wyatt farm in

Doddridge County, West Virginia. Even though this family of nine grew only two-thirds of its food needs, Wyatt used part of his limited land and labor to grow thirty pounds of tobacco. Other marginal staple farmers faced even greater food deficits, like the John Youst household of Marion County, West Virginia. Even though they cultivated only half of their food needs, they opted to apply part of their labor time to produce twenty pounds of tobacco. John Chevalley of Berkeley County, West Virginia, was an even more extreme case. The Chevalley household chose to use their fourteen acres to produce nothing except three hogs and $600 worth of garden vegetables that were marketed in the nearby town. Since they generated less than one-quarter of their annual household food requirements, they must have exchanged cash or labor for survival needs.[11]

Land Concentration as a Deterrent to Subsistence Agriculture

If indeed the subsistent homesteader was unusual in antebellum Southern Appalachia, what accounts for the absence of this type of agricultural production? Contrary to nostalgic stereotypes, subsistence farming was *not* motivated as much by ideological choices on the part of producers as it was by their shortages of land, labor, and capital. Much of the explanation for the scarcity of subsistence farmers lies in the region's inequitable landholding patterns. Several researchers have documented the extent to which land was out of the reach of many ordinary nineteenth-century families on other American frontiers. Still, the conventional perception is that preindustrial Appalachia was characterized by "the prevalence of small-scale agriculture." However, that view is faulty. As we have seen, antebellum Southern Appalachians competed for land with two layers of absentee and resident resource monopolizers. As a direct consequence of the capitalistic restructuring of land tenure, the region's farm acreage was heavily concentrated into the hands of the largest landholders in every Appalachian geographical zones. In 1860 in the region as a whole and in the Appalachian counties of South Carolina, Tennessee, and West Virginia, the top decile of farm operators owned more than half of the farm acreage while the bottom half controlled less than 12 percent of the resources. This same pattern was also evident in the other sectors of the region. In the Appalachian counties of Georgia, Kentucky, Maryland, North Carolina, and Virginia, the wealthiest decile of farm operators engrossed more than two-fifths of the farm acreage, leaving only one-seventh of the resources available to the poorer bottom half of the farm households. Even those middling farmers holding 200 to 499 acres acquired less than their proportionate share of the available agricultural land area.[12]

Such resource concentration occurred all over the region. For instance, farm lands in twelve counties of Appalachian Virginia were cut up into immense estates that were "held by a few individuals who derive[d] large incomes from them, whilst the generality of the people [we]re but in a state of

Table 5.2. Who Owned Appalachian Farm Land (1860)?

A. Distribution of Owner-Operated Farms by Acreage

Appalachian Counties of	% of Owner-Operated Farms in Each Size Category			
	1–99	100–199	200–499	500+
Alabama	29.9	23.4	36.4	10.3
Georgia	20.0	31.3	39.9	8.8
Kentucky	18.4	28.7	33.1	19.8
Maryland	24.1	38.9	29.6	7.4
North Carolina	13.3	32.4	33.3	21.0
South Carolina	—	35.3	41.2	23.5
Tennessee	11.9	28.3	41.1	18.7
Virginia	15.3	33.2	28.8	22.7
West Virginia	21.4	31.4	31.4	15.8
Region	17.9	30.6	34.2	17.3

B. Distribution of Farm Acres Owned in Each Size Category

Appalachian Counties of	% of All Acres Owned by Each Size Category			
	1–99	100–199	200–499	500+
Alabama	6.4	12.5	34.7	46.4
Georgia	4.3	16.6	45.1	34.0
Kentucky	3.1	13.1	22.4	61.4
Maryland	4.2	16.7	31.8	47.3
North Carolina	2.4	12.7	29.4	55.5
South Carolina	—	13.4	30.5	56.1
Tennessee	1.8	11.3	19.4	67.5
Virginia	2.3	12.2	23.1	62.4
West Virginia	4.9	21.9	21.1	52.1
Region	3.4	15.8	21.7	59.1

Source: Derived from analysis of farm sample ($N = 3,447$) drawn from the 1860 Census of Agriculture enumerator manuscripts; see Table A.3 for sampling details.

mediocrity." In similar fashion, only a small minority (12.7 percent) of the parental households of 474 Appalachian Civil War veterans owned more than 500 acres; yet they monopolized nearly two-thirds of the farmland in their counties. Landholding patterns in Cherokee communities paralleled the elite concentration typical of white Appalachians; the wealthiest 8 percent of Indian households monopolized nearly half the available land area.[13]

The extent of farmland concentration becomes evident when the actual holdings of poorer farmers are examined. Even though holders of fewer than 100 acres comprised nearly one-fifth of the region's farm owners (see Table 5.2), they controlled less than 4 percent of the agricultural land. Thus, the region's poorest farm owners held fewer than one of every twenty-five acres. In Appalachian Tennessee and Appalachian Virginia, the bottom decile of farm owners held land at relatively negligible levels, controlling less than 2 percent of the total acreage. Conditions were even worse in northern Alabama, where subsistence producers owned little more than one-half an acre out of every one hundred. In western North Carolina and West Virginia, subsistence producers comprised nearly one-fifth of the owner households, but they owned only 4 to 8 percent of the farmland. In antebellum Southern Appalachia, farmland was concentrated into the hands of those farmers who were cultivating crops for the marketplace. Nearly two-thirds of the agricultural acreage was monopolized by holders of more than 500 acres, and one-fifth of the farmland was monopolized by a tiny plantation elite.

Moreover, farmland ownership was most concentrated in those sections of Southern Appalachia where agricultural production was made most difficult by rugged terrain. In the region's most mountainous counties, two-thirds of the agricultural acreage was monopolized by one-fifth of the owners, those holding more than 500 acres. Consequently, mountain farms averaged 518 acres in size. In mountainous Monroe County, Tennessee, for instance, less than 8 percent of the farms were smaller than 100 acres, and they encompassed less than 2 percent of the total farmland. In contrast, the county's 107 owners who held more than 500 acres monopolized more than one-third of all the farm acreage. Similarly, little more than one-tenth of the region's ridge-valley owners controlled more than three-fifths of the agricultural acreage in those counties; farms situated in ridge-valley terrain averaged 398 acres. While the entire region's largest farms averaged nearly 1,220 acres, larger farms situated in ridge-valley terrain averaged more than 3,400 acres.[14]

In antebellum Southern Appalachia, only the typical Cherokee farm corresponded to the romantic stereotype of small family homesteads. Nine-tenths of the pre-Removal Cherokee households operated farms averaging less than 14 acres; another small fraction controlled landholdings ranging between 50 and 99 acres. Among white Southern Appalachians, however, less than one-fifth of the region's owners operated farms smaller than 100 acres. Indeed, the small farmstead was very rare in the Appalachian counties of North Carolina, Tennessee, South Carolina, and Virginia. Moreover, less than one-tenth of the parents of Appalachian Civil War veterans owned farms smaller than 100 acres, and this small group of households controlled less than 2 percent of the total farmland.[15]

Contrast these patterns to public land policy in the Midwest. After 1832, an outlay of $50 could buy 40 acres. As a result, most of that region's farms were smaller than 160 acres, and land was fairly evenly distributed among farmers. Moreover, it was not unusual for farms to be small enough to operate as subsistence producers. In Southern Appalachia, however, antebellum landholding patterns *discouraged subsistence agriculture* by concentrating farm acreage under the control of larger farmers and by relegating poorer households to the worst terrain. Land was just too dear and farm-establishment costs too expensive to be afforded by those propertyless households at the bottom, those most likely to be subsistence producers. With concentrated land ownership, even access to the most hilly and mountainous sections—those areas that we might presume to be cheaper—were limited because these were the places in which capitalist investments were being made in antebellum extractive industries and tourist resorts.[16]

Southern Appalachia's Surplus Producers

By 1860, Southern Appalachia produced about 8 percent of the country's wheat and corn, 7 percent of its tobacco, 3 percent of its cotton, 6 percent of its cattle, and a little less than one-tenth of total swine production—or an average of 137 bushels of wheat, 615 bushels of corn, 1,298 pounds of tobacco, and 19.5 bales of cotton per farm owner. In sharp contrast to the stereotype of a backward, laggard region, most of Southern Appalachia's farm owners *exceeded* national averages in per capita production of wheat, corn, and hogs and were equivalent to national averages in their per capita production of tobacco and cattle. Moreover, they fell only slightly below national averages in per capita production of cotton (see Table 5.3).[17]

Even more significant is a comparison of the region's agricultural output with that attained by all the southern states. For all crops except cotton, Southern Appalachia's farm owners cultivated at a level that far exceeded output by southern farms. Appalachians generated seven times the per capita wheat production of the South as whole, four times the per capita corn production, twice the per capita tobacco production, two and one-half times the per capita cattle production, and three times the per capita swine production. Most surprisingly, Southern Appalachia fell only a fraction below southern per capita production of cotton, the crop usually believed to have been absent due to the region's more rugged terrain and shorter growing season.[18]

Zone Specialization in Crops
Internally, there were zone differences in the types of major crops grown and the levels of production. Western North Carolina fell below national per capita production in all food crops; West Virginia was equivalent to national averages only in the production of wheat. East Kentucky fell behind national averages in its grain crops while northern Georgia and western Maryland produced cattle and hogs at levels below national per capita averages. Only in the production of wheat, tobacco, and cotton was there any significant impact of terrain upon agricultural output, for these crops were more often grown in

Table 5.3. Agricultural Production of Southern Appalachia, 1860

Appalachian Counties of	Wheat Total Bushels Grown	Wheat Bushels per Capita	Corn Total Bushels Grown	Corn Bushels per Capita	Tobacco Total Pounds Grown	Tobacco Pounds per Capita
Alabama	583,472	3.2	6,501,510	35.9	131,097	0.7
Georgia and South Carolina	989,412	5.6	6,503,061	34.8	570,928	3.4
Kentucky	665,874	3.5	8,930,523	46.4	616,573	3.2
Maryland	1,946,672	18.3	1,913,300	18.0	389,150	3.7
North Carolina	565,959	1.9	4,452,047	15.3	946,836	3.3
Tennessee	2,660,162	6.8	16,974,448	43.4	944,923	2.3
Virginia	4,927,659	10.5	12,504,844	26.7	24,615,739	52.5
West Virginia	2,268,118	6.0	7,733,397	20.6	2,179,091	6.0
Region	14,607,328	6.7	65,513,130	29.9	30,418,410	13.9

Appalachian Counties of	Cotton Total Bales Grown	Cotton Bales per Capita	Cattle Total Number	Cattle Number per Capita	Swine Total Number	Swine Number per Capita
Alabama	83,291	0.5	133,479	0.7	331,578	1.8
Georgia and South Carolina	26,647	0.2	98,075	0.5	323,240	0.7
Kentucky	—	0	138,875	0.7	394,474	2.1
Maryland	—	0	52,572	0.5	79,948	0.8
North Carolina	3,054	0.1	99,454	0.3	298,120	1.0
Tennessee	8,295	0.1	327,199	0.8	729,325	1.9
Virginia	170	0	337,630	0.7	591,057	1.3
West Virginia	125	0	282,329	0.8	334,751	0.9
Region	112,582	0.1	1,469,613	0.7	3,082,493	1.4

Source: Calculated using aggregated totals from the published 1860 censuses of Agriculture and Population.

the region's ridge-valley counties where large coves, valleys, and river bottom-lands were located. However, terrain disparity accounted for little per capita difference in the production of corn, cattle, and hogs across the region.[19]

Still, the region's geographical zones did specialize in different combinations of grains, livestock, and staples. The Appalachian farm owners of Alabama and Georgia opted to cultivate most of the region's cotton, with high production also in a few counties of Appalachian Tennessee. These cotton-raising areas produced wheat at levels below regional averages, but they exceeded regional averages in their production of corn, cattle, and hogs. Even though staples were cultivated to some extent in every geographical zone of Southern Appalachia, only the farm owners of Appalachian Virginia were significant tobacco producers, cultivating this staple crop at a level that was two and a half times the national per capita averages and five times the southern per capita averages. Western North Carolina ranked second in the region in per-owner production of tobacco while falling well below regional averages in grain and livestock production. Western Maryland specialized in wheat production, each farm owner averaging three and a half times as much of that crop per year as did the average Southern Appalachian farm owner. At the same time, western Maryland fell below regional averages in its production of all other crops. In contrast to all the other zones, West Virginia fell well below regional averages in its per capita production of all crops. East Kentucky barely exceeded regional averages in corn production, but that zone's farms fell below regional averages in per-owner cultivation of wheat, tobacco, cattle, and hogs.

Who Were the Surplus Producers?

In short, most Southern Appalachian farm owners produced agricultural surpluses, as we can see from an examination of average household production and consumption of grains and livestock. The region's typical farmowner household produced 752 corn equivalencies but consumed for its subsistence only 185 bushels of that output, thereby generating three times more wheat, corn, cattle, and hogs than were necessary to meet minimal survival needs. On average, then, the region's farm owners consumed less than onequarter of their total annual grain and livestock production. In the Appalachian counties of Alabama, Georgia, South Carolina, and Tennessee, farm owners consumed, on average, less than one-fifth of their food crop production. Similarly, Appalachian farm owners of Maryland and Virginia utilized less than one-quarter of their food crops for household subsistence. After meeting subsistence and crop reproduction requirements, East Kentucky farm owners cultivated two-thirds to seven-tenths of their crops as surpluses. West Virginia's farm owners absorbed a greater proportion of their crops for subsistence than did households in other Appalachian zones. Even these Appalachians, however, produced twice as much grain and livestock as they needed for minimal survival needs.[20]

Who, then, were these surplus producers? Nearly nine-tenths of the region's farm owners consumed less than one-fifth of their total food crop production or grew staple crops; used laborers other than family members; had assets well above minimal survival needs; and often drew on income from nonagricultural endeavors. Surprisingly, little more than half of the region's surplus-producing farm owners were nonslaveholders (Table 5.1). Clearly, however, the vast majority of the surplus producers were operating small to middling farms (see Table 5.4).

Table 5.4. Who Produced Agricultural Surpluses (1860)?

A. Grains, Cattle, and Swine

Appalachian Counties of	% of Total Corn Equivalencies Produced		
		Slaveholding Owners	
	Nonslaveholding Owners	Small to Midsize	Plantations
Alabama	27.9	38.7	33.4
Georgia and South Carolina	21.4	27.4	51.2
Kentucky	57.9	32.8	9.3
Maryland	66.4	21.5	12.1
North Carolina	19.5	47.8	32.7
Tennessee	56.7	34.4	8.9
Virginia	13.0	38.4	48.6
West Virginia	49.9	30.3	19.8
Region	43.8	36.6	19.6

B. Staple Crops

Appalachian Counties of	% of Owners Producing Staple Crops	% of Total Tobacco or Cotton Produced		
			Slaveholding Owners	
		Nonslaveholding Owners	Small to Midsize	Plantations
Alabama	52.3	12.3	38.4	49.3
Georgia and South Carolina	28.9	16.6	44.8	38.6
Kentucky	27.2	51.2	40.0	8.8
Maryland	5.3	—	15.8	84.2
North Carolina	41.0	21.3	49.9	28.8
Tennessee	17.8	10.0	66.5	23.5
Virginia	33.6	14.3	38.6	47.1
West Virginia	13.1	44.4	55.6	—
Region	29.6	27.5	49.1	23.4

Source: Derived from analysis of sample of farms ($N = 3{,}447$); see Table A.3 for sampling details.

Nonslaveholders played a much more significant role in the region's output of grains, cattle, and hogs. Farm owners using free laborers dominated grain and livestock production in East Kentucky, western Maryland, Appalachian Tennessee, and West Virginia. Contrary to long-standing stereotypes, however, that one-third of Appalachian farmers who held slaves produced more than one-half of the region's total output of major food crops and meat. In western North Carolina and Appalachian Virginia, less than one-fifth of the corn, wheat, cattle, and hogs were grown by nonslaveholders, followed closely by the Appalachian counties of Georgia, South Carolina, and Alabama, where nonslaveholders cultivated little more than one-fifth to one-fourth of these crops. Just as they had monopolized the region's tobacco and cotton production, nearly one-fifth of the wheat, corn, beef, and pork were grown by that small fraction of the region's farm owners who applied extensive slave labor to their large landholdings.

Three of every ten Southern Appalachian farm owners cultivated cash staple crops, averaging nearly 1,300 pounds of tobacco and 19.5 bales of cotton per farm. In East Kentucky and western North Carolina, grain and livestock production fell below regional averages. Yet three-tenths to two-fifths of the farm owners opted to cultivate staples rather than grains, averaging 174 to 274 pounds of tobacco and 7.9 bales of cotton. Even in West Virginia, which had the lowest per capita food production in the region, thirteen of every one hundred farm owners cultivated cash crops, averaging nearly 100 pounds of tobacco per producer.[21]

In the Appalachian counties of Georgia, South Carolina, and Alabama, three-tenths to one-half of the farm owners were producing staple crops, averaging 236 pounds of tobacco and 28 bales of cotton. Fewer farm owners in east and middle Tennessee opted to produce staples; still, nearly one-fifth of them were larger producers who averaged 316 pounds of tobacco and 62 bales of cotton annually. In Appalachian Virginia, more than one-third of the farm owners planted tobacco, averaging 1,100 pounds per owner. Even in western Maryland, where less than one of every seventeen farm owners cultivated staples, those who did so were the largest tobacco producers in the region, averaging more than 1,800 pounds per owner.

Slaveholding was typical of those Southern Appalachian farm owners who cultivated cotton and tobacco. Nearly three-fourths of the region's staple crops were grown on farms where unfree laborers were utilized (Table 5.4). In the Appalachian counties of Alabama, Georgia, Maryland, South Carolina, North Carolina, Tennessee, and Virginia, nearly nine-tenths of the tobacco and cotton production came from slaveholding farms. In contrast, a much higher proportion of staple crop production was generated by nonslaveholders in East Kentucky and West Virginia, where one-half or less of the total tobacco production was cultivated by slaveholders. Clearly, however, the slaveholding farms dominated the region's antebellum staple crop production.

While most Appalachian slaveholders owned fewer than nine unfree laborers, nearly eight of every one hundred farm owners applied the labor of more than ten slaves to cultivation of more than five hundred acres (Table 5.1). Though small in number, Appalachian plantations generated a disproportionate share of the region's agricultural production. This tiny segment of Appalachian farms produced nearly one-fifth of the regional output of grains and livestock. Plantations located in the Appalachian counties of Alabama, Georgia, the Carolinas, and Virginia cultivated one-third to one-half of the total grain and livestock grown in those areas. Similarly, staple crops were also heavily concentrated among the plantation elites. Appalachian plantations accounted for nearly one-quarter of the regional output of tobacco and cotton. In the Appalachian counties of Alabama, Georgia, South Carolina, and Virginia, plantations accounted for one-half to three-fifths of the staple crop production. The most extreme case was western Maryland, where a small number of large slaveholders produced four-fifths of the tobacco, averaging 2,400 pounds each.

Agricultural Production for Export

In the nineteenth century, some parts of the globe were still "external arenas," outside the reach of international trade flows and the sociopolitical changes that accompanied integration into the capitalist world system. Southern Appalachia is viewed by most scholars as one such external arena that somehow remained a precapitalist enclave within a competitive national economy. The conventional wisdom is that cultural resistance to capitalism, rugged terrain, and the lack of transportation networks prevented the growth of an export economy. Fundamentally, then, Southern Appalachia has been conceptualized as a self-contained farm economy in which neighbors in small communities exchanged domestic produce and work skills and never became dependent upon external trade.[22]

Such premises vastly oversimplify the structure of Southern Appalachia's local economies and assume a degree of physical isolation that was indeed never absolute. In fact, the transition to capitalism was proceeding at an uneven pace throughout Southern Appalachia. As we have seen, the region's farmers were *not* predominantly small subsistence producers eking out a meager living on forbidding terrain. Instead, the vast majority of the region's agricultural households aggregated several labor mechanisms in order to produce surpluses. To determine how Appalachian farmers disposed of their surpluses, I shall explore two questions in the following sections. First, did the region generate surpluses at a level in excess of local consumption needs and for which there were inadequate community markets? Second, did the region generate certain commodities specifically for distant markets?

Did Southern Appalachia Export Food Crops?

When a geographical area is integrated into capitalist trade flows, agricultural production provides opportunities for surplus accumulation that are not evident in subsistence economies. The precapitalist farmer concentrates upon production for survival and reproduction of the household unit. But the capitalist entrepreneur *rationalizes* the production process to achieve three concurrent economic goals: (1) acquisition of the minimal basic needs of the family; (2) production of sufficient surpluses to permit commodity sales in markets; and (3) accumulation of sufficient surplus to supply the raw materials and equipment to reinvest in future surplus production.[23]

It is this quest for profit from exchanged commodities that sets capitalism apart from precapitalist societies. Subsistence economies secure survival largely through the households' labor outside the market and through minimal exchanges in local trading networks. Moreover, little is produced that is not consumed in the local communities. In order to assess the extent to which insular subsistence production typified antebellum Southern Appalachia, it is necessary to quantify whether the region's counties were producing agricultural commodities above and beyond the requirements to meet their local consumption. To accomplish this, aggregated corn equivalencies were allocated to supply the needs of all free and slave citizens, to feed all livestock, to allow for waste, and to reserve the means to generate future crops. When this statistical procedure is completed, we can estimate how Appalachian counties disposed of their grain and livestock production.[24]

Nineteenth-century Southern Appalachians were, indeed, *not* precapitalist peasants, for they were utilizing less than one-third of their food crop production on the farms to supply subsistence needs and to make crop reinvestments (see Table 5.5). About another one-quarter of Appalachian food crops were absorbed to supply food and whiskey to local nonfarm households and to sustain nonagricultural livestock. Even after allowing for local survival needs, livestock rations, waste, and future crop reservations, *two-fifths* of the total grain, hog, and cattle production of Appalachian counties was still unused. In other words, Appalachian counties produced one and one-half times more food grains and meats than were required to meet local subsistence and reinvestment demands.

While subsistence production carries the connotation of "minimum basic needs," we should view this level of surplus commodity production as a "quest for profits." The region's farmers were certainly doing more than "makin' do and gettin' by," to use a popular Appalachian expression. In reality, they were producing crops at levels that required the aggregation of many nonfamily labor mechanisms. Therefore, it is not reasonable to assume that such production occurred accidentally or that these farmers wasted such large surpluses. In fact, Southern Appalachian counties were generating food surpluses at levels that were *double the global average*. In the nineteenth-century world economy, the typical agricultural community exported only about one-fifth of its annual food harvest. It is obvious, therefore, that Southern Appalachia must have been sending grain and livestock surpluses to distant external markets.[25]

Contrary to popular mythology, Southern Appalachian counties had available for export nearly 6,500,000 bushels of wheat; more than 26,000,000 bushels of corn; more than 1,000,000 hogs; nearly half a million cattle; more than 90,000 horses and mules; more than 30,000,000 pounds of tobacco; and

Table 5.5. Orientation to Market Production: How Farmers Disposed
of Their Grain and Livestock Production

| | % of Total Corn Equivalencies Utilized | | | |
| | Consumption on Farms | | Production for Market | |
Appalachian Counties of	Farm Household Subsistence	Reinvested to Generate Surpluses[a]	Sales in Local Markets[b]	Exports out of County[c]
Alabama	25.2	24.9	24.3	25.6
Georgia	21.5	14.2	34.8	29.5
Kentucky	23.8	17.5	19.9	38.8
Maryland	9.6	11.1	24.5	54.8
North Carolina	25.3	12.0	26.6	36.1
South Carolina	24.3	15.1	37.8	22.8
Tennessee	17.5	18.3	20.7	43.5
Virginia	14.0	10.3	25.4	50.3
West Virginia	22.7	13.2	26.6	37.5
Region	18.9	13.3	26.1	41.7

Sources: Calculated by applying ratios derived from enumerator manuscript samples to aggregated data from the published censuses of Population and Agriculture.
[a]Farm subsistence and reinvestment estimated from analysis of the farm sample ($N = 3,447$); see Table A.3 for sampling details. Reinvestment includes food for farm slaves, feed for surplus farm livestock, plus seed reservations, waste allowance, and herd retention required to reproduce the same level of crops in the next year.
[b]Includes food and whiskey for nonfarm households and slaves, feed for nonagricultural livestock, plus seed reservations, waste allowance, and herd retention required to reproduce the same level of locally marketed surpluses in the next year. For methods, see Appendix.
[c]Percentage of surplus corn equivalencies available for export out of the county after all other local uses are met and after exclusions for a 5 percent waste allowance, reservations of seed, and herd replacements for future production. This export surplus includes amounts fed to itinerant livestock drives.

121,542 bales of cotton (see Table 5.6). On average in 1860, every Appalachian farm owner produced enough to export from the region 36.4 bushels of wheat, 147.9 bushels of corn, nearly six hogs, and more than two cattle. Although there is no precise census count of the levels of production, there is also ample evidence that poultry and other livestock derivatives (e.g., lard) were part of the regular export trade from the region. Because there were shortages of butter and cheese in the South and East, some parts of the region exported these commodities to the Tidewater, to northeastern cities, and to the lower South.[26]

Table 5.6. Appalachian Grain and Livestock Exports, 1860

A. Grain Exports from the Region[a]

Appalachian Counties of	Wheat		Corn	
	Bushels	% Total	Bushels	% Total
Alabama	149,369	25.6	1,664,387	25.6
Georgia	274,929	29.5	1,719,158	29.5
Kentucky	257,027	38.6	3,465,043	38.6
Maryland	1,066,776	54.8	1,048,488	54.8
North Carolina	204,311	36.1	1,607,189	36.1
South Carolina	13,099	22.8	153,993	22.8
Tennessee	1,157,171	43.5	7,383,885	43.5
Virginia	2,478,613	50.3	6,289,937	50.3
West Virginia	850,544	37.5	2,900,024	37.5
Region	6,451,839	39.2	26,232,104	44.2

B. Livestock Exports from the Region[b]

Appalachian Counties of	Hogs		Cattle	
	No.	% Total	No.	% Total
Alabama	72,746	21.9	24,398	18.3
Georgia	73,958	24.7	18,794	20.6
Kentucky	131,169	33.3	38,473	27.7
Maryland	37,547	46.9	20,570	39.1
North Carolina	92,231	30.9	25,635	25.8
South Carolina	5,999	22.9	1,441	21.4
Tennessee	271,888	37.3	101,625	31.1
Virginia	254,788	43.1	121,257	35.9
West Virginia	107,581	32.1	75,593	26.8
Region	1,047,907	34.0	427,786	29.1

Source: Using aggregated county data from the published Census of Population, I allocated grain and livestock for consumption by the entire local population of humans and livestock.

[a]Once I had determined the corn equivalencies available for export, I reconverted those amounts into their original crop values in wheat, corn, hogs, or cattle. These are more conservative export estimates than can be derived from any other cliometric approach. I have allocated grains to four types of local use that have been ignored by earlier studies.

[b]I retained 14.3 percent of the surplus hogs and 28.6 percent of the surplus cattle for herd replacement; see Battalio and Kagel, "Structure."

Table 5.7. External Trade and Agricultural Labor Time

Appalachian Counties of	% Total Labor Time Invested in Crops			
	Consumed on Farms		Produced for Market	
	Farm Household Subsistence	Reinvested to Generate Surpluses	Sales in Local Markets	Exports out of County
Alabama	21.5	21.2	20.7	36.6
Georgia	20.3	13.5	32.9	33.3
Kentucky	23.8	17.4	19.9	38.9
Maryland	10.0	10.6	24.5	54.9
North Carolina	25.0	11.9	26.3	36.8
South Carolina	23.8	14.8	37.0	24.4
Tennessee	17.4	18.1	20.6	43.9
Virginia	13.7	9.9	24.8	51.6
West Virginia	22.6	13.2	26.5	37.7
Region	18.4	14.2	24.1	43.3

Source: Ratios from Table 5.5 were applied to aggregated crop data from the published Census of Agriculture. Then these distributions were multiplied by estimated labor hours required to produce a unit of each crop. The estimated labor times required for the antebellum production of crops were derived from Holmes, *Supply of Farm Labor*, pp. 62–69.

Orchard fruits also comprised part of the region's regular external trade. In Alabama, one hundred wagon loads of apples and peaches were exported yearly from Jefferson and Blount Counties to Mobile. From "great big orchards," Greenup County, Kentucky, "barreled and shipped apples" down the Ohio River. East Tennesseans regularly exported dried fruits. Apple cider was hauled to Alexandria and Richmond markets from the Shenandoah Valley while east Kentuckians, Shenandoah River farmers, and East Tennesseans exported peach brandy.[27]

What, then, of the argument that these surpluses were generated only as a coincidental part of the overall subsistence-oriented goals of the producers? By examining the allocation of labor time by Appalachian farmers, we can assess the likelihood that they were cultivating export crops by accident. In reality, Appalachian farmers utilized less than one-fifth of their total crop production time to cultivate the foods that were required for subsistence and reinvestments on the farms (see Table 5.7). Instead, Appalachian farmers applied more than three-quarters of their labor time toward the generation of surpluses. Most importantly, Appalachian farmers applied twice as many labor hours toward the cultivation of export surpluses as they allocated toward the generation of minimum basic needs. Obviously, then, production for export was a planned segment of the region's total agricultural output.

Did Appalachian Farmers Export Nonfood Crops?

In addition to their meat sources, Appalachian farmers produced four other types of livestock with an eye toward export profits: horses, mules, sheep, and poultry. One of every two farm owners was producing a horse or mule for export (see Table 5.8). Because of their strength and resilience, mules could "always be sold for ready cash in the South" where cotton and sugar planters were willing to pay 10 to 15 percent more for mules than for draft horses. Commentators reported that the South was "indebted to Kentucky" for its annual "Great droves" of horses and mules, part of which were reexported out of New Orleans, Mobile, and Charleston to West Indies plantations. Similarly, Tidewater tobacco planters obtained their supplies of work animals from western Virginia and East Kentucky in annual drives that were "enormous" and "increasing."[28]

By the early 1840s, East Kentucky was exporting to Deep South markets 4,396 horses and 3,177 mules yearly through the Cumberland Gap. East Kentucky mules were also transported via Louisville to midwestern markets. Down the Ohio River, they were reexported through St. Louis, an intermediate hub for mules. Planters of East Tennessee and western North Carolina also bred horses and mules for export to South Carolina and Alabama. By 1860, there were nearly 39,000 mules and horses passing through Knoxville for southern markets (Table 5.8). Because their stock was inferior to upper South breeds, the exported mules of northern Alabama "command[ed less prices [than those from Kentucky and Tennessee] when driven to the plantations of South Carolina and Georgia." Still, the Appalachian counties of Alabama exported more than 4,000 horses and mules per year. Though their exports were much less significant, the Appalachian counties of Maryland, Virginia, and West Virginia also exported to the Tidewater nearly 36,000 horses and mules yearly.[29]

After world beef and pork prices became increasingly erratic during the 1840s, Appalachian sheep production expanded dramatically. In 1860, sheep were just as crucial to the generation of agricultural exports as were all other livestock, except swine. In fact, the region had 1.1 sheep for every head of cattle, and there was one sheep for every two hogs. In West Virginia, where there were 1.6 sheep to every head of cattle, sheep drives and wool exports were more important than the beef industry. Sheep raising and wool production also exceeded beef production in the Appalachian counties of Georgia, Kentucky, and North Carolina, and there were just as many sheep as cattle in the Appalachian counties of South Carolina, Tennessee, and Virginia.[30]

In contrast to their other livestock, Appalachian farmers did not raise sheep

Table 5.8. Major Nonfood Crop Exports, 1860

A. Staple Crop Exports[a]

Appalachian Counties of	Tobacco (pounds)	Cotton (bales)
Alabama	131,097	83,291
Georgia	546,855	25,708
Kentucky	616,573	—
Maryland	389,150	—
North Carolina	946,836	3,014
South Carolina	24,073	939
Tennessee	944,923	8,295
Virginia	24,615,739	170
West Virginia	2,179,091	125
Region	30,394,337	121,542

B. Export of Horses and Mules from the Region[b]

Appalachian Counties of	Number Exported
Alabama	4,275
Georgia	4,320
Kentucky	12,411
Maryland	2,601
North Carolina	6,808
South Carolina	525
Tennessee	26,241
Virginia	19,732
West Virginia	13,230
Region	90,143

Source: Aggregated from published Census of Agriculture.

[a]Production aggregated from published 1860 Census of Agriculture.

[b]To arrive at a conservative estimate of horse and mule exports, I assumed that antebellum farmers sold the same proportion of their herds as did their postbellum counterparts. The 1910 published Census of Agriculture reports an aggregated county count of horses and mules sold; I used these counts to calculate what proportion of the total county herds were exported.

as a food crop. Even though it was cheaper to produce, wool averaged five times the price per pound that cotton brought on world markets. Because wool was just as crucial as cotton to the emergent textile industries of the American Northeast and Europe, it is not surprising that Southern Appalachians produced 21.2 pounds of wool for every bale of cotton exported from the region. As early as 1835, there were many substantial flocks of sheep in the Shenandoah Valley and in the West Virginia counties of Brooke, Hancock,

Jefferson, Berkeley, Preston, and Webster, where sheep breeding and wool growing comprised a leading industry. In upper West Virginia, farmers considered sheep to be "the most profitable animal [they could] pasture."[31]

A few Appalachians exported hay to the lower South; and many Appalachian farmers collected poultry feathers for trading with local stores. Merchants processed feathers into mattresses and pillows to be exported as luxury items to the lower South. One East Tennessee merchant had a "feather hole" in the floor; underneath the trap door, the store kept a bed tick attached to a square chute into which bartered feathers were dumped. When full, these bed ticks were exported downriver to New Orleans. Some larger farms even raised special breeds of fowl for their decorative plumage. For example, the Ferry Hill Plantation of western Maryland raised peafowls; their large colorful feathers were exported by canal boat to Baltimore, where they were made into fans and dusters.[32]

By 1850, the British cotton industry was consuming 900 tons of raw cotton daily, and the United States was exporting nearly 200 million pounds of tobacco to Europe. By 1860, Southern Appalachia was generating more than 120,000 bales of cotton per year. Most of the region's production came from the Appalachian counties of Alabama and Georgia (Table 5.8), where farm owners averaged nearly 1,400 pounds of the staple each, followed by East Tennessee and western North Carolina, where farm owners averaged only 400 pounds. Southern Appalachian farms also produced more than 30 million pounds of tobacco, which left the region in two forms—in hogsheads of leaf and as manufactured twists and plugs. Appalachian Virginia's farm owners produced more than 600 pounds of tobacco each while farm owners in the rest of the region averaged only 42 pounds of tobacco.[33]

Mapping Agricultural Exports

No Appalachian county consumed all of its food crops. As Map 5.1 illustrates, a majority of the region's counties were engaging in external trade in agricultural commodities. Only six of the Appalachian counties were producing few agricultural surpluses for external export. However, although they were exporting their agricultural crops at a level below the global average, they were *not* subsistent. These counties were Fannin, Lumpkin, and Rabun in Georgia; Wilkes in North Carolina; Cumberland in Tennessee; Buchanan in Virginia; and Webster in West Virginia. They exported less than one-fifth of their total grains and livestock and cultivated few or no staples. A second group of thirteen counties exported grains and livestock at levels well above the global average. These counties exported more than two-fifths of their total grains and livestock, but they cultivated no tobacco or cotton.

More than one-half of the region's counties (116) predominantly exported grains and livestock, averaging less than 200 pounds of staples per farm. On average, these counties exported a little more than two-fifths of their food

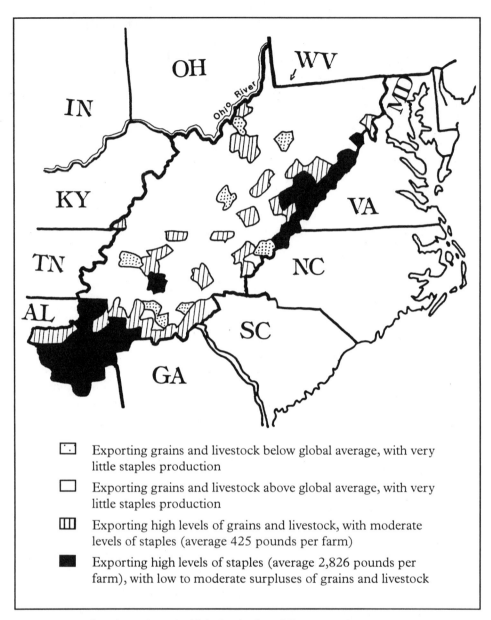

Map 5.1. Southern Appalachia's Agricultural Exports, 1860
Source: Cliometric techniques applied to aggregated data from U.S. Census Office, *Agriculture of the United States in 1860* (Washington, D.C.: Government Printing Office, 1864).

crops, and they bolstered their export profits by cultivating small amounts of cotton or tobacco. A fourth group of counties exported high levels of grains and livestock but also produced moderate levels of staple crops. These thirty counties generated enough food crops to export one-third of their total production, but they also averaged 425 pounds of staples per farm.

The market orientation of a fifth tier of Appalachian counties is very clear. These counties specialized in the production of staples, with grains and livestock playing a secondary role. Eight of these counties produced only enough grains and livestock to export about one-fifth of their total corn equivalencies; however, they opted to utilize their farmland to cultivate 2,613 pounds of staples per farm. Another nineteen counties exported nearly one-third of their food crops but still generated nearly 3,0000 pounds of staples per farm. However, agricultural crops were not the only commodities being produced for external trade.

Close Linkage between Agriculture and Manufacturing

To maximize their own profits, the region's capitalist elites and absentee speculators kept local manufacturing closely linked to the processing of raw agricultural commodities for export. Firms involved in the agriculturally linked manufacture accounted for nearly three-fifths of the gross annual output of all Appalachian industries (see Table 5.9). One of the top three industrial categories in every geographical zone, agricultural processing took six forms in Southern Appalachia: milling flour and cornmeal, distilling grains into liquor, packing beef and pork, finishing livestock hides into leather products, manufacturing tobacco plugs and twists, and producing textiles from cotton and wool. Contrary to the stereotype of a lone farmer completing these functions on a part-time basis, these agriculturally linked manufactories were government-licensed commercial ventures that absorbed two-fifths of the region's manufacturing labor force.[34]

Manufacture of Agricultural Raw Materials
The average Appalachian mill utilized only 1.4 laborers to generate an annual gross of $8,747, and its goods were quality-controlled by state-funded inspection stations. More than one-third of the mills were situated in giant industrial complexes that were comprised of grist, flour, and saw mills, an iron forge, (sometimes a paper mill), and a distillery. Typical of these commercial ventures was the four-story flour mill in Cass County, Georgia, which generated 250 barrels of flour daily. These large mills grossed nearly $16,000 annually and stimulated the growth of distribution towns, like Wellsburg and Wheeling, West Virginia. Similarly, Hagerstown, Maryland; Knoxville, Tennessee; Staunton, Virginia; and a commercial belt of four towns in Frederick County,

Table 5.9. Top Three Industrial Activities, 1860

Appalachian Counties of	Laborer Definition		Output Definition	
	Sector	% of Total	Sector	% of Total
Alabama	1. Extractive	30.5	1. Processing	38.0
	2. Leather	16.2	2. Extractive	29.3
	3. Artisan	15.5	3. Leather	11.3
Georgia and South Carolina	1. Extractive	25.3	1. Processing	35.7
	2. Artisan	20.6	2. Extractive	17.5
	3. Processing	17.1	3. Household	14.8
Kentucky	1. Extractive	58.0	1. Extractive	45.9
	2. Processing	17.3	2. Processing	30.1
	3. Leather	12.6	3. Leather	15.8
Maryland	1. Extractive	34.4	1. Processing	41.4
	2. Leather	17.9	2. Leather	25.3
	3. Processing	8.3	3. Extractive	15.3
North Carolina	1. Processing	38.2	1. Processing	58.8
	2. Extractive	21.9	2. Leather	12.8
	3. Leather	16.2	3. Extractive	11.3
Tennessee	1. Extractive	46.6	1. Processing	41.8
	2. Processing	15.0	2. Extractive	32.7
	3. Leather	11.1	3. Leather	8.8
Virginia	1. Processing	30.7	1. Processing	61.1
	2. Extractive	26.5	2. Extractive	13.2
	3. Leather	12.7	3. Leather	8.5
West Virginia	1. Extractive	36.9	1. Processing	32.8
	2. Building	15.6	2. Extractive	25.8
	3. Processing/	9.8	3. Building	11.3
	Textiles	9.7		
Region	1. Extractive	35.5	1. Processing	43.7
	2. Processing	17.5	2. Extractive	22.7
	3. Leather	11.8	3. Leather	12.1

Source: Derived from aggregate totals in the published 1860 Census of Manufacturing. "Processing" refers to the processing of agricultural commodities. Percentages represent the proportion of all manufacturing laborers or the proportion of total manufacturing gross in each sector.

Virginia, emerged as wheat-processing centers for adjacent rural areas. The 177 large firms of western Maryland and 58 merchant mills in Page and Shenandoah Counties, Virginia, represented the region's most highly commercialized milling.[35]

The region's typical distillery employed only three laborers, but it produced an annual output of just under $7,300. However, 15 percent of these firms were larger commercial enterprises grossing an average $37,017 per year. One of the ten largest firms in East Kentucky was a Greenup County distillery with a workforce of twenty-five. Four commercial distilleries in Ohio and Marshall Counties, West Virginia, occupied ninety-seven workers and grossed more than $70,000 each. Even though livestock comprised such a significant part of the region's agricultural production, meatpacking did not develop very extensively. Only three large commercial firms packed beef and pork, including one in Madison County, Kentucky, that employed eighty laborers to gross $216,000 and one in Hamilton County, Tennessee, that applied fifty-four workers to generate an output of $130,000. Thus, regional activities around livestock exporting were characterized by *asymmetrical integration* into the world market. Livestock processing stimulated several multiplier mechanisms and ancillary industrial spinoffs that might have supported development in the mountain communities. However, these multipliers and the value added in the manufacturing process were transferred from Southern Appalachia to those distant trade centers that specialized in meatpacking for export.[36]

The processing of staples was also significant to regional manufacturing. Cotton ginning occurred only in northern Alabama and northwestern Georgia, with two large firms averaging eighteen laborers and $16,500 annual gross. Tobacco, however, was manufactured in every geographical zone except northern Alabama and East Kentucky. This industry was comprised of eighty-five firms that employed some of the region's largest labor forces. Averaging twenty-two wage laborers per firm and numerous uncounted slaves, tobacco manufacturers averaged $8,509 each. Wheeling, West Virginia, was one of the country's largest producers of plug tobacco, and other large firms operated in northern Georgia and western North Carolina. In Appalachian Virginia, twenty-eight firms each employed more than twenty-two laborers and grossed $11,865; another twenty-five firms used similar large labor forces to generate an output of nearly $19,000 annually. Western Maryland, Appalachian Tennessee, and West Virginia also manufactured cigars, plugs, and smoking tobacco, but these firms were medium-size operations, averaging only twelve to fifteen workers and an annual gross of $4,328.[37]

As an ancillary industry to the region's livestock production, the tanning of leather and the production of finished leather goods (e.g., boots, shoes, harnesses, saddles) expanded into the third most important manufacturing sector. Only one-tenth of these producers fit the stereotype of small independent artisans who applied family labor to earn less than $1,000 a year. Instead, more than three-fourths of Appalachian leather manufactories were medium-size firms in terms of their annual output and employed fewer than nine laborers each. Employing more than one-tenth of the region's manufacturing labor force, most of these enterprises engaged fewer than three workers to gross an average $3,895 yearly.

However, eighty-five of the region's leather manufacturers were large enough to average an output of $22,033 annually. Concentrated in western Maryland and in four counties of West Virginia, seventy-two large firms each applied five workers to produce $23,452 worth of leather goods. Situated in Greenup County, Kentucky; in Ohio County, West Virginia; and in Morgan County, West Virginia, the region's largest leather manufacturers averaged workforces of twenty-one and annual outputs of $52,788. Thirteen other large regional leather manufacturers were situated in Whitfield County, Georgia; in Hamilton and Warren Counties, Tennessee; and in Roanoke and Rockbridge Counties, Virginia.[38]

By capitalizing upon regional production of wool and cotton, textile producers comprised the fourth most important category of Southern Appalachian industry. Absorbing 8 percent of the region's manufacturing labor force and 5 percent of the total annual gross, textile industries encompassed the manufacture of cloth; calico printing; wool carding; the manufacture of staves, shooks, and headings for women's undergarments; and the production of finished clothing, mittens, hats, and caps. By national standards, the 299 Appalachian textile manufacturers were medium-size operations that averaged six laborers and an annual gross of $5,433. More than half the region's total textile labor force were women.[39]

Two-thirds of the textile manufacturers were small artisan shops: wool carders, milliners, tailors, and hatters. However, one-third of the firms were larger operations that required labor forces of fourteen or more and generated outputs of at least $12,475 yearly. Located in only eleven of the region's counties, twenty-two cotton mills averaged thirty-one laborers and an annual gross of $32,000 each. Found in Coosa County, Alabama; in Chatooga County, Georgia; and in Brooke and Ohio Counties, West Virginia, the region's largest cotton mills averaged seventy-one laborers and marketed $42,842 worth of goods each year.[40]

Concentrated in only five counties, thirty-one clothing factories averaged fifteen workers and a yearly gross of $8,000. The region's largest clothiers were located in Allegany County, Maryland (where six factories employed 108 laborers), and in Ohio County, West Virginia (where two factories required 197 laborers). Some Appalachian factories were famous throughout the South for their manufacture of jeans, like the Warren County, Tennessee, company that perfected Faulkner's Jeans or the Habersham County, Georgia, plant whose women laborers were "remarkably skilful in weaving jeans." Similarly, the Abram's Creek Manufactory of Blount County, Tennessee, produced the well-known Chilhowee cotton that was popular with slaveholders; Senator John Calhoun's South Carolina factory manufactured Pendleton blankets and saddle cloths, an unusual blend of cotton and wool.[41]

Even the region's output of small tools and hardware was linked to agriculture. About 7 percent of the region's manufacturing labor force produced tools, hardware, household equipment, wagons, and carts in blacksmith shops and small facilities. In addition, there were forty-three medium-size manufacturers of agricultural implements, two-thirds of them concentrated in western Maryland and Appalachian Virginia. By far the most famous antebellum manufacturer of agricultural implements was Cyrus McCormick of Rockbridge County, Virginia, whose factory was, by 1860, building 6,000 wheat reapers yearly. In fact, about one-half of the region's output of agricultural implements and small tools left their counties of origin for regional and distant markets.[42]

Exports of Agricultural Byproducts

As early as the mid-1700s, the Appalachian counties of the northern neck of Virginia and the Potomac Valley were exporting wheat and flour to Europe and the West Indies; by the early 1800s, northern West Virginia wheat was "celebrated in foreign markets for its superiority." Western Maryland's primary export was flour shipped to Baltimore for reexport to foreign markets. By 1860, more than 800,000 barrels of flour were being exported from the Appalachian counties of Maryland and Virginia to eastern and Tidewater markets; and West Virginia was exporting an additional 253,516 barrels to the same trade centers (see Table 5.10).[43]

By the late 1840s, the superiority of the flour of the lower part of the region was also being heralded in Europe. One Liverpool newspaper advertised that "Samples of flour from the mills of Knoxville have been received in this market equal in every respect to the best from any other quarter. . . . Tennessee, Northern Georgia, and the Western Carolinas thus promise to become one of the chief granaries of the world and of a large part of this vast region, Charleston is the natural market."[44]

In its 1840 report, the Western and Atlantic Railroad reported that the export of flour had become significant in northern Georgia, especially for Cass, Walker, and Murray Counties. Etowah Mills was "stimulating the production of wheat to an unprecedented extent," and Georgia brands were "already esteemed among the best in the market." In 1843, South Carolina alone imported 52,000 barrels of Appalachian flour. Between 1855 and 1860, Charleston and Savannah exported 292,000 barrels of flour and 1,925,000 bushels of wheat, most of it shipped from the Appalachian counties of Tennessee, North Carolina, and Georgia to northeastern destinations.[45]

On average, each Appalachian farm owner could supply enough surplus grain to permit local mills and distilleries to process for export 1,058 pounds

Table 5.10. Manufacturing of Local Wheat and Corn, 1860

Appalachian Counties of	Flour and Grist Mills Barrels Exported		Distilleries Gallons Exported
	Flour	Meal	
Alabama	9,595	126,877	10,000
Georgia	12,277	61,834	44,667
Kentucky	4,626	75,155	301,822
Maryland	374,217	—	1,198,200
North Carolina	8,627	67,842	66,211
South Carolina	—	—	—
Tennessee	67,392	454,447	317,889
Virginia	454,379	530,234	927,656
West Virginia	253,516	297,035	1,190,593
Region	1,184,629	1,613,424	4,057,038

Source: Quantities aggregated from the 1860 Census of Manufacturing enumerator manuscripts. I assumed that all of the output of these commercial mills and distilleries was exported since grains have already been allocated to meet local consumption of food and whiskey.

(5.4 barrels) of flour. East Tennessee was shipping nearly 70,000 barrels of flour to New Orleans and Charleston, and the Appalachian counties of Alabama, North Carolina, and Georgia were sending nearly 30,500 barrels to the same markets. Likewise, nearly 4,700 barrels of flour were exported from East Kentucky via the Ohio River to New Orleans.[46]

In addition to flour exports, the average Appalachian farm owner could supply enough surplus grain to permit local mills and distilleries to process for export 1,588 pounds (8.1 barrels) of meal and 26 gallons of whiskey or malt liquor. In 1860, the region's manufacturers also utilized local grains to process for export more than 1,600,000 barrels of meal, a staple food for the laborers on plantations in the lower South, the West Indies, and South America. Moreover, whiskey distillation offered an efficient way for transporting surplus grain since spoilage and aging were not problematic, and the surplus production could be warehoused for long periods to wait for rises in market prices. By 1819, New Orleans was already receiving 2 million gallons of Appalachian whiskey yearly, most of it arriving by flatboat down river. By 1860, American adults imbibed an average of 3 gallons of whiskey each annually, and whiskey was used by planters to reward slave performance. In 1860, Southern Appalachia produced enough surplus corn to export more than 4,000,000 gallons of whiskey (Table 5.10). Corn whiskey was exported from throughout the region while malt liquors were manufactured by thirteen brewers in five counties of Maryland, West Virginia, and Virginia. Moreover, three Appalachian counties of Kentucky, Virginia, and West Virginia exported rectified liquors that gained national notoriety. For instance, Monongalia County, West Virginia, began the production in 1791 of Old Monongahela Rye Whiskey, which became highly popular in the northeast through its marketing via Pittsburgh and Philadelphia.[47]

Appalachian manufactories also processed livestock into export commodities. Two large meatpacking plants in East Kentucky and East Tennessee exported more than 18,000 barrels of pork and nearly 7,000 barrels of processed beef to New Orleans. Another important derivative commodity produced by the Appalachian meatpacking hubs was lard. After export to New Orleans, Charleston, or Baltimore, Appalachian lard was restamped in its barrels as "sperm oil" (a whale by-product). Then these barrels were shipped to European markets for consumption as fuel. In addition, nearly one-half of the region's output of leather products ended up in regional and distant markets. For example, a few large western Maryland and West Virginia firms specialized in the production of leather commodities for export to Baltimore and eastern markets.[48]

In addition to foodstuffs, Appalachian manufacturers exported commodities derived from the region's staple crops. Eighty-five firms in the Appalachian counties of Georgia, Maryland, North Carolina, Tennessee, Virginia, and West Virginia manufactured 6,633,514 pounds of tobacco twists and plugs for export to northeastern and European markets. In addition, several Appalachian counties were utilizing 2,461,198 pounds of cotton and 1,126,277 pounds of wool to manufacture cloth, about one-half of which was exported to regional and distant markets. East Tennessee's Chilhowee cloth and South Carolina's Pendleton cotton-wool blend were popular with planters in the lower South who needed cheap, durable fabrics for slave clothing. By 1860, there were a few large wool manufactories in West Virginia and Virginia that absorbed much of the local wool production to produce textiles for export to Tidewater cities. Two Appalachian counties were also famous for their export of jeans.[49]

In fact, the regional manufacture of agricultural raw materials was heavily oriented to external trade. The total gross value of the region's output of flour, meal, whiskey, meat provisions, and manufactured tobacco accrued from exports to distant markets. In addition, nearly one-half of the output of Appalachian leather products, agricultural implements, small tools, and textiles was sent to markets outside the counties in which those goods were produced. All told, then, more than four-fifths of the gross value of the region's agriculturally linked manufactures derived from exports to non-Appalachian regional markets or to distant coastal trade centers.[50]

However, regional activities were characterized by asymmetrical integration into the world market, for Appalachian counties exported most of their agricultural surpluses as raw materials (see Table 5.11). Nine-tenths of the

Table 5.11. How Southern Appalachia Exported Its Agricultural Surpluses

Crop	% Manufactured Locally[a]	% Sold to Itinerant Livestock Drives[b]	% Exported as Raw Commodities
	Available Export Surpluses Utilized		
Corn[c]	34.5	21.6	43.9
Wheat[c]	30.8	—	69.2
Hogs	3.3	—	96.7
Cattle	1.4	—	98.6
Tobacco	21.6	—	78.4
Cotton	5.0	—	95.0
Wool	32.2	—	67.8

Source: Aggregated from detailed tables in Dunaway, "Incorporation."
[a]Derived from Dunaway, "Incorporation," Tables 9.6, 9.7, 9.8, 9.9, 11.5.
[b]Derived from Dunaway, "Incorporation," Table 11.2.
[c]Average for region excludes western Maryland and West Virginia where large commercial millers utilized all local grains and imported additional supplies from Ohio and Pennsylvania. For statistical detail, see Dunaway, "Incorporation," Table 9.6.

surplus livestock left the region "on the hoof" because few meatpacking firms operated in Southern Appalachia. Similarly, almost all the cotton and three-quarters of the tobacco left the region in unprocessed form. Similarly, only about one-third of the region's surplus corn, wheat, and wool was manufactured prior to export. As a result, 1860 Southern Appalachians transported to distant markets 6,572,163 bushels of raw corn and 1,120,006 bushels of raw wheat.[51] Despite the close linkage between agriculture and manufacturing, most crop surpluses left the region as raw materials. Consequently, the value added in the finishing process and the multiplier mechanisms and ancillary industrial spinoffs that might have supported sustainable development in the mountain communities were transferred from Southern Appalachia to distant trade centers where manufacturing was more diversified.

Summary

Despite its long-standing popularity, the "subsistent homesteader" stereotype conceals the real complexity of preindustrial agrarian economic structure. Contrary to popular historiography, precapitalist farming was not characteristic of antebellum Southern Appalachia. Indeed, the "subsistent homesteader" was unusual in the region during this period. In reality, subsistence agriculture was deterred in Southern Appalachia by two structural barriers. First, the minority of owners who operated farms larger than 500 acres engrossed nearly three-fifths of the region's agricultural acreage. Second, subsistence farmers lacked control over the labor resources needed to generate larger units of production. In short, subsistence agriculture was *not* the typical mode of production of antebellum Southern Appalachia.

Quite the contrary, the expansion of subsistence farming was impeded by spatial competition with larger capitalist farms. As a direct consequence of the capitalistic restructuring of land tenure, the region's farm acreage was heavily concentrated into the hands of the largest landholders. In the region as a whole, the bottom half of the population controlled less than 12 percent of the resources. While smallholders comprised nearly one-fifth of the region's farms, they controlled less than 4 percent of the agricultural land. In short, antebellum landholding patterns discouraged subsistence agriculture by concentrating farm acreage under the control of the largest surplus producers and by relegating poorer households to the worst terrain.

Contrary to conventional stereotypes, antebellum Southern Appalachia was not a "subsistence refuge region." Overwhelmingly, the farmers of this region were producing for the market and were striving to become ever larger and wealthier in their holdings. In reality, nine-tenths of the Appalachian farm owners produced agricultural surpluses, and the average farm consumed less than one-quarter of its total annual grain and livestock production for subsistence. Not a single regional sector consumed all its locally produced crops. On average, Appalachian counties produced one and one-half times more food grains and meats than were required to meet local needs. Contrary to popular stereotype, Appalachian farmers engaged in external trade and exported large surpluses of grains, livestock, tobacco, cotton, orchard fruits, and wool.[52]

Southern Appalachia's local economies replicated the spatial organization common to societies impacted by the spread of capitalist relations. Smaller, subsistence producers eking out a minimal survival and middling farmers producing grains and livestock for the market existed side by side with larger planters who "employed a large labour-force made up of those who had no option but to work for others." As a result, antebellum agriculture was not just a single homogeneous type of production; the region's farms actually ranged from small subsistence producers to plantations. This diversity was replicated all over the region; not a single county was comprised entirely either of subsistent or surplus producers. In its uneven and erratic development, the emergence of agrarian capitalism in Southern Appalachia mirrored global patterns. Throughout the region, antebellum farms were operated to meet four functions: (1) production of the subsistence requirements of local farm households; (2) growth of surplus grains and meat that were reinvested to generate more profitable market commodities; (3) cultivation of food crops for local markets comprised of nonfarm families, commercial and industrial establishments, and nonagricultural livestock; and (4) production of large cash crops for export.[53]

In its spatial organization, Southern Appalachia also exhibited another key characteristic of capitalist agrarian peripheries. The "creation of large-scale economic units" accompanies incorporation into the capitalist world economy, and the pressure toward larger units of production was evident in the Appalachian countryside. Despite terrain barriers, farmland was heavily concentrated into the hands of the largest producers, thereby deterring access to land by the region's subsistence farmers. Like other agrarian peripheries of the nineteenth-century capitalist world economy, Southern Appalachia was heavily impacted by "gentlemanly capitalism" based on "landed wealth." Those who monopolized landed property held the dominant economic and sociopolitical positions in the region's local economies, and the wealthiest planter-merchant elites stood at the pinnacle of local status.[54]

As a peripheral formation undergoing incorporation into the nineteenth-century world system, Southern Appalachia was handicapped by two economic distortions. In contrast to core sectors, this region had a relative *abundance* of labor but a *scarcity* of local capital. Second, incorporation into the capitalist world economy generated in Southern Appalachia "the destruction of the crafts and the development of agrarian capitalism without accompanying industrialization." In western Europe and in the American Northeast, "landed property [w]as progressively los[ing] its dominant position in the economy and in society." In Southern Appalachia, however, the transition to capitalism was accompanied by a historic strengthening of the economic position of the landed.[55]

Consequently, capitalism as it was unfolding in antebellum Southern Appalachia was only a *stunted* version of the historical process that had evolved in the richer sectors of the world economy. In the core, three historical steps had accompanied the transition to capitalism: (1) the separation of rural laborers from the means of production; (2) the transformation of these workers into a *waged labor force*; and (3) the separation of manufacturing from agriculture.[56]

Clearly, more than half of Southern Appalachia's rural labor force had been severed from the land, the primary means of production, and they were being gradually proletarianized. As in other peripheries of the global economy, there was an inverse relationship between a household's access to land and its integration into the waged labor market. Propertyless households were three times more likely to be engaged in wage-earning occupations than farm owners. However, the third stage of economic development had not been attained. Instead, the region underwent the type of "modernization" that has typified much of the Third World. As has historically been the case in the peripheries of the modern world system, Southern Appalachia never fully experienced the final step in the transition to capitalism, for the region's antebellum agriculture and manufacturing were never fully separated. Instead, locally dominant agrarian-merchant elites and absentee speculators sank the region's limited investment capital into enterprises that were complementary to those activities stimulated by integration into the world market.[57]

As a result, the region's manufacturing remained closely linked to agriculture. Little wonder, then, that the processing of farm crops and livestock required two-thirds of the nonextractive industrial labor force and generated more than eight-tenths of the region's annual manufacturing gross. Like other peripheral areas of the world economy, Southern Appalachia specialized in light manufacturing and consumable goods—industries that either relied on imported technological knowledge or fostered the emergence of only low-level mechanization. There are fewer economic spinoffs and multipliers associated with raw materials production than with more diversified manufacturing. Thus, antebellum Southern Appalachia—like other peripheries of the world economy—experienced slower economic growth than the core sectors of the capitalist world system, culminating in a wide economic gap between this region and the rest of the United States.[58]

6

DIGGERS OF THE COUNTRY:

INDUSTRIAL PRODUCTION FOR EXPORT

The Distorted Industrialization Process

By 1860, there were 6,019 industrial enterprises in Southern Appalachia, employing 23,357 laborers. However, industrialization as it unfolded in Southern Appalachia differed fundamentally from the historical process that characterized core regions of the nineteenth-century world economy. Rather, the region's industrial development was stunted and distorted, as evidenced by three historical trends. Because Appalachian industries were capitalized at lower levels than other American manufactories, these regional enterprises exploited smaller labor forces to generate outputs at the same levels as average medium-size firms nationally (see Table 6.1). Second, regional industries developed unevenly, with heavy concentration into a few geographical areas and few spinoffs outside those small enclaves. Third, the region's industry developed primarily around the production of export commodities that involved the manufacture of agricultural surpluses and the processing of timber and mineral ores for distant markets.[1]

Low Capitalization of Industries

Significantly, capital investments were made in the region's antebellum manufacturing at a per capita level that was only one-half the national average. Even though Southern Appalachia was not far behind the Midwest in its average capital investments in 1860, nearly three-quarters (159) of the region's counties were characterized by capital investments in manufacturing that fell below averages for the South as a whole (see Map 6.1). Moreover, 48 (22.3 percent) of those laggard counties had minimal industrial development, as evidenced by the investment of less than $3.00 per capita into manufacturing enterprises.[2]

Table 6.1. Regional Comparisons of Manufacturing Firms, 1860

A. Classification by Annual Gross Output[a]

Size	% Distribution of Firms		
	Midwest	South	Southern Appalachia
Small	16	18	13
Medium	66	62	72
Large	18	20	15

B. Classification by Number of Laborers[b]

Size	% Distribution of Firms		
	Midwest	South	Southern Appalachia
Small	52	54	86
Medium	39	35	7
Large	9	11	7

Sources: Appalachian estimates from Table 6.2. Midwestern and southern estimates derived from Bateman and Weiss, "Comparative Regional Development," Table 3.

[a] Size categories are drawn from Bateman and Weiss, "Comparative Regional Development." Small firms produced less than $1,000 annual output. Medium firms produced between $1,000 and $10,000 annual output. Large firms produced more than $10,000 output.

[b] Size categories are drawn from Bateman and Weiss, "Comparative Regional Development." Small firms employed fewer than five employees. Medium firms employed five to ten employees. Large firms employed more than ten workers.

Consequently, Appalachian manufactories utilized smaller labor forces than average American enterprises. When categorized according to the size of their workforces, nearly nine-tenths of the region's manufacturers were small firms employing fewer than five full-time laborers. Less than 7 percent were large enough to need more than ten free workers (see Table 6.2). Consequently, Southern Appalachia fell behind other regions of the country, including the South as a whole, in its development of larger factories. Instead, manufacturing firms that required fewer than five workers typified more than three-quarters of the region's counties.[3]

However, when these same firms are analyzed according to the value of their capital investment and their annual output, little more than one-tenth of them were small enterprises by national standards. Instead, nearly three-fourths of them are medium-size operations. Another 15 percent were large enterprises involving more than $10,000 invested capital to generate more than $10,000 annually in marketable goods. To show the extent to which

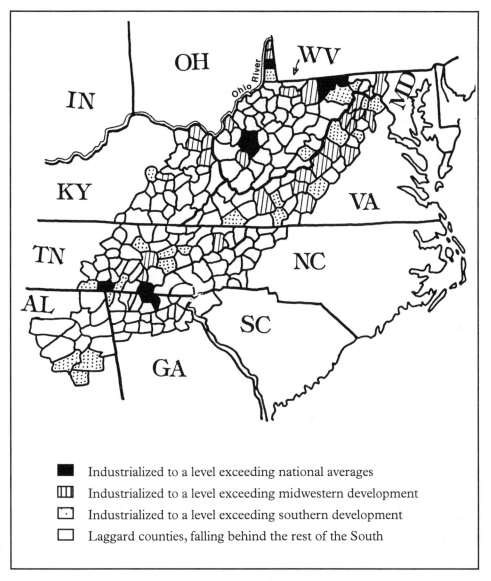

Map 6.1. Southern Appalachia's Industrializing Counties, 1860
Source: Aggregated data from U.S. Census Office, *Manufactures of the United States in 1860* (Washington, D.C.: Government Printing Office, 1865).

Appalachian manufacturing had developed essentially at the medium-size level, it is important to compare counties (see Map 6.2). Significantly, only twenty-three counties (less than 11 percent) were characterized by manufacturing that fit the stereotype of small artisan enterprises that were capitalized with less than $1,000 and that sold less than $1,000 per year in goods or

Table 6.2. Size Distribution of Manufacturing Firms, 1860

A. Distribution of Firms According to Output

Appalachian Counties of	% of Firms in Size Category		
	Small	Medium	Large
Alabama	5.5	78.8	15.7
Georgia and South Carolina	14.6	68.9	16.5
Kentucky	3.6	81.6	14.8
Maryland	2.5	67.3	30.2
North Carolina	26.9	70.0	3.1
Tennessee	19.6	71.1	9.3
Virginia	16.1	69.2	14.7
West Virginia	10.1	76.3	13.6
Region	13.3	71.7	15.0

B. Distribution of Firms According to Employment

Appalachian Counties of	% of Firms in Size Category		
	Small	Medium	Large
Alabama	86.5	6.8	6.7
Georgia and South Carolina	75.7	11.6	12.7
Kentucky	75.5	12.2	12.3
Maryland	78.1	16.7	5.2
North Carolina	93.6	2.0	4.4
Tennessee	91.1	4.2	4.7
Virginia	88.9	5.6	5.5
West Virginia	84.7	5.5	9.8
Region	86.2	7.1	6.7

Sources: Derived from analysis of all county enumerator manuscripts for the 1860 Census of Manufacturing ($N = 6,014$). In order to make interregional comparisons, I drew size definitions from Bateman and Weiss, "Comparative Regional Development." See Table 6.1 for explanation of size categories.

services. At the other extreme, thirty-four counties (15.8 percent) were typified by local industries that were established with more than $10,000 capital investment and produced commodities worth more than $10,000 per year. Nearly three-quarters of the region's counties were characterized by local manufacturing enterprises that were medium-size in terms of capital investment and annual gross but that generated few employment opportunities for local laborers. Thus, Appalachian manufactories exploited smaller labor forces to produce the same amount of goods as did the average medium-size firms nationally. Consequently, industries were not expanding rapidly enough to absorb the growing surplus rural labor force in Southern Appalachia.

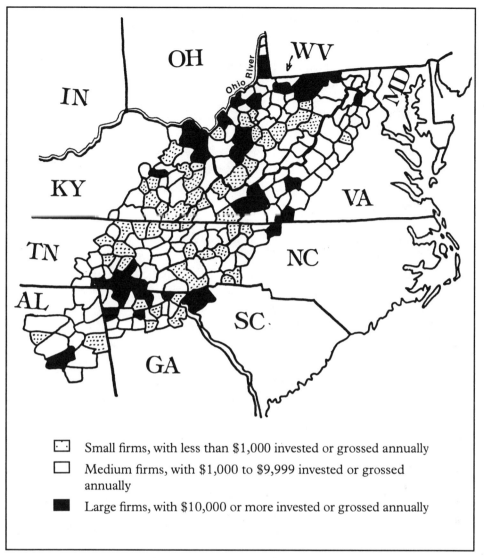

Map 6.2. Typical Size of Manufacturing Firms, 1860
Source: Aggregated data from U.S. Census Office, *Manufactures of the United States in 1860* (Washington, D.C.: Government Printing Office, 1865).

Uneven Development of Industry

Antebellum Southern Appalachia was also handicapped by a second historical trend. Industrialization was proceeding at an uneven pace throughout the region, resulting in centralization into a few enclaves. While most of the region developed enterprises requiring fewer than five laborers, one-fifth of the Appalachian counties attracted larger firms. There were twenty-five counties in

which local industries averaged medium-size labor forces of five to nine workers. Industries requiring ten or more workers were typical of only twenty
Appalachian counties.[4]

Thus, the laggard development pattern did not hold for all counties of the
region. In sharp contrast to the rest of Southern Appalachia, western Maryland exhibited per capita investments in manufacturing that were one and
one-half times the national average. West Virginia had developed the region's
second most extensive manufacturing, with average per capita investments
one and one-quarter times the regional average. Furthermore, twenty-three
counties (10.7 percent) were characterized by per capita investments in manufacturing that exceeded southern averages while twenty counties (9.3 percent) surpassed the Midwest in their average per capita investments in industrial development. Surprisingly, there were thirteen counties in which per
capita investments in manufacturing exceeded national averages.

Map 6.1 makes clear that the region's most significant industrial development was heavily concentrated into a few enclaves. In northern Alabama, only
two counties exceeded southern averages in per capita investments; the other
eleven counties (84.6 percent) fell behind the South as a whole. In Appalachian Georgia, one county exceeded national averages and one surpassed the
South in per capita investments; however, twenty-two counties (91.7 percent)
fell behind the South in industrial development. In East Kentucky, one county
surpassed national per capita investment averages, four had moved ahead of
midwestern averages, and one exceeded southern averages; yet twenty-one
counties (77.8 percent) fell behind the South. In western Maryland, Allegany
County surpassed national averages in per capita investments, and Frederick
County had moved ahead of midwestern averages, but Washington County
had fallen behind southern averages.

All of the counties of western North Carolina and Pickens County, South
Carolina, had fallen behind southern averages in per capita investment. In
Appalachian Tennessee, two counties surpassed national averages in per capita investments, three had moved ahead of the Midwest, six exceeded southern averages, but twenty-nine counties (72.5 percent) lagged behind the
South. In Appalachian Virginia, two counties surpassed national averages, ten
counties had moved ahead of the Midwest, nine counties exceeded southern
averages, but nineteen counties (47.5 percent) lagged behind the South. In
West Virginia, six counties surpassed national averages, two counties had
moved ahead of the Midwest, four counties exceeded southern averages, but
thirty-seven counties (75.5 percent) lagged behind the South.

One group of counties had, by 1860, industrialized to a level that exceeded
midwestern development but still fell below national averages. In twenty-eight
Appalachian counties, per capita investments in manufacturing were greater
than those in the antebellum Midwest. In these local communities, one-fifth to

A large Ohio County, West Virginia, manufacturer. (Courtesy Library of Congress)

one-third of the free adult male population was employed full time in manufacturing. A second group of counties had industrialized to a level that exceeded southern development but still fell below Midwestern and national averages. In twenty-three Appalachian counties, per capita investments in manufacturing were greater than was typical of the antebellum South as a whole. In these local communities, one-tenth to one-fifth of the free adult male population was employed full time in manufacturing.

As Map 6.1 illustrates, more than one-quarter of the region's counties were industrializing much more rapidly than was typical of the region as a whole. Six counties had industrialized to levels that exceeded national averages. In Fannin County, Georgia; Marion and Polk Counties, Tennessee; Allegany County, Maryland; and Kanawha and Ohio Counties, West Virginia, per capita investments in manufacturing exceeded or were equivalent to local per capita investments in agriculture. The Ohio County glass works depicted in Illustration 6.1 was typical of the largest manufacturers in these industrializing counties. To support the region's most industrialized enclave, three dollars were invested in Polk County, Tennessee, manufacturing for every dollar invested in farms. These industrial boom areas absorbed one-third to two-fifths of their free adult male populations into manufacturing.

It is clear, then, that industrial booms characterized only a few regional zones while most of Southern Appalachia accrued little economic benefit from those poles of rapid growth. Moreover, the antebellum Appalachian industrial base had not diversified significantly into commodities that would sustain long-term economic growth. Less than one-quarter of the region's industrial gross was generated by manufacturers that were not linked into the region's specialization in raw agricultural and extractive materials. This small sector consisted of a limited array of enterprises that manufactured building materials, household goods, paper, and mechanical equipment. Nineteen of the region's counties specialized in the manufacture of building materials in medium to large factories, and this industry was the second-largest employer in West Virginia. Even though Southern Appalachia was a major exporter of cement, bricks, sashes, doors, and blinds, the region's most important building commodities were nails and spikes.[5]

Nearly three hundred Appalachian firms manufactured household goods: baskets, brooms, carpets, furniture, cabinets, glassware, mattresses, pottery, soap, candles, and metalware. Although such enterprises gained little ground in Southern Appalachia, a few counties reported heavy industries engaged in highly technical mechanical production. Probably the country's first "defense contract" was initiated with the Halls Rifle Works in Harpers Ferry, West Virginia. In addition, railroad cars, millstones, industrial bellows, machinery, and steam engines were produced in fourteen counties. Because of the need to import the necessary technology from the Northeast and the Midwest, paper milling comprised the region's least-developed industry.[6]

In addition to being centralized geographically, industrial development was disproportionately concentrated into the extraction of raw materials, a type of economic expansion that did not stimulate sustained growth. Thus, extractive enterprises absorbed more laborers than any other manufacturing sector and generated the region's second-highest annual gross (Table 5.9). Extractive activities comprised the most significant form of industry in the Appalachian counties of Alabama, Georgia, Kentucky, Maryland, Tennessee, and West Virginia and the second most important in western North Carolina and Appalachian Virginia.

In sharp contrast to the rest of the nation and the South, the region's antebellum industrial development was heavily concentrated into low-wage mining, quarrying, smelting, intermediate ore processing, and timbering. As Table 6.3 shows, more than one-third of the region's nonagricultural workers were absorbed by extractive industries, with even greater capture of the labor force in northern Alabama, East Kentucky, and Appalachian Tennessee. More significantly, nearly three-fifths of the region's manufacturing investments were in extractive industries while only about one-quarter of the na-

Table 6.3. Concentration of Manufacturing into Extractive Industries, 1860

Region	% of Manufacturing Labor Force	% of All Manufacturing Capital
United States	20.3	26.5
Appalachian counties of		
Alabama	40.8	66.5
Georgia	18.4	44.6
Kentucky	54.8	75.1
Maryland	32.8	63.9
North Carolina	21.8	25.2
South Carolina	37.5	21.6
Tennessee	41.5	64.4
Virginia	26.9	31.1
West Virginia	37.5	58.6
All of Southern Appalachia	34.7	56.1

Source: Calculated using aggregated county and national statistics from the published 1860 Census of Manufacturing.

tion's manufacturing capital was invested in these kinds of economic development. By 1860, Southern Appalachia was exhibiting uneven and erratic development of export enclaves that could exploit mineral resources that were in demand on world markets.[7]

Manufactured Exports for Distant Markets

Southern Appalachia's nonagricultural manufactures were absorbed by three types of markets: local consumers near production sites; regional towns and merchants within 100 miles of the production sites; and distant markets. Only about one-quarter of the gross value of the region's total output accrued from sales in the county of production or at adjacent regional markets. Instead, three-quarters of that gross value derived from exporting to distant southern or midwestern markets. About one-half of the region's output of household goods, tools, and hardware was sold to residents of the counties in which these commodities were manufactured. Three-quarters of the region's output of building materials and paper remained in the local communities. Within one hundred miles of the production sites, regional markets absorbed another one-quarter of the tools, hardware, building materials, and household goods.[8]

As a result, only about one-quarter of the small tools, textiles, building materials, and household goods ended up in distant markets. Northern Alabama and western North Carolina sent sashes, doors, and blinds to consumers in the lower South while East Kentucky and two Virginia counties produced bricks and cement for export. To fill the special orders of distant planters, northern Georgia and northern Alabama constructed fancy carriages while western North Carolina and northern Georgia produced furniture. Out of East Tennessee and West Virginia, the lower South and Midwest received large quantities of nails and spikes. Cotton and woolen cloth, iron household goods and tools, pottery, and an array of patented drug products were also exported to distant markets by Appalachian manufacturers. Wheeling, West Virginia, even exported glass containers to be used by food companies in eastern cities. Some regional manufacturers exported intermediate components to be utilized by distant manufacturers to generate finished commodities. For instance, Frederick, Maryland, supplied to Baltimore industries 138,000 chair tops and 5,000 locust ship pins.[9]

In contrast, the region's manufacture of industrial machinery was oriented entirely to distant markets. Southern Appalachia's rifles, railroad cars, industrial bellows, and steamboat engines were destined for distant markets. For example, Southern Appalachia exported 12,000 rifles annually from the national armory at Harpers Ferry. Steamboat engines originated in northern Alabama, northern Georgia, and West Virginia while railroad cars and industrial equipment were manufactured in East Tennessee, northern Georgia, and West Virginia.[10]

Extractive Exports for Distant Markets

Nearly one-half of the region's antebellum extractive output was generated for out-of-county markets, and some extractive industries were produced solely for distant manufacturing centers. The region's large coal and copper firms were oriented entirely to external markets. Only in western Maryland, East Kentucky, and a few West Virginia counties was there any local consumption of coal—not by households but primarily in the production of salt or iron for export. Predominantly coal left the county of origin for regional industries or for export to distant urban centers. All of the region's antebellum gold production accrued to absentee Americans, to the national mint, and to European markets. In the case of Appalachian salt and iron production, only about one-third of the total production was absorbed by local communities. Probably one-half or more of those commodities was exported outside the county of origin to regional and distant markets. In addition, Southern Appalachia's lead, manganese, saltpeter, and ginseng production was used entirely outside the region.[11]

In addition to external trade with the lower South and the Midwest, Appalachian counties engaged in distant exporting to other regional markets. In 1860, four of the region's counties supplied salt to the lower South, the Midwest, and most of the other Appalachian counties. Moreover, only 80 of the

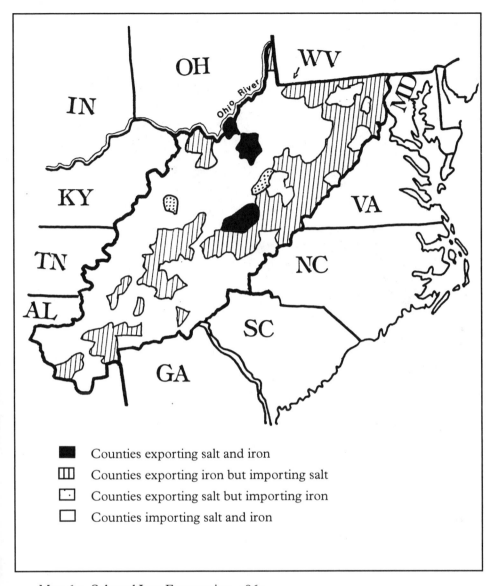

Map 6.3. Salt and Iron Exportation, 1860
Source: Aggregated data from U.S. Census Office, *Manufactures of the United States in 1860* (Washington, D.C.: Government Printing Office, 1865).

region's counties produced their own iron; the other 135 counties imported this essential metal from within the region, often from industrial sites located at a great distance (see Map 6.3). Forty-three counties exported one-third or more of their total iron production from large year-round forges, furnaces, bloomeries, and rolling mills while four counties supplied salt to distant mar-

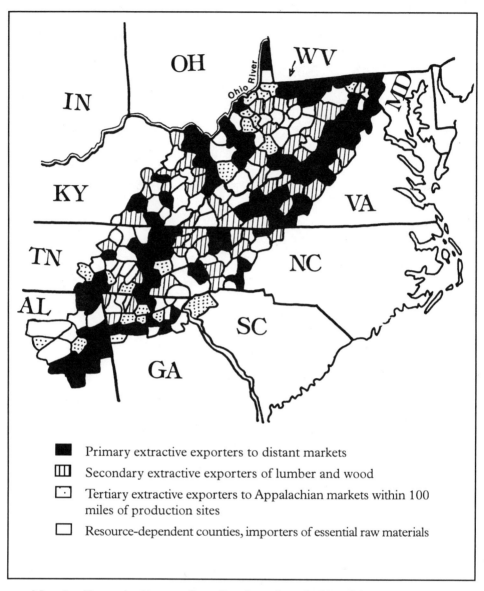

Map 6.4. Extractive Exports from Southern Appalachia, 1860
Source: Aggregated data from U.S. Census Office, *Manufactures of the United States in 1860* (Washington, D.C.: Government Printing Office, 1865).

kets. In this sense, then, salt and iron were significant export commodities to nearby, intermediate, and distant markets.

In contrast to the agricultural exporters, which were fairly evenly distributed across the region, extractive exportation was heavily concentrated in certain counties. More than one-third of the region's counties were relatively resource dependent. Twenty-two Appalachian counties were tertiary extractive exporters that transported one-third or more of their lumber and wood products via river networks to regional and distant markets. These counties generated no extractive exports other than timber products and were dependent upon other Appalachian counties for their supplies of iron and salt. The fourth group of sixty-two Appalachian counties were totally dependent upon outside sources for imports of essential raw materials.

However, eighty of the region's counties shipped raw materials to distant markets before the Civil War (see Map 6.4). In addition to the sections that exported iron or salt to distant markets, thirty-three other counties exported extractive ores to distant markets. Gold was exported from fifteen counties during the 1830s and 1840s while thirteen Appalachian counties supplied much of the nation's copper production. Wythe County, Virginia, exported lead beginning in the eighteenth century while two Appalachian counties supplied the nation's entire production of manganese. From another twenty-five Appalachian counties, coal was exported to fuel distant industries and to supply urban centers.

Another fifty-one Appalachian counties were secondary extractive exporters that supplied regional markets, usually within a one-hundred-mile radius of the production sites. These smaller industries generated iron, salt, coal, lumber, marble, stone, and petroleum products for adjacent markets. Thirty-six counties produced iron in small amounts, part of which was exported across county lines to supply nearby markets (Map 6.3). For example, the iron manufacturers of western North Carolina predominantly served a narrow target area of less than one hundred miles, exporting only a small segment of their production to urban centers in South Carolina and to Augusta or Athens, Georgia. Small salt operations in Washington County, Virginia, and Mercer County, West Virginia, supplied adjacent areas.[12]

In some instances, extractive resources were exported to fuel other intraregional industries. For example, coal and lumber were floated by river from several West Virginia counties to the salt furnaces located on the Ohio River. The production of kerosene is another example of a resource supplied to intraregional markets. In the late 1850s, a New York firm imported a new kind of Vienna lamp that made it possible to use kerosene for household lighting. Subsequently, a few East Kentucky and West Virginia producers supplied nearby towns with door-to-door deliveries in horse-drawn tank wagons. Similarly, West Virginia's natural gas was piped to adjacent towns where it was used to operate streetlights.[13]

America's First Gold Rush

Early in the nineteenth century, the nation's first gold rush erupted in the interior southern hills. An 1829 gold discovery in the Cherokee Nation triggered the mania for the yellow mineral. Within a year, 3,000 whites were prospecting illegally on ancestral Indian lands in Georgia and Tennessee. After the forced removal of the Native Americans, state land lotteries attracted 12,000 gold seekers to one northern Georgia county. Speculators subdivided their lottery grants, leasing their gold lots in tiny parcels on a share-crop basis. Newspapers and archival records from 1830 to 1855 document that there were nearly 10,000 free and slave laborers in the gold fields of seventeen Appalachian counties of Alabama, Georgia, North Carolina, South Carolina, Tennessee, and Virginia. In fact, Southern Appalachia led the country in gold production until the California boom of the 1840s. Even as late as 1850, there were still forty-seven active gold mines in Southern Appalachia, requiring eight to sixty laborers each.[14]

In addition to placer and water-pressure surface mining, huge barges were used to dredge gold from northern Georgia riverbottoms. One large company constructed "a boat with a diving bell attached to it for the purpose of . . . collecting gold from the bed of water courses." However, northern Georgia was not the only geographical zone in which antebellum gold mining boomed. In northern Alabama, 3,000 people in shacks and tents produced $183,500 worth of gold from placer mines in Clay, Coosa, and Talladega Counties. Four enterprises exploited the gold deposits of Pickens County, South Carolina, while placer washing generated $2,500 worth of gold per year from the Tellico Plains area of Monroe County, Tennessee. In western North Carolina, planters and farmers worked their gold deposits with slaves or sharecroppers, and there were 2,800 "diggers of the country" in Burke County alone. Between 1829 and 1860, gold was also dug in Fauquier, Greene, and Amherst Counties in Virginia.[15]

Although it is impossible to place a precise value on these exports, archival sources offer some insight into the extent of the extraction of surplus out of the region. Between January and October of 1830, northern Georgia mines exported $230,000 worth of gold to Augusta while the private mint at Gainesville manufactured 50,000 gold coins in a short period. By 1843, the Lumpkin County mint was annually processing more than $3 million (in contemporary values) worth of gold for export to the national mint at Philadelphia. From the Nacoochee Valley of northeast Georgia, one merchant purchased and exported $1.5 million worth of gold in a thirty-year period. Between 1834 and 1839, thirty-four companies operated by investors from Great Britain, New York, and New England exported to Europe $6,000,000 worth (in contemporary values) of Appalachian Virginia gold for use in art works and jewelry. Between 1829 and 1860, the Philadelphia mint coined $3,000,000 worth (in contemporary values) of gold harvested from Fauquier, Greene, and Amherst Counties.[16]

Antebellum Iron Manufacturing

Some of the largest industrial complexes in antebellum Southern Appalachia were engaged in iron manufacturing. Established in eighty-four (39.1 per-

Table 6.4. Iron Manufacturing, 1860

Appalachian Counties of	1860 Census Count		Uncounted Firms		Corrected Total	
	Firms	Laborers	Firms	Laborers	Firms	Laborers
Alabama	4	98			4	98
Georgia	3	64	8	451	11	515
Kentucky	15	345	4	92	19	437
Maryland	4	144	2	1,123	6	1,267
North Carolina	7	37	3	16	10	53
Tennessee	41	404	34	788	75	1,192
Virginia	49	686	12	168	61	854
West Virginia	21	596	43	1,204	64	1,800
Region	144	2,374	106	3,842	250	6,216

Sources: Aggregated from the published Census of Manufacturing and numerous archival and published sources. The corrected count of iron manufacturers may still be low because census returns were not made for 28 (10%) of the region's counties, and I could not locate adequate archival records to check every missing county that had iron deposits or furnaces at earlier antebellum periods. Moreover, the count of laborers is far too low because slaves were not included. At least 106 firms were uncounted according to these sources: Lesley, *Iron Manufacturer's Guide*; *Atlanta Daily Intelligencer*, 8 April 1859; *Rome Courier* (Ga.), 3 March 1860; White, *Statistics of Georgia*; Bouwman, *Traveler's Rest*, p. 155; Smith, "Historical Geography," pp. 231–34; "Old Kentucky Iron Furnaces"; Eubank, "Iron Industry in Kentucky"; Ellwanger, "Estill Springs," p. 53; Allen, "Mount Savage Iron Works"; Harvey, *Best-Dressed Miners*; Lewis, *Coal, Iron, Slaves*, pp. 26–33, 49–51; Cappon, "Iron Making," pp. 335–36; Hoskins, *Anderson County*, p. 36; Safford, *Geological Reconnaissance*, pp. 51–55; Burns, "Blount County Coves," p. 64; Van Benthuysen, "Sequent Occupance of Tellico"; MacArthur, *Knoxville: Crossroads*, p. 40; Bruce, *Virginia Iron Manufacture*, p. 452; Capron, "Virginia Iron Furnaces," pp. 10–18; Wayland, *History of Shenandoah*, chap. 14, pp. 236, 241; Barbour County, Miscellany Papers No. 1115; Iron Furnaces Typescript; Anderson Papers; Blakemore Papers; Sanders and Greene Papers and Notebooks, 1820–64.

cent) of the region's counties, Appalachian bloomeries, furnaces, forges, and rolling mills produced nearly one-fifth of the country's total iron in 1840. Employing 6,216 free laborers (and numerous uncounted slaves), the region's 250 iron manufacturers turned out pig iron, blooms, castings, bar iron, and railroad iron (see Table 6.4). Only about one-quarter of the Appalachian iron manufacturers were small artisans employing fewer than five workers. Rather, these firms averaged an annual gross of $19,154 with twenty-five workers.[17]

Although the region's antebellum iron production comprised only a small segment of the total national production, the plantation economy was dependent upon iron exports from Southern Appalachia. Even before the Revolutionary War, iron was being exported by river out of western Maryland. For most of the antebellum period, one western Maryland firm held the national monopoly on the production of heavy iron rails for the westward-advancing railroads; prior to this facility, the rails were imported from England. Other Maryland manufacturers operated progressive facilities to speed iron production for eastern, southern, and foreign markets. In 1853, for instance, Frederick County exported 2,450,000 pounds of pig iron and five tons of blooms.[18]

Since western Maryland established its first iron furnaces in the early 1700s, that Appalachian zone made some of the country's most important technical advances in the antebellum iron production process, including the use of coke to fire blast furnaces. By 1860, this zone's six major complexes averaged 211 laborers (exclusive of slaves) and an annual gross of $35,692. Located on 11,000 acres in Frederick County, the George's Creek facility consisted of four blast furnaces with steam power, molding houses, and a foundry, steam hammer, puddling furnace, and rolling mill. However, with investments of $1.5 million, the Mount Savage Iron Works of Allegany County was the most heavily capitalized facility of its kind in the United States. As "the only establishment extensively engaged in the manufacture of heavy railroad iron," Mount Savage employed 900 laborers (including slaves) at the peak of its prosperity in the 1850s. The largest iron complex in Southern Appalachia, Mount Savage kept active three blast furnaces, a refinery with seventeen puddling furnaces and six reheating furnaces, a rolling mill, and a foundry. In addition, the firm owned its own spur rail line, a road, and 300 laborer houses.[19]

However, Southern Appalachia's largest iron manufacturing district was situated in northeastern Kentucky on the Ohio River. From there, 23,724 tons of iron were exported annually via flatboats to the Blue Grass Basin, the Midwest, and New Orleans. The principal consumers of Hanging Rock pig iron were the foundries, rolling mills, and forges in urban centers. East Kentucky iron fueled secondary manufactories at Cincinnati, Pittsburgh, Wheeling, Louisville, and in the Mississippi Valley and the Midwest. In addition to smaller facilities in Nelson, Lawrence, and Menifee Counties, there were sixteen large iron complexes in Boyd, Carter, Estill, and Greenup Counties that averaged twenty-three laborers and an annual gross of $38,064. Ashland emerged as a boom town after the establishment of the Buena Vista Iron Furnace in Boyd County, and at one time there were fifty furnaces in Greenup, Kentucky. One of the country's first manufacturing districts to rely on steam power, the Hanging Rock District generated a mean annual production that was four times greater than that of iron producers in the rest of the country. As a result, three-fourths of the state's production derived from this district, making Kentucky the third-largest iron producer in the nation in 1860. East Kentucky's iron towns also intensified external trade flows in the other direction. For example, the eleven furnaces and five forges of Greenup County imported nearly $750,000 worth of trade goods for resale to their laborers and local communities.[20]

Only one-third of Appalachian Virginia's iron manufactures were recast into commodities for consumption within a one-hundred-mile radius. Instead, the bulk of that zone's cast or bar iron was exported to distant markets. Between 1840 and 1850, the Great Valley expanded its production to meet increased demands for pig iron from Tidewater urban-industrial centers. From eight southwest and Blue Ridge Virginia counties iron traveled down the James River and Kanawha Canal to Lynchburg and Richmond, which dominated iron reexport to New York. However, those Appalachian areas also traded as far south as Greensboro, North Carolina. Shenandoah, Frederick, Warren, Page, and Rockingham Counties sent their iron down the Shenandoah Valley to the railroad terminus for export to Baltimore, Philadelphia, and Wilmington.[21]

Iron manufacturing in Appalachian Virginia encompassed ten small firms using fewer than five free laborers, nineteen medium producers employing six to ten workers, and thirty large complexes averaging twenty free laborers each. Established in the early 1700s, many of the Virginia iron facilities had disappeared or declined by the middle of the nineteenth century. By 1860, the largest facilities were centralized in Augusta, Botetourt, Franklin, Frederick, Loudon, Page, Patrick, Rockbridge, Shenandoah and Wythe Counties. Typical of these large complexes were the Washington Iron Works, the Marlboro Iron Works, the Lucy Selina, the Etna Furnace and Buffalo Forge, the Catawba Iron Works, and the Glenwood Furnace, six iron manufacturers that engrossed 145,075 acres.[22]

Easy river access also stimulated the early expansion of the East Tennessee iron industry. Even in the late 1700s, upper East Tennessee iron and ironware were being exported on twenty-five-ton flatboats to the Mississippi Valley. By the 1820s, upper East Tennessee nail manufactories were marketing their product to adjacent counties by wagon, and "Quantities of nails [we]re also furnished for other markets down the rivers, as far as Huntsville, and even Florence, Alabama." In the early 1830s, upper East Tennessee iron was finding its way by wagon to Lynchburg, the Valley of Virginia, and the Cumberland Plateau. Knoxville emerged as the redistribution hub; there a large secondary manufactory produced for export railroad bridge parts, engines, boilers, and farm equipment. From southeastern Tennessee, iron was exported down river via Chattanooga to Alabama, Mississippi Valley, and Missouri destinations. By 1860, East Tennessee ranked third in national bloomery output because that zone's commodity was cheaper than that of Ohio. East Tennessee furnaces supplied about two-thirds of their production to secondary regional manufactories—like northern Georgia's Etowah Mining and Manufacturing Company—for fashioning into commodities for reexport to the lower South.[23]

With its twenty furnaces and fifty-five forges, Appalachian Tennessee generated 2,150 tons of blooms, pig iron, castings, and bar iron in 1850. Heavily concentrated in five counties of upper East Tennessee were, by 1840, fifty-four furnaces and forges. The largest of these, Sullivan County's Bumpass Cove mines and the Embree Iron Works encompassed 70,000 acres. This extensive complex consisted of several mines, a furnace, a rolling mill, a mill dam, two forges, a nail factory, a sawmill, plus facilities for making charcoal and mining limestone. Built in 1824 on 9,000 acres, Carter County's O'Brien Furnace employed slaves to operate a furnace, a forge, two bloomeries, and a water-driven hammer. Established around 1830, Greene County's Bright Hope Industrial complex mined and smelted ore, manufactured cast and wrought iron, and operated a paper mill, a pottery, a distillery, and flour and grist mills. Typical smaller operations that produced about twelve to fifteen tons annually were the Laurel Bloomery of Johnson County, an iron and milling complex in Sevier County, and Amerine Forge of Blount County. At Knoxville, the Maxwell Iron Works employed 250 laborers who produced iron for railroad bridges, engines, and boilers. Situated on 30,000 acres in southeastern Tennessee, the Tellico Iron Company utilized 300 workers to manufacture 800 tons of iron per year.[24]

In contrast to most of the rest of the region, West Virginia was characterized by small to medium-size iron facilities, only four of its counties having large complexes. By 1860, more than seventy West Virginia iron furnaces and forges had disappeared. For example, Monongalia County's thirty-five large iron manufacturers dwindled between 1810 and 1860 to only thirteen small to medium furnaces. Between 1810 and 1850, that zone's largest facilities were centralized on the Ohio River. There eight Ohio County firms averaged sixty-four laborers and generated an annual output of $83,928, the most profitable iron manufacturers in the entire region.[25]

Three external markets received West Virginia iron exports. Hauled to Morgantown by mule teams, northern counties floated "sows" and "pigs" by river to Pittsburgh. Eastern counties sent cast iron overland by wagons, down the Shenandoah Valley to the railroad terminus for shipping to northeastern destinations. The largest exports were produced along the Ohio River for markets further south and in the Midwest. In addition to iron exports, West Virginia was one of the country's largest nail producers. Flatboats stopped at one point to take on empty kegs, filled them with nails from the forge mills at the next stop, then transported them down the Ohio River.[26]

Only western North Carolina and seventeen counties of other geographical zones were characterized by small iron producers. Nearly two-thirds of the region's iron manufacturers were large year-round facilities that annually marketed an average of nearly $40,000 worth of iron and typically employed at least thirty-eight laborers. Four northern Alabama firms averaged twenty-five laborers each to produce $16,573 worth of iron. Even larger industries predominated in northern Georgia, where firms combined several ancillary functions. That area's largest facility was the Etowah Mining and Manufacturing Company, a massive 12,000-acre industrial complex comprised of two blast furnaces, a rolling mill, and a flour mill. Operated night and day the year round, this company produced twelve to fifteen tons daily, employed 300 laborers (including slaves), and paid out an annual $90,000 payroll.[27]

In the Appalachian counties of Alabama, Georgia, and North Carolina, most of the iron production was carried by turnpike, river, or rail to regional markets within a two-hundred-mile radius. Western North Carolina iron was absorbed by local or regional buyers within a one-hundred-mile radius of the production sites. Unique in the South, northern Georgia's Etowah Company complex was an integrated system of mining, manufacturing, and transportation. Relying on its own coal mines and railroad spur, this Appalachian company produced iron castings and bellows from local coal, iron, and charcoal. Then its water-powered rolling mill transformed them into railroad iron to be shipped to distant southern points. Other Georgia firms exported their cast iron or pig iron to secondary manufactories within Georgia or Alabama. Because Alabama iron consumption exceeded internal production, Appalachian output was easily marketed within the state at downriver secondary manufactories and towns. In fact, Alabama was dependent upon iron imports from East Tennessee and northern Georgia.[28]

Antebellum Salt Manufacturing
One of the first resources of the region to be exported to other parts of the country was salt derived from several West Virginia furnaces, from two facilities in southwest Virginia, and from East Kentucky. By 1810, Southern Appalachia led the nation in salt production. By the late eighteenth century, salt was being manufactured in Clay County, Kentucky, and in the Kanawha Valley, Braxton County, and the Clarksburg area of West Virginia. With its twenty commercial salt works averaging twenty-six laborers and grossing $22,594 each, the region was second only to New York in this industry in 1860 (see Table 6.5).

By the early nineteenth century, Abingdon, Virginia, had been transformed into a manufacturing and commercial center "in consequence of the salt works." As a result, southwestern Virginia had become "a place of considerable resort of, and importance to, all the western country." That zone's salt works sent spring shipments by flatboats down the Holston River; Knoxville merchants regularly advertised for wagoners to haul the commodity from those salt works. From Knoxville, Virginia, salt was reexported to southeastern Tennessee, Alabama, and New Orleans. By the 1840s, one southwestern Virginia operation had expanded to five furnaces of eighty-four kettles each. There were only two salt works in production in that zone by 1860—a small furnace in Washington County employing five laborers to gross $20,000 and

Table 6.5. Salt Manufacturing, 1860

Appalachian Counties of	1860 Census Count		Uncounted Firms		Corrected Total	
	Firms	Laborers	Firms	Laborers	Firms	Laborers
Kentucky	6	74	2	25	8	99
Virginia	2	55			2	55
West Virginia	12	390	2	65	14	455
Region	20	519	4	90	24	609

Sources: Aggregated from the published Census of Manufacturing and numerous archival and published sources. This corrected count of salt manufacturers is probably fairly accurate since it accounts for the region's counties that contained major salt deposits and since counties with frontier salt wells were checked in other sources. In addition, this count is in agreement with documents about salt wells used by the Confederacy during the Civil War. However, the count of laborers is far too low because slaves were not included. The Kanawha Valley salt furnaces owned or leased 1,497 slaves in 1860. Four salt wells of Clay and Pulaski Counties of Kentucky and Mason County, West Virginia, were uncounted according to these sources: Moore, "Historical Geography," p. 43; Stealey, "Salt Industry of Great Kanawha"; *Wheeling Intelligencer*, 27 December 1854; J. Q. Dickinson and Company Papers; "Salt Manufacturing in Mason County"; Hansford Papers; Business correspondence of John D. Lewis, 1840–60, Lewis Family Papers; Luke Willcox Diary.

a large firm in Smythe County that utilized fifty workers to gross $52,000 annually.[29]

In East Kentucky, salt manufacturing began in Clay, Floyd, Greenup, Lewis, and Pulaski Counties. By 1840, however, the fifteen wells of Clay County had become the most important production area. Initiated from two small 1802 establishments, the Clay County salt industry grew to fifteen wells in 1845, producing 250,000 bushels, and the boom town of Manchester was promoted as the "Athens of the West." By 1850, salt manufacturing had all but died out in Lewis, Floyd, and Greenup Counties. There still remained, in 1860, eight East Kentucky salt furnaces, averaging twelve laborers and an annual gross of $6,865 each (Table 6.5).[30]

Although Virginia and Kentucky salt was predominantly marketed to adjacent Appalachian counties, these two zones also exported directly and indirectly to more distant markets. Even on the frontier, East Kentucky salt was exported by river via Nashville to planter markets; was sent overland by wagon to the Blue Grass Basin; or was carried out by packhorse through the Cumberland Gap to Virginia, Tennessee, and North Carolina. Regional meatpacking facilities depended on Kentucky salt for the processing of their reexport meat provisions. In the early 1800s, Greenup County maximized its

Ohio River location to export 89,200 bushels of its salt to Louisville and Cincinnati, much of which was absorbed by meatpackers preparing provisions for the New Orleans market. Within Appalachia, meatpacking facilities in Madison County, Kentucky, and in Knoxville also depended upon East Kentucky salt. By 1846, fifteen Clay County furnaces were producing 200,000 bushels, much of which was transported great distances overland by ox-drawn wagons or packhorses or by river southward.[31]

However, Southern Appalachia's largest salt exporters were situated in Kanawha and Mason Counties, West Virginia. Southern grocers could not "do better than to send to the salt mines of Virginia for pure table salt," *DeBow's Review* proclaimed. In 1810, West Virginia furnaces were already producing 540,000 bushels annually, much of which was sent on log rafts down the Ohio River. By 1817, thirty wells and twenty furnaces extracted nearly 700,000 bushels per year. By 1828, salt was big business in West Virginia; there were sixty-five wells sunk along ten miles of the Kanawha River. With a labor force of 471, these manufacturers produced a total of 787,000 bushels of salt each year. By 1835, the industry had grown to nearly 3,000 laborers (counting slaves). Charleston emerged as the center of this industry, sporting the fine homes of the salt barons along its Front Street. Kanawha salt production expanded to 3,000,000 bushels by 1846.[32]

As a result, this economic sector stimulated ancillary development of adjacent lumber, coal, and natural gas resources and triggered the expansion of cooperage, blacksmithing, boat building, and shipping. In addition, the West Virginia salines "used $47,600 worth of agricultural produce each year; 1,695,000 bushels of coal; 142 tons of iron; and 130,000 salt barrels worth $32,000" and "paid $8,000 a year to blacksmiths, $7,950 to mechanics." By 1852, 400 flatboats per year carried 3 million Kanawha Valley bushels to be marketed in Ohio, Illinois, Indiana, Iowa, Missouri, Tennessee, and Kentucky. To export salt from Mason County, West Virginia, tram roads were constructed from the salt furnaces to the boat landings: barrels were rolled down the trams and loaded onto packet boats and barges for transport down the Ohio River.[33]

The orientation of the region's large salt producers to fluctuations in distant markets is historically clear. When prices fell due to oversupply in distant markets, the Kanawha Valley salt firms linked themselves into a monopolistic cartel to regulate production and fix prices. In an 1817 contractual agreement, the participating companies agreed to sell salt only through their new association at its fixed prices. A ceiling of 450,000 bushels was set, and a production quota was assigned to each firm. All salt was to be of "good quality and nailed in good and sufficient barrels" that were delivered monthly to the association. Furthermore, any salt remaining unsold at year's end could never be marketed at prices lower than those set by the cartel.[34]

To maximize profits between 1817 and 1854, the Kanawha salines kept in effect a series of such supply and price-fixing arrangements. In their attempts to exert monopolistic pressures on the market, these West Virginia manufacturers withheld salt when demand was low, raised prices suddenly when demand was high, refused to sell to firms that bought salt from rivals, and lobbied Congress for the passage of tariffs on foreign salt. To effect a monopoly on the external flow of salt, three large trading companies were formed to decrease the activity of independent companies. Systematically, credit was overextended to these small producers; then the cartel seized their mortgaged furnaces.[35]

In addition to their monopolistic control over supply, the salt cartel sought to expand the geographical range of its market. In 1830, the cartel created a spinoff factorage to act as the distribution arm of the industry. The Dickinson-Armstrong Company acted as commission merchant to export Kanawha salt. When this approach failed, the Kanawha cartel began to consign its salt to wholesale agents in Maysville and Louisville, Kentucky, and in Cincinnati. This strategy rationalized distribution since the largest market for Kanawha salt was the pork-packing industry concentrated in those Ohio River towns. Once the wholesalers maximized advertising and river shipping, Cincinnati emerged as the major center for reexporting West Virginia salt to St. Louis, Memphis, and New Orleans. This move made for more efficient capture of river markets, centralized control of salt sales, and facilitated shipping to a greater number of distant ports. Unfortunately, the greatest profits accrued to the distant wholesalers, not to the Appalachian producers.[36]

In addition to their exports, West Virginia salt manufacturers triggered expansion of external trade through their imports from distant locations. Salt furnaces required ancillary support from a number of other industries; therefore, in the 1830s, the salines imported 185 tons of iron from Pittsburgh and Ohio. In addition, the company stores stocked for resale to their laborers foodstuffs, dry goods, agricultural produce, and groceries, predominantly shipped from Philadelphia and Baltimore. However, West Virginia's salt industry had declined, by 1860, to only fourteen manufacturers in Kanawha, Marion, Mercer, and Mason Counties, averaging thirty-three laborers and an annual gross of $28,224 each (Table 6.5). Even though salt manufacturing was not established there until 1849, Mason County quickly outstripped the production of its predecessors, and the Kanawha salines were in decline by the mid-nineteenth century.[37]

Antebellum Coal Mining

By using river, canal, and later railway linkages, four major Appalachian zones exported coal before the Civil War: several West Virginia counties, western Maryland, a few East Kentucky counties, and a few East Tennessee counties. In 1820, the United States was sixth in the world in coal production, and three-quarters of the country's exports were supplied by the mines, banks,

Table 6.6. Coal Mining, 1860

Appalachian Counties of	1860 Census Count		Uncounted Firms		Corrected Total	
	Firms	Laborers	Firms	Laborers	Firms	Laborers
Alabama	4	54		146	4	200
Georgia	3	14			3	14
Kentucky	17	105			17	105
Maryland	8	705			8	705
Tennessee	6	309	5	234	11	543
Virginia	1	12			1	12
West Virginia	16	682			16	682
Region	55	1,881	5	380	60	2,261

Sources: Aggregated from the published Census of Manufacturing and numerous archival and published sources. The corrected count of coal mines may still be low because census returns were not made for 28 (10%) of the region's counties, and I could not locate adequate archival records to check every missing county that had coal deposits. Moreover, the count of laborers is far too low because slaves were not included. At least five firms and numerous laborers were uncounted according to the following sources. Coal laborers were underreported for northern Alabama: see *De Bow's Review* 10 (1851): 73–76. Major coal operations of Grundy, Franklin, Anderson, and White Counties in Tennessee were uncounted: see Siler, *Tennessee Towns*, p. 88; Chitty, "Brief History of Sewanee"; Seeber, "History of Anderson," pp. 48–49; Seals, *History of White County*, p. 50.

and pits of southwestern Virginia, western Maryland, and West Virginia. By 1860, however, Southern Appalachia contributed less than one-fifth of the country's total production, encompassed only 12.7 percent of all the nation's mines, and earned less than 8 percent of the nation's total gross from coal. Concentrated in only twenty-five (11.6 percent) of the region's counties, sixty coal mines averaged thirty-seven laborers and an annual gross of $26,959 each (see Table 6.6). By 1860, four-fifths of the region's coal was being sent to regional, midwestern, and southern markets far from the production sites.[38]

During early stages of development, Appalachians dug coal from outcrops and wagoned the commodity to waterways. At river landings, it could be sold to dealers who operated fleets of flatboats. Regional coal deposits were discovered and mapped in the 1700s. Thus, early-nineteenth-century speculators bought up Appalachian lands adjacent to rivers or major creeks when they were rumored to contain "A Coal Bank that appear[ed] valuable." To exploit their investments, frontier landholders opened crude coal pits to permit "digging by the bushel." In 1822, for instance, an Owsley County, Kentucky, land agent managed "pits" and "banks" for absentee speculator Robert

Wickliffe. He marketed coal "sometime at 50 cents per hundred bushels when anyone want[ed] to raise a load." In addition, he rented two coal banks on half-shares "by the year generaly on the creeks of the river"—not a very profitable method for Wickliffe, he lamented, since he was forced "chiefly to collect according to law."[39]

By 1816, coal was being extracted from huge underground shafts in western Maryland. Producing "Coal in Abundance of an excellent quality," one such coal pit "led in horizontally & had many turnings & windings & the earth & rocks above from 20 to 30 feet thick supported & kept up by having columns of Stone Coal for the same to rest on. . . . this Cave had a masterly & superb appearance, the passages or streets . . . let a Cart and horse in with Ease & when Loaded goes out easyly." Commercially significant by 1820, western Maryland's coal mining involved thirty chartered companies between 1828 and 1850. By the 1840s, 672,000 tons of coal per year were leaving western Maryland by canal boats and rail, much of it to be reexported from Baltimore to Cuba and France. By 1860, Allegany County reported eight large mines averaging eighty-eight workers to generate an annual output of $58,053 each.[40]

The earliest coal exports from East Kentucky were generated by small producers at open pits. Some Blue Grass planters utilized slaves to mine coal at absentee East Kentucky pits, shipping the ore by flatboats to Frankfort. In that Appalachian zone, there was very little local use of coal. Instead, producers maximized their profits by sending their commodity to distant markets. In the late 1830s, East Kentucky coal was selling for less than three cents per bushel at the pit but bringing five times that price in the Blue Grass towns. Even in the early 1800s, Lexington and Frankfort consumed 18,000 bushels of East Kentucky coal annually, hauled in wagons or shipped on special canoes or flatboats. By 1840, an estimated 1,000,000 bushels of coal moved annually across the Cumberland, Kentucky, and Big Sandy Rivers. Hazard emerged as the head of navigation on the Kentucky River, which carried most shipments to the Blue Grass Basin and a minority to steamboats on the Ohio for reexport to Mississippi and Louisiana.[41]

East Kentucky coal was also exported to fuel the Nashville foundries and rolling mills. One Appalachian entrepreneur arranged annual fleets of boats to carry coal via the Cumberland River. It was not unusual for the Nashville industries to order 100,000 to 150,000 bushels at a time. After the miners transported the coal to creek edges, flatboaters hauled 3,500 bushels of coal each to steamboat landings on the Cumberland River for reexport to New Orleans and Nashville.[42] In the 1830s, one such steamboat captain wrote to an East Kentucky flatboater:

We will be there on the first rise without doubt or defalcation. I would be glad if you and Mr. Withers would [arrange] as much freight at the river as you could on our first trip as it is always scarce the first round. I am afraid that freight [to New Orleans] is some higher than it was last year but it is not the fault of the up River Boats. Freight to Nashville will be about the same it was the past season. . . . I do hope the River will rise before long. For I think the Coal is scarce at least it [is] selling very high.[43]

Such annual Nashville shipments averaged 2,100 tons in the 1830s, but Kentucky coal was also exported via the Big Sandy River for reexport from Maysville to Cincinnati.[44]

Appalachian Tennessee's earliest coal extractions were made from small banks discovered in the Smoky Mountains. Commercial coal mining had begun in Roane County by 1814 and had expanded into several other counties by 1830. Small mines emerged also in Morgan and Anderson Counties; however, this area's first real coal boom began in the late 1830s with the establishment of large-scale operations. As early as 1830, East Tennessee mines hauled coal by wagon to landings on the Clinch River. Special flatboats, barges, and steamboats then moved the coal to Kingston and Knoxville for redistribution downriver. A coal boom burst upon Anderson County in the 1840s. In 1836, the Bon Air Coal Company opened three White County mines on 11,000 acres, followed shortly after by the opening of four large mines in mountainous Marion County, which by 1860 employed 300 laborers and grossed $408,662. In the late 1840s, the Sewanee Mining Company (a subsidiary of the Tennessee Iron and Coal Company) captured large landholdings in Franklin, White, Grundy, and Sequatchie Counties to initiate large, heavily capitalized operations. River and rail connections at Chattanooga permitted the export of coal to Charleston, Mobile, and New Orleans.[45]

Developed initially to fuel salt manufacturing in the Kanawha Valley, twenty-five companies had been incorporated in West Virginia by 1860, one of the largest being the British-financed Winifrede Mining and Manufacturing Company. In one year's time, thirty-three salt manufacturers consumed 5,658,250 bushels of coal. Thus, "coal mining on the Kanawha River was a completely integrated function of salt production operations," so there were only two independent coal producers in the entire county in 1850. Consequently, Southern Appalachia's largest antebellum coal producers were located in nine counties of West Virginia. In 1860, two Boone County mines employed 180 laborers while two Mason County mines utilized 280 workers. Large mines requiring 45 to 50 laborers operated in Brooke County and in Preston County. In addition, nine medium-size mines were active in Hancock, Kanawha, Marion, Ohio, and Putnam Counties, these facilities averaging only 13 miners each.[46]

To maximize external trade linkages, West Virginia firms used slides, wagons, wooden tramways, and narrow-gauge railroads to get their commodity to the Ohio River, the major conduit for export. At the river, steam-powered tugboats moved the barges that transported coal to Louisville and Cincinnati for consumption and reexport. Due to "the long continuance of low water" in the fall of 1858, the Winifrede Mining Company had on hand "some $14,000 worth of coal mined and loaded ready for market." West Virginia firms also exported cannel coal to be consumed as home heating fuel in the Midwest and lower South.[47]

Copper Mining and Smelting

Copper was extracted from Southern Appalachia beginning in the 1830s with the opening of a western Maryland mine. Between 1844 and 1848, the Front Royal Mining and Copper Company, the Shenandoah Copper Mining Company, and the South Shenandoah Copper Company mapped and began to exploit veins of Warren, Rappahannock, Page, Shenandoah, Madison, Greene, and Rockingham Counties in Virginia. At the "spur of the Blue Ridge . . . called Stony Man" in Page County, northern adventurers used engines and slaves to exploit a mine and run a smelting mill. In the 1850s, a small copper mining operation was initiated in Cherokee County, Georgia. By 1860, there were also copper mining and smelting firms in Fannin County, Georgia; Alleghany County, North Carolina; and Carroll and Fauquier Counties, Virginia. These large extractive firms averaged twenty-three laborers and an annual gross of $11,689 each.[48]

When a new copper strike occurred nine years after the forced removal of the Cherokees, few white resettlers had yet located in the southeastern Tennessee mountains. The mineral find came as a by-product of the Chestatee River gold rush when a prospector panned a Polk County tributary. News of the strike attracted national and international attention, particularly in Baltimore and London. Prospecting boomed in 1851, and land speculation intensified in "the Switzerland of America," (as *De Bow's Review* tagged mineral-rich East Tennessee. By 1855, international attention was "fast being directed to the copper interests" of East Tennessee. In one mountainous county, "capitalists and miners [we]re investing in lands and bringing forth the heretofore hidden mineral to so surprising a degree as almost to be declared fabulous." Between 1850 and 1854, thirteen major copper sites were opened; by 1860, there were 671 households in the county, three-quarters of which were engaged in copper mining. By far the largest Appalachian copper mining operations in 1860, two Polk County firms employed 405 laborers and grossed $404,000. With $2,700,000 invested in land and facilities, Union Consolidated Mining and Isabella Mining were two of the country's most heavily capitalized industries.[49]

In fact, the country's largest antebellum copper exports came from two adjacent mountainous counties in southeastern Tennessee and northwestern Georgia. Appalachian copper was extracted entirely for distant markets, for there were no secondary processing facilities in the region. By 1860, four

Appalachian counties exported nearly $600,000 worth of copper, primarily to northeastern and European ports. From several mine locations, ore was hauled forty-five miles by mule trains or floated on the river to Cleveland for rail shipping to New York, Baltimore, and Cuba. Ore amounting to 14,291 tons and valued at more than $1 million was shipped in 1850, much of it to Savannah for reexport to Liverpool.[50]

Timbering and Lumber Exports

Perhaps the most extensive antebellum extractive industry was timbering and lumber manufacture. The leather, coal, iron, and salt industries spurred ancillary forest exploitation. In the Kanawha Valley, the antebellum salt manufacturers leased thousands of acres to produce their barrels, wooden pipelines, and plank tramways. Throughout the region, timberlands were consumed to produce the charcoal that fired iron furnaces, to generate bark for leather tanning, and to provide beams for shoring up coal mines. Thus, merchant mill complexes typically included a sawmill that charged tolls for its services.[51]

Moreover, it was not unusual for the largest farmers to operate commercial sawmills on shares with skilled tenants. For example, one East Tennessee gentleman-farmer leased his sawmill "for four years on condition that [the tenants] saw 1,000 feet of plank a year" for him. Others gradually cut over their wooded parcels as a winter source of income. For example, the Ferry Hill Plantation used tenants and slaves to timber its western Maryland woodlands in order to market fuel, lumber, and fence railings to nearby townspeople and to barges on the Erie Canal.[52]

By 1860, the Census of Manufacturing identified 991 lumber operations in 150 (70 percent) of the region's counties; it is likely that there were sawmills in every county. A profitable business venture requiring only $60 to $500 in mechanical parts, Appalachia's early water-powered sawmills averaged two laborers and an annual gross of $2,007 each. However, larger operations characterized counties adjacent to iron, coal, or salt production, as was the case in Polk County, Georgia; Owsley County, Kentucky; Allegany County, Maryland; and Roane County, Tennessee. By 1835, the largest Appalachian lumber companies relied on circular saws powered by steam, and there were fifteen West Virginia firms applying this technological advance. In Pickens County, South Carolina, the largest manufacturing activity was such a progressive lumber mill. Utilizing fifteen laborers, this firm grossed $12,000 per year by marketing its production to Savannah for reexport to England. The most extensive operations paralleled the sawmill located in Kanawha County. Powered by a twenty-two-foot-high waterfall, it produced 30,000 to 40,000 board feet daily, using logging crews organized into swampers (road makers), choppers (workers who cleared limbs and brush), sawyers, loaders, and teamsters.[53]

Appalachian lumber was exported from the production sites in two ways:

intermediate marketing to adjacent regional towns and river shipping of lumber to southern towns. Within a one-hundred-mile radius, counties with river access sent timber, charcoal, and tanning bark to supply regional salt, iron, leather, cooperage, and furniture manufactories. In addition, cordwood was supplied to adjacent towns, and timber was transported to boat-building facilities. River towns also sent shingles, scantling, and finished lumber to distant trade centers on the Mississippi and Ohio Rivers, which were the major national conduits for antebellum timber movement. The treeless Midwest absorbed part of the surpluses from East Kentucky and West Virginia; however, once at seaports, Appalachian exports were redistributed to northeastern cities or to western Europe. By the early 1850s, New York City was importing 438,388 tons of timber annually for urban and industrial expansion, most from the southern ports of Charleston, Mobile, Savannah, and New Orleans. Because timber had already been cut over in western Europe, there was also a booming reexport trade to British ports.[54]

Beginning in the early 1800s, timber was being exported from several Appalachian Virginia counties to the Tidewater, the Northeast, and to Baltimore for reexport to the West Indies. To augment the output of river counties, inland West Virginia companies floated logs to Ohio River boatyards, sawmills, and manufactories. On a single rise of the Little Kanawha River, 400 rafts of timber were floated to the Ohio. Much of this aggregated production was finished for reexport to southern and midwestern markets. In fact, some West Virginia sawmills specialized in the processing of pine for southern markets. From northern counties, logs were rafted to Pittsburgh.[55]

From East Kentucky, timber rafts followed the Big Sandy River to be marketed at Louisville. Tanning bark, railroad cross ties, cords of wood, shingles, staves, barrels, and semifinished wood also moved from the Appalachian counties into the Blue Grass Basin. In addition, lumber was shipped on Kentucky River flatboats to Ohio River landings for reexport. Even in landlocked western North Carolina, the secretary of the navy advertised for "lumber to be supplied from that region and delivered" in New York and Philadelphia.[56]

East Tennessee counties along the Tennessee River network shipped annual lumber rafts to Chattanooga for reexport by steamboat to Alabama and Mississippi Valley destinations. From the Clinch Valley of upper East Tennessee and southwestern Virginia, 1,000 rafts per year headed south for reexport out of Knoxville and Chattanooga. By 1834, a Maine company was undertaking massive lumbering on the northwestern edge of Appalachian Georgia. As a result, Savannah emerged as a major national timber entrepôt that reexported surpluses to England.[57]

Other Mineral Exports

Even the most mountainous areas did not escape extractive exploitation. Appalachian saltpeter fueled the production of gunpowder in southern and northeastern manufactories. From a location "pent up amidst Cloud Caped Mountains," alum was packed and hauled down steep, rough grades to a crude turnpike leading to Knoxville, where it was reexported by rail or river to northeastern canneries. Alum Cave, located on the highest peak in the Smoky Mountains, attracted the attention of the Epsom Salts Manufacturing Company, which bought up 10,050 acres and established camps to mine the sheer bluffs. Southern Appalachia also exported the country's only antebellum manganese for use in northeastern steel manufacturing. Even water from Appalachian mineral springs was bottled and exported to distant markets.[58]

In the eighteenth century, speculation was flamed by the search for lead and silver in some of the most rugged terrain of present-day West Virginia and southwestern Virginia. By attracting British capital and equipment in the 1750s, the governor and three other powerful planters syndicated a 1,000-acre mine in present-day Wythe County. After the Continental Congress appointed a 1775 committee "to enquire in all colonies after virgin lead, leaden ore, and the best methods of collecting, smelting, and refining it," new mining operations emerged in Rockingham, Montgomery, and Botetourt Counties.[59]

Because the metal was imported regularly from Europe, Southern Appalachia's early antebellum production of lead was crucial to the emerging nation. Early federal documents indicate the national excitement over locating dependable domestic supplies. In 1790, the secretary of the Treasury reported that "A prolific mine of it has long been open in the southwestern parts of Virginia. . . . This is now in the hands of individuals, who not only carry it on with spirit, but have established manufactories of it at Richmond."[60]

Laboriously by wagon and river, lead was exported from southwestern Virginia to Richmond and Philadelphia, beginning in the early 1800s. From the furnace "the lead [wa]s transported one hundred and thirty miles along a good road, leading through the peaks of Ottie and Lunch's ferry, whence it [wa]s carried by water about the same distance to [the foundry at] Westham, where [after smelting] it f[ou]nd its way by James River and the Potowmac to the markets of the Eastern States." Although smaller mines were exhausted by 1820, two large industrial descendants of the eighteenth-century mines had expanded, by 1860, to require 165 free laborers (and numerous uncounted slaves), in order to generate an annual gross of $61,000.[61]

Ginseng and Herbs

The trade in Appalachian ginseng was initiated during the eighteenth-century fur trade. On the frontier, the Cherokees received ten cents per pound in store merchandise for their ginseng. Then Charleston merchants shipped the herb to the London-based East India Company for reexport to China. Between 1784 and 1860, a small group of New York brokers traded American ginseng for Chinese tea to be marketed in the United States. Soon after the Revolutionary War, George Washington reported that his West Virginia survey party "met with many mules and pack horses laden with ginseng going east." Similarly, in 1784, pack horses of ginseng moved frequently from western Maryland to Baltimore. In the 1820s, a Pickens County, South Carolina, merchant sent to Savannah and Charleston "about 1000 pounds of gensing, and several hogsheads of snakeroot." This store also bought from the Cherokees pinkroot "made up into bundles of about one pound each," which were then pressed into 600-pound hogsheads for export. In West Virginia, some farmers domesticated ginseng in their corn fields, and one Virginia planter exported about $1,000 a year in "roots" from this kind of cultivation.[62]

Charleston, Baltimore, and New Orleans shipped ginseng to New York for reexport; after 1840, Louisville and Cincinnati engaged in this trade as well. Charleston, West Virginia, and Winchester, Virginia, merchants exported ginseng, yellow root, mayapple root, and snakeroot for nearly ten times the value they allowed local customers in barter. One West Virginian recalled that "the Pittsburgh and Eastern merchants always let on that the back settlements never brought in anything but ginseng and snakeroot to market." One western North Carolina merchant exported 30,000 pounds accumulated in one year's store trades. By 1840, Appalachian ginseng was becoming scarcer, but the region exported $83,273 worth of the herb in that year—nearly one-fifth of the country's total supply.[63]

Extractive Exports to Regional Markets

In addition to their exports to distant national and international markets, Southern Appalachian counties shipped several extractive commodities to consumers within a one-hundred-mile radius of production sites.

Antebellum Petroleum and Natural Gas

The region's natural gas was first marketed commercially in 1841 to provide a new source of city street lighting. Transported through large wooden pipes, gas also fueled the salt furnaces. By 1860, the fuel was being extracted by five firms of Allegany and Frederick Counties in Maryland; Augusta County in Virginia; and Ohio and Taylor Counties in West Virginia. These small to medium-size companies averaged seven laborers and grossed $8,840 each. Despite these meager showings, the speculation in West Virginia gas lands and leases attracted significant attention from local and absentee investors; these antebellum activities would form the basis for a second early-twentieth-century boom.[64]

After the import of Vienna lamps had popularized kerosene as a source of household lighting, American petroleum boomed in 1859. As the first stage of the petroleum industry in the United States, kerosene was produced by only thirty-four companies in 1859, one-third of them located in Southern Appalachia. In any area where there was believed to be oil, frantic land speculation transformed the isolated Pennsylvania countryside into derrick-filled boom towns like Titusville and Oil City.[65] Simultaneously, the petroleum mania spread into West Virginia and East Kentucky. Hidden at the end of one county's 1860 Census of Population, rare comments document the region's antebellum oil boom. Describing a belt forty miles long by twenty miles wide in Wirt County, the enumerator reported that

> Petroleum has been known for many years to exist here and has been worked on a small scale. . . . Recently it was discovered in some old salt wells which had been standing unworked for years. . . . One well is now yielding from 12 to 15 barrels of pure oil per day and the quantity gradually and daily increases. Other wells are being bored for oil—some of which promise to yield richly. . . . There can be no doubt but the oil is abundant and inexhaustible for generations to come. . . . The excitement here in relation to oil is running high and bids to rival the California gold fever and well it may, as investments in oil lands and oil privileges gives far more certainty in realizing larger profits for small investments. If the wells now being sunk yields [sic] as much as those that are now worked, in a few years we shall produce not a million but millions of dollars worth of the purest petroleum that was ever mined.[66]

In this same county, a boom town consumed a large farm on the Little Kanawha River, and a Philadelphia journalist commented: "The Rathbone farms began to look like a city of the forest, and where the sheep and cattle were wont to live in undisturbed content derricks and cisterns, and barrels and scaffolds, formed a busy and exciting scene." In less than a year between 1859 and 1860, Wirt County generated one million gallons of oil. Likewise, in Wood County, the Burning Springs field alone consumed thousands of former farm acres. Emergent towns, like Volcano and Mannington, became centers of the booming oil industry as early as 1857 as the speculative fever spread into the counties of Boone, Brooke, Cabell, Clay, Fayette, Kanawha, Logan, Marion, Monongalia, Nicholas, Ohio, Ritchie, Tyler, Wayne, and Wood.[67]

Although petroleum extraction came a little slower to East Kentucky, the speculation in oil lands continued throughout the Civil War. As a result of a boom beginning in 1859, the town of Catlettsburg "rapidly improv[ed] in wealth and population." Since few skirmishes actually occurred in East Kentucky, investors were able to move quickly when they saw the conflict winding down. Only three months after the war's end, a Pike County merchant had built a second hotel to accommodate the influx of outsiders; at that time, "houses [were] going up on every vacant lot." With great optimism, the capitalist assessed the town's "promising" economic prospects. "There are to be several changes in town," he reported, "and we are expecting a greater rush than ever of oil hunters this coming season."[68]

Seriously undercounted by the antebellum census, small to medium-size quarrying operations were sprinkled throughout the region. The 1860 Census of Manufacturing reported only thirty-five quarries in fourteen counties of Southern Appalachia, averaging five laborers and an annual gross of $4,266 each. Seven large firms extracted marble and granite from quarries in Talladega and Etowah Counties, Alabama; Pickens County, Georgia; and Lewis County, Kentucky. Operation of the dual sites of the Rock Springs Quarry Company was the most important economic activity in Etowah County, Alabama. Knoxville, Tennessee, entrepreneurs operated the country's second-largest quarry and one of the largest plants for producing finished marble. At nearby Rogersville was located the first southern quarry to mechanize its operations with derricks and channeling machines in the 1850s. Medium-size firms specialized in marble production in all three western Maryland counties, in three East Tennessee counties, in three Appalachian Virginia counties, and in Harrison County, West Virginia. In addition, slate and limestone were harvested by ten small Frederick County, Maryland, firms and from two large quarries located in Polk County, Georgia.[69]

Even massive extractive resources were exported from the mountainous region. For use in building planter homes, marble and stone were shipped from many Appalachian counties to regional towns with river access. Several mule teams hauled marble boulders to the river's edge for export on flatboats. In fact, two-thirds of the region's marble output was probably consumed by distant planters. Strangely enough, one Tidewater store offered, as part of its regular merchandise, stones quarried in the distant Blue Ridge Mountains.[70]

Pooling an Industrial Labor Force

Industrialization was introduced to those areas of the nineteenth-century world economy where there were concentrations of unpropertied people. Because the very poverty of its workforce gave capitalism a competitive advantage, Southern Appalachia was such a periphery. As we have seen, a sizeable segment of the region's population was severed from the land and forced to sell its labor power. Beginning as early as 1830, the economic gambling of absentee speculators and regional elites changed the face of the land and restructured the lives of working people. As a result, the antebellum Southern Appalachian countryside "teemed with non-peasants and hummed with manufacture."[71]

Proletarianization of Farmers and Women

In peripheral communities of the world economy, many farm households become semiproletarianized, even though they are never totally divorced from production on the land. In order to eke out their livelihoods, such households are compelled to move back and forth between economic arenas, continually shuffling external wage labor, household production for the market, exchange activities in the informal sector, and subsistence agriculture. During the early stages of proletarianization in the United States, small farm households utilized external wages to try to sustain their agricultural way of life. Increasingly, however, such families were drawn into reliance upon full-time wage work.[72]

By the mid-nineteenth century, this historical process was clearly underway in Southern Appalachia. Nearly two-fifths of the region's farm operators were semiproletarianized by 1860. Such households either worked for a share of the crop production or were engaged in full-time second occupations for monetary wages (Table 4.2). The region's larger towns attracted these rural laborers. For instance, a Knoxville, Tennessee, editor described the annual influx from the countryside of those seeking to pick up odd jobs at nearby industries. Many poor and ragged men were "seen every day lounging on the street corners." However, the dependence of Appalachian farm households on wage earning varied with their access to opportunities for producing their subsistence on the land.[73]

By 1860, 15 percent of the region's tenant farmers and two-fifths of the sharecroppers reported that one or more household members were earning wages in a second nonfarm occupation. Because they were most likely to be "food-deficient" each year, the sharecroppers were becoming proletarianized at a rate nearly three times that of the more productive tenant farmers. Across the region, there was some disparity from one geographical region to another. Landless farmers in Appalachian Georgia, South Carolina, Tennessee, Virginia, and West Virginia were slightly more likely to be employed in second jobs that their counterparts in western Maryland, northern Alabama, or western North Carolina, the fewest second wage earners occurring among landless farmers in East Kentucky.[74]

Because they retained greater access to the land needed to provide their subsistence, farm-owner households were entering second nonfarm occupations at a rate that was less than half that for landless farm operators. However, one of every five Appalachian farm owners was finding it necessary, by 1860, to combine agriculture and wage labor. About one-tenth of the region's farm owners reported agriculture as their primary occupations, with nonagricultural wage earning used to subsidize total family resources. Yet another one-tenth of the farm owners were heads of household who had left agriculture to earn full-time wages, leaving farming to be a secondary, subsistence activity of wives and children. In upcountry South Carolina, for instance, "several hundred poor native whites . . . had deserted farms and rented lands for employment in the [cotton and flour] mills." As early as 1838 in western Maryland, George's Creek Coal and Iron Company reported that local farmers "continue to apply to us faster than we can give places to them."[75]

The 1860 census provides only a conservative estimate of the pace at which Southern Appalachia's farm operators were becoming proletarianized, for these records do not reflect the extent to which agricultural households engaged in part-time wage earning. The Civil War veterans report a widespread pattern of industrial employment during the off-season. For instance, one Cherokee County, Georgia, farmer dug gold and operated a still for winter wages. Southern Appalachia's farm owners also timbered, constructed rafts or trade wagons for merchants, worked as grist or sawmill laborers, and hired out to artisans.[76]

In addition to the invisible labor that Appalachian females provided to subsidize the farm work of their husbands and fathers, some Appalachian women were integrated into market activities that were overtly defined as income generating. Some farm women sought to increase their household income by taking on wage labor in mining and in the manufacture of textiles and glass. By 1860, 6 percent of the region's factory and mining jobs were filled by women. In western North Carolina, women comprised nearly one-fifth of the factory laborers (primarily in textiles and tobacco manufacturing).[77]

Perceived Labor Scarcities and Labor Migration

Despite the empirical availability of a surplus landless labor force in the region, Southern Appalachia's industrialists bemoaned local scarcities of cheap, skilled labor. Most southern capitalists believed that "any good system of management" necessitated laborers who comprehended that the employer "is to govern absolutely" while the worker "is to obey implicitly." For this reason, Appalachia's wealthiest elites stereotyped local landless poor laborers as a recalcitrant and "unmanageable" lot who "just picked up and moved on when they felt like it." In order to overcome these perceived local scarcities and to widen their margins of profit, Appalachian manufacturers sought to centralize a steady, year-round supply of skilled laborers under their legal control. Rather than creating new job opportunities for resident workers, these capitalists reached out into the international labor market to secure workers. Initially, the region's manufacturers purchased and hired slaves as their cheapest source of labor. By 1840, however, Appalachian manufacturers required skilled artisans, the most expensive "laborer-elite" among slaves. Then these capitalists exploited the desperate living conditions of European laborers to recruit immigrant artisans bound by contract to the companies that imported them to the United States.[78]

Heavily dependent on such labor-pooling strategies were the copper mines of Ducktown, Tennessee; the coal mines in Marion County, Tennessee; the iron industry of western Maryland; and the coal operators of the Kanawha Valley, West Virginia. These Appalachian industries utilized a contractual system to import immigrant laborers, thereby recruiting to the region several thousand Cornish, Irish, Welsh, Italian, and German families. In western Maryland, nine-tenths of the miners were foreign-born, two-thirds of them recruited from Scotland, Ireland, and Germany. Five thousand German and Irish workers broadened the industrial labor force of Wheeling, West Virginia, and immigrant ironworkers dominated the Hanging Rock District of East Kentucky. The labor strategies of mining operations in East Tennessee were typical. At the Ducktown copper mines, the workers were "mostly white North Carolinians" and "several hundred Cornish men" who were "constantly coming" from Cornwall, where they had been engaged by the companies to have "their expenses out paid, and forty dollars a month wages."[79]

In addition to immigrants contracted for mining enterprises, hundreds of international laborers were recruited into Southern Appalachia to complete the dangerous work associated with antebellum canal and railroad construction. As the Chesapeake and Ohio Canal advanced across western Maryland, numerous shantytowns of Irish and German laborers emerged. After labor shortages delayed completion of the Blue Ridge and Virginia Central Railroad, Corkian and northern Irish laborers were contracted from Europe to construct tunnels through the mountains.[80]

Summary

It is clear that the transition to industrial capitalism was underway in Southern Appalachia by the early nineteenth century. Rather than being isolated or autonomous from the international economy, this region seemed to be replicating many of the characteristic patterns of development that had advanced to a higher technological level in other parts of the capitalist world economy. In some respects, the region's nineteenth-century manufacturing mirrored capitalist development that had occurred in the European core of the world system more than a century before. Just as England had previously experienced the "slow progress of mechanization," Southern Appalachia was undergoing capitalist expansion "rooted in a sub-soil of small-scale enterprises."[81]

In addition, the region paralleled historical capitalism in the European core in the emergence of three major structures for manufacturing: artisan shops that depended on small manual labor forces (e.g., hatters); small manufactories and mills that combined manual labor with mechanization (e.g., flour mills); and factories that centralized large labor forces in utilizing machinery (e.g., glass factories). In its governmental subsidization of early manufacturing and in "the presence of a rapidly growing proletariat in the countryside," this inland region also replicated historical capitalism as it had already unfolded in western Europe. In short, Southern Appalachia was not unlike the European core or other regions of the United States in the "vast multiplication of small rural industries based on small to medium accumulation of capital."[82]

Three historical trends occurred as capitalist industry emerged in antebellum Southern Appalachia. First, small artisan shops operated by independent producers disappeared in the face of competition from larger factories and imported commodities. Simultaneously, skilled artisans were absorbed as wage laborers in larger, more centralized capitalist enterprises. Moreover, the importation of distant commodities (like clothing, machinery, and household goods) ruined Appalachian crafts "without their being replaced by local industrial production." Consequently, the region's crafts were displaced more rapidly than new employment openings were created by local manufacturing enterprises.[83]

Second, incorporation into the world economy generated the development of manufacturing in a very uneven pattern throughout the region. Investments were made in the region's antebellum manufacturing at a per capita level that was only one-half the national average. In their investments in new manufacturing enterprises, three-quarters of the region's counties fell behind the rest of the South. Appalachian elites made wealthy by trade in "manufactured goods from the center, and in [raw] products destined for the center, invest[ed] their profits not in industry, which would be unprofitable, given the foreign competition, but in the purchase of land. . . . The attraction exerted on capital by land ha[d] the effect of limiting the rate of accumulation. It is in this sense that it is correct to say that 'the land is a bottomless pit for savings.'" However, one-quarter of the Southern Appalachian counties were industrializing much more rapidly, some at levels exceeding national averages. Despite this uneven development, capitalist restructuring was evident in the regionwide pressure toward "the creation of large-scale economic units" that could profitably produce commodities for the world market. Large factories were scattered throughout the region, and company towns were structured to centralize and control the labor forces.[84]

The capitalist world system continually demanded new sources of raw materials to sustain the expansion of diversified manufacturing in its richer regions. Beginning in the sixteenth century, the western European core was impelled by its thirst for mineral wealth to push the boundaries of the world system into new frontiers. As part of that global expansion, external explorers began in the seventeenth century to identify and map Southern Appalachia's pockets of profitable resources that might supply raw materials essential to future core growth.[85]

Consequently, articulation with the world market triggered capitalist speculation in Appalachian mineral lands, and hoarding of the region's natural resources by absentee investors spanned the entire antebellum period. In sharp contrast to the rest of the United States, Southern Appalachia's antebellum manufacturing investments were heavily concentrated in low-wage mining, quarrying, smelting, intermediate ore processing, and timbering. As a result, extractive industries comprised the region's predominant employer of nonagricultural laborers and accounted for the second most important industrial category in terms of annual gross. Consequently, the emergence of diversified manufacturing was deterred by investment of capital, labor, and infrastructure into production of agricultural and extractive materials for export to world markets.

By 1860, Southern Appalachia had already experienced a series of boom and bust cycles triggered by the dependence of local economies upon the availability of profitable distant markets for their raw materials. The expansion and heavy capitalization of the region's extractive industries was neither accidental nor autonomous. Local elites "cashed the industrial potential of their territories" by gambling their own wealth accumulation and by syndicating absentee investments into Appalachian minerals for which there was a demand in national and international markets. Iron ore fueled the proliferation of bloomeries, forges, furnaces, rolling mills, naileries, machine shops, tool factories, and numerous secondary enterprises, making iron production the leading industry of the nineteenth-century world economy. In addition, western Europe voraciously devoured Appalachian gold and copper while the region's iron, lead, manganese, and saltpeter were greedily sought by the growing industrial cities of the American Northeast. At the same time, the Deep South demanded steady supplies of Appalachian iron, stone, marble, and timber. After 1840, Southern Appalachia's deposits of coal, oil, and natural gas were tapped as ancillary fuel resources to make possible increased output of salt, one of the region's primary exports to the markets of the Midwest and Deep South.[86]

In the richer sectors of the nineteenth-century world system, capital was invested in all branches of production. In sharp contrast, local and absentee promotion of the extraction of Southern Appalachia's natural resources deterred the development of core-type diversified manufacturing throughout the region. "The dominant classes engendered by such economies tend to invest available capital in infrastructure and exchange rather than in industry." Consequently, two structural distortions occurred as peripheral capitalism expanded throughout the region. First, there was a propensity toward the two branches of industry (light manufacturing and extractive) closely associated with the processing of raw materials—types of economic development that do not generate the spinoffs and multipliers required to foster the kind of sustained growth that occurs in the core regions of the capitalist world economy. Second, there was local and absentee focus upon those activities that produced exports rather than upon the utilization of raw materials to spur local industrial development.[87]

Yet there was nothing economically unique about the manner in which the capitalist core drained off Southern Appalachia's natural resources. Nor was there anything historically peculiar about the negative side effects that impacted Southern Appalachia as it underwent incorporation into the capitalist world economy. "By creating in the periphery, in the sectors that are of interest to it, organizations for mining and industrial processing on the scale required by modern technique, the center *everywhere* blocks the path for the development of a [diversified] industrial capitalism capable of competing with it."[88]

7

THE SPATIAL ORGANIZATION

OF EXTERNAL TRADE

Specialization Zones in the World Economy

During the nineteenth century, the world's geographical regions were hierarchically integrated into a framework of production processes structured
around three interdependent specializations: zones to produce export commodities; support zones to supply food or raw materials to the export areas
and their urbanizing centers; and support zones from which laborers emigrated to the export centers. None of these zones was totally independent
from the other areas, for self-sufficiency was to be found only at the level of
the entire capitalist world system.[1]

As the transition to capitalism unfolded in India, West Africa, the Ottoman
Empire, and Russia, there was "considerable geographic concentration of
particular crops in certain tracts." In this way, those areas cultivating staple
exports for external markets could acquire cheap survival provisions and
labor from contiguous regions. Thus, the emergence of cash-crop zones stimulated the expansion of market-oriented food production in adjacent zones.
In South America, the Caribbean, and the West Indies, there developed a
"continuous interplay of plantations and small-scale yeoman agriculture." In
order to maximize access to international markets, the Europeans concentrated their plantation systems along the coasts. To supply food to the coastal
plantations, a second type of "production regime" was adapted to the inland,
more mountainous terrain. In those zones, smaller-scale farms and manufacturing enterprises generated grains, livestock, and extractive commodities to provender the coastal export centers. There were some areas without
easy market access where high capital or labor investments were risky. Because of the high demand in the global metropoles, such "unprofitable" vast
inland tracts were transformed into the "livestock frontiers" of the nineteenth-
century world economy. In addition, extractive industry emerged in the in-

land mountains of the New World colonies, replicating the pattern that western Europe had followed in its own transition to capitalism.[2]

Appalachian Articulation with the World Economy

On a world scale, Southern Appalachia's role was not that different from many other such peripheral fringes at the time, including inland mountain sections of several Caribbean islands, Brazil, the West Indies, and central Europe. Incorporation into the capitalist world economy triggered within Southern Appalachia agricultural, livestock, and extractive ventures that were adapted to the region's terrain and ecological peculiarities. Yet those new production regimes paralleled activities that were occurring in other sectors of the New World that had been colonized by western Europe. In fact, several production regimes were developing unevenly throughout the region. Some Appalachian counties specialized in the cultivation of tobacco or cotton for export. Fundamentally, however, Southern Appalachia was a "support zone" that supplied raw materials to other agricultural or industrial export regions of the world economy.[3]

On the one hand, this inland region exported foodstuffs to other peripheries and semiperipheries of the Western Hemisphere, those areas that specialized in cash crops for export to the core. It is not by accident that the region's surplus producers concentrated their land and labor resources in the generation of wheat and corn—often in terrain where such production was ecologically unsound. Appalachian agriculture was neither irrational nor precapitalist; crops were planned and cultivated in response to distant market prices. The demand for flour, meal, and grain liquors was high in plantation economies (like the North American South and most of Latin America), where labor was budgeted toward the production of exotic staples, not foods. Nor was it a chance occurrence that Southern Appalachians specialized in the production of livestock, as did inland mountainous sections of other zones of the New World. The demand for meat, work animals, meat derivatives, and leather was high in those peripheries and semiperipheries of the world economy that did not allocate land to less profitable livestock production.

On the other hand, Southern Appalachia was also a production regime that supplied raw materials to the emergent industrial cores of the American Northeast and western Europe. The appetite for Appalachian minerals, timber, cotton, and wool was great in those industrial arenas. In addition, regional exports of manufactured tobacco, grain liquors, and foodstuffs provisioned those sectors of the world economy where industry and towns had displaced farms. Antebellum journalists believed the cotton South was dependent upon the upper South for grain, cattle, hogs, horses, and mules. However, the needs of the lower South were insufficient to absorb the entire surplus output from the upper South. Even without the Appalachian counties, the South and Southwest were self-sufficient in grain and livestock production in 1860. For example, Mississippi Valley residents consumed only two-thirds of the flour and beef, three-quarters of the corn, and 86 percent of the pork received at New Orleans between 1858 and 1861.[4]

Instead, much of the Appalachian surplus received in southern ports was reexported to the urban-industrial centers of the American Northeast and to foreign plantation zones of the world economy. By the 1840s, the northeastern United States was specializing in manufacturing and international shipping, and that region's growing trade and production centers were experiencing food deficits. Consequently, by 1860, three-fourths of the upper South's grain received at southern seaports was being reexported to the Northeast. In return for raw ores and agricultural products, southern markets—including the mountain counties—consumed nearly one-quarter of the transportable manufacturing output of the North and received a sizeable segment of the redistributed international imports (e.g., coffee and tea) handled by northeastern capitalists.[5]

Beginning in the 1820s, Great Britain lowered tariff rates and eliminated trade barriers to foreign grains. Subsequently, European and colonial markets were opened to North American commodities. Little wonder, then, that flour and processed meats comprised the country's major nineteenth-century exports or that more than two-thirds of those exports went to England and France. Outside the country, then, Appalachian commodities flowed to the manufacturing centers of Europe, to the West Indies, to the Caribbean, and to South America. Through far-reaching commodity flows, Appalachian raw materials—in the form of agricultural, livestock, or extractive resources—were exchanged for core manufactures and tropical imports.[6]

In the nineteenth-century American Southeast, "the world of commerce was in effect a triangle with one apex on the near-by coast, at Charleston or Savannah, a second in the Tennessee-Ohio region, say at Knoxville, Nashville, or Cincinnati, and a third in the district of metropolitan commerce, Baltimore or New York." At the local level, production for export stimulated the development of towns and villages that served as the intermediate hubs for forwarding commodities to the outside world. "The movement from farm to market generated employment opportunities and attendant urban systems that varied with the particular staple involved and the technique of marketing."[7]

On the one hand, sectors of the world economy were interdependent around product specializations; trade revolved around exchange of the resulting variety of export commodities. On the other hand, the world economy must be organized to mobilize those goods between geographically distant areas. Thus, zones were differentiated not only by their production regimes but also by their roles in the distribution process. Spatially, the villages, towns, and cities of the capitalist world economy were hierarchically structured into interlocking networks of "production zones," "distribution zones," and "consumption zones." Interconnected by networks of oceans, rivers, canals, turnpikes, roads, and later railroads, these three layers of distribution points made international trade possible. How, then, was Southern Appalachia integrated into this global system?

The Spatial Articulation of Trading Centers

Antebellum Appalachian towns and villages were hubs of commercial inter-action with other regional communities and with distant territories. Capitalis-tic trading triggered a network of commodity chains in which "urbanizing" centers subsumed nearby smaller towns, villages, and hamlets. Consequently, the region's larger towns gradually became "foreign bodies" in their local economies, "looking beyond [their] narrow surroundings and out towards the greater movement of the outside world, receiving from it rare, precious goods unknown locally, which [they] sent in turn to smaller markets and shops."[8]

In this way, the region's fragile town economies were integrated into the spatial organization of the capitalist world system. For it was through these towns and villages that the region's trade goods moved. Export commodities were centralized in these towns because public inspection stations, banking, merchants, and manufacturers were located there. Thus, the layer of smaller villages and towns moved commodities to towns that had better access to transportation or were more commercialized. For example, many small river villages temporarily warehoused goods that were to be forwarded to larger towns. Reeds' Landing, located in Greenup County, Kentucky, was such "a public trading place and shipping place. In bad weather they kep' the grain an' things they was going to ship in the warehouse."[9]

From these smaller towns, trade goods moved to larger regional trading hubs that provided "export linkages" for the distant transport of bulky or perishable produce and "import linkages" for the wholesale distribution of foreign commodities. For example, Tidewater Virginia grain brokers received regular consignments from farmers in several Blue Ridge counties through Lexington, Milton, and Warren, three Appalachian towns with access to the James River and Kanawha Canal. Such small towns were intermediate dis-tribution points for large volumes of trade goods moving out of and into the Appalachian hinterlands. Consider, for example, three tiny East Tennessee towns. In the 1840s, the little community of Jonesboro imported merchandise "direct from Baltimore through the Lynchburg market, and cotton and sugar and other heavy articles [were] imported from Charleston, Hamburg and Augusta, at least $14,000.00 annually, independent of . . . something like 25,000 lbs. of coffee, sugar, etc., annually imported into Washington County from the same places by the farmers and other traders" in exchange for agricultural produce. Further southeast, merchants in the towns of Kingston and Athens expended nearly $170,000 annually to import goods by land "from the Eastern markets and groceries from the South," to purchase salt from southwestern Virginia, and to transport agricultural produce downriver via Chattanooga to Alabama and Mississippi markets.[10]

Appalachian Bulking Centers

Situated at major transportation crossroads, the region's larger towns functioned as "bulking centers" for adjacent smaller villages, agricultural hinterlands, and extractive enclaves. Cumberland and Hagerstown, Maryland; Staunton and Winchester, Virginia; Wheeling, Morgantown, and Charleston, West Virginia; Knoxville and Chattanooga, Tennessee; and Rome, Georgia, were regional distribution centers for the export of Appalachian commodities and for the import of foreign goods back into the countryside (see Map 7.1). In a sense, then, these centralized towns served as first-level "distribution zones" for large adjacent agricultural, manufacturing, and extractive "production zones."[11]

Located at the northern tip of West Virginia, the Ohio River town of Wheeling developed into the largest antebellum town in Southern Appalachia. In 1832, the town already housed 5,200 inhabitants because it was "the principal depot for the supply and commerce" of West Virginia, Pennsylvania, and the Midwest. Because it was a natural gateway linking the West to the Northeast, Wheeling was a major distribution point for the flow of foreign immigrants and trade commodities. In addition to being a boat-building center, Wheeling was a railroad terminus, the turnpike nexus for the west-to-east flow of livestock drives, and the convergence point for post roads from Philadelphia, Baltimore, and Virginia. Because of its prime location and its early development of wholesale distribution facilities, Wheeling rivaled Pittsburgh as the focal point for the east-west and north-south flows of commerce.[12]

By the 1830s, Wheeling had grown into the nation's largest exporter of nails and spikes, and the city outstripped all other iron centers in its export of manufactured by-products to international markets. In 1840, Wheeling was receiving inland grains, then reexporting more than half its flour, whiskey, and manufactured products to lower Mississippi River markets and the West Indies. Downriver below Wheeling, other Ohio River towns developed into secondary bulking centers. Wellsburg was an important milling center while Charleston grew up as the center of the salt export industry. Further inland, Morgantown capitalized upon its Monongahela River location to function as a feeder point for goods traveling to Pittsburgh, then eastward.[13]

Because of its strategic location on the National Turnpike and its later access to canal and railroad transport, Cumberland, Maryland, was the major bulking center between the northwestern Appalachian counties and Baltimore. As a regional wholesale hub, Cumberland was exporting fifty boatloads per week of coal and flour as early as 1828. Across the bridge leading into the town, "lines of carts and wagons, in close succession, and heavily loaded with coal, stone, iron, etc. crossed almost daily, together with droves on full rune."[14]

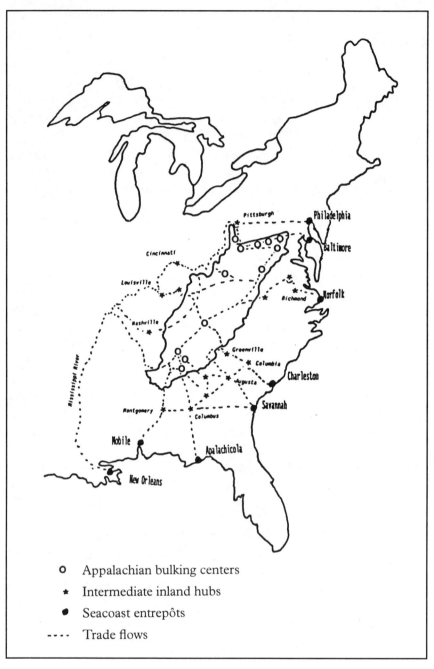

Map 7.1. Southern Appalachia's External Trade Routes

Antebellum Wheeling, West Virginia. (Courtesy Library of Congress)

To the east of Cumberland, Hagerstown emerged as an intermediate processing center. There merchant mills and commercial distilleries purchased
large quantities of western grains, then reexported flour, whiskey, and malt
liquor to Baltimore. As the hub lying closest to Baltimore, Frederick was the
major railroad terminus that redistributed goods between West Virginia, western Maryland, and the Atlantic seaboard. After the railroad opened in 1831,
"a vast quantity of flour and other products arrived at Frederick brought
down the [National Turnpike] in wagons to be carried to Baltimore by rail. In
one day in April 1832 . . . $50,000 worth of goods arrived in Frederick from
Baltimore consigned not only to Frederick merchants, but to those of Middle-
town, Hagerstown, Harper's Ferry [West Virginia], Charlestown [Maryland]
and others farther west." As a result of its commercial success, Frederick
expended public funds in the 1840s to install gas street lighting and to convey
"in pipes through the city the most salubrious waters of the best springs of the
mountains."[15]

At the top of the Shenandoah Valley, Winchester acted as a bulking center
and travel nexus. By the late 1700s, the town had grown to thirty stores and
eleven inns. An eighteenth-century commentator observed that Winchester
merchants "obtain their goods from Philadelphia, Baltimore, and Alexandria,
but principally from Philadelphia, and dispose of them to people of the town,
of the neighborhood, and of the back country. Multitudes come down every
spring and return loaded with the products of Europe and the West Indies, but
principally with salt and iron. . . . You would be astonished at the multiplicity
of cattle which pour through this town from the backcountry [i.e., West Vir-
ginia] to the north."[16] By the early 1800s, Winchester was the most important
Appalachian town west of the Blue Ridge. By 1848, eastbound trains exported
from there 20,000 barrels of flour; 2,011 tons of iron; and 158 tons of manganese. For redistribution into the countryside, westbound trains brought back

into the town 8,360 tons of merchandise; 1,176 tons of coal; and 4,076 tons of "plaster" (an imported fertilizer). In an attempt to expand its external trade in the 1850s, Winchester sent a three-man commission to lobby London, Manchester, and Liverpool factors about the advantages of direct European commerce with the town.[17]

Situated east of the Blue Ridge Mountains in about the middle of the Shenandoah Valley, Staunton was, by the late 1700s, "a place by no means inconsiderable, carrying on much trade with the farther mountain-country." In addition to its significance as a redistribution point for Appalachian exports moving northward or to Richmond, it was also a nexus for travel to the mountain spas and for the flow of livestock drives up the valley. As the home for four academies, a state lunatic asylum, and the institute for the deaf, dumb, and blind, the town also served as a regional public service hub.[18]

In the southern sector of the region, Knoxville, Tennessee, served as the primary bulking center. Situated at the heart of the Tennessee River system and major road linkages to Nashville and the Carolinas, the town was an important commercial distribution point. As early as 1809, eighteen different boat companies and regular stage lines transported goods and people to distant northeastern, western, and southern points. Throughout the antebellum period, Knoxville was the focal point for the flow of livestock drives out of the rural hinterlands of East Kentucky, southwestern Virginia, and East Tennessee. Destined for Charleston, Mobile, or New Orleans, cattle, hogs, and mules flowed westward through the Carolinas or southward down the river. In addition, upriver communities shipped iron, nails, lumber, agricultural produce, coal, whiskey, flour, cornmeal, tobacco, and cotton for warehousing and redistribution by the town's commission merchants. Knoxville was even the hub for the export of southwestern Virginia salt so that, by 1857, forty to fifty salt boats brought the commodity to the town's warehouses each year. Specially constructed steamboats reexported the coal centralized at Knoxville from several neighboring counties.[19]

By 1850, Knoxville was "a business place of considerable importance." Four wholesale commission merchants redistributed throughout East Tennessee and southwestern Virginia the dry goods, groceries, gypsum, and guano that had originated at Baltimore, Philadelphia, New Orleans, and Charleston. Knoxville's annual export trade grew from 100 flatboats per year in 1839 to more than 300 flatboats, several regular steamboats, and a major railroad terminus by 1856. In fact, the town's export trade boomed so much that local newspapers complained that store lots were "cheaper on Broadway in New York, or Market Street in Philadelphia."[20]

As "the business on the river increas[ed] every year," upper East Tennesseans packed their raw wheat and corn into 150-pound cotton bags to be floated down the Clinch River. Boats were built especially for this purpose. At Knoxville, "the grain merchants would come out on the boat and make offers

Antebellum Knoxville, Tennessee. (From *Scribner's Monthly*, May 1874)

for the grain and you sold to the best man. The grain was bagged before loading. The men who unloaded it formed a line and two men laid it on their shoulders and they carried it off the boat. Then the boat itself could be sold." Because of its central river location, Knoxville emerged as a major milling center and a wholesale warehouse nucleus for the reexport of flour, meal, and whiskey.[21]

After 1840, Chattanooga emerged as a second major bulking center further south on the river near the Tennessee-Georgia-Alabama boundaries. Because of its river and railroad linkages, Chattanooga developed into a major meat-packing and wholesale distribution hub for the reexport of Appalachian commodities to the Charleston, Mobile, and New Orleans markets. Like Knoxville, Chattanooga was the focal point for several keelboat companies that organized wharves to receive goods for transport. By 1853, the town boasted eight forwarding and commission merchants, two wholesale grocers, and a coal dealer.[22]

Located near the Georgia-Alabama state line on the Coosa River, Rome emerged as a major regional trading hub. By way of the river, Rome exported goods through Gadsden and Montgomery, Alabama, to Mobile. For those Alabama farmers seeking to send goods to the East Coast, Rome acted as an intermediate point for the railroad movement of goods through Augusta to Charleston. Because of its strategic location, Rome acted as the clearinghouse for the produce of the rich Coosa Valley and the northeastern Alabama towns. In sharp contrast to other Appalachian trading hubs, Rome emerged as an important cotton-slave distribution center that "warehoused" and auctioned export commodities centralized there from northern Alabama, northern Georgia, and southeastern Tennessee. By 1860, Rome retail outlets were handling $340,565 worth of imported commodities. Northeast of Rome, the railroad nexus of Dalton emerged near the Tennessee-Georgia state line. To access the coast by means of the Western and Atlantic Railroad, "immense quantities or produce [we]re brought [t]here by wagons" from southeastern Tennessee, southwestern North Carolina, and northeastern Georgia.[23]

Intermediate Inland Distribution Centers

From these Appalachian bulking centers, exports were shipped to several intermediate inland distribution centers. Appalachian livestock and extractive commodities were exported through two major transshipment centers in the Northeast and the Midwest. To the west, Cincinnati expanded its pork-packing for southern markets. From West Virginia and East Kentucky along the Ohio or Monongahela Rivers, commodities traveled southward to Cincinnati or northward to Pittsburgh. As a major redistribution point for commodities destined for Memphis, St. Louis, or New Orleans, Cincinnati became a dominant force in the export of Appalachian pork and salt. To the northeast, Pittsburgh specialized in the redistribution of live cattle to eastern beef packers. As a link on the routes to Philadelphia and New Orleans, Pittsburgh attracted livestock, extractive commodities, and farm provisions from West Virginia, western Maryland, and East Kentucky. Pittsburgh was also the primary nucleus for northeastern goods to be imported into East Kentucky or West Virginia. By packhorse or wagon, goods moved from Philadelphia to Pittsburgh, where they were transported down the Ohio River to West Virginia towns or to Louisville for inland redistribution.[24]

By the early nineteenth century, commodities moved from the Appalachian counties of Virginia and the eastern West Virginia panhandle to several inland transshipment points. In the late 1700s and early 1800s, the region's tobacco, wheat, and iron were consigned to Fredericksburg or Williamsburg. After 1830, Lynchburg emerged as an intermediate distribution point for southwestern Virginia wheat. By 1840, Petersburg was the center of a Tidewater consuming region that required 15,000 Appalachian hogs per year. That city was also a major hub for processing tobacco and grains, and its five large cotton mills made the town one of the major textile producers of the South. In addition, its numerous wholesale grocers and commission merchants served Appalachian farmers as far away as western North Carolina.[25]

Still, the most significant inland Virginia transshipment point was Richmond, which began attracting trade from the Appalachian counties in the early 1800s. After 1830, Richmond became increasingly important as the intermediate trade center for the Appalachian counties of western Virginia and East Kentucky. Linked by water, turnpikes, and railroads, Richmond was a central nexus for the movement of goods in all geographical directions. As a major inland meatpacking center, Richmond imported livestock from the southwestern counties of West Virginia, from East Kentucky, and even from upper East Tennessee. Second only to Baltimore, Richmond was one of the South's most important grain distribution centers. By 1840, the city boasted twenty-one large merchant mills that imported Appalachian grains. In addition, the Richmond Tobacco Exchange accepted consignments, inspected hogsheads, and warehoused and auctioned Appalachian staple production.[26]

Many Appalachian Virginia planters and manufacturers dealt with the several large commission merchants in Richmond to export their tobacco, wheat, or iron. Claiming that their "establishments [we]re set up more particularly with a view of doing a Western Country business," Richmond commission houses also advertised regularly in East Tennessee, West Virginia, and East Kentucky newspapers. Promising that "Western produce [would be] received and sold on commission," Richmond factors promised that return goods would be "received and forwarded to the West with fidelity and despatch."[27]

East Kentucky commodities traveled through three major inland distribution points. Close at hand was Lexington, which sat at the heart of the state with major turnpike and rail linkages. Lexington was a major wholesale center for trade in cotton, tobacco, saltpeter, and hemp. By river and roads, East Kentucky farm produce and extractive commodities were shipped to Louisville. Because this Ohio River port was an important inland meatpacking center, East Kentucky was heavily dependent upon Louisville as the transshipment point for its livestock exports to New Orleans. By way of the Cumberland River, southeastern Kentucky exports were sent to Nashville, Tennessee, which was linked by river and rail to the distant ports of Charleston and New Orleans.[28]

From northern Alabama and northern Georgia, commodities were sent by river to Montgomery and Wetumpka in the center of the state for reexport to the coast. From northern Georgia, the Cherokee Nation, Pickens County, South Carolina, and southeastern Tennessee, trade flowed to Augusta, Georgia. As a major inland tobacco inspection center, Augusta offered significant advantages. Turnpike and river linkages made it possible for the town's commission houses to monitor market prices at either of the port cities of Mobile, Alabama, or Savannah, Georgia. Secondarily, Athens and Macon redistributed Appalachian goods to Savannah, the primary port for upland cotton and tobacco. Northern Georgia's cotton often flowed through Columbus, which was linked by the Chattahoochee River to the Gulf port of Apalachicola, Florida.[29]

From upland South Carolina, western North Carolina, East Tennessee, and East Kentucky, trade wagons and livestock drives aimed for Greenville, South Carolina, the major intermediate distribution center for reexport further south and to the coast. Because of the lack of eastern turnpike or river access, western North Carolinians were more economically linked to Greenville than to the Tidewater counties of their home state. For southern planters traveling to or from Appalachian summer resorts, Greenville was the terminus for making transportation connections. However, that town played an even more important role as the regional hub for the interstate movement of livestock. The economic significance of Appalachian livestock drives is evidenced by the naming of the major Greenville hotel as the Kentucky-Tennessee Drover Inn. An 1840s traveler observed that "there [we]re 60,000 hogs; 7,000 sheep; 6,000 horses and mules; 600 cattle; 800 wagons; and 1,500 horsemen passing through Greenville District annually from the West on their way to Augusta, Columbia, Charleston, and the middle districts of South Carolina." While Greenville specialized in the distribution of livestock, Columbia, South Carolina, served as the intermediate distribution hub for the export of cotton out of the Appalachian Carolina counties. From Greenville and Columbia, commodities moved overland or by river to Charleston.[30]

Linkages to Seacoast Entrepôts

From these inland transshipment points, Appalachian exports finally arrived at one of several southern or northeastern seacoast entrepôts (Map 7.1), from which these goods were redistributed inland to nearby consumers or were shipped by ocean to distant domestic or foreign markets. By the 1840s, specialized commodity exchanges operated in the nation's larger cities, such as the Commercial Exchange of Philadelphia, the Charleston Cotton Exchange, the New Orleans Lumber Exchange, or the Baltimore tobacco and wheat exchanges. Before 1850, Boston, Philadelphia, and Baltimore were domestic commission centers for American textiles. Four such major coastal centers processed and reexported Appalachian grains, cotton, tobacco, hogs, cattle, or livestock by-products: Philadelphia, Baltimore, Charleston, or New Orleans.[31]

Initially, the Cherokee fur trade cemented the trade linkage between Southern Appalachia and Charleston. By the early 1800s, the ultimate destination for much of the external trade of East Tennessee, East Kentucky, western North Carolina, upland South Carolina, and northern Georgia was "carried on, in a great measure, with Charleston. . . . The articles they carr[ied] there consist[ed] chiefly in short cotton, tobacco, hams, salt butter, [bees]wax, . . . and cattle. They t[ook] in return, coarse ironware, tea, coffee, powder sugar, coarse cloths, and fine linen, but no bar iron, the upper country abounding in mines of that metal. . . . They also br[ought] salt from the seaports. . . . The carriage of these goods [wa]s made in large waggons."[32]

Even more significant to Southern Appalachia's external trade was New Orleans. With its 300 large factors and many smaller brokers and commission merchants, this Louisiana entrepôt specialized in the consignment of sixty-five different types of agricultural produce for redistribution to other southwestern markets; to the northeastern ports of Baltimore, Philadelphia, New York, and Boston; and to foreign ports in the West Indies, Latin America, and Europe. From inland markets in 1860, New Orleans received 5,000 tons of beef; 3,000,000 bushels of corn; 50,000 tons of pork; and 7,000,000 bushels of wheat. Linked to New Orleans via Cincinnati or Louisville, East Kentuckians exported grains, livestock, and tobacco to the southern coast. From East Tennessee alone in 1830 "ninety thousand bales of cotton were sent down the Tennessee River to New Orleans."[33]

In the Northeast, Baltimore and Philadelphia were the two major seaports that reexported Appalachian commodities and from which Appalachians received imports. East Kentucky, western North Carolina, and East Tennessee merchants made annual or semiannual trading trips, and Appalachian newspapers frequently advertised the availability of a "general assortment of well chosen goods from the markets of Philadelphia and Baltimore." In the 1840s, a typical large East Tennessee merchant wagoned 22,000 pounds of imports from Baltimore and received by water from Philadelphia 340,000 pounds of dry goods. As a major meatpacking entrepôt, Philadelphia was the final destination for a large segment of the upper Appalachian livestock exports. In their external trade patterns, East Kentucky, West Virginia, and East Tennessee were closely linked to the Pennsylvania port, and western North Carolinians received more imports from Philadelphia than from the Tidewater region of their own state.[34]

Baltimore became increasingly important to the export of grains, livestock, and ores from the Appalachian counties of Virginia, northeastern West Virginia, and western Maryland. After 1827, Baltimore was the second most important entrepôt for the movement of flour out of the United States. In return for flour exports to South America and Europe, Baltimore sent Appalachians imported coffee, sugar, copper derivatives, silver products, and northeastern manufactured dry goods.[35]

However, it was another unusual South American import that tightened the trade linkage between Baltimore and Southern Appalachia. Beginning in 1844, two London factors held monopolies in the export of guano, bird droppings from islands off the coast of Peru. Utilizing three agents at Baltimore, those factors marketed to Appalachian farmers this rich new fertilizer. By 1853, regional agricultural societies could report that "Wheat, which was formerly considered so precarious a crop that its culture was almost abandoned, has now, by improved husbandry, . . . and the best of all fertilizers, *guano*, become our greatest staple, in the production of which we can defy the competition of the world." In return for bags of Baltimore guano, steamboats received wheat from the Appalachian counties of Virginia, West Virginia, and Maryland. At river landings, workers toted bags of the smelly import from the deck while "granaries on the river bank, with short troughs, or spouts, running into the hold of the vessel" reloaded the steamboat with wheat.[36]

Baltimore recognized the significance of Appalachian wheat, as is evidenced by changes in Maryland milling regulations. When Baltimore tightened inspection standards to compete with New York flour exports, western

Maryland millers complained about the increased expense and lobbied for relief. Subsequently, the Maryland legislature decentralized flour inspections to Frederick and Hagerstown in order to serve those Appalachian counties exporting wheat by these routes. To attract grain shipments from western Maryland, the state subsidized the extension of the Baltimore and Ohio Railroad and the Chesapeake and Ohio Canal into the Appalachian hinterlands. Because of easy access to these transport networks, West Virginia was more tightly linked in its external trade to Baltimore than to eastern Virginia.[37]

In addition, Southern Appalachia was linked to five other secondary seaports. From Alexandria and Norfolk, Virginia; Savannah, Georgia; Mobile, Alabama; and Apalachicola, Florida, Appalachian goods were shipped to other seaports that were engaged in foreign trade. Beginning in the late 1700s, the Appalachian Virginia counties accounted for 15 percent of the export trade of eastern Virginia ports. By 1860, Mobile was importing 9,000 tons of pork; 500,000 bushels of wheat; 500,000 bushels of corn; and 300 tons of beef, a large segment of which derived from the Appalachian counties of Alabama, Georgia, and Tennessee. Out of Savannah, the grain and livestock surpluses of the Carolinas, Tennessee, and Georgia were reexported, primarily to Charleston or New Orleans. From Apalachicola, northern Georgia cotton was shipped to New England for reexport to Liverpool.[38]

Appalachian Waterway Networks

If, then, commodities must flow back and forth between zones of production, zones of distribution, and zones of consumption, the system for moving those goods must be highly rationalized. Since Southern Appalachia was part of the integrated national and international system, the region developed antebellum transportation networks to effect the efficient flow of commerce. Contrary to long-standing stereotypes, the flow of global exchanges led to the expansion of "the economic infrastructure of markets, roads and currencies" in this inland region. Access to distant trade centers and the expansion of external trade were the primary motivations for public funding of antebellum internal improvements in Southern Appalachia. River channeling, canals, bridges, ferries, and the construction of major state turnpikes or toll roads were justified by public officials as investments essential to commerce. State governments neglected streams or roads that were used predominantly by local travelers in favor of infrastructure that would make extractive sites more accessible to trade routes or that would link Appalachian farmers and merchants to outside markets.[39]

External Trade Routes by Water

Throughout most of the antebellum period, rivers comprised the dominant medium for accomplishing interregional trade throughout the United States, and less than one-third of the total land area of Southern Appalachia lay outside the reach of these waterways. Two-thirds of the region's counties were intersected by fourteen navigable river systems and two canals, which linked them into the broader system of national waterways that fed ultimately to the Atlantic or Gulf seacoasts (see Map 7.2). Even though it was inland, the region was not landlocked in mountainous isolation. Instead, the region's external trade was effected through interconnected networks of major rivers, secondary tributaries, state turnpikes, and county roads.[40]

Seven of the region's counties were connected directly to the Atlantic Ocean, either through river systems or canals. In the northern tier, the Chesapeake and Ohio Canal connected western Maryland directly to the coast. At the southeastern extreme, the Tugaloo and Savannah Rivers linked four Appalachian counties of Georgia and South Carolina directly into the Atlantic Ocean. One-third (67) of the Appalachian counties were situated within the Ohio River Basin and linked to the Gulf of Mexico, either because of their geographical location or through access to secondary tributaries that fed into the Ohio River. Twelve West Virginia counties and three East Kentucky counties lay immediately upon the Ohio. Another thirty-three West Virginia, East Kentucky, and East Tennessee counties enjoyed secondary access to the Ohio River because they were traversed by the Monongahela, the Kanawha, the Guyandote, the Tug, the Kentucky, the Big Sandy, and the Cumberland Rivers, which fed into the Ohio. To the south, the Tennessee River system meandered through the valleys and mountains of thirty-three Tennessee, Georgia, and Alabama counties, ultimately to connect with the Ohio River.[41]

In the northern tier of Appalachian counties, the Shenandoah and Potomac Rivers and the Chesapeake and Ohio Canal linked together into a network that drew eighteen Appalachian counties of Virginia, West Virginia, and Maryland into the wider system of national commerce. In addition, another seven Appalachian counties of Virginia were connected to Richmond and to the Atlantic Coast by way of the Roanoke River and the James River and Kanawha Canal. At the southern extreme, twenty-three Georgia and Alabama counties were embraced by the Coosa River, which fed into the Alabama River at Montgomery to link this zone of Southern Appalachia to Mobile and the Gulf of Mexico.[42]

Of all the Appalachian waterways, only two tributaries remained unnavigable during the antebellum period. Even though it fed into the Ohio River indirectly through its linkage to the Kanawha, the New River received no state funding to alleviate blockages at several shoals. Thus, it was of little or no utility to the seven West Virginia, Virginia, and North Carolina counties that it bisected. Jutting out of the Smoky Mountains, the French Broad arm of the Tennessee River system remained too shallow and rugged to be utilized by the three counties through which it passed.[43]

A complex system of external and local trade emerged in every part of the

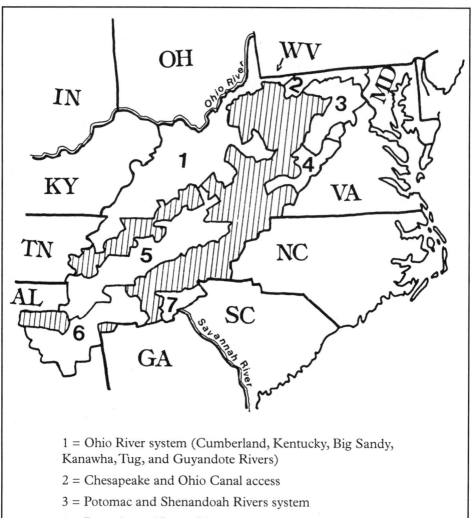

1 = Ohio River system (Cumberland, Kentucky, Big Sandy, Kanawha, Tug, and Guyandote Rivers)

2 = Chesapeake and Ohio Canal access

3 = Potomac and Shenandoah Rivers system

4 = Roanoke and James Rivers and Kanawha Canal

5 = Tennessee River system

6 = Coosa River system

7 = Tugaloo and Savannah Rivers system

⊞ Overland transport required from these counties

Map 7.2. Southern Appalachian Waterways

Steamboating grain down the Tennessee River. (From *Harper's Monthly*, August 1858)

region traversed by navigable rivers. Along these waterways, more than five hundred small communities became landings for commercial activity and boat construction. Even natural sites like large caves were transformed into boat landings and warehouses. Most of the river systems were improved with canals, locks, sluices, or dams to bypass shoals and falls. Around these points, trade communities boomed. Probably the most famous was Muscle Shoals of the Tennessee River, where the federal government funded the development of a canal. Because of the interruption in the flow of commodities, merchandise was transferred to canal boats or barges for transshipment to steamboats.[44]

Licensed by county courts as public monopolies, hundreds of local ferries played a crucial part in the flow of commodities from inland areas to the river systems. Since they were transshipment points between wagon and water transport, ferry sites stimulated the emergence of adjacent inns, warehouses, stores, and manufactories. As the "staging areas" for downriver flatboat movements, ferries were often collection points for agricultural or extractive exports and for the redistribution of imported goods.[45]

In short, Appalachian rivers were the avenue for the most rapid transport of bulky agricultural, extractive, or manufactured commodities out of the region. Even on the Appalachian frontier, farmers and merchants exported their produce great distances by means of river craft, as is evident from this 1821 newspaper article about the transport of commodities down the Tennessee River:

> There arrived at Montgomery [Alabama] a flat bottomed boat loaded with flour. The wheat of which the flour was made in Washington County, Virginia. . . . The speculator started with ninety-three barrels of flour. He descended the Holston 300 miles, and, entering the Tennessee River, he descended that river 150 miles, arriving at the Hiwassee . . . he ascended that river 40 miles until he reached the Oco[ee] which he descended ten miles. Here the flour was transported twelve miles across the country to O'Dear's Landing to Connussawga. Here he built a flatboat on which he freighted the flour into the Coosa, and down that river to Montgomery—a two months trip.[46]

Several types of river craft linked together the region's major waterways, canals, and ferries. For unidirectional transport downriver, local companies constructed flatboats, tobacco canoes, broad horns, and Kentucky boats. To permit round-trip downstream-upstream travel, exporters relied on larger keelboats or packet boats and—after 1840—more versatile steamboats. The flow of Appalachian commodities often involved the use of all three types of craft. Flatboats and arks carried goods out of tributaries where larger boats could not float safely. Dams were opened to fill canal locks with enough water to permit two types of boats to pass. Human laborers poled bateaux up and down the James River and Kanawha Canal. On the Chesapeake and Ohio Canal, mules pulled cables that drew narrow barges and tows through the locks to the river. Hooked to circular rope and pulley systems, large flat ferry boats were propelled back and forth by horses stationed on each riverbank. These smaller craft carried commodities to transshipment sites for transfer to larger packets or steamboats, forming an interdependent network of shipping methodologies that used different parts of the rivers.[47]

By 1840, all the major navigable Appalachian rivers and many of the secondary tributaries were regularly served during seasons of high waters by steam towboats, packet boats, and larger steamboats. As the primary vehicle for antebellum export trade, Appalachian steamboats averaged twelve round trips annually, many losing only ninety days per year due to unnavigable rivers. In 1835, the downriver steamboat trade on the Ohio River totaled nearly $15 million, at least half that amount deriving from the Appalachian counties of the Ohio Basin.[48]

Export by flatboat down the Tennessee River. (From *Harper's Monthly*, August 1858)

There is much evidence that river craft were constructed jointly along many of the backwaters of the region. Along the West Virginia tributaries feeding into the Ohio River, flatboats for downriver runs were "built along the shores of the river, but more frequently on its tributary streams, and often on the smaller rivers and creeks, far inland, and at points beyond the reach of all ordinary navigation. Here they l[ay], with their cargoes, waiting until the annual rise of water . . . when they [we]re floated off, with their immense freights." Along the Cumberland River in East Kentucky and middle Tennessee, preparations for the annual run of river craft was a communitywide effort. The residents "buil[t] large flat boats say from 70 to 85 feet long [and] 24 feet wide, buil[t] them on the banks of the river, bottom side up, turn them over on the bank after well corking and ictchin [pitching] them well and then launching the boat in the river, ready for finishing. All this work by man power, say from 40 to 50 men from all over the county asked in to turn and put the boat in the river."[49]

Export by river was highly rationalized, however, for this mode of transportation required skilled specialists. Because professionals were needed to construct boats and to freight goods to market, some large farmers and merchants kept such workers on annual labor contracts. A large flatboat required four laborers and a pilot who were contracted for a four- to six-week period; some professional flatboaters made three or four round trips yearly from Appalachian rivers to distant markets. Trained slaves also operated boats to inland regional markets, like Richmond, Lynchburg, Augusta, Savannah, or Columbia. Larger planters and merchants often managed their own keelboats, canal boats, or packet boats, taking their neighbors' goods to market for a commission. River wharves, landings, and warehouses were owned and operated by companies that accepted goods on consignment for transport to distant markets. For example, James King and Company plied the Tennessee with keelboats and steamers, averaging one trip monthly. On all the Appalachian rivers, boatyards developed as points for accumulating commodities for export or for wholesale distribution. State legislatures created as public monopolies numerous navigation companies that were authorized to make river improvements, construct boats, operate landings for tolls, and accept payment to transport passengers and commodities by river. On the Ohio River and its tributary rivers, several cartels were formed among canal and steamboat companies to control freight rates and to maximize profits related to external transport.[50]

By examining antebellum reports of activity on some of the region's waterways, we can get some idea of the extent of the Appalachian river trade. The "great quantities of produce floating down" the Ohio from Wheeling and other West Virginia towns has been well documented. By means of its North River connector to the James River and Kanawha Canal, Rockbridge County, Virginia, exported $20 million worth of agricultural produce, iron, timber, and manufactured commodities to Richmond. In the 1850s, these shipments annually averaged 150,000 bushels of corn; 60,000 gallons of whiskey; nearly 20,000 barrels of flour; and 2,226 tons of iron. One entrepreneur in "the business of Boating Flour and other produce to market" transported 5,623 barrels along the Shenandoah River to Harpers Ferry, where the commodities were transferred to the railroad for shipment to Baltimore. By 1847, Appalachians were exporting by way of the Kentucky River 13,203 tons of goods; 20,754 passengers; nearly 3,000 hogs; and more than 11,000 kegs of pork, beef, and lard.[51]

Contemporary newspaper accounts indicate that most of the bulk corn received at New Orleans was shipped by flatboats from the Appalachian counties of Kentucky and Tennessee. Before the railroad, the "growing prosperity" of East Tennessee was "mainly attributable to the river trade" with New Orleans and Mobile. By the 1840s, there were, in addition to regular steamboats, "annually flatboats down the French Broad and Holston Rivers, hundreds of arks and flatboats from the upper counties, laden with Iron, nails, castings, brandy, whisky, flour, &c. destined for the Alabama and other markets . . . also hundreds of rafts and boards, plank, and scantling."[52]

By utilizing Tennessee River transport out of Knoxville, numerous wholesalers and manufactories filled "orders from a distance . . . promptly and punctually" and "shipped everywhere" an array of unusual products like paper, patent medicine, agricultural tools, wrought-iron fences, lumber, meat provisions, cloth, coal, marble, furniture, carriages, and iron. By 1839, Knoxville was wholesaling annually $800,000 worth of dry goods and groceries that had been imported by river from distant markets. South of Knoxville, thirty-nine steamboats operated on the short Coosa River system, fed by hundreds of "dry land boats" that carried cotton, tobacco, iron, and foodstuffs from streams too shallow for larger craft.[53]

Overland Transportation Networks

Connecting to these waterways, several networks of state turnpikes and county roads linked Appalachian communities into the flow of national commerce. Fifty-nine Appalachian counties relied solely on major river access. However, more than one-half (117) of the region's counties were traversed by major thoroughfares that carried livestock droves and trade goods to distant markets in other states (see Map 7.3). Two major national turnpikes crisscrossed Southern Appalachia. Running east to west, the National Turnpike linked Baltimore to the Ohio River at Wheeling, then proceeded into the Midwest. From Philadelphia via Hagerstown, Maryland, the Great Philadelphia Wagon Road proceeded down the Valley of Virginia to link with East Kentucky's Wilderness Road and routes into East Tennessee. Interlinked with these national turnpikes were several major Appalachian livestock and wagon routes that connected the region to Philadelphia, Baltimore, Richmond, Louisville, and cities in the Deep South. With more than three-quarters of its land area linked by major trade routes to interstate thoroughfares, pre-1850 Southern Appalachia was no more isolated from the national economy than were most rural areas of New England or much of the Midwest.[54]

Except for connections into a few Appalachian counties of Maryland, Virginia, and West Virginia, most of Southern Appalachia lacked railroad service during the antebellum period. But by 1855, railroad development had occurred in fifty-three of the region's counties, linking the region even more firmly to Baltimore, Philadelphia, Richmond, Louisville, Nashville, St. Louis, and Charleston. However, this new phase of internal improvements did not open up the most isolated sectors of Southern Appalachia. Following established trade patterns, railroads were constructed in counties that already had major river and turnpike connections (Map 7.3), leaving thirty-nine of the Appalachian counties with no outside linkages except ill-kept county roads.[55]

Overland Transport of Commodities

Throughout most of the antebellum period, Southern Appalachians relied on five techniques of direct transport: packhorses, stages, wagons, boats, and overland drives. During the frontier years, residents of the most rugged terrain exported iron bars, salt, ginseng, furs, whiskey, and a variety of produce by packhorses. Stagecoaches also hauled commodities to and from farms,

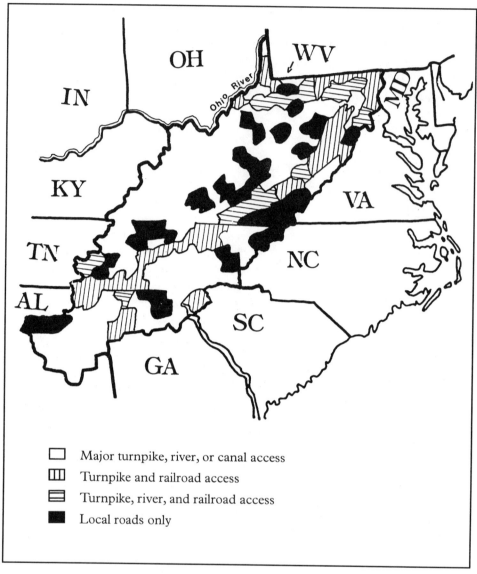

Map 7.3. Transportation Networks, 1850–1860

merchants, and towns along their routes. People who lived along major roads
sent their goods to market by passing wagoners or stages that brought imports
on their return trips.[56]

As roads and turnpike connections improved, however, the more typical
method of overland trading was transport by wagons. The region's major
thoroughfares were busy places, filled with "jostling processions of freight
wagons." Along the Appalachian turnpikes and roads of Maryland, Virginia,

and West Virginia, "wagons were so numerous that the leaders of one team had their noses in the box at the end of the next wagon."[57]

In the 1830s, an observer commented about the lower Appalachians that "Any one traveling in the mountains at this time will see long lines of six-horse teams constantly employed on almost impassable roads, hauling bacon and other heavy articles to the Southern states, and returning with loads of foreign goods." Out of East Kentucky, overland wagoning was probably more important than any other form of transport. Because of their poor road linkages with the Tidewater, western North Carolina counties wagoned "full three-quarters of all that sold of the produce of the land" to South Carolina and Georgia markets, hauling back "foreign goods for home consumption" from the points where raw materials had been sold.[58]

Farmers or merchants could transport commodities themselves, or they could advertise in newspapers to hire wagoners. Cherokee farmers sold nearly one-third of the corn they produced so that, in the 1820s, "wagon loads of corn [were] going from the nation to the different states." While some individual farmers or merchants may have transported their goods in this way, most consigned their goods to three different types of freighting professionals. Exporters could engage "sharpshooters" who hired out to haul goods to any location specified or "regulars" who hauled over the same routes throughout the year. Several Civil War veterans reported that their Appalachian fathers or brothers worked full time as wagoners. One such Catoosa, Georgia, freighter "wagon Hauled wheat to Chatanoog, hauled goods from Nashville, [and] Hauld Salt from Saltworks in Kentucky." Another regional wagoner worked the year round, "hauling produce of all kinds from Tennessee to Georgia."[59]

In addition to such independents, local companies operated "line teams" that specialized in long-distance hauling and freight. It was not unusual for larger farmers or merchants to operate their own line of wagons and to hire drivers on annual contracts. About twice a year, Appalachian merchants made regular trading trips to distant towns, exporting commodities and hauling back imported items for local retailing. Larger merchants who made monthly or bimonthly trading trips kept wagoners in their regular employ. Thus, their surcharges from this long-distance hauling could be maximized. An antebellum journalist observed that East Tennessee merchants "realize[d] a profit of 70% from almost every article" they wagoned to or from Baltimore and Philadelphia.[60]

Appalachian manufacturers often disposed of their products by sending their own trade wagons to peddle their commodities in distant communities. For example, a Preston County, West Virginia, firm patented and sold in Maryland, Virginia, and the Midwest a washing and wringing machine, a mowing machine, and a threshing machine. Trade wagons traveled from farm to farm in Virginia, Maryland, West Virginia, and the Midwest peddling the reapers manufactured by Rockbridge County inventor Cyrus McCormick.

Hundreds of wagons were sent by Appalachian manufacturers to peddle plug or twist tobacco to retailers in the Deep South or the Midwest. Out of East Tennessee and East Kentucky, meatpackers sent regular "pork wagons" south to peddle their wares to plantation owners. Frederick Olmsted reported "meeting two great Tennessee bacon wagons" of this sort in western North Carolina headed south. In 1843, South Carolina imported 5,000 hogsheads of Appalachian bacon, about half of which arrived in these trade wagons.[61]

Annual Livestock Drives

Long-distance livestock drives formed another annual mechanism for the overland export of Appalachian commodities to southern and eastern markets. Drives from southwest Virginia to the Northeast began in the eighteenth century. By 1750, West Virginians were "driving hogs over the Blue Ridge" to eastern markets. By the 1820s, large droves of 700 to 800 hogs were driven east from West Virginia and western Maryland along the Cumberland Road, where one traveler reported that "For the past week, I have met two or perhaps three of these hordes daily . . . yet these apparently overflowing supplies are . . . much smaller than usual." By 1860, nearly 400,000 hogs were being exported each year from the Appalachian counties of Virginia, Maryland, and West Virginia, many of them sent overland to eastern markets.[62]

In the early 1800s, hogs were being exported from the Big Sandy region of East Kentucky to Ohio River towns. Already in 1802, Louisville was reexporting to New Orleans 72,000 barrels of dried pork annually. By the 1820s, East Kentuckians were bypassing the Louisville meatpackers in order to accrue greater profits through a new marketing technique. As one contemporary journalist observed, "Large droves of livestock, especially hogs, are now driven every year . . . to Baltimore, in preference to being packed on the spot and sent down the river . . . to the New Orleans market." In 1838, 68,764 hogs were also driven through the Cumberland Gap, headed south via the French Broad trail to South Carolina and Georgia. By 1860, East Kentucky was exporting 131,169 hogs, mostly to southern markets.[63]

In the 1840s, East Tennessee farmers were importing European breeds to improve the quality of their exports. An early commentator surmised that "On the Bottom Land of the French Broad River from Newport to Dandridge, a distance of from twenty-five to thirty miles . . . from 20 to 30,000 hogs are annually fattened for market, exclusive of Horses, Mules, and Cattle." From Cocke, Jefferson, and Greene Counties, there were as many as twenty-five to forty hog drives per year eastward along the French Broad. From isolated mountainous Cocke County alone, "five thousand head of hogs [we]re annually driven . . . to the southern market." Across the French Broad trail of western North Carolina, 150,000 to 175,000 hogs were moved each year, organized in droves of 300 to 1,000. By 1850, 81,000 hogs yearly passed through Asheville. By 1860, western North Carolina and East Tennessee were

Southwestern Virginia hog drive headed to Richmond. (From *Harper's Monthly*, October 1857)

exporting more than 764,000 hogs, at least half of them overland via the French Broad trail.[64]

In the early 1800s, the Cherokees exported large herds of hogs to southern Georgia planters while the central and Tidewater counties of North Carolina were importing large droves of Appalachian hogs. During the 1840s, another 80,000 hogs were driven each year from East Tennessee, northern Alabama, and northern Georgia to Chattanooga, a regional meatpacking hub. After 1850, Chattanooga shipped by rail to Charleston 12,213 live hogs per year. By 1860, more than 150,000 hogs were being exported from the Appalachian counties of Alabama, Georgia, and South Carolina, many of them sent overland to Chattanooga for reexport.[65]

The first drove of cattle out of Southern Appalachia was sent in 1805 from

Blue Ridge Virginia cattle drive headed north. (From *Harper's Monthly*, February 1855)

western Virginia to Baltimore. By 1860, more than 200,000 cattle were exported from the Appalachian counties of Virginia, Maryland, and West Virginia, primarily to eastern markets. In the early 1800s, East Tennessee farmers were already "rear[ing] a great deal of cattle, which they t[ook] four or five hundred miles to the seaports belonging to the southern states." By 1860, East

Tennessee was sending more than 100,000 cattle per year to southern markets. Prior to their removal, the Cherokees specialized in exporting cattle, at the rate of 200 per year to the Northeast and 800 per year to the plantation South. By 1860, more than 45,000 cattle per year were being exported from those areas where the Cherokees had once lived. By 1838, East Kentucky was exporting 4,540 cattle yearly through the Cumberland Gap to eastern markets. Although East Kentucky exported most of its hogs and mules to the South, nine-tenths of its cattle went to eastern markets up the Virginia Valley. Still, a few of East Kentucky's cattle were exported to planters of the Blue Grass and western Tennessee. By 1860, East Kentucky's cattle exports had grown to nearly 40,000 per year.[66]

In the early 1800s, horses were being exported from East Kentucky via the Big Sandy and Kentucky Rivers to New Orleans. Predominantly, however, mules and horses were exported overland since drives were cheaper than water shipment. One early traveler observed that "the Southern States, and in particular South Carolina, are the principal places destined for the sale of Kentucky horses. They are taken there in droves of fifteen, twenty or thirty at a time, in the early part of winter. . . . They usually take eighteen or twenty days . . . to Charleston. The distance, which is about seven hundred miles, makes a difference of twenty-five or thirty percent in the price of horses." Because of its "decided market advantage," Knoxville was a regional hub for the shipment of mules from East Tennessee and East Kentucky to Mississippi, Louisiana, Georgia, and Alabama. From Knoxville via the French Broad River trail, "not less than 10,000 horses and mules . . . [went] down every year for sale to the purchasers in the Atlantic states . . . as many as 500 at a time frequently passing though Greenville [South Carolina] in a single day." By 1860, Southern Appalachia supplied nearly 90,000 horses and mules to the lower South, primarily driven overland.[67]

Annual turkey drives formed another type of export mechanism. Contemporary sources indicate that numerous flocks of turkeys in droves of 400 to 600 crossed the French Broad trail to the slaughterhouses of Spartanburg for reexport to Charleston. Turkeys were also transported from West Virginia to Baltimore and Philadelphia, and the Valley of Virginia sent turkeys to Richmond. For instance, one Patrick, Virginia, slaveholder raised turkeys "in de 500 lots" for export. Southeastern Tennessee and northern Georgia turkeys were also driven to Chattanooga, where they were processed for reexport.[68]

Although the export of live sheep was not very significant in the total picture, there were sizeable drives from several West Virginia and Virginia counties. From Berkeley, West Virginia, 6,000 sheep were "annually sent to Baltimore." There were also great drives of Appalachian sheep into Illinois, Wisconsin, and Missouri between 1844 and 1845 for reexport via St. Louis to Missouri and Texas markets.[69]

Summary

When an external arena underwent incorporation into the capitalist world system in the eighteenth or nineteenth centuries, three major structural changes were set in motion. First, the mode of production was rationalized so that more efficient and more profitable units were effected. More centralized enterprises were put in place, as evidenced by Southern Appalachia's tendency toward larger farms, extractive company towns, and the displacement of small artisan-based manufacturing. Second, these larger economic enterprises stimulated greater coercion of laborers, with increased reliance on a new interplay of free and unfree labor mechanisms, as we have seen in the utilization by Southern Appalachian capitalists of a labor force comprised of slaves, several categories of coerced workers, and wage laborers. Third, capitalist incorporation of a zone triggered the emergence of new exports and imports that replicated patterns in the capitalist world system.[70]

Spatially, the nineteenth-century world economy was organized into three types of specialization zones. Production zones, distribution zones, and consumer zones were integrated into interdependent trade relationships. In its antebellum economic development, Southern Appalachia replicated several patterns that were occurring in other sectors of the world economy that had been colonized by western Europe. As was also the case in other New World peripheries, there developed an "economic symbiosis" between the coastal plantations and this inland mountainous zone. As the transition to capitalism unfolded, the adjacent southern plantation economy stimulated the expansion of market-oriented food production and laborer surpluses in the inland mountains. The Appalachian "production regime" consisted of smaller-scale farms and manufacturing enterprises that generated foodstuffs and surplus laborers to underpin the coastal export zones. Like other New World peripheries, Southern Appalachia utilized vast land areas to become one of the "livestock frontiers" of the nineteenth-century world economy; extractive industries emerged in these inland mountains, replicating the pattern that western Europe had followed in its own transition to capitalism.

However, Southern Appalachia also had economic linkages to other sectors. In addition to its external trade connections to the plantation South, the region was incorporated into the world economy as a peripheral fringe that produced raw materials and foodstuffs to provender the plantation economies of the West Indies and South America and the emergent urban-industrial metropoles of the core. Out of southern coastal entrepôts, Appalachian raw agricultural produce, light manufactures, and extractive commodities were reexported to the American Northeast and to western Europe in exchange for core manufactured goods and tropical imports.

To effect this external trade, layers of markets were connected between small Appalachian towns, regional trading hubs, inland trade centers, and seacoast entrepôts. Spatially, these centers of commerce were linked by means of networks of waterways, turnpikes, and county roads. Since three-quarters of the land area of Southern Appalachia was situated in counties with direct access to these transportation systems, the region's external trade was highly rationalized around commercialized wagoning, boating, and overland drives. From the frontier years, raw materials and semiprocessed commodities flowed across county, state, and international boundaries in a relatively unimpeded fashion. External trade was increasingly mobilized along regional transportation circuits that linked with established paths to core areas of the world economy.

THE PERVASIVE REACH OF

GLOBAL COMMODITY CHAINS

The Spatial Organization of Commodity Chains

Were there parts of Southern Appalachia isolated from the reach of the market economy? Were counties with no major rivers or turnpikes excluded from global commodity chains? Farms in those counties without access to major rivers or turnpikes may have produced somewhat lower levels of agricultural exports (see Table 8.1). Still, these were not subsistent zones that generated only the survival needs of their residents. Instead, the notion that the terrain of Southern Appalachia isolated farming communities from distant markets has been grossly overstated.

Because waterways and bottomlands were essential in the cultivation and export of wheat, farms in counties without access averaged less than half the export grain that was raised on farms in counties linked to major transportation networks. In the production of other agricultural commodities, however, the availability of transport was of much less significance. Farms in counties without access averaged 43.4 fewer bushels of corn or 76 fewer pounds of tobacco than their counterparts in counties with good turnpike and river connections. However, the average production of export hogs and cattle in counties lacking access varied little from that of counties having direct trade connections. Surprisingly, Appalachian farmers did not predicate their production of cotton upon the availability of transport. Farms in counties without access to major rivers or turnpikes actually averaged nearly twice as many pounds of cotton as farms in those areas with good transportation linkages. Despite their lack of rivers and turnpikes, farmers of western North Carolina, a few mountainous East Tennessee counties, Alabama's mountainous Jackson County, and several rugged northern Georgia counties generated sizeable amounts of cotton and tobacco. In short, Appalachian farms pro-

Table 8.1. External Trade and Access to Transportation Networks

| | Average Exports per Farm | |
Agricultural Commodity	Counties without River or Turnpike Access	Counties with River or Turnpike Access
Wheat (bu.)	29.2	56.4
Corn (bu.)	130.2	173.6
Hogs	8.3	8.8
Cattle	4.0	3.9
Tobacco (lbs.)	238.6	314.4
Cotton (lbs.)	437.8	225.8

Source: Total export production in Table 5.6 and Table 5.8 divided by the aggregated total number of farms reported in the published 1860 Census of Agriculture.

duced crops for export even in those counties which lacked good direct trade route linkages.

What, then, of those counties that were very mountainous? What of those sections of Appalachian counties that were shut off from major trade routes by terrain? An examination of mountain gaps provides insight into the mechanisms by which these areas achieved access to trade routes. The Appalachian mountain chain is interrupted by numerous gaps and passes. In the lower Blue Ridge Mountains, for example, there are thirty-one such Virginia gaps, averaging only 6.1 miles apart, while there are sixty-three North Carolina passes, averaging less than 4 miles apart. Moreover, families living in some mountainous and hillier sections were not isolated from waterways or roads. For instance, four major roads crossed the mountains east to west, and the Shenandoah River linked those sections to the eastern seaboard. Many early mountain roads followed the long, even "flats" of the ridges to reach these gaps, for the upper limits of many Appalachian mountain areas are surprisingly level, not rugged or uneven.[1]

As a result, mountain gaps became focal points for economic activity and bulking points for commodity transport to trade routes. Extractive operations, grain mills, tanneries, sawmills, distilleries, stagecoach stops, inns, taverns, livestock stands, and stores were centralized at the gaps. To facilitate future transport to market, livestock were often kept in rock-fenced pens in mountaintop meadows near the gaps. In Virginia, turnpikes crossed at four gaps to link to the Valley of Virginia turnpikes, the James River and Kanawha Canal, and regional trading hubs. In North Carolina, wagon roads followed down from the gaps toward trading towns in the foothills and valleys and toward the French Broad drover pike. In the Smoky Mountains, cove communities established wagon roads into Knoxville and drover trails to connect down the French Broad Valley to South Carolina. Obviously, then, the Appalachian mountains were not formidable obstacles that locked communities away from the world. Instead, the system of interconnected gaps, trails, roads, turnpikes, and rivers integrated even these out-of-the-way places into the flow of external trade.[2]

Commodity Chains between Peripheries

Spatially, external trade can take place because transportation networks and centralized trading hubs exist. However, market linkages are much more complex than this level of focus would imply. As Wallerstein explains, the transition to capitalism stimulated "the widespread commodification of processes—not merely exchange processes, but production processes, distribution processes, and investment processes—that had previously been conducted other than via a 'market.' And in the course of seeking to accumulate more and more capital, capitalists have sought to commodify more and more of these social processes in all spheres of economic life. . . . Nor has it been enough to commodify the social processes. Production processes were linked to one another in complex commodity chains."[3] In reality, then, linkages between distant metropoles, trading hubs, and rural hinterlands of the world economy are effected through *commodity chains*—a complex network of labor, production, and distribution processes. The entire global chain for a single commodity comprises four large networks of actors: raw materials suppliers, producers, exporters, and marketers. Examination of these internetwork relationships will permit us a closer look at the micro-level operations of the world economy, for we can situate within a commodity chain the spatial position and economic risk of a single human actor. In this way, we can assess historically the extent to which real antebellum Southern Appalachians became involved in or withdrew from the capitalist world economy.[4]

Let us begin by taking a close look at the commodity chain for one of the region's earliest industries. As Figure 8.1 illustrates, a West Virginia salt furnace drew raw materials inputs from iron, timber, natural gas, and coal producers, some of which were "vertically integrated" in the sense that the salt furnace owned these ancillary industries. Labor was drawn from leased slaves and from low-paid immigrant wage laborers whose subsistence derived from housing, food, salt, coffee, and dry goods that were advanced by the company store against their wages. In exchange for salt from the company store, local coopers supplied the barrels used to pack the commodity for export. To acquire salt, local farmers hauled raw agricultural produce and meats to the company store, which, in turn, advanced these foodstuffs to the furnace's labor force.[5]

To market its product, the salt furnace consigned its output to commission merchants at Louisville and Cincinnati who forwarded it to midwestern and southern buyers. At Cincinnati, Appalachian salt provided a vital input to the

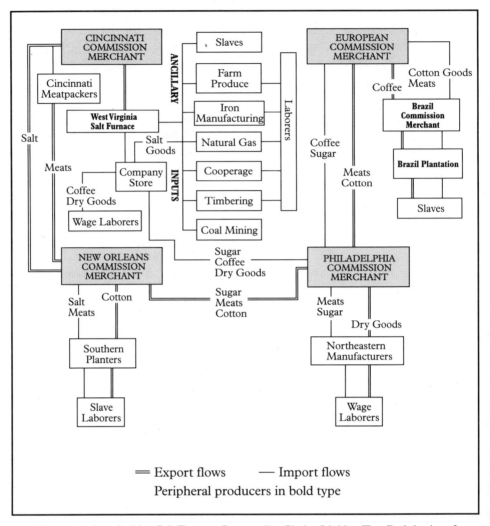

Figure 8.1. Appalachian Salt Export: Commodity Chains Linking Two Peripheries of the World Economy

meatpacking industry, which exported via New Orleans processed pork to southern, northeastern, and international destinations. Out of Cincinnati, then, the Appalachian commodity proceeded forward in two forms: as raw salt and as an invested input in another industrial export. After consignment by the Cincinnati commission merchant to a New Orleans commission merchant, salt was sold to inland southern and southwestern merchants and planters. However, only a segment of the total meat production was absorbed by the slave laborers who produced sugar and cotton. From New Orleans, then, Appalachian salt proceeded forward in disguised form: as ancillary investments in other commodities produced for the world market.

After consignment by the New Orleans commission merchant to a Philadelphia commission merchant, part of the cotton, meats, and sugar—which now carried the combined investments of Appalachian salt laborers, midwestern meatpacking laborers, transport laborers, and southern slaves—were exported to European factors who marketed cotton, meats, and sugar to textiles manufacturers. At the farthest end of the commodity chain, European factors consigned English cotton goods and reexported part of the meats to a South American commission merchant. Imported European cotton goods and American meats—which ultimately carried the combined labor investments of Appalachian salt workers, midwestern meatpackers, southern slaves, and European mill workers—were exchanged to Brazilian plantations that generated coffee and sugar, part of which flowed backward via the European factor to the Philadelphia commission merchant.

In addition to exporting to international markets, the Philadelphia commission merchant marketed to northeastern manufacturers part of the meats and sugar derived from New Orleans. Relying on company-store advances of imported meats and sugar, northeastern wage laborers generated dry goods. Through turnpike and river networks, the middleman shipped directly to the company store of the West Virginia salt furnace northeastern dry goods and Brazilian sugar and coffee—which, in addition to the labor needed to move them, aggregated the labor investments of Appalachian salt workers, midwestern meatpackers, southern slaves, European mill workers, and South American slaves.

At the macro level, this illustration emphasizes the complexity of a commodity chain between two distant peripheries that were exporting raw produce. It certainly becomes clear that neither Brazil nor Southern Appalachia were autonomous from the global economy. Moreover, it is obvious that the entire commodity chain could not have functioned if there had not been in place "political structures accommodative of these exchanges." At the micro level, this approach permits us to identify the many layers at which laborers made investments in commodities from which "nonproducing" distributors captured the profits.[6]

Subsistence Producers and the World Economy

Suppose, however, we begin at even a more micro level with an Appalachian subsistence farmer who generated very little surplus for marketing, as depicted in Figure 8.2. Most of the crops and livestock produced on a farm smaller than one hundred acres would have been consumed for survival. Purchases and trading would have been very minimal, with never more than one-fifth of the total crop production entering local exchange networks. Despite the limited wealth of this family and despite their restricted market activity, the operation of commodity chains would have absorbed even these subsistence producers into the capitalist world economy.[7]

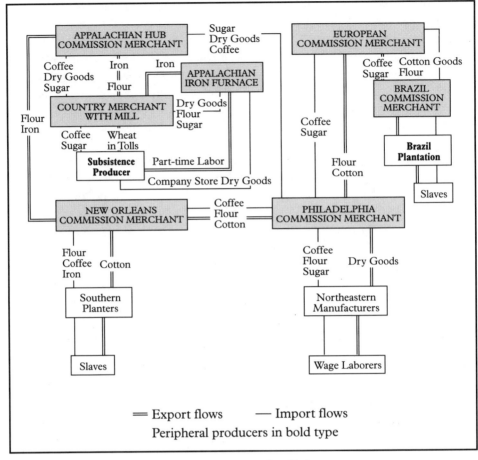

Figure 8.2. Pervasive Reach of Global Commodity Chains

Let us begin the commodity chain with the kind of barter exchange that some scholars have erroneously posited outside the realm of capitalist relations. We shall assume that this subsistent farmer paid one-eighth of the grain in tolls to the miller who ground the flour to be consumed by the family. By accepting wheat in exchange for store goods, the merchant-miller accumulated surplus grain that was processed into flour. Part of the flour was supplied, along with imported dry goods, to provision the laborers at a local iron furnace, where the subsistent farmer provided part-time labor during the off-season. Iron accepted in trade and surplus flour were consigned by the merchant-miller to a commission merchant located at one of the region's trading hubs, who shipped it, in turn, to a New Orleans commission merchant. Out of the seaport, flour and iron were sold to inland southern and southwestern merchants and planters. However, only a segment of the total flour was absorbed by the slave laborers who produced sugar and cotton for the global market.[8]

After consignment by the New Orleans commission merchant to a Philadelphia commission merchant, part of the flour and cotton was exported to European factors who marketed it to textiles manufacturers. At the farthest end of the commodity chain, European factors consigned English cotton goods and reexported part of the flour to a South American commission merchant. Imported European cotton goods and American flour were exchanged to Brazilian plantations that generated coffee and sugar, part of which flowed backward via the European factor to the Philadelphia commission merchant.

In addition to exporting to international markets, the Philadelphia commission merchant marketed to northeastern manufacturers part of the flour and sugar derived from New Orleans. Relying on company-store advances of imported flour and sugar, northeastern wage laborers generated dry goods. Through turnpike and river networks, the Appalachian commission merchant transported from Philadelphia dry goods and Brazilian sugar and coffee. From the Appalachian trading hub, the local merchant-miller imported northeastern dry goods, along with Brazilian coffee and sugar—the commodities used, in the first place, to acquire export iron. At its extreme bottoms on each end, this commodity chain links together exploited peripheral laborers whose accumulated investments of productive work transformed raw materials into valuable export commodities.

Is this Appalachian household self-sufficing and totally independent of the world economy? Is this a "peasant" household with roots in the soil and cultural resistance to capitalism? The *mentalité* of the farmer is largely irrelevant, for it would have been almost impossible for such a subsistence producer to be totally free of the capitalist economy. Even if our subsistent farmer supplied only a few hours each week toward production of export iron to receive from the furnace company store only small amounts of imported dry goods, and even if only a few purchases of coffee and sugar were made each year, then this Appalachian was still part of a far-reaching capitalist trade network. Only total isolation from all market exchanges—including reciprocal barter with neighbors—would have guaranteed autonomy from the world economy. The subsistence producer stopped being "precapitalist" as soon as he or she engaged in a chain of exchanges that involved even one actor that was linked into the capitalist economy. Rather than thinking that it was so difficult for such a subsistence producer to be involved in external trade, it becomes hard to create a scenario in which such households could avoid the pervasive reach of global commodity chains. A complete commodity chain consists of so many elements that the intricate networks of interconnected linkages encompass a majority of households worldwide.[9]

Can sectors of local economies remain outside the realm of capitalist relations, even after capitalism has become the dominant mode of production? Braudel has this observation: "I believe in the virtues and the importance of a market economy, but I do not think of this economy as excluding all other forms." In peripheral zones, capitalism is based primarily on economic activities geared toward external markets. For that reason, capitalism "tends to become not exclusive, but only dominant." In fact, the pattern of transition to peripheral capitalism is "fundamentally different from that of the transition to central capitalism. The onslaught from without, by means of trade, carried out by the capitalist mode of production upon the precapitalist formations, causes certain retrogressions."[10]

Internally, there is a "disarticulation" between the subsistence and export sectors so that external trade grows much faster than the subsistence sector. When "not all links in the chain are in fact commodified," the export sector drains off labor and capital from subsistence producers to augment production for external markets. Moreover, infrastructure and state priorities are directed toward expansion of external trade, to the neglect of local roads and services. Progress in the export sector, therefore, blocks economic growth in local market activities, and subsistence agriculture is actually deterred. Because of such pressures from the transition to capitalism, the true subsistence sector of Appalachian local economies was, by 1860, very small, as we have seen from examination of farms; manufacturing was becoming increasingly centralized in capitalist factories. Even the communal Cherokees had been absorbed into the commodity chains of external trade. Indeed, there were probably Appalachians who rarely traded in formal markets and even more who engaged in external trade indirectly through middlemen. However, those who rarely participated in the export sector did not stop it from developing, nor were they in positions of economic and political control.[11]

Consequently, while we may speak of a minority of Appalachians who engaged in economic activities that seem to have been barely touched by the complex global commodity chains, we cannot generalize that entire local economies were "noncapitalist." In reality, the pressures were already great in antebellum Southern Appalachia for people to have money, and families did not acquire cash without participating in the dominant capitalist economy. By doing so, these households became "semiproletarianized"—like the region's agricultural wage laborers, tenant farmers, and Cherokees—only imperfectly absorbed into the circuits of the economy, often unemployed, but still exploited by the region's capitalistic surplus producers.

The Role of Middlemen in External Trade

Southern Appalachia's semiproletarianized households more often engaged in short "decentralized commodity chains" in *local* markets where producers and buyers either dealt directly with one another or utilized one layer of rural merchants. However, those simpler commodity chains were not disconnected from more complex linkages, as we have seen from the example about how a subsistence farmer was absorbed by the world economy. The simpler, decentralized chains intersected at a few points with "centralized commodity chains," those far-flung networks by which local products were exported to distant markets. There are numerous distribution networks for centralizing commodities at regional and distant export markets. As commodities flow forward, exporters and marketers do not increase the value of the finished product itself, for the initial labor investment never changes. However, there are several points in the external trade process where "nonproducing" distributors control the flow of economic surplus throughout the commodity chain, with a great deal of profit expropriated by "middlemen traders."[12]

Types of Middlemen

Antebellum trading from rural hinterlands was much more structured and rationalized than most scholars have perceived. Appalachian producers could reach distant markets through linkages with several different types of middlemen traders who warehoused commodities for export. By the 1830s, several layers of retailers, brokers, speculators, dealers, wholesalers, and forwarding agents had emerged to offer "ancillary services connected with marketing." The existence of this layer of nonproductive profiteers is powerful evidence of the extent to which external trade had been rationalized and made more efficient. The farther the production zone was from the consumption zone, the greater the number of layers of distribution agents that had to be involved in the commodity forwarding process. Figure 8.3 illustrates the array of possible marketing strategies available to an Appalachian exporter.[13]

While larger producers utilized direct transport techniques or consignment to commission merchants, Southern Appalachia's middling to smaller producers relied upon a number of local marketing strategies. In reality, a high proportion of the region's farmers did not participate in the direct export of their own surpluses; instead, they disposed of their surpluses to one or more layers of local middlemen who warehoused commodities for export to distant markets; these included operators of livestock stands; local merchants, peddlers, and transportation termini; local elites who speculated in export trading; local manufacturers who bought agricultural crops for reprocessing and export; and itinerant buyers, speculators, drummers, or agents for distant commercial distributors.

The Importance of Commission Merchants

For the region's largest surplus producers, the most significant link in the flow of external trade was the distant *commission merchant* who accepted Appalachian goods on consignment, made advances to the shipper on credit,

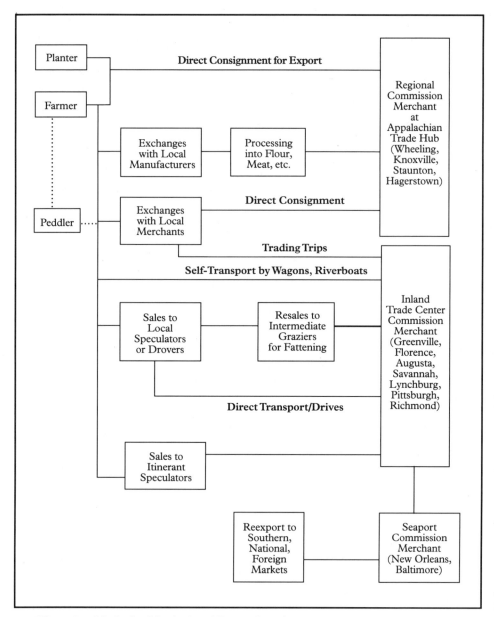

Figure 8.3. Methods of Agricultural Export from Southern Appalachia

obtained imports for the seller, and handled running accounts. Commission merchants based in Charleston, Augusta, New Orleans, Philadelphia, Baltimore, Louisville, and Cincinnati advertised regularly in Appalachian newspapers. Even railroads acted as commission merchants by accepting shipments on consignment. Rather than being isolated in a rural hinterland without interest in the outside world, Appalachian elites kept a running correspondence with commission houses in Richmond, Louisville, Charleston, New Orleans, Baltimore, Philadelphia, and New York; they were attuned to supply, demand, and price fluctuations in the world economy. When demand was high, distant commission merchants contacted their clients in the Appalachian countryside, soliciting shipments of flour, wheat, tobacco, or cotton. By 1850, most of Southern Appalachia's manufactured tobacco was being consigned to New York factors by way of Richmond or Norfolk houses. Distant commission merchants also marketed extractive exports for Appalachian salt, iron, copper, and coal producers.[14]

These distant capitalists provided several crucial ancillary services associated with external trade and, thereby, achieved a high degree of control over the economic affairs of Appalachian producers. In the Tennessee Valley

> Agricultural products moved out of the interior down the rivers to New Orleans and other ports on the Gulf of Mexico, whereas manufactured products came into the interior through Atlantic ports, such as Philadelphia, Baltimore, and Alexandria, down the valleys by wagon to the navigable rivers, and downstream to distributing points. . . . Money accumulated in the New Orleans banks to the credit of the up-country banks in behalf of [Appalachian farmers or manufacturers and], was transferred to east-coast towns to facilitate western purchases of manufactured articles.[15]

Consequently, it was the distant factor who controlled the marketing process, influenced supply and demand, effected the prices received, and manipulated the backward flow of cash or goods to the seller. However, the factor was also in a position to put distant clients at an economic disadvantage. In an attempt to stabilize Virginia tobacco prices, for example, Tidewater factors lobbied for legislation to apply a discriminatory selection process to Appalachian leaf. Claiming that transmontane tobacco was inferior, public inspectors (who were also the factors) segregated hogsheads from West Virginia, western North Carolina, and East Kentucky. As a result of the "Western Tobacco" label, Appalachian leaf was auctioned by commission houses at lower prices than Tidewater exports. To bypass this sectional pricing mechanism, West Virginians and East Kentuckians mislabeled their own hogsheads or shipped their tobacco down the Ohio River to New Orleans factors.[16]

To get their commodities to market, many Southern Appalachians dealt with an intermediate layer of commission merchants—forwarding agents located either in nearby towns outside the region (like Lexington or Lynchburg) or at the Appalachian trading hubs (like Chattanooga or Wheeling). At the regional level, large commission houses were in operation, by 1840, in the major Appalachian trading hubs—five in western Maryland, seven in East Tennessee, and four in Wheeling, West Virginia. These large commercial operations offered ancillary services to expedite export of extractive ores, manufactured goods, and farm crops out of the region and to arrange the distribution of imported commodities into the Appalachian countryside. For instance, Boothe and Dews of Knoxville advertised in numerous southern newspapers that "Every description of dry goods and groceries, stationary, cotton yarn, iron castings, nails, lead, and country produce, will be received and promptly attended to, and sold with dispatch and care. [Live]stock of all kinds, and every species of property wished to be sold in this market, will be promptly attended to and sold on the shortest notice."[17]

From a farm in Jefferson County, Tennessee, peach and apple brandy, corn whiskey, gin, rye, molasses, tree sugar, and tobacco "were barreled, sent down the river" and consigned to such a forwarding agent at Knoxville who, in turn, arranged shipping to a New Orleans commission merchant. To receive imports, the farmer wrote the Knoxville agent and initiated the same system in the reverse direction. Without leaving his rural home, the East Tennessean simultaneously sent produce to Deep South consumers and derived in return northeastern dry goods, European wines, South American coffee, or Indian teas. In addition to these large commercial operations, smaller merchants and traders—like Virginia's Thomas Adams, John Orr, or James Blanton—were operating in most Appalachian communities. One East Tennessee backcountry merchant accepted local iron on consignment, which he shipped south by flatboats. Similarly, professional cattle drovers, hog traders, and mule dealers acted as middlemen who contracted to drive to market the livestock belonging to one or more farmers or merchants.[18]

Intermediate Marketing Strategies

In addition to consigning their commodities to commission merchants, Appalachian producers also engaged in "intermediate marketing strategies." Agricultural produce or livestock was exported out of the county to intermediate regional points, from which the commodities would be resold farther away. For example, manufacturers marketed salt and iron in this fashion. From Wheeling, Frederick, Winchester, Staunton, Knoxville, and Chattanooga, livestock brokers reexported to distant cities the herds that had been driven from East Kentucky, West Virginia, western Maryland, and upper East Tennessee. For instance, East Kentucky mules were marketed to Knoxville dealers who fattened them for reexport to the Deep South.[19]

Another type of local broker was the "grazier," who invested in livestock drives that had originated in other parts of Southern Appalachia. Smaller farmers of the more rugged counties drove cattle and hogs into the region's valleys and grassy mountain meadows "where they were sold to grain raising farmers who fattened them for market. . . . The mountain cattle were customarily purchased when three or four years of age, 'roughed' through the first winter on cornstalks and wheat straw, fattened in the summer and fall on clover pasture and grain, and then driven to the markets of Baltimore and Philadelphia." This class of larger farmers engaged in systematic stock breeding to utilize their large landholdings with the minimal investment in labor. By buying up droves from adjacent Appalachian counties, several Virginia, East Tennessee, West Virginia, and western North Carolina graziers specialized in this pattern of export production of cattle, hogs, and sheep. In the upper Blue Ridge, graziers even engaged tenants to tend large herds pastured in the mountain meadows.[20]

Beginning in the late 1700s, East Kentucky speculators transported young or lean cattle "in droves of from two to three hundred" to the Shenandoah Valley and the northeastern edge of West Virginia, "where they s[old] them to graziers, who fatten[ed] them in order to supply the markets of Baltimore and Philadelphia." Graziers "realize[d] 50 to 60 percent" profit on their speculation. For instance, one Winchester trader annually toured the East Kentucky countryside, aggregating large droves of cattle and horses "at a trifling expense." Subsequently, he drove them to Winchester graziers for temporary fattening before export to Philadelphia or Baltimore.[21]

Sales to Livestock Stands

In addition to direct transport, consignment to commission merchants, or intermediate export, Appalachian producers could sell their commodities to local middlemen, like the merchants who operated "livestock stands." By the 1820s, several major drover trails crisscrossed Southern Appalachia, linking the border states to national markets. The Wilderness Road and Cumberland Gap linked Kentucky to routes leading to the eastern seaboard and to southern routes through North Carolina. The connector between Wheeling and Pennsylvania's Three Mountain Trail, the Cumberland Road, western Virginia's Northwestern Turnpike, and the Great Kanawha Turnpike provided midwestern access to eastern cities. By 1808, regular cattle drives were passing from Ohio over the Kanawha route to eastern markets. By 1826, there were more than 60,000 hogs a year passing from Ohio across the Kanawha route to eastern markets. Border livestock also moved to the Atlantic South down the Tennessee River valley or across the French Broad trail in western North Carolina.[22]

Following these routes, about 1,355,000 hogs; 100,600 cattle; and 86,870 horses and mules were herded annually to distant markets through Southern Appalachian counties. Highly rationalized for maximum efficiency, herds averaging 120 to 200 livestock traveled ten to twenty miles daily. At one-day intervals along the drover trails, commercial livestock stands provided lodging and food for the travelers where the herds were stabled, penned, or pastured each night. By the early 1800s, the Cherokees were operating "stock stands" and taverns to cater to the itinerant livestock droves that passed through the Nation headed south. Some Appalachian towns—like Bean Station, Benton, or Crossville in Tennessee—were economically dependent upon the itinerant drover trade while smaller stands emerged at ferries, turnpike crossroads, and near mountain gaps. For example, fifteen livestock stands operated between East Tennessee and Asheville. Each stand provisioned thirty to one hundred drives per year, feeding 3,000 to 10,000 livestock. At the peak of the season at one western Maryland drover inn, "there would be thirty six-horse teams on the wagon yard, one hundred Kentucky mules, in an adjacent lot, one thousand hogs in other enclosures, and as many fat cattle."[23]

These itinerant drives consumed about 5,672,186 bushels of Appalachian corn every year, and each Appalachian farm owner could dispose of 32 bushels of surplus corn in this manner. Consequently, more than one-fifth of the region's corn exports left the region "on the hoof." In the upper zones of Southern Appalachia, farmers disposed of a sizeable segment of their export corn through sales to livestock stands. Western Maryland fed four-fifths of its export corn to these itinerant drives, followed by West Virginia, where farm owners utilized nearly half of their export corn in this manner, and Appalachian Virginia, where nearly one-third of the export corn was fed to traveling livestock herds. In the Appalachian counties of Georgia and North Carolina, less than one-fifth of the export surplus was consumed by these drives; but less than one-tenth of the export surplus was required to provender the drives passing through East Kentucky, East Tennessee, and northern Alabama.[24]

Sales to Local Merchants

Preindustrial Appalachian commerce has been stereotyped as an egalitarian system of reciprocal exchanges of equivalent items between independent producers. In the popular scenario, the center of this barter economy "was the local merchant who exchanged retail commodities for surplus agricultural products and extended credit." Supposedly, this form of commerce "reinforced the autonomy of the local market system and provided mountain communities with considerable freedom from the fluctuations of the national cash economy." This image is vastly oversimplified and flawed, for Appalachian merchants were profit driven and oriented to prices in distant trading centers. For a large segment of the Appalachian farming community, participation in external trade came *indirectly* because antebellum marketing was effected through "triangular trading" between producers, local merchants, and distant markets. Local merchants acted as the first layer of export-import linkages between the Appalachian countryside and the capitalist world economy. Recent archival research indicates that Southern Appalachia's country merchants were much more involved in national networks of credit and commerce than most scholars have thought. In western North Carolina, for example, a national mercantile agency regularly rated the credit standing of local merchants who traded in eastern cities.[25]

Typically, Appalachian merchants engaged in multiple enterprises, often operating mills, distilleries, or livestock stands—all of which warehoused local commodities for export. Some Appalachian merchants operated chain stores for distant companies seeking to expand their markets. In addition to the stationary store, there were four other types of merchants who operated as middlemen. In remote areas, some merchants operated traveling wagon stores. A "fraternity of moving Merchants" bought goods wholesale in nearby towns for peddling in the countryside and on county court days; or they peddled the wares of distant manufacturers, like those financed by New England tinware and clock producers. Floating stores and huckster boats frequented the region's major rivers, stopping to trade all along the routes. Orders were delivered to specific farms, and all sorts of produce were received in trade. At boatyards, canals, ferries, and railroads, merchants bought and sold goods.[26]

Country stores purchased their dry goods from distant eastern or southern cities, sending in return "the produce of the country, which they b[ought] of the cultivators, or t[ook] in barter for their goods." Lumber, furs, hides, all sorts of produce, butter and cheese, feathers, flour, whiskey, slaves, and all sorts of crafted items appear in the account books of Appalachian stores. In addition to the barter process, Appalachian merchants engaged in a number of aggressive speculative strategies. Quite often, Appalachian merchants vigorously sought certain commodities for which they had ready distant markets.[27]

Many large merchants speculated in livestock, buying up hogs or cattle for store credits, then driving large herds to distant markets. The proprietors of regional livestock stands were typically also the merchants. These country stores advanced goods to farmers to be paid in corn in the fall. Each year prior to the drives, local farmers hauled wagonloads of corn to the merchant for resale to the large itinerant herds. Wool was also collected for export. It was common for western Virginia producers to wrap small amounts of wool "in a blanket and carry it to the nearest little country town, where they [we]re at the mercy of one or two speculators" who bought the commodity for export at one-half or less of its market value.[28]

In less developed counties, farmers went "to their nearest tradin' point [to] sell cotton," either to country stores or cotton exchanges. Local farmers sold their cotton to the merchant who consigned the commodity to a New Orleans, Mobile, or Charleston factor. In return, the commission merchant advanced two-thirds to three-fourths of the expected sales value to the merchant in the form of "bills of exchange." The Appalachian storekeeper imported goods from the commission house equivalent to the value of those bills of exchange. It was these goods which the merchant advanced on credit to local cotton producers, against the local contract price for their cotton.[29]

Sales to Local Speculators

Appalachian producers could also dispose of their surpluses by selling them to local speculators who purchased on credit from their neighbors extractive commodities, agricultural produce, or livestock. After contracting to accept certain amounts at specified below-market prices, these traders then exported to distant towns, accruing considerable profits. On the Appalachian frontier, Cherokees found ready buyers for their stolen horses among local speculators who shipped them south. One early East Kentuckian initiated his enterprise "on a speculation with a Boat loaded with corn tobacco bacon & laird bound to the port of Knew Orleans." Cyrenius Wait speculated in East Kentucky pork, salt, and coal that he exported on his flatboat fleets to Nashville. For resale to his community, he imported from Louisville exotic commodities like opium.[30]

Kentucky and Tennessee breeders bought up mules through trading at stables and on court days, then resold them to professional drovers when they were mature enough for export. In order to buy up local produce for export to New Orleans, a group of East Tennesseans operated their own wharf, warehouse, and steamboat out of Blount County. To fill a contract with an English purchaser for the Dublin markets, an East Tennessee country merchant traded in "commodity futures." Before the crops had matured in the fields, he contracted to purchase from many farms between the Clinch River and Chattanooga enormous amounts of corn. After harvest, the producers delivered the grain to the river's edge for transport by flatboats to New Orleans. Many annual livestock drives were organized by brokers and professional drovers— like West Virginians Daniel McNeill or Jacob W. Marshall and North Carolina's William Lenoir—who bought up local livestock for a contracted below-market price. One East Tennessee broker maximized his profits from such business by investing in an upland South Carolina farm. If the prices were too low at Charleston, he fattened the East Tennessee livestock at the intermediate point, waiting for prices to rise.[31]

Another type of local speculator was the "wholesale merchandiser." Appalachian newspapers regularly announced the arrival of Baltimore, Philadelphia, or Richmond goods that were being wholesaled, with "great allowance made to those who buy to sell again." Some of these capitalists specialized in "import linkages" in the trading process. For example, a Boyd County, Kentucky, merchant acquired Philadelphia goods for Appalachian retailers and company stores, passing on to the purchasers charges for freight, storage, advertising, commission fees, and specie discounts. Other wholesalers accrued their profits by redistributing imports to smaller country merchants in exchange for agricultural produce that they shipped to distant markets to procure dry goods. On the Nolichucky River of East Tennessee, Alfred Jackson warehoused agricultural produce and iron to export to Baltimore and Philadelphia, where he secured the wholesale dry goods that he resold to a chain of Appalachian retail outlets.[32]

Sales to Itinerant Speculators

In addition to resident middlemen, Southern Appalachians could sell export surpluses to itinerant buyers, speculators, and drummers. State and county regulations are evidence that there routinely appeared in the region commercial drummers for distant wholesale dry goods merchants and manufacturers. These drummers visited country retailers, collected debts, and arranged transport or credit linkages between Appalachian merchants and distant wholesalers. In this manner, Alexandria, Richmond, and Norfolk tobacco buyers traveled into the Appalachian countryside to buy up tobacco at below-market prices.[33]

Cincinnati and Baltimore meatpackers regularly sent agent-drovers into the East Kentucky and West Virginia countryside to buy up herds for export to their markets. With financing from distant manufacturers, "stock purchasers" bought up East Kentucky and West Virginia cattle or hogs for export to Louisville or the East. In the 1820s, for example, there appeared in upper West Virginia "eight or ten Drovers in paires, from New York & Pennsylvania [who] purchased a considerable Number of Cattle. . . . it [wa]s thought more than half of the Cattle in the country [we]re purchased."[34]

At numerous river towns and wharves, itinerant speculators competed for local supplies of grain, flour, dried fruits, whiskey, lumber, bacon, eggs, and butter to be exported to New Orleans. In many Appalachian counties of Alabama and Georgia, itinerant traders bought up local cotton for distant commission houses. For example, Heard and Simpson of Augusta sent agents into northern Alabama, northern Georgia, and southeastern Tennessee during the 1850s to buy up cotton at cheap prices.[35]

When there was a sudden demand for a scarce commodity, coast wholesalers sent agents inland to locate supplies. Trading in commodity futures had its forerunner in this pattern of antebellum trading, for these itinerant buyers often invested in immature crops or livestock. To fill distant demand, they would "option" grain crops of local farmers who contracted to sell to them at specified below-market prices. In middle Tennessee, one such trader speculated on "cotton futures," optioning the growing crops in the fields. He reported to his Augusta factor that he could "buy some cotton there at ten cents all round, and let them have their own time to deliver it, and it is the only possible terms on which we can get it, inasmuch as Cotton is getting quite scarce, I am determined on going back in that section, and buy all I can, which I hope may be four or five hundred bales."[36]

In addition to sales to the various types of middlemen, Appalachian farmers could market their grains, livestock, hides, furs, cotton, tobacco, and wool to local manufacturers who exported flour, meal, liquors, tobacco plugs or twists, meat provisions, leather products, and textiles. Because these export commodities were closely regulated and inspected to meet distant-market standards, the producers were highly centralized within Southern Appalachia. Only 34 of the region's counties may be described as "vertically diversified" (see Map 8.1). In these areas, twenty or more firms exported agricultural commodities in manufactured forms, accruing local benefits from the value added in processing. These largest exporters were heavily concentrated along major rivers in the Appalachian counties of Tennessee, Virginia, West Virginia, and Maryland. For the rest of the region, heavy production of agricultural exports was centralized in a few counties, including Talladega, Alabama; Madison, Kentucky; and Rutherford and Yancey Counties, North Carolina. In sharp contrast to these developed zones, nearly two-thirds (132) of the region's counties were only minimally vertically diversified. While these areas absorbed a small segment of the available export surpluses in the production of manufactured exports, they were still transporting most of their agricultural produce in raw forms. The rest of the counties (49) were totally horizontally integrated; that is, those areas exported only raw produce without any intermediate processing to increase their market value.[37]

The image of every farmer milling and distilling at small individual facilities is romantic but historically erroneous. Mills were licensed monopolies, and their technology was complex; often millwrights and mill machinery were imported from great distances. Grain processing was also closely regulated; every Appalachian state specified product standards and weights. Authorized inspection towns enforced uniform packing, grading, and branding of flour. In Tennessee, for example, exporters were required to barrel the flour and place it on river boats for export within three days of milling. In addition to the processing of flour and meal, regional enterprises also generated whiskey and malt liquor from the surplus grains. Corn whiskey was produced throughout Southern Appalachia. However, several counties of Maryland and Virginia generated high levels of malt liquor while West Virginia created the famous Monongahela Rye Whiskey.[38]

Because manufactories were highly centralized in a few geographical areas, grain flowed from adjacent counties into these production zones, where the raw materials were transformed into intermediate commodities of higher value at distant markets. However, there was considerable variation from one zone to another in the extent to which grains were exported in the raw form. Most counties of the region were horizontally integrated into the world economy because local producers transported raw grain surpluses, the form

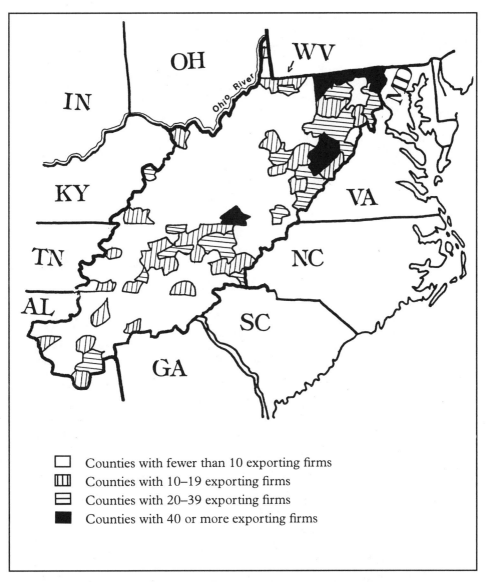

Map 8.1. Firms Exporting Processed Agricultural Commodities, 1860
Source: Aggregated data from U.S. Census Office, *Manufactures of the United States in 1860* (Washington, D.C.: Government Printing Office, 1865).

of lowest value at distant markets. The Appalachian counties of Alabama, Georgia, Kentucky, North Carolina, South Carolina, and Tennessee shipped three-quarters or more of their available export wheat and corn in raw form (see Table 8.2).

At the other extreme, the region's primary flour-milling zone was fifteen

Table 8.2. Methods for Exporting Grains

A. Corn Exports[a]

Appalachian Counties of	Sold to Livestock Stands	Sold to Local Manufacturers to Process Exports		Raw Corn Exported (Imported)
		Whiskey	Meal	
Alabama	116,960	15,000	609,010	923,417
Georgia	468,178	67,001	296,803	887,176
Kentucky	268,884	452,733	360,744	2,382,682
Maryland	868,140	1,797,300	—	(1,616,952)
North Carolina	268,884	99,317	325,642	913,346
South Carolina	—	—	—	153,993
Tennessee	713,470	476,834	2,181,346	4,012,235
Virginia	1,777,230	1,391,484	2,545,123	576,100
West Virginia	1,348,200	1,785,890	1,425,768	(1,659,834)
Region	5,829,946	6,085,559	7,744,436	6,572,163

B. Wheat Exports[b]

Appalachian Counties of	Total Flour Barrels Exported	Bushels of Wheat Sold to Local Mills to Process Export Flour	Bushels of Raw Wheat Exported (Imported)
Alabama	9,595	43,178	106,191
Georgia	12,277	55,247	218,682
Kentucky	4,626	20,817	236,210
Maryland	374,217	1,683,977	(617,201)
North Carolina	8,627	38,822	165,489
South Carolina	—	—	13,099
Tennessee	67,392	303,264	853,907
Virginia	454,379	2,044,706	433,907
West Virginia	253,516	1,140,822	(290,278)
Region	1,184,629	5,330,833	1,120,006

Sources: Calculated by applying ratios derived from manuscript samples to aggregated data from the published Censuses of Population and Agriculture.

[a]Corn for livestock stands from Dunaway, "Incorporation," Table 11.2. Corn exports from Table 5.10 were converted using these ratios: 1 barrel meal required 4.8 bushels corn; 1 gallon whiskey required 1.5 bushels corn; see Battalio and Kagel, "Structure of Antebellum Agriculture"; Dabney, *Mountain Spirits*, p. 51. Raw corn exports were calculated by subtracting these forms of export from the total available export grain in Table 5.6.

[b]Wheat exports from Table 5.10 were converted using these ratios: 1 barrel flour required 4.5 bushels wheat; see Battalio and Kagel, "Structure of Antebellum Agriculture." Raw wheat exports were calculated by subtracting these forms of export from the total available export grain in Table 5.6.

counties of West Virginia and western Maryland, where 378 mills and distilleries produced more output than local grain production could supply. Because of their locations on major national trade routes, these two zones were *importing* supplementary raw grains from Virginia, West Virginia, Pennsylvania, and Ohio. Western Maryland manufactories generated enough flour, whiskey, and malt liquor to require one and one-half times the surplus wheat and one and three-quarters times the surplus corn available from local farmers. Consequently, Maryland manufacturers imported from other areas more than 600,000 bushels of wheat and more than 1,600,000 bushels of corn (Table 8.2). In similar fashion, West Virginia manufactories processed enough flour, meal, and liquor to need one and one-third times the surplus wheat and one and one-tenth times the surplus corn that could be bought from local producers; thus, they must have imported nearly 300,000 bushels of wheat and more than 1,600,00 bushels of corn. Wellsburg and Wheeling alone exported 300,000 barrels of flour annually down the Ohio River.[39]

The second most important zone of export grain processing was twenty Appalachian Virginia counties where 563 mills and distilleries absorbed more than three-quarters of the available export wheat and more than two-thirds of the available export corn. Heavily centralized in eighteen counties of the region's third most significant grain-processing zone, 364 East Tennessee mills and distilleries absorbed only about one-quarter of the available export wheat and nearly two-fifths of the available export corn to generate flour, meal, and whiskey for the New Orleans market. Grain processing was less advanced in East Kentucky or western North Carolina, where nine counties dominated the export of flour, meal, and whiskey. East Kentuckians processed less than one-tenth of their available export wheat and less than one-fifth of the available export corn. Similarly, less than one-fifth of the wheat and little more than one-quarter of the corn were exported out of western North Carolina in manufactured form. Even though northern Alabama and northern Georgia exported most of their grains in raw form, the Coosa River Valley developed into an important manufacturing zone, from which 104 mills and distilleries centralized in fourteen counties exported flour, meal, and whiskey to the Mobile market (Map 8.1).

In addition to their sales of grains to local manufacturers, Appalachian farmers could also dispose of tobacco, cotton, and wool to local export producers. Nearly every Appalachian planter who "raise[d] tobacco to any extent [wa]s a manufacturer; but there [we]re some who ma[d]e a business of it, and purchase[d] the article in the leaf from their neighbors." However, only twenty-three of the region's counties exported manufactured cigars, twists, or plugs. In Appalachian Virginia, Georgia, and North Carolina, it was not unusual for a small factory to be combined with a general merchandise store, like those in Patrick, Franklin, and Cumberland Counties of Virginia. However, one-third of the country's cigar manufacturing occurred in Southern

Appalachia, and slave laborers were utilized in several larger tobacco factories. In northern Georgia, all of the local tobacco was absorbed to manufacture twists and plugs for export, but the farmers of northern Alabama, East Tennessee, and East Kentucky exported almost all of their tobacco as leaf. In between these two extremes, Appalachian manufacturers of Maryland, North Carolina, and Virginia transformed into the more valuable plugs, cigars, or twists only one-fifth to two-fifths of the total exports.[40]

Appalachian farmers followed similar patterns in their handling of cotton and wool exports. Less than 5 percent of the region's cotton and about one-third of the region's wool were transformed into cloth prior to export. Appalachian wool exporters of Alabama, Georgia, Kentucky, South Carolina, and Tennessee were horizontally integrated into the world economy while West Virginia produced cloth from about two-fifths of its wool. The Appalachian counties of North Carolina and Tennessee manufactured one-third to one-half of their cotton before export, but the greatest vertical integration characterized western Maryland and Virginia, where most of the local wool was manufactured into cloth before export.[41]

In their exports of livestock, Southern Appalachians were almost totally horizontally integrated into the world economy. With meatpacking facilities centralized in only three of the region's counties, Southern Appalachia transported more than nine-tenths of its export livestock "on the hoof." By doing so, Appalachians stimulated the expansion of manufacturing in adjacent export zones. Blue Grass Kentucky, Tidewater Virginia, upland South Carolina, and Baltimore, Philadelphia, and Cincinnati processed great quantities of Appalachian hogs, turkeys, and cattle into preserved meat provisions, ready for long-term, international transport. To achieve this production, these arenas also imported Appalachian salt and barrels—thereby draining away from the region the wealth accumulation that might have accrued from the value added during local processing of those raw materials.[42]

Summary

As the transition to capitalism proceeded, regional productive processes and infrastructure were spatially reorganized to effect the articulation of rural Appalachian producers with distant consumer markets. Country merchants, hinterland villages, trading hubs, transportation networks, and distant metropoles were integrated into an interlocking web of exchange flows that' absorbed most Appalachians within the pervasive reach of global commodity chains. The economic dominance of the export sector encouraged the development of Appalachian commerce and towns at a pace that far outstripped the emergence of local manufacturing. In fact, the external trade in several types of raw materials actually deterred the "vertical diversification" of local Appalachian economies. When commodities were exported in the raw forms to a distant destination, the receiving zone captured the trade's operating institutions and allied industries at the expense of the production zone and drained away the value added to the commodities through processing. For example, Southern Appalachia never developed any extensive regional facilities for processing meat or copper prior to export. Instead, annual drives of livestock on the hoof and massive transfers of raw ore fueled meatpacking in adjacent zones (like Louisville or Cincinnati) and stimulated the proliferation of allied copper industries in the Northeast and Europe.

This "horizontal integration" further slowed development of Appalachian manufacturing and internal markets because it stimulated external trade in the reverse direction. Finished goods were bought from distant markets, even when such commodities might have been manufactured locally from available raw materials (e.g., shoes and fabrics). More significantly, technology for manufacturing and industry (e.g., mills) were imported from distant trade centers, as were many of the livestock breeds, foreign plants, and fertilizers that Appalachian farmers employed to increase their agricultural output.[43]

The expansion of external trade in Southern Appalachia was characterized by another form of economic restructuring. Producing the surplus commodities or constructing infrastructure are not enough to effect articulation with the world economy. As part of the incorporation process, commodity transportation processes were highly rationalized, and a new layer of nonproducing "commodity distributors" emerged to move goods between distant points. Their role was to activate linkages between layers of markets and to keep capital mobile between metropoles. Without these actors at the micro level, the far-reaching commodity chains could not span the globe with exports and circle back again to deliver imports to the original exporting producers.

What enlivened the transition to capitalism was the creation of layers of markets that broke the direct connection between producers and buyers. "Long chains of merchants took position between production and consumption," and these middlemen traders expropriated high profits for their nonproductive services. To facilitate external trade, there emerged several types of commission merchants, wholesalers, retailers, intermediate processors, speculators, and shippers. At one level, these middlemen effected the exchanges between raw material suppliers or intermediate processors and the distant manufacturers that finished the products. At another level, commission merchants, wholesalers, and retailers constructed the extensive trade chains between food suppliers or manufacturers and distant consumers.[44]

Even when Appalachians engaged in direct transport of their products, they never moved their commodities to the final consumer destinations. Instead, Appalachians marketed their goods at intermediate points to middlemen who forwarded them along the global chain. At the local level, many smaller Appalachian producers penetrated the distant market only indirectly, by selling their export surpluses to merchants, manufacturers, and speculators who propelled the commodities outward. Because of their domination of the region's external trade, commission middlemen drained off 10 to 15 percent of the surpluses that might have accrued to the original producers. An even larger drain of regional capital was effected by speculators who originated from external metropoles. These middlemen bought up regional raw materials far below market prices, resold them for sizeable profits, and drained away much of the external trade wealth that might have accumulated within Southern Appalachia.

9

APPALACHIAN COMMUNITIES AND

NONECONOMIC ARTICULATION WITH

THE CAPITALIST WORLD SYSTEM

Looking at the Big Picture

Up to this point, my discussion has focused upon the intricacies of Southern Appalachia's market linkages and upon the historical transformations in its dominant mode of production. I have attacked the popular image of preindustrial Appalachia as an undeveloped society shut away from the outside world. On the one hand, the picture is incomplete in most conventional accounts because analysts fail to take into consideration those Cherokees who lived as a racially and legally segregated "region of refuge" on the fringes of dominant Appalachian society. On the other hand, these local economies were much more complex and diverse—both internally and across the region—than they are typically portrayed. Appalachian towns, villages, and counties were not simply agrarian hinterlands. Indeed, the countryside was a mosaic of agriculture, industry, commerce, and town life.[1]

While the region's local communities were differentiated by the degree to which they had diversified their development, every Appalachian subzone had some mix of the three major economic sectors. In fact, the shift to non-agricultural activities began in this region much earlier than has previously been recognized. Even as early as 1820, more than one of every seven of the region's free heads of household were employed outside farming. Over the forty-year period, new commercial and industrial sectors emerged and expanded at an uneven pace. Thus, by 1860, nearly two-fifths of the region's free households were earning income from nonagricultural activities, either as their sole occupations or as pursuits supplemented by agriculture. Surprisingly, more than one-third of Southern Appalachia's free labor force had left farming.[2]

The analysis is incomplete, however, if we leave the theoretic lens focused narrowly upon the expansion of Appalachian economic activities. Beginning in 1700, the local institutions that dominated in Southern Appalachia were articulated with the structural dynamics of the capitalist world system. This long incorporation process entailed a reformulation of the "trinity of arenas of social action"—the economy, the state, and the culture.

All economic activity assumes socio-cultural rules and preferences, and works within political constraints. Furthermore, markets are socio-political creations. . . . All political activity serves the end of ensuring or pursuing economic advantage or need as well as the reinforcement of socio-cultural objectives. And socio-cultural activity is itself made possible and explained by economic and political location, and serves ends that are ultimately defined in these terms. . . . [H]uman activity within a given world-system moves indiscriminately and imperceptibly in and among all three arenas.[3]

While it is artificial to treat these elements of the incorporation process as though there were discernibly autonomous, I have done so here simply as a matter of organizational convenience and clarification. In the sections that follow, we shall examine more closely the mechanisms by which Southern Appalachia's *political and cultural institutions* were subordinated to the drives of the capitalist world system. However, social institutions are not the only elements to be irrevocably altered by incorporation. When an external arena is absorbed, its *natural and human resources* are reorganized as factors of production and exploited to maximize outputs for global commodity chains. People are reordered into centralized workforces, and their lives reflect their location within the hierarchical division of labor. Still, there is one other crucial piece in the complicated explanation. The *environment* comprises a fifth layer that we must peel back if we are to understand the long historical process through which Southern Appalachia was peripheralized and impoverished.

Political Articulation with the Capitalist World Economy

The expansion of capitalism is accompanied not only by economic reorganization but also by the reformulation of the local political structure. Before an area can be incorporated into the network of world production processes, the first major stumbling block that must be overcome is political resistance. The intrusion of the world economy into an external arena triggers the creation of political mechanisms that can facilitate the participation of that zone within the global division of labor. "The transition from a self-regulating and self-producing political authority to a political authority enmeshed in a global political network is a fundamental rupture. The very radical nature of this transition is indicated by the different spatial boundaries between economic and political spheres; pre-capitalist modes of production had coterminous economic and political domains, while the secret of modern capitalism is its multiple political structures cross-cutting a unified economic division of labor."[4]

Political institutions provide the matrix within which a capitalist economy can be built and expanded. Thus, another political obstacle that must be overcome is the existence of archaic regulations and institutions that deter the expansion of capitalism. Historically, Southern Appalachia could not be articulated with the structures of the world system until indigenous political resistance had been overcome. Moreover, land tenure had to be reformulated to permit capitalistic trading in natural resources. Subsequently, the local states enacted legislation that facilitated capitalistic monopolization of the region's land and resources.

Political Facilitation of Capitalism

In order to be fully integrated with the world system, a new zone must develop rationalized and centralized structures of governance characterized by three features. First, the new local-state assumes "jurisdictional responsibility within the interstate system for a defined geopolitical area." Second, this new local government must be strong enough to overcome any internal resistance to the flows of people and commodities from outside its border. On the other hand, however, this local-state must remain "weak enough in relation to other jurisdictions (mainly core) to be incapable of blocking such flows." In this fashion, Euro-American settlers established new county and local-state structures in Southern Appalachia to replicate those that had developed as subordinate units throughout the emergent frontiers of the United States.[5]

Because Appalachian elites dabbled in multiple economic pursuits, they formed counties and local-states that would act as catalysts for economic growth. The region's wealthiest families routinely combined farming, retail trade, and the professions with their speculations in land and slaves and their intrigues in state or national politics. Because they participated within the inner circles that controlled state governments, the region's wealthiest families exploited their political positions to "jump-start" their speculative projects. These powerful profit seekers acted as catalysts for expansion into enterprises that were linked to production of raw materials in demand on the world market. Little wonder, then, that local governments licensed as public monopolies new privately held towns, transportation infrastructure, or banks. Public markets were operated under government scrutiny while weights and measures, tolls, and pricing procedures were standardized locally. In order to facilitate external trade, local governments funded internal improvements and established inspection procedures to standardize export commodities. In addition, local governments enacted labor control laws, including regulation of slavery, tenancy, vagrancy, pauperism, and wage controls.

Finally, local governments regulated credit. For instance, debt collection was the compelling reason for the creation of public regulatory mechanisms in the Watauga settlement, a speculative venture that is touted in popular mythology as a bastion of frontier equality. "Being apprehensive" that their new community "might become a shelter for such as endeavored to defraud their creditors," the Wataugans, "by consent of the people, formed a court." Similarly, the Talladega, Alabama, court assisted unscrupulous merchants to cheat local Indians out of their small farms. When groceries and rum advanced on credit accumulated in unpaid debts, merchants acquired warrants from the court to authorize the sheriff to confiscate Cherokee lands on behalf of the creditors and to auction off the debtors through the poorhouse.[6]

The Role of the State in Industrial Development

Political structures and laws were modified not only to promote external trade and the flow of credit and commerce but also to speed the development of industry. In addition to licensing functions and the granting of virtual public monopolies, local and state governments often directly subsidized emergent enterprises. Outright grants were made to expedite the formation of export manufacturing, as was the case with upper South Carolina cotton mills. To spur antebellum industry, state governments made interest-free loans, granted land bounties, and enacted protective tariffs to discourage the competitive import of externally manufactured commodities. For instance, a special Maryland act imposed duties on imported glass so that the Bremen Glass Manufactory of Frederick County "might with some encouragement be firmly established." Lobbied by a powerful Kanawha Valley cartel, the U.S. Congress enacted a similar tariff on foreign salt in order to protect the prices afforded West Virginia manufacturers.[7]

Huge land grants were made to nascent manufacturers, and states cut land prices to favored developers of new mines and furnaces. In the early 1800s, even the federal government engaged in this practice. A huge southeastern Tennessee tract was reserved for the establishment of a frontier iron complex. Thomas Jefferson insisted that this public monopoly must not "be conducted on account of the United States" because there were "private individuals ready to erect" and to profit from the new manufactory. Tennessee acts rewarded 10,000 acres to iron manufacturers while North Carolina offered to them a land bounty of 3,000 acres. Kentucky and Virginia made similar land grants to encourage salt manufacturing.[8]

New extractive industries were further bolstered by state tax abatements for as long as ninety-nine years; many of them were powerful enough to circumvent county taxation as well. For instance, western Maryland's George's Creek Coal and Iron Company stressed to the court its past history of state relief as evidence of its right to be exempted from local property reassessments. Subsequently, the judge issued a permanent injunction barring the county from equalizing company tax rates with the ratios imposed on resident farmers. Public funds were also utilized to make direct loans to aid the establishment of extractive industries or to cushion them from economic recessions. For example, the Pactolus Iron Works was constructed after the legislature loaned the industrialist the entire school fund of East Tennessee; this company was further assisted with five other subsequent fiscal relief bills. In addition, public funds were applied to build roads and to improve river navigation near the region's extractive industries.[9]

Beginning in the late 1700s, land jobbers and local agents were paid by northeastern capitalists "to hunt the Land" of Southern Appalachia for mineral deposits. By 1810, the region's gold, copper, lead, iron, salt, silver, coal, and saltpeter were being extracted in quantities significant to the country's economic growth. Beginning in the late 1820s, every Appalachian state funded antebellum geological surveys as a strategy to attract mineral developers. By 1860, for example, Kentucky had completed three such surveys; Tennessee had funded eight. Moreover, national investors employed geologists and engineers to locate and map major ore veins, most of which lay in northern or southern Appalachia.[10]

As a result of public mapping, speculative interest in Southern Appalachia's mineral lands was kindled repeatedly throughout the antebellum period. Many eastern capitalists hoarded their Appalachian investments until after the Civil War. For example, the descendants of William Cathcart hoarded a Revolutionary War grant of 33,280 western North Carolina acres until the early 1900s.[11] Local communities promoted their natural resources and appealed for absentee speculation. In 1854, for instance, an East Tennessee newspaper reported that

> Thousands of acres of land in East Tennessee, where this coal and iron so much abound, might now be purchased for less than fifty cents per acre. . . . there are soon to be radiating from Knoxville railways to the North, South, East, and West, over which the iron may be transported with profit to any market in the United States. . . . Here then is the place to "put money"—in the coal and iron lands; not that there are not large profits to be realized from a more complete development of our marble quarries, zinc and lead mines; but iron has ever been, and must continue to be, an article absolutely indispensable.[12]

Appalachian elites, like the Means family of East Kentucky, agglomerated huge tracts of coal, oil, and timber lands in every county, forming the land basis for the postbellum industrial boom. Throughout the region, governmental insiders—like David Goff, Gideon Camden, Henry Gassaway Davis, Arthur I. Boreman, George Cookman Sturgiss, and Stephen B. Elkins of West Virginia—exploited their state and congressional positions to acquire Appalachian holdings that they could resell or syndicate with distant speculators. New connectors penetrated the region after 1850, triggering engrossment of vast mineral tracts by the railroad companies, as the Baltimore and Ohio Railroad Company did in western Maryland. Empowered by state governments to improve Appalachian waterways, several private companies exploited their positions to agglomerate large landholdings. For example, the Virginia Assembly chartered a New York–financed navigation company in 1849, funding it to clear the Guyandotte River of obstacles. Primarily interested in timberland, the company cleared the stream minimally for logging, buying up large parcels along its banks.[13]

Moreover, state governments flamed the speculative fervor with national and international offers of large tracts of tax-delinquent lands for sale at extremely low prices. In 1857, for example, Virginia advertised a schedule of Appalachian properties "amounting in all to more than 2 and a ½ million acres, and for which the price asked [wa]s 12 and ½ cents an acre." Later that same year, Virginia made a second offering of 300,000 of its western coal lands for sale at only fifty cents per acre.[14]

Cultural Articulation with the Capitalist World Economy

In addition to the subordination of economic and political institutions to the drives of global capitalism, there must be a restructuring of the local culture. In Southern Appalachia, this transition occurred over two long epochs—the displacement of the precapitalist society and the reformulation of a new culture by those settlers who emigrated to the frontier from other zones of the world system. The ideological dominance of capitalist values was initially secured through the dramatic reshaping of the indigenous traditions and institutions. During the colonial period, international trade linked Cherokee villages inexorably into the European world system. The Appalachian communal economy was transformed into a putting-out system that exported slaves, ginseng, and deerskins. Once the fur trade and warfare assumed primacy, laborers were increasingly drawn away from subsistence production, thereby escalating Cherokee dependency on trade goods. No aspect of Cherokee life was left untouched by the new capitalist relations of production. Despite internal resistance to domination, Cherokee culture and traditions were irrevocably altered.[15]

Stage One: Creation of an Internal Region of Refuge
After the Revolutionary War, the status of the Cherokees within Southern Appalachia was downgraded even further into a racially and legally segregated "region of refuge." To appease settlers, the federal government initially established in southeastern Tennessee two "fur factories." There the Indians exchanged pelts for imported trade goods that were sold at "68 percent advance over the marked cost." Thomas Jefferson envisioned such trade linkages

as the best strategy for furnishing the Cherokees "all the necessaries and comforts they may wish," thereby encouraging them "to run in debt for these beyond their individual means of paying." Once trapped in this dilemma, they would "always cede lands to rid themselves of debt."[16]

When the fur factories failed, the federal government instituted its "civilization program." Subsequently, the Cherokees were coerced to abandon their communal economies in order to engage in the types of agricultural, craft, and trading activities occurring among white settlers on the Appalachian frontier. Ironically, then, the Cherokees had come full circle in their cultural collision with capitalism. Traditionally, they had been agriculturalists until they were acculturated by the British in commercial hunting. When their hunting clashed with the expansion of settler farming, the Americans pressured them toward sedentary agriculture.

> The processes involved in the expansion of the capitalist world economy—the peripheralization of economic structures, the creation of weak state structures participating in and constrained by an interstate system—involved a number of pressures at the level of culture: Christian proselytization; the imposition of European language; instruction in specific technologies and mores; changes in the legal codes. . . . There were two main motives behind these enforced cultural changes. One was economic efficiency. If given persons were expected to perform in given ways in the economic arenas, it was efficient both to teach them the requisite cultural norms and to eradicate competing cultural norms. The second was political security. It was believed that if the so-called elites were "westernized," they would be separated from their "masses," and hence less likely to revolt.[17]

To speed acculturation, the Indian agency subsidized the schools of missionaries who educated Cherokee children to take on "all the arts of civilized life" and to earn their livelihoods through "husbandry and the labors of the field." By 1822, it had become "a principle of sound policy in the government of the United States to disband Cherokee settlements [from villages to dispersed dwellings], and to encourage the plantation system." By 1826, the cultural transition from commercial hunting to sedentary agriculture was complete. The Cherokees had abandoned their villages in favor of dispersion "over the face of the Country on separate farms." Cherokee elite John Ridge boasted to the U.S. secretary of war:

> there is not to my knowledge a solitary Cherokee to be found who depends upon the Chase [i.e., hunting] for subsistence. Every head of a family has his own farm and house. . . . The principal portion of our trade consists in Hogs and horned Cattle. Skins formerly were sold in respectable quantities, but that kind of trade is fast declining and becomes less reputable. Cherokees on the Tennessee River already commence to trade in Cotton and

grow it on large plantations for which they have experienced flattering profit. Preparation is making . . . to cultivate the Cotton for market which will soon be a Staple commodity of traffic for the Nation.[18]

Moreover, the Indian agent had compelled the Cherokees to discontinue the *gadugi* customs by which they engaged in communal agriculture and public grain stores. Thus, Ridge could also report that Cherokee "laws to govern the labour of the Citizens who acted in concert in cultivating their patches have disappeared long since."[19]

Because the United States had "the sole and exclusive right of regulating their trade," all aspects of economic interaction with the Cherokee "were purposefully developed so as to effect change in Cherokee culture." As the Cherokees expanded their market production at federal instigation, they were forced into increased dependency upon food supplies allocated against their federal annuity payments for prior land cessions. By 1820, the Cherokees were probably the most acculturated of the Native American groups; they had adapted a national council patterned after the American legislative and juridical system, and they had developed their own written language. Throughout the antebellum period, native Appalachians were confined to a territorially and racially segregated "region of refuge" that was politically dominated by and economically dependent upon the white society around them. Despite their accommodation and voluntary change, the Cherokees were forcibly removed in 1838.[20]

Settler greed for territory was culturally guised as a humanitarian effort to relocate indigenous Appalachians to western wilderness areas that were more suitable to their "barbaric" lifestyle. The Cherokee "hunter state" could survive "only in the vast uncultivated desert," President Monroe proclaimed. Arguing that federal policy toward the Cherokees was "not only liberal, but generous," President Jackson laid out the master plan for the "ethnic cleansing" of Southern Appalachia. To save the "savages" from "utter annihilation" and to make way for "the settled, civilized Christian," the United States would send the Indians "to a land where their existence m[ight] be prolonged." What "good" American, he chastised, "would prefer a country covered with forests and ranged by a few thousand savages to our extensive Republic, studded with cities, towns, and prosperous farms, embellished with all the improvements which art can devise or industry execute, occupied by more than 12,000,000 happy people, and filled with all the blessings of liberty, civilization, and religion?"[21]

Those few Cherokees who remained in Appalachia held an anomalous status in southern race relations. They were not recognized as citizens of the states in which they squatted, nor were they permitted the legal right to own property. In 1860, only nine of the residents of Quallatown in western North

Carolina held deeds to their parcels. Cherokee culture had been transformed into a mixture of traditionalism and cultural adaptations from white settlers.[22]

Stage Two: Creation of a New Cultural Division of Labor

Let us be clear about the historical reality. There was no peculiar or unique "Appalachian" culture in existence prior to the expansion of capitalism into this new zone of the world system. In fact, the repeopling process brought to this first American frontier immigrants from several national and ethnic backgrounds, and the region's settler capitalism grew out of the amalgamation and diffusion of these varied cultures. Can we accurately speak, then, of a homogeneous Appalachian "folk society" that characterized preindustrial Southern Appalachia? On the contrary, the region's new population was the result of the synthesizing of cultural traits from the English, Irish, Scotch-Irish, Welsh, Corkians, French Huguenots, Germans, Italians, African Americans, several Native American populations, and smatterings of several other ethnic groups. There is no evidence in primary sources that antebellum Appalachians identified themselves as a region unified by a common culture that was distinct from the rest of the South. Moreover, external travelers did not describe a "peculiar folk" who resided in the southern mountains. Journalists sometimes criticized the impoverished living conditions, the customs of specific resident groups like the Irish or the Cherokees, or the "uncommodious" travel accommodations or transportation infrastructure. But they did *not* document a unique Appalachian culture that was isolated from or resistant to the capitalist society that was developing in the rest of the United States. In short, there is no archival corroboration for the existence of a "strange and peculiar" Southern Appalachian "subculture" that "challenged America's notions of progress."[23]

What is more evident than cultural differentiation between Southern Appalachia and the rest of the United States is the vast *internal cultural division of labor* between the region's elites and the masses of the population. Capitalism gives birth to a cultural sphere predominantly divided along class lines. Consequently, articulation with the world system created in Southern Appalachia a peripheral *comprador bourgeoisie* that was tied by kinship to elites in other parts of the South and that remained loyal to external political and economic schemes. Because those regional elites embraced the capitalist values dominant in the core, they aspired to rise to the economic level of southern merchant-planters. Since wealth, land, and political power were heavily concentrated into their hands, this Appalachian minority could utilize their local positions to sustain within their communities an exploitative division of labor.[24]

In the nineteenth-century capitalist world system, the attainment of land and wealth were the social indicators of "high culture." The aspiration of all rising groups was to gain enough wealth to become part of the leisured,

Table 9.1. The Cultural Division of Labor in Southern Appalachia

Cultural Categories Ranked in Order of Social Esteem	% All Households	Average Household Wealth ($)	% Household Heads Illiterate
"High-cultured Southern Gentlemen"			
Wealthiest slaveholders, merchants, and industrialists	2.5	74,265	0
Professional and gentlemen farmers	0.9	52,635	0
"The Respectable"			
Middling farm owners and cash renters, government officials, clergy	25.8	6,600	0
Small farm owners	5.4	4,328	7.9
Small shop owners and artisans	4.6	2,292	0
"The Marginally Respectable"[a]			
Subsistence or marginal farm owners	3.5	489	32.7
Skilled wage laborers	3.1	368	26.3
"The Poor White Trash"[b]			
Landless farm operators and annual contract laborers on farms	14.1	98	46.4
Common laborers	24.4	83	49.6
Immigrant wage laborers	11.7	72	25.8
Unstably employed whites	1.9	79	74.1
"The Disreputable Rabble"			
Free blacks	1.4	55	69.8
White paupers	0.7	0	80.9

Source: Derived from analysis of sample of 3,056 households drawn from the 1860 Census of Population manuscripts. Cultural categories were derived from the responses of the 474 Appalachian Civil War veterans.

[a] Skilled laborers include wage laborers with specialized skills (e.g., millwright or engineer), store clerks, teachers.

[b] Common laborers include unskilled nonagricultural laborers and agricultural day laborers.

landed upper class. While Appalachian elites comprised only 3.4 percent of the region's households, they were well educated, and their material consumption reflected their average household wealth of $63,450 (see Table 9.1). Little wonder, then, that their views of "respectability," "thrift," and "cultural refinement" dominated local society. Appalachian elites "were in separate and distinct classes," according to the son of a Meigs, Tennessee, large slaveholder. Yet those "Southern gentlemen always recognized *worth* and *merit* under all circumstances, and mingled freely with those who were *respectable* and *honourable*." The acknowledgement of those positive cultural characteristics hinged, of course, upon the extent to which persons of lower status "were of equal intelligence, refinement and education," thereby making such equality an impossible achievement in Southern Appalachia. Culturally, the working classes were stigmatized because "the larger land and slave-owners did not regard manual labor as respectable for a gentleman." A Charleston, West Virginia, minister showed the extent to which elite stereotypes were dominant in the local society when he wrote, "To work with our hands is contrary to the pride of this life and to the customs." Similarly, the wife of a Frederick County, Virginia, small slaveholder lamented that "it almost broke [her] heart" to see her sons "work as hired labourers for other people."[25]

A second tier of "respectable" categories comprised slightly more than one-third of the region's households. These families included middling farm owners and cash renters, government officials, and clergy who averaged $6,600 in assets, followed by small farm owners and shopkeepers who were slightly less literate and had acquired only about half the wealth of the group slightly above them. Having accumulated less than $500 in assets, the next layer of "marginally respectable" Appalachians consisted of those subsistence farm owners and a small slice of landless skilled wage workers (e.g., engineers and teachers). Because they either held land or were educated, these families were "respectable" only so long as they exhibited their commitment to rise in the social scale. Even though they were set apart distinctively from the region's "high culture," these "respectable" fractions emulated the stereotypes, materialistic values, and community agendas of the Appalachian elites.

Southern Appalachia's elite and "respectable" families culturally affirmed the notion that anyone could be economically mobile, even someone from the worst of circumstances, simply "by applying himself." Examination of the responses of 474 Appalachian Civil War veterans provides a unique look at social perceptions of antebellum mobility. Three-quarters of the landed Appalachians were convinced that laborers experienced few difficulties in buying a farm or business. In their denials of any class distinction except that between "hard-working people" and the "shiftless poor," the Appalachian petty bourgeoisie embraced the dominant capitalist myth that laborers could rise from poverty with relative ease and frequency. The hegemonic philosophy of the day was that "discredit must attach itself to those who are unfortunate and poor. A Man, in America, is not despised for being poor in the outset . . . but every year which passes, without adding to his prosperity, is a reproach to his understanding or industry." By using culturally coded affirmations that they helped those who were "respectable" and "deserving," Southern Appalachia's petty capitalists acknowledged that they blamed those labeled as "poor white trash" for their own impoverishment.[26]

The cultural antithesis of the "respectable" classes was the precarious lifestyle endured by the poorest three-fifths of the region's households who averaged less than $100 in accumulated wealth. Although they comprised a majority of the region's resident households, the most culturally degraded group were these landless workers. These families were seven times more likely than landed Appalachians to be lacking in the "cultural capital" that was reflected in literacy and education (Table 9.1). In sharp contrast to the dominant cultural ideology, nine-tenths of the laborers believed there was "no chanc for a poor man" because "the big land owners controlled everything and kept the poor man down." "Respectable" Appalachians constructed social images that reflected the views that were dominant throughout the nineteenth-century western core. People of "low culture" were differentiated by genetic endowment or by the failure to acquire "cultural capital" (i.e., education, attire, speech, social connections, and pursuit of materialist goals).[27]

On the one hand, slavery was rationalized by Appalachian owners as a system that saved these unfree laborers from the destitution and savagery of the African wilds and "civilized" them away from their biological weaknesses. Furthermore, all the "respectable" and poor white Appalachians abhorred "the disreputable rabble," that tiny community segment of free blacks and white paupers. On the other hand, there was a cultural "contempt on the part of thriving nonslaveowners and thrifty slave-owners for the thriftless known as 'poor white trash.'" Wage differentials were justified by Appalachian industrialists on the basis of *ethnic* indicators of innate skill levels and worker malleability, and company-town operators did not hesitate to use force to quell laborer resistance to such cultural derogation. Unskilled and very often illiterate, poor rural laborers were culturally stigmatized as "a distinct and rather despicable class," with whom "respectable" Appalachians "wanted to have as little to do with as possible."[28]

The Appalachian laborer was culturally demeaned "as being no better than a slave and was treated as one." Antebellum commentator Frederick Olmsted summarized this hegemonic class prejudice as he had heard it from a southwestern Virginia slaveholder:

"Our white hands are not, in general, a bit better than the negroes." He employed several white hands and paid them ten dollars a month; and they wanted the same whether they were hired by the year or only for the summer. They didn't care to work for any great length of time without a change. They were very stupid at work, almost as much so as the negroes, and could not be set to do anything that required the least exercise of judgement, unless he stood over them constantly. . . . There was much that was inconvenient and unpleasant in employing whitemen, especially where they were employed with negroes. His white hands were seated with us at the breakfast table; coarse, dirty, silent, embarrassed.[29]

In the view of "respectable" Appalachians, "such white folks brought that opprobrium upon themselves by being too lazy to work and too thriftless to save." Even slaves came to disparage the lowly station of laboring poor Appalachians, who were described this way in one narrative:

> Many of these white people live in wretched cabins, not half so good as the houses which judicious planters provide for their slaves. . . . These people do not occupy the place held in the north by the respectable and useful class of day labourers. . . . The slaves generally believe, that however miserable they may be, in their servile station, it is nevertheless preferable to the degraded existence of these poor white people. . . . If it were possible for any people to occupy a grade in human society below that of the slaves . . . certainly the station would be filled by these white families, who cannot be said to possess anything in the shape of property.[30]

In short, the idealization of wealth and the derogation of "working for a living" unfolded as cultural expressions of peripheral capitalism in Southern Appalachia. Attributions of status served as cultural legitimations of the inequitable division of labor. Moreover, "respectable" Appalachians idealized the *cultural distance* between those who engrossed the region's resources and those who were impoverished.[31]

By directing attention away from "dominant structural realities, such as those associated with . . . resource exploitation or class-based inequalities," culture provides "a convenient mask for other agendas of change and throws a warm glow upon the cold realities of social dislocation." The causes for the inequities are posited in the weaknesses of those at the bottom, not in the exploitation of those who held the resources at the top. Another central feature of this cultural imperialism is its role in hiding inequality from view—under the guise of "the good of the people." Cultural affirmations serve to maintain the prevailing order of inequality through the shaping of beliefs about capitalism's legitimacy and immutability. Consequently, the dominant cultural ideology is integrated into the "way of life" of the poorest classes. The capitalist ideology of progress is so pervasive that the affected peoples do not resist the economic and political activities that exploit them but become "quiescent in the face of inequalities."[32]

On the other hand, "the discourse upon the culture of the Appalachian region" emanated from the dominant society and was manipulated to the benefit of external political and economic interests. Just as Appalachian elites viewed their poorer neighbors with disdain, the planter-elites who controlled southern legislatures labeled their mountain residents as culturally laggard. In an 1853 letter, for example, a western North Carolina elite described his middling neighbors as "mountain boomers and backwoods folks" because they were at odds with the political interests of his Tidewater allies. When Appalachians resisted the dominant agenda for "progress" being advanced within their states, they were disparaged for their backwardness. Internally and externally, a system of cultural ideologies rationalized the inequalities that were evident in peripheries like Southern Appalachia. The concept of a universal set of capitalist values "came to serve as one of the pillars of the world system as it historically evolved. The exaltation of progress, and later of 'modernization,' summarized this set of ideas, which served less as true norms of social action than as status-symbols of obeisance and of participation in the world's upper strata." Absentee speculators and local elites cloaked their economic agendas for the region and their vested interests in the location of internal improvements in symbolism of "social good" and "civilization." This cultural ethos was comprised of four elements: the concept of "common purpose" to downplay social inequalities, the promise that benefits would be attainable through hard work, a prophecy of progress, and a restructuring of traditional relationships with the environment. In the final two sections, we shall examine the mechanisms by which human and natural resources were rearticulated to be compatible with the drives of the capitalist world system.[33]

Labor Articulation with the World Economy

Competition for land operated as a significant historical pressure toward the formation of a low-wage rural labor force. In this way, access to land became a significant mechanism in "anchoring labor relations," for the labor force was subordinated to the dictates of those who engrossed the region's resources and guided its economic development. Throughout the antebellum period, Appalachian land was heavily concentrated in the hands of two layers of monopolizers. In the late eighteenth century, the bottom half of resident households owned less than one percent of the acreage. Thus, nearly three-fifths of the frontier Appalachian households were unpropertied, and there was little accretion in land ownership between 1810 and 1860. In short, landless Appalachians either sold their labor to survive, or their labor was legally contractualized (i.e., slaves and paupers) to surplus producers.

Contrary to popular stereotype, only two-fifths of Southern Appalachian farm owners relied solely on family laborers. The majority of the region's agricultural producers exploited labor through the operation of several free and coerced labor mechanisms. By 1860, nearly two-thirds of the region's agricultural households were semiproletarianized into coerced labor arrangements or into unstable wage employment. On the one hand, farm owners exploited three types of coerced workers: slaves, Cherokee squatters, and indentured paupers. On the other hand, farm owners captured the labor of eight types of wage and nonwage workers from the large population of landless free households. In order to produce surpluses for the world market, these agrarian capitalists centralized, rationalized, and restricted the mobility of this ethnically diverse labor force by organizing their land into multiple uses.

From the frontier years, Appalachian farm owners maximized control over different groups of laborers by organizing their land into symbiotic arrangements. Even small to medium-size farm owners split up their holdings to place tenants adjacent to their own fields. In this way, labor could be more closely controlled and maximized, and slavery and tenancy could be functionally related through the spatial organization of farms. In eighteenth-century East Kentucky, for example, landholders opened the new country by combining the labor of slaves and tenants. One farmer, for instance, produced large grain surpluses by subdividing his large holdings into a small plantation and parcels for "40 Tennants who pa[id] 12 bushels of corn to the acre."[34]

The region's large farms continued such practices until the Civil War. For example, western North Carolinian Thomas Lenoir utilized numerous slaves and tenants, all managed by an overseer. Similarly, the Ferry Hill Plantation of western Maryland was subdivided into quarters and garden patches for twenty-five slaves, tracts for three tenant farmers, a small cropper parcel with a cottage and garden plot, the landholder's buildings and fields, and a ferry. In addition, the planter housed many of his numerous white farm laborers in his nearby townhouses.[35]

A rare archival find illustrates the manner in which Appalachian farm owners systematized land uses. As the antebellum plat map in Figure 9.1 shows, a 1,000-acre East Kentucky farm was subdivided into eighteen tracts. With its direct access to the turnpike and the railroad, this small plantation produced grains, livestock, and tobacco for export. The presence of a tollgate (S) indicates that the farm owner also collected turnpike fees; the parcel nearest the tollgate (D) was utilized by the tollgate keeper, who also grew grains on shares. Adjacent to the owner's "mansion" (A) with three slave dwellings were a woodland tract (B) and the centrally located parcel (F) upon which the farm manager resided. Farther away from the owner's parcel were four small tenant farms with houses (I, L, M, N) and a 100-acre cash-renter parcel (E) with a house and two slave dwellings. Originally, this cash parcel had been the home of relatives who cropped on shares, but it was empty at the time this plat map was drawn. In most instances, the owner specified the crops to be cultivated on each parcel and permitted none of the tenants, except the cash renter, to produce tobacco.

Even though there were no houses on them, five other parcels ranging in size from 16 to 115 acres (D, H, Q, R, K) were leased to sharecroppers and annual-contract laborers who boarded with the owner or with other tenants. Two tiny parcels (O, P) were made available to "cottage tenants" who boarded with the owner or farm manager, supplying their labor in exchange for subsistence and use of the garden plots. Two parcels (C, J) were reserved as pasture and meadow and leased on shares to tenants raising cattle. In fact, a

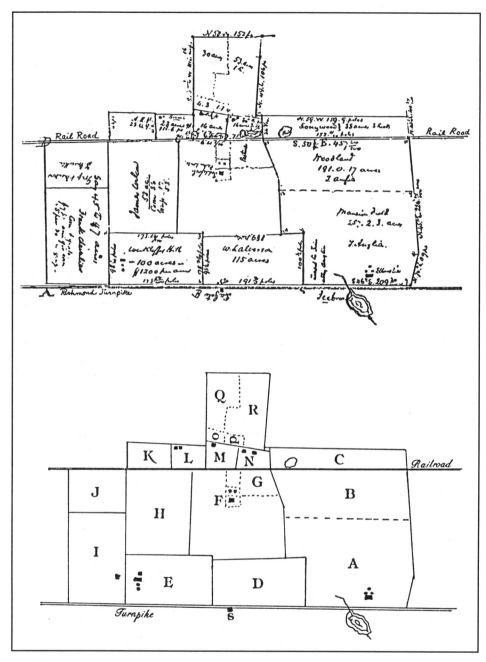

Figure 9.1. Antebellum Subdivision of an East Kentucky Plantation
Source: Ellerslie estate contracts and plat map, 12 June 1857, Wickliffe-Preston Papers, Martha I. King Library, University of Kentucky.

tract near the farm manager (G) consisted of a pasture with an area for loading livestock on trains, evidence of the extent to which this farm was exporting cattle and hogs.[36]

It was common for slaves, white hired hands, and tenants to work the fields together, either under the supervision of the owner or of an overseer. "They all worked together whites and colored." One western North Carolina slave reported that his master "had plenty o' poor white trash help, what wuked fer flour, meal, syrup, en fer anything else he'd give 'em as pay fer dey work." An East Kentucky slave commented that his owner kept six slaves in the fields. Even though he leased out six other slaves, "he hired a lot of help and had white tenants besides the land he worked with slaves." On a western Maryland plantation, slaves and white hired hands worked in small squads under "lead men." Wheat-cradling crews typically consisted of seven laborers, quite often a mix of hired hands, slaves, and tenants. After the wheat was cradled, other crews stored it. At Ferry Hill, for example, one small slave squad loaded and hauled wheat from the field while another small squad of white laborers loaded the grain into the barn. "Bad planned and poorly managed Negroe dictation," the planter commented in his journal at the end of the workday, indicating that the work had been under the supervision of a slave driver. On one East Tennessee plantation, the land owner

> used both slave labor and white sharecroppers. [The] family only bought slaves who had special skills. The first three generations . . . owned slaves who were brickmasons, carpenters, blacksmiths, coopers, tinsmiths, and wheelwrights. They also owned slaves who knew a lot about horses and livestock raising. . . . Usually, [the] slaves handled more specialized chores. Not many slaves were used to work the plantation fields on a routine basis. Most of the actual field preparation, plowing, planting, and crop-tending was done by white croppers and tenants.[37]

This intensive spatial organization of land and labor is made clear in an 1860 description of how the countryside appeared when the holdings of slave-owners were comingled with the rented parcels of poorer tenants. In northern Alabama, Frederick Olmsted reported that the countryside was "well-populated by farmers, living in log huts, while every mile or two, on the more level and fertile land, there [wa]s a larger farm, with ten or twenty negroes at work. A few whites [we]re usually working near them, in the same field, generally plowing while the negroes hoe."[38]

In addition to subdividing land between those sections cultivated by the owner and those utilized by tenants, slaveholders structured the spatial organization of their farms to keep tight controls over their laborers. A Murray County, Georgia, slave commented that the owner's home, weaving shed, kitchen facilities, slave quarters, farm buildings, mill, and tanning yard "made a little town itself." Usually, slave quarters were situated behind the owner's house or in the back, in rows or a circle to make it easier for the owner or overseer to make "de rounds evvy night." Interspersed with other land uses were small lots set aside for the household gardens of workers. For instance, more than one-third of the Appalachian slaves reported that their masters permitted them to cultivate small subsistence garden patches at night or on Saturday afternoons. One Walker County, Alabama, slave recalled that their master erected platforms near the slave cabins upon which a fire was kept "so dey hab light to wuk dey own l'il plot and garden at night."[39]

Debt Peonage as Agrarian Labor Control

While enslavement and physical oppression were the mechanisms utilized to coerce black laborers, *debt peonage* was the land owner's best strategy for controlling free landless laborers. The region's low annual incomes from agricultural labor did not allow "for one day's want of employment of the husband, or one day's sickness of him or his wife!" Consequently, Southern Appalachian legal practices kept antebellum landless farmers, particularly the croppers, dependent upon the owners. State and county laws regulated tenancy, allowing the owner to hold a lien against the tenant's possessions and work time. In their contractual arrangements with landless farm operators, owners exercised their "right to distrain" (i.e., to seize the renter's property for the debt). Typical of this practice were the antebellum tenancy contracts of William Preston, which included the standard clause that "no crops or property shall be sold, or removed from the place, unless with the consent of the landlord: and that he shall have a lien on all crops, cattle, and other property upon the place." Often landlords stretched this legal right one step further to control the tenant's crop-selling process. Jefferson, for instance, required his tenants to agree that "their tobacco shall be delivered at certain warehouses in [his agent's name] so that [Jefferson] may receive the money from the purchaser."[40]

Nineteenth-century laws also permitted landlords to initiate court action for delinquent debts. First, the farm owner secured an "attachment to restrain for rent" from a local court, through proceedings in which the tenant was not heard. Then an arrest warrant was issued to insure that the tenant would "answer the [landlord's] complaint of a plea of debt." Four settlement strategies were legally open to the indebted tenant or laborer: (1) execute a note to the landlord for the indebtedness; (2) sign a labor contract agreeing to work for a specified time period to repay the debt; (3) borrow funds from a third party, with interest, to pay the debt; or (4) dispose of all assets to pay the landlord. Because "a debtor could be arrested, placed in prison and kept there . . . so long as he failed to surrender his estate for the satisfaction of his debts," the sheriff, more often than not, seized and auctioned all the laborer's household possessions or tools. If totally destitute, the tenant was jailed until

State of North Carolina,
COUNTY.

To the Sheriff of the said County, or any one of the Constables thereof or other lawful officer
    WHEREAS

hath complained before me,   one of the Justices of
the Peace, in and for said County, that
is justly indebted to him in the sum of   Dollars and
                      Cents, due the   day of
and delays payment thereof. These are therefore to command you to take the body of
the said   if he be found in said County; and to bring
him before me, or some other Justice of the said County, within thirty days from the date
hereof, (Sunday's accepted,) to answer the said complaint; when and where do you return
how you have executed this WARRANT. Given under my hand and seal, this
day of   in the year of our Lord 18

                                                         J. P.

Antebellum arrest warrant for a delinquent debtor. (Courtesy Duke University
Library)

the family signed a promissory note, agreeing to work for the landlord until
the debts were paid.[41]

An equally effective mechanism for sustaining debt peonage was the landlord's total control over the "running accounts" of tenants and farm workers.
The owner charged for rent on a tenant's house and land, pasturage for
livestock, cash advances, food and household provisions, and damages to
fields or tools. Toward the tenant's indebtedness, the owner credited cash
payments, labor at a daily rate, produce, the wife's manufactures or services,
and the boarding of the owner's hired hands.[42]

Because of the shortage of currency, tenants rarely received money for
labor, services, or produce. In lieu of cash, nineteenth-century farmers signed
handwritten one-year promissory notes. For example, when the Aldie Plantation made its annual settlement with a laborer named Fry, the farm owner
paid him only ten dollars, "giving him [a] due bill for the balance eighty odd
dollars." Tenants handed over these accumulated "due bills" to their landlords, to be credited against their running accounts. It was customary for the
landlord to "discount" such notes of a neighboring farmer by crediting only
90 percent or less of its face value against the tenant's indebtedness. In addition, landlords never credited interest due on such notes, so this amount
accrued to the land owner as extra profit. At "settling up" time, any notes (and
their accumulated interest) left unpaid by adjacent farmers were charged
toward the running indebtedness of the tenant![43]

Landlords held full control over the settling-up process, and they were heartlessly creative in their manipulation of tenant accounts. Most landless heads of household could neither read nor write (Table 9.1), and they had little legal standing in local courts to resist the owner's claims. As the only record of tenant labor, many farm owners followed the practice of signing daily work "chits"—hours worked were recorded on small slips of paper and initialed by the owner or the overseer. To receive full credit for labor, the tenant had to collect these chits for six to twelve months and present them for credit at settling-up time. In addition, some landlords used an ingenious double-entry system; they recorded questionable debits every time labor, cash, or goods were credited to the tenant's account. Landlords inflated charges for food or rent at whim and valued the labor of various workers at whatever rate they pleased. Land taxes, county school expenses, poll taxes, and road fees were also charged to tenants.[44]

Another tactic that kept landless workers indebted was the custom of employers to pay laborer accounts with merchants and then debit these charges against their wages. For instance, Noland's Mill advanced flour to local laborers that was charged, in the name of the worker, to the account of the employer. In East Kentucky, store debts and doctor bills were charged against the monthly wages of a farm laborer. The Ferry Hill Plantation of western Maryland also handled laborer accounts this way. The owner reports in his journal, for example, that "Lewis Fletcher called with a Claim on M. Shellman [one of his hired laborers] which I paid." In fact, the Ferry Hill owner even charged bills from the town washerwoman against the wages of his laborers.[45]

On the other side of the spectrum, farm owners often paid their laborers or tenants in merchant vouchers. Even though the employer had agreed to pay for a subscribed amount of store goods in lieu of wages, local stores often discounted their value. In fact, the store treated these vouchers like instruments of credit. Since customers buying on credit paid a higher cost per item than cash patrons, laborers paid inflated prices for goods, thereby receiving less than full value of their wage vouchers.[46]

Antebellum newspapers commented on the plight of agricultural laborers caused by the credit and debt procedures legitimated by state laws. Speaking to the North Carolina General Assembly, an 1845 politician lamented:

A large portion of the laborers of North Carolina are tenants occupying yearly leases. Under the operation of the present law, as soon as the tenant pitches his crop and prepares his land, a constable comes and levies upon the growing crop, it is sold for a mere song, the creditor gets a few cents in the dollar of his debt; the other creditors are deprived of making their debts. . . . Hard is the lot of these poor men who have large families to support and pay debts besides, with a small portion of what they can raise by their own hands from a barren soil. But how harder does this lot become when even the scanty crop which they force from the sterile old fields of their landlords is taken.[47]

The Emergence of Company Towns

Like their agrarian peers, Appalachian industrialists organized their holdings into spatial arrangements that permitted the maximum exploitation of cheap laborers. What characterized Southern Appalachia's antebellum extractive industries was not their production for small homogeneous rural communities but rather their orientation toward export to distant markets. Consequently, large *enclaves of industrialism* were concentrated into a few subregional "zones of intensive capitalist effort." Concomitant with the region's integration into the worldwide hierarchy, antebellum Southern Appalachia numerous large-scale economic units were constructed. Many of these enterprises triggered the birth of industrial boom towns that later "busted" in the face of global recessions or competition with other supply zones (e.g., Appalachian mining towns after the discovery of California gold). Extractive plantations and company towns centralized huge labor forces, captured at first from among landless Appalachians and slaves. Subsequently, these industrial enclaves turned to the global economy to recruit even cheaper, more skilled miners and artisans, thereby stimulating the contractual importation of European immigrants into the region.

With laborers supplied from such a broad array of ethnic backgrounds, antebellum manufacturers established tight controls by aggregating worker families into communities adjacent to factory or mining sites. In fact, *centralized development* was typical of Southern Appalachia's antebellum manufacturing, extractive, and transportation industries. Because mining, timbering, railroad construction, and canal digging were typically situated in isolated settings, the provision of laborer shelter was essential. Small operations housed laborers in tiny shacks and brought in supplies from distant towns. For example, an East Tennessee Epsom salts company operated out of numerous tent camps erected on the side of steep Mount LeConte. Similarly, makeshift huts for immigrant proletarians sprinkled the countryside around transportation projects. For example, "a great many Irish cabins on each side of the mountains" housed railroad construction workers near Rockfish Gap, Virginia, in the 1850s.[48]

Laborer communities were also established around merchant mills, large factories, mines, and quarries. In order to keep control over its large force of immigrant workers, Halls Rifle Works constructed a compound at Harpers Ferry, West Virginia. This centralization permitted the factory to summon workers at sunrise by sounding a bell. An antebellum traveler surmised that, during the factory's early years, its "tavern, one store, & a warehouse on the Potomac, with a number of dwelling houses, [we]re a handsome monopoly to [one family]." By the 1840s, the rifle works had been expanded to include

The company town at Harpers Ferry, West Virginia. On one side of the river are the railroad and factory buildings, flanked by a canal for barges. On the opposite side of the river are employee houses. (Courtesy Library of Congress)

three warehouses, an office, ten workshops, four machine shops, three annealing houses, five sheds for coal and lime, and nearly two hundred dwellings for laborers. Laborers were provided garden patches, and church services were held in the factory; but there was no school.[49]

Southern Appalachia's antebellum iron industry was structured around two systems of production. The first type was a furnace or forge that operated six months or less by using free laborers during the fall and winter months. Centralized control over capital, natural, and human resources was crucial to profitable operation of antebellum extractive industries. Thus, from the frontier years, the region's economic elites invested in a second type of industrial enclave that operated year round by using a labor force of slaves supervised by free managerial and artisan personnel. This spatial organization was most pronounced in the region's iron industry. "The large consumption of raw materials necessitated that the ironmaster administer a large landholding in order to insure a timely supply of iron ore, charcoal, and limestone. As a consequence, the blast furnaces, especially those linked with a forge and/or rolling mill, were among the largest industrial establishments with respect to capital investment, employment, and size of landholding."[50]

More than two-fifths of the region's iron manufacturers were of the second type—the iron plantation—which spatially organized its centralized labor force to exploit large landholdings. Typical of this strategy were the Etowah Mining and Manufacturing Company, the Tellico Iron Company, the Embree Iron Works, the Lucy Selina, the Oxford Iron Furnace, and the Ice's

Ferry complex, which controlled from 12,000 to 40,000 acres in the Appalachian counties of Georgia, Tennessee, Virginia, and West Virginia. In Botetourt, Wythe, Page, and Shenandoah Counties of Virginia, one-third to one-quarter of the total land area was monopolized by the largest iron plantations; similar patterns of land concentration occurred where these complexes were situated in other zones of the region.[51]

At least fifty-one furnaces and forges in Virginia, forty-three in Tennessee, and sixteen in West Virginia were systematized as industrial plantations. Appalachian Virginia and West Virginia furnaces averaged fourteen free laborers (Table 6.4) and seventy purchased or hired slaves, with unfree laborers comprising three-fourths of the workforce on iron plantations. From the late 1700s, Virginia furnaces advertised for "Sundry Hier'd Negroes for Extra Labour." The Oxford Iron Furnace of Bedford County employed 220 slaves in 1811; the Cumberland (Maryland) Forge utilized 44 in 1796; the Clifton Forge and the Lucy Selina Furnace of Alleghany County used 90 slaves in 1827; the Bath Iron Works employed 70; and the Buffalo Forge of Rockbridge County required 114 slaves in 1840. Slaves were even utilized regularly at smaller operations in Botetourt, Page, and Wythe Counties in Virginia as well as at iron works in Estill County, Kentucky, and at the Monongalia Iron Forge in West Virginia. In other parts of the region, unfree laborers comprised only one-fifth to one-third of the total furnace workforce. Iron plantations in Appalachian Tennessee were the smallest in scope, usually employing an average sixteen free laborers and eight slaves.[52]

In Virginia and West Virginia, Appalachian iron plantations averaged 12,146 acres and sometimes were so extensive that—like the Glenwood Iron Works—they spilled over into other adjacent counties. Typically, these enclaves were large merchant mill complexes. Enterprises like the Marlboro Iron Works or the Monongalia Iron Forge integrated iron and other manufacturing functions with agriculture. In addition, such communities often operated ancillary enterprises, such as a rolling mill, foundry, sawmill, flour mill, grist mill, lime kiln, barrel factory, or distillery. Some ironmasters also processed cloth, leather, or salt and cut cordwood for resale. Besides their industrial facilities, these plantations encompassed warehouses, company stores, laborer housing, and the ironmaster's mansion. In addition, toll roads were often integrated into the spatial organization of the complex. Within the large landholding, there would be several farms, at least one of which was operated for the furnace by a landless farm manager. Secondary to industry in economic importance, agriculture "provided all or part of the furnace community's food and provender, with the degree of involvement in farming depending upon the ironmaster's objectives." At many furnaces, ironworkers supplemented their food supply by planting gardens and tending a few animals on lands allocated to them on a share-tenancy basis.[53]

The largest of these complexes was the Ice's Ferry Iron Works in Monongalia County, West Virginia, which employed 1,700 slave and free laborers at its peak between 1838 and 1848. The firm combined five furnaces, a forge, a refinery, a rolling mill, a nailery, a powder works, blacksmith shops, a tavern, a hotel, a large store, a cooper shop, a firebrick kiln, a flour mill, and wagon shops. In addition, the company developed one of the most complex transportation networks utilized by regional industries. A system of tramways ran back through the mountains, linking mining sites to processing plants. Rails with affixed wooden cross ties were laid on graded roadbeds to permit iron ore, coal, and timber to be hauled in horse-drawn trucks to the blast furnaces.[54]

Situated on 12,000 acres in four northern Georgia counties, Etowah Mining and Manufacturing was probably the second-largest iron plantation in Southern Appalachia. Consisting of a furnace, forge, foundry, rolling mill, flour mill, grist mill, and sawmill, Etowah employed 500 to 600 laborers (one-third of them slaves). Integrated into its spatial organization was an ancillary coal mine in adjacent Dade County and a railroad spur line linking the complex to the coast. In contrast to Virginia enclaves, which averaged only 75 to 250 inhabitants, Etowah was populated, at its peak, by 2,000 to 4,000. More like an industrial town than a plantation, the complex housed laborers in company-owned dormitories and tenements; a combination school-church, a bordello, a post office, and a brewery served Etowah families. Even though farms augmented the food supply and laborers were supplied with garden spots, agriculture played a minor role on this plantation. Instead, this complex placed greater emphasis on retailing imported goods; Etowah's $90,000 annual payroll was disbursed as vouchers credited to laborer accounts at the company store or bank.[55]

Smaller size and less dependence upon slave labor were not the only characteristics that distinguished Tennessee iron plantations from those in Virginia or Georgia. A few operations—like the Embree Iron Works of Sullivan County—integrated as many economic roles as Etowah or Virginia enclaves. However, most Tennessee enterprises were more narrowly specialized, usually engaging in only one or two ancillary functions from among a forge, rolling mill, farm, or grist mill. In this zone, iron manufacturing and agriculture were probably of equal economic significance, for the plantations coordinated work activities and land use to insure seasonal compatibility. "The ironmaster-planter operated the furnace so that (1) iron making would not interfere with [farming] seasons, (2) labor could be shifted to the industry when free from agriculture, (3) iron-ware was manufactured in time to meet the spring and fall needs of the farmer and planter."[56]

Such large complexes centralized slave and free laborers to process grains, lumber, coal, and iron on large plantations. However, a second type of industrial enclave emerged in antebellum Southern Appalachia—company-owned boom towns, which were more dependent upon immigrant and free local laborers. For example, the region's 1830s gold rush triggered the hasty development of a series of villages around the "strike" zones. Almost overnight, boom towns appeared throughout the 150-mile gold belt of northern Georgia. A national newspaper reported in 1831 that Gainesville, "a small village on the border of the gold region," was experiencing "phenomenal growth" around 3,000 workers at two large mining areas where "merchants took in $120,000.00 worth of gold."[57]

After the establishment of the federal mint in 1836, Dahlonega became the regional center for Georgia, Tennessee, and South Carolina gold production. The mint town consisted of one hundred laborer dwellings, eighteen retail shops, twelve law offices, five taverns, and a newspaper—all either leased or operated by the parent company. In Gilmer County, the 1845 Whitepath Mining Camp was a temporary shack and tent camp for 700 laborers who leased gold lots from the company and maintained running accounts at company shops. Similar shantytowns sprang up at two gold camps in northern Alabama. In Appalachian Virginia, log tenements were constructed for workers, and small shantytowns were sprinkled all through the dispersed gold fields in the 1830s.[58]

By far the largest and most tightly controlled antebellum company towns were associated with Southern Appalachia's production of iron, coal, salt, and copper. Integrated workforces of slaves, free residents, and immigrant laborers were common in the region's extractive industries. Around the Kanawha Valley salines in 1818, a town of slum shanties housed 800 to 1,000 slaves and transient white laborers. By 1830, there were twenty dwellings, three stores, two churches, a hotel, a post office, a cooper shop, a barber shop, and a tailor shop. To conserve cash and to gain high profits on retail markups, the salt manufacturers paid wages by issuing weekly store vouchers.[59]

In order to attract immigrant "Mechanics, Miners, Boatmen," coopers, blacksmiths, and other workers to isolated rural areas, West Virginia coal operators constructed small mining villages comprised of coal chutes, railroad spurs, sawmills, mechanical shops, laborer housing, and a company store adjacent to the mine openings. For example, Coal River and Kanawha Mining and Manufacturing built a school and small worker cabins. Even though the board of directors lamented that agriculture "should not be the object of a Coal Company," Coal River Cannel Coal farmed 150 acres, mostly to provide hay and grains for livestock.[60]

Similarly, the large coal mines in Marion, Grundy, and Franklin Counties in Tennessee and the large copper-mining operations in Polk County, Tennessee, and Fannin County, Georgia, established company villages in isolated rural settings. By recruiting immigrant contract laborers and western Carolina artisans, the Ducktown copper mine employed 500 men and boys who resided in a town of forty-two dwellings, a blacksmith shop, and a company store. The nearby Union Consolidated Mining Company operated a boom town comprised of twenty-eight laborer houses, two company stores, a school, a carpenter shop, a blacksmith shop, two ore sheds, the company office, and barns and stables.[61]

Because they required steady and reliable supplies of labor, many Appalachian iron manufactories "colonized [laborers] in cabins erected in rows about the furnace." Northern Georgia's Habersham Iron Works and Nobles Iron Foundry rented boardinghouse rooms or small log cabins to laborers and sold them supplies at company stores. In the Hanging Rock Iron District of East Kentucky, the owners established company villages that typically consisted of fifty to seventy-five cabins, a boardinghouse, a general store, and a school and church. Heavily dependent upon immigrant laborers, these industrial enclaves averaged populations of 386. Laborers were housed in one-story, one-room cabins with rear appendages in which they kept chickens and cows. Managerial personnel resided in much more opulent homes located a short distance from the furnaces.[62]

Thirteen antebellum company towns were established in western Maryland to specialize in iron production. In Allegany County, 900 immigrant laborers occupied 300 company houses; the enclave's population grew to 5,000 by 1853. Maryland and New York Iron and Coal established a village of twenty laborer houses, a school, and a store while Maryland Mining developed a community of 800 people in seventy dwellings at Eckhart. By 1853, Cumberland Coal and Iron had grown into a company town of 152 laborer houses, sixteen large farms, two churches, a school, two stores, and numerous industrial facilities. To accommodate expansions to new mines between 1825 and 1857, these manufacturers laid out eight additional company-owned villages.[63]

Comprised of dwellings for 700 people, a company store, a church, a school, and several industrial buildings, George's Creek Coal and Iron Company controlled its holdings with absolute authority. The company's "Rules of the Lonaconing Residency" empowered its superintendent to regulate the behavior, on and off the job, "of all persons in the service of the company." Laborers were required to work every day except Sundays and Christmas; absences were "punished by abatement from the wages" or by dismissal. The sunrise-to-sunset workday was signaled by "tolling the great bell of the company." Brawling, quarreling, fighting, gaming, and intoxication were forbidden, and the "company expect[ed] all persons in its service to observe an orderly and decorous conduct."[64]

Debt Peonage to Control Industrial Laborers

By permitting employers closer control over the entire lives of laborers, antebellum legal practices restricted the free mobility of workers. The civil rights of nineteenth-century laborers were tightly delimited by legislation and by frequent judicial rulings. Typically, American courts applied the English rule of an "assumed annual hiring," and employers operated under the principle that a contract for labor was "entire." Thus, a worker hired for a stated job or period of time was not legally entitled to be paid for any labor performed until the job or term was completed. Moreover, American courts took the view that, by signing such a long-term contract, the laborer gave to the employer control over all his or her labor for the specified period. Using this principle, employers deducted from annual wages so-called "lost work time" and brought court-enforced judgments to confiscate the laborer's wages from other employment. In short, antebellum laws "expressed the employer's proprietary interest not only in the worker's labor performed under the contract but also in all labor that might be performed by the worker's person, under a different contract."[65]

Moreover, nineteenth-century laws imposed strong constraints upon debtors; the courts punished laborers when they left an employer without settling their unpaid debts. Consequently, workers could not legally leave their employers until they had fully discharged several categories of indebtedness, including transportation costs for their importation into the United States; damages to company tools or property; cash advances made by the employer; and all expenses incurred by the employer in sustaining the daily subsistence of the worker's household (i.e., advances against wages for food, housing, and medical care).[66]

Relying on these legal sanctions, Southern Appalachian manufacturers restricted the mobility of their laborers through the operation of a debt peonage system that was just as confining as antebellum tenant farming. Company towns kept close surveillance over the lives of their laborers. In the gold towns, immigrant diggers earned ten dollars a month in gold dust, from which living expenses were deducted by company stores. At mining and iron complexes, companies paid weekly or monthly wages with script or vouchers redeemable at village stores and shops; laborers rarely saw cash. Consequently, Hanging Rock company stores retailed over $1,290,500 in goods each year, earning a markup profit of 75 to 100 percent. West Virginia's Winifrede Mining and Manufacturing invested $3,208 for laborer's houses but collected back one-third of that amount within a few months. With minimal outlay in buildings and inventory, the Winifrede company store retailed $57,632 in less than a year while the Western Mining and Manufacturing Company's store transacted nearly $15,000 annually in retail sales to workers.[67]

In addition to store purchases, company stores added rent, county poll taxes, and medical expenses to the laborers' running accounts. At George's Creek Coal and Iron, the company superintendent controlled house rental rates and the tenure of leases, requiring "every tenant of the company . . . to preserve neatness and cleanliness about his premises." Monthly settlements were made with laborers; from wages were "deducted the amount of the accounts against [the laborer] at the store, mills, and post office, and his contributions for the doctor and school fund." When the company doctor complained that "the people want[ed] so much medicine that he ha[d] lost money," the company began to withhold fifty cents per month from wages to cover their medical services. The company even controlled laborer voting. On an 1839 election day, "a general permission [wa]s given to voters to absent themselves for that purpose." Company supervisory personnel were "sent with instructions . . . to control the vote of the Lonaconing voters in obedience to the company's interests."[68]

Since merchants were also often the owners of smaller industrial enterprises, local store account books reflect the manner in which the wages of laborers were handled. Each laborer contracted to work for one year; then store accounts were opened for the household. Food and clothing advances were made against wages, either through company-owned stores or through community merchants. Each laborer's account reflected *charges* for boarding, food, salt, clothing, and cash advances for taxes and *credits* for labor or home manufactures sold to the store. Most of the worker accounts ran for several years; very rarely did a laborer receive any remaining cash wages at settling-up time each year. More typically, laborers began the new year indebted to their employers, and sheriff's bonds were issued for the arrest of any laborers who left employment without paying off indebtedness. Such labor-control tactics were the custom of the day, for similar techniques are found in the records of merchants all over the region, beginning during the frontier years and continuing throughout the antebellum period.[69]

Environmental Articulation with the Capitalist World Economy

At the same time that human resources are restructured into units of efficient production, ecological exploitation unfolds as another cultural expression of peripheral capitalism. Land plays a dialectical role in the expansion of capitalism. First, land is stationary *territory* over which wars are fought with the resident peoples to make cultural and political articulation with the world system possible. Conversely, land is also a mobile investment *commodity* from which rents, sales, and brokerage trading in natural resources are utilized to generate market and environmental articulation with the world system. At the same time, land is central to economic growth—the essential "infrastructure," as it were, for development of the agriculture, industry, and commerce that will become interdependent with other structural tiers of the world economy. In order for capitalists to incorporate external arenas into the world economy, those frontiers must pass through a full-circle rearticulation with the structures of the world system. An essential prerequisite for capitalist expansion is the "anchoring of settler property relations," which is accomplished in three historical phases. The land must first be depopulated; then it is contractualized so that it is transformed from a natural resource into a marketable commodity. Finally, the land is resettled and exploited as an essential element of the production process.[70]

The Dialectical Role of Land

Between 1600 and 1860, the capture of territory played a crucial role in the articulation of Southern Appalachia with the capitalist world system. Beginning in the eighteenth century, the commodification of land propelled the incorporation of Southern Appalachia into the capitalist world economy. Half a century before the American Revolution, southern planters and eastern merchant-investors expropriated vast territories of Southern Appalachia from the Native American groups who lived and hunted there. In the econo-cultural rearticulation that followed, new settlers displaced the Tuscaroras, the Shawnees, the Senedos, and the Toteros and forcibly engrossed the ancestral lands of the Cherokee Nation. Once the frontiers had been depopulated of their Native American inhabitants, speculator and settler capitalism expanded into the region.

In addition to the extermination of the politico-cultural resistance of indigenous peoples, capitalist incorporation hinges upon the rearticulation of land tenure into forms that permit individual wealth accumulation and demographic growth. "Evolution of tenurial forms is a hallmark of involvement in the capitalist world-economy, since . . . the commercialization of land [is] a necessary element in the liberation of all factors making possible the endless accumulation of capital." In Southern Appalachia, the commodification of land could not proceed until the feudalistic landholding institutions had been politically restructured into public policies that could make possible private property relations and short-term tenancy. Subsequently, frontier land was contractualized into "paper" capital (grants, bounties, warrants, surveys, deeds) that could be transferred from one owner to another and priced in the market place. In addition, the "rights" of owners of this capital were protected and guaranteed by state policies that were enforced by public sanctions. Once land was transformed into paper capital that could be transferred between buyers and sellers over great distances, capitalistic trading hastened incorporation. In addition, speculative towns became the focal points for external trade connections and the resale of imported goods, thereby pulling the region further into the commodity chains of the capitalist world economy.[71]

Subsequently, heavy speculation in Appalachian land continued throughout the antebellum period. Because states implemented policies favorable to engrossers, absentee investors monopolized three-quarters of the region's land area during the frontier years. Consequently, the regional environment was subordinated to the drives of the capitalist world economy in such a way that more wealth from trading in the region's land resources accumulated in other zones than in Southern Appalachia. In that way, exploitation of Appalachian lands contributed toward the expansion of the world economy at the expense of the region in which those natural resources lay. Moreover, long-term hoarding by absentees slowed the rate at which resources trickled down to cultivators of the soil and transferred decision-making power about the region's environment into the hands of distant speculators.

Agricultural Degradation

Slash and burn, tear down and clear—these are the development techniques that characterized the expansion of global capitalism into new frontiers between the seventeenth and nineteenth centuries. In similar fashion, antebellum engrossers viewed Southern Appalachia's natural resources as commodities to be bought, leased, and sold in the marketplace. Land was acquired because it might produce space for towns, agricultural exports, tourist resorts, or natural resource extraction. The quick return of profits was deemed more crucial to economic progress than was the conservation of plentiful resources. Moreover, the land and its natural assets were defined as *valueless* until they were transformed into new products that were marketable. In the wake of such a consumptive mentality, wasteful agricultural and industrial practices decimated the wildlife, exhausted and polluted soil and water, destroyed the region's virgin forests, and triggered annual flooding and epidemics.[72]

The first natural resources to be depleted were the region's plant and animal wildlife. Well before 1800, hundreds of new plant and animal species had been introduced into the Appalachian countryside, irrevocably altering the regional environment and disrupting the ecological balance. Companies moving to new frontiers "would kill 3, 4, 5, or half a dozen buffaloes, and not take half a horse load from them all." The fur trade and legally mandated bounties for "pests" like red squirrels, foxes and hawks, and cougars and wolves quickly diminished the numbers of many animals in the region. By 1775, bears, panthers, wolves, deer, buffalo, and wildcats were extinct throughout most of Southern Appalachia. In addition, several native herbs like ginseng had been harvested for export to the point of near-extinction by the mid-1800s.[73]

Following a "semisedentary" style of agriculture, the region's larger farmers moved ever westward when lands were wasted by years of tobacco, wheat, or cotton production. The two favored strategies for overcoming depletion of the soil only further degraded the environment. In order to offset diminishing yields, some Appalachian farmers applied more laborers to cultivate more acres. Most, however, abandoned "old fields" and broke "new grounds" from adjacent forests. As early as the eighteenth century, plantation agriculture and tenancy had exhausted the soil in the northern sector of Southern Appalachia. In western Maryland, the ground was never plowed deeper than two or three inches and was rarely manured when growing tobacco. On grain farms, corn was planted the first year, "then wheat for 6 or 7 years without interruption, or as long as the soil [would] bear any."[74]

As early as the 1790s, many Appalachian Virginia lands had been butchered by tobacco and wheat production. An eighteenth-century report on the northern Shenandoah Valley criticized the intensive overcropping of fields. On most of the farms of Fauquier County by 1786, the "earth [wa]s more than halfworn," and Albermarle County was "a scene of desolation that baffle[d] description—farm after farm . . . worn out, washed and gullied, so that scarcely an acre could be found in a place fit for cultivation." As early as 1790, an English traveler observed that throughout much of the upper Shenandoah Valley, areas of good crops were "so intermixed with extensive tracts of waste land, worn out by the culture of tobacco, and which [we]re almost destitute of verdure, that on the whole the country ha[d] the appearance of barrenness." In southwestern Virginia, similar environmental degradation was already evident in the late eighteenth century. One Revolutionary era traveler reported that "On the sides of the mountain, where the ground has been worn out with the culture of tobacco, and the water has been suffered to run in the same channel for a length of time, it is surprising to see the depth of the ravines."[75]

Even those who specialized in grains depleted the land. In the 1830s and 1840s, Appalachian farmers "plant[ed] the land every alternate year in corn, and sow[ed] it in wheat or rye in the autumn of the same year . . . and whilst the corn [wa]s yet standing in the field, so as to get a crop from the same ground every year, without allowing it time to rest or recover, [this practice] exhaust[ed] the finest soil in a few years. . . . Many of these fields ha[d] been abandoned altogether, and [we]re overgrown by cedars." By the 1840s, Charles Dickens reported that, because of such intensive cultivation, much of the farmland around Roanoke was "little better than a sandy desert overgrown with trees."[76]

Land jobber Uria Brown reported that the soil was already "Compleatly worn out" by 1816 in several northwestern West Virginia counties. By the 1830s, West Virginia farmers were cultivating tobacco in the hills where "but two crops [could] be raised on the same ground." As early as 1818, cotton cultivation had "impoverished the land" in most of upcountry South Carolina; the president of the state agricultural society predicted that another few decades of the typical farming methods would transform the Appalachian county into "a desert with deep-washed gullies." This system of "miserable husbandry" had, by the 1820s, also impoverished the soils of East Tennessee, where "manuring for any field-crop [was not] ever practised."[77]

Sparse use of fertilizers, the custom of deep tillage, and "an exhaustive process perpetuated by raising too much corn" had resulted in deep erosion throughout East Tennessee. For example, one large upper East Tennessee farmer claimed that "he ha[d] never once in his sixteen years here let his land lie fallow." By the mid-1800s, much farmland in several counties of western North Carolina had already "washed into gullies as deep as the Shapes of the hills would Admit of." These practices continued throughout the antebellum period; by 1860, northern Alabama followed the same overcropping techniques. There farmers cultivated wheat and corn "for a long series of years on the same ground" without any fertilizer; then they abandoned old fields once they became "intersected by deep red gullies."[78]

Still an even more long-term environmental disaster was wreaked upon the region's virgin forests. Antebellum capitalists devalued the trees as a source of wealth because land could only be incorporated into the economic cycle once the forests no longer stood in the way. In fact, white settlers believed that the presence of forests was a reliable test of the soil's fertility; thus, they disdained to farm in the vast fertile "barrens" of Frederick County, Maryland, parts of East Kentucky, and parts of West Virginia.[79]

Continuing the tradition established in Europe, Southern Appalachian farmers annually burned over woodlands to create pastures. Near Wheeling, West Virginia, an 1819 traveler reported that the air was daily filled with "smoke arising from burning barrens and prairies which are yearly at this time set on fire." In addition, "new grounds" were initially cleared by felling, burning, and girdling trees; then corn, wheat, tobacco, or cotton was planted among hundreds of stumps. Throughout Southern Appalachia, farmers cleared the sides of hills and mountains, creating vast tracts of eroded lands. Near the Peaks of the Otter in Blue Ridge Virginia, for instance, trees were left standing on the top of the mountain, "but the sides were cultivated."[80]

Within a few years after resettlement, the primeval "cane breaks" of the Appalachian countryside were destroyed by the cattle and hogs, and "the meadows encroach[ed] continually upon the forests." By the 1840s and 1850s, massive soil erosion was evident along major livestock trails. In those counties, farms were cultivated intensively to supply grain to drovers, and pastures were overtaxed for the great annual drives. Overgrazing woodlands with great herds of cattle and hogs had wasted the greater portion of western North Carolina timber by the mid-1800s. Similarly, the forests of East Kentucky, middle Tennessee, and the Kanawha Valley of West Virginia had been devastated. "No timber larger than small bushes" remained in much of upper middle Tennessee; the Kanawha Valley was filled with "dismal looking places with bare, unhospitable-looking mountains, from which all the timber ha[d] been cut."[81]

Industrial Degradation

Agriculture was not the only economic activity that abused the environment. Antebellum industries were also villains in the destruction of the Southern Appalachian forests. Tanneries devoured wood and bark, and the iron furnaces incinerated thousands of acres of trees to prepare their charcoal. By 1816, clearing practices had made an "Extensive now Barren" graveyard of thousands of acres in western Maryland and northern West Virginia. "The Aleghany as well as its Surrounding Mountains are ruined & kept poore," reported Uria Brown, "by the raskally practice of seting fire to the same every 2 or 3 years."[82]

To provide the 360 bushels of charcoal necessary for one day's operation of an iron furnace, an acre of virgin oaks and hardwoods was cut. In addition to triggering frequent forest fires, charcoal hearths eroded, sterilized, and stripped the topsoil, creating scattered plots of barren ground throughout iron-producing counties. In the antebellum period, many forests of Appalachian Virginia were clear-cut several times to fuel adjacent iron furnaces. An 1814 salt producer burned up ninety-four acres of trees over the seven-year operation of a small furnace. A larger blast furnace, like the one in Bartow County, Georgia, swallowed the nearby forests voraciously; one hearth could be fired only three or four times from an entire acre of trees. Subsequently, in such areas the huge virgin hardwoods were replaced by scrub oak, cedar, weed trees, vines, and bushes.[83]

In the 1830s, 10,000 acres around Morgantown, West Virginia, were burned over to produce charcoal for the iron furnaces. Similarly, the Hanging Rock iron district of East Kentucky consumed an acre of timber for every 6.7 tons of iron. Thus, by 1850, East Kentucky iron facilities were destroying 3,541 acres of forests each year. In the Smoky Mountains of East Tennessee, "to keep a smelting furnace in operation making about twenty tons of metal per week, require[d] 7,000 to 10,000 acres of common mountain land." Every East Tennessee county near a furnace denuded its virgin forests to fuel iron manufacturing; many forests had already been cut over twice by the Civil War. In the upper Shenandoah Valley, 32,000 acres were repeatedly cut over. Similarly, 18,000 acres of western North Carolina forests disappeared in the wake of iron furnaces. Even in the hills of upper South Carolina in the 1840s, "the whole country," for miles on either side of the iron works, had been "laid waste, presenting as far as the eye c[ould] reach, the most desolate gloomy appearance. The lands having all been bought up by the Company for the sake of fuel."[84]

Antebellum salt furnaces also devoured hundred of acres of virgin trees, left huge gaping holes, and gutted fields "diging for Oar." One salt manufacturer devoured 1,200 bushels of coal daily per furnace, and, by the mid-1800s, there were fifty-two salt producers in West Virginia. In addition to the devastation left from digging coal in open ore banks and underground shafts, salt manufacturing heavily polluted soil, water, and air. The ground near the salt works was galled where escaping brine had killed vegetation, and the process "blackened the air and rendered [it] unpleasant to the lungs and senses."[85]

Even more devastating was the copper mining in East Tennessee and northern Georgia. The roasting process released sulfur dioxide into the air, killing all the vegetation and polluting adjacent streams. Forty-seven square miles of timber were stripped, either by the gas or to fuel the smelting. Adjacent lands became barren, as vegetation did not return to soil corrupted by the poisonous discharges from the furnaces and mines. Thus, two entire counties were engulfed in vast gullies.[86]

Probably the most injurious antebellum industry occurred in Appalachian Georgia, where itinerant gold miners laid waste to thousands of acres of valleys within a few years. Rich coves were segmented by diverted, dirty streams and defiled with thousands of gravel piles and uprooted trees. In Lumpkin County, all the streams had been polluted to a deep yellow and were mutilated by digging. In addition, "large brooks and even an occasional river ha[d] been turned into a new channel and deprived of their original beauty. And, all the hills in the vicinity of Dahlonega [we]re riddled with shafts and tunnels." In his 1847 journal, Feastonhough assessed the extent of the damage: "To obtain a small quantity of gold for the wants of the present generation, the most fertile bottoms are rendered barren for countless generations. . . . By and by, when the gravel in the valleys is all dug out and washed, they will take to the hills, which will be violated and ransacked in a similar manner, and what was once a paradise will become a desert."[87]

In addition to destroying streams, gold mining washed away entire hills in northern Georgia and western North Carolina. Piped as far as twenty miles through elevated canals, water was dumped with great force onto the face of the mountains, tearing to pieces the rock and land on the surface. One large gold-mining company acquired a monopoly on the water of the Chestatee River so that it could utilize hydraulic techniques to mutilate 20,000 acres.[88]

Besides their impact upon the countryside, antebellum industries made Appalachian towns into dangerous environments. Forest destruction, mill dams, canal projects, channeling, and other changes to the region's major rivers triggered frequent flooding. Appalachian towns were also sites of frequent epidemics. Practically every summer between the 1830s and the 1850s, parts of the region were ravaged by cholera carried by the itinerant hog drives. About once every five years, smallpox struck. One antebellum traveler described West Virginia towns along the Ohio River as "without exception, unhealthy" because of "annual visitations of discentary, flux, pleuracy, and various species of intermittent fevers."[89]

Living conditions were inhumanly bad in the industrial boom towns. In Auraria, Georgia, miners rented tiny cabins in which they could not even stand. Trash and dead animals were left to accumulate in the streets and alleys; consequently, the community was scourged repeatedly with epidemics of measles, scarlet fever, and cholera. According to an 1833 letter, exaggerated newspaper accounts had "drawn a multitude of persons" to that area "with the full calculation of getting rich. From the number therefore wanting employment it makes [gold] lots of value very hard to obtain. . . . There is in this village . . . about 1,000 inhabitants. A third of which must starve this summer." Salt laborer Booker T. Washington described living conditions at a

West Virginia boom village. His family resided "in the midst of a cluster of cabins crowded closely together; and as there were no sanitary regulations, the filth about the cabins was often intolerable."[90]

Industrial towns were unhealthy, but they were also unsafe. Mining "dwarfed" the healthy development of child laborers and exposed adult workers to very dangerous working conditions. "There was always the danger of being blown to pieces by a premature explosion of powder, or of being crushed by falling slate." For example, Virginia and West Virginia coal operations depended heavily upon slave laborers who "worked day and night," often in waist-deep water that was drawn off on Sundays "to keep the works below from being flooded." Similarly, the company town at George's Creek, Maryland, averaged one to four laborer accidents daily, ranging from methane inhalation to avalanches to being blown up by dynamite.[91]

In addition to their devastating and wasteful practices, Appalachian industries encroached unabated onto adjacent farm lands. Every Appalachian state enacted legislation granting to antebellum extractive industries special privileges with respect to land use. State laws specified procedures by which entrepreneurs could confiscate the acreage they needed to build roads or railroads, to obtain timber, and to have access to streams. Salt producers enjoyed the "right of eminent domain" to secure wood and to transport brine across the property lines of nearby farmers. Typically, the local sheriff assembled a jury to determine nominal damages when landowners sustained property losses. Moreover, county courts granted legal immunity to iron works seeking to build dams on streams. Farms destroyed by subsequent flooding were simply condemned and sold to the company for less than their undamaged values. In this fashion, for instance, one East Tennessee iron works petitioned the county court to "acquire" 3,000 acres of farmland.[92]

Summary

Typically, world-systems analysts focus upon the mechanisms by which the economy, governance, and labor of an external arena are subordinated to the drives of global capitalism. We have seen that Southern Appalachia was incorporated as a peripheral fringe of the southern plantation economy and of the American Northeast. The advance of settler capitalism into this region unfolded in two historical phases. Initially, the precapitalist mode of production was displaced by the intrusion of the international fur trade. Subsequently, settler capitalists generated agricultural and extractive raw materials for export to distant markets. Political institutions provide the matrix within which a capitalist economy can be built and expanded. In Southern Appalachia, social change occurred in two major historical stages: overcoming indigenous resistance and the creation of new forms of settler governance. The intrusion of the world economy into Southern Appalachia triggered the creation of political structures that facilitated the participation of that zone within the global division of labor. Moreover, counties and local-states engaged in policies and fiscal practices that were aimed at promoting the types of agriculture, commerce, and industry that spurred the local expansion of peripheral capitalism.

In addition to the transformation of economic and political structures, people are reordered into centralized workforces, and their lives reflect their location within the hierarchical division of labor. Initially, the intrusion of the world system into Southern Appalachia stimulated the redefinition of indigenous Cherokees as marketable slaves and later as captors of unfree laborers. As settler capitalism advanced, land served as the mechanism for anchoring labor relations; a large landless semiproletariat was aggregated from several categories of free, coerced, wage, and nonwage workers. To control this ethnically diverse workforce, Appalachian entrepreneurs centralized them into capitalist enclaves (including farms with subdivided land uses, company towns, and industrial plantations) that were designed to maximize the exploitation of cheap laborers. Moreover, debt peonage and public regulation of labor were utilized to restrict laborer mobility and to quell resistance to low wages.

In addition to examining the mechanisms by which the economy, the state, and labor were subordinated to the drives of the capitalist world system, I have focused upon two elements of the incorporation process that are typically overlooked by world-systems analysts. On the one hand, world-systems theory has been criticized for its inadequate consideration of culture. While Wallerstein has begun to direct recent attention to considerations of culture, his focus has been upon the thrust of the world system toward global cultural hegemony and resistance to that ideological dominance. Chase-Dunn virtually dismisses the relevance of culture to the incorporation process: "the capitalist world-economy is integrated more by political-military power and market interdependence," he claims. Typically, the research of world-systems analysts has emphasized the trend toward world cultural integration while ignoring examination of cultural change that occurs when an external arena is captured.[93]

By looking at incorporation from the perspective of the affected zone, we can more closely examine the role of culture in this long process. Within Southern Appalachia, cultural articulation with the capitalist world system unfolded in two historical stages. Through a "civilizational project" that spanned 150 years, the Euro-Americans supplanted the indigenous culture. As the displacement unfolded, a new cultural division of labor was established among those settlers who repopulated the land area. Contrary to popular stereotype, there is no archival evidence for the existence of a "peculiar folk society" within antebellum Southern Appalachia; instead, the area was repeopled by immigrants from several other capitalist zones of the world system. What was more evident than cultural differentiation between Southern

Appalachia and the rest of the United States was the vast internal cultural division of labor. Because the values and agendas of capitalist elites were dominant in local communities, their cultural ideologies legitimated an inequitable division of labor that permitted the engrossment of regional resources by a tiny minority. Wealth accumulation was idealized and "working for a living" was demeaned; moreover, the dominant ideology was that impoverishment resulted because of the faults of the victims, not because of their exploitation at the hands of capitalist elites. In addition, absentee speculators and local elites cloaked their development agendas for the region in symbolism of "social good" and culturally degraded Appalachian opponents for standing in the way of "progress."

Except for limited attention to ecological degradation as a side effect, world-systems analysts have not focused upon the articulation of local environments with global capitalism. It is clear from this investigation of the first western frontier of the United States that environment plays a critical role in the transition to capitalism. There can be no new economy or society without the capture of indigenous lands, without the restructuring of land tenure, or without the contractualization of land into a paper commodity (e.g., deeds) that can be marketed. Moreover, that land and its natural endowments are commodities over which absentee speculators competed to accumulate wealth that spurred the development of other distant regions. Most important, it is the environment that must be exploited to achieve all agricultural and industrial development; thus, capitalist innovators rationalize massive degradation and wasteful disruption of the ecological balance.[94]

It is clear, then, that we should examine the transition from external arena to capitalist zone over the *longue durée*. Moreover, we must not focus the theoretic lens too narrowly upon the integration of institutions. Not only are local structures transformed, but natural and human resources are reallocated. Figure 1.1 provides a visualization of all the elements that should be studied. Beginning in 1700, the local institutions that dominated in Southern Appalachia were articulated with the structural dynamics of the capitalist world system. This long incorporation process entailed a reformulation of the economy, the local state, and the culture. However, social institutions were not the only elements to be irrevocably altered. Once this external arena was absorbed, its natural and human resources were reorganized as factors of production and exploited to maximize outputs for global commodity chains.

10

ECONOMIC CRISIS AND

DEEPENING PERIPHERALIZATION

The Historical Process

By 1840, Southern Appalachia's indigenous peoples had been displaced, and the entire land area had been incorporated into the expanding capitalist frontiers of the United States. However, one constant element in the capitalist world system is "the shifting location of economic activity and consequently of particular geographic zones in the world-system. . . . Alterations in the relative economic strength of localities, regions, and states can be viewed as a sort of upward or downward 'mobility,' . . . a movement measured in relation to other states within the framework of the interstate system." Consequently, Southern Appalachia was, by 1850, losing ground in relation to more recently incorporated zones within the interstate system. After 1840, the terms of trade became more and more disadvantageous for Appalachian exports. Even though world prices for regional export commodities declined after 1840, the volume of imports steadily increased. Overuse and exhaustion of the land contributed to agricultural stagnation and worse living conditions for the region's landless laborers. Even though the region's population increased, its production of food crops declined.[1]

The region's economic dependence on richer zones was cemented, as local elites acted like a *comprador bourgeoisie* to syndicate absentee investment capital for local enterprises. Consequently, the region's resources and nonagricultural enterprises were heavily controlled by absentees, and its commerce was virtually in the hands of foreigners located in distant trade centers. Despite intensified political rivalries with the richer nonmountainous sections of their home states, most Appalachian elites aligned themselves with the planter-merchant aristocracies of their home states. As a result, Appalachians steadily fell behind other Americans in wealth accumulation, in literacy, and in the development of transportation infrastructure.

Deepening Polarization

By 1860, the region's economy had virtually stagnated. In addition to a declining trade position in the global economy, Southern Appalachia experienced a one-sided pattern of development in which capital was primarily invested in land, slaves, and areas of export activity. Expansion of home markets was deterred by the focus on external trade in raw agricultural produce and extractive commodities, an economic orientation that also prevented the emergence of new industrial technology and diversified manufacturing. As a result, local Appalachian economies were "disarticulated" such that agrarian and commercial capitalism remained dominant, without stimulating the level of industrialization that was occurring in other sections of the country and in the European core. All these factors deepened the region's peripheral position within the world economy and exacerbated its polarization from other sections of the United States.

Inequality in Appalachian Communities

Incorporation into the capitalist world system stimulated three structural distortions of local Southern Appalachian economies. First, landed property holders progressively strengthened their dominant position because land and the means of production were heavily concentrated in the hands of a few local elites. During the late 1700s, nearly three-fifths of this region's resident households were unpropertied. Strikingly, Southern Appalachians were 1.7 times more likely to be landless than their counterparts in the northern sector of the Appalachian Mountains. In comparison to New England during this era, resident households were twice as likely to be unpropertied on the Southern Appalachian frontier.[2]

The small minority of Appalachian capitalists accumulated wealth by leasing or selling tracts to settlers, by acting as agents for absentee engrossers, or by holding natural features that were attractive as resorts. Land was the basis for the capital accumulation required for the development of local industry and commerce. Local elites utilized their landed estates to profit from legally mandated towns, toll roads, ferries, railroads, canals, mills, and iron foundries that were operated as publicly subsidized monopolies. Yet land also provided the economic basis for the structuring of polarized local economies in which the wealthy landed gentry amassed a majority of the acreage while more than half the settler households remained landless.[3]

The concentration of regional land resources into a few hands meant that Southern Appalachian farm operators were more likely to be tenants than were their counterparts in the United States as a whole and in the rest of the South. In 1860, for instance, farm operators in the Appalachian counties of Tennessee were 2.1 times more likely to be unpropertied than their counterparts in the western counties of the state. By comparison, there were 1.4

tenant farmers in Southern Appalachia to every landless farm operator in the Midwest. Most striking, however, is the comparison of this peripheral zone with the northeastern core. While two of every five Southern Appalachian farms were cultivated by landless operators, fewer than one of every twenty-five northeastern farms was run by a tenant. In short, Southern Appalachian farm operators were 5.4 times more likely than their core United States peers to be unpropertied.[4]

These landless Appalachians formed the human pool from which the region's agricultural semiproletariat and wage-earning proletariat would be drawn, for the means of production, other than land, were also unevenly distributed. In the region as a whole, only slightly more than half of all free households owned land, cash assets, slaves, retail facilities, artisan shops, professional skills, or manufacturing plants (see Table 10.1). The rest of the free population were selling their labor power to subsist. When the region's Cherokee and slave households are added to the ranks of nonowners, we see that *more than half* of Southern Appalachia's households lacked access to the economic resources that would have permitted them to be land-owning cultivators or "independent commodity producers."

A second structural distortion resulted because the region's influential elites guided development toward economic activities and public infrastructure improvements that would bolster their profits from exports. Out of this mentality there derived an asymmetric manufacturing sector propelled by boom-to-bust cycles of processing of the region's raw materials that were in demand in distant markets. It was no accident that the processing of agricultural surpluses and mineral ores received such attention, for the manufacturing sector was dominated by the region's agrarian and commercial elites. This *comprador bourgeoisie* invested their own wealth and channeled absentee capital into enterprises that strengthened their profit levels through distant trade linkages. Consequently, Southern Appalachia's antebellum regional economy was characterized by a structural distortion toward *tertiary* activities. Retail trade, petty commodity production in small shops, and travel capitalism grew much more rapidly than did the industrial base.

The third structural distortion occurred because employment opportunities expanded much too narrowly to accommodate Southern Appalachia's large landless rural labor force. Since three-fifths of the region's free households neither owned nor rented farmland (Table 3.7), at least one-quarter of Southern Appalachia's households consisted of "historically forgotten" families who were "urbanized" by 1860. In three-quarters of the region's nonindustrializing counties, the nonagricultural labor forces were overwhelmingly engaged in "nonproductive tertiary activities" in towns and villages. As a result, the region's towns masked *hidden unemployment* by absorbing poorer Appalachians into informal commodity production; seasonal or part-time employment in surplus transport to distant markets (e.g., "rivermen"); non-

Table 10.1. Ownership of Means of Production by Southern Appalachians, 1860

A. Free Households Only

Appalachian Counties of	Owners[a]		Laborers[b]		Total No. of Households
	No.	%	No.	%	
Alabama	14,620	57.9	10,644	42.1	25,264
Georgia and South Carolina	11,796	44.9	14,501	55.1	26,297
Kentucky	19,633	64.3	10,881	35.7	30,514
Maryland	9,159	50.0	9,159	50.0	18,318
North Carolina	12,273	54.0	10,476	46.0	22,749
Tennessee	32,031	53.8	27,539	46.2	59,570
Virginia	36,671	58.8	25,724	41.2	62,395
West Virginia	27,569	44.1	34,961	55.9	62,530
Region	163,752	53.2	143,885	46.8	307,637

B. All Free and Unfree Households

Appalachian Counties of	Owners[a]		Laborers[b]		Total No. of Households
	No.	%	No.	%	
Alabama	14,620	51.8	13,584	48.2	28,204
Georgia and South Carolina	11,796	34.8	22,057	65.2	33,853
Kentucky	19,633	59.7	13,233	40.3	32,866
Maryland	9,159	47.7	10,060	52.3	19,219
North Carolina	12,273	47.2	13,740	52.8	26,013
Tennessee	32,031	48.3	34,271	51.7	66,302
Virginia	36,671	44.2	46,300	55.8	82,971
West Virginia	27,569	41.9	38,114	58.1	65,683
Region	163,752	46.1	191,359	53.9	355,111

Source: Calculated by applying ratios derived from enumerator manuscript samples to aggregated data from the published Census of Population.
[a]Proportions of owners derived from sample (N = 3,056) drawn from Census of Population enumerator manuscripts. These proportions were then multiplied by the total number of free households aggregated from the published Census of Population.
[b]All Cherokee and slave households were counted as nonowners.

wage service jobs (e.g., washerwomen, operators of boardinghouses); wage labor in inns, resorts, or hotels; and public transport (e.g., stage drivers, canal and railroad workers). The region's towns and villages virtually teemed with these semiproletarians who survived by pooling several adult incomes from nonagricultural and nonindustrial "odd jobs" and from erratic petty commodity production.[5]

With the gradual diversification away from a totally agrarian society, those

Appalachians who lacked access to economic resources were transformed into a capitalistic labor force. Proletarianization is a contradictory and unstable process in which rural producers are severed from the land and then are pressured into the marketplace to maintain household consumption levels. Once commodity purchasing becomes essential, the rural household must widen its base of wage income. In nineteenth-century America, those who became full-time wage laborers in nonagricultural occupations had first been "stripped of their means of production—freed or deprived, that is, of all alternate ways of supporting themselves."[6]

As in other peripheries of the global economy, there was an inverse relationship between a household's access to the means of production and its integration into the wage labor market. Landless households were three times more likely to be engaged in wage-earning occupations than farm owners. However, the transformation to wage labor was being slowed. On the one hand, the region's nascent manufacturing generated inadequate employment opportunities to absorb the surplus laborers. In recruiting the cheapest, most skilled laborers for their enterprises, the region's manufacturers relied heavily upon slaves and immigrants, bypassing much of the large pool of rural workers in the Appalachian countryside. On the other hand, capitalist labor recruitment strategies were instituted. Complete proletarianization was slowed by mechanisms like debt peonage and legal sanctions that restricted credit and mobility.[7]

Overwhelmingly, Southern Appalachia's mid-nineteenth-century nonagricultural households were employed in small enterprises, as was typical of the entire United States of that era. Two-fifths of the region's nonagricultural households were engaged in manufacturing or extractive production while more than one-quarter of them were involved in commerce and trade or the professions. The wealthiest among them were the region's merchants, bankers, insurance agents, commission merchants, land brokers, lawyers, doctors, part-owners of transportation companies (e.g., railroads or canals), and government officials. Typically, Southern Appalachia's *commercial elites* consisted of individuals who also ranked among the largest planters and farmers in their local communities. At a middling level were those who operated small shops, hotels, taverns, and restaurants and other petty capitalists who populated the region's towns and villages. Centered in the region's towns, most of these households never engaged in agriculture. Through cultural rearticulation with the world system, the region's entrepreneurs sought cheaper labor from distant zones. Consequently, much of the industrial labor force was comprised of immigrant groups—including Cornish, Welsh, Irish, German, and Italian laborers, of indentured laborers, and of black slaves.[8]

Still, at least one-third of the nonagricultural households were not clearly linked in the census manuscripts to an economic sector. Such laborers were part of the landless households that were semiproletarianized. Unemployed three to four months of the year, they worked at whatever was available. Part of the year, such laborers might be employed in unskilled manufacturing or mining jobs. At harvest time, they could hire out as short-term day laborers. The poorest town households hired themselves out as stage drivers, wagoners, mail carriers, boat hands, store clerks, livestock drovers, or common laborers. Part of the time, these common laborers joined the small segment of nonagricultural households that scraped meager existences from activities in the informal economy. Like the rest of the United States in this era, every Southern Appalachian community had its gamblers, prostitutes, bawdy houses, washerwomen, wood choppers, and others who survived by participating in the informal economy.[9]

Political Polarization within Local-States

However, the local interests of Appalachian counties were subordinated to the drives of the capitalist world economy. The planter zones of the Appalachian states became dominant within the state legislatures, and they were relatively secure and resistant to challenges from the contradictory needs of those aspects of community life that were not oriented toward export to the world market. Throughout the latter two decades of the antebellum period, Appalachian counties were polarized within their state governments. Antebellum newspapers lamented, for example, that western North Carolina had "been borne down by the unequal influence of the East." Free public primary schooling was one of the major issues over which Appalachians and their state counterparts battled consistently during the antebellum period. With the exception of western Maryland, which provided widespread schooling for the poor, none of the Appalachian states provided free public education. In their resistance to higher taxation, the planter-controlled legislatures repeatedly voted down bills to create funding for public schools. Since elites paid for their children to be educated at exclusive academies, they refused to be taxed to benefit those great numbers who made up the middling and lower classes. The result of this sectionalism was growing illiteracy in the Appalachian counties. In 1840, white Appalachian adults were 2.2 times more likely than other Americans and 1.5 times more likely than other southerners to be illiterate.[10]

Still, universities and academies received public support because Appalachian elites aligned themselves with the interests of the planters. The class conflict between Appalachian Virginians and eastern Virginians was typical of the controversy throughout the region. West Virginia elites opposed support of public primary schools on the grounds that outsider-teachers would corrupt the youth. An 1856 editorial mirrored the interests of the Tidewater planter class in its warning that "No person [should] be employed to teach and instruct Virginia youths unless he be of the 'Manor born'. . . the influence exerted in the trans-Alleghany by Yankee teachers is entirely too great, and it behooves every true Virginian to correct this evil. No education is better than bad education.[11] While opposing public funding of primary schooling for the majority of West Virginians, Appalachian elites sang the praises of the University of Virginia because it was educating Southern students "with similar thoughts, with like principles, who are united by a common devotion to Southern rights, to Southern institutions, to Southern manners and Southern chivalry. . . . it is uniting the young men of the South together and making them more and more attached to her peculiar institutions.[12]

Ironically, the primary source of state funds for education were the sales of tax-delinquent lands—most of which lay within the Appalachian counties. Even though most of the state educational budget was allocated to support the University of Virginia, less than 10 percent of that school's students came from counties west of the Blue Ridge.[13] An 1841 West Virginia educational conference offered this criticism:

> A splendid university has been endowed accessible only to the sons of the wealthy planters of the eastern part of the state and to the southern states. . . . The resources of the Literary Fund are frittered away in the endowment of an institution whose tendencies are essentially aristocratic and beneficial only to the very rich. . . . The men of small farms are left to their own means for the education of their children. They cannot send them to the University, and they are prohibited, if they would, from joining in the scramble for the annual donation to the poor.[14]

The sectional split over state funding of internal improvements was just as rancorous. Consistently, the state Legislatures funded transportation projects in those counties dominated by the planters, and the Appalachian counties paid a higher proportion of taxes than their share of internal improvements. For instance, Tidewater politicians defeated western North Carolina bids for improved roads from the 1830s onward. "Nature has supplied us with the means of reaching a good market," they objected to the western representatives, "and we will not be taxed for your benefit." Similarly, East Tennesseans saw themselves as "mere supplicants at the gate of the Nashville temple" where the legislature was under the control of the "Middle Tennessee aristocracy." By the late 1830s, the state had subscribed $277,000 for turnpike construction, all in the planter-dominated counties of middle and West Tennessee.[15]

In every Appalachian state, the sectional rivalry over internal improvements resulted in the funding of roads, canals, river channels, and railroads that benefited non-Appalachian counties. Railroad construction in the non-Appalachian counties of these Southern states *surpassed* national averages. However, Appalachian counties received less than one-half mile of track for every mile laid in the planter-dominated areas.[16] By 1860, there were ten miles of railroad for every 10,000 residents in the United States, but railroads were only developing half that fast in Southern Appalachia.

In the half-century between 1810 and 1860, inequality in the ownership of wealth remained relatively constant throughout the rest of the United States. In sharp contrast, there was growing internal polarization between Southern Appalachian elites and the rest of the region's residents. In the early nineteenth century, the top decile of the region's households controlled a little less than three-fifths of the total wealth reported in county tax lists (see Table 10.2). By 1860, the top decile of families were monopolizing nearly three-quarters of the total regional wealth. This pattern of growing inequality characterized every geographical zone of Southern Appalachia, with western Maryland and East Tennessee exhibiting the greatest increases in the proportion of resources engrossed by elites.[17]

In addition, Southern Appalachians were increasingly polarized from the rest of the country. Regional wealth drained away to distant metropoles due to high levels of absentee control over resources and the predominance of external trade activities. Consequently, Southern Appalachians did not accumulate wealth at the level that was characteristic of the country as a whole. By 1860, Southern Appalachia was one of the poorest geographical sections of the United States. Each Appalachian averaged $265 in accumulated wealth other than slaves, but the average American owned nearly twice that level of assets. Moreover, Appalachian households had acquired only three-fifths of the wealth that typified other Southern families.[18]

Residents of the region's most mountainous terrain—in East Kentucky and western North Carolina—owned only one-fifth of the wealth accumulated by a typical American. Appalachians living in hill-plateau terrain and in the Appalachian counties of Alabama, Georgia, Maryland, South Carolina, Tennessee, and West Virginia had acquired only about one-third of the assets typical of other Americans. Even the region's richest residents—those situated in ridge-valley terrain and in the Appalachian counties of Virginia—had accumulated only about one-half to three-quarters of the wealth levels of their counterparts in the rest of the United States. The declining economic status of Southern Appalachians is also evidenced by the proportions of the populations that were impoverished. In 1860, Southern Appalachian households were nearly twice as likely to be poor as families in the country as a whole.[19]

Deepening Economic Crises

Between 1815 and 1850, there was a global contraction in world trade. By the latter part of this downward cycle, the American Northeast had risen to core status in the world system, pulling the plantation South to the semiperipheral level. There are two mechanisms by which a capitalist economy can grow and

Table 10.2. Increased Wealth Inequality, 1810–1860

Appalachian Counties of	% of Total Wealth Owned by Top 10% of Households	
	1790–1810	1860
Alabama	n.a.	74.9
Georgia	n.a.	63.7
Kentucky	56.1	69.8
Maryland	43.7	76.3
North Carolina	53.2	70.1
South Carolina	65.8	76.8
Tennessee	44.7	75.4
Virginia	62.0	76.8
West Virginia	64.9	81.9
Region	56.2	71.6

Sources: Frontier wealth estimates were derived from analysis of the 1790–1810 tax list samples ($N = 10,264$); see Appendix for sampling techniques and methodology. Wealth estimates for 1860 were derived from analysis of sample of households ($N = 3,056$) drawn from the 1860 Census of Population enumerator manuscripts.

expand: reduce costs or eliminate competitors. However, Southern Appalachia held no monopolistic control over production of any of the commodities it exported. Consequently, three factors had, by 1860, eroded the competitive position of Southern Appalachia in the world economy. National and global prices declined for the major agricultural commodities exported from the region. Second, grain and livestock exports became "redundant" in the southern trade centers where they were sold, resulting in lowered prices. Excluding Appalachian production, the South and Southwest generated enough food crops to meet their own internal needs; thus, Appalachian exports were heavily dependent upon the demand for reexports to the industrial Northeast, to distant international plantation economies, and to the European core. As the world system and the United States incorporated new arenas, there were periodic global oversupplies of most of the commodities marketed by Appalachians. Finally, lack of access to railroads weakened the region's trade position after 1845. Because other regions of the United States improved their transportation infrastructure faster than Southern Appalachian counties, the external demand for Appalachian commodities changed. As the railroads advanced more rapidly into the Midwest, Southern Appalachia fell further and further behind in infrastructure to support external trade, and the flow of western livestock and agricultural produce into eastern and southern markets generated competition for Appalachian commodities.[20]

As the European core and the American Northeast shifted to different suppliers, Southern Appalachia entered a long downswing. In the wake of the structural predominance of agrarian and commercial capitalism, the region experienced an agrarian crisis. "Moreover, capitalist forms of agriculture cause the excessive agricultural labor force to be thrown out of employment. In the precapitalist systems, the whole population . . . has the right of access to land, but as capitalist forms develop, this right is lost. An increased proportion of landless peasants, and the driving of ever larger numbers of them right out of production, with the consequent appearance of unemployment, are the results of this process.[21] Because there were insufficient employment opportunities outside agriculture for the increasing population, pressure on the land intensified.

Between 1840 and 1860, agriculture stagnated in Southern Appalachia while agricultural production in the entire United States steadily expanded. In contrast to a 6.2 percent increase nationally, per capita food-crop production declined or stagnated in every geographical sector of Southern Appalachia (see Table 10.3). Concomitantly, there was an increase in the proportion of the region's farms that were "food deficient." During this same period, however, the Appalachian populations were expanding. In western North Carolina, for instance, the population nearly tripled after the 1838 removal of the Cherokees opened new lands to resettlement. During the same two decades, per capita food-crop production fell more than 60 percent in those counties.[22]

Like producers in other nineteenth-century agrarian peripheries, Southern Appalachians reacted to their worsening economic position by withdrawing from distant markets and by turning their attention inward to internal marketing of surplus commodities. In 1860, Appalachians were exporting a smaller proportion of their surplus food crops than they had marketed in distant cities in 1840 (Table 10.3). On the one hand, this agricultural stagnation "represented a shift toward subsistence production, involution if you will, but not a negation of the capitalist mode of production. They represented precisely an intelligent adjustment to market conditions, a way for the capitalist entrepreneurs . . . to optimize profits (or minimize losses) in a weak market—a global reduction of inventory and an overall stagnation in production."[23]

Consequently, economic contraction did not cause Appalachians to abandon production for distant markets. At the same time that per capita food-crop production was declining, Appalachian farmers *deepened* their linkages to global markets in two ways. First, Appalachian elites intensified their efforts to attract absentee investments into local resorts, transportation projects, and extractive industries—economic sectors that were heavily dependent upon external trade. Second, Appalachian farmers shifted greater amounts of their land and labor resources into the production of wheat, tobacco, and cotton,

Table 10.3. Agricultural Stagnation, 1840–1860

Appalachian Counties of	Population[a]	% Increase (Decline), 1840–1860		
		Per Capita Food Crop Production[b]	Exported Grains and Livestock[c]	Per Capita Staples Production[d]
Alabama	110	(26.5)	(4.1)	33.5
Georgia	138	(14.5)	(47.5)	195.4
Kentucky	80	2.9	62.9	0.0
Maryland	31	(16.0)	(40.9)	(17.4)
North Carolina	178	(61.4)	(45.8)	72.5
South Carolina	37	(14.6)	(29.1)	28.4
Tennessee	40	(18.2)	(14.5)	1,153.5
Virginia	29	(25.2)	(41.2)	19.3
West Virginia	51	(44.6)	(78.6)	577.8
Region	54	(33.5)	(28.3)	82.2

Source: Aggregated population and crop data calculated from the published censuses.
[a]Calculated using aggregated county totals from the published 1840 and 1860 Censuses of Population. The Appalachian counties of Alabama, Georgia, and North Carolina show the most dramatic increases because new land frontiers opened there after the 1838 removal of the Cherokees.
[b]County totals for wheat, corn, cattle, and hogs were aggregated from the published 1840 and 1860 censuses, then converted to corn equivalencies. To estimate per capita production, total corn equivalencies were divided by total population; then the proportion of change was calculated.
[c]Based on aggregated county crop and population totals from the published 1840 and 1860 censuses, cliometric techniques were applied to determine the corn equivalencies available for export after allocation of food and whiskey for residents, feed for livestock, future seed reservations, and waste allowances. Then export levels in both years were used to calculate the degree of change.
[d]County totals for tobacco and cotton production were aggregated from the published 1840 and 1860 censuses. To estimate per capita production, pounds of tobacco and cotton were added together, then divided by total population; then the proportion of change was calculated.

even in terrain that would not bear such intensive cultivation. With the exception of East Kentucky and western Maryland, Southern Appalachians nearly doubled their staple crop production between 1840 and 1860. In fact, the Appalachian counties of Georgia, North Carolina, Tennessee, and West Virginia were increasing their tobacco or cotton production at levels that far exceeded the national increase of 39.4 percent over the twenty-year period. Over these two decades, East Tennesseans expanded their staple crop production nearly twelve times while West Virginians increased their 1860 tobacco production to a level that was six times their 1840 output. By shifting away from grains and tobacco, the Appalachian counties of Georgia nearly tripled their 1840 output of cotton. After converting from livestock and grains, western North Carolina farmers almost doubled their output of cotton and tobacco. Even in northern Alabama; Pickens County, South Carolina; and Appalachian Virginia, where decades of staple production had exhausted the soil, farmers expanded their cotton and tobacco production at levels only slightly below the national average.[24]

Dominance of External Trade

Southern Appalachia's regional economy was articulated with the structures of the capitalist world system in two historical stages. First, the precapitalist mode of production was eroded and undermined during the colonial period. On the colonial frontier, the region's indigenous population specialized in the production of furs and wild herbs for the European core. After the Revolutionary War, settler capitalism spread throughout this vast land area. Clearly, antebellum Southern Appalachia had been incorporated and was well into the transition to capitalism as its dominant mode of production. However, the predominance of raw-material exports did not change with the subsequent establishment of new economic activities by Euro-American settlers. By 1860, this large regional economy was generating for export five categories of raw commodities: grains, livestock, staples, semiprocessed products, and unfinished extractive materials. While the conventional view is that preindustrial Southern Appalachia was overwhelmingly agrarian, a different picture emerges when we examine the gross value of the region's export commodities. By 1860, Southern Appalachia was already one of the world economy's "extractive enclaves," for the total value of the region's exported light manufactures and extractive resources exceeded the value of any other single category of exports. Livestock and grains comprised the region's second and third most important exports while staples (tobacco or cotton) generated the smallest segments of the total external trade volume. However, the *combined value* of all three types of agricultural exports did not greatly surpass the value of exports from the manufacturing-extractive sector.[25]

Internally, there was great economic diversity within the region. By 1860, three zones—the Appalachian counties of Maryland, Virginia, and West Virginia—were predominantly exporting manufactured and extractive commodities. Cotton and tobacco comprised the primary export for only one Appalachian zone—northeastern Alabama. In all other sectors of the region, grains or livestock were the most significant exports. Even though Southern Appalachia was not a single-crop economy, there was one common characteristic among its exports at every historical stage during the antebellum period. Overwhelmingly, this periphery exported to the world economy raw materials to fuel the productive systems of other more advanced zones. Even its light manufactures were processed as low-level commodities (e.g., leather and bar iron) to be finished in the manufactories of distant markets or to be utilized in the refinement of other more profitable products. The economic spinoffs and multipliers associated with the export of such raw materials are less than those associated with diversified manufacturing. Consequently, peripheries of the world economy—like Southern Appalachia—experienced slower, more erratic growth.[26]

Moreover, the export of intermediately processed commodities prevented the development of "backward linkages" in the manufacturing sector. By exporting its intermediately processed commodities (like bar iron, leather, wool), this region never developed a crucial economic linkage because it lost much of the derived expansive multiplier effect. In those zones of the world economy receiving Southern Appalachia's transfers, the processing of raw materials stimulated the invention of productive equipment or technology, elements crucial to sustained growth. This dependence upon export of primary commodities "limited the potential spread effects of available forward linkages by transferring processing" to other zones. As a result, the expansion of domestic processing was further deterred by the increased importation of goods that competed with local craft production. Finally, the predominance of raw exports diverted capital investment into the provision of infrastructure geared to facilitate external trade—to the detriment of local needs.[27]

In addition to the capital drain associated with export of raw materials, Southern Appalachia's regional economy was distorted in another way. Core zones are articulated with the world market as integrated systems that have a balance between production for internal and external markets. Core economies deepen capital investments in production for domestic consumption at the same time that they broaden their export activities. In contrast, peripheral capitalism stimulates a one-sided pattern of development in which external trade expands much more rapidly than does internal commerce.[28]

On the one hand, Appalachians chose distant markets for their commodities because "exports offer a higher level of profitability." As a result, much of the town life of Appalachian communities was oriented toward linkages into external trade systems. In exchange for raw produce, Appalachian merchants imported dry goods and luxury consumer items for retailing in local markets. Manufacturing and extractive development were oriented toward processing of commodities for export more often than for local consumption; however, most of the productive technology was imported from outside the region. On the other hand, wealth from those export profits was concentrated into the hands of a minority of the largest owners of the means of production who kept wages low in order to maximize their returns. Low incomes and limited wealth accumulation, in turn, further deterred local demand for Appalachian commodities. Consequently, the dominance of external trade stimulated importation of finished goods (like tools, machinery, shoes, fabrics) that might have been produced locally from the raw materials that were leaving the region. In short, the greater emphasis upon external trade than upon internal markets resulted in a productive structure that was not capable of "generating self-sustained economic development" in Southern Appalachia.[29]

Deterrence of Internal Markets

In the core zones of the modern world system, the capitalist mode of production is based on the historical expansion and deepening of internal markets. At the periphery, on the other hand, the extension of capitalism is motivated from without. Consequently, trade and commerce develop around outward-oriented structures of exchange, and expansion of home markets plays only a secondary role. In nineteenth-century peripheral formations, incorporation into the world system fostered local economies dominated by agrarian capitalists and ancillary commercial capitalists. As a result, local commerce developed around a limited array of economic endeavors that complemented the integration of these elites into global export networks and commodity chains. Thus, local commercial enterprises proliferated much faster than did investments in new manufacturing.

Following this global pattern, Southern Appalachia's towns emerged as the geographical nuclei for exchange between the Appalachian countryside and distant trade centers. As was the case with other peripheral zones of the world system, Southern Appalachia's local commerce was dominated by three complementary and overlapping capitalist factions: agricultural surplus producers, many of whom engaged in multiple speculative pursuits; a local commercial bourgeoisie centralized in the region's towns and comprised of merchants, bankers, manufacturers, professionals, slaveholders, and top government officials; and an "urban" community of petty capitalists that consisted of a kaleidoscope of independent artisans, service trades, and petty commodity producers. Even though one-quarter of the region's population resided in towns and villages, local commerce and internal markets were growing much more slowly in Southern Appalachia than in other parts of the country.[30]

Throughout the antebellum period, Southern Appalachia remained heavily dependent upon externally controlled banks and credit linkages. In the antebellum South, banking was carried on through one of three types of institutions: private ventures chartered by state legislatures as public monopolies; private unincorporated companies that operated banks as minor parts of extensive commercial enterprises; and public banks through which the state sold bonds. Because of their status as public monopolies, antebellum southern banks were powerful economic institutions that received deposits, made loans, and issued paper currency with minimal public scrutiny.[31]

After 1840, little more than one-tenth of the region's counties were served by externally controlled branch banks that were centralized in twenty-four of

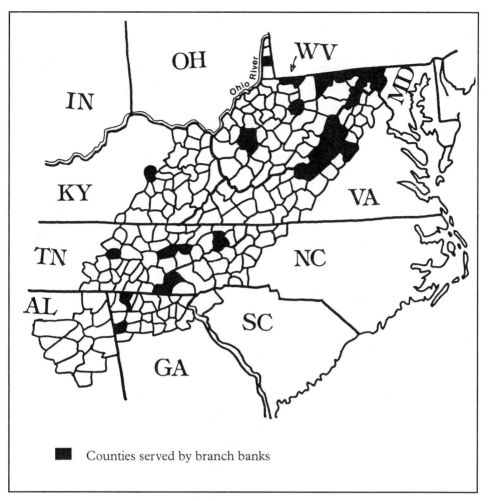

Map 10.1. Absentee-Controlled Banking in Southern Appalachia

the region's larger towns (see Map 10.1). There were no banks in the Appalachian counties of Alabama or South Carolina, and the only bank in western North Carolina did not open until 1859. The number of Tennessee banks declined from twenty-two in 1838 to fourteen in 1846, eliminating facilities at eight smaller Appalachian towns. After the creation of the state-subsidized institution in the early 1830s, banking was concentrated in the western end of the state. After nearly a decade of public complaints, branches of the Bank of Tennessee were finally opened in four Appalachian Tennessee towns.[32]

Controlled out of Louisville, the only East Kentucky bank was located in Madison County. Only three banks served the vast territory of northern Georgia. Similarly, the entire land area of West Virginia was served by Tidewater banks centralized in only five towns. In Appalachian Virginia, branch banks were located in only six of the northern Valley counties, neglecting the entire land area of southwestern Virginia. Only in western Maryland were banking operations relatively decentralized into all three counties.[33]

Throughout Southern Appalachia, scarcities of currency and fluctuations in the money market were triggered by absentee-controlled banks. The region's absentee-controlled banks issued paper notes payable at distant cities. For example, the Bank of East Tennessee issued specie against banks located in the planter-dominated western counties. The stockholders of these distant institutions "frequently inflated the currency, reaped the benefits of the resulting business boom," and then ceased operations. Moreover, "during such periods of depression, the banks transferred their available capital to various commercial cities of the East and then charged their noteholders from three to ten percent premium for exchange. In other words, the banks first depreciated their own papers by refusing to pay it, and then after having depreciated it, they bought it at three to ten percent discount, paying for it with checks on Eastern banks instead of with gold."[34] Prior to 1830, state governments did not penalize these private banks when they failed to redeem their bank notes. Consequently, paper currency was heavily discounted in value, the further the holder might be from the redemption city or the weaker the economic reputation of the issuing institution. For these reasons, it was essential for merchants to rely upon a regularly updated *Counterfeit Detector and Banknote List*.[35]

Discounting of private currency had several negative effects on the region's commerce. First, Appalachians holding paper notes from an unstable, suspended, or failed bank often lost the entire value of the money they had accumulated. Second, farmers or manufacturers who sold their commodities in distant markets experienced economic losses. Paper currency was discounted as much as 12 percent in their local markets. Moreover, Appalachians paid inflated prices for goods in distant cities since western currency was discounted or refused by distant merchants. Third, the market value of Appalachian commodities fell or rose in response to fluctuations in the national and global economies. When there was a moratorium on bank specie payments, prices fell drastically. When new banks proliferated and more currency was printed, market values inflated dangerously.[36]

In general, Appalachians who resided in counties without banks encountered great difficulty when they transacted business using paper money. For instance, residents of early-nineteenth-century West Virginia could not pay their state land taxes because "the treasury at Richmond [Virginia] would not receive their [Pennsylvania bank] paper & the people C[ould] not get money that w[ould] be taken for taxes."[37] An 1840 traveler between Virginia and Kentucky provides this assessment of the difficulties encountered in utilizing antebellum currency across state lines:

Started from Virginia with Virginia money; reached the Ohio River; exchanged $20 Virginia note for shinplasters [privately issued paper notes] and a $5 note of the Bank of West Union . . . reached Tennessee; received a $100 Tennessee note; went back to Kentucky; forced there to exchange the Tennessee note for $88 of Kentucky money; started home with the Kentucky money. In Virginia and Maryland compelled, in order to get along, to deposit five times the amount due, [i.e., to pay five times the priced value in Kentucky currency] and several times detained to be *shaved* at an enormous percent [i.e., forced to sell notes at a discount higher than customary rates]. At Maysville, wanted Virginia money; couldn't get it. At Wheeling exchanged $5 note, Kentucky money, for notes of the Northwestern Bank of Virginia; reached Fredericktown [Maryland]; there neither Virginia nor Kentucky money current; paid a $5 Wheeling note for breakfast and dinner; received in change two $1 notes of some Pennsylvania bank, $1 Baltimore and Ohio Railroad, and balance in Good Intent shinplasters; 100 yards from the tavern door all notes refused except the Baltimore and Ohio Railroad; reached Harpers Ferry; notes of Northwestern Bank in worse repute there than in Maryland; deposited $10 in hands of agent; in this way reached Winchester; detained there two days in getting shaved. Kentucky money at twelve percent, and Northwestern Bank at 10.[38]

Rather than being the institution that kept rural communities isolated and autonomous from the national economy, "country stores" were the intermediaries between the hinterlands and distant markets of the capitalist world economy. In antebellum Southern Appalachia, however, commercial enterprises were emerging in the region at an uneven pace that was only about one-third of that of the rest of the country. By 1840, there was one retail store for every 297 persons in the United States. In Southern Appalachia, however, there was only one retail store for every 618 people. However, this slow level of development was not homogeneous across Southern Appalachia (see Map 10.2). Surprisingly, six of Southern Appalachia's industrializing counties exceeded the rate of development that was occurring in New England, where there was one retail store for every 219 persons. In another fifteen of the region's counties, retail facilities were emerging at a pace that matched or exceeded the national average.[39]

Slightly behind the national pace, three Southern Appalachian counties were developing faster than the Midwest, where there was one store for every 346 persons. Commercialization of the South as a whole was proceeding at a much slower pace, the entire section averaging one store for every 453 people. Fifteen Appalachian counties were behind national averages but ahead of the rest of the South, with an average of one store for every 405 persons. However, four-fifths of the Appalachian counties were developing retail institutions at a level far behind that of the rest of the country and of other American regions.[40]

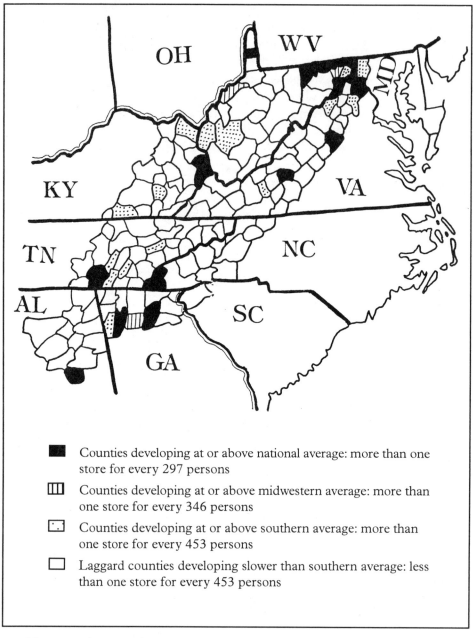

Map 10.2. Commercialization of Southern Appalachia, 1840
Source: Aggregated data from U.S. Census Office, *Compendium of Enumeration*

This slow commercialization was occurring because Southern Appalachia's local commerce was not primarily fueled by enterprises that generated strong home markets. Instead, local merchants accumulated higher profits through the exchange of Appalachian raw materials for distant imports, commodities they then retailed to local customers at high markups. Moreover, since the region's financial institutions were externally oriented and absentee-controlled, this segment of local commerce generated no economic spinoffs for Appalachian communities. More significantly, two of the region's most lucrative "home" markets depended upon access to external customers. Transient livestock drives comprised a major "home" market for surplus grains; yet the stability of this flow of buyers was determined entirely by fluctuations in external market demands and by changes in the transportation technology that linked Appalachian communities to outside networks. Another important segment of local commerce was travel oriented.

Dependence on Travel Capitalism

The region's inns, hotels, and mineral spas drew their profits almost exclusively from those passing through Appalachian counties while the region's stage lines, toll roads, canals, and railroads also drew a significant segment of their livelihood from external customers. Nearly one-half of the region's counties were heavily dependent upon a "tourism industry" that prospered or declined as a direct reflection of business cycles in the Northeast, in the Deep South, and in western Europe—the external markets from which Appalachian communities attracted travelers to their livestock trails or their natural wonders. More than one-third of the Appalachian counties relied on grain sales and inns for itinerant livestock drives while sixty-six of these local economies attracted tourists to their 134 mineral spas (see Map 10.3).[41]

Widely respected periodicals like *De Bow's Review* chastised well-to-do southerners to "cease their annual migrations to the North" where they "squander[ed] millions, which, if retained at home, would [have] give[n] new life to every branch of [southern] domestic employment." Trade journals claimed that the South had "watering places that need but *fashion* to make them equal, if not superior to Saratoga or Cape May, with none of the [political] disadvantages." Rather than traveling to the alien North, southern tourists could find in their own inland mountains "health, pleasure, intellectual pastime, and fashion, when it was vainly imagined they existed only afar off." Besides, reminded the *Southern Literary Messenger*, "the very difficulties of getting there have had the effect of rendering the society more exclusive." Southerners were stoutly informed that the highlands of the southern states contained "some of the wildest and most beautiful scenery that ever inspired a poet; spots sequestered from the busy routine of commercial life, where the spirit m[ight] find repose and revel in a satisfied sense of the grandeur and loveliness of Nature."[42]

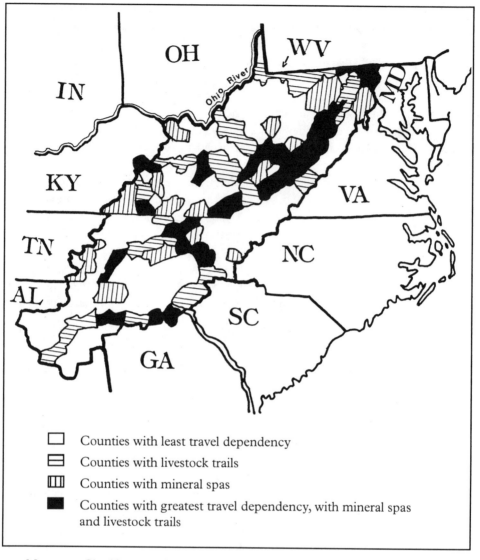

Map 10.3. Significance of Travel Capitalism in Southern Appalachia
Source: Dunaway, "Incorporation," Table 8.5.

Compelled by the sectional "stay-at-home" campaign fomented by the regional press, planter families trekked annually into the southern mountains to avoid the hot, sultry months that bred epidemics of cholera and yellow fever in their more humid home climates. The social season at the Appalachian mineral springs catered to Deep South planters who traveled the same circuit every year, many of whom constructed elaborate absentee homes in the vicin-

A medium-size spa. (Courtesy Library of Contress)

ity of their favorite watering spots. Since "taking the cure" required at least three weeks, spa-goers visited four or five resorts during "the season," a luxury afforded only by the wealthy. Moreover, visits to the mineral springs offered important political opportunities for powerful Deep South planters separated by miles during the rest of the year. At Appalachian summer resorts, wealthy planters and professionals comingled with powerful politicians, "communicating to each other the information they br[ought] from their respective countries."[43]

Widely promoted by regularly published medical endorsements and travel books, many of the Appalachian springs emerged as "celebrated resorts of fashion and abodes of health." Publications by renowned travel critics, like John Moorman, provided information for distant pilgrims wanting to make connections into the mountains. By the late 1840s, tourists could combine road, railroad, steamboat, canal, and stage connections to reach the mountains "with far greater ease, safety and expedition." Travel routes, the medicinal applications for the waters, and the round of entertaining activities were advertised regularly in northeastern and southern newspapers. By the 1830s, a Richmond newspaper foresaw that the "high prices of cotton and tobacco in the South and the superabundant capital in the North, will bring multitudes to the mountains who have never before experienced the incalculable value of these fountains of health." The prediction was accurate; by 1835, the Appalachian resorts were being annually patronized by 10,000 to 15,000 tourists. By 1840, these summer resorts were among the wealthiest commercial enterprises in Southern Appalachia. Moreover, travel capitalism further stimulated landholding by absentees and channeled a disproportionate share of public funds into transportation infrastructure that would link regional livestock trails and resorts to distant trade centers.[44]

Economic growth cannot occur when consumption expands faster than production, as occurred in Southern Appalachia between 1840 and 1860 (Table 10.3). In this circumstance, expensive imports must grow more rapidly than internal production for export, resulting in an even further drain of capital away from the region. Since producers marketed more of their commodities internally at lower prices (Table 10.3), their exports declined and their profit margins narrowed, as did the capital available for reinvestment in commerce, industry, or infrastructure. Because the region's agriculture and manufacturing remained closely linked, agricultural stagnation slowed industrial expansion. On the one hand, local elites accumulated less capital to reinvest in Appalachian enterprises. On the other hand, much of the local manufacturing was centralized in the processing of agricultural commodities for export. Consequently, manufacturing enterprises grew much more slowly than agriculture in good economic times, and industry stagnated when agriculture did. Finally, local food-crop production was not always sufficient to meet the needs of the region's industrializing counties; consequently, Appalachian company towns and industrial enclaves (like West Virginia's salt works or East Kentucky's iron district) imported much of the food for their labor forces from distant cities.

Appalachian manufacturing was concentrated in small and middle-size firms to a much greater extent than was true of the rest of the United States. The region's manufacturing firms averaged only about four laborers while the national average was more than nine workers per manufacturing enterprise. As in other peripheral areas of the world economy, Southern Appalachia's industries developed in an uneven and inequitable pattern that concentrated industry in a few counties, sprinkled most of the counties, and left a few counties only minimally industrialized. While fifty-six of the region's counties were industrialized at levels equivalent to midwestern averages or higher, three-quarters of the Appalachian counties lagged behind midwestern and national averages.

The typical Appalachian firm produced less than one-half of the national average in annual gross output because the region's manufacturing enterprises were established with only seven-tenths of the average fixed-capital investment that typified the rest of the country. The explanation for this pattern of development lay in the "disarticulation" between economic sectors. In the core regions of the world system, capital was allocated to all branches of production, resulting in sectors that were economically "articulated." In 1860, the American Northeast was investing one dollar in manufacturing for every 84 cents put into farms (see Table 10.4). In sharp contrast, investments in peripheral areas of the world system are concentrated in land and in areas of export activity. In Southern Appalachia, local and absentee capital was over-

Table 10.4. Economic Investments by Sector, 1860

U.S. Zone	No. of Dollars Invested in Slaves for Every Dollar Invested in		No. of Dollars Invested in Farms for Every Dollar Invested in Manufacturing and Extractive Firms
	Manufacturing	Farms	
United States	3.73	0.57	6.58
Northeast	n.a.	n.a.	0.84
Appalachian counties of			
Alabama	45.91	2.52	18.22
Georgia	28.36	1.29	22.05
Kentucky	5.70	0.42	13.45
Maryland	0.83	0.17	4.90
North Carolina	34.87	0.86	40.48
South Carolina	37.59	1.11	33.76
Tennessee	6.10	0.51	11.97
Virginia	18.15	0.73	24.90
West Virginia	2.22	0.19	11.88
Southern Appalachia	9.15	0.65	14.11

Sources: Investments in manufacturing and farms aggregated from county totals in the published 1860 Censuses of Manufacturing and Agriculture. U.S. slave values and investments in slaves aggregated from county totals in Lee, "Westward Movement of Cotton Economy," Appendix. Slaves older than 69 were not valued as investments.

whelmingly sunk into agriculture, slaves, travel capitalism, and extractive enclaves—those sectors stimulated by the region's integration into the world market.[45]

Therefore, too little surplus remained for investment in manufacturing and mining. For every 1860 dollar allocated to the region's manufacturing sector, $14.11 was invested in agriculture. As a result, capital was invested in Appalachian farms at a level that was more than twice the national trend. Comparisons with the northeastern core are even more startling. While agricultural and manufacturing investments per capita were relatively equal in the Northeast, per capita investments were made in Appalachian agriculture twelve times more often than they were made in manufacturing. For every dollar invested in northeastern farms, $16.80 was sunk into Southern Appalachia's agricultural sector.

In contrast to northeastern sectors that were growing at a relatively even pace, Southern Appalachia was dominated by agrarian capitalism, and less than 5 percent of regional investments fostered the growth of manufacturing

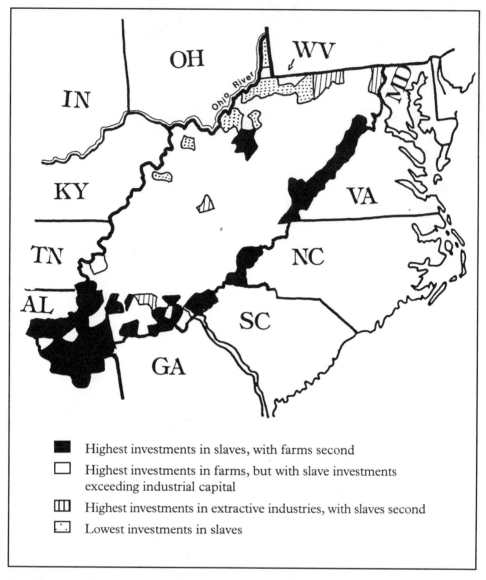

Map 10.4. Investments by Economic Sectors, 1860
Sources: Aggregated county totals from U.S. Census Office, *Agriculture of the United States in 1860* (Washington, D.C.: Government Printing Office, 1864); U.S. Census Office, *Manufactures of the United States in 1860* (Washington, D.C.: Government Printing Office, 1865). Slave investments from Susan P. Lee, "The Westward Movement of the Cotton Economy, 1840–1860" (Ph.D. diss., Columbia University, 1975), Appendix.

Queen of mountain spas: West Virginia's White Sulphur Springs. (From *Harper's Monthly*, August 1855)

and extractive enterprises. Appalachian elites "made wealthy by *comprador* trade in manufactured goods from the center, and in exotic products destined for the center, invest[ed] their profits not in industry, . . . but in the purchase of land. . . . The attraction exerted on capital by land ha[d] the effect of limiting the rate of accumulation. . . . The purchase of land mean[t] a loss for the economy comparable to the hoarding of gold." Three-quarters of the Appalachian counties exhibited the highest concentration of fixed capital in farms; however, regional investments in slaves far surpassed capital allocations to the development of manufacturing.[46]

Thus, Appalachian slavery "present[ed] an obstacle" to the shifting of resources into industry. Even though Southern Appalachia had a much lower incidence of slavery than the rest of the South, investments in unfree laborers had a significant impact upon the development of regional manufacturing. In reality, nearly two-fifths of the region's combined fixed assets were tied up in slaves. In the region as a whole, only 65 cents was sunk into slaves for every dollar invested in farms, but Southern Appalachians sank $9.15 in slaves for every dollar allocated to the development of manufacturing or extractive firms (Table 10.4). Moreover, slaves were the most important investment sector in nearly one-fifth of the region's counties (see Map 10.4). In fact, there were only eleven Appalachian counties in which slaves were the least significant investment sector. As a result of the predominance of agriculture and slavery, there were only four Appalachian counties in which extractive investments exceeded or equaled resource allocations to agriculture and surpassed the capital invested in slaves. The astonishing reality is that Southern Appalachia might have paralleled the American Northeast in its development trajectory if local elites had invested their capital in diversified manufacturing rather than slaves.[47]

Still another distorted investment pattern deterred the development of diversified manufacturing in Southern Appalachia. Absentee speculators and local elites invested heavily in travel capitalism, a sector of local economies entirely dependent upon cyclical trends in the world economy. For every

Table 10.5. Investment Concentration into Travel Capitalism

Appalachian Counties of	Reported Value of Enterprises		
	Manufacturing	Extractive	Mineral Spas
Alabama	523,762	669,318	160,000
Georgia	427,622	546,459	1,185,000
Kentucky	894,725	1,143,372	790,340
Maryland	2,620,521	3,348,775	240,000
North Carolina	180,802	231,048	375,000
South Carolina	—	100,460	—
Tennessee	1,973,023	4,243,952	874,939
Virginia	2,469,338	3,152,578	1,852,812
West Virginia	3,229,686	4,127,229	1,236,000
Region	12,319,479	17,563,191	6,714,091

Sources: Manufacturing and extractive investments aggregated from the published 1860 Census of Manufacturing. Spa investments aggregated from county tax lists, census manuscripts, company archival records, and numerous secondary sources for 134 Appalachian resorts. For a detailed list of these spas by county, see Dunaway, "Incorporation," Table 8.5.

dollar invested in industry, 25 cents was sunk into mineral spas (see Table 10.5). However, these watering places were often the most heavily capitalized enterprises in their home counties. For instance, White Sulphur Springs was worth nearly twice as much as the entire value of all Greenbrier County manufactories. Similarly, Buena Vista, Esculapia, Patton's, and Montvale Springs each were individually worth more than the value of all the manufacturing firms in the four Appalachian counties where they were located. On average, Appalachian spas were valued at $50,105. However, the region's extractive industries averaged only $12,592 in assets, compared with only $2,800 property valuation for manufacturing enterprises. In northern Georgia, $1.22 was sunk into travel capitalism for every dollar invested in industry. Similarly, 91 cents was allocated to western North Carolina's resorts for every dollar put into industry. In East Kentucky, investments in resorts almost equaled the total assets of nonextractive industries. In short, the region's dominant classes and absentee speculators invested "available capital in infrastructure and exchange rather than in industry. Political institutions [we]re largely adapted to control access to natural resources. Neither [wa]s geared to the protection or rational exploitation of the resources on which the economy is based."[48]

Consequently, two structural distortions occurred as peripheral capitalism expanded throughout the region. First, there was a propensity toward the two branches of industry (light manufacturing and extractive) closely associated with the processing of raw materials—types of economic development that do not generate the spinoffs and multipliers required to foster the kind of long-term growth that occurs in the core regions of the capitalist world economy. Second, there was local and absentee focus upon those activities that either produced exports or were geared toward external consumers and travelers. Inadequate funds were targeted toward local manufacturing of the region's raw materials or toward industrial expansion for internal markets. While local elites concentrated their investments in land and slaves, most of the region's resorts, largest manufacturers, and extractive enclaves were owned by absentee capitalists. Thus, the region's largest industries were concentrated in extraction of natural resources because capital was disproportionately invested in those absentee-owned enterprises that were producing gold, iron, salt, copper, lead, lumber, and other profitable exports for the southern semi-periphery, the American Northeast, and international markets.

Exploitation of Southern Appalachia's mineral and natural resources began late in the eighteenth century. Capitalist speculation in Appalachian mineral lands was initiated even before resettlement, and hoarding of the region's natural resources by absentee investors spanned the entire antebellum period. Consequently, extractive industries comprised the region's predominant employer of nonagricultural laborers and accounted for the second most important industrial category in terms of annual gross. In sharp contrast to the rest of the United States, Southern Appalachia's antebellum manufacturing investments were heavily concentrated into low-wage mining, quarrying, smelting, intermediate ore processing, and timbering.

The stunting effects of economic emphasis upon extractive industry are made clear by a comparative look at regional investments. By 1860, Southern Appalachia paralleled the national average in the proportion of its resources allocated to agriculture; however, the region was investing a disproportionate share of its resources in slaves and extractive industries. The Appalachian pattern of development was a glaring contrast to that unfolding in the northeastern core. The predominant northeastern sectors were diversified manufacturing and agriculture, with less than 7 percent of the total fixed capital allocated to extractive industries. For every dollar allocated to extractive enterprises, the Northeast assigned more than seven dollars to diversified manufacturing, thereby absorbing 90 percent of its manufacturing per capita into enterprises that generated the kinds of spinoffs and multipliers essential to sustain economic growth. The Southern Appalachian development trajectory exhibited the opposite trend. More than half of all the manufacturing capital was invested in extractive industries, devouring $1.27 in mining, smelting, quarrying, or timbering for every dollar allocated to light manufacturing. Absent from the Appalachian portfolio were investments in a growth-generating diversified industrial base.[49]

By 1840, another important historical step in the transition to capitalism was occurring in antebellum Southern Appalachia. In the face of shifts toward modern, centralized factories, the region was undergoing "deindustrialization." As a peripheral formation undergoing incorporation into the nineteenth-century world system, Southern Appalachia was handicapped by two economic distortions. In contrast to core sectors, this region had a relative *abundance* of labor but a *scarcity* of local capital. Furthermore, incorporation into the capitalist world economy generated in Southern Appalachia "the destruction of the crafts and the development of agrarian capitalism without accompanying industrialization."[50]

Between 1810 and 1860, Southern Appalachia's manufacturing became much less significant to national economic growth. In 1810, the region was producing $42.40 worth of manufactured goods per capita annually—a level that was nearly twice the national average. By 1860, the situation had reversed itself. Over the fifty-year period, the per capita manufacturing gross generated in the entire country nearly tripled. In contrast, Southern Appalachia's production declined by nearly two-thirds per capita. In 1810, for instance, this region supplied a significant segment of the country's gold and salt and was the nation's most important iron-producing region. However, by 1860, the Appalachian trade position with respect to these commodities had shifted precipitously downward. Although a number of causes were responsible for the decline of Appalachian manufacturing, global competition was the overriding factor. The deindustrialization of Southern Appalachia can be largely explained by the inability of the region's manufacturers to compete for markets.[51]

After 1829, American iron facilities upgraded technology to anthracite, a production system that was more efficient and less costly than the charcoal process that typified Appalachian enterprises. Moreover, Appalachian production was heavily dependent upon slave laborers, who proved to be more costly than immigrant workers. The demise of hundreds of smaller furnaces and bloomeries resulted from lowered federal tariffs on foreign imports and the region's inaccessibility to railroads. By the early 1840s, the American Northeast was being "largely supplied with Russian, Swedish, and English bar iron," and foreign iron could be purchased in the South at a lower cost than Appalachian iron. Consequently, the 195 iron facilities operating in Southern Appalachia in 1840 had dwindled to 142 by 1860, a decline of 27.2 percent during a period when the total number of American iron producers expanded 40.9 percent.[52]

Although the region's gold mines had once held a monopoly on national demand, this industry was also quickly displaced by California and western production. Likewise, the region's coal exports became increasingly redundant over this fifty-year period. The quantity of Appalachian coal that came "more in competition with the foreign coal, also bituminous, was gradually increasing until 1834. As soon, however, as the effects of the Compromise bill of 1832 began to be felt, it lingered for several years without much variation, and then commenced declining annually, and continued to decline up to 1842, while the foreign trade increased in a corresponding, but much greater ratio, up to 1841."[53]

Due to lobbying by southern planters for cheaper salt prices, the federal tariff on foreign salt was cut in half in the 1830s and repealed in the 1840s. In addition, salt manufacturers faced steadily increasing costs to acquire the slave laborers upon whom they were heavily dependent. In the face of competition from European and western producers, Appalachian salt manufacturers faced steady declines in prices and profits. After 1850, the expanding railroad network in the Midwest "brought about a westward shift in slaughtering and packing which allowed Chicago to surpass Cincinnati" as the center of the country's meatpacking industry. With this westward shift of markets, the salt producers of West Virginia, southwest Virginia, and East Kentucky faced dwindling demand from Cincinnati and New Orleans. In addition, the introduction of ice refrigeration to cool packing rooms and refrigerated railroad cars slowed demand for Appalachian salt. By 1854, Southern Appalachia's salines were "a vanishing industry."[54]

Simultaneously, two historical trends occurred in Southern Appalachia. On the one hand, incorporation into the world economy generated the development of manufacturing in a very uneven pattern throughout the region. Investments were made in the region's antebellum manufacturing at a per capita level that was only one-half the national average. In their investments in new manufacturing enterprises, three-quarters of the region's counties fell behind the rest of the South. However, one-quarter of the Southern Appalachian counties were industrializing much more rapidly, some at levels exceeding national averages. Despite this uneven development, capitalist restructuring was evident in the regionwide pressure toward "the creation of large-scale economic units" that could profitably produce commodities for the world market. Large factories were scattered throughout the region, and company towns were structured to centralize and control the labor forces.

On the other hand, the development of industry in Southern Appalachia fell far behind the national average and even slightly behind the southern average. By 1860, nearly three-fifths of all American adult laborers were employed outside agriculture, primarily in industrial occupations. In contrast, little more than two-fifths of Appalachian adult laborers were employed outside agriculture, predominantly in occupations other than industry where they experienced long periods of unemployment and low wages. However, regional development was grossly uneven. In their shift to nonagricultural occupations, the Appalachian counties of Maryland and Virginia exceeded national averages while northern Georgia and West Virginia fell only slightly behind the rest of the country. In sharp contrast, only one of every four adult laborers in the Appalachian counties of Alabama, Kentucky, North Carolina, South Carolina, and Tennessee were employed outside agriculture—at the same time that one of every 1.7 American adult workers earned their living in nonagricultural occupations.[55]

In the face of competition from larger factories and imported commodities, small artisan shops operated by independent producers were disappearing. Moreover, skilled artisans were being absorbed as wage laborers in larger, more centralized capitalist enterprises. By 1860, for example, more than half of the country's flour was being produced in the Mississippi Valley and the Midwest, dramatically increasing market competition with Appalachian millers. As a result, Southern Appalachia's smaller milling artisans were driven out of business. Between 1840 and 1860, there was a considerable decline in the number of Appalachian cooper shops and flour, grist, paper, and saw mills, accompanied by a trend toward larger merchant mills and the centralization of multiple milling functions at urban centers.[56]

As we have seen, the region's antebellum manufacturing enterprises employed smaller labor forces than were characteristic of industries in the rest of the nation. Moreover, the importation of distant commodities, like clothing, machinery, and household goods, ruined Appalachian crafts "without their being replaced by local industrial production." Consequently, the region's crafts were displaced more rapidly than new employment openings were created by new centralized manufacturing enterprises.[57]

Surplus Drains from the Region

Because of the region's environmental and market articulation with the world economy, distant capitalists drained surpluses away from Southern Appalachia, removing the potential for its economic growth. First, expropriation of surplus value from the marketing of Appalachian lands augmented the capital used to finance the distant commerce and industrial advances of other regions, especially the Northeast. Second, the region's towns, resorts, transportation infrastructure, commercial enterprises, and extractive industries were heavily concentrated in the hands of absentee owners who expropriated the profits without reinvesting in the region. More than two-thirds of the region's mineral spas were owned by absentees, and two-fifths of the region's frontier town lots were held by distant speculators.[58]

More significantly, the region's industries were heavily concentrated into the hands of absentee owners (see Table 10.6). Nearly three-fifths of the Appalachian manufacturing and extractive enterprises were fully or partially owned by nonresidents. Nearly nine-tenths of the extractive producers and more than two-thirds of the agricultural processors were absentee controlled.

Table 10.6. Absentee Ownership of Manufacturing and Extractive
Industries, 1860

A. By Type of Commodity Produced

Type of Production	No. in Sample	Absentee-owned Enterprises[a]	
		No.	%
Agricultural processing	123	85	69.1
Extractive	89	77	86.5
Artisan/building trades	66	16	00.0
Tools and hardware manufacturing	41	12	29.3
Household goods manufacturing	25	12	48.0
Textiles manufacturing	23	10	43.5
Leather manufacturing	15	5	33.3
Building materials manufacturing	15	7	46.7
Industrial machinery manufacturing	2	2	100.0
Paper manufacturing	1	1	100.0
Totals	400	227	56.8

B. By Size of Manufacturing Firm

Size of Manufactory	No. in Sample	Absentee-owned Enterprises[a]	
		No.	%
Small firms	53	13	24.5
Medium firms	287	154	53.7
Large firms	60	60	100.0
Totals	400	227	56.8

Source: Derived from analysis of a systematic sample with a random-number start of firms drawn from the 1860 Census of Manufacturing by selecting every fifteenth entry from the enumerator manuscripts. Since it encompasses nearly 7 percent of the region's firms, this sample is large enough to obtain estimates of percentages that are within plus or minus less than five percentage points of actual population values.
[a]The residency of firm owners was checked in the 1860 Census of Population manuscripts; alphabetized listings were utilized at several archives and libraries. In some instances, the residency of owners was identified in secondary sources. Firms were counted as absentee-owned when total or part ownership rested with nonresidents.

Moreover, all the region's large firms were held by nonresidents, encompassing manufacturers in every sector except artisan trades. In fact, locally controlled firms were concentrated among the small artisans, building trades, and those enterprises involving investments of less than $1,000; such firms did not generate the kinds of spinoffs and multipliers essential to generate sustained economic growth.

A fourth cause of surplus drains was the unequal rate of exchange in the international market. Southern Appalachia remained on the under side of the global exchange process because its raw materials were valued too low to offset the prices demanded by the core for its manufactured goods and exotic international imports. Differential wage rates in the center and the periphery are the primary sources of this dilemma. A regional comparison will clarify the point. In 1860 laborers in the northeastern core were earning wages that were 1.3 times greater than those received by Southern Appalachian farmhands or industrial laborers. For example, a northeastern worker could purchase Appalachian flour by investing 26 percent less labor time than the mountain farmhand and industrial laborer invested in the production process. In contrast, an Appalachian would have labored 1.3 hours to purchase a northeastern import that was produced in one hour.[59]

Consequently, differential wage rates—low in Southern Appalachia, high in the northeastern core—rendered high rates of surplus expropriation from the region. The outcome of this uneven and imbalanced hierarchy was an unequal exchange process in which the economy of Southern Appalachia was continually weakened by expansion of the northeastern or European core and the semiperipheral South. Export prices and import values were controlled by the core to maximize the profits that fueled its economic growth. Because the region was economically stagnant, Southern Appalachia fell farther and farther behind every time the prices for its export commodities declined or the costs of its distant imports increased.[60]

External trade effected surplus drains from the region in two other ways. On the one hand, all Appalachian banks were externally owned. Since Appalachian paper money and specie were heavily discounted at the distant financial centers, 10 to 12 percent of potential regional wealth circulated away each year. On the other hand, Appalachians rarely transported their exports directly to the final consumer destinations. Instead, Appalachians marketed their goods at intermediate points to middlemen who forwarded them along the global chain. At the local level, many smaller Appalachian producers penetrated the distant market only indirectly, by selling their export surpluses to merchants, manufacturers, and speculators who propelled the commodities outward. Because of their domination of the region's external trade, commission middlemen captured 10 to 15 percent of the surpluses that might have accrued to the original producers; this wealth was reinvested in the purchase of manufactured goods and exotic imports from the core. An even larger drain of regional capital was effected by speculators who originated from external metropoles. These middlemen bought up regional raw materials at prices far below market, resold them for sizeable profits, and drained away much of the external trade wealth that might have accumulated within Southern Appalachia.

Once we factor in the distribution costs for exporting and importing commodities, we can see that the average Appalachian was at a serious disadvantage. On the one hand, as much as one-quarter of the sales value of export commodities might be absorbed by middlemen, commission merchants, transportation, and specie discounts. On the other hand, Appalachians experienced parallel drains when they imported distant commodities. Due to external transportation surcharges and specie discounting, the market value of imports was inflated as much as 40 percent. To purchase an imported commodity that required one hour of work by a laborer in the northeastern core, an Appalachian industrial laborer was required to work 1.6 hours, but an Appalachian farmhand had to invest 2.9 hours. For these reasons, the mechanisms of unequal exchange caused the Appalachian population to grow poorer, even when they improved their productivity or shifted their exports in reaction to changes in the world economy.[61]

In addition to wealth expropriation caused by land speculation and unequal exchange, capital flight was another source of surplus drain from Southern Appalachia. First, the region's elites poured their savings into luxury imports and into investments outside the region. Second, distant speculators withheld vast tracts of Appalachian land outside the local productive process, in effect "banking the land" somewhere else and keeping it idle. Third, the value added during the manufacturing of Appalachian exports of raw grains, livestock "on the hoof," and raw extractive ores accrued to other regions. Fourth, Appalachians purchased technology advances from the core, including machinery, industrial specialists (e.g., millwrights, ironmasters), livestock breeds, and fertilizer imports. Finally, capital flight occurred through the mechanisms of a number of *disinvestments* made by absentee owners of the region's resources. Most of the time, profits were not reinvested in Appalachian communities. However, when absentees reinvested locally, they developed extractive industries or tourist resorts—enterprises that kept wages low, polluted the environment, and prevented the growth of the internal market. In addition, absentee investors drained away the base for building Appalachian infrastructure and education when they received tax abatements or government subsidization. When they exhausted nonreplenishable resources, absentees permanently weakened the wealth base of the region, carrying the value of that natural capital to the core. Moreover, when absentees degraded the Appalachian environment, the costs for reclamation or for subsequent side effects were passed on to residents, once again draining away the wealth base to benefit external capitalists. Because absentees held disproportionate influence over local politics, they caused disinvestment in another way. By lobbying for transportation networks that favored the development of extractive industries and resorts, absentees absorbed capital away from infrastructure that would have benefited Appalachian residents.

The Deepening Peripheralization
of Southern Appalachia

If Southern Appalachia had remained outside the capitalist world economy, as the conventional wisdom informs us, this region would have been characterized by an agricultural sector that produced for local consumption and a manufacturing sector that specialized in craft production for internal exchange.[62] On the contrary, this peripheral zone was producing much more food than was essential for internal markets; its artisan crafts were rapidly disappearing in the face of centralized factories, and it had already emerged as a low-wage extractive enclave. "Peripheralization of an area means turning the use of local resources—in land, in subsoil resources, and in labor—toward the production of items that maximize the process of overall capital accumulation within the world-economy. This involves not only the production of cash-crops, ores, or transformed products for sale on the world market, but production of the foodstuffs necessary to sustain the work force, and production (or reproduction) of the labor to work in market-oriented production organizations."[63] In reality, Southern Appalachia had been fully incorporated into the capitalist world economy by 1860, and its peripheralized position within the international division of labor was deepening. Increasingly after 1840, local elites and absentee investors channeled capital into the region's mineral resources, into export-oriented industry and transportation systems, and into travel capitalism.

By 1860, Southern Appalachia had experienced a series of "boom and bust" cycles triggered by the dependence of local economies upon the availability of profitable distant markets for their raw materials and upon the flow of external tourists into its mountain resorts. In response to core demand, Appalachians shifted to high production of grains and livestock, and later to tourism, tobacco, and cotton, only to experience a declining trade position when they could not compete successfully for markets with other zones of the world economy. Moreover, local elites "cashed the industrial potential of their territories" by gambling their own wealth accumulation and by syndicating absentee investments into Appalachian minerals for which there was a demand in national and international markets.[64]

Yet Southern Appalachia never completed the transformation to the kind of capitalism that characterized the core. Instead, this region's transition to peripheral capitalism was uneven and made up of phases of temporary growth, followed by sudden blockages to autonomous and self-sustained growth. In short, the process of peripheralization reproduced "the structures that perpetuate peripheral capitalism and block[ed] the emergence of core capitalism." Like other peripheries of the capitalist world system, the antebellum Southern Appalachian economy manifested three structural distortions. First, the region was oriented toward outside markets; its internal markets were atrophied. The region's deepening peripheralization was accompanied by an "increase in the density and connectedness of the networks that link[ed] its units of production to the 'outside' world." At the same time, its local commerce (evidenced by slower development of retail stores and banking) stagnated, except in those large towns that were conduits for external trade and importation.[65]

Second, the integration of Southern Appalachia into the broader world division of labor was marked by the creation of export-oriented production processes that relied upon cheap labor. Deepening of the capitalist process involved the emergence of enterprises that sought to keep production costs cheap by combining several forms of wage and nonwage labor.[66] Exacerbated by the concentration of land that accompanied the unfolding of peripheral capitalism, low wages and long periods of unemployment marginalized the bottom half of the Southern Appalachian population. Lacking any control over the means of production, several categories of free and coerced, wage and nonwage laborers made up a growing landless semiproletariat, many of whom experienced unstable work lives that jeopardized their day-to-day survival. To complicate matters, poor Appalachians lost the class struggle over funding of public schools, and illiteracy escalated throughout the region at a pace that far surpassed the rest of the country.

The region's deepening peripheralization was also evidenced by a third structural distortion. Appalachian local economies were dominated by and dependent upon the core at every historical stage of their development. The type of capitalism that unfolded in Southern Appalachia was characterized by much greater *sectoral unevenness* than was found in the northeastern or European core. Investments were concentrated into those activities that were geared to the export of raw materials and travel capitalism, and those economic sectors could not generate diversified manufacturing or sustained growth.[67] Southern Appalachia's situation was made even more precarious because its production processes were not reoriented toward *direct* linkages with core areas of the world economy. Indirectly, through southern coastal entrepôts, Southern Appalachia supplied foodstuffs and raw materials to provender the urban-industrial centers of the American Northeast and western Europe. Consequently, those intermediate distribution points drained away much of the accumulated value of the region's surplus production. Moreover, areas like Southern Appalachia were only *indirectly* essential to the core as "support zones" for other peripheries or semiperipheries that generated staple crops or precious metals in demand in the core. Simultaneously, then, the economic fate of such zones is inexorably bound to the core and to those other export zones that it supplies. An economic downswing in the global demand for southern cotton, tobacco, or sugar or a decline in demand for the raw materials reexported by southern coastal entrepôts triggered even worse economic reverberations for the peripheral Appalachian fringe.

Because of its dependence on absentee capital and external trade flows, the region tended to lose a steady economic rhythm. The growth rate of the core and of the adjacent plantation South dictated that of the peripheral Appalachian fringe. Thus, antebellum Southern Appalachia was the scene of spurts of rapid growth in one sector while the rest of the economy stagnated. Prosperous in one era because regional exports were essential to the core, the region's agriculture and extractive industries later fell into hopeless decay when the center's interest shifted to different products or to different supply zones. Handicapped by stunted infrastructure and industry, Southern Appalachia was increasingly polarized from the rest of the United States. The basis for its future growth—its land and mineral resources—had been degraded, squandered, or hoarded in response to periodic changes in commodity demand by the core. In short, economic cycles in the world system, not the logic of internal development, were the driving force and the determinant of the direction and pace of regional development on the first western frontier of the antebellum United States.

APPENDIX: ESSAY ON QUANTITATIVE METHODS

Frontier Land and Wealth Patterns

The Basic Methods

Complex and tedious methods are required to research Southern Appalachian land ownership and wealthholding patterns during the frontier period because there is no single source of land records. While deeds comprise the type of public record that is most consistently available, they are of little utility for a project of this scope. Because they are recorded chronologically by parcel and because holdings are not aggregated for each owner, one must scrutinize the deeds over many years to ascertain, with certainty, whether any one owner held land. For this entire period, deeds are recorded in nonalphabetical order in all states, and the availability of name indexes is sporadic. Thus, to aggregate land holdings and transfers for a single name, one would have to check every annual county list of deeds over a period of about twenty-five years. Moreover, antebellum property holders were often slow in filing deeds at distant courthouses. To complicate matters, many other early Southern Appalachian public records have been lost or destroyed. The 1790–1800 census records have been lost entirely for Virginia and Tennessee and partially for other counties in Southern Appalachia.[1]

Consequently, it has been necessary to adapt data collection methods that permit the use of numerous state, county, and national sources from multiple archives. County tax lists offer the best archival source for researching frontier land distribution in a large region like Southern Appalachia. First, the tax manuscripts were roughly alphabetized, and information was collected and recorded for households within designated districts. Second, tax lists permit the aggregation of total landholdings for each owner, a procedure not possible when deeds are utilized. Third, many of these lists are accessible on microfilm or in published form. However, it is not possible to find in existence a complete set of records for any single year for all counties of Southern Appalachia.

It is necessary, therefore, to devise distinct sampling techniques for each state subgrouping of records. In most instances, I drew systematic samples, with random-number starts, by devising distinct methods for each state subarea. Tax lists for five 1800–1801 Kentucky counties, representing three-quarters of the Appalachian land area, were systematically sampled. For Tennessee, all available, complete tax lists between 1790 and 1810 were systematically sampled; these eleven counties embraced about three-fifths of the Appalachian land area. For Virginia and West Virginia, I included in the universe every county for which 1800 tax lists and 1800 land books were available. Thus, tax lists for ten Virginia counties, representing two-thirds of the Appalachian land area, and twelve West Virginia counties, encompassing 90 percent of the Appalachian land area, were systematically sampled. Representing about one-half of the Appalachian land area for western North Carolina, 1800–1815 tax lists for three counties were systematically sampled because they were the only extant legible lists. In two cases, the entire available lists were utilized. For western Maryland, the entire 1804 Washington County tax list was analyzed. Deeds were utilized only in the instance of

Table A.1. Frontier Land Record Sampling: Summary

A. Researching Resident Land Distribution[a]

Appalachian Counties of	Total No. of Households in Land Records	No. of Households Sampled
Georgia	495	495
Kentucky	3,164	1,047
Maryland	2,016	2,016
North Carolina	3,205	1,068
South Carolina	1,379	1,379
Tennessee	7,492	1,022
Virginia	16,018	1,144
West Virginia	9,645	1,052

B. Researching Absentee Ownership: Second Sample Utilized[b]

Appalachian Counties of	Total No. of Households in Land Records	No. of Households Sampled
Georgia	220	220
Kentucky	489	489
South Carolina	312	312
Virginia	10,926	1,360
West Virginia	8,334	1,675
Grand Totals	63,695	13,279

Sources: Manuscript county tax lists.

[a]No Alabama records before 1830. Regional ratios were calculated by weighting based on proportion of land area situated within each state subregion in this era. At the 95 percent confidence interval, the Kentucky, North Carolina, Tennessee, Virginia, and West Virginia samples are large enough to obtain estimates of percentages that are within plus or minus less than three percentage points of actual population values. For frontier maps, see Thorndale and Dollarhide, *Map Guide*. For Georgia, every household in the 1820 Habersham County census was cross-matched with deeds. For Kentucky, a systematic sample with a random-number start from the 1800–1801 tax lists for Knox, Madison, Pulaski, and Wayne Counties, representing three-quarters of the Appalachian land area. For Maryland, all taxpayers included in the 1804 Washington County tax list. For North Carolina, a systematic sample with a random-number start from the Ashe, Burke, and Surry county tax lists for 1800–1815. For South Carolina, all households in the 1790 Pendleton District census were cross-matched with deeds. For Tennessee, a systematic sample with a random-number start from 1790–1810 tax lists for the counties of Anderson, Blount, Carter, Grainger, Hawkins, Jefferson, Knox, Rhea, Sullivan, Washington, and White, representing three-quarters of the Appalachian land area. For Virginia, a systematic sample with a random-number start from the 1800 personal tax lists for the counties of Albermarle, Amherst, Augusta, Bath,

the one South Carolina county where landholders were cross-matched with the 1790 census.[2]

In order to measure absentee land ownership, separate samples were required for the Appalachian counties of Kentucky, Virginia, and West Virginia. Virginia maintained separate tax lists for personal tax and land. To check absenteeism, it was necessary to draw a separate sample from the land books that was then cross-matched with the personal tax lists. Beginning in 1800, the Kentucky Land Office maintained separate records for absentees; nonresidents do not appear on county tax lists. To avoid this complication, the 1792–1793 tax lists for two counties were cross-matched with the 1790 census. As a result, 13,279 frontier households were scrutinized in early county tax manuscripts. Table A.1 provides a summary of the frontier land-record methods and the tax-list sampling completed for frontier households. Since most of the records were organized by districts, a single name might occur more than once in the county. Consequently, a search was made for each selected name in every district of the county to insure that landholdings were aggregated for each owner.

Identifying Residency of Landholders

When utilizing these early tax lists, one must be careful to distinguish residents from absentee landowners. Absentee landholders were isolated through several techniques. First, names could be cross-matched with available census lists or, in the case of Virginia, with personal tax lists. In most Appalachian counties, residents were legally required to pay poll taxes. Households not paying poll taxes were scrutinized for ownership of wealth other than land. Absentee owners were assumed to be those taxpayers who paid no poll tax and who held no property other than land. Third, the tax enumerators sometimes identified landholders as absentees.[3]

Bedford, Botetourt, Fauquier, Franklin, Frederick, and Wythe and from the 1792 list for Russell, representing most of the Appalachian land area. West Virginia did not yet exist as a separate state; however, county records permit an approximation of West Virginia trends. For West Virginia, a systematic sample with a random-number start from the 1800 personal tax lists for the counties of Berkeley, Brooke, Greenbrier, Hampshire, Hardy, Harrison, Kanawha, Monogalia, Monroe, Pendleton, Randolph, and Wood, representing all except one county.

[b]For Maryland, North Carolina, and Tennessee, same sample as Part A above. At the 95 percent confidence interval, all these samples are large enough to obtain estimates of percentages that are within plus or minus less than three percentage points of the actual population value. Regional ratios were calculated by weighting based on proportion of land area situated within each state subregion in this era. For Georgia, all surnames in the Habersham County deeds were cross-matched with the 1820 census. For Kentucky, all taxpayers included in the county tax lists for Madison and Floyd Counties, 1792–93. Absentees not reported on later frontier tax lists, but recorded only at state level. For South Carolina, 1789–92 Pendleton District deeds were cross-matched with the 1790 census, using surnames. For Virginia, a systematic sample with a random-number start from the land books of the counties listed above; names of land owners were then cross-checked against the personal tax lists of the same year. For West Virginia, a systematic sample with a random-number start from the land books of the counties listed above; names of land owners were then cross-checked against the personal tax lists of the same year.

Several problems emerge when one attempts to determine taxpayer residency by cross-matching lists. First, the early censuses provide only the names of heads of household. However, the tax lists might reflect land for other family members. In the case of deceased male heads of household, the land might be listed in the name of the wife or several children. If land were deeded by a father to an unmarried son, the child's name would not appear on the census list. Therefore, when checking residency, I assumed that landowners were residents when they had a surname that recurred in the county census list. This is somewhat problematic since it denies the possibility of migration by segments of the same family or the inheritance of estates by nonresident children. Given the nature of this project's exploration of absentee holdings, however, I felt it essential to follow methods that might tend to overcount the residents rather than the nonresidents.

Controlling for Landless Kin of Owners

Nineteenth-century county tax lists collected information about the populace by situating the description of taxpayers into specific dwellings and districts. Enumerators proceeded geographically from one dwelling to the next, listing each household in the order in which they were encountered. When studying the extent of landlessness, however, these lists pose a peculiar difficulty. Because of the legal requirement that all males older than twenty-one years of age pay a poll tax, the tax assessors sometimes enumerated unmarried sons or other related males as a separate entry from the household in which they actually resided.

To avoid an undercount of owners, I scrutinized carefully each sampled landless household. The enumeration order aids the identification of landless kin of owners since these persons are typically listed immediately before or after the landowner. When using published lists, I had the benefit of genealogical footnotes to link such persons to the correct households. When such landless kin were selected in the sampling process, I aggregated these persons with the rest of the appropriate owner household in which they actually dwelled.[4]

Mid-Nineteenth-Century Patterns of Land, Occupation, and Wealth

Samples from 1860 Census Manuscripts

Because they provide extensive detail about land ownership, wealth accumulation, occupations, and agricultural production, the 1860 census enumerator manuscripts are the best primary source for antebellum information on all Southern Appalachian counties. In order to analyze patterns of land ownership, occupation, and wealthholding among all regional households, I drew one systematic sample of 3,056 households from Schedule I (Population) of the manuscripts by selecting every hundredth entry. As Table A.2 demonstrates, the derived household sample is closely representative of the region's population distribution into state and terrain subareas. In addition, this sample represents nearly one percent of all the region's households in 1860.

In order to analyze household characteristics and production patterns among the region's farms, I drew a second systematic sample with a random-number start of 3,447 farms from Schedule IV (Agriculture). To insure that the sample included enough farms to permit subregional comparisons, I selected 333 farms for Alabama by drawing every twenty-fifth farm, 301 farms for Georgia (every seventeenth farm), 344 farms for Kentucky (every seventh mountain farm and every twenty-third hill-plateau farm), 302 farms for Maryland (every twelfth farm), 302 farms for North Carolina (every twenty-first farm), 325 farms for South Carolina (every fourth farm), 514

Table A.2. 1860 Census Manuscript Sampling: All Households

A. Distribution by States

Appalachian Counties of	Total Households		Sample Households	
	No.	%	No.	%
Alabama	25,264	8.2	254	8.3
Georgia	23,345	7.6	235	7.7
Kentucky	30,514	9.9	286	9.4
Maryland	18,318	6.0	182	6.0
North Carolina	22,749	7.4	228	7.5
South Carolina	2,952	0.9	30	0.9
Tennessee	59,570	19.4	597	19.5
Virginia	62,395	20.3	618	20.2
West Virginia	62,530	20.3	626	20.5
Region	307,637	100.0	3,056	100.0

B. Distribution by Terrain Type

Terrain Type	Total Households		Sample Households	
	No.	%	No.	%
Mountainous	57,059	18.6	572	18.7
Hill-Plateau	148,072	48.1	1,478	48.4
Ridge-Valley	102,506	33.3	1,006	32.9
Totals	307,637	100.0	3,056	100.0

Sources: Sample drawn from the 1860 Census of Population manuscripts. Total households aggregated from the Appalachian county totals in the published 1860 Census of Population. At the 95 percent confidence interval, this sample is large enough to obtain an estimate of a percentage that is within less than three percentage points of the actual population value. Terrain distinctions are mapped and described in *Appalachia*, pp. 9–11.

farms for Tennessee (every twenty-eighth farm), 517 farms for Virginia (every twenty-fifth farm), and 509 farms for West Virginia (every twenty-fourth farm). To calculate cumulative farm statistics for state or terrain subregions or for the region as a whole, I weighted each geographical category according to the actual proportion of total farms (aggregated from published county census data) located in each subregion (see Table A.3). This sample represents nearly 3 percent of all Southern Appalachian farms; therefore, it is closely representative of the region's farm distribution by state and terrain subareas.[5]

Methods for Identifying Landless Farmers

Because the 1860 census did not ask heads of household if they owned land, farm owners are not directly distinguishable from landless farmers. Consequently, it is necessary to determine land ownership by comparing several elements of information collected for each household on Schedules I and IV. To determine whether a particular farm operator owned land, it is necessary to cross-match farm sample names from

Table A.3. 1860 Census Manuscript Sampling: Farm Households

A. Distribution by States

Appalachian Counties of	Total Farms		Sample Farms	
	No.	Proportion	No.	Proportion
Alabama	13,552	.0940	333	.0966
Georgia	11,145	.0773	301	.0873
Kentucky	17,631	.1223	344	.0998
Maryland	4,659	.0323	302	.0876
North Carolina	12,232	.0849	302	.0876
South Carolina	1,301	.0091	325	.0943
Tennessee	28,026	.1945	514	.1491
Virginia	27,139	.1883	517	.1500
West Virginia	28,430	.1973	509	.1477
Region	144,115	1.0000	3,447	1.0000

B. Distribution by Terrain Type

Predominant Terrain Type	Total Farms		Sample Farms	
	No.	Proportion	No.	Proportion
Mountainous	29,997	.2081	602	.1746
Hill-Plateau	68,886	.4780	1,823	.5289
Ridge-Valley	45,232	.3139	1,022	.2965
Region	144,115	1.0000	3,447	1.0000

Sources: Sample drawn from the 1860 Census of Agriculture manuscripts. Total farms aggregated from the published Census of Agriculture. When calculating cumulative statistics for the region as a whole or for state or terrain subregions, I weighted each geographical subregion according to its actual proportionate share of farms or of farm land. At the 95 percent confidence interval, this sample is large enough to obtain an estimate of a percentage that is within less than three percentage points of the actual population value. Terrain distinctions are mapped and described in *Appalachia*, pp. 9–11.

Schedule IV with household names in Schedule I. Schedule IV contains all farm operators, reporting acres of improved land, acres of unimproved land, cash value of farm, value of farming implements, number and value of livestock, and quantity of agricultural commodities produced. In addition to several other categories of information, Schedule I reports for each household the "value of real estate owned."

Several conventional techniques utilized by 1860 census enumerators provide us with clues about land ownership. First, since "value of real estate" was reported on Schedule I, any farmer listed on that schedule without real property was landless. Enumerators frequently labeled landless farmers, using terms like "tenant," "renter," "cropper," or "farm laborer." In several Southern Appalachian states, enumerators omitted acreage, value of farm implements, and farm value for tenants.[6]

The 1860 census collected information about the populace by situating the description of residents into specific dwellings and districts. Enumerators proceeded geographically from one structure to the next, thereby treating "households" and residents of physical "dwellings" as synonymous entities. Because of this procedure, an extended family residing in separate dwellings upon the same farm were enumerated as distinct, unrelated households. The value of the farm and of real estate were designated for one dwelling while the other households were identified as owning no real estate. As a result, the children, parents, or other relatives who supplied labor on a family farm might appear in the census as landless. To avoid an undercount of owners, I scrutinized carefully each selected landless household. The enumeration order facilitates the identification of landless kin of owners since these households are typically enumerated immediately before or after the owners. When a selected landless household appeared to be part of an extended family residing in separate dwellings on a family farm, I aggregated characteristics for all pertinent households, treating them as a single "owner" household.

The enumeration order is studied carefully to identify extended families. Landless kin whose names appear at a great distance from the owners (often in a different district) in the enumeration order are counted as nonowners. In those instances, the enumeration order seems to indicate they were residing in a dwelling located on nonfamily land and at a great geographical distance from the relatives. In short, these persons were providing their labor to a farm on nonfamily land, and they were operating as households independent from their kin.

Measuring Subsistence and Surplus Production

Estimating Farm Production and Consumption

The Census of Agriculture manuscripts provide rich quantitative details that permit close assessment of production and consumption levels by Appalachian farm households. In order to compare farm production levels, it is first necessary to find a way to standardize the varied crops and livestock into a single measure. The following methods were applied to permit the estimation of production and consumption at two levels: for individual farms and for entire counties. Earlier studies have devised methods for converting food crops and meat sources into their equivalent nutritional value in corn. Major food crops and livestock were converted into corn equivalencies, using nutritional-value ratios. Overall, Southern farmers produced insignificant amounts of peas, beans, oats, rye, barley, buckwheat, and hay. In contrast, many Southern Appalachian counties cultivated high levels of these crops to utilize as feed supplements for livestock. Since conventional methods ignore these crops as nutritional resources for livestock, I converted these crops using ratios from 1910.[7]

Earlier studies have provided extensive study data on human and animal consumption levels in the antebellum South. Based on these earlier sources, this research allocated three and one-half pounds of meat and one and one-quarter pecks of grain to each adult weekly, which converts into 24.8 annual corn equivalencies in grains, potatoes, peas or beans, and meat for each adult (fifteen years of age or older). Half that amount was allowed to children younger than fifteen. In addition to meat supplied from hogs, oxen were butchered at about eight years of age; thus, about one of every six oxen were utilized for food annually. In addition, about two of every five sheep were slaughtered each year for food. Thus, when I calculated the total corn equivalencies available for the food supply, I included one-sixth of the total number of oxen and two-fifths of the total number of sheep.[8]

In addition to human consumption, one must take into account feeds for livestock. Antebellum southern livestock practices were characterized by neglect and near-subsistence feeding levels. Except during fattening, hogs, cattle, swine, and sheep were left to forage for their feed during most months of the year. During the winter months, they were supplemented with hay, coarse fodder, peas, beans, and pumpkins. Moreover, only 69.5 percent of all livestock were ever grain-fed; the rest consumed forage only. However, corn allocations were made for cattle, hogs, horses, mules, oxen, and sheep.[9]

Overall, my estimates of surpluses and exports are conservative because I allowed for several subsistence exigencies for which other analysts have not usually accounted. In addition to food requirements, I allocated three gallons of whiskey annually per adult, allowing 1.5 bushels to produce each gallon.[10] To cover the cost of mill or distillery tolls, I added 10 percent to the amounts of grain required for household subsistence. In addition, the subsistent household would need to reserve seed for the next year's essential food crops and to reserve part of the livestock for herd replacement. Thus, 5 to 13 percent of crops were reserved as seeds.[11] To allow for the next year's production, one of every seven surplus swine was retained for herd replacement. In addition, 28.6 percent of the surplus cattle were retained for herd replacement. Since I assumed that sheep and oxen were consumed at low levels and were not exported, it was not necessary to allow for herd replacements. Finally, I deducted 5 percent of the corn and wheat production as having been lost due to spoilage or waste, even though existing studies ignore such crop losses.[12]

Space does not permit elaboration about cliometric debates over the precise amounts that should be allocated for human and livestock consumption. My calculations of exports at the county level present a much more conservative estimate than can be obtained by applying the methods used in any of the earlier studies. My food allowances for humans exceed or equal all these studies; however, I have varied my allocation of feeds to reflect the near-subsistence production methods of Appalachian farmers and graziers. Still, my calculation achieves lower counts of exports than those obtained by applying higher livestock feed levels. Earlier cliometric studies have not allocated grain for four local uses that are accounted for in my calculations: local whiskey consumption, subsistence milling tolls, seed reservations, and waste allowances. Moreover, most analysts have not reserved part of the surplus cattle and hogs for herd replacements, as I have.[13]

Distinguishing Subsistence and Surplus Producers

Using these procedures, I calculated production and consumption levels for major food crops for each sampled farm household and for every Appalachian county. I determined whether each farm was a subsistence or surplus producer based on the proportion of the total production remaining after subsistence requirements were met. Subsistence producers are defined as those farmers who:

1. *Have limited market dependency.* Subsistence households consume 80 percent or more of their food crops and livestock. In addition, they produce no major amounts of marketable staple crops (tobacco or cotton).[14]

2. *Control the means of production.* Subsistence farmers own no more than ninety-nine acres. They are not landless, but they do not hold large surpluses of land.[15]

3. *Are neither proletarians nor petty capitalists.* Subsistence farmers report no external wage-earning, artisan, or business source of nonagricultural income.

4. *Do not utilize paid or coerced laborers.* Subsistence farmers utilize no labor mechanism other than family members.

In short, a subsistence farmer is overwhelmingly dependent upon the land for survival and has few sources of money.

Surpluses Used for Reinvestments

In order to maintain conceptual precision, it is also necessary to distinguish carefully between those crops that were consumed for household subsistence and those food crops that were reinvested to produce more profitable marketable commodities. In reality, grains and meats were produced for three distinct functions: to provide household subsistence needs, to reinvest in the production of surpluses, and to generate profits through exchange. Thus, real surplus production consists of the sum total of all commodities produced or accumulated by the household—in excess of the needs for survival of the kinship unit.

The corn equivalencies used by a farm to generate surpluses are not essential to the survival of its household members. A farm geared to subsistence production relies on family labor and does not have the means to afford external labor sources. Therefore, the food consumed by the nonfamily laborers who produce surpluses is not part of subsistence (i.e., the food consumption of slaves, tenants, or paid laborers). Similarly, the feed for surplus livestock and seed reservations (stored to produce next year's surplus crops) are utilized in the production of marketable commodities, not to sustain the household. I designated as subsistence requirements the grain feeds necessary to sustain consumed livestock and one or two work stock (horses, mules, or oxen). Feed requirements above subsistence levels were considered crop reinvestments utilized to generate livestock surpluses.

Abbreviations Used in Notes

Census MSS	Census Enumerator Manuscripts, 1860, for Appalachian Counties
CWVQ	*The Tennessee Civil War Veterans Questionnaires*
De Bow's	*De Bow's Review*
FHPJ	*Ferry Hill Plantation Journal*
Hunt's MM	*Hunt's Merchants Magazine and Commercial Review*
Olmsted, *JBC*	Olmsted, *A Journey in the Back Country*
Olmsted, *JSS*	Olmsted, *Journey in the Seaboard Slave States*
Slave	Rawick, *The American Slave*
Slave I	Rawick, *The American Slave: Supplement I*
Slave II	Rawick, *The American Slave: Supplement II*
Wallerstein, *HC*	Wallerstein, *Historical Capitalism*
Wallerstein, *MWS1*	Wallerstein, *The Modern World-System I*
Wallerstein, *MWS2*	Wallerstein, *The Modern World-System II*
Wallerstein, *MWS3*	Wallerstein, *The Modern World-System III*

Chapter One

1. Mooney, "Myths of Cherokee," pp. 23–29. Goad, "Copper," p. 56.

2. For government landholding, see Appalachian Land Ownership Task Force, *Who Owns Appalachia?*, pp. 35–38. On antebellum exploration and tourism, see Dunaway, "Incorporation," chaps. 2, 8. Roosevelt, *Winning of West*, p. 231, wrote of the Watauga Association: "They were the first men of American birth to establish a free and independent community on the Continent."

3. Hofstadter, *Age of Reform*, pp. 23–25, 30. Hofstadter, "Myth of Yeoman," p. 43.

4. Mood, *Early Writings of Turner*, p. 187. Vincent, "Retarded Frontier," p. 1. On self-sufficiency, see Appalachian Land Ownership Task Force, *Who Owns Appalachia?*, p. 80.

5. Fox, "Southern Mountaineer," p. 390. Roberts and Roberts, *Where Time Stood Still*, p. 128; Pearsall, *Little Smoky Ridge*, p. 127. Kephart, *Our Southern Highlanders*, p. 329; Raine, *Land of Saddle Bags*, p. 240; Beaver, *Rural Community*.

6. For an idealization of Appalachia, see Kirby, *Rural Worlds Lost*. For overviews, see Badham, "Sociology"; Buttel and McMichael, "Sociology." On egalitarian preindustrial America, see Tocqueville, *Democracy in America*, 2:258; Szymanski, *Class Structure*, pp. 195–203.

7. Headlee, *Political Economy*, p. 3. On freeholders, see Buttel and Newby, *Rural Sociology*, p. 93; Lipset, *First New Nation*, p. 130. On Appalachian traits, see Dykeman, "Appalachia in Context"; Banks, "Emergence"; Gaventa, *Power and Powerlessness*;

Opie, "Where American History"; Eller, *Miners, Millhands*; Billings, Blee, and Swanson, "Culture, Family," p. 158.

8. Eller, *Miners, Millhands*, p. 4. For the argument that Appalachia was undeveloped prior to industrialization, see Gaventa, *Power and Powerlessness*, p. 49; Simon, "Uneven Development," p. 183; Matvey, "Central Appalachia." On lack of infrastructure, see Deakin, "Appalachia." On internal barriers to development, see Kaplan, *Blue Ridge*, p. 22; Dykeman, "Appalachia in Context"; Banks, "Emergence." For a critical survey of this literature, see Stotik, "Political Economy."

9. Billings, Blee, and Swanson, "Culture, Family," p. 160. Schlotterbeck, "Plantation and Farm," abstract. Eller, "Land and Family," p. 95. See also Pudup, "Limits of Subsistence," p. 72.

10. Gaventa, *Power and Powerlessness*, p. 48. Eller, "Land and Family," p. 84. Folk society, subculture of poverty, and regional development theses of the 1960s and 1970s posit the following as the causal mechanisms for retarded development: a traditional way of life maladapted to the modern age; a pathological, "analgesic subculture as a dysfunctional response to modernity"; and an absence of the entrepreneurial values and work ethic necessary for the "takeoff" into competitive production. Even though they are currently frowned upon by most academics, these three theoretical models continue to shape public policy formation for the Appalachian region. For proponents of these cultural theses, see Caudill, *Night Comes to Cumberlands*; Ball, "Poverty Case"; Weller, *Yesterday's People*; Matvey, "Central Appalachia," pp. 122–29; Billings, Blee, and Swanson, "Culture, Family," pp. 163, 167.

11. Billings, Blee, and Swanson, "Culture, Family," p. 158. Simon, "Uneven Development," p. 183. On the postbellum transition to capitalist agriculture, see Ford, *Origins*; Weiman, "Farmers and Market," p. 627; Hahn, *Roots*, p. 169.

12. Caudill, *Night Comes to Cumberlands*, p. 325. Eller, *Miners, Millhands*, p. xxiv. Simon, "Uneven Development"; Gaventa, *Power and Powerlessness*; Nyden, "Internal Colony," p. 34; Lewis, Johnson, and Askins, *Colonialism in Modern America*.

13. For the traditional view, see Bidwell, "Rural Economy"; Bidwell and Falconer, *History of Agriculture*. For the radical view, see Post, "American Road," p. 38; Mosley, "Founding Fathers"; O'Connor, "A Note"; Kelly, "Independent Mode"; Szymanski, *Class Structure*, pp. 195–203; Kulikoff, "Transition to Capitalism," p. 144; Mann, *Agrarian Capitalism*.

14. Sellers, *Market Revolution*, p. 5. For theoretical clarification of the *household mode of production*, sometimes called *simple commodity production*, see Friedmann, "Household Production"; Merrill, "Cash Is Good"; Henretta, "Families and Farms"; Clark, "Household Economy"; Mutch, "Colonial America." Henretta, *Origins*, p. xxiii. Rothenberg, "Market and Farmers," pp. 283–314. Brown, *Modernization*, p. 114. North, *Economic Growth*, p. 213. Hoffman, *Economy of Early America*, pp. 45–87; Foner, *New American History*, pp. 51–72. Cochran, *Frontiers of Change*, pp. 44–48. Bruchey, *Roots*, pp. 90–91. Rothenberg, "Emergence of Capital." Prude, *Coming of Order*, chap. 1; Clark, *Roots*, chap. 1; Dublin, "Rural Putting-out"; Baker and Izard, "New England Farmers," pp. 51–52.

15. Dowd, *Twisted Dream*, pp. 46–47, 165. Hoffman, *Economy of Early America*, p. 191. North, "Location Theory," pp. 244–45. Hartz, *Liberal Tradition*, p. 89. Grant, *Democracy in Connecticut*; Battis, *Saints and Sectaries*; Lemon, "Household Consumption"; Bushman, *From Puritan to Yankee*; Lockridge, *New England Town*. Perkins, "Entrepreneurial Spirit," p. 186. Lemon, "Early Americans," p. 130. Lemon, *Best Poor Man's Country*, pp. 27–29. Appleby, "Commercial Farming," p. 840. Mancall, *Valley*, pp. 182, 228. Pruitt, "Self-Sufficiency," p. 363. Agnew, *U.S. in World*, p. 101. See also Clemens, *Atlantic Economy*; North, "Sources"; North and Thomas, "Economic The-

ory"; Shepherd and Walton, *Shipping*; Shammas, "How Self-Sufficient?"; McCusker and Menard, *Economy of British America*, p. 71; Coclanis, *Shadow of Dream*, pp. 49, 51; Otto, *Southern Frontiers*, p. 4.

16. For a critique of this national focus, see Buttel and McMichael, "Sociology," p. 105.

17. For the thesis that the discourse on Appalachia emanates from the dominant culture, see Shapiro, *Appalachia on Our Mind*; Batteau, "Appalachia and Culture"; McKinney, "Political Uses"; Whisnant, *All That Is Native*; Cunningham, *Apples on Flood*, p. 117.

18. Bohm, *Wholeness and Order*, p. 173. Prigogine, "Time, Structures," p. 780. Wallerstein, "World-System Analysis: Second Phase," pp. 291, 293.

19. Wallerstein, *MWS1*, pp. 347–48.

20. Clark, *Roots*, p. 15. On long-distance trade that is not capitalistic, see Wallerstein, *MWS3*, p. 130. Hopkins and Wallerstein, "Capitalism and Incorporation," pp. 776–77.

21. Mitchell, *Commercialism and Frontier*, p. 3. Otto, *Southern Frontiers*, p. 4.

22. Lamar and Thompson, *Frontier in History*, p. 7.

23. Arrighi, "Peripheralization," 161. Hopkins and Wallerstein, "Capitalism and Incorporation," p. 771; Wallerstein, "Crisis as Transition," p. 15; Wallerstein, *Politics*, p. 404; Wallerstein, *MWS1*, p. 349; Wallerstein, *HC*, p. 773.

24. Braudel Center Research Working Group, "Cyclical Rhythms," p. 485; Wallerstein, *MWS2*, pp. 233–34; 167.

25. Wallerstein, "Crisis as Transition," pp. 18–21; Wallerstein, *Politics*, pp. 16–17; Amin, *Accumulation*, p. 136; Amin, *Class and Nation*.

26. Wallerstein, *HC*, p. 32; Wallerstein, *MWS1*, p. 7.

27. Wallerstein, *MWS2*, p. 257.

28. Wallerstein, *Capitalist World-Economy*, p. 34; Wallerstein, *Politics*, p. 15; Wallerstein, *MWS2*, pp. 101–9; Wallerstein, *MWS1*, p. 281; Hopkins and Wallerstein, "Capitalism and Incorporation," p. 773.

29. Wallerstein, *MWS1*.

30. Wallerstein, *HC*, chap. 1; Hopkins and Wallerstein, "Commodity Chains"; Wallerstein, *Capitalist World-Economy*; Frank, *World Accumulation*; Wallerstein, *MWS2*, pp. 169, 175, 266.

31. Wallerstein, *MWS3*, p. iv. Wallerstein, *MWS2*, p. 88. By 1830, the European peasantry had been replaced by an agricultural proletariat; see Worsley, *Three Worlds*, pp. 94–95. See Chapter 3 for a map of the Appalachian resettlement eras.

32. Frank, *World Accumulation*, p. 194. Agnew, *U.S. in World*, pp. 27–28.

33. Agnew, *U.S. in World*, p. 28. Wallerstein, *MWS2*, pp. 238–39.

34. Agnew, *U.S. in World*, p. 26; Frank, *World Accumulation*, p. 219.

35. Williams, *Capitalism and Slavery*, pp. 51–52.

36. Agnew, *U.S. in World*, p. 27; Frank, *World Accumulation*; Wallerstein, *MWS2*. Naval stores included pitch, turpentine, tar, and hemp, which were needed by the European shipbuilding industry.

37. Chase-Dunn, "Development," pp. 208–9.

38. Henretta, "Families and Farms," p. 9.

39. "Over small groups of the natives who lived adjacent to the colonial settlements of the Europeans, the rights of a protectorate were gradually assumed"; see Osgood, *American Colonies*, 1:257.

40. For theoretical discussion, see Aguirre-Beltran, *Regions of Refuge*.

41. Agnew, *U.S. in World*, p. 25.

42. Frank, *World Accumulation*, pp. 179, 200.

43. Walls and Billings, "Sociology," p. 135.

44. Martin, "Incorporation," p. 854. I have added culture to the levels of social change delineated by Hopkins and Wallerstein, "Capitalism and Incorporation," p. 773. Wallerstein, "Crisis as Transition," p. 15; Wallerstein, *Politics*, p. 404; Wallerstein, *MWS1*, p. 349; Wallerstein, *HC*, p. 32.

45. Arrighi, "Peripheralization," p. 162.

46. Wallerstein, *Capitalist World-Economy*, pp. 69–70. Martin, "Incorporation," pp. 854–55.

47. Cox, *Capitalism as System*, p. 297. Braudel, *Afterthoughts*, pp. 62–64. Hopkins and Wallerstein, "Capitalism and Incorporation," pp. 776. Amin, *Accumulation*, pp. 37–38.

48. Hopkins and Wallerstein, "Capitalism and Incorporation," p. 777.

49. Phillips, "Incorporation," p. 781. Braudel, *Civilization and Capitalism*, 2:251. For theory on land tenure, see Wallerstein, *MWS1*.

50. Wallerstein, *Unthinking Social Science*, p. 237.

Chapter Two

1. Smith, *Seventeenth-Century America*, pp. 34, 39. Folmsbee and Lewis, "Journals of Pardo Expeditions," p. 115. King, *Cherokee Nation*, p. 46. For a brief overview of all three Spanish expeditions into Cherokee country, see Mooney, "Myths of Cherokee," pp. 23–29. For a map of the 1539–43 Spanish expedition, see Shaffer, *Native Americans*, p. 88. Goad, "Copper," pp. 50, 56. Extracts from this chapter appeared previously in *Review of the Fernand Braudel Center*; see Dunaway, "Southern Fur Trade."

2. Bouwman, "Native Americans," p. 4. Smith, *Archaeology*, p. 112.

3. Smith, *Archaeology*, p. 25. Williams, "Indians," p. 32. Information on Mississippian chiefdoms from Cherokee Indian Museum, Cherokee, North Carolina; Sears, "State," pp. 109–25; "Etowah," pp. 54–67.

4. Smith, *Archaeology*, p. 145. Williams, "Indians," pp. 35–36.

5. On the extended Caribbean, see Wallerstein, *MWS2*, pp. 241, 102, 167. Evans, *General Map*; Doddridge, *Notes*; Scharf, *History of Western Maryland*; Royce, *Cherokee Nation*; Peters, *Guidebook*; Lord, *Blue Ridge Guide*, 1:139.9 and 2:383.5; Couper, *History of Shenandoah*, 1:543; Maxwell, "Use and Abuse," pp. 84–85, 102; Lord and Lord, *Historical Atlas*, p. 19. Cotterill, *Southern Indians*; De Vorsey, *Indian Boundary*; Morgan, *League of Iroquois*.

6. Eliades, "Indian Policy," pp. 106–7. For detailed historical overviews of the three-sided international rivalry among the Cherokees during the colonial era, see Hamer, "Anglo-French Rivalry"; Crane, *Southern Frontier*; Corry, "Indian Affairs"; Robinson, *Southern Frontier*; De Vorsey, *Indian Boundary*.

7. Glen to Dinwiddie, January 1755, in *Records in British P.R.O.*, 26:222. For a discussion of preemptive colonization, see Wallerstein, *MWS2*, p. 237. For a history of the world economy, see Wallerstein, *MWS2*, pp. 241, 102, 167. Religious zeal was a significant factor in the preemptive colonization of southwestern Indians; see Hall, *Social Change*. Similar efforts were made by the Spanish among the Indians of Florida. However, few such missionary attempts were made among the Appalachian indigenes during the colonial period. In contrast to the Spanish, the British politically resisted attempts by clerics to send missionaries among the Indians of the Southeast; see Logan, *History of Upper Country*, 1:259–79; Clowse, "Charleston Export Trade," pp. 89–95. See also Eliades, "Indian Policy," p. 9.

8. Jacobs, *Edmund Atkin Report*, p. 48.

9. *South Carolina Gazette*, 4 June 1754. Jacobs, *Edmund Atkin Report*, p. 3. Glen to Dinwiddie, in *Virginia Gazette*, 18 August 1751.

10. Hewatt, *Historical Account*, 1:491. *Colonial Records of S.C.: Documents*, 1:52. *Historical Collections of S.C.*, 2:480.

11. Williams, *Early Travels*, pp. 124–25. Jacobs, *Diplomacy*, pp. 26–27, 123–24, chap. 8. Shaw, "British Administration," p. 9; see also pp. 70, 166–67.

12. Alden, *John Stuart*, p. 4. Indian Commissioner, 1708, in *Records in British P.R.O.*, 5:196. *Mississippi Provincial Archives*, 2:23.

13. British colonial records, cited in De Vorsey, *Indian Boundary*, p. 11. *Colonial Records of S.C.: Documents*, 1:53. Logan, *History of Upper Country*, p. 471. For example, the British charged the Cherokees sixteen heavy, dressed skins for a gun, but they charged the Creeks twenty-five skins for the same weapon. See *Colonial Records of S.C.: Journals*, pp. 269, 281.

14. Sellers, *Charleston Business*, p. 170. Crane, "Tennessee River," pp. 3–18. Franklin, "Virginia and Cherokee," p. 31.

15. Ward, *"Unite or Die,"* p. 156. On intertribal warfare, see Goodwin, *Cherokees*, pp. 102–3.

16. *Mississippi Provincial Archives*, 2:573–74.

17. For example, the 1730 and 1751 British treaties required the Cherokees to assist against the enemies of the English; see *Colonial Records of N.C.*, 3:129–33; *Colonial Records of S.C.: Documents*, 1:187. For other examples of this treaty policy, see Willis, "Colonial Conflict." For an overview of intertribal warfare, see Mooney, "Myths of Cherokee," p. 38. See, for example, the 1707–8 scheme in Crane, "Tennessee River," p. 18. Caldwell, "Southern Frontier," p. 40; Williams, *Timberlake's Memoirs*, pp. 38–40; Corry, "Indian Affairs," pp. 113–32; Robinson, *Southern Frontier*, pp. 185–200.

18. *Journal of John Herbert*, p. 22. *Colonial Records of S.C.: Documents*, 1:290; for arms sales to the Creeks a few months earlier, see p. 249. On the arms race, see Cotterill, *Southern Indians*, pp. 22–25.

19. Williams, *Timberlake's Memoirs*, p. 93.

20. Strickland, *Fire and Spirits*, pp. 11–12; 24–26. The rule of the White organization can be characterized as benevolent paternalism. Decisions were generally unanimous, and direct coercion or overactive leadership were strongly devalued; see Fogelson and Kutsche, "Cherokee Cooperatives," pp. 91–92. Gearing, "Cherokee Organizations," pp. 5–9. On the resolution of disagreements, see Malone, *Cherokees*, p. 26.

21. *Journal of Proceedings*, p. 18. For example, the 1721 treaty specified a principal chief for the Cherokees; see Bloom, "Acculturation," p. 338. In a 1727 meeting with the Lower Towns, Colonel Herbert told the Cherokees "that the Warrior of Keewohee had a Com'icon to Com'and all the people of the Lower Towns wch. [he] produced to them & told them that they must allways remember to Obey him as their Comander"; see *Journal of John Herbert*, p. 14. The French and Spanish also used commissions to try to centralize control over the Cherokees; see Corkran, *Cherokee Frontier*, p. 13; Logan, *History of Upper Country*, 1:480–81. The 1763 proclamation designated the "Beloved Men" process as the required leadership for British-allied Indians; see Shaw, "British Administration," p. 30. On regional storehouses, see Mereness, *Travels*, p. 109. On town relocation, see Cotterill, *Southern Indians*, pp. 28–29.

22. Williams, *Early Travels*, pp. 122–26.

23. For discussion of the "tribal half-government," see Gearing, "Cherokee Organizations"; Goodwin, *Cherokees*, pp. 113–14; Corkran, *Cherokee Frontier*, pp. 15–16. As smallpox spread devastation in the Cherokee country, the war chief accused the English of bringing this disease to his people in the trade goods they sold. During the

ensuing period of internal and external strife, the warrior element gained ascendancy. See Satz, *Tennessee's Indian Peoples*, p. 60.

24. *Colonial Records of S.C.: Documents*, 1:188. Rutman, *Old Dominion*, p. 31.

25. Gearing, "Cherokee Organizations," p. 122.

26. For precontact economic history, see Fogelson and Kutsche, "Cherokee Cooperatives," p. 93; Lewis and Kneberg, "First Tennesseeans," p. 88; Lawson, *History of North Carolina*, pp. 219–20; Wright, *Only Land They Knew*, p. 10.

27. Bloom, "Acculturation," p. 341; Carlson, "America's Drug Connection," pp. 233–35. Anderson, "Cherokee Clay"; Morrison, "Virginia Indian Trade"; Silver, *A New Face*, pp. 83–84, 74. On Indian slavery, see Snell, "Indian Slavery," p. 97. On the deerskin trade, see Corry, "Indian Affairs," pp. 27–28; Brown, "Early Indian Trade," p. 124.

28. The majority of slaves exported from South Carolina in the early 1700s were Indians; see Snell, "Indian Slavery," p. 94; Sellers, *Charleston Business*, p. 174. On the development of slavery marketing among the Cherokees, see Thornton, *Cherokees*, p. 19; Buchanan, "Relations," pp. 19–20; Reid, *Better Kind of Hatchet*, p. 24; Milling, *Red Carolinians*, p. 269n.

29. *Records in British P.R.O.*, 5:197. Crane, "Tennessee River," p. 15; King, *Cherokee Nation*, pp. 68–70.

30. On furs as a luxury export in the world market, see Wolf, *Europe and People*, p. 173. On the development of the leather industry, see Phillips, *Fur Trade*, 1:7 and 2:105; Andrews, *Colonial Period*, 4:105; Chapman, *Tellico Archaeology*, p. 100.

31. Gray, *History of Agriculture*, 1:129. Corry, "Indian Affairs," p. 32. England's Navigation Acts of the 1660s enumerated colonial products that must be shipped on English ships and sold to English buyers; see Wallerstein, *MWS2*, p. 236. On deerskins as a major Southern export, see Sellers, *Charleston Business*, p. 170. On intercolonial competition, see Ward, *"Unite or Die,"* pp. 150–89; Rutman, *Old Dominion*, pp. 29–32; Phillips, *Fur Trade*, vol. 2, chap. 21. The southern colonies held monopolistic control over the Indian trade during the following periods: South Carolina: 1710–14, 1721–35; Virginia: 1714–21; Georgia: 1735 to Revolutionary War; Maryland was the only southern colony that had no part in expansion through Indian trade. On the Indian trade as capital accumulation for the development of other economic activities, see Bernard, "Analysis of Mercantilism," p. 51. Fur trading also occurred in other parts of Southern Appalachia. As early as 1707, a fur trading post was established at Harpers Ferry, West Virginia, to trade in luxury furs and deerskins brought by the Iroquois and other Indian groups out of Pennsylvania and western Maryland. See Moler, "Traders Settle," p. 24.

32. Logan, *History of Upper Country*, 1:382–84. Clowse, "Charleston Export Trade," pp. 62, 167–69. *De Brahm's Report*, p. 95. Phillips, *Fur Trade*, 1:173, 341–42, 426.

33. Clowse, "Charleston Export Trade," p. 48. Virginia even used duties on deerskins to fund the establishment of William and Mary College; see Rutman, *Old Dominion*, pp. 29–32.

34. Wallerstein, *MWS3*, p. 130. Destinations of deerskin exports were calculated using raw data in Clowse, "Charleston Export Trade," pp. 230–31. On trade commodities, see Rivers, *Sketch of History*, p. 234; Lauber, "Indian Slavery," pp. 173–74; Bloom, "Acculturation," p. 336; Sellers, *Charleston Business*, pp. 78–79; Phillips, *Fur Trade*, 1:426.

35. Phillips, *Fur Trade*, 1:170. Fitzhugh, *Cultures in Contact*, p. 272. Such monopolies were politically opposed by merchants, however, and private trading was reinstated after only brief periods of public monopolization; see Eliades, "Indian Policy," pp.

119–20. A Virginia company held the Crown monopoly from 1714 to 1721; South Carolina and Georgia companies were later granted the Crown monopoly over the entire southern Indian trade; see Phillips, *Fur Trade*, 1:85–88. Crane, *Southern Frontier*, p. 143. For example, the Virginia Assembly encouraged explorations into the Blue Ridge in the late 1600s by granting monopolistic licenses "to discover the Mountains and Westward parts of the country"; see Williams, *Early Travels*, p. 18. A Boston merchant reported in the late 1600s that "The French are reported to be very diligent in the discovery of the lakes and land behind New England, Virginia and Carolina. . . . They have designes of improving these discoveries and planting people in the most commodious passages"; see letter of Richard Wharton, 23 January 1676, in *Mississippi Valley Historical Review* 21 (1934): 255–56. For discussion of these early explorations, see also Phillips, *Fur Trade*, 1:163–77.

36. *Colonial Records of Georgia*, 1:561. *Writings of Colonel Byrd*, p. 235. On Byrd's trade, see Phillips, *Fur Trade*, 1:177.

37. Williams, *Early Travels*, p. 137. *Statutes at Large of S.C.*, 4:168–88. On the decline of Virginia trade, see *Executive Journals*, 4:1–2; Spotswood to Lords of Trade, 1 February 1720, in *Official Letters of Spotswood*, 2:331. On the emergence of Carolina trade, see Meriwether, *Expansion*, pp. 191–93; Sellers, *Charleston Business*, pp. 170–71.

38. For a theoretical discussion of putting-out systems, see Wallerstein, *MWS2*, pp. 193–96. Because putting-out was the forerunner of the factory system, direct producers worked out of their own domiciles. Putting-out systems were dependent upon foreign merchant capital. Direct producers received credit advances from a merchant, who thereby retained the right to purchase the end product at a fixed rate and who took charge of transporting the product to market. The direct producer worked only part time, combining the putting-out with other economic roles. Operation of the system resulted in chronic indebtedness of the producers to the merchant.

39. Bernard, "Analysis of Mercantilism," pp. 55–56. Clowse, "Charleston Export Trade," p. 47.

40. Rothrock, "Carolina Traders," p. 8. Brown, "Early Indian Trade," p. 125; Williams, *Early Travels*, p. 119; *Journal of Commons House*, 29 April 1761. Goodwin, *Cherokees*, pp. 95–98. Blackmun, *Western North Carolina*, 1:62–63. Logan, *History of Upper Country*, 1:434.

41. Bienville to Maurepas, 23 April 1735, in *Mississippi Provincial Archives*, 1:262. *Colonial Records of S.C.: Journals*, p. 191.

42. Corkran, *Cherokee Frontier*, p. 6. *Journal of John Herbert*, p. 5. On trader profits, see Williams, *Timberlake's Memoirs*, p. 87. Rothrock, "Carolina Traders," pp. 9–10; Corry, "Indian Affairs," p. 41; see also Williams, *Early Travels*, p. 137. On trading debts, see *Journal of Commons House*, 13 June 1711.

43. Jacobs, *Edmund Atkin Report*, p. 35.

44. Wilcox, "Skins, Rum, and Ruin," p. 59. On the worldwide use of alcohol by the core to control the poorer laborers of peripheries, see Wallerstein, *MWS2*, pp. 140–41. On trader abuses, see *Colonial Records of S.C.: Journals*, p. 205. On overplus tactics, see Logan, *History of Upper Country*, 1:473.

45. Goodwin, *Cherokees*, p. 120. On reprisals for Cherokee stealing, see *Journal of John Herbert*, pp. 18, 28. Treaties with the British typically included agreements to make restitution for any harm done to traders in Cherokee villages; see, for example, the 1733 treaty in *South Carolina Gazette*, 1–8 June 1734. On actions against deceased debtors, see Logan, *History of Upper Country*, 1:473.

46. King, *Cherokee Nation*, pp. 26–28. On the proletarianization of Cherokees by traders, see *Colonial Records of S.C.: Journals*, p. 272; Logan, *History of Upper Country*, 1:262–64; Crane, *Southern Frontier*, p. 128. On fort construction, see *Colonial Records*

of S.C.: Documents, 1:195. On labor loss due to rum and weapon production, see Woodward, *Cherokees*, p. 35.

47. Gulick, *Cherokees*, p. 89. Williams, *Timberlake's Memoirs*, p. 68. *Journal of John Herbert*, p. 28. For greater detail about *gadugi* traditions, see Fogelson and Kutsche, "Cherokee Cooperatives," pp. 93–97; also see Williams, *Early Travels*, pp. 260–61; *Adair's History*, p. 462; Bartram, *Travels*, p. 510. On female labor in skin preparation, see Swanton, *Indians of Southeast*, p. 259.

48. For a theoretical discussion of disarticulation, see Amin, *Accumulation*, pp. 390–94. On declines in Cherokee agriculture, see Wright, *Only Land They Knew*, p. 221; *Colonial Records of S.C.: Journals*, pp. 168, 192, 170, 198, 195, 144, 276. Corn was sold to the Cherokees at a 150 percent profit; see *Colonial Records of S.C.: Journals*, p. 209. See also Shaw, "British Administration," pp. 71–72; Fant, "Indian Trade Policy," p. 219. For example, in 1751 the Lower Towns broke up and moved to the Overhills villages; see *Colonial Records of S.C.: Documents*, 1:118–19, 151.

49. *Adair's History*, p. 456. Williams, *Timberlake's Memoirs*, pp. 77–78; Swanton, *Indians of Southeast*, pp. 491–95, 565; Satz, *Tennessee's Indian Peoples*, p. 17; Reid, *Better Kind of Hatchet*, pp. 29–31; Smith, *Archaeology*, pp. 20, 52, 83; Smith and Williams, "Trade Material," pp. 42–49; Logan, *History of Upper Country*, 1:465. Stone, "Captain Demere," pp. 17–24.

50. Williams, *Early Travels*, p. 112. Catesby, *Natural History*, 2:xi. Population declines resulted in increased dependence upon European weapons; see *Colonial Records of S.C.: Documents*, 1:255. Declines in agricultural and livestock production also increased Cherokee dependence upon the British for food; see Logan, *History of Upper Country*, 1:290.

51. Williams, *Early Travels*, pp. 142–43. For a theoretical discussion of trade-induced acculturation, see Smith, *Archaeology*, p. 117.

52. *Colonial Records of S.C.: Documents*, 3:321–23 and 1:196–97. Bernard, "Analysis of Mercantilism," p. 55. John Stuart's 1764 report, in De Vorsey, *Indian Boundary*, p. 12. For a similar appraisal of this era, see *Executive Journals*, 6:215.

53. Cox, *Capitalism as a System*, p. 297. De Brahm's Report, p. 109; For a discussion of the notion that capitalism entails the "commodification of everything," see Wallerstein, *HC*, chap. 1. On clan revenge, see Cotterill, *Southern Indians*, p. 11; Satz, *Tennessee's Indian Peoples*, pp. 30–31. On the adaptation of European tactics, see Bloom, "Acculturation," p. 343; Terrell, *Traders*, p. 193; Lewis and Kneberg, "First Tennesseeans," p. 76; Eliades, "Indian Policy," p. 14. See also Williams, *Timberlake's Memoirs*, p. 78; *Colonial Records of S.C.: Documents*, 1:332; Demere to Lyttelton, 18 August 1757, "South Carolina Indian Affairs," 6:74–78.

54. *Executive Journals*, 6:279. *Adair's History*, pp. 158–59. Cotterill, *Southern Indians*, p. 17. *Colonial Records of S.C.: Documents*, 1:54–55; 158–59. Strickland, *Fire and Spirits*, p. 54.

55. Perdue, *Slavery and Evolution*, p. 31. *Carolina Chronicles of LeJau*, pp. 59–60. Bloom, "Acculturation," pp. 344, 8. Bartram, *Travels*, p. 186.

56. Walthall, *Prehistoric Indians*, p. 190. Goad, "Copper," pp. 63–64. Among the Cherokees, neutral old men acted as traders with the coastal Indians; see Jones, *Antiquities of Indians*, p. 243; Rau, *Ancient Aboriginal Trade*, p. 388. On precontact trade items, see Swanton, *Indians of Southeast*, p. 737; Terrell, *Traders*, pp. 49–67. On present-giving and pricing customs, see Reid, *Better Kind of Hatchet*, p. 35; Rich, "Trade Habits," p. 44. On trade as a communal activity, see Jablow, *Cheyenne*, pp. 47–49.

57. On trade as individual exchange, see Wolf, *Europe and People*, p. 163. On commodification of Cherokee agriculture, see Reid, *Better Kind of Hatchet*, p. 129; Strickland, *Fire and Spirits*, p. 44; Goodwin, *Cherokees*, p. 114.

58. On wampum, see Carr, *Dress and Ornaments*; Weeden, "Indian Money," pp. 19–20; Swanton, *Indians of Southeast*, p. 484. On tobacco, see Terrell, *Traders*, pp. 70–71; Mooney, "Myths of Cherokee," p. 439. The Cherokees were introduced to rum by traders who sold them mouthfuls from buckskin; see Lawson, *History of North Carolina*, p. 238; also see Thornton, *Cherokees*, pp. 65–66. On commodification of religious roles, see Reid, *Better Kind of Hatchet*, p. 29.

59. Long, "Small Postcript," p. 26. On failure to complete burials, see Logan, *History of Upper Country*, 1:329–30. On the emergence of inheritance practices, see Malone, *Cherokees*, p. 29.

60. Williams, *Timberlake's Memoirs*, pp. 76–77. Wright, *Only Land They Knew*, pp. 218–19.

61. Long, "Small Postcript," pp. 19–20. On the manipulation of intercolonial competition, see Bouwman, "Native Americans," p. 8. In 1751, the Cherokees secured price concessions from South Carolina after sending a trade delegation to Virginia; see *Colonial Records of S.C.: Documents*, 1:105–10; Corkran, *Cherokee Frontier*, pp. 32–33; Milling, *Red Carolinians*, pp. 281–82. On broken promises, see, for example, *Colonial Records of S.C.: Documents*, 1:43.

62. Wolf, *Europe and People*, p. 174. Logan, *History of Upper Country*, 1:463. *Colonial Records of S.C.: Documents*, 1:76. *Calendar of Virginia State Papers*, 1:283. For examples of internal dissension, see *Colonial Records of S.C.: Documents*, 1:175; Eliades, "Indian Policy," p. 260; Corkran, *Cherokee Frontier*, pp. 16–17, 50–51, 72–73; Williams, "Fort Robinson," p. 26; Bloom, "Acculturation," p. 330; Goodwin, *Cherokees*, p. 103; Milling, *Red Carolinians*, pp. 274–75, 281. On nativist movement, see Reid, *Better Kind of Hatchet*, p. 196; Strohfeldt, "Warriors," pp. 10–11. On resistance tactics, see Corkran, *Cherokee Frontier*, p. 26; *Kentucky Gazette*, 4 April 1788 and 12 April 1788; Buchanan, "Relations," pp. 63–64; Milling, *Red Carolinians*, pp. 308–10, 294–95.

63. Wallerstein, *HC*, p. 82. Strickland, *Fire and Spirits*, p. 45. On British tactics in dealing with Cherokee elites, see Logan, *History of Upper Country*, 1:422, 309; *Colonial Records of S.C.: Journals*, pp. 236–37; Alden, "Cherokee Archives," p. 241n. On the 1721 treaty meetings, see Bloom, "Acculturation," p. 338.

64. *Colonial Records of S.C.: Documents*, 1:45.

65. Kupperman, *Settling*, p. 170. For an example of such British paternalism, see *Colonial Records of S.C.: Documents*, 1:518–19. On the politico-cultural significance of such language to the British, see Kupperman, *Settling*.

66. On depopulation, see Logan, *History of Upper Country*, 1:510, 519; Thornton, *Cherokees*, p. 87. On the disintegration of Coosa, see Ethridge, "Flintlocks," pp. 15–16.

67. Lawson, *History of North Carolina*, p. 238. Thornton, *Cherokees*, p. 63. Duffy, "Smallpox," p. 335; Dobyns, *Their Number Become Thinned*, Tables 25 and 27; Bloom, "Acculturation," p. 346.

68. Thornton, *Cherokees*, pp. 44–45. Chapman, *Tellico Archaeology*, p. 118. Mooney, "Myths of Cherokee," p. 36.

69. British colonial records, in De Vorsey, *Indian Boundary*, p. 100. Cotterill, *Southern Indians*, p. 32; Duffy, "Smallpox," p. 335. *Records in British P.R.O.*, 31:302; Thornton, *Cherokees*, pp. 21, 29–30; Swanton, *Indians of Southeast*, p. 223.

70. On the early settlement of Cherokees along the coast and in Virginia, see Pickett, *History of Alabama*, 1:154. On Cherokees as urbanites, see Wright, *Only Land They Knew*, pp. 14, 228–29. On town relocation, see *Colonial Records of S.C.: Documents*, 1:256–57.

71. Goodwin, *Cherokees*, p. 112. Smith, *Archaeology*, pp. 142–45. On the movement of towns to improve trade linkages, see *Colonial Records of S.C.: Documents*, 1:186;

Ivers, *Colonial Forts*, p. 3; Bloom, "Acculturation," p. 333; De Vorsey, *Indian Boundary*, p. 50; McPherson, *Journal of Egmont*, p. 158. See also Goodwin, *Cherokees*, pp. 116, 103.

72. On the diminution of Cherokee settlements, see Thornton, *Cherokees*, pp. 24–25, 29, 51. On changes in internal structuring of villages and land-use patterns, see Dickens, *Cherokee Prehistory*, p. 15. After the Revolutionary War, Cherokee settlement patterns continued to be altered by the pressures of white encroachment; the Cherokees finally abandoned towns for dispersal on isolated farms, like frontier whites; see Wilms, "Cherokee Settlement," pp. 46–53.

73. Hudson, "Natural Balance," p. 54. Catesby, *Natural History*, 2:xi–xii. On the Cherokee notion of natural balance, see also Mooney, "Myths of Cherokee," p. 446; Goodwin, *Cherokees*, pp. 147–48. For a detailed discussion of the impact of the European market mentality upon the southeastern Indian environment, see Silver, *A New Face*, chap. 4.

74. Bartram, *Travels*, pp. 263–64. *De Brahm's Report*, p. 80. *Historical Collections of S.C.*, 2:482. On the depletion of buffalo and deer, see Logan, *History of Upper Country*, 1:17; Goodwin, *Cherokees*, pp. 98–99. In addition, the salt operations of the Shawnees in West Virginia consumed large forest areas and produced massive pollution; see Maxwell, "Use and Abuse."

75. Cotterill, *Southern Indians*, p. 13. Bloom, "Acculturation," p. 328; Lewis and Kneberg, "First Tennesseeans," p. 3. Reid, *Law of Blood*, chap. 13. Orchard, *Penn Wampum Belts*, p. 11.

76. For regulation against white settlement, see Logan, *History of Upper Country*, 1:178–79. Land cessions were calculated using treaty records and maps in Royce, *Cherokee Nation*.

77. Letter dated 1 March 1689, in Williams, *Early Travels*, p. 93. The British planned expeditions into Southern Appalachia as early as 1649; see Williams, *Dawn of Tennessee*, p. 9.

78. Williams, *Timberlake's Memoirs*, p. 73. George Washington, for example, was just such a speculator; he capitalized upon his role in the French and Indian War to locate desirable holdings; see *Writings of Washington*, 3:1–2; 47–48; 157. On hunter encroachments, see *South Carolina Gazette*, 14 July 1759 and 30 October 1762; *Journal of Grand Council*, 16 September 1756 and 31 October 1766; Logan, *History of Upper Country*, 1:28–31; *Records of Moravians*, 1:46–47, 50, 58; *State Records of North Carolina*, 23:218–19; *Colonial Records of Georgia*, 8:167; Byrd, *Histories of Dividing Line*, p. 157. On the expansion of farms and land speculation by British officers, see Logan, *History of Upper Country*, 1:431–37. Information on boundary negotiations is from De Vorsey, *Indian Boundary*; acreage calculations are based on maps and treaty records in Royce, *Cherokee Nation*.

79. Williams, *Timberlake's Memoirs*, p. 166. On the importance of trading paths in stimulating settlement, see Meriwether, *Expansion*, pp. 162–65. For examples of land cessions related to trade agreements, see *Executive Journals*, 6:363–66; *Colonial Records of S.C.: Documents*, 1:519–20; Logan, *History of Upper Country*, 1:398–99, 495–98; Carter, "British Policy," pp. 45–46; Franklin, "Virginia and Trade," p. 38; Cotterill, *Southern Indians*, p. 29. Calculations of total acreage of land cessions are based on treaty records and maps in Royce, *Cherokee Nation*. On Creek cessions to get better prices, see Cotterill, *Southern Indians*, p. 27. For examples of settlers following the opening of trading paths, see *Colonial Records of S.C.: Documents*, 1:10, 193, 494–96.

80. De Vorsey, *Indian Boundary*, pp. 162–63. Derthick, "Boundary Line," p. 116 and chap. 3. Information on trading debts is from Hagy and Folmsbee, "Lost Archives," pp. 122, 114–16. Acreage calculations are based on treaty records and maps in

Royce, *Cherokee Nation*. Rate of exchange is from Wright, *Only Land They Knew*, p. 95.

81. Wallerstein, *MWS2*, pp. 47, 102, 167, 241.

82. Ibid., p. 158.

83. Hopkins and Wallerstein, "Concluding Note," p. 902. For discussion of "nominal" and "effective" incorporation, see Hopkins and Wallerstein, "Capitalism and Incorporation." Wallerstein, *MWS2*, p. 102, notes that in the period 1600–1700, "a major European reexport trade of colonial products was developed by England, a vast new profitable *entrepot* trade." For example, Cherokee ginseng was reexported to China to be exchanged for luxury goods. Cherokee clay was coveted by the British to use in the manufacture of Wedgewood porcelain, a cheaper replica of Chinese luxury imports.

84. For a brief theoretical discussion of "unequal exchange," see Wallerstein, *HC*, pp. 31–32.

85. According to Wallerstein, *HC*, p. 25, "What was new under historical capitalism was the correlation of division of labour and valuation of work. . . . Under historical capitalism there has been a steady devaluation of the work of women (and of the young and old), and a corresponding emphasis on the value of the adult male's work."

Chapter Three

1. 1763 Proclamation, in Kappler, *Indian Affairs*, 4:1172. Ford, *Writings of Washington*, 2:220. Abbott, "American Land System." Hinsdale, "Western Land Policy." Norona, "Fry's Report."

2. Mulkearn, *George Mercer Papers*, p. 144. De Vorsey, *Indian Boundary*; Hamer, *Tennessee*, 1:241. Henderson, "Pre-revolutionary Revolt," pp. 203–4. Livermore, *Land Companies*, pp. 74–82; Harris, *Land Tenure System*, pp. 301–2. Royce, *Cherokee Nation*.

3. The headright system required recipients to settle a certain number of heads of colonists on the land granted. Quitrents were paid by such colonists to the proprietor. Under the feudal escheat system, land reverted either to the proprietor or to the state in the absence of legally recognized heirs. Alienation fines were charged by proprietors when land was transferred among freeholders, who paid quitrents and did not own the land in the modern sense. Wallerstein, *MWS3*, p. 6. Ford, "Colonial Precedents," pp. 57–58; Giddens, "Land Policies," pp. 147–59. Lands vacated, deserted, or without visible heirs generally escheated to the proprietary. Tenements escheated to the lords of manor when tenants failed to pay quitrents. See Gould, "Land System," p. 31. Harris, *Land Tenure System*, p. 220. Hening, *Statutes of Virginia*, 1:305–29.

4. Mitchell, *Commercialism and Frontier*, p. 82n. Harris, *Land Tenure System*, p. 245; Mitchell, *Appalachian Frontiers*, p. 116. Henderson, "Pre-revolutionary Revolt," p. 194.

5. Mulkearn, *George Mercer Papers*, pp. 145–46. Deane, "Role of Capital," p. 364; Deane is describing the "capital widening" process. The Ohio Company of Virginia was exempted from quitrents for ten years in its attempts to settle West Virginia holdings; see Mulkearn, *George Mercer Papers*.

6. I purposely utilize the concepts of "repopulation" and "resettlement" to avoid the racially derogatory stereotype that these emigrants, rather than Native Americans, were the first residents of these lands. For information on settlement phases, see Gray, *History of Agriculture*, 1:119–26. The names given the areas mentioned are those found on current maps.

7. Treat, *National Land System*, p. 179. The Preemption Act did not become law until 1841, and the Homestead Act was not passed until 1862; see p. 388.

8. The largest of these estates included Ross and Bryan Grant (100,000 acres); Borden Grant (925,000 acres); Roanoke Grant (100,000 acres); Beverly Manor (118,491 acres); Patton Grant (120,000 acres); Carter Grants (100,000+ acres); the manor of Lord Fairfax (100,000+ acres); Van Meter and Kercheval Grants (40,000 acres); McKay and Heyd Grant (100,000 acres); Peyton Randolph (400,000 acres); Bernard Moore (100,000); Hiscock and Griffin (100,000 acres); and Thomas Lewis (100,000 acres). For greater detail, see Kemper, "Settlement"; *Kegley's Frontier*, p. 245; Mitchell, *Commercialism and Frontier*, p. 65; Bennett, "Early Settlement," p. 22; Mitchell, *Appalachian Frontiers*, pp. 109–10. Harris, *Land Tenure System*, pp. 299–300; Livermore, *Land Companies*, pp. 74–82; Anderson-Green, "New River Frontier," pp. 416–18; Abernethy, *Western Lands*, p. 5; Kessel, "Germans," p. 95; Gould, "Land System," pp. 86–87. For example, Daniel Dulaney acquired 16,550 acres, which he surveyed into 100- to 300-acre parcels for sale or lease to German emigrants; see Land, "Land Speculator."

9. Hunt, *Writings of Madison*, pp. 15–17. Soltow, "Land Speculation," p. 111. In Table 3.1, resident surnames were identified by cross-comparing tax lists with census lists or by looking for the payment of local poll taxes. Absentee owners were assumed to be those landholders whose names appear on tax lists but not on census lists or those whose surnames appear as landholders but who pay no poll tax or any other taxes. Female landholders were assumed to be residents since they were exempted from poll taxes and since their husbands' or sons' names usually appeared in the census lists.

10. *Annals of Congress*, 4th Cong., 1st sess., p. 340. Scalf, *Kentucky's Last*, pp. 469–70. Letter from W. Price, Virginia Land Office, 15 January 1795, in *Calendar of Virginia State Papers*, 7:424. Friedenberg, *Life, Liberty*, pp. 99–103, 113–15, 130–32.

11. All grants made before 1810 in the counties of Randolph, Monongalia, and Hampshire were aggregated from *Sims Index*. Residents were identified by using an alphabetical statewide listing; see Bridges, *Virginians in 1800*.

12. Because absentee landholders do not appear on Kentucky county tax lists after 1796, I utilized the early tax lists for Floyd and Madison Counties. Beginning in 1797, nonresident lands were recorded with the State Auditor (not in the counties where they lay), and absentee taxes were paid directly to the State Treasury. Thus, I could not locate any extant records of nonresidents. Taff, *History of State Revenue*, pp. 17–18. The names of several well-known resident large landholders (e.g., the Clays) do not appear at all in county tax lists, or their names appear in some years but not others. It is likely that county tax assessors extended this exclusionary treatment to wealthy absentees as well. Governor's Message, in *Kentucky House Journal*, 1869, p. 5. Gates, "Tenants," p. 5. Teute, "Land, Liberty," pp. 234–36. For more information about East Kentucky, see Dunaway, "Incorporation," Table 3.6. See also Friedenberg, *Life, Liberty*, pp. 213–21.

13. Keith, "Three Blount Brothers," pp. 108–10; 278–90; 296–98.

14. "John Brown's Journal," pp. 285, 295, 298–99, 303, 313; see also pp. 284–313.

15. Billington, *Westward Expansion*, p. 203. The Earl of Granville held the only colonial grant that encompassed parts of western North Carolina, including much of Randolph, Buncombe, and Haywood Counties to the Tennessee state line. Granville had located a land office at Edenton and sold parcels through agents. After the Revolutionary War, this grant was declared forfeit by the Supreme Court, and the lands were largely redistributed. References are to present-day county boundaries in western North Carolina. Information on grants was aggregated from Smathers, *Land Titles*; Deyton, "Toe River Valley"; Bennett, "Burke County," p. 9; Blackmun, *Western North*

Carolina, 1:164–65. John Blount was the brother of William Blount, delegate to the Constitutional Convention and first governor of the Territory South of the River Ohio; see Keith, "Three Blount Brothers." In Virginia and North Carolina, "there was almost no difference between the legislative and executive state leaders and the western land speculators"; see Friedenberg, *Life, Liberty*, pp. 357–58.

16. "John Brown's Journal," pp. 284–313.

17. Every land transaction in the 1789–92 deeds for Pendleton District, South Carolina, was categorized by sales procedure. The deeds are available in published form; see Hendrix, *Pendleton County Deed Book*. When not specified in the deeds, residency of buyers and sellers was identified by using the 1790 census; see U.S. Census Office, *Heads of Families*.

18. *Nashville Whig and Tennessee Advocate*, 20 September 1818. Braudel, *Civilization and Capitalism*, 1:485–97. "The speculative town became the norm as the [American] frontier moved westward"; see Lingeman, *Small-Town America*, p. 34. For a partial list of speculative frontier towns, see Dunaway, "Incorporation," chap. 8.

19. Ford, "Colonial Precedents," p. 38. Calk's Journal and Plan of the Town Called Boonsborough, Calk Papers. Scalf, *Kentucky's Last*, pp. 94, 105. Robertson, *Petitions*, pp. 48–52, 127–28. *Kentucky Gazette*, 18 October 1788. Morrison, "Frontier Forts," pp. 131–39. Mulkearn, *George Mercer Papers*, pp. 164–78, p. 147. *Kegley's Frontier*, p. 322. *De Bow's* 27 (1859): 407–19. Land, "Land Speculator." Chalkey, "Before the Gates," p. 190. Blackmun, *Western North Carolina*, 1:161. Smathers, *Land Titles*, pp. 29, 42. Toulmin, *Western Country*, p. 45. Wayland, "Germans of Valley," pp. 40–44.

20. *Maryland Gazette*, 8 September 1747. Wilhelm, "Local Institutions," pp. 408–18. Land, "Land Speculator," pp. 199–200.

21. "John Brown's Journal," p. 280. *Maryland Gazette*, 7 April 1763; Mulkearn, *George Mercer Papers*, p. 449.

22. Mitchell, *Appalachian Frontiers*, pp. 117–18. Coxe, *Statement of Manufactures*, p. 314n. *Kegley's Frontier*, pp. 424–25; Peters, *Guidebook*; Salmon, *Washington Iron Works*; Cohen, *Historic Springs*. Head and Etheridge, *Neighborhood Mint*, chap. 1. Chitty, "History of Sewanee." Bouwman, *Traveler's Rest*; Scruggs, "Northeast Georgia"; Wellman, *Kingdom of Madison*, chap. 6; Marlowe, "Winchester Springs," pp. 33–38.

23. Data are from analysis of town lots in 1790–1810 county tax lists. Town plat and 1820 census, in Kimsey, *Early Records: Habersham*, pp. 145, 190–92. Jackson, *North Georgia Journal*, p. 12. Mitchell, *Commercialism and Frontier*, p. 84.

24. Names of land barons were aggregated from 1790–1810 county tax list manuscripts. The Louisa Company and the Yazoo Companies were syndicates of merchant and planter capitalists; see Livermore, *Land Companies*.

25. Eller, *Miners, Millhands*, p. 4.

26. For Palmyra, see Keith, "Three Blount Brothers," pp. 296–98.

27. The Maryland anomaly is discussed in a later section. Numerous sources were used to categorize absentee holders, including several genealogical and census listings as well as Laidley, "Large Land Owners," p. 243; Abernethy, *Western Lands*, p. 228; Scalf, *Kentucky's Last*, pp. 181–82; Arbuckle, "John Nicholson," pp. 482–83; Livermore, *Land Companies*; Bennett, "Early Settlement," p. 22; Soltow, "Land Speculation." Military land warrants encouraged land engrossment because of the manner in which these bounties were awarded. The acreage was staggered to reflect the status of the soldier so that the wealthiest officers acquired the largest grants of 2,000 acres and more; see Harris, *Land Tenure System*, pp. 255–67. For information about brokerage houses, see Swierenga, "Western Land Business." There was extensive brokerage trading in military warrants because most soldiers sold their land bounties; see *Ameri-*

can *State Papers: Public Lands* 7:333–76; Friedenberg, *Life, Liberty*, pp. 177–86. For the practice of dodging, see Sakolski, *Land Bubble*, pp. 36, 42, 52–53.

28. 1787 letter, Calk Papers. *Kentucky Gazette*, 21 April 1792. Two early journals kept by land speculators who operated on the Southern Appalachian frontier have been published but virtually ignored by Appalachian scholars. On speculation in North Carolina and Tennessee lands in 1795, see "John Brown's Journal." An 1816 journal about speculation in western Maryland, Virginia, and West Virginia lands is "Uria Brown's Journal."

29. "Uria Brown's Journal," p. 346. Similar land jobbers were found in the Midwest of this era; see Gates, "Role of Land Speculator."

30. Letter, 28 July 1850, Maxwell Papers. Hammon, "Land Acquisition," p. 315; Teute, "Land, Liberty," p. 226. See also 1826–42 transcripts and letters in the Goff Papers.

31. Letters dated 2 January 1854 and 18 February 1840, Levassor Papers. As a public surveyor, Washington mapped much of the Virginia and West Virginia area where he amassed an estate of 29,754 acres; see *Writings of Washington*, 37:295–302. Calk laid off the town of Boonsborough, thereby acquiring prime town lots and linkages to nearby river lands; see entries of April 1775 in "William Calk, His Journal," Calk Papers.

32. Quarrier to Levassor, 7 July 17 1855, Levassor Papers. Sakolski, *Land Bubble*, p. 32. Teute, "Land, Liberty," p. 225. "Uria Brown's Journal," pp. 365–66. Brown subsequently hired the clerk "as Agent over these several tracts of lands."

33. Letter dated 18 November 1854, Levassor Papers. Agreement dated 29 July 1808, McCoy Papers. In the mid-1800s, West Virginia merchants Samuel Tolbert (Lewis County) and John Rogers (Monongalia County) acted as agents for out-of-state landowners; see Talbott-Tolbert Papers and Rogers Papers. Hammon, "Land Acquisition," pp. 308–10; Thwaites, *Early Western Travels*, 3:278. "Uria Brown's Journal," p. 363.

34. "Uria Brown's Journal," pp. 153–54. "Report from the State Auditor's Office," 28 December 1816, Kentucky Land Office Records: Nonresident Land Owners, 1792–1843.

35. Population densities were calculated using aggregated county statistics in 1810 *Census of Population* and in Anderson, *American Census*, pp. 90–96; for revealing maps of the intraregional disparities in population density, see pp. 93–95. Population densities were then compared with proportions of absentee-held land in Table 3.1. Obviously, the threat of Indian warfare does not account for these disparities in resettlement, for Tennessee and the Carolinas encroached on the Cherokee Nation and experienced post-Revolutionary incursions. Moreover, distance from the coast does not account for the differences. Several counties of Virginia and West Virginia are closer to the coast but were less populated than western Maryland. Age of the settlement area does not account for these differences either. The oldest settlements were located in Virginia and West Virginia, but the population density does not reflect a steady influx of emigrants there.

36. *Writings of Washington*, 28:393. The 1810 population density for the entire United States was 9.1 persons per square mile. The 1810 population density of Frederick County, Maryland, was 45.2 persons per square mile. The two Frederick counties are roughly equidistant to the Atlantic Coast.

37. Huth and Pugh, *Talleyrand in America*, p. 144. In the 1780s, Maryland lands were selling at an average price of five pounds (more than $20) per acre; see Harris, *Land Tenure System*, p. 247. Gould, "Land System," pp. 62–63. In addition, Maryland allocated military claims by lottery; Virginia did not; see Soltow, "Land Inequality," pp.

282, 290n. For North Carolina and Tennessee military bounties, see *Laws Relative to Lands*, pp. 35–40. In Virginia, the land office and taxation were centralized at Richmond. Uria Brown reported in his 1816 journal that "the Western counties of Virginia is in a half state of Insurrection with the Southern Counties of said State . . . the treasury at Richmond would not receive their [local bank] paper & the people Cannot get money that will be taken for taxes." Richmond officials accepted only paper currency from banks chartered in Virginia or Maryland, and these distant institutions were inaccessible to many residents of West Virginia; see "Uria Brown's Journal," pp. 362–63. Virginia restricted land grants to Anglican Church members and to slaveholders; the land companies lobbied the Virginia Council for legislative changes to permit early land sales to groups like the Germans. See Harris, *Land Tenure System*, pp. 249, 334, 351–52. In 1782, Kentucky squatters petitioned the Virginia Assembly to require grantees to cultivate and improve the land; see Robertson, *Petitions*, pp. 66–68. However, Virginia never legislated any requirement more than nominal evidence of seating (constructing a makeshift cabin; use of the land by tenants) to retain legal possession. Hopkins, *Papers of Henry Clay*, 1:898.

38. *Writings of Washington*, 28:436–37.

39. Abdy, *Residence and Tour*, 3:89. In 1730, Virginia grantees resold Valley lands for six times the purchase price; see Abernethy, *Three Virginia Frontiers*, p. 55. In 1793, western Maryland agricultural lands within fifteen miles of town were selling for $16 to $24 per acre; see Toulmin, *Western Country*, p. 54. In Tennessee, lands sold for $2 per acre until the 1820s, with much higher prices for river lands. Only the worst mountain acreage sold cheaply at 12.5 cents per acre; see Whitney, *Land Laws of Tennessee*, pp. 58–61.

40. Robertson, *Petitions*, pp. 63, 67–68. "Governor's Message," *Kentucky Senate Journal*, 1828, p. 3. Porter, "Backcountry to County," p. 338. Smith, "Letter," p. 93. All land grants between 1787 and 1800 in the counties of Knox, Madison, Pulaski, and Wayne were aggregated from Jillson, *Kentucky Grants*. Settlers were identified by utilizing a statewide alphabetical listing; see Clift, *"Second Census."* A "settler" was defined as a landholder who resided in the county where the Appalachian lands were located. A similar pattern emerged in West Virginia, where post-Revolutionary settlers owned less than 13 percent of the total acreage in three counties; see Dunaway, "Incorporation," Table 3.2; Abernethy, *Western Lands*. Only 33.5 percent of all land grants in Kentucky were settler and preemption claims; see Hammon, "Land Jobbers," pp. 250, 259.

41. For examples of local planters who invested in Appalachian lands, see Skipwith Papers; *Thomas Jefferson's Farm Book*; "Journal of John Sevier." Information about landholdings of Jefferson and Gallatin were aggregated from 1800 county tax lists for Albermarle and Monongalia Counties, Virginia. For maps and plats of Gallatin's lands, see Hansford Papers. For information about Lenoir, see Bennett, "Early Settlement," p. 22. Also see Friedenberg, *Life, Liberty*, pp. 248–60.

42. Craven, "Soil Exhaustion," p. 62. Frontier land concentration was derived from analysis of 1790–1810 county tax list samples. Care was taken to distinguish the landless sons of property holders from other landless households; see Appendix. For analysis of frontier land concentration in East Tennessee, see Soltow, "Land Inequality," p. 286. See also map of Frederick and Jefferson Counties, Virginia, 1809.

43. "Memorandum of Austin's Journey," pp. 525–26. For a similar account of Appalachian South Carolina in this era, see Bacot, "South Carolina," p. 692. See also Teute, "Land, Liberty," pp. 238–39. Southern Appalachia's landless rate is parallel to other regions of the United States in this era. For instance, 50 percent of Pennsylvania (1798) and 55 percent of Ohio (1810) males were landless; see Soltow, "Land Inequal-

ity," pp. 277–78. Toulmin, *Western Country*, p. 80; Mitchell, *Commercialism and Frontier*, pp. 70, 88; *Farmer's Register* 5 (1803): 334. These landless households moved so often that very few of their names appear in the same county tax lists from one year to the next. Over half the people in one tax list were missing from the next year's list; see Hsiung, "Isolation and Integration in East Tennessee."

44. *Writings of Washington*, 28:199, 355; 27:344.

45. Gould, "Land System," p. 82. McNall, "John Grieg," p. 528; Scalf, *Kentucky's Last*, p. 95; Spence, *Land of Guyandote*, p. 75; Hammon, "Land Acquisition," pp. 302, 308. Teute, "Land, Liberty," pp. 194–97.

46. Thwaites, *Early Western Travels*, 3:279–80. Dater, "Albert Gallatin," p. 29. Danhof, "Farm Making Costs." *Executive Journals*, 6:552–54. *Documentary History*, 2:225–26. On the treatment of squatters, see also Abernethy, *Western Lands*, pp. 90, 218; Gates, "Tenants," pp. 11–14; Teute, "Land, Liberty," p. 153. On poor relief, see Smathers, *Land Titles*, p. 68; Harris, *Land Tenure System*, p. 246.

47. Henretta, "Families and Farms," p. 24.

48. "Autobiography of Lincecum," p. 448. Turtle-at-Home to Meigs, 1 October 1809. Louis-Phillipe, *Diary of Travels*, pp. 66, 99. The Records of the Cherokee Indian Agency indicate the extent of the Cherokees' problems with illegal settlers on their lands. Encroachers were discussed in the following letters or reports. *Tennessee*: A List of White Settlers, 22 April 1809; Address to Intruders, 23 April 1809; Names of Intruders, 10 February 1813; List of Settlers, 1 June 1813; Bogs to Meigs, 20 February 1807; Lowrey to Settlers of Franklin County, 1 February 1813; Meigs to Macrae, 17 June 1803; Meigs to Macrae, 26 August 1803; Meigs to Millridge, 17 November 1803; Pathkiller to Meigs, 7 July 1819; Meigs to John C. Calhoun, 6 September 1819. *Alabama*: List of Intruders, 23 May 1809; Drew to Alabama, 12 January 1807; Hicks to Meigs, 7 July 1819. *North Carolina*: Adair to Meigs, 12 September 1813; Adair and Aunechee to Meigs, 2 March 1813; Hicks to Meigs, 18 February 1815; Hicks to Meigs, 7 July 1819. *Georgia*: Adair to Meigs, 12 September 1813; Alexander to Meigs, 22 February 1805; Meigs to Kingsbury, August 1803; Vamel to Meigs, 25 March 1805.

49. *Huntsville Republican*, 21 January 1818. In addition to his land speculation, Coffee traded in Illinois salt, operated five boats to act as a commission merchant between Nashville and New Orleans, exported slaves to Natchez, and held interests in a store, cotton gin, boatyard, tavern, and racetrack; see Chappell, "Life and Activities." For a description of Coffee's corruption, see Chappell, "Some Patterns," pp. 467–68.

50. Letter dated 18 November 1818, Campbell Papers, Duke University. Chappell, "Some Patterns," p. 472; Livermore, *Land Companies*, pp. 146–62; Whitaker, "Muscle Shoals"; *American State Papers: Public Lands* 7:548–49.

51. *American State Papers: Public Lands* 5:376–81. Such prime lands sold from $4 to $13.25 per acre; see Rohrbough, *Land Office Business*, pp. 110–11. Powell, "Description," pp. 112–13. Allman, "Yeoman Regions," p. 139. See also Rohrbough, *Land Office Business*, chap. 5.

52. Letter dated 8 January 1819, Campbell Papers, Duke University. Allman, "Yeoman Regions," p. 139.

53. On Indian removals, see Foreman, *Indian Removal*. Smathers, *Land Titles*, pp. 82–85; Hamer, *Tennessee*, 1:255. Lands worth less than fifty cents were not surveyed off but were reserved for later disposition.

54. These lands were purchased from Peet and Gilbert in the early 1900s to become the home of Champion Fiber Company, which is still located on this tract; see Smathers, *Land Titles*, p. 96. Hamer, *Tennessee*, 1:261; Chapter 25, Public Laws of 1850–51, *Code of 1883 of North Carolina*, 2:101–5.

55. I checked the residency of all 381 lottery grantees for Habersham County, Georgia, between 1821 and 1829. Cross-comparisons were made between Deed Book A and the 1820 and 1830 census lists in Kimsey, *Early Records: Habersham*.

56. McNall, "John Grieg," pp. 527–29; Levassor Papers; Summers, "James Swan's Lands"; Dater, "Albert Gallatin." For example, analysis of 1900 county land books shows that Charleston and Wheeling were heavily absentee-owned.

57. For planter investments, see Account Book, 1803–22, Barbour Papers; Warrick-Miller Papers, 1816–42; Means-Seaton Papers, 1818–39; Wickliffe-Preston Papers. For mineral investments, see letters dated 29 September 1856 and 14 February 1859, Temple Papers; letters and agreements after 1830 in Johnson Newlon Camden Papers, Marshall Papers, and Middleton Correspondence. For mineral speculation in East Tennessee, see Armstrong, *History of Hamilton*, pp. 105–8, 149; Holt, *Claiborne County*, pp. 16–17; Hoskins, *Anderson County*, p. 33; Lillard, *History of Bradley*, pp. 42–43; Nicholson, *Grundy County*, p. 28. For a typical antebellum promotional survey, see Troost, *Fifth Geological Report*.

58. Virginia Senate Chamber to Maxwell, 24 March 1853, Maxwell Papers. For instance, O. P. Temple of East Tennessee and Lewis Maxwell and David Goff in West Virginia were land agents for absentee landholders; see Temple Papers, Maxwell Papers, and Goff Papers. See also lease agreements and letters in McCoy Papers and Rogers Papers.

59. Virginia Senate Chamber to Maxwell, 8 February 1853, Maxwell Papers. One Philadelphia landowner wrote to West Virginia agent McCoy: "Please continue thy care of these lands and advise us of such Internal Improvements and Geological developments as may tend to enhance their value." See letter dated 15 February 1839, McCoy Papers.

60. Undated emigrant prospectus entitled "Colonies in Western Virginia" and plat map labeled "1st Western Virginia Colony," with 1845 letters of Louis Chitti, Levassor Papers. On other frontiers, see Waples, "Farm Ownership"; Bogue and Bogue, "Profits"; Bogue, *From Prairie*; Swierenga, *Pioneers*. Also see earlier discussion of the marketing tactics of the John Gray Blount Land Company dealing in Tennessee and North Carolina lands; Keith, "Three Blount Brothers."

61. Hopkins and Wallerstein, "Capitalism and Incorporation," pp. 776–77. For theory, see Frank, *Dependent Accumulation*, p. 161.

62. For town detail, see Dunaway, "Incorporation," Table 8.1, Figures 8.1 and 8.2.

63. To distinguish them from laborers, "cash renters" have been counted here with farm owners. Cash renters typically held wealth, slaves, and other means of production. Not reflected in Table 3.7 were agricultural laborers who resided in the households of farm operators. Laborers who resided on farms, but who did not have dwellings separate from their employers, were enumerated by 1860 census-takers as though they were members of the households of their employers. This category of wage laborers is discussed in a later section. Because of this enumeration method, the figures in Table 3.7 are not inflated by the unmarried sons of farm owners who hired themselves out as temporary wage laborers. Such individuals were enumerated in the 1860 census as members either of their parents' households or of their employers' households and, therefore, "disappear" when the labor force is assessed in terms of households rather than individuals.

64. Innes, *Work and Labor*, p. 248. Also see Clark, *Roots*, pp. 306–7.

65. Findings were derived from an analysis of Appalachian veterans surveyed in *CWVQ*. The quotations are from *CWVQ*, pp. 1063, 878. For information about agricultural wage rates, see pp. 1, 46, 801, 940, 966, 1946, 2165. Nearly 50 percent

(238) of the veterans were poor, defined as those who described their parents as landless with very limited assets or as struggling owners of small farms.

66. *Augusta Chronicle*, 24 September 1819. *CWVQ*, pp. 64, 1932; 1057.

67. *CWVQ*, p. 699. Innes, *Work and Labor*, p. 248.

68. *CWVQ*, pp. 801, 22, 801, 1235, 94, 1946. Appalachian wealthholding patterns derived from analysis of sample of 3,056 households drawn from the 1860 Census of Population manuscripts.

69. Innes, *Work and Labor*, pp. 251, 127. Almost all of the Civil War veterans reported the same pattern of schooling in every section of Southern Appalachia; see, for example, *CWVQ*, pp. 5, 9, 13, 20, 897, 1080, 1229, 1360, 1922, 2013, 2086. For an Appalachian example, see the contract for subscription school dated 7 July 1845, Freeman Papers. Hamer, *Tennessee*, pp. 356–57. *North Carolina Standard*, 3 August 1853. Appalachian wealthholding patterns were derived from analysis of a sample of 3,056 households drawn from the 1860 Census of Population manuscripts.

70. Stewart, "Land Tenure," pp. 10–11. See also Atack, "Agricultural Ladder," p. 14; Winters, "Agricultural Ladder," p. 37.

71. Eller, "Land and Family," p. 87. On inheritance, see Gray, Stewart, and Turner, "Farm Ownership," p. 562. For inheritance patterns, 474 Appalachian Civil War veteran questionnaires were analyzed in *CWVQ*. On national inheritance patterns, see Gates, *Frontier Landlords*; Chandler, *Land Title Origins*; Friedenberg, *Life, Liberty*; Soltow, *Men and Wealth*.

72. On Kentucky land-granting restrictions, see Jillson, *Kentucky Land Grants*, i–xi. For difficulties in becoming a landowner on American frontiers, see McNall, *Agricultural History*, pp. 240–41; Hofstadter and Lipset, *Turner and Sociology*, pp. 105, 115–16; Henretta, "Families and Farms," pp. 8–10.

73. For the Lenoir leases, see Reid, "Antebellum Rental Contracts," pp. 71–73.

74. *CWVQ*, p. 392. Calculations were based on a systematic probability sample of 3,056 households drawn from the 1860 Census of Population manuscripts for all nine state subregions. Of the 1,398 landless households, 14.2 percent were 24 or younger; 32.9 percent were between 25 and 34; 19.2 percent were between 35 and 46; 15.9 percent were between 47 and 54; and 17.8 percent were 55 or older. Atack, "Agricultural Ladder," p. 16, argues that "Rising entry costs seem the most likely explanation for why starting out as an owner-occupant was an increasingly remote dream for the young, but as these farmers aged they seem to have been able to advance more rapidly up the ladder than earlier generations."

75. This mountainous county was computer selected from the counties for which a frontier county tax list and the 1860 census manuscripts were available. Both sets of records were computerized and alphabetized to permit longitudinal tracking. Households were grouped by surname, and each surname group was tracked in both sets of records. To check for inheritance, 1801 landless heads of household with the same surname as landholders were tracked again in the 1860 census.

76. Oral history collected by the author. McKenzie, "From Old South," p. 120. For similar accounts, see the oral histories of Frank Harmon and Melvin Proffitt, Appalachian Oral History Project.

77. Wallerstein, *MWS3*, chap. 4.

78. Ibid., chap. 2.

79. Ibid.

80. Kenwood and Lougheed, *Growth of International Economy*.

81. Otto, *Southern Frontiers*, chap. 1, discusses the connection between expansion of the southern frontiers and world-market conditions.

Chapter Four

1. Wallerstein, *Capitalist World-Economy*, p. 265. Amin, *Accumulation*, pp. 15–16; Frank, *Dependent Accumulation*, p. 161.

2. Braudel, *Civilization and Capitalism*, 2:59. Innes, *Work and Labor*, pp. 106–9. Petrusewicz, "Wage-Earners," pp. 489–90.

3. Luxemburg, *Accumulation*, p. 358. Munslow and Finch, *Proletarianisation*, p. 5. Wallerstein and Martin, "Peripheralization," p. 194; Amin, *Accumulation*, pp. 15–16; Frank, *Dependent Accumulation*, p. 161; Roseberry, "From Peasant," p. 83. Labor markets were not a creation of the Industrial Revolution; rather, capitalist labor markets were initiated in predominantly agricultural economies. See Braudel, *Civilization and Capitalism*, 2:52; Rothenberg, "Emergence of Farm Labor"; Wallerstein, *MWS1*, p. 127. Wallerstein, *Politics*, p. 290; Wallerstein, *Capitalist World-Economy*, pp. 147–48; Amin, "Social Characteristics," p. 46; Wallerstein, *MWS1*, chap. 2.

4. On the notion of family labor, see Eller, "Land and Family," p. 87.

5. I identified the resident laborers in farm households in several ways. First, enumerators consistently listed such laborers as the last entries for the households in which they resided and identified them with such terms as "hired hand" or "farm laborer." Second, these laborers typically had different last names from their employers, and they were most often single and younger than forty-five years of age. Third, enumerators often specified that such laborers were not family members. Since it was possible that family members might have had different surnames than the household head, I scrutinized carefully these characteristics: age, evidence of other family members with same surname, wealth, and enumerator comments. If the person had wealth of more than $50 or appeared to be too old or too young to work, I considered those persons family members. In most instances, however, paid laborers (and incidentally "bound" laborers) stand out from the family members.

6. On tenants as coerced laborers, see Mendenhall, "Southern Tenancy."

7. Arrighi and Saul, *Essays*, p. 69. Wallerstein and Martin, "Peripheralization," p. 196.

8. Janvry and Vandeman, "Patterns," p. 67. Smith, Wallerstein, and Evers, *Households*, pp. 81–82.

9. McDonald, "Specifications," p. 43. Entry dated 13 January 1858 in Benjamin Johnson Barbour Memorandum Book, Barbour Papers. The notion of "finding" appears in early New England and southern law; see Morris, *Government and Labor*, p. 109. Similar contractual provisions appear in the antebellum contracts of the Lenoir plantations in western North Carolina; see Reid, "Rental Contracts," p. 76.

10. For households as income-pooling units, see Smith, Wallerstein, and Evers, *Households*, pp. 37–55.

11. Bizzell, *Farm Tenancy*.

12. On inheritance, see Chapter 3. My finding of little intrafamily tenancy is supported by other studies; see, for example, Bode and Ginter, *Farm Tenancy and Census*. In the early 1900s, only 13 percent of southern tenants rented farms owned by relatives; see Gray, Stewart, and Turner, "Farm Ownership," p. 529.

13. Agreement between Nathan Dehart and Morgan Dehart (1857), in Browder, "The Cherokee Indians," p. 297. *FHPJ*, p. viii. Court case of Floyd v. Floyd (1850), cited in Ford, "Social Origins," pp. 102–3.

14. Hopkins and Wallerstein, *Processes*, p. 163. Lenin, *Development of Capitalism*, p. 203.

15. *Code of State of Georgia*, p. 408. Ruling of Georgia Supreme Court, cited in Bode and Ginter, *Farm Tenancy and Census*, p. 94.

16. On planters as semisedentary, see Craven, "Soil Exhaustion." I utilized several types of information from the farm census manuscripts to distinguish statistically between these categories of landless farm operators, including ownership of work stock; ownership of farm tools; size of parcel; household wealth; identifying labels or comments made by the census enumerators; types and amount of crops and livestock produced; and the degree to which the household was food deficient in its crop production. In addition, comparisons were drawn between tenancy and labor contracts located in archival and primary sources.

17. Agreements dated 10 March 1803 and 24 April 1805, McCoy Papers. Bliss, "Rise of Tenancy," pp. 431–33. Toulmin, *Western Country*, p. 50.

18. July–August 1786, Jonathan Clark Notebook. Knowlton, "Journal of Crawford," p. 9. "Uria Brown's Journal." Benjamin Johnson Account Book, 1801–6, Barbour Papers. Des Champs, "Early Days," pp. 209–10; "David Stuart's Report," pp. 283–92; *Thomas Jefferson's Farm Book*, p. 165; Thwaites, *Early Western Travels*, 3:58–59; Reid, "Rental Contracts."

19. Bliss, "Rise of Tenancy," p. 435. Account Books and Memoranda, 1777–1800, Muse Papers. Dickson Papers, 1815–60. Ewin Papers. Letters of Samuel T. Tolbert, Talbott-Tolbert Papers. George W. Smith Papers, 1831–42. Correspondence and pocket diary of James Wilson, 1800–1820, Wilson and Stribling Papers. Correspondence of William McCoy, Sr., McCoy Papers. Correspondence about tenant ejectments from absentee owner's land in Lewis County, 1803–26, Boardman Papers. Letter dated 23 August 1853, Maxwell Papers. Letters and agreements, 1828–67, Tavenner and Withers Papers.

20. Agreements and letters pertaining to Lee and Estill Counties, 1787–1841, Wickliffe-Preston Papers and Alves Papers.

21. Harris to Christie, 11 April 1797.

22. Thwaites, *Early Western Travels*, 3:279–80.

23. "Albermarle," pp. 44–45. Olmsted, *JBC*, pp. 258–59. A Virginia planter also engaged in this type of tenant parceling; see entries dated 17 December 1806–21 January 1807, Benjamin Johnson Account Book, 1801–7, Barbour Papers. The following elites, drawn from the 1860 Census of Agriculture manuscripts, are typical of Appalachian gentleman farmers: J. J. Woodward, lawyer (Talladega, Alabama); William Henderson, minister (Cass, Georgia); James Hoff, physician (Mason, West Virginia); Robert Elsom, merchant (Albermarle, Virginia); James Smith, manufacturer (Franklin, Virginia); W. S. Reed, physician (Warren, Tennessee); Amos Harrill, merchant (Rutherford, North Carolina); Lewis Brummer, miller (Frederick, Maryland); Nelson Read, merchant (Allegany, Maryland); William Long, physician (Clinton, Kentucky). Usually among the wealthiest households in their communities, these men, on the average, owned twenty-two slaves and held estates other than farms valued at $23,425.

24. *CWVQ*, pp. 318, 814, 202. For use of terms, see Rosengarten, *All God's Dangers*, p. 466; Woofter, *Landlord and Tenant*, p. 10.

25. Economic characteristics of tenant farmers are derived from analysis of the farm sample.

26. Smith, *Review*, p. 25. Reid, "Rental Contracts," p. 75.

27. Reid, "Rental Contracts," p. 77. Lease dated 11 February 1835, McCoy Papers.

28. *Thomas Jefferson's Farm Book*, p. 119. For parallel tenancy procedures in a later period, see Reid, "Rental Contracts."

29. Reid, "Rental Contracts," p. 76. Lease dated 11 February 1835, McCoy Papers. Leases dated 13 March 1842–12 June 1857, Wickliffe-Preston Papers. On the "thirds and fourths system," see *Proceedings of Agricultural Convention*, pp. 5–8; Mangum, *Legal Status*, pp. 12–13, 22–23.

30. Letter dated 20 January 1843, Wilson-Lewis Papers.

31. Calling card of Charles Town Real Estate and Finance Company, Forsythe Papers. Lambert, *Undying Past*, chap. 11. Lord, *Blue Ridge Guide*, 1:272.6, 2:339.5, 2:417.8, 2:422.4.

32. Sharecropping is historically rooted in land tenure mechanisms that originated in medieval Europe; see Byres, "Historical Perspectives." Scholars who have studied land speculation on the American frontier report that early American tenants were more like sharecroppers than present-day tenants. See Harris, *Land Tenure System*, p. 340. Morris, *Government and Labor*, p. 212; Orser, *Material Basis*, 38.

33. Georgia Supreme Court ruling, cited in Brooks, *Agrarian Revolution*, p. 67. Applewhite, "Sharecropper," pp. 136–38. On paying wages as crop shares, see *Code of State of Georgia*, pp. 436–38. For South Carolina's 1833 law defining croppers as wage laborers, see Orser, *Material Basis*, pp. 56–57.

34. Articles of Agreement dated 31 December 1847, Henry W. Jones Papers.

35. *Writings of Washington*, 28:185–86. *Thomas Jefferson's Garden Book*, p. 265. Belting involved clearing wooded land by cutting trees so that they would die, then planting among the stumps; see pp. 74, 464. See also letters and account books about property rentals and plantation management, Monroe Papers, 1790–1846 (Albermarle, Virginia); Anderson Papers, 1850–58 (Botetourt, Virginia).

36. Address from Pathkiller to Indian Agent, 2 November 1819, Records of Cherokee Indian Agency. *Proceedings of Agricultural Convention*, pp. 5–8. Malone, "Cherokee-White Relations," p. 12.

37. *CWVQ*, p. 45. Lanman, *Letters*, p. 62. See also Thwaites, *Early Western Travels*, 3:279–80.

38. Analysis of sample derived from 1860 census manuscripts. The term "cropper" appears frequently in census manuscripts for Appalachian counties in Virginia, West Virginia, North Carolina, and middle Tennessee.

39. Census MSS: Agriculture.

40. Lenoir Plantation contracts, in Reid, "Rental Contracts." *Thomas Jefferson's Farm Book*, p. 166. *Thomas Jefferson's Garden Book*, pp. 202, 265, 267, 270. See also account entries in Miller Farm Records; *CWVQ*, pp. 293, 621, 665, 769, 1460, 2174; contracts in Wickliffe-Preston Papers; 1840s contracts and account entries in Wilson-Lewis Papers. Economic characteristics of sharecroppers were derived from analysis of the farm sample.

41. The following farm account books were useful: Plantation Accounts of Alexander Henderson, 1798–1810, Henderson-Tomlinson Papers; 1853 Farm Account Book, Meredith Papers; Correspondence and Receipts, 1841–50, McClaugherty Papers; Farm Account Book, 1831–50, Courtney Papers; Plantation Account Books, Campbell Papers, West Virginia University; diary of farming operations, 1851–60, Clarke Papers. Patterns of tobacco and cotton sharecropping are evident in these manuscripts: Mallory Diary, 1843–60 (Talladega, Alabama); Ridgeway Plantation Diaries, 1828–29, 1830–34, 1838–39, 1842–44 (Albermarle, Virginia), Minor Notebooks; Frederick County, Virginia, Plantation Account Books, 1810–50, Bryarly Papers. For patterns of sharecropping in connection with livestock operations in Haywood, North Carolina, see 1840–58 letters in Lenoir Papers.

42. Letter dated 10 June 1841, Wilson-Lewis Papers. "Diary of Nathaniel Reinhardt," in Marlin, *History of Cherokee*, p. 51. Economic characteristics of sharecroppers are derived from analysis of the farm sample.

43. Moore, *Calhoun Boy*, p. 8; see also pp. 5–7.

44. Mason, *John Norton*, pp. 486–88. For correspondence with overseers, see Yancey Papers, 1835–60; Carter Papers, 1825–58; Berrien Papers, 1851–55.

45. *Thomas Jefferson's Garden Book*, pp. 190–91, 202, 158, 255; *CWVQ*, pp. 1520, 390. Reid, "Rental Contracts," p. 76. McDowell Papers, 1830–46; General Edmund Jones Papers, 1796–1844.

46. Census MSS: Agriculture. On Fannin County copper mining, see Thompson, *Touching Home*, pp. 124–32; Census MSS: Manufacturing, Fannin County, Georgia.

47. Letter dated 14 December 1840, Wilson-Lewis Papers. Overseer agreement dated 29 July 1838, Wickliffe-Preston Papers. Correspondence of John F. Howard, 1850, about farm managed at Congo, West Virginia, Howard Papers. Correspondence with overseers at estates in Rockbridge County, Virginia, 1830–46, McDowell Papers. Correspondence with overseers in Cherokee County, Alabama, and Floyd County, Georgia, 1825–58, Yancey Papers. Correspondence with overseers in Murray, Georgia, 1825–58, Carter Papers. Correspondence with overseers in Clarksville, Georgia, 1851–55, Berrien Papers. Wilkes County, North Carolina, farm account books, 1796–1844, General Edmund Jones Papers. *Thomas Jefferson's Farm Book*, pp. 76, 95. Account entries for Greene County, Virginia, farm manager Henson, 21 December 1858, Benjamin Johnson Barbour Memorandum Book, Barbour Papers. Farm manager contracts, 1828, 1838, 1839, and 1844, Wickliffe-Preston Papers.

48. Entries dated 1829, 1838, 14 February 1855, and 8 March 1855 in Accounts, Wickliffe-Preston Papers. *Thomas Jefferson's Farm Book*, pp. 393, 401, 459–60; *Thomas Jefferson's Garden Book*, p. 357. Olmsted, *JBC*, pp. 258–59. Census MSS: Agriculture.

49. Olmsted, *JBC*, pp. 208–9. On timber cutting on shares, see letter dated 30 December 1835, Wilson-Lewis Papers; *FHPJ*, p. xii. Coal pits on Owsley County farms were rented on a half-share basis; see letter dated 6 January 1822, Wickliffe-Preston Papers.

50. Orser, *Material Basis*, pp. 142–43.

51. Cottage tenants appear in the manuscripts as those landless farm households that were food deficient but cultivated only small amounts of corn and vegetables, kept no livestock, held no wealth, and owned neither work stock or farm implements.

52. Atkeson and Atkeson, *Pioneering*, pp. 26–27.

53. Innes, *Work and Labor*, p. 112. *FHPJ*, pp. 21–22, 25. Agreements dated 13 March 1842 and 15 February 1846, Wickliffe-Preston Papers. Beasley is labeled a "renter-washwoman" by the 1860 census enumerator in McMinn, Tennessee. "Vineland," pp. 95–111.

54. Entry dated 25 May 1858, Benjamin Johnson Barbour Memorandum Book, Barbour Papers. Agreement dated 15 February 1846 and letter dated 21 December 1840, Wickliffe-Preston Papers. *FHPJ*, pp. 18, 22, 25.

55. Census MSS: Agriculture.

56. Lord, *Blue Ridge Guide*, 1:8.5, 2:349.2, 2:368.2.

57. Lambert, *Undying Past*, pp. 138–39.

58. *Knoxville Gazette*, 24 September 1792. "John Brown's Journal," pp. 289, 305–6. Entry dated July–August 1786, Jonathan Clark Notebook. In East Kentucky, such squatters were legally liable for the payment of rents and damages to the party declared the new legal owner; see Hammon, "Land Acquisition." Jillson, "Big Sandy," p. 246.

59. Census MSS: Agriculture.

60. Census MSS: Population, Greene County, Tennessee. On vagrancy laws, see Wisner, *Social Welfare*; Orren, *Belated Feudalism*, pp. 76–77; Morris, *Government and Labor*, pp. 6–16. On squatters in the Alabama mountains, see Olmsted, *JBC*, p. 219. The Georgia and Virginia squatters were selected from Census MSS: Agriculture.

61. *CWVQ*: pp. 243, 395, 780, 801, 940, 1387, 1435, 1670, 1858, 1404. Lambert, "Oconaluftee," p. 421. Olmsted, *JBC*, p. 278. Smith, *Review*, p. 57. *FHPJ*, pp. xiv–xvi,

46, 55, 58–59. "Journal of John Sevier," p. 246. 1846 diary, Wilson-Lewis Papers. Advances of food charged against wages, Col. Benjamin Johnson Account Book, 1801–6, and 13–14 January 1858 entries, Benjamin Johnson Barbour Memorandum Book, Barbour Papers. Data about unemployment of day laborers derived from analysis of Census of Population manuscript sample. Wallace, *South Carolina*, pp. 498–99.

62. Olmsted, *JBC*, p. 260.

63. *Thomas Jefferson's Farm Book*, p. 159. From the farm sample, I estimated the proportion of farm owners reporting resident farm laborers and an average number of laborers per farm. These proportions were then multiplied by the number of farm owners reported in Table 3.7.

64. *CWVQ*, pp. 10, 405. *Thomas Jefferson's Farm Book*, pp. 161, 165–66. Aldie Plantation entries dated 31 December 1858 and 1 January 1860, William N. Berkeley Ledgers, 1854–60, Berkeley Papers. *FHPJ*, p. 35. Reid, "Rental Contracts." Agreements of 1828–58, Wickliffe-Preston Papers. *Documentary History*, 2:275–76. Annual contract laborers appear in Ridgeway Plantation Diaries, 1828–29, 1838–39, 1842–44 (Albermarle, Virginia), Minor Notebooks; Plantation Account Books, 1854–58 (Frederick, Virginia), Bryarly Papers; various receipts and bills, 1838–46, Kidwiler Papers; Mallory Papers (Talladega, Alabama). The 1860 census asked adults to report the number of months they were involuntarily unemployed during the previous year; I estimated the level of unemployment for wage farm laborers using that information from my census samples.

65. Munslow and Finch, *Proletarianisation*, p. 2. Chase-Dunn, *Global Formation*, p. 233. For greater statistical detail regarding the Appalachian labor force, see Dunaway, "Incorporation," Table 4.2.

66. Analysis is based on raw census data in Browder, "The Cherokee Indians," pp. 197–214, 218–19. State laws in Tennessee, North Carolina, and Georgia prohibited the purchase or ownership of land by nonwhites; see Owl, "Eastern Band," pp. 89–90. Even though the 1860 census enumerators were instructed not to report any Indian households, Cherokees appear in the 1860 census manuscripts for several counties of East Tennessee, western North Carolina, and northern Georgia. Typically, these households are identified as either "illegal squatters" or as "farming on shares." In Monroe County, Tennessee, the original Cherokee owner of a ferry and mill is listed in the 1860 census manuscripts as a "farm laborer" for the new white owner.

67. Lossiah, "Story of My Life," pp. 90–92.

68. The slave count was aggregated from 1860 published county census of population.

69. For greater statistical detail regarding the Appalachian labor force, see Dunaway, "Incorporation," Table 5.13.

70. "Employment of the Indigent," *Journal of Commerce*, 20 November 1847. Townsend, "Dissertation," pp. 403–4, 415. *Mechanics Free Press*, 18 October 1828. While contemporary popular usage may limit the term "indentured" to immigrant laborers, I am applying it here in the legal sense that was customary in antebellum documents and newspapers. In so doing, I hope to correct popular myths about the sources of indentured labor.

71. "Employment of the Indigent," *Journal of Commerce*, 20 November 1847. Klebaner, "Poor Relief," pp. 310–15. The 1860 Census of Population manuscripts contain information for poorhouses (which averaged between two and eleven inmates) in the following counties: Calhoun, DeKalb, and Jackson, Alabama; Letcher, Kentucky; Cherokee, North Carolina; Rutherford and Surry, North Carolina; Pickens, South Carolina; White, Tennessee; Fauquier, Warren, and Wythe, Virginia. Only two counties reflected a tendency to institutionalize paupers; the poorhouses in Alleghany

and Frederick Counties, Maryland, housed ninety-eight and forty-one inmates respectively.

72. Crowther, *Workhouse System*. Morris, *Government and Labor*, pp. 314–89. On methods of handling paupers, see Overseers of the Poor, 1850–54, Raleigh County Archives; Record of Poor Funds, 1859, Summers County Archives; Record of the Overseer of the Poor, 1835–57, Marshall County Archives; Poor Funds, 1831–32, Harrison County Tax Book; Overseers of the Poor, 1861, Brooke County Archives; Poor Relief Records, Augusta County, Virginia, 1791–1822, Tapp Papers; Staunton, Virginia, Poor Records, 1770–1872; Bradley County, Tennessee, Poor Commission. On the indenturement of destitute children, see correspondence of Florence Fleming, 1858–63, Fleming Papers; apprenticeship indentures of 1828 and 1846, Krebs Papers. On Appalachian Alabama, see Brewer, "History of Coosa," pp. 37–41; and "Reminiscences of Olden Times, 1809–1850" and "The Centennial History of Winston County," Cather Collection. Scharf, *History of Western Maryland*, 2:1347. Johnson, *Antebellum North Carolina*, pp. 257, 690–96, 704. Taylor, *Antebellum South Carolina*, p. 86.

73. Buncombe County petition, cited in Johnson, *Antebellum North Carolina*, pp. 584–85. Taylor, *Antebellum South Carolina*, p. 87.

74. *Registers of Free Blacks*, Augusta entries, nos. 1, 29, 39, 48, 50, 51, 52, 85, and Staunton entries, nos. 6, 29, 31, 33, 52, 63, 79. Free Negro Register, Monroe County Archives. Indenturement of free blacks appears in the poorhouse records previously mentioned for the following counties: Raleigh and Brooke, West Virginia; Augusta and Staunton, Virginia; Bradley, Tennessee.

75. Census MSS: Agriculture, Calhoun, Alabama, no. 719; Wayne, Kentucky, no. 590; Magoffin, Kentucky, no. 311; Rockbridge, Virginia, no. 802. For greater statistical detail regarding indentured laborers, see Dunaway, "Incorporation," Table 4.11.

76. Evans, "Morse's Report," p. 70. Thwaites, *Early Western Travels*, 3:301. *Slave*, 10 (5): 211. Pendleton County, West Virginia, Apprenticeship Indenture, Harry F. Temple Typescripts. Wallace, *South Carolina*, p. 382; *CWVQ*, pp. 1705, 996–97; 1560.

77. Oral history collected by the author. See also *CWVQ*, p. 1499.

78. Egypt, Masuoka, and Johnson, "Unwritten History," p. 106. *Slave*, 7:45–47. *Slave II*, 3:672, 9:3870. See also *CWVQ*, p. 246; *Slave*, 6:155, 12:350.

79. Oral history collected by the author.

80. *Slave*, 12:350. *Slave II*, 12:311–12. Eqypt, Masuoka, and Johnson, "Unwritten History," p. 10; *Slave II*, 6:2282; 2 (2): 50; 12:350.

81. *Slave*, 13:81.

82. Hopkins and Wallerstein, "Capitalism and Incorporation," p. 777. Mies, Bennholdt-Thomsen, and Werholf, *Women*, p. 29.

83. Gutkind, *Third World Workers*, p. 181.

84. Oral history collected by the author. For entries of livestock or produce received by physicians in payment of annual medical accounts, see Physician's Account Book, 1833–39, Laisley Papers; Physician's Daybook, 1855–60, Marmaduke Dent Papers. *CWVQ*, pp. 1229, 1609, 1640, 1682. *FHPJ*, pp. 22, 66.

85. Olmsted, *JBC*, pp. 208–9. *CWVQ*, p. 1229; *FHPJ*, p. 73.

86. Boydston, "Daily Bread," p. 22. *FHPJ*, pp. 15–17, 19, 22, 25, 33, 41, 65. Agreement dated 1 November 1828 and letter dated 26 May 1840, Wickliffe-Preston Papers.

87. *CWVQ*, p. 1401. Agreement dated 1 November 1828, Wickliffe-Preston Papers. On using landless wives to make clothes for the plantation owner and slaves, see Aldie Memorandum Book, 1838–50, Berkeley Papers. Johnson, *Weaving Rag Rugs*, pp. 6–18.

88. *CWVQ*, p. 270.

89. Phillips, "Incorporation," p. 802.

Chapter Five

1. Pearsall, *Little Smoky Ridge*, p. 127. Even contemporary world-systems theorists have made the mistake of viewing Appalachia in terms of this stereotype. Chase-Dunn, *Global Formation*, p. 210, comments that "Appalachia has long been a subsistence refuge region."

2. See, for example, Hofstadter, "Myth of Yeoman"; Merrill, "Cash Is Good"; Henretta, "Families and Farms"; Hedley, "Rural Structure"; Shammas, "How Self-Sufficient?"

3. On barter, see Braudel, *Civilization and Capitalism*, 1:447–48. Tenant farmers or sharecroppers should not be thought of as subsistent. In the case of these landless farmers, the landowner holds legal control over the means of production. In these instances, agricultural commodities are produced for profitable sale in local or distant markets. Moreover, the landowner "remunerates" tenant laborers with crop shares. In short, we should think of tenant farmers and sharecroppers as coerced wage laborers. See Brooks, *Agrarian Revolution*; Wright, *Old South*, p. 102; Woodman, "Agriculture and Law."

4. Wallerstein, Martin, and Dickinson, "Household Structures," p. 438. Wallerstein, *HC*, pp. 23–24. For the argument that subsistence production is precapitalist activity, see Boydston, "Daily Bread"; Stauth, "Capitalist Farming"; Clark and Haswell, *Economics*. For the argument that subsistence production occurs within the capitalist system, see Marx, *Capital*, 1:274, 276–77, 431. Also see Hopkins and Wallerstein, "Patterns," pp. 111–46.

5. The assets level that distinguishes poor antebellum households from their wealthier peers has been determined to be $100; see Soltow, *Men and Wealth*, chap. 3. A turn-of-the-century study determined that a farmer needed 100 acres to produce survival needs for the average mountain farm family in 1900; see U.S. Department of Agriculture, *Agriculture*. To produce its subsistence needs during the eighteenth century, an American family of five needed 73 acres: 8 acres for crops, 35 acres for livestock support, 15 acres pasture, and 15 acres woodland; see Lemon, "Household Consumption." In line with these two studies, I utilized 100 acres as the maximum size for a subsistent Appalachian farm. For a similar conceptualization of subsistence, see Headlee, *Political Economy*, p. 2.

6. On reinvestments, see Table 5.5.

7. Census MSS: Agriculture, Roane County, West Virginia. In addition to the other factors mentioned above, household consumption was taken into account to identify subsistence producers. Household consumption includes food for family members; grains to feed consumed livestock and one work animal; seed reservations for the next year's subsistence needs; and a waste allowance. To estimate consumption, annual production of major food crops, grains, swine, and cattle were converted to corn equivalencies (see Appendix).

8. Analysis of farm sample.

9. On the difficulty of locating pure subsistence, see Wilk, *Household Ecology*, pp. 7–8.

10. Clark and Haswell, *Economics*, p. 71; Wallerstein, Martin, and Dickinson, "Household Structures," pp. 440–41. Bernstein, "African Peasantries," pp. 421–43.

11. Census MSS: Agriculture, Berkeley County, West Virginia.

12. Eller, *Miners, Millhands*, pp. 11–12. Appalachian land distribution was derived from analysis of a systematic probability sample of 3,447 farm households drawn from Census MSS: Agriculture. Total sample farm acres = 479,322.

13. Weld, *Travels*, p. 113. Analysis of questionnaire responses by all Civil War veterans from Appalachian counties (n = 474) in *CWVQ*. Wilms, "Cherokee Land Use," pp. 161–62.

14. Farmland distribution for Monroe County was derived from analysis of all farms (n = 1,238) enumerated in the 1860 Census of Agriculture manuscripts. Regional trends are from analysis of farm owners in the 1860 farm sample.

15. Wilms, "Cherokee Land Use," pp. 161–62. Analysis of questionnaire responses by all Civil War veterans from Appalachian counties (N = 474) in *CWVQ*. For greater statistical detail, see Dunaway, "Incorporation," Table 5.2.

16. For midwestern trends, see Atack and Bateman, "Land and Development," p. 291. On the cost of establishing new antebellum farms, see Danhof, "Farm Making Costs." Antebellum speculation in mineral and resort lands is detailed in Chapters 3 and 6.

17. National per capita crop production was aggregated using statistics in U.S. Census Office, *Agriculture in 1860*: corn = 26.7 bushels; wheat = 5.5 bushels; cotton = 0.17 bales; tobacco = 13.8 pounds; hogs = 1.1; cattle = 0.7.

18. Southern per capita crop production was aggregated using data published in ibid.: corn = 8.1 bushels; wheat = 0.9 bushel; cotton = 0.13 bale; tobacco = 6.5 pounds; hogs = 0.5; cattle = 0.3.

19. Aggregated from county statistics in ibid. For greater statistical detail, see Dunaway, "Incorporation," Table 5.6.

20. For statistical detail, see Dunaway, "Incorporation," Table 5.7.

21. Crop production averages were derived from analysis of the farm sample drawn from Census MSS: Agriculture.

22. Kaplan, *Blue Ridge*, p. 22; Banks, "Emergence," p. 190; Gazaway, *Longest Mile*, p. 64; Billings, Blee, and Swanson, "Culture, Family," p. 158.

23. Fox-Genovese, "Antebellum Households," pp. 222–23; Chevalier, "Nothing Simple," p. 157.

24. For theoretical distinctions between precapitalist and capitalist societies, see Marx, *Capital*, 1:281; Wallerstein, *HC*, p. 15; Sahlins, *Stone-Age Economics*, p. 303; Elwert and Wong, "Subsistence Production," p. 504; Vellenga, "Women"; Bernstein, "African Peasantries." When estimating corn equivalencies available for export, 5 percent of the total grain production was deducted to allow for waste or losses; 5 to 13 percent of grain production was reserved as seeds for future crops; 14.3 percent of the total hog production and 28.6 percent of the total cattle production were deducted to allow for herd replacement. For these methods, see Battalio and Kagel, "Structure."

25. For global averages in agricultural production, see Wallerstein, *MWS3*, p. 142.

26. On poultry exports, see Smith, *Review*, p. 2; Hilliard, *Hog Meat*. In the early 1800s, East Kentucky butter was sent in barrels via Louisville and New Orleans to the Caribbean; see Thwaites, *Early Western Travels*, 3:245. In the 1830s and 1840s, Tidewater Virginia purchased large quantities of butter and cheese from its western counties; see *Farmer's Register*, 2 (1800): 611; Kemper, "Settlement," p. 179. In the 1840s, Fauquier County, Virginia, produced cheese, and the Valley of Virginia shipped butter to eastern markets; see Gray, *History of Agriculture*, 2:838. In 1843, South Carolina purchased $255,000 worth of East Tennessee and western North Carolina butter and cheese; see *Carolina Planter* 1 (1844–45): 42; *Farmer's Register* 4 (1802): 711.

27. *Slave II*, 9:3878–81. Hilliard, *Hog Meat*, p. 199. Smith, *Review*, p. 2. "David

Stuart's Report," p. 289; Thwaites, *Early Western Travels*, 3:242; Raulston and Livingood, *Sequatchie*, p. 99. Lambert, *Undying Past*, p. 97.

28. *Report of Patents, 1851*, p. 133. *Report of Patents, 1850*, p. 188. Lamb, "The Mule," pp. 24, 33. *Farmer's Register*, 2 (1800): 611.

29. Olmsted, *JBC*, pp. 223–24. *Frankfort Daily Commonwealth*, 15 March 1842. Ashton, "Jack Stock," p. 2. Mitchell, *Appalachian Frontiers*, p. 227. Letters, 1815–38, Lenoir Papers. *CWVQ*, p. 1655.

30. For antebellum trends, see Wentworth, *America's Sheep Trails*, p. 72. Only in the Appalachian counties of Alabama and Maryland did the production of cattle exceed the production of sheep in 1860. Calculations are based on aggregated county totals from U.S. Census Office, *Agriculture in 1860*.

31. *Report of Patents, 1851*, p. 334. For average prices, see Cole, *Wholesale Commodity Prices*. Wool and cotton prices were calculated from aggregated county totals in U.S. Census Office, *Agriculture in 1860*. On Virginia and West Virginia sheep raising, see Caldwell, *History of Brooke*, p. 146. For records of sheep growers, see Beall Papers and Ware Papers. Dodrill, "Cross Creek," pp. 32–33; McCrum, "Aurora," p. 26; Gray, *History of Agriculture*, 2:834–35. Estate inventory, 1853, Berkeley Papers.

32. In 1843, South Carolina imported 24,826 bundles of Appalachian hay; see *Carolina Planter* 1 (1844–45): 42; *Farmer's Register* 4 (1802): 6, 93. On feathers, see Smith, *Review*, p. 2; Clayton, "Deery Inn," *FHPJ*, p. 59.

33. On national exports to Europe, see *Report of Patents, 1851*, pp. 461–62; U.S. Census Office, *Statistical View*.

34. For greater statistical detail, see Dunaway, "Incorporation," Table 6.1.

35. *Mountain Visitor* (Townsend, Tennessee), 10 August 1990, p. 9; "Uria Brown's Journal," pp. 273; 281–83; 360. Laprade Account Books, 1839–60. Mill and distillery accounts, Nadenbousch Papers. White, *Statistics*. *Wheeling Intelligencer*, 12 April 1879. Wayland, *History of Shenandoah*, p. 274. Details in this section about industrial activity were derived from analysis of Census MSS: Manufacturing and from aggregated county totals in U.S. Census Office, *Manufactures in 1860*.

36. Census MSS: Manufacturing and aggregated county data in the published census. *Knoxville Gazette*, 22 May 1794.

37. Census MSS: Manufacturing and aggregated county data in the published census. On Wheeling, see Johnson and May, *Over the Counter*, p. 96.

38. Census MSS: Manufacturing and aggregated county data in the published census.

39. Ibid.

40. Ibid. The following counties had antebellum cotton mills: Coosa, Alabama; Chatooga, Georgia; Frederick, Maryland; Surry and Caldwell, North Carolina; Pickens, South Carolina; Warren and Washington, Tennessee; Albermarle, Virginia; Ohio and Brooke, West Virginia.

41. Hale, *Early History of Warren*, p. 33; White, *Statistics*, p. 300. *Knoxville Register*, 22 June 1853; Wallace, *South Carolina History*, p. 381. Details about industrial activity were derived from analysis of Census MSS: Manufacturing and aggregated county totals in U.S. Census Office, *Manufactures in 1860*.

42. U.S. Census Office, *Manufactures in 1860*; Rockbridge County, Virginia, Historical Society. For statistical detail, see Dunaway, "Incorporation," Table 9.5.

43. Gouger, "Northern Neck," p. 76; Skaggs, "John Semple"; Rice, *Allegheny Frontier*, p. 321. Williams, *History of Washington*, p. 157.

44. Reprinted in *De Bow's* 19 (1855): 228–29.

45. White, *Statistics*, p. 92. *Carolina Planter* 1 (1844–45): 42; *Farmer's Register* 4 (1802): 6, 93. Lindstrom, "Southern Dependence," p. 109.

46. Barrels of flour and meal contained 196 pounds; see Cole, *Wholesale Commodity Prices*.

47. To determine farm-owner averages, total county export surpluses were divided by the number of farm owners and cash renters reported in Table 3.7. Dabney, *Mountain Spirits*, p. 72. *Niles Register* 20 (1821): 63. Gusfield, *Symbolic Crusade*, p. 75. Details about whiskey and liquor production are from Census MSS: Manufacturing. Sayre, "Morgantown."

48. For greater statistical detail about leather, tool, and meat exports, see Dunaway, "Incorporation," Tables 9.5 and 9.7. On lard, see De Bow, *Industrial Resources*, 1:377. On leather, see Johnson and May, *Over the Counter*, p. 106; Williams and McKinsey, *History of Frederick*, 1:277–78.

49. For wool sales in the period 1831–47, see Miller Farm Records. *FHPJ*, p. 34. Warren, Tennessee, and Habersham, Georgia, were famous jeans producers; see Census MSS: Manufacturing. For greater statistical detail about manufactured tobacco and textile exports, see Dunaway, "Incorporation," Tables 9.8, 9.9, 9.5.

50. For statistical detail, see Dunaway, "Incorporation," Table 9.5.

51. Raw grain exports were derived from Ibid., Table 11.5. The disadvantages to the region of this asymmetrical integration are discussed in greater detail in Chapter 8.

52. Chase-Dunn, *Global Formation*, p. 210.

53. Worsley, *Three Worlds*, p. 94. For functions of capitalist agrarian farms, see Wallerstein, *MWS3*, p. 138.

54. Wallerstein, *MWS3*, p. 153. Cain and Hopkins, "Gentlemanly Capitalism," pp. 503–4. Amin, *Accumulation*, p. 195 observes that, in contrast to economic development in the peripheries, "landed property has progressively lost its dominant position in the economy and in society" of core regions.

55. Amin, *Accumulation*, p. 195. For the dominance of landed elites in the peripheral formations, see pp. 192–95.

56. Marx, *Capital*, 1:747–48.

57. Ibid., 1:176.

58. For parallels with other peripheries, see De Janvry, *Agrarian Question*; Ward, *Women Workers*, pp. 25–47. For theory regarding spinoffs and multipliers, see Hirschman, *Strategy*.

Chapter Six

1. Industries were aggregated from U.S. Census Office, *Manufacturing in 1860*, with certain esoteric categories like dentistry and photography excluded from the totals. For a parallel discussion of antebellum industrial development in the entire South, see Parker, "Southern Development"; Bateman and Weiss, "Comparative Regional." Throughout this chapter, the term "gross" refers to the gross value of manufactured goods.

2. Average capital invested per firm: United States, $7,170; New England, $12,456; Middle Atlantic, $8,164; Midwest, $5,216; South, $4,847; Southern Appalachia, $4,967. Capital invested per capita: United States, $37; New England, $82; Middle Atlantic, $52; Midwest, $19; South, $11; Southern Appalachia, $18. Derived from aggregated totals in the published 1860 Census of Manufacturing. For statistical detail, see Dunaway, "Incorporation," Table 6.4.

3. Average size of manufacturing firms has been calculated for several regions in Bateman and Weiss, "Comparative Regional." These interregional averages were utilized to categorize by employment and gross. The 1860 census labor counts are for free

wage laborers; the census did not report the number of slaves employed at various manufacturing and extractive firms.

4. The following Appalachian counties were characterized by medium-size firms, which averaged five to nine laborers. Alabama: Coosa, Shelby; Georgia: Bartow, Hall, Polk, Whitfield; Kentucky: Boyd, Clay, Estill, Lawrence, Pulaski, Madison; Maryland: Frederick, Washington; North Carolina: Watauga; Tennessee: Warren; Virginia: Bedford, Franklin, Roanoke; West Virginia: Brooke, Hancock, Mercer, Preston, Ritchie. Manufacturing firms averaged more than ten laborers in the following Appalachian counties. Georgia: Chatooga, Fannin, Floyd; Kentucky: Greenup; Maryland: Allegany; North Carolina: Surry; Tennessee: Campbell, Hamilton, Marion, Meigs, Polk; Virginia: Patrick, Smythe, Wythe; West Virginia: Boone, Kanawha, Marshall, Mason, Ohio, Wood.

5. One of the country's earliest nail factories was established in Washington County, Tennessee, and the Old Forge Nail Factory of Washington County, Maryland, employed 200 white laborers and 60 slaves in the mid-nineteenth century. Still, the country's largest antebellum nail and spike producers were located in West Virginia, where one firm in Marshall County employed 299 laborers; three firms in Ohio County utilized 502 workers. Detail about industrial activity was derived from analysis of Census Enumerator Manuscripts, 1860, for Appalachian Counties: Census of Manufacturing, and from aggregated county data in the published census. Artisan and building trades have been excluded. Williams, *History of Washington*, 1:246.

6. Most of the housewares firms were small to medium in size, averaging four laborers. However, the country's largest glass factories operated in Ohio County, West Virginia, where two firms employed 240 laborers. Although they are seriously undercounted in the 1860 census, Southern Appalachia was regionally renowned for its varieties of pottery. Firms in northern West Virginia, the Shenandoah Valley, middle Tennessee, and northern Georgia produced redware, ceramics, crockware, and jugs for local consumers and for export. Jefferson, *Wheeling Glass*. Caldwell, *History of Brooke*, p. 144. "Pottery," pp. 23–29. Monongalia Historical Society, *Morgantown*, p. 21. Rice and Stroudt, *Shenandoah Pottery*. Webb, "Pottery," pp. 100–112. White, *Statistics*. Scruggs, "Northeast Georgia." Elrod, *Historical Notes*, p. 165. Because Halls Rifle Works at Harpers Ferry invented the first breech-loading rifle and the earliest arms with interchangeable parts, this town became the site for the U.S. Armory. As such, the company was heavily subsidized by the federal government, which, in the 1850s, expanded the facility into a massive complex of workers' houses around a modern factory and several warehouses. Smith, *Harpers Ferry*. Railroad cars were manufactured in Knox County, Tennessee, and in Hampshire County, West Virginia. Millstones were engineered in Claiborne County, Tennessee. Industrial bellows were cast in Ohio County, West Virginia; and Rockbridge County, Virginia, produced wheels, hubs, and felloes. The heaviest industrial machinery and steam engines were produced in Calhoun and Coosa Counties, Alabama; in Floyd, Union, and Whitfield Counties, Georgia; in Allegany and Frederick Counties, Maryland; in McMinn and Hamilton Counties, Tennessee; in Wythe County, Virginia; and in Ohio County, West Virginia. Four steam engine plants were concentrated in the cities of Wheeling and Wellsburg, West Virginia. Ambler, *History of West Virginia*, p. 208. Wheeling, West Virginia, paper mills imported drying fans from a firm in Cincinnati. Even though paper milling was little developed in Southern Appalachia, the country's first paper bags were manufactured in Brooke County, West Virginia. Wrapping paper, newsprint, and blank books were produced at medium-size facilities in only eight Appalachian counties. One East Tennessee factory periodically engaged trains of 500 horses and mules to transport from Baltimore and Cincinnati the rags needed to make

paper. Letter dated 29 January 1851, Paper Mills Letter. Caldwell, *History of Brooke*. *WPA Guide to Tennessee*, p. 329. Details about industrial activity were derived from analysis of Census MSS: Manufacturing and from aggregated county data in U.S. Census Office, *Manufactures in 1860*.

7. For national and regional comparisons, see Bateman and Weiss, "Comparative Regional."

8. For greater detail about the methods used to estimate the magnitude of exports going to various markets, see Dunaway, "Incorporation," Table 9.5.

9. Census MSS: Manufacturing. Johnson and May, *Over the Counter*, p. 106. Williams and McKinsey, *History of Frederick*, 1:277–78.

10. On rifles, see Harpers Ferry Typescript. Census MSS: Manufacturing.

11. For greater statistical detail about extractive exports, see Dunaway, "Incorporation," Table 9.4. On iron export levels and markets, see Smith, "Historical Geography," pp. 114–19.

12. Blethen and Wood, "Antebellum Iron"; Smith, "Historical Geography."

13. On kerosene and natural gas, see Yergin, *The Prize*, pp. 23–26.

14. Lord, *Blue Ridge Guide*, 2:330.9; Young, "Southern Gold Rush," p. 373. *Niles Weekly Register* 39 (1830): 106. *Southern Banner* (Athens, Georgia), 7 April 1843. Near Dahlonega, one such landowner found a deposit and then "went to leasing small sections, which [we]re worked by a good many men, giv[ing him] a decent living"; see Lanman, *Letters*, p. 15. Fauquier County, Virginia, was the only county for which gold mining was reported in the 1860 census. However, no manufacturing returns were made for several Georgia counties where gold mining occurred. Even though the U.S. Mint was located there, no manufacturing return was made for Lumpkin County, Georgia. The following counties had active gold mines in 1850: Alabama: Coosa (2), Talladega (2); Georgia: Hall (5), Habersham (10), Cherokee (4), Lumpkin (4), Fannin (1); North Carolina: Burke (1), Rutherford (1), Surry (1); South Carolina: Pickens (4); Tennessee: Monroe (3); Virginia: Fauquier (5), Greene (3), Amherst (1). See Sakowski, *Touring*, p. 151; White, *Statistics*; Thompson, *Touching Home*, pp. 46–47; Peters, *Guidebook*, p. 34; Roberts, *Gold Seekers*, pp. 59–65, 150.

15. *Western Herald* (Auraria, Georgia), 9 April 1833. Killion and Waller, *Slavery Time*, p. 99. Jackson, *North Georgia Journal*, pp. 158–59. Roberts, *Gold Seekers*, pp. 59–65, 150. Van Benthuysen, "Sequent Occupance," p. 26. Green, "Forgotten Industry." Diary, Barbour Papers. *CWVQ*, pp. 2239–40. "Diary of Geological Tour," p. 46. Sakowski, *Touring*, p. 151. *De Bow's* 18 (1855): 241–42. U.S. Census Office, *Mines and Quarries*, pp. 168–69, 200–201, 276, 307, 317.

16. *Niles Weekly Register* 39 (1830): 106. Jackson, *North Georgia Journal*, p. 107. Exhibit at Dahlonega, Georgia, Gold Museum. Georgia Historical Commission Marker no. 154-9. Green, "Forgotten Industry"; Green, "Gold Mining of North Carolina"; Green, "Gold Mining in Virginia." Roberts, *Gold Seekers*, pp. 60–61. *De Bow's* 18 (1855): 241–42.

17. Cappon, "Trend."

18. Smith, "Historical Geography," map, p. 4. Williams, "Washington County," pp. 347–48. *American Railroad Journal* 15 September 1842, pp. 161–64; *Niles Weekly Register* 47 (14 September 1844): 20. *Cumberland Alleghanian*, 27 September 1845. Gutheim, *Potomac*, pp. 212–13.

19. *Cumberland Alleghanian*, 27 September 1845. The 1820 census reported that the western Maryland iron works had "been in profitable operation for sixty years." In 1860, iron manufactories were active in these western Maryland counties: Allegany (1), Frederick (2), Washington (2). See *Kentucky Gazette*, 15 April 1797. Crapster, "Hampton Furnace." Depew, *One Hundred Years*, p. 232. Harvey, "Frontier Iron-

works." *Niles Weekly Register* 48 (15 November 1845): 172. Allen, "Mount Savage," p. 36. *Cumberland Civilian*, 29 January 1847.

20. Russell Papers. Smith, "Historical Geography," pp. 201, 248–58. Moore, "Historical Geography," pp. 49–51. Iron manufactories were active in these East Kentucky counties: Boyd (2), Carter (2), Estill (3), Greenup (9), Lawrence (2). See "Old Furnaces of Kentucky"; Census MSS: Manufacturing, Kentucky counties; journals and papers, 1849–59, Means-Seaton Papers; notes to 1849 diary, Hilton Diaries; Moore, "Historical Geography," pp. 49–51; Coleman, "Kentucky Furnaces."

21. Smith, "Historical Geography," pp. 70, 114–19, 101–2. Bruce, *Virginia Iron*, p. 134. "Lucy Selina's Charcoal," p. 31. Toulmin, *Western Country*, p. 36. Salmon, *Washington Iron Works*, pp. 34, 53–55. Cappon, "Trend," pp. 372–73.

22. Iron manufactories were active in these Appalachian Virginia counties: Albermarle (1), Alleghany (2), Augusta (4), Bedford (1), Botetourt (2), Carroll (1), Craig (1), Fauquier (1), Floyd (1), Franklin (2), Frederick (1), Grayson (1), Lee (1), Loudon (1), Nelson (1), Page (2), Patrick (1), Pulaski (2), Roanoke (1), Rockbridge (4), Rockingham (6), Shenandoah (8), Smythe (1), Warren (2), Washington (1), Wythe (5). See "Old Furnaces of Kentucky." Dabney, "Jefferson's Albermarle," pp. 187–88. Bruce, *Virginia Iron*, pp. 453–56. "Diary of Geological Tour," p. 28. Wayland, *History of Shenandoah*, chap. 14. Account books for pig iron furnace, 1820–64, Sanders and Greene Papers and Notebooks. Shenandoah Iron Works documents, Blakemore Papers. Cloverdale Furnace documents, Anderson Papers. Pine Forge data, Pennybacker Daybook. Smith, "Historical Geography," p. 93. Salmon, *Washington Iron Works*, p. 34.

23. Williams, "Journal of Deaderick," pp. 131–32. Hersch, "Iron Industry," pp. 17–21. Belissary, "Industrial Philosophy," p. 52. Smith, "Historical Geography," p. 313. Nave, "History of Iron," pp. 95–97. *Atlanta Daily Intelligencer*, 8 April 1859. Williams, "Early Iron Works," pp. 43n, 46n. "Journal of John Sevier," p. 26n. *Railroad Advocate*, 4 July 1831. Cappon, "Trend," p. 371. MacArthur, *Knoxville*, p. 40. *Tennessee Historical Markers*, p. 89. Van Benthuysen, "Sequent Occupance," pp. 12–15.

24. Iron manufactories were active in these Appalachian Tennessee counties: Anderson (1), Hancock (1), Hamilton (1), Grainger (1), Jefferson (1), McMinn (1), Sevier (1), Union (1), Blount (2), Campbell (4), Claiborne (3), Knox (2), Monroe (2), Rhea (3), Roane (4), Washington (2), Carter (5), Greene (4), Sullivan (2), Johnson (12). See Safford, *Geological Reconnaissance*, pp. 51–55; Fink, "Bumpass Cove Mines"; Van Benthuysen, "Sequent Occupance," p. 18. Belissary, "Industrial Philosophy." Nave, "History of Iron," p. 54. Hunt, "Pactolus Iron." *Tennessee Historical Markers*, pp. 47, 56–57, 62, 74, 79. MacArthur, *Knoxville*, p. 40.

25. Iron manufactories were active in these West Virginia counties: Berkeley (1), Brooke (1), Greenbrier (1), Hancock (10), Hardy (9), Jefferson (11), Kanawha (1), Marion (1), Mason (1), Monongalia (13), Ohio (8), Preston (2), Wood (1). See Ambler, *History of West Virginia*, p. 208. Monongalia County Land and Legal Papers; Preston County Papers; clipping on iron furnaces, Barbour County, Miscellany Papers No. 1115; Greenville Mining and Manufacturing Company letters, Hagans Papers; Barbour County Manuscripts and Articles. "Iron Industry in Jefferson County." *West Virginia: Centennial*, p. 62.

26. Barbour County Typescript. Smith, "Historical Geography," pp. 116–17. Hamilton Family Typescript. Census MSS: Manufacturing. Morel, "Early Iron." On nails, see Ice's Ferry Typescript.

27. Iron manufactories were active between 1850 and 1860 in the following counties: Alabama: Calhoun (1), Cherokee (1), Shelby (2); Georgia: Cass (2), Dade (1), Fannin (1), Floyd (1), Habersham (3), Murray (1); North Carolina: Surry (1), Cher-

okee (5), Watauga (2), Ashe (2). For western North Carolina iron manufacturers, see "Diary of Geological Tour," pp. 22–23; Sakowski, *Touring*, pp. 30–31, 205; *The Star*, 21 February 1811; Cappon, "Iron Making," pp. 342–43; Blethen and Wood, "Antebellum Iron." For Alabama, see Census MSS: Manufacturing. For Georgia, see Bouwman, *Traveler's Rest*, p. 155; Marlin, *History of Cherokee*, p. 149; Coleman, *History of Georgia*, p. 172; Elrod, *Historical Notes*, p. 19; *Rome Courier* (Georgia), 3 March 1860; *Atlanta Daily Intelligencer*, 28 April 1859.

28. Cappon, "Trend," pp. 372–75. Blethen and Wood, "Antebellum Iron." Jackson, *North Georgia Journal*, pp. 14–15. Smith, "Historical Geography," pp. 313–14.

29. "General Slade's Journal," p. 45. White, "Salt Industry," p. 238. *Wheeling Intelligencer*, 27 December 1854. Donnally and Steele Kanawha Salt Works Records. Goodall, "Manufacture," p. 235. Lanman, *Letters*, p. 158. *Knoxville Register*, 30 April 1834. *Hunt's MM* 39 (1858): 430–33.

30. White, "Salt Industry," pp. 238–41. The following East Kentucky counties had active salt furnaces in 1860: Clay (6), Pulaski (1), Lawrence (1); see published Census of Manufacturing. Moore, "Historical Geography," p. 41. Talley, "Salt Lick Creek."

31. Thwaites, *Early Western Travels*, 3:247; White, "Salt Industry," p. 241. Pulaski County salt went by flatboat to Nashville in the 1830s; see Wait Papers. Moore, "Historical Geography," pp. 41–44. *Knoxville Register*, 4 July 1831. Parr, "Kentucky's Overland Trade." For greater statistical detail about 1860 salt exports, see Dunaway, "Incorporation," Table 9.4.

32. *De Bow's* 18 (1855): 680. *Wheeling Intelligencer*, 27 December 1854. Donnally and Steele Kanawha Salt Works Records. Goodall, "Manufacture," pp. 235–37. "Historical Sketch," Dickinson Papers. Cohen, *Kanawha Images*, p. 37.

33. Pease, "Great Kanawha," pp. 192–93, 180. Carpenter, "Ward Diary," p. 45. Cohen, *Kanawha Images*, p. 37; Mosby, "Salt Industry," p. 133. "Salt Manufacturing in Mason County."

34. Agreement dated 10 November 1817, Dickinson Papers.

35. On tariffs, see Pease, "Great Kanawha," pp. 191–93. On the salt cartels, see Hunter, "Studies," pp. 50–77. On the 1845–55 era, see Stealey, "Salt Industry," chap. 8.

36. Receipts, 1851–52, Ruffner-Donnally and Company Records; Kanawha Salines Account Book, 6–9 March 1827, Ruffner Papers; letters of John D. Lewis, 1840–60, Lewis Papers; Hansford Papers; Willcox Diary, 1843–54. Stealey, "Salt Industry," pp. 124–27, 131–33, 158–59, 510–12, 517.

37. Stealey, "Salt Industry," chap. 6; pp. 145, 473–76, 526. 598–99. Petition dated 27 January 1835, Legislative Petitions of Kanawha County. "Salt Manufacturing in Mason County."

38. U.S. Census Office, *Census for 1820*; Depew, *One Hundred Years*, p. 179.

39. Goddard Diary. Letter dated 6 January 1822, Wickliffe-Preston Papers. For greater statistical detail about coal exports, see Dunaway, "Incorporation," Table 9.4. On early coal pits, see Lewis, *Coal, Iron, Slaves*, p. 48; Wait Papers; Scharf, *History of Western Maryland*, pp. 1342, 1441. Coal was discovered by land companies in East Kentucky and upper East Tennessee in 1750. See Jillson, "History of Coal," p. 1.

40. "Uria Brown's Journal," pp. 348–49. *Cumberland Civilian and Telegraph*, 9 and 23 June 1859. Lewis, *Coal, Iron, Slaves*, p. 49. Census MSS: Manufacturing.

41. Letter dated 6 January 1822, Wickliffe-Preston Papers. Goddard Diary, pp. 12–13. Jillson, "History of Coal," p. 30. *Kentucky House Journal*, 1837–38, p. 468; 1838–39, Appendix: 24. Verhoeff, *Kentucky River*, pp. 172–79.

42. Letters dated 7 February 1837 and 29 August 1861, Wait Papers. Verhoeff, *Kentucky River*, p. 178.

43. Letter dated 28 November 1833, Wait Papers.

44. Moore, "Historical Geography," pp. 52–56. Bill of lading, 1858, Maysville, Kentucky, Papers.

45. Hoskins, *Anderson County*, p. 36. *De Bow's* 10 (1851): 73–76. Gauding, "Water Transportation," pp. 99–100. Seeber, "History of Anderson," p. 49. Siler, *Tennessee Towns*, pp. 88, 50. McCormick, "Development of Coal." Burns, "Blount County Coves," p. 59. *WPA Guide to Tennessee*, p. 67. U.S. Census Office, *Census for 1820*, and U.S. Census, *Fifth Census*. Seeber, "History of Anderson County," pp. 48–49. Seals, *History of White*, p. 50. Census MSS: Manufacturing. *Nashville Republican Banner*, 4 October 1867.

46. Stealey, "Salt Industry," p. 392. Pease, "Great Kanawha," p. 183. Lewis, *Coal, Iron, Slaves*, p. 46. Winifrede Mining and Manufacturing Company Documents. Rice, "Coal Mining," p. 415.

47. Letter from Winifrede Company dated 9 October 1858, Holland Papers. Pease, "Great Kanawha," p. 183. Toothman, *Great Coal Leaders*, p. 260. Lewis, *Coal, Iron, Slaves*, p. 47. Account books for Coal River and Kanawha Mining and Manufacturing Company, 1851–58, and Winifrede Mining and Manufacturing Company, 1850–58; Kanawha County Archives.

48. *Narrative of Bethany Veney*, pp. 33–34. *Hunt's MM* 5 (1841): 54. Wayland, *History of Shenandoah*, p. 291. Marlin, *History of Cherokee*, pp. 149–50.

49. *De Bow's* 18 (1855): 408. Olmsted, *JBC*, p. 242. Ansted, "On Ducktown." *De Bow's* 14 (1853): 620. *Goodspeed's History*, p. 805. Census MSS: Population and Manufacturing, Polk County, Tennessee.

50. For greater statistical detail about copper exports, see Dunaway, "Incorporation," Table 9.4. Pearre, "Mining," pp. 21–22. Lambert, *Undying Past*, p. 82. *Goodspeed's History*, p. 805. Mellen, "Old Copper Road," *Knoxville Sentinel*, 22 October 1921. Campbell, *Upper Tennessee*, pp. 25, 46. Young, "Origins of Copper Industry," p. 133. Green, "Gold Mining of North Carolina," p. 148. *De Bow's* 18 (1855): 408.

51. Stealey, "Salt Industry," pp. 385–86; Rogers Papers.

52. *Calendar of Tennessee Draper Collection*, p. 612; *FHPJ*, pp. xii, 8, 12, 27, 54, 59, 98.

53. On the costs of starting a sawmill, see Depew, *One Hundred Years*, p. 196. Martin, *New Gazetteer*, p. 60. Sawmill account books, Hall Papers and Moreland Papers. Clarkson, *Tumult on Mountains*, p. 17.

54. Williams, *Americans and Forests*, pp. 177–81. Coleman, *History of Georgia*, p. 170. Eisterhold, "Charleston"; Eisterhold, "Savannah"; Eisterhold, "Lumber"; Gosse, *Letters*.

55. Lambert, *Undying Past*, p. 97. Wayland, *History of Shenandoah*, p. 267. Low, "Merchant and Planter," pp. 308–18. *Louisville Democrat*, 1 May 1860. Ambler, *History of West Virginia*, p. 198. Murphy, "Transportation," pp. 17–19. Tally book of rafts on Little Kanawha River, 1856, Lynch Papers; Bradford Noyes Recollections; Shahan Letter; diary entries and letters, 1860, George W. Johnson Papers; Barbour County Typescript. Hulbert, *Historic Highways*, 9:76. Hunter, *Steamboats*, p. 108. Clarkson, *Tumult on Mountains*, p. 17.

56. Hunter, *Steamboats*, p. 58. Verhoeff, *Kentucky River*, pp. 187–92. Green Papers. Clark, "Early Lumbering." *Western Sentinel*, 3 June 1859; *People's Press*, 17 June 1859.

57. Campbell, *Upper Tennessee*, p. 7. Livingood, "Chattanooga," p. 160. Hunter, *Steamboats*, p. 58; Hoskins, *Anderson County*, p. 36. Coleman, *History of Georgia*, p. 170.

58. 1854 letter, cited in Jenkins, "Mining," p. 81. Gauding, "History of Water," pp. 99–100. "Fairfax in the Mid-1800s," *Knoxville News-Sentinel*, 30 July 1989. Livesay Papers, p. 68. Plater, "Building," p. 49n. *WPA Guide to Tennessee*, p. 434. Tarkington,

"Saltpeter Mining"; Hill and DePaepe, "Saltpeter Mining," p. 262. Donnelly, "Bartow County." Semes, "200 Years at Rockbridge," p. 49. Jenkins, "Mining of Alum," pp. 78–87.

59. *Journals of Continental Congress*, 4:185. Hecht, "Lead Production," p. 174.

60. *American State Papers*, 5:139.

61. Ashe, *Travels*, p. 74. Thomas Jefferson held an interest in Westham Foundry; see "Letters to Jefferson," p. 124.

62. Owl, "Eastern Band," p. 106. Hardacre, *Woodland Nuggets*, p. 34. Hulbert, *Historic Highways*, 11:42. Mills, *Statistics*. Spence, *Land of Guyandote*, pp. 161–65. James Barbour Account Book, 1802–22, Barbour Papers.

63. Ice's Ferry Typescript. Hardacre, *Woodland Nuggets*, pp. 37–47. William P. Grohse Typescripts, p. 7. Woodbridge Mercantile Company Records, Woodbridge-Blennerhassett Papers; McNeel Papers; Marshall Papers, 1852–60. Kemper, "Settlement," p. 179. *De Bow's* 26 (1858): 705. Aggregated county totals for the 1840 sale of ginseng are reported in U.S. Census Office, *Compendium*.

64. Pease, "Great Kanawha," p. 183. For Wadestown area land sales and leases, see Garrison and Company Records; for Monongalia County gas fields, see Memorandum Book, 1858–65, Moreland Papers.

65. Eight kerosene plants in five West Virginia counties averaged twenty-three laborers each while two East Kentucky plants averaged ten laborers and an annual gross of $14,000 each. West Virginia's largest kerosene processors were concentrated in Kanawha County, where four firms grossed more than $60,000 each. Census MSS: Manufacturing. Yergin, *The Prize*, pp. 23–25.

66. Census MSS: Population, Wirt County, West Virginia, enumerator's note.

67. John R. Young, "A Visit to the Oil Regions of West Virginia, Ohio, and Pennsylvania," *Forney's Philadelphia Press*, 5 December 1864. Newspaper clippings, Rathbone Papers; Sharp, "Oil Field of Wood and Ritchie"; letters and documents on land speculation, Levassor Papers; Parkersburg Town Council Journals; "The Saga of Red Neck Nellie and West Virginia's Wild Volcano," Metheny Papers; "A Short History of Mannington," Mockler Papers; history of Hancock-Brooke County area, Campbell Typescripts; papers of Charles L. Lewis, Sr., Lewis Papers; Hughes Stock Certificates; historical notes on Guyandotte Valley, Lambert Papers; letters on Monongalia County oil lands, 1858–59, Sturgiss Papers; Sisterville and Tyler County Scrapbook, Thistle Papers; entries and letters, 1851–65, Clarke Papers; letters and transcripts regarding 1850–65 court cases about oil wells, Boreman Papers.

68. Letters dated September 1865 and 15 February 1866, Forsythe Papers.

69. *History of Etowah*, p. 250. *WPA Guide to Tennessee*, pp. 67–68. Census MSS: Manufacturing.

70. For greater statistical detail about marble and stone exports, see Dunaway, "Incorporation," Table 9.4.

71. Tilly, "Flows," p. 126. Braudel, *Civilization and Capitalism*, 3:601.

72. For theory, see Wallerstein, *Capitalist World-Economy*, p. 264. Rothstein, "New Proletarians," p. 223.

73. *Knoxville Standard*, 12 May 1846.

74. Landless farmer characteristics were derived from analysis of the farm sample drawn from census manuscripts. The extent of proletarianization was estimated using manuscript information about nonfarm occupations reported by members of farm households.

75. *De Bow's* 27 (1859): 695. "Lonaconing Journals," p. 29. For greater statistical detail, see Dunaway, "Incorporation," Table 6.5.

76. *CWVQ*, pp. 1608, 1285, 898, 1474, 1866. Olmsted, *JBC*, pp. 247–49. "Journal

of John Sevier," pp. 241, 243, 249. *Knoxville Argus and Commercial Appeal*, 21 January 1840. Letters (1850s), Baker Papers. Laborer agreement, 1853, Wickliffe-Preston Papers. Account Book, 1836–55, Lightburn Papers. Account Book, 1850–53, Hall Papers. Fairmont General Store Records. Accounts, 1830s, John J. Davis Papers.

77. For greater statistical detail, see Dunaway, "Incorporation," Table 6.6.

78. 1833 journal, cited in Levine, *Half Slave*, 30. Quantitatively, there was a large surplus of landless laborers in the region. Moreover, oral histories from this period indicate that there was a scarcity of work opportunities for such workers. Antebellum merchants and manufacturers still lamented the "scarcity" of laborers. To these industrialists, local laborers were unusable because they could not control them totally.

79. Olmsted, *JBC*, pp. 243–44. Harvey, *Best-Dressed Miners*, pp. 20–24. Turner, "Early Virginia Railroad." Williams, *West Virginia*, p. 50. Smith, "Historical Geography," p. 233.

80. Sanderlin, *Great National Project*, pp. 118–22. Turner, "Early Virginia Railroad," pp. 325–34.

81. Samuel, "Workshop," pp. 8, 47.

82. Saville, "Primitive Accumulation," p. 251. Wallerstein, *MWS3*, p. 78; on the role of the state in bolstering early industry in Europe, see pp. 94–118.

83. On deindustrialization, see Amin, *Accumulation*, p. 391.

84. Ibid., p. 177. Wallerstein, *MWS3*, p. 149. For detail about Appalachian company towns, see Chapter 9.

85. On booms and busts, see Chase-Dunn, *Global Formation*, p. 209. For theory of global expansion, see Wallerstein, *MWS1*.

86. Wallerstein, *MWS3*, p. 78; also see p. 26.

87. Chase-Dunn, *Global Formation*, p. 234; also see p. 205. See Amin, *Accumulation*, pp. 170–75, 391–92; Hirschman, *Strategy of Economic Development*.

88. Amin, *Accumulation*, p. 378, emphasis added.

Chapter Seven

1. Wallerstein, "Incorporation," pp. 15–19.

2. Habib, *Agrarian System*, p. 56; Gough, "Agrarian Relations," p. 32. Mintz, "Caribbean," p. 917; Frank, *World Accumulation*, p. 123. Duncan-Baretta and Markoff, "Civilization." Kriedte, Medick, and Schlumbohm, *Industrialization*, pp. 14, 24. Wallerstein, *MWS2*, pp. 193–96. For an extensive overview, see Wallerstein, *MWS3*, chap. 3.

3. For other peripheries, see Wallerstein, *MWS3*.

4. *De Bow's* 19 (1855): 229. Lindstrom, "Southern Dependence," p. 113. Southern deficits are based on analysis of food-crop production and consumption for the non-Appalachian counties of Alabama, Georgia, Kentucky, Maryland, North Carolina, South Carolina, Tennessee, Virginia, Arkansas, Louisiana, Florida, Texas, and Mississippi. Fishlow, "Interregional Trade," p. 189.

5. Lindstrom, "Southern Dependence," pp. 112–13. Billington, *Westward Expansion*, pp. 399–402. These imports included hardware, fabrics, clothing, leather goods, soap and candles, glass, household goods, drugs, machinery, and paper; see Uselding, "Note."

6. Holtfrerich, *Interactions*, i–xvi. Johnson, Van Metre, Huebner, and Hanchett, *History of Commerce*, p. 606.

7. Phillips, *History of Transportation*, p. 393. Earle and Hoffman, "Staple Crops," p. 9.

8. Braudel, *Civilization and Capitalism*, 2:117.

9. *Slave II*, 9:3879. On town economies, see Wallerstein, *MWS3*, pp. 148–49; Meillassoux, *Indigenous Trade*, pp. 96–98.

10. *Railroad Advocate*, 4 July 1831. "Letters to Jefferson," p. 130.

11. On "bulking centers," see Wallerstein, *MWS3*, p. 148.

12. Fleming, "Western Virginia," p. 18. Thwaites, *Early Western Travels*, 12:51. Haites, Mak, and Walton, *River Transportation*, p. 5. Allen, *Western Rivermen*, pp. 34, 67. Wentworth, *America's Sheep Trails*, p. 58. Dodrill, "Cross Creek."

13. May, *Principio*, pp. 99–119. *Wheeling Intelligencer*, 12 April 1879. Caldwell, *History of Brooke*, p. 123; Stealey, "Salt Industry."

14. Scharf, *History of Western Maryland*, 1:1339.

15. Williams and McKinsey, *History of Frederick*, 1:231. Lowdermilk, *History of Cumberland*, pp. 311–13, 316, 370–72, 438–47. Williams, *History of Washington*, pp. 155–56. *Frederick Examiner*, 17 October 1849.

16. Toulmin, *Western Country*, pp. 57–58.

17. *Travels in Virginia*, pp. 121–22. Norris, *Lower Shenandoah*, p. 190. Turner, "Railroad Service," p. 244. *Richmond Enquirer*, 27 April 1857.

18. Schoepf, *Travels*, 2:69. Also see Smyth, *Tour of U.S.A.*, 2:156. At Staunton, Appalachian flour was packed for shipment to Richmond; see Buni, "Rambles," p. 108n. Armstrong, "Urban Vision," pp. 177–78.

19. Gray, *History of Agriculture*, 2:840. Lamb, "The Mule," p. 23. Verhoeff, *Kentucky Mountains*, p. 101. *Knoxville Register*, 2 January, 3 April, 2 June 1836; 13 January 1841; 3 April 1839; 24 April 1856; 17 December 1857. Gauding, "History of Water."

20. *De Bow's* 27 (1859): 416. *Knoxville Register*, 15 June 1819, 24 May 1837, 3 April 1839, 24 June 1846, 15 May 1856. *Knoxville Whig*, 28 February 1857.

21. Livesay Papers, pp. 16, 19–20. See also *CWVQ*, p. 1117.

22. Camp, *Sequatchie County*, p. 29. Govan and Livingood, *Chattanooga Country*, pp. 104, 138.

23. White, *Statistics*, p. 440. Battey, *History of Rome*, 1:94, 108–12, 262. *History of Etowah*, p. 21. *Slave*, 7:141.

24. For a map showing the location of major Appalachian towns in relation to these external hubs, see Lord and Lord, *Historical Atlas*, frontispiece. Mabry, "Antebellum Cincinnati." Walsh, "Spatial Evolution." Burford, "Steam Packets." List of steamboats, 1830–60, Thistle Papers; Diary, January 1–March 20, 1864, Porter Papers; R. H. Hendershot Shipping Bills, 1850–54. Thwaites, *Early Western Travels*, 3:145. Verhoeff, *Kentucky River*, p. 67.

25. Siener, "Staples Rates." Yowell, *History of Madison*, p. 113. Wayland, *History of Shenandoah*, p. 139. Armstrong, "Urban Vision," chap. 3, pp. 73, 129. *Report of Patents, 1851*, p. 213. Gray, *History of Agriculture*, 2:840. Wyatt, "Industry." Blunt, "Warehouses," pp. 16–21. Henderson, "Cotton Mills," pp. 176–85. Letter dated 2 September 1858, Henry W. Jones Papers.

26. "Albermarle in 1815," p. 43. Also see "Letters to Jefferson," p. 128; letters, 1790–1830, Hook Papers. Coleman, "Richmond's Second Market," pp. 8–13. Pease, "Great Kanawha." Scalf, *Kentucky's Last Frontier*, p. 115; Livingood, "Tennessee Valley," p. 24. Depew, *One Hundred Years*, p. 267. Buni, "Rambles," p. 108n. Robert, "Auction System," pp. 170–82.

27. *Knoxville Gazette*, 10 March 1811. Letters, 1790–1830, Hook Papers. Letters, 1852–66, Clark Papers. Morton, *History of Rockbridge*, pp. 170–71. Gold, *History of Clarke*, pp. 15, 19, 23. Rawlings, *Albermarle*, pp. 112–13.

28. Clark, "Trade between Kentucky," chaps. 2–3. Letters of John Wesley Hunt, 1776–1849, Hunt-Morgan Papers. Walsh, "Spatial Evolution," pp. 1–22. *Kentucky*

Statesman, 30 November 1852. Douglas, *Steamboatin'*, map. Bacon, "Nashville's Trade," pp. 30–36.

29. White, *Statistics*, p. 92. Ritchie, *Sketches*, p. 252. Phillips, *History of Transportation*, pp. 126, 54–55. *Goodspeed's History*, p. 802. Taylor, *Antebellum South Carolina*, p. 14. Willoughby, *Fair to Middlin'*, chap. 1. Curry, "Reminiscences of Talladega." Brewer, "History of Coosa." Boozer, "Jacksonville." "Reminiscences of Olden Times, 1809–1850," "Brief Historical Sketch of St. Clair County," and "The Centennial History of Winston County," Cather Collection.

30. "Pamphlet Report of Proceedings of a Railroad Convention at Laurensville, South Carolina, 1846," cited in Phillips, *History of Transportation*, p. 372. Brown, *State Movement*, pp. 8–12. Lesesne, "Nullification," pp. 13–24. *The Mountaineer*, 3 March 1843. Taylor, *Antebellum South Carolina*, p. 14.

31. Duboff, "Telegraph," p. 259. Depew, *One Hundred Years*, p. 557. Henlein, *Cattle Kingdom*, pp. 130–35, 152, 154.

32. Thwaites, *Early Western Travels*, 3:300. On Charleston trade linkages, see also Mills, *Statistics*, p. 677; Ashe, *History of North Carolina*, p. 406; *American Husbandry*, 1 (1775): 431; *South Carolina Gazette*, 30 November 1770; Klein, *Unification*. White, *Statistics*, p. 92.

33. Smith, *Review*, pp. 17–18. Stephenson, "New Orleans," pp. 161–74. Clark, "Grain Trade," pp. 131–42. Hilliard, *Hog Meat*, pp. 121, 204–15.

34. *Knoxville Gazette*, 31 December 1791. Chenault, "Early History," p. 148. *Impartial Review and Cumberland Repository*, 25 August 1808. John Wallace Journal, 1786–1802. Olmsted, *JBC*, p. 250. Holt, *Claiborne County*, pp. 21–24. Phillips, *History of Transportation*, p. 185. *Kentucky Gazette*, 18 February 1798. *CWVQ*, p. 84. Robinson, *Southern Colonial Frontier*, p. 248. Livingood, "Tennessee Valley," p. 24. *Travels in Virginia*, pp. 121–22. Mitchell, "Shenandoah Frontier," pp. 469–70.

35. Sharrer, "Merchant Millers," p. 142. Rutter, "South American Trade."

36. *American Farmer*, 9 (1854): 347. *De Bow's* 26 (1859): 276. Rutter, "South American Trade," p. 41n. *De Bow's* 12 (1850): 203; 13 (1852): 627–28. *American Farmer* 9 (1853): 110.

37. Browne, *Baltimore*, pp. 84–85. Porter, "From Backcountry," p. 347. Caldwell, *History of Brooke*, p. 117. Buni, "Rambles," p. 108n. Williams, *History of Washington*, p. 157. *FHPJ*, p. 77n.

38. Malone, "Falmouth," pp. 695–96. Earle and Hoffman, "Staple Crops," pp. 16–17. Hilliard, *Hog Meat*, p. 209. Lewis, "Valley," pp. 315–16. Willoughby, *Fair to Middlin'*.

39. Northrup, "Compatibility," p. 361. The rationale for antebellum Appalachian internal improvements has been well documented; see Weaver, "Internal Improvements"; Ambler, *Sectionalism*; Spencer, "Transportation"; Verhoeff, *Kentucky Mountains*; Verhoeff, *Kentucky River*; Littlefield, "Maryland Sectionalism"; Rice, "Internal Improvements"; Fischer, "Internal Improvement"; Catton, "Study"; Boughter, "Internal Improvements"; Delfino, "Elites"; Jeffrey, "Internal Improvements"; Martin, "Internal Improvements"; Heath, *Constructive Liberalism*, pp. 243–53; Inscoe, *Mountain Masters*, chaps. 6–7; Folmsbee, *Sectionalism*; Folmsbee, "Turnpike Phase"; Evans, "Roads"; Hunter, "Turnpike Construction"; Allen, "Turnpike System."

40. On rivers as major antebellum U.S. conduits, see Haites, Mak, and Walton, *River Transportation*, p. 11.

41. Bouwman, *Traveler's Rest*. Banta, *Ohio*. Verhoeff, *Kentucky River*. Clark, *Kentucky*. Wiley, *Monongahela*. Bissell, *Monongahela*. Pease, "Great Kanawha." Spencer, "Transportation." Westfall, "Internal Improvements," Murphy, "Transportation." Ambler, *History of Transportation*. Douglas, *Steamboatin'*. Gauding, "History of Wa-

ter." Rollins, "Tennessee River." Tennessee Valley Authority, *History of Navigation.* Davidson, *Tennessee.* Campbell, *Upper Tennessee.* Applewhite, "Navigation."

42. Stevens, *Shenandoah.* Davis, *Shenandoah.* Niles, *James.* Gutheim, *Potomac.* Dunaway, "James River." Harlow, *Old Towpaths.* Woodlief, *In River Time,* pp. 100–125. Jones, "Economic Influence." Hulbert, *Historic Highways,* 13:81–85. Reynolds, *Coosa River.*

43. Kirby, "Canalization," p. 269. Dykeman, *French Broad.*

44. In East Tennessee, for example, a large cave was transformed into a warehouse and loading area for trade goods; see "The Rock House," *Knoxville News Sentinel,* 3 January 1993. On Appalachian canals, see Trout, "Goose Creek," pp. 31–34.; Simms, "John Jordan," p. 23. Niemi, "Canals," p. 515; Dupre, "Ambivalent Capitalists," pp. 215–40. Druyvesteyn, "James River"; *FHPJ,* vii–xxi. *History of Etowah,* p. 19; Coleman and Hemphill, "Boats Beyond," pp. 8–13; Woodlief, *In River Time;* Gauding, "History of Water," pp. 72–75; *American State Papers: Miscellaneous,* 1:73, 809; Tennessee Valley Authority, *History of Navigation,* pp. 58–65; Harpers Ferry Typescript; Coleman, "Kentucky Steamboats," p. 309.

45. For example, ninety such communities developed around trade functions on the Tennessee River tributaries; see Holmes, "Ferry Boats," p. 68. Moore, "Ferry Crossings"; Watson, "Ferry," pp. 249–50; "West Virginia Ferries," pp. 172–73; Spencer, "Transportation," pp. 12–13; Wayland, *History of Shenandoah,* p. 266.

46. *Montgomery Republican,* 3 March 1821. See also John Halley, "Journal of Trips to New Orleans." *American State Papers: Miscellaneous,* 1:813–17.

47. Carson, "Transportation," pp. 26–38. Terrell, "James River," pp. 180–91. Haites and Mak, "River Transportation." Haites and Mak, "Social Savings." Haites, Mak, and Walton, *River Transportation.*

48. Gamble, "Steamboats." Burford, "Steam Packets." Teuton, "Steamboating." Coleman, "Kentucky River." Spencer, "Transportation," pp. 12–15. *Rome Courier,* 3 March 1860. *History of Etowah,* p. 19. Norris, *Lower Shenandoah,* chap. 20. Reynolds, *Coosa River,* pp. 101–10. There was limited and irregular steamboating on the Tennessee, Kentucky, Big Sandy, and Kanawha Rivers until after 1830s; see Haites, Mak, and Walton, *River Transportation,* p. 51; Campbell, *Upper Tennessee;* Hunter, *Steamboats,* p. 217; Mak and Walton, "Steamboats," p. 623. Hall, *Notes,* p. 249. For archival lists of steamboats, see Boreman Papers; Thistle Papers; John W. Clarke Papers; letters, 1840–60, Fleming Papers; 1836 list in Kanawha County Archives.

49. Hall, *Notes,* pp. 31–32. *CWVQ,* pp. 624–25.

50. *CWVQ,* pp. 1009, 624–25. Entries, 1831–47, Miller Farm Records. Davidson, *Tennessee,* pp. 209–12. Coffey, "Into the Valley," p. 162. *FHPJ,* p. 39. Commercial landings, warehouses, stores, and taverns operated at places like McNair's Boat Yard on the Conasauga, Hildebrand's Boat Yard on the Ocoee, the boatyard at Kingsport on the Tennessee, and numerous boatyards on Ohio Basin rivers; see Lewis, "Valley"; Ahern and Hunt, "Boatyard Store," pp. 257–77. Gauding, "History of Water," pp. 41–44. Hunter, "Studies."

51. "Letters of 1831–32," p. 225. *Rockingham Register,* 16 January 1841. See also Hall, *Notes;* Haites and Mak, "River Transportation." Rector, "Westward down the Ohio." Coleman and Hemphill, "Boats Beyond," p. 10. Clark, "Trade between Kentucky," p. 4.

52. *Report of the Board of Internal Improvement,* p. 3. Smith, *Review,* p. 18. Lindstrom, "Southern Dependence," p. 111n.

53. "Made in East Tennessee" (East Tennessee Historical Society exhibition). *Knoxville Gazette,* 11 May 1842. *Knoxville Argus and Commercial Appeal,* 2 June 1839. Reynolds, *Coosa River,* p. 112.

54. Major Appalachian turnpikes and roads have been well documented for every zone of the region; thus, details about specific roads will not be repeated here. For an early map of major roads for the entire region, see Melish, *Traveler's Directory*. For maps of major livestock drover routes, see Henlein, *Cattle Kingdom*, p. 102; Hilliard, *Hog Meat*, p. 194. For turnpike information, see Cooke, "Road System"; Ierley, *Traveling National Road*; Rouse, *Great Wagon Road*, map; Arthur, *Western North Carolina*, pp. 239–40; Bouwman, *Traveler's Rest*; Davis, *Shenandoah*; Dykeman, *French Broad*; Folmsbee, "Turnpike Phase," p. 46; Harlow, *Old Towpaths*; Heath, *Constructive Liberalism*, p. 251; Hulbert, *Historic Highways*, vol. 9; Hunter, "Turnpike Construction," p. 193; Kincaid, "Wilderness Road," p. 45; Kirby, "Canalization"; Niles, *James*; Reynolds, *Coosa River*; Bissell, *Monongahela*; Spencer, "Transportation"; Templin, "Making a Road," pp. 80–87; Tennessee Valley Authority, *History of Navigation*; Verhoeff, *Kentucky River*; Lord, *Blue Ridge Guide*; Martin, "Internal Improvements," pp. 21–25; Verhoeff, *Kentucky Mountains*, pp. 100–133; Williams, *History of Frederick*, 1:181; Durrenberger, *Turnpikes*; Norris, *Lower Shenandoah*; Wayland, *History of Shenandoah*, pp. 261–75; Hunter, "Turnpike Movement"; Pawlett, *Roads of Virginia*; Wayland, *Valley Turnpike*; Braake, "James River," pp. 27–54.

55. For a detailed map of all southern railroads, see Phillips, *History of Transportation*, back pocket. Map, 1853, Baltimore and Ohio Railroad Records. Ambler, *History of Transportation*, p. 187. On railroad development, see Tanner, *Canals and Railroads*; Haney, "Congressional History"; Brown, *State Movement*; Reizenstein, "Baltimore and Ohio"; *History of Etowah*, p. 169; Scharf, *History of Western Maryland*; Johnson, *Antebellum North Carolina*, p. 26; Weaver, "Internal Improvements," pp. 323, 413; Couper, *History of Shenandoah*, 2:728–32; *De Bow's* 13 (1852): 87.

56. Such transactions are detailed, for example, in Claiborne County, Tennessee, Stagecoach Book. Rouse, *Great Wagon Road*, p. 195.

57. *Harper's* 59 (November 1879): 804. Rouse, *Great Wagon Road*, pp. 167–75. *Hagerstown Mail*, 31 March 1837.

58. Hayne, "Address." Newsome, "Colton's Report," pp. 217–18. Todd, "How Pioneers."

59. *Cherokee Phoenix*, 22 September 1830. *CWVQ*, pp. 74–75, 389. *Kentucky Gazette*, 24 May 1788; *Knoxville Register*, 3 December 1824. Wilms, "Cherokee Land Use," p. 106.

60. Smith, *Review*, p. 54, see also p. 24. The owner of the Fotheringay Plantation in Montgomery County, Virginia, operated the Alleghany Turnpike and kept in operation a line of long-distance wagon freighters; see Wood, "Alleghany Turnpike," p. 308. For other accounts of regular trading trips, see Allman, "Yeoman Regions," p. 428; Gauding, "History of Water," pp. 26–31. Letters dated 24 July 1833, 12 February 1860, 12 September 1860, 7 February 1839, 15 May 1849, Holland Papers. Ray Diary. Dickinson Papers. Letter dated 15 November 1854, Chapin Papers. Wallace Journal, 1786–1802. Forsythe Papers. Also see *CWVQ*, p. 1272; *Knoxville Standard*, 31 March 1846; Royall, *Southern Tour*, vol. 1, entry for 1 May 1828; "Thomas Lenoir's Journey," p. 158; Hilliard, *Hog Meat*, p. 281; Taylor, *Antebellum South Carolina*; Gray, *History of Agriculture*, 1:123–24; Williams, "Washington County," p. 353; Malone, "Falmouth."

61. Olmsted, *JBC*, p. 267. Clark, "Trade between Kentucky," p. 44. Hagans Papers. Dolan, *Yankee Peddlers*, pp. 250–51. Letter to Editor, *Southern Planter*, 11 (1851): 355–56. Letters on peddling manufactured tobacco, 1830–45, Penn Papers. Robert, *Tobacco Kingdom*, p. 222. *Carolina Planter* 1 (1844–45): 42; *Farmer's Register* 4 (1802): 711, 6, 93.

62. *Atlantic Monthly* 26 (1827): 170. Discussion of Appalachian livestock exports is derived from Table 5.6. Royall, *Sketches*, p. 71. *Documentary History*, 2:287.

63. *North American Review* 20 (1825): 99. Thwaites, *Early Western Travels*, 3:44–47. Verhoeff, *Kentucky Mountains*, p. 127n. Also see Table 5.6.

64. Smith, *Review*, p. 8. Morris, *Tennessee Gazetteer*, p. vi. Burnett, "Hog Raising," p. 99. Dykeman, *French Broad*, pp. 141; 147–49. *Report of Patents for 1851*, p. 563. Also see Table 5.6.

65. Hamilton, "Minutes," p. 46. *Farmer's Journal* 2 (1814): 83; *The Arator* 1 (1842): 183. Phillips, *Life and Labor*, pp. 144–45. Olmsted, *JBC*, p. 224. Hilliard, *Hog Meat*, p. 218. See Table 5.6.

66. Thwaites, *Early Western Travels*, 3:281. Depew, *One Hundred Years*, p. 225. Bays, "Cattle Herding." *Cherokee Phoenix*, 22 September 1830, 27 August 1831. Verhoeff, *Kentucky Mountains*, p. 127n. Clark, "Trade between Kentucky," pp. 53–54. Mitchell, *Appalachian Frontiers*, pp. 227. See Table 5.6.

67. Thwaites, *Early Western Travels*, 3:244–45. Smith, *Review*, p. 7. Buckingham, *Slave States*, 2:203. Toulmin, *Western Country*, p. 112. *Report of Patents, 1851*, p. 29. Lamb, "The Mule," p. 23; *Report of Patents, 1849*, p. 179. See Table 5.6.

68. *Slave*, 11 (2): 208. Dykeman, *French Broad*, pp. 139–40. Buzzell, "Economic Picture," p. 65. Seals, *History of White*, p. 58; Camp, *Sequatchie County*, p. 29.

69. Wentworth, *America's Sheep Trails*, p. 77.

70. Wallerstein, *MWS3*, pp. 136–37.

Chapter Eight

1. The upper Blue Ridge is now Shenandoah National Park; see Lambert, *Undying Past*, p. 87. The lower Blue Ridge now comprises the Blue Ridge Parkway in Virginia and North Carolina. Gaps calculated using Lord, *Blue Ridge Guide*.

2. Examples of ridge-top roads include Flat Laurel Gap, Locust Gap, and Rocking Horse Gap in the Blue Ridge Mountains; see Lord, *Blue Ridge Guide*, 2:408.4, 2:433.3, 2:435.3. For the Smoky Mountains coves, see Dunn, *Cades Cove*.

3. Wallerstein, *HC*, pp. 15–16.

4. For four major networks in commodity chains, see Gereffi and Korzeniewicz, "Commodity Chains," pp. 45–67.

5. Comparable commodity chains could be constructed for Southern Appalachia's other extractive industries or manufacturers. For historical detail about salt, see Stealey, "Salt Industry"; Mosby, "Salt Industry."

6. Phillips, "Incorporation," p. 789.

7. Hopkins and Wallerstein, "Commodity Chains," p. 159; Wallerstein, *HC*, p. 23; Hopkins and Wallerstein, "Patterns," pp. 127–29; Ulshofer, "Household," pp. 190–91.

8. On milling tolls as precapitalist barter, see Eller, "Land and Family."

9. Hopkins and Wallerstein, "Commodity Chains," p. 159; Wallerstein, *HC*, p. 23; Hopkins and Wallerstein, "Patterns," pp. 127–29.

10. Braudel, *Afterthoughts*, p. 44. Amin, *Accumulation*, pp. 360, 390.

11. Wallerstein, *HC*, p. 16. Amin, *Accumulation*, pp. 392–93. Braudel, *Civilization and Capitalism*, 3:541.

12. On decentralized and centralized chains, see Vellenga, "Women."

13. On ancillary marketing services, see Bruchey, "Marketing Change," pp. 217–25.

14. *Knoxville Argus and Commercial Appeal*, 2 June 1839 and 1 December 1840. *Knoxville Register*, 3 November 1847, 25 October 1848, 20 June 1849. *Knoxville Register*, 25 October 1848. *Knoxville Register*, 20 June 1849. *Knoxville Register*, 3 November 1847. For commission merchant correspondence with Appalachians, see letters dated

14 August 1801; 19 January 1802; 27 February 1801; 30 April 1802; 6, 14, and 17 August 1802; 2, 22, and 27 September 1802, Downey Papers; letters dated 23 June 1820, 3 November 1825, 21 May 1828, 12 September 1829, 21 January 1828, 15 September 1831, 28 August 1833, 24 June 1836, 28 July 1837, 17 February 1842, 29 August 1845, 1 April 1859, Dickinson Papers; letters, 1857–58, Nathaniel Hunt and Company Papers; letters from New Orleans, 1843–50, Timberlake Papers; letter dated 29 January 1841, Scott Papers; entries, 1859, Henry B. Jones Diary. See also Allman, "Yeoman Regions," p. 428; Robert, *Tobacco Kingdom*, pp. 222–25; Harvey, "William Alexander," pp. 26–36; Mosby, "Salt Industry," pp. 32–33; Malone, "Falmouth."

15. Tennessee Valley Authority, *History of Navigation*, pp. 51–53.

16. Robert, *Tobacco Kingdom*, pp. 62, 142; *Richmond Daily Dispatch*, 4 December 1857.

17. *Knoxville Argus and Commercial Appeal*, 21 January 1840; *Decatur Register*, 21 January 1840. Appalachian commission merchants were enumerated in the 1840 census. Todd, "How Pioneers." Verhoeff, *Kentucky River*, pp. 63, 204; *Thomas Jefferson's Farm Book*, pp. 256–57. Jones, "Middlemen."

18. *Slave I*, 5 (1): 214. Adams Account Books; Blanton Papers, 1830–69; Orr Papers. *Knoxville Register*, 9 May 1849. McKee, "Jackson." Caswell Diary, p. 22. Parr, "Kentucky's Overland Trade." Goddard Diary. Olmsted, *JBC*, pp. 223–24, 262. *CWVQ*, pp. 587, 1655, 1881. Bays, "Historical Geography." McCrum, "Aurora," p. 26. Harrison, "Recollections," p. 291. Dykeman, *French Broad*, p. 141.

19. *Frankfort Daily Commonwealth*, 15 March 1842.

20. Gray, *History of Agriculture*, 2:840. For graziers, see 1840s entries, Lenoir Papers; McNeill Papers; Chapin Papers, 1792–1857; Gatewood Papers, 1866–69; McNeel Papers; Martin Papers; Price Papers, 1858–60; Sloan Brothers Papers, 1827–35; Miller Farm Records, 1831–47. Mitchell, *Appalachian Frontiers*, pp. 127–49. Lambert, *Undying Past*, pp. 131–44.

21. Thwaites, *Early Western Travels*, 3:244–47. Buckingham, *Slave States*, 2:40; see also 2:530–33. Olmsted, *JBC*, p. 274. Toulmin, *Western Country*, pp. 111–12.

22. Ambler, *History of West Virginia*, p. 201. For major routes to northeastern cities, see Henlein, *Cattle Kingdom*, p. 102. For major routes between the border states and the Deep South, see Leavitt, "Livestock Industry." Hilliard, *Hog Meat*, p. 194.

23. Oral history, cited in Searight, *Old Pike*, pp. 142–43. For statistical and methodological detail about itinerant livestock drives and grains utilized at livestock stands, see Dunaway, "Incorporation," Table 11.2. See also Henlein, *Cattle Kingdom*, p. 119; Olmsted, *JBC*, pp. 268–69. *Cherokee Phoenix*, 23 October 1836. *Tennessee Historical Markers*, pp. 12, 92, 107. Siler, *Tennessee Towns*. *WPA Guide to Tennessee*, p. 312. Smith, *Review*, p. 27. Burnett, "Hog Raising," p. 99. Dykeman, *French Broad*, pp. 147–49.

24. Estimates are based on statistical detail from Dunaway, "Incorporation," Tables 11.2, 4.3.

25. Eller, "Land and Family," p. 95. Mancall, *Valley of Opportunity*, p. 230, found a similar pattern of indirect participation in external trade in Pennsylvania. Johnson and May, *Over the Counter*, p. 27. Wood, "Mercantile Activity."

26. Letters, 1798–1806, and Mercantile Company Records, Woodbridge-Blennerhassett Papers; Hagans Papers. Plater, "Building," pp. 45–50. Malone, "Falmouth," pp. 693–703. Diary, 1818–19, Wait Papers. Letter book and accounts, 1801–9, Hook Papers. Mitchell, *Appalachian Frontiers*, pp. 150–65. Rawlings and Hemphill, "Reminiscences," pp. 55–68. Beeman, "Trade and Travel," p. 176. *Western Carolinian*, 15 March 1834. *Chattanooga Gazette*, 16 May 1844. Atherton, "Itinerant Merchandising," pp. 36, 49–50, 55. Sutcliff, *Travels*, pp. 90–91. Hunter, *Steamboats*, p. 342. Spen-

cer, "Transportation," p. 9. Henderson, "Century of Progress," p. 73. Gamble, "Steamboats." Atkeson and Atkeson, *Pioneering*, pp. 30, 33–34, 38. Henry Boswell Jones Diary.

27. Thwaites, *Early Western Travels*, 3:266.

28. *Southern Planter* 7 (1847): 90. Mercantile Company Records, Woodbridge-Blennerhassett Papers. Friend, "Frontier Pendleton," p. 97. Dykeman, *French Broad*, p. 143. Garrison and Company Papers.

29. *Slave*, 2 (1): 229. Allman, "Yeoman Regions." Morgan, "Old Salem," pp. 3–6. Woodman, *King Cotton*, chaps. 7–8.

30. Diary, 1846, Wilson-Lewis Papers. Siler Papers. *CWVQ*, p. 2231. Olmsted, *JBC*, 2:65–67. Robert, *Tobacco Kingdom*, pp. 94–117. *American State Papers*, 4:535. "Journal Kept on the Trip to New Orleans in 1804," Calk Papers. Letters dated 28 November 1833, 7 February 1837, 5 July 1837, Wait Papers.

31. Clark, "Trade between Kentucky," pp. 37–39. "The Mollie Garth," *Knoxville New Sentinel*, 6 July 1921. McKee, "Alfred Jackson." Account books, Lenoir Papers. Letter dated 1 November 1820, McNeill Papers. Letters, 1852–60, Marshall Papers. Hill, *Herbert Walters Story*, pp. 11–24.

32. *Knoxville Gazette*, 28 January 1792. Commission Sales Book, 1849, Means-Seaton Papers. McKee, "Jackson."

33. Hollander, "Anti-Drummer," pp. 479–500. Letter dated 23 May 1834, Winn Collection. Letter dated 13 January 1850, Mallett Papers. Letter dated 9 April 1846, Eiler Letter Book. *Hunt's MM* 1 (1830): 37–41. *Carolina Watchman*, 14 April 1853. Also see Jones, "Middlemen," pp. 13–18. Soltow, "Scottish Traders," pp. 111–17.

34. Letter dated 24 February 1823, McNeill Papers; see also 2 July 1812, 13 June 1814, and 1 November 1820. Henlein, *Cattle Kingdom*, pp. 112–13. Walsh, "Pork Merchant," pp. 127–37.

35. *Kentucky Gazette*, 15 December 1787. Neale Manuscript. Quinn Typescript, p. 28. Grohse Typescript, p. 7; Verhoeff, *Kentucky River*, p. 67. Jillson, "Big Sandy Valley," p. 252. Allman, "Yeoman Regions," p. 425. Kemper, "Settlement," p. 179n. Abernethy, "Early Development," p. 317. Letters dated 11, 13, 22, 28, and 30 September; 8 and 11 November 1858; 29 January, 1 February, 11 April 1859; and 27 January 1860 in Heard Papers.

36. Letter dated 27 January 1859, Heard Papers. See also Keith, "Three Blount Brothers," pp. 161–64.

37. On inspection of agricultural exports, see Gray, *History of Agriculture*, 2:604, 606, 608, 706, 736, 771–72, 841; Peterson, "Milling," pp. 97–108; Lander, "Milling." On vertical and horizontal diversification, see Maizels, *Commodities*, pp. 236–41.

38. Peterson, "Milling." Malt liquor was produced in the counties of Alleghany and Frederick, Maryland; Frederick, Virginia; Ohio and Brooke, West Virginia; famous Monongahela Rye Whiskey was produced in the Morgantown area. See U.S. Census Office, *Manufactures in 1860*.

39. The West Virginia counties dominant in grain milling and distilling were Berkeley, Brooke, Greenbrier, Hampshire, Hardy, Jefferson, Marion, Monongalia, Monroe, Nicholas, Pendleton, and Wetzel.

40. Martin, *New Gazetteer*, p. 258. For statistical detail, see Dunaway, "Incorporation," Table 9.8. Elliott and Nye, *Virginia Directory*, pp. 111, 175. Larger factories included Moorman and Peters (Bedford, Virginia) and Matthews and Wright (Bedford); John S. Hale (Franklin, Virginia) averaged annual production of 150,000 pounds. Details are from Census MSS: Manufacturing.

41. For statistical detail, see Dunaway, "Incorporation," Table 9.9.

42. For statistical detail, see ibid., Table 9.7.

43. Lenemer, "Improved Cattle," pp. 79–92. Clark, "Trade between Kentucky," pp. 46–56. For imports of fertilizers, see "Simply the Stolen," p. 25. *Hill's Almanac and State Register.*

44. Braudel, *Afterthoughts*, p. 53.

Chapter Nine

1. For an example of the conventional view of preindustrial Appalachia, see Eller, *Miners, Millhands.*

2. Diversification had advanced to the greatest extent in western Maryland and Appalachian Virginia, where nearly two-thirds of the free households earned all or part of their livelihoods outside agriculture. Similarly, in West Virginia and the Appalachian counties of Georgia and South Carolina, more than one-half of the households earned all or part of their incomes from activities other than farming. At the other end of the spectrum, the least diversified local economies of East Kentucky, western North Carolina, and Appalachian Tennessee absorbed only one-fifth to one-quarter of their labor forces into nonagricultural sectors. These estimates are derived from analysis of the household sample ($n = 3,056$) drawn from Census MSS: Population. For statistical detail, see Dunaway, "Incorporation," Tables 12.2, 12.3.

3. Wallerstein, "World-System Analysis: Second Phase," p. 292.

4. Martin, "Incorporation," pp. 855–56.

5. Hopkins and Wallerstein, "Transformations," 131–32. For an overview of the process of creating local governance on the frontiers of this era, see Rohrbough, *Trans-Appalachian Frontier*, chap. 5.

6. Ramsey, *Annals of Tennessee*, 134–35. Antebellum sheriffs spent more time assisting with commerce than in preventing crimes; they issued summons, administered oaths, and wrote and served warrants connected with debt collection in addition to recording livestock brands and auctioning slaves at public markets. See, e.g., Hamilton District Court Papers. Vandiver, "Pioneer Talladega Minutes," pp. 29, 61–63.

7. Tariff act, cited in Oland, "New Bremen," p. 260. County courts fostered the establishment of mills and distilleries by granting to a few operators the monopolistic use of streams and the legal right to collect publicly regulated tolls; see Holt, "Economic Beginnings," pp. 117–19; Lander, "Milling"; Charles L. Campbell Typescripts; and *Documentary History*, 2:346. Owen, *Story of Alabama*, p. 599; Wallace *South Carolina History*, p. 381. On the salt tariff, see Mosby, "Salt Industry," pp. 23–26.

8. *American State Papers* 4:752–53. Holt, "Economic Beginnings," pp. 115–16; Blethen and Wood, "Antebellum Iron." Moore, "Historical Geography," p. 41. Stealey, "Salt Industry," chap. 2.

9. Nave, "History of Iron," p. 7. "Lonaconing Journals," p. 41. Hunt, "Pactolus." Eubank, "Iron Industry," pp. 13–14; Moore, "Historical Geography," p. 41. A road was constructed between Dumplin Iron Works in Jefferson Company and Knoxville in the early 1800s; see "Thomas Lenoir's Journey," p. 158. A canal connected seven Rockbridge, Virginia, iron furnaces to the James River; see "100 Historic Sites." The saltworks owner was commissioned by the Virginia legislature to oversee road and river improvements in several counties adjacent to his southwestern Virginia operations; see Ahern and Hunt, "Boatyard Store," p. 259.

10. "Uria Brown's Journal," p. 364. Analysis of 1810 and 1820 manufactures in Coxe, *Statement of Arts*, and U.S. Census Office, *Digest of Accounts*. For antebellum geological surveys, see Owen, *Third Report*; Troost, *Fifth Geological Report*. Taylor, *Statistics of Coal.*

11. On Cathcart, see Chapter 3.

12. *Knoxville Register*, reprinted in *De Bow's* 17 (1854): 303.

13. The extensive land speculation in coal, oil, gas, salt, and timber lands between 1840 and 1865 is documented in Kentucky Iron, Coal, and Manufacturing Company correspondence, Means-Seaton Papers; map of Kanawha Valley coal fields, Mintz Papers; Deakins Papers; Edwards Papers; Great Kanawha Coal, Oil, and Metallurgic Company Papers; correspondence of Charles C. Lewis, Sr., Lewis Papers; Memorandum Book, 1858–65, Moreland Papers; Ewin Papers; Worley Papers; Business Papers of James H. Carroll, 1840–60, Pierce Papers; estate papers of John Nuttall and newspaper articles, Nuttall Papers; Middleton Correspondence; correspondence and contract, 1857–65, Collins Papers; Gideon D. Camden Papers, 1805–60; Goff Papers; Henry Gassaway Davis Papers; Boreman Papers; Sturgiss Papers; Elkins Papers. Also see Burns, "Blount County Coves," p. 62; Ellis, *Frontier in Development*, pp. 194–95. On mineral land speculation by transportation companies, see Fairbanks and Hamill, *Coal Mining Industry*, p. 38; Spence, *Land of Guyandotte*, p. 162.

14. *New York Evening Post*, 26 February 1857. Smith, "Antebellum Attempts," pp. 210–13.

15. On cultural change during the colonial era, see Chapter 2.

16. *American State Papers: Indian Affairs*, 7:326–64; 2:520–21. "Letters of Benjamin Hawkins," p. 253. Letter of Jefferson, 1809, quoted in Williams, *Beginnings*, p. 63.

17. Wallerstein, *HC*, p. 82.

18. Sturtevant, "John Ridge," pp. 81–82. Evans, "Morse's Report," p. 68.

19. Sturtevant, "John Ridge," p. 81. Regarding *gadugi*, see Fogelson and Kutsche, "Cherokee Cooperatives."

20. *American State Papers: Indian Affairs*, 1:124. Ford, "Cherokee Contact," p. 118; on food advances against annuities, see pp. 101–2. Bloom, "Acculturation." All of the characteristics specified by Aguirre-Beltran, *Regions of Refuge*, chaps. 1–2, can be applied to the Cherokees.

21. Richardson, *Messages of Presidents*, 2:585–86; 3:1082–85.

22. Finger, *Eastern Band*, pp. 50–56, 80–81.

23. *Encyclopedia of Southern Culture*, pp. 1138, 1389. To search for perceived cultural disparities between the mountain South and the rest of the South or the United States, I scrutinized the Appalachian slave narratives, the Civil War veteran questionnaires, twenty-one outsiders' journals of travel in the region, two lengthy plantation journals, and five collections of condensed diaries by outsiders visiting the region.

24. Wallerstein, *Geopolitics*, p. 84. Analysis of the Civil War veteran questionnaires shows that middling farmers and merchants tended to agree with most of the value judgments of the elites about economic opportunities and work habits of the local poor. For detail, see Dunaway, "Incorporation," Table 4.4.

25. Quotes from *CWVQ*, pp. 911, 1448, 317, 1670, emphasis added. Carpenter, "Henry Dana Ward," 10 July 1846 entry. McDonald, *Woman's Civil War*, p. 238. See also *CWVQ*, pp. 44, 107, 698–99, 858–60, 973, 1009, 1022, 1090, 1129, 1166, 1285, 1404–6, 1416–17, 1423, 1428, 1446–47, 1453, 1494, 1608, 1823, 1932. Glickstein, *Concepts*, 217–19. Olmsted, *JBC*, p. 238.

26. Grund, *Americans*, pp. 172–73. The discussion on social mobility is derived from analysis of the survey responses of all 474 Appalachian respondents in *CWVQ*. For greater statistical detail, see Dunaway, "Incorporation," Table 4.4. For an extensive discussion of this ideology about laborers, see Glickstein, *Concepts*, pp. 32–52, 86–92.

27. *CWVQ*, pp. 801, 1235.

28. Olmsted, *JSS*, p. 84. For the views of a Winchester, Virginia, slaveholder, see McDonald, *Woman's Civil War*, pp. 80–81. On ethnic wage differentials, see "Lona-coning Journals," pp. 30–38, 44; *Baltimore Sun*, 9 January and 21 April 1854. When the Chesapeake and Ohio Canal Company paid differential wages to laborers based on ethnicity, labor riots erupted in 1838. The "military [was] sent off to quell" the unrest, in the process burning the laborer shantytown in Washington County, Maryland. Subsequently, state courts convicted twenty immigrant labor leaders; see *FHPJ*, p. 49; Sanderlin, *Great National Project*, pp. 118–22.

29. Olmsted, *JBC*, pp. 275–76. *CWVQ*, p. 107. For the dominant view of the landless poor on the frontier, see Klein, "Ordering the Backcountry," pp. 678–79.

30. Ball, *Slavery*, pp. 290–91.

31. *CWVQ*, pp. 698–99. Appalachians paralleled capitalist views dominant throughout the United States and Europe in this era; see Glickstein, *Concepts*, pp. 32–52, 86–92.

32. Whisnant, *All That Is Native*, p. 260. Gaventa, *Power and Powerlessness*, p. 256. Poulantzas, *Political Power*, pp. 214–15. Wallerstein, *HC*, pp. 84–87.

33. Letter, 1853, cited in Johnson, *Antebellum North Carolina*, p. 62. Wallerstein, *HC*, p. 83. Gaventa, *Power and Powerlessness*, pp. 61–62. See the sectionalism discussion in Chap. 10.

34. Letter from Harris to Christie, 11 April 1797.

35. Reid, "Rental Contracts," p. 76. For Tennessee farms, see *CWVQ*, pp. 621, 625. *FHPJ*, vii–xxi.

36. Contracts and plat map, 1857–59, Wickliffe-Preston Papers.

37. *CWVQ*, p. 542. *Slave I*, 5:285–86; 14:332. Oral history collected by the author and verified in family records. See also *CWVQ*, pp. 13, 595, 698, 819, 1022, 1913. Olmsted, *JBC*, pp. 273–74; *FHPJ*, pp. xiv–xvi, 72.

38. Olmsted, *JBC*, p. 208.

39. *Slave II*, 3:672.

40. Carey, "Essays," p. 171. Contract dated 12 June 1857, Wickliffe-Preston Papers. *Thomas Jefferson's Farm Book*, p. 164. For state and county laws, see Banks, *Economics*; Gray, *History of Agriculture*; Mendenhall, "Southern Tenancy." For an 1833 tenancy law that drew sharp legal distinctions between renters and croppers, with the cropper being viewed as a wage laborer, see Orser, *Material Basis*, pp. 55–56.

41. Owen, *Story of Alabama*, 2:600. Arrest warrants in Henry W. Jones Papers; Frederick County, Virginia, Court Papers; Washington County, Tennessee, Court Records; Holland Papers; Hook Papers. Also see Johnson, *Antebellum North Carolina*, p. 654; Williams and McKinsey, *History of Frederick*, 1:209. Court records in Braxton County Archives; court records in Brooke County Archives. For an overview of ante-bellum legal practices, see Applewhite, "Sharecropper."

42. On landlord accounting practices, see Miller Farm Records; Wilson-Lewis Papers; Campbell Typescripts; Courtney Papers; Cupp Papers; Hall Papers; court records in Braxton County Archives; court records in Brooke County Archives; Wick-liffe-Preston Papers; Forsythe Papers; Harkins Papers; John Graham Record Book. Also *FHPJ*; Reid, "Rental Contracts." For a specific tenant account, see the 1847 account of Augustus Sprague, Miller Farm Records.

43. Entry dated 1 January 1860, William N. Berkeley Ledger, Berkeley Papers. Entries for tenants and laborers in Aldie Memorandum Book, 1838–50, and William N. Berkeley Ledger, Berkeley Papers; Mallory Diary, 1843–60; Plantation Account Books, 1813–63, Bryarly Papers; Farm Account Book, 1853, Meredith Papers; Farm Account Books, 1831–50, Courtney Papers.

44. Tiny labor chits were found in several of the farm records cited above. For a

double-entry system of this sort, see William N. Berkeley Ledgers, 1854–85, Berkeley Papers. For variations in charges and wages, see letter dated 10 June 1841, Wilson-Lewis Papers; Minute Book of Low Dutch Company, Beers Collection. Entries for 1831–47, Miller Farm Records, indicate that the farm owner credited amounts to tenant accounts for boarding his hired laborers, then charged a higher boarding cost against the wages of the laborer. In western Maryland and western Virginia, tenants paid fees to support schools their children could not attend.

45. *FHPJ*, p. 44; also see p. 80. Account of Horace Luckett, Noland's Mill Ledger, Berkeley Papers. Letter dated 15 February 1846, Wickliffe-Preston Papers.

46. Store records, 1830s, Forsythe Papers. Merchant's Day Book, 1854–55, Orr Papers; Sherrill Account Book, 1845–47; Ledger of Samuel D. Thorn, Shingleton Records.

47. *North Carolina Standard,* 15 January 1845.

48. Buni, "Rambles," p. 89. "Lonaconing Journals," p. 78. Tarkington, "Saltpeter Mining," pp. 17–25. Jenkins, "Mining of Alum," pp. 78–87.

49. Harpers Ferry Typescript; *Virginia Free Press,* 10 September 1842. See also Williams, *West Virginia,* pp. 47–48; Smith, "John Hall," pp. 28–32; A large complex developed around the North Wales Mill in Fauquier County, Virginia, in the eighteenth century; see Plater, "Building North Wales Mill," pp. 45–50. One of the region's earliest full-blown company towns was established in 1785 around the Bremen Glass Manufactory in Frederick County, Maryland. Financed by German investors, Bremen was one of the largest industrial settlements of that time. In addition to three glass factories, a sawmill, and several grist mills, the company provided dwellings and retail shops for 400 people; see Oland, "New Bremen Glass," pp. 255–72.

Throughout the antebellum period, there were mill communities in Lonesome Valley, Powell Valley, and Barren Creek in Appalachian Tennessee. Around Mitchell's Mill in White County, Tennessee, a small village for thirty to forty hands was constructed. Small laborer villages even grew up around the region's small potteries, like several communities in middle Tennessee and West Virginia. The town of Glencoe was founded as a worker community for large quarries in Etowah County, Alabama. Around a large paper mill in Claiborne County, Tennessee, 120 houses and a rural village were built to accommodate workers. See *WPA Guide to Tennessee,* pp. 25, 329; Seals, *History of White,* p. 57; Webb, "Pottery," pp. 110–12; *History of Etowah,* p. 250.

50. Stealey, "Salt Industry," pp. 32–33. On the two types of southern iron furnaces, see Douglas, *Coming of Age,* pp. 261–64.

51. Smith, "Historical Geography," pp. 93, 303; Ice's Ferry Typescript; *Atlanta Daily Intelligencer,* 8 April 1859.

52. Account book for Redwell Iron Furnace, cited in Wayland, *History of Shenandoah,* p. 244. Smith, "Historical Geography," p. 106. Lewis, *Coal, Iron, Slaves,* pp. 27–9. Account books of Sanders-Greene Pig Iron Furnace, Sanders and Greene Papers and Notebooks; Shenandoah Iron Works correspondence, 1849–61, Blakemore Papers; Cloverdale Furnace correspondence, 1850–58, Anderson Papers; Tayloe Iron Furnace, Iron Furnaces Typescript; Account Book of Monongalia Iron Forge, Maxwell Papers; slave inventories for King Saltworks (Washington County), 1838–63, White Papers; "Negro Book," 1839–59, Weaver-Brady Iron Works and Grist Mill Papers (mines, furnaces, and forges, in Rockbridge, Rockingham, Botetourt Counties); Davis Iron Manufacturing Company Papers; Breckinridge Papers; Etna Furnace Company Account Book.

53. Smith, "Historical Geography," pp. 98–99; for an excellent discussion of Virginia iron plantations, see pp. 91–123. For a map of the Glenwood Plantation showing

locations of furnace, several farms, and landholdings in three counties, see p. 95. Average size was estimated using 1860 census records and archival sources.

54. Ice's Ferry Typescript.

55. *Atlanta Daily Intelligencer*, 8 April 1859; Jackson, *North Georgia Journal*, p. 13. For the average size of Virginia enclaves, see Smith, "Historical Geography," p. 103.

56. Smith, "Historical Geography," p. 306.

57. *U.S. Telegraph*, 4 May 1831. Exhibit at Gold Museum, Dahlonega, Georgia.

58. Exhibit at Gold Museum, Dahlonega, Georgia. Green, "Georgia's Forgotten Industry," p. 222; Green, "Gold Mining in Virginia." Young, "Southern Gold Rush," p. 389. Roberts, *Gold Seekers*, p. 61.

59. Starobin, *Industrial Slavery*, p. 138. Pease, "Great Kanawha," pp. 199–200. Washington, *Up from Slavery*, p. 26. Mosby, "Salt Industry," p. 48. Stealey, "Salt Industry," p. 399.

60. *Kanawha Valley Star*, 26 September 1859, 31 May 1859, 9 June 1857. *Charter of Coal River*, p. 39.

61. Thompson, *In Touch*, pp. 80, 94.

62. "Furnaces and Forges," pp. 190–92. Bouwman, *Traveler's Rest*, p. 155. *Rome Courier*, 3 March 1860. Smith, "Historical Geography," pp. 231, 235, 245.

63. Allen, "Mount Savage," pp. 67–68.

64. "Lonaconing Journals," p. 37.

65. Orren, *Belated Feudalism*, pp. 78–84.

66. Ibid.

67. Roberts, *Gold Seekers*, p. 61. Smith, "Historical Geography," pp. 231, 235, 245. Company Ledger, 1851–58, Winifrede Mining and Manufacturing Company Documents. *Kanawha Valley Star*, 26 September 1859.

68. "Lonaconing Journals," pp. 37, 26, 59. Thompson, *In Touch*, pp. 80, 94.

69. For a company account, see Pocket Account Book for Mill, 1836–55, Lightburn Papers. For labor accounts in stores, see Merchant's Ledger, 1854–60, Burnside Papers; Thorn Ledger, 1849–51; account books, 1796–1867, Hagans Papers; account books, 1858–60, Garrison and Company Records; Sherrill Papers (Haywood County, North Carolina); Rhodes Papers (Loudon County, Virginia); Pennybacker Papers (Shenandoah County, Virginia); daybooks and account books, 1837–67, Foster Papers (Wilkes County, North Carolina); daybook, 1854–55, Orr Papers (Fauquier County, Virginia); and Mason County Account Book (Kentucky).

In Preston County, West Virginia, Jacob Guseman operated a fulling mill, sawmill, gristmill, and other manufactories at Muddy Creek; accounts were opened for milling laborers at Guseman's general store. Cash wages were never actually paid, and sheriff's bonds were issued for the arrest of any laborers who left Guseman's employ without paying off indebtedness. Guseman also recorded amounts received from the public auction of confiscated household belongings of "dilitary" laborers. See Muddy Creek Ledgers and Daybooks, 1836–60, Guseman Records.

An East Kentucky sawmill operator opened accounts for his timberers, loggers, and rafters at his general store. Laborers signed a legal contract to work for one year, boarded in his shacks, and received wages in *vouchers* for store purchases. One laborer named Browning signed on to cut timber, make rafts, and run logs downriver. When he became ill, Browning continued to live in a shack that housed several other unmarried timberers. Frustrated with such a "worthless" worker, the manufacturer terminated his contract after only four months and called upon the laborer to "settle up." Credited to the 1849 account of this timberer was only $15.00 in wages, but the employer charged him $34.60 for rent, food advances, and four months of washing and $12.00 "to me & family taking care of you when you was sick 4 wks." See Browning account, 1849, Account Books, Forsythe Papers.

70. On "anchoring" concept, see McMichael, "Settlers."

71. Wallerstein, *MWS3*, p. 158.

72. On environmental degradation associated with the expansion of capitalism in western Europe, see ibid., p. 142; Wallerstein, *MWS1*, pp. 44–45, 193, 281; Wallerstein, *MWS2*, pp. 43, 99–100, 133, 210; Braudel, *Civilization and Capitalism*, 1:366–67.

73. *Documentary History*, p. 229. On environmental change during the colonial era, see Chapter 2. On wildlife destruction, see Deyton, "Toe River," pp. 451–54; Bacot, "South Carolina."

74. Harper, "Development," p. 16. Craven, "Soil Exhaustion"; Otto, *Southern Frontiers*, pp. 135–36. A quarter of the emigrants into northern Alabama between 1816 and 1820 were planters with ten or more slaves who had moved from the seaboard South in search of fresh lands; see Allman, "Yeoman Regions," pp. 92. Rochefoucauld-Laincourt, *Travels*, 2:116; Harris, *Land Tenure System*, p. 343; Moore, "Historical Geography," p. 123.

75. *Farmer's Register* 1 (1799): 150. Weld, *Travels*, p. 116. *Travels in Virginia*, p. 104."David Stuart's Report," p. 287. On Fauquier County, see entries dated July–August 1786, Clark Notebook.

76. Ball, *Slavery*, pp. 50–51. Coombs, *America Visited*, p. 323. See also Olmsted, *JBC*, p. 222.

77. "John Brown's Journal," pp. 358–60. Entry dated June 1832, Ray Diary. Agricultural Society speech, 1818, in Mendenhall, "Southern Tenancy," p. 118. *Atlantic Monthly* 23 (1823): 172.

78. Killebrew and Safford, *Introduction*, p. 598. Louis-Phillipe, *Diary*, p. 61. "Journal of Surry," p. 511. Moore, *Calhoun Boy*, p. 22. See also Nesbitt and Netboy, "Bent Creek Forest," p. 123.

79. A similar devaluation of forest wealth occurred in western Europe; see Braudel, *Civilization and Capitalism*, 1:364. *American State Papers: Public Lands* 1:6; "John Brown's Journal"; Porter, "Backcountry to County," pp. 336–37.

80. Thwaites, *Early Western Travels*, 12:200–205. Buni, "Rambles," p. 100.

81. Thwaites, *Early Western Travels*, 3:257, 268. "Thomas Lenoir's Journey," p. 159. Royall, *Sketches*, p. 25. Gray, *History of Agriculture*, 2:840. Michaux, *Travels*, pp. 182–90. "Diary of Geological Tour," p. 40. Kemper, "Settlement," p. 170; "John Brown's Journal," p. 359; "Journal of Surry," p. 528; Durr, *Economic Problems*, pp. 69–70; Otto, *Southern Frontiers*, chap. 1; Nesbitt and Netboy, "Bent Creek Forest," pp. 123–24; Dykeman, *French Broad*, p. 151. *Kentucky Gazette*, 21 March 1822.

82. "John Brown's Journal," p. 47.

83. Morel, "Early Iron," p. 18; Laidley, "Large Land Owners," pp. 244–45; *Atlanta Daily Intelligencer*, 18 April 1859; Round, "Wilderness."

84. Troost, *Fifth Geological Report*, p. 37. *Laurensville Herald* (South Carolina), 11 May 1849. Ice's Ferry Typescript. Smith, "Historical Geography," pp. 221–26. Nave, "History of Iron," p. 5; Van Benthuysen, "Sequent Occupance," p. 15; Pickel, "History of Roane," p. 51. Lambert, *Undying Past*, pp. 77–78. Blethen and Wood, "Antebellum Iron."

85. *New England Magazine*, September 1832, pp. 222–27. "John Brown's Journal," p. 362; Cohen, *Kanawha Images*, p. 37. Stealey, "Salt Industry," p. 386; Pease, "Great Kanawha," p. 182.

86. Thompson, *In Touch*, pp. 107, 135.

87. Lanman, *Adventures*, 1:343–44. Feastonhough, *Canoe Voyage*, 2:255.

88. Exhibit at Gold Museum, Dahlonega, Georgia. Green, "Georgia's Forgotten Industry," p. 225. Green, "Gold Mining of North Carolina," p. 151.

89. Ashe, *Travels*, p. 69. On floods, see Goddard Diary, p. 23; Hall, *Notes*, pp. 31–34; entry dated April 1852, Ray Diary; clippings about 1829 and 1855 floods, Ruffner Papers. On epidemics, see Williams and McKinsey, *History of Frederick*, 1:212–15; Beckley Papers; entries dated September 1832–May 1833, Ray Diary; *Kingston Gazetteer*, 30 September 1854; Lowdermilk, *History of Cumberland*, pp. 370–79; *Carolina Watchman*, 1 March and 18 October 1836.

90. Bryan, "Letters," p. 343. Washington, *Up from Slavery*, p. 26.

91. Stampp, *Peculiar Institution*, p. 108. Washington, *Up from Slavery*, pp. 38–39. *Report of the Board of Directors of the Cannel Coal Company of Coal River, Virginia*, 1855, p. 9, Rosencrans Papers. "Lonaconing Journals."

92. Moore, "Historical Geography," p. 41. "Lonaconing Journals," p. 39n. Nave, "History of Iron," pp. 10–19.

93. Chase-Dunn, *Global Formation*, p. 88. For critiques, see Chirot and Hall, "World-System Theory"; Robertson and Lechner, "Problem of Culture"; Worsley, *Three Worlds*; Robertson, *Globalization*, chap. 4. For traditional world-systems analysis, see Wallerstein, *Geopolitics*, pp. 158–83.

94. There is no attention to environment in either of Wallerstein's three volumes in the *Modern World-System* series; moreover, Chase-Dunn, *Global Formation*, provides no synthesis of writing done about the topic within this perspective. Only three articles in the *Review of the Fernand Braudel Center* address ecological degradation; see Feder, "Odious Competition"; Crosby, "Biotic Change"; and Barbosa, "World-System and Brazilian Amazon."

Chapter Ten

1. Wallerstein, *MWS2*, p. 179.

2. For Southern Appalachia, see Table 3.3. For northern Appalachia, see Slaughter, *Whiskey Rebellion*, p. 65. For New England, see Henretta, "Families and Farms," p. 7.

3. See Tables 3.3 and 3.4.

4. For Southern Appalachia, see Table 4.2. The studies with which I compared rates did not control for the landless kin of owners; therefore, I utilized the tenancy rate calculated by method 1. All rates were calculated for 1860. In the northeastern U.S., 6.8 percent of the farms were operated by tenants; see Yang, "Farm Tenancy," p. 139. For Tennessee, see Winters, "Agricultural Ladder," Table 1. In the Midwest and the South, 27 percent and 32.4 percent of farms were operated by tenants respectively; see Atack, "Agricultural Ladder," Table 1.

5. For Appalachians in towns, see Dunaway, "Incorporation," Table 8.1 and Figure 8.2.

6. Gordon, Edwards, and Reich, *Segmented Work*, p. 56. Munslow and Finch, *Proletarianisation*, p. 140.

7. See Dunaway, "Incorporation," Tables 4.7 and 4.10.

8. For statistical detail, see ibid., Table 12.4.

9. Census MSS: Population indicates the number of months in which adults were unemployed during the previous year. For more detailed discussion of informal economy, see Dunaway, "Incorporation," chap. 8.

10. *Raleigh Register*, 10 July 1850. On the sectional rivalry over education, see Johnson, *Antebellum North Carolina*, pp. 76–79; Taylor, *Antebellum South Carolina*, chap. 1; Ambler, *Sectionalism*, chap. 9; Lacy, *Vanquished Volunteers*, chap. 4; Coleman,

History of Georgia, p. 121; Norris, *Lower Shenandoah*, pp. 213–20; Heath, *Constructive Liberalism*, chap. 13; Rohrbough, *Trans-Appalachian Frontier*, pp. 57–60, 309; Williams, *History of Washington*, pp. 226–53; Olmsted, *JBC*, pp. 331–37; *CWVQ*, pp. 51, 270, 461, 530, 819, 970, 1230, 1235, 1302, 1387, 1417, 1419, 1423, 1435, 1544–45, 1609, 1611, 1749, 1786, 1904–5, 1944, 1995, 2035, 2247. For statistical detail, see Dunaway, "Incorporation," Table 12.6.

11. *Kanawha Valley Star*, 2 December 1856.

12. Ibid., 12 July 1859.

13. *Kanawha Republican*, 25 January 1842.

14. "Account of the Clarksburg Educational Convention of September 8–9, 1841," in *U.S. Commissioner of Education Report*, 1:435.

15. Legislative speech, 1835, in Ashe, *History of North Carolina*, p. 324. *Jonesborough Whig*, 8 December 1841. Lacy, *Vanquished Volunteers*, p. 110.

16. Weaver, "Internal Improvements." Ambler, *Sectionalism*. Spencer, "Transportation." Verhoeff, *Kentucky Mountains*. Verhoeff, *Kentucky River*. Littlefield, "Maryland Sectionalism." Rice, "Internal Improvements." Fischer, "Internal Improvement Issues." Boughter, "Internal Improvements." Delfino, "Antebellum Elites." Jeffrey, "Internal Improvements." Martin, "Internal Improvements." Heath, *Constructive Liberalism*. Folmsbee, *Sectionalism*. Hunter, "Turnpike Construction." Folmsbee, "Turnpike Phase." Allen, "Turnpike System." Brown, *State Movement*. For statistical detail, see Dunaway, "Incorporation," Table 12.7.

17. On U.S. wealth, see Soltow, *Men and Wealth*, p. 112.

18. Wealth statistics were aggregated from U.S. Census Office, *Population of the U.S. in 1860*.

19. For statistical detail, see Dunaway, "Incorporation," Table 12.6. "Poor" is defined as a household reporting total wealth less than $100; see Soltow, *Men and Wealth*.

20. On trade contraction, see Kondatrieff, "Long Waves"; Braudel Center Research Working Group, "Cyclical Rhythms," p. 499. On U.S. regional shifts, see Wallerstein, *MWS3*, chap. 4. On the impact of railroad development in other regions, see Parr, "Kentucky's Overland Trade." Leavitt, "Livestock Industry," pp. 29–55; Stealey, "Salt Industry," pp. 563–65.

21. Amin, *Accumulation*, p. 381.

22. On food-deficient farms, see McKenzie, "From Old South," pp. 52–53.

23. Wallerstein, *MWS2*, p. 137.

24. On crop shifts, see Gray, *History of Agriculture*, 2:695. Ford, "Social Origins," p. 332. McKenzie, "From Old South," pp. 39–42. *Richmond Semi-Weekly Examiner*, 9 October 1857. *Richmond Daily Dispatch*, 4 January 1859.

25. For greater statistical detail about the gross values of major categories of exports, see Dunaway, "Incorporation," Table 9.20.

26. On multipliers and spinoffs, see Chase-Dunn, *Global Formation*, p. 233.

27. On forward and backward linkages, see Frank, *Dependent Accumulation*, pp. 117–18.

28. Amin, *Accumulation*, pp. 175–80.

29. Ibid., p. 175; Frank, *World Accumulation*, p. 123.

30. Town sectors were derived from analysis of the households sample drawn from Census MSS: Population.

31. Schweikart, *Banking*, pp. 21, 120. Ashe, *History of North Carolina*, 1:199. Wallace, *South Carolina History*, pp. 372–73. Connelley and Coulter, *History of Kentucky*, 1:513–14. Hall, *Notes*, p. 286. Owen, *Story of Alabama*, pp. 594–96. *Niles Weekly Register* 11 (1827): 336. Scharf, *History of Western Maryland*, 2:1179–80. Campbell, *Development*, p. 32. Dewey, *State Banking*, p. 143.

32. Brantley, *Banking*, vol. 1. Schweikart, *Banking*, pp. 100–103, 128–29. *Knoxville Register*, 21 March 1832. *Nashville Union*, 29 June 1838. Hillsman, "Bank of Tennessee," pp. 16–17. Campbell, "Branch Banking," pp. 39–40.

33. Hall, *Notes*, p. 286. Schweikart, *Banking*, pp. 109–11, 122–23. Bryan, "History of Banking," pp. 43, 78, 112–13.

34. Campbell, *Development*, pp. 148–49.

35. Dewey, *State Banking*, pp. 76–77. Morton, *History of Rockbridge*, p. 106.

36. When the Bank of Tennessee failed in the 1830s, the bank's Dandridge agent reported in his journal that "We have a good deal of money in the bank, but not the kind we want. . . . The branches of the Bank of East Tennessee at Jonesboro have suspended. The Bank at Knoxville still pays out. This failure will injure many people in East Ten." See Caswell Diary, pp. 20–21.

Cyrenius Wait, an East Kentucky trader, lost nearly 10 percent of the value of the paper currency that he sent to pay for distant commodities. His Louisville factor informed him that "We have been compelled To sell 80$ Tennessee and Alabama money for which we credited you $70.70 and we enclose your 5$ Bank of Florida note which cannot be used here at any price. Your a/c [account] is credited with $185.70 being the Nett proceeds of the Two Hundred Dollars Enclosed. We are sorry you Shall lose so much on the remittance but it as well as can be done." Letter dated 11 January 1837, Wait Papers.

During the bank panic of the 1830s, an East Kentucky diarist reported that "In the fall of 1836 [there] was [a] Remarkable . . . sudden Rise in all articles of trade. the old united states Bank was put down by Jackson's party. new Banks sprang up all over the united states which put a large quantity of paper money in circulation. property of every description rose high. pork rose from $2.50 to five dollars neat. lands and negroes and horses rose to nearly double their former value. everybody was on the high road to fortune and speculation." See Goddard Diary, p. 7.

37. "Uria Brown's Journal," p. 363.

38. Travel diary, 1840, cited in Dewey, *State Banking*, p. 111.

39. Rates of commercial development were calculated by using aggregate county, regional, and national totals from the published 1840 census. The total population was divided by the number of retail stores. Aggregated statistics for Maine, Massachusetts, Vermont, Rhode Island, New Hampshire, and Connecticut characterize New England.

40. Aggregated statistics for Ohio, Illinois, and Indiana characterize the Midwest.

41. For a detailed list of mineral spas and information about livestock trails, see Dunaway, "Incorporation," Table 8.5 and chap. 10. For trail maps, see Henlein, *Cattle Kingdom*.

42. *De Bow's* 10 (January 1851): 107; see also 21 (1856): 323–29. *De Bow's* 21 (September 1856): 323. *Southern Literary Messenger* 17 (June 1851): 378.

43. Feastonhough, *Excursion*, 1:94. The following planter manuscript collections report regular visits to Appalachian resorts: Bridges Papers; Grattan Papers; Bills Papers; Race Diary; Williams Papers; Pettigrew Papers; Turrentine Papers; Clay Papers; Ellis and Munford Papers; Fraser Papers and Account Books; Law Papers; McCay Papers; Rutherford Papers and Letter Books; White Family Papers; Taveau Papers; John Horry Dent Farm Journals and Account Books, 4:70; For other planters who frequented Appalachian resorts, see Brewster, "Summer Migrations." For construction of absentee-owned cottages near springs, see Reniers, *Springs of Virginia*, pp. 96–113; Berdan, "Spa Life," p. 113. For a typical diary of such an elite tour, see Shepard, "Trip."

44. *De Bow's* 14 (1853): 49–54. Nashville, Chattanooga, and St. Louis Railway,

"Summer Resorts 1909," promotional brochure, cited in *Franklin County Historical Review* 2 (1970): 3. *Richmond Whig*, 19 June 1837. Moorman, *Virginia Springs*, map and p. 1. Pencil, *White Sulphur Papers*, p. 35. *Richmond Whig*, 21 January 1851. Annual report of Western and Atlantic Railroad, 1848, cited in White, *Statistics*, p. 92. *Raleigh Southern Weekly Post*, 2 July 1853; *Lancaster Ledger* (South Carolina), 25 August 1858. Lanman, *Letters*, p. 125. Olmsted, *JBC*, p. 251. *Kentucky Statesman*, 14 September 1855 and 20 July 1858. *Tri-weekly Commonwealth* (Frankfort, KY), 21 June 1852. Ellwanger, "Estill Springs." Coleman, *Springs of Kentucky*, p. 53. "Summer Travel in the South," *Southern Quarterly Review* 18 (September 1850): 32. Wright, "Montvale Springs," p. 59. Thorne, "Watering Spas," pp. 321–25.

45. On disarticulation, see Amin, *Accumulation*, pp. 175–77, 393–95.

46. Ibid., p. 177.

47. Goodloe, *Inquiry*, p. 59. Combined fixed assets were the sum of investments in farms, farm implements, manufacturing/extractive, and slaves, aggregated from county totals in the published 1860 Censuses of Agriculture and Manufacturing and 1860 slave investments in Lee, "Westward Movement," Appendix.

48. Chase-Dunn, *Global Formation*, p. 234. For methods in estimating assets of travel and industrial enterprises, see Table 10.5.

49. For statistical detail, see Dunaway, "Incorporation," Table 12.10.

50. Amin, *Accumulation*, p. 195.

51. For statistical detail, see Dunaway, "Incorporation," Table 12.11. "Gross" refers to gross value of manufactured goods.

52. *Hunt's MM* 6 (1842): 529. Regarding iron decline, see Salmon, *Washington Iron Works*, pp. 61–70; Coleman, "Old Kentucky Furnaces," p. 239; Blethen and Wood, "Antebellum Iron"; Harvey, "Frontier Iron Works," p. 166; Cappon, "Trend," p. 377; Smith, "Historical Geography," pp. 126–34, 258–64, 276–78, 323–25; "Lonaconing Journals," p. 68. Comparative statistics were aggregated from the published 1840 and 1860 censuses.

53. *Hunt's MM* 8 (1843): 386.

54. Moore, "Historical Geography," pp. 44–45. *Wheeling Intelligencer*, 27 December 1854. On salt decline, see Pease, "Great Kanawha"; Stealey, "Salt Industry"; Cummings, *American Ice Harvests*, pp. 59–61.

55. For statistical detail, see Dunaway, "Incorporation," Table 12.4.

56. Peterson, "Milling," p. 105.

57. Amin, *Accumulation*, p. 391.

58. In the household sample drawn from the 1790–1810 county tax lists, 68 of the 169 sampled town lots were absentee-owned. For resort ownership, see the sources detailed in Chapter 7.

59. Northeastern wages were aggregated from U.S. Census Office, *Statistics of the United States*, p. 512. Appalachian wages were estimated from a sample of 3,056 households from Census MSS: Population. Emmanuel, *Unequal Exchange*, pp. 196–99.

60. For theory, see Wallerstein, *Capitalist World-Economy*, pp. 34–37.

61. For theory, see Amin, *Accumulation*, pp. 31–32.

62. For theory, see Arrighi, "Peripheralization," p. 173.

63. Wallerstein and Martin, "Peripheralization," p. 194.

64. Wallerstein, *MWS3*, p. 78.

65. Chase-Dunn, "Development," p. 189. Arrighi, "Peripheralization," p. 163.

66. For theory, see Hopkins and Wallerstein, "Capitalism and Incorporation," p. 773.

67. For theory, see Amin, *Accumulation*, pp. 136, 178, 299, 390–93; Amin, "Social Characteristics."

Appendix

1. Space does not permit an extended discussion of all statistical and archival methodology. The most important approaches are presented here and throughout the notes. Methods are also explained in the notes to several of the tables. In addition to the manuscript methods discussed here, quantitative data were aggregated from several published censuses, and many archival and primary sources were utilized. However, those approaches are not summarized here. In addition to the manuscript samples discussed here, a sample was also drawn from the Census of Manufacturing manuscripts; that methodology is summarized in Table 10.6. For greater detail about quantitative methodology, primary and archival sources, and statistical analysis of wealthholding, see Dunaway, "Incorporation," Appendix A.

2. The Appalachian land area of Alabama and Georgia was Indian territory until after 1820. Although West Virginia did not yet exist as a separate state, it is possible to isolate the appropriate county tax lists.

3. Since women were not liable for poll taxes, female-headed households were scrutinized carefully. Women were counted as residents except when no property other than land was reported and there was little evidence that the owners lived in structures on the land or when the enumerator identified them as absentees.

4. I developed this methodological adaptation in response to critiques from some scholars who argued that the only landless people in Appalachia were the extended kin of landowners who were actually residing and working on family farms and, thereby, supposedly waiting to inherit the family farms. By controlling for the landless kin of owners, I can demonstrate that landlessness occurred even when one accounts for extended households on family farms. Similar steps were followed in assessing landless households selected from the 1860 census manuscripts.

5. Microfilmed copies of census manuscripts were secured from several archives or were utilized on site at several regional archives. Only nine farm households had to be dropped from the sample because they could not be cross-matched with Schedule I. Alphabetized indexes for the Census of Population were sometimes used to speed cross-matching; however, it was usually simple to cross-match by following the parallel enumeration order for the two schedules.

6. I replicated the enumeration conventions that are identified by Bode and Ginter, *Farm Tenancy and Census*, chap. 2.

7. I converted food crops to corn equivalencies using these 1860 ratios: 1 bu. wheat = 1.3 bu.; 1 bu. potatoes or yams = .25 bu.; 1 lb. rice = .01 bu.; 1 beef = 2.25 bu.; 1 hog = 5 bu.; 1 sheep = .5 bu; 1 ox = 14.4 bu. The count of beef cattle does not include milk cows. I converted crops to corn equivalencies using the following 1910 ratios: 1 bu. buckwheat = .9 bu.; 1 bu. barley = .9 bu.; 1 bu. rye = .85 bu.; 1 bu. oats = .9 bu.; 1 bu. peas or beans = 1.2 bu.; 1 ton hay = 48.8 bu. For 1860 ratios see, Battalio and Kagel, "Structure"; Hilliard, *Hog Meat*, p. 273n. For 1910 ratios, see Jennings, *Consumption*.

8. An "adult" is defined as a person sixteen years of age or older. A "household" is defined as those persons residing in the same dwelling who are related by kinship ties or living as a family unit. Human consumption levels are based on annual allowances per adult of 13 bushels of corn, 2 bushels of wheat, 2.2 swine, and one beef per household; see Hilliard, *Hog Meat*. For food consumption of sheep and oxen, see Battalio and Kagel, "Structure," p. 36. Poultry were not allocated as part of regular food allowance since the census did not record kinds or numbers produced. For whiskey allowances and production, see Gusfield, *Symbolic Crusade*, p. 75; Dabney, *Mountain Spirits*, p. 51n.

9. I allocated the following annual bushels of corn to livestock: cattle 2.25 bu; hogs 5 bu; horses 21.6 bu.; mules or oxen 14.4 bu; sheep 0.5 bu; see Battalio and Kagel, "Structure," pp. 28–30. For livestock husbandry, see Gray, *History of Agriculture*, chap. 35; Cathey, "Agricultural Development," chap. 9. For the proportion of livestock fed on pasturage and forage only, see U.S. Department of Agriculture, *Agricultural Statistics*.

10. The following seed reservations were made: corn, 5 percent; oats, 10 percent; potatoes/yams, 10 percent; rye, 11 percent; wheat, 13 percent; peas/beans, 5 percent. For information on seed reservations, see Battalio and Kagel, "Structure," p. 28n. In the actual calculation, I allowed an additional 5 percent to account for potential loss or wastage. This is a very conservative approach since archival sources indicate that most antebellum farmers producing surpluses purchased new seeds each year.

11. On calculation of herd replacement ratios, see Battalio and Kagel, "Structure," p. 36.

12. For each farm household, consumption is subtracted from total crop production (both expressed in corn equivalencies) to determine how much of the total production remains as surplus.

13. For comparisons, see Battalio and Kagel, "Structure"; Hilliard, *Hog Meat*; Gallman, "Self-Sufficiency"; Hutchinson and Williamson, "Self-Sufficiency"; Fogel and Engerman, *Time on Cross*, 1:115–18, 2:97; Sutch, "Care and Feeding"; and Kahn, "Linear Programming." For greater discussion, see Dunaway, "Incorporation," Appendix.

14. A turn-of-the-century study determined that 100 acres were needed to produce a family's survival needs; see U.S. Department of Agriculture, *Agriculture*, p. 190.

Manuscript Sources

Annapolis, Maryland
Maryland State Archives
  Appalachian County Tax List Manuscripts

Chapel Hill, North Carolina
Southern Historical Collection, University of North Carolina Library
  Walter Alves Papers
  John McPherson Berrien Papers
  John Houston Bills Papers
  John Luther Bridges Papers
  Farish Carter Papers
  William G. Dickson Papers
  H. B. Eiler Letter Book
  Peachy R. Grattan Papers
  Stephen B. Heard Papers
  Nathaniel Hunt and Company Papers
  General Edmund Jones Papers
  Thomas Lenoir Family Papers
  Peter Mallett Papers
  James Mallory Diary
  Pettigrew Family Papers
  "Plantation Instructions" (typescript)
  George Wesley Race Diary
  Jacob Siler Papers
  Willis R. Williams Papers
  Benjamin Cudworth Yancey Papers

Charlottesville, Virginia
University of Virginia Library
  Barbour Family Papers
  Alfred Beckley Papers
  Berkeley Family Papers
  James Breckenridge Papers
  John Buford Papers
  Byers Family Papers
  William D. Cabell Papers
  W. W. Davis Iron Manufacturing Company Papers
  Dickinson Family Papers
  Holland Family Papers
  John Hook Papers

James River and Kanawha Canal Company Papers
Keith Family Papers
General Joel Leftwich Papers
Lewis, Anderson, and Marks Family Papers
McDowell Family Papers
Massie Family Papers
Callohill Mennis Papers
James Monroe Papers, 1790–1846
Nelson County Business Ledgers
Negro Book, 1850–1862
Page-Walker Family Papers
Bowker Preston Papers
Rust Family Papers
Virginia Letters Collection
Weaver-Brady Iron Works and Grist Mill Papers
White Family Papers

Durham, North Carolina
Duke University Library
Thomas Adams Account Books, 1768–1808
Francis Thomas Anderson Papers
Daniel Baker Papers
N. L. Blakemore Papers
James Blanton Papers
Samuel, Richard, and Rowland Bryarly Papers
Campbell Family Papers
George W. Clark Papers
Clement Claiborne Clay Papers
Samuel Smith Downey Papers
Charles Ellis and George Wythe Munford Papers
Alfred M. and John A. Foster Papers
Mary D. Fraser Papers and Account Books
Henry W. Jones Papers
Michael Kidwiler Papers
Henry Clay Krebs Papers
William LaPrade Account Books, 1839–1860
William Law Papers
Thomas Lenoir Papers
Henry Kent McCay Papers
James McDowell Papers
Mary Singleton McDuffie Papers
Hugh Minor Notebooks
Battaile Muse Papers
John Quincy Adams Nadenbousch Papers
John M. Orr Papers
Green W. Penn Papers
Benjamin Pennybacker Daybook
Poor Relief Records, Augusta County, Virginia, 1791–1822
H. I. Rhodes Memorandum Book
John Rutherford Papers and Letter Books

Richard W. Sanders and John W. Greene Papers and Notebooks
Samuel P. Sherrill Account Book
Vincent Tapp Papers
Augustin Louis Taveau Papers
Cabell Tavenner and Alexander Scott Withers Papers
William H. Thomas Papers
John W. Timberlake Papers
Michael H. Turrentine Papers
Josiah William Ware Papers
Thomas White, Jr., Papers
Philip J. Winn Collection

Knoxville, Tennessee
East Tennessee Historical Society
   Appalachian County Tax List Manuscripts
   "Made in East Tennessee: Agriculture and Industry in the Great Valley, 1780–
      1940" (1989 exhibition)
McClung Collection, Lawson-McGhee Public Library
   Hamilton District Court Papers
   Paper Mills Letter, 1851
   "South Carolina Indian Affairs" (typescripts)
Tennessee Valley Authority Library
   Quinn, Edythe A. "History of the Little Tennessee River Valley" (typescript)
University of Tennessee Library
   Browder, Nathaniel C. "The Cherokee Indians and Those Who Came After:
      Notes for a History of Cherokee County, North Carolina, 1835–1860" (type-
      scripts)
   William R. Caswell Diary, 1856
   O. P. Temple Papers

Lexington, Kentucky
Martha I. King Library, University of Kentucky
   Appalachian County Tax List Manuscripts
   Buckner Family Papers
   William Calk Papers
   J. Winston Coleman Papers on Slavery
   Forsythe Family Papers
   Francis M. Goddard Diary, 1834–1850
   John Graham Record Book
   Halley, John. "Journal of Trips to New Orleans," 1789 and 1791
   Hilton Family Diaries
   Hunt-Morgan Family Papers
   Kentucky House Journal
   Kentucky Senate Journal
   Joseph and Archibald Logan Papers
   Means-Seaton Papers
   "Old Furnaces of Kentucky." Typescript.
   Scott Family Papers
   Cyrenius Wait Papers
   Wickliffe-Preston Papers

Lexington, Virginia
Washington and Lee University Library
   Etna Furnace Company Account Book, 1854–1857
   Henry Boswell Jones Diary

Louisville, Kentucky
Filson Club
   Jayne Bergen Beers Collection
   Jonathan Clark Notebook
   Willis and Lafayette Green Papers, 1818–1860
   Letter from Harris to Christie, 1797
   Mason County Account Book, 1797–1799
   Frank B. Russell Papers, 1849–1860
   Peyton Skipwith Papers
   John Wallace Journal
   Warrick-Miller Papers

Montgomery, Alabama
Alabama Department of Archives and History
   William H. Cather Collection

Morgantown, West Virginia
West Virginia Collection, West Virginia University
   Baltimore and Ohio Railroad Records
   Barbour County, Miscellany Papers No. 1115
   Barbour County Manuscripts and Articles
   Barbour County Typescript
   C. H. Beall Papers
   Alfred Beckley Papers
   Arthur I. Boreman Papers
   Daniel Boardman Papers
   Braxton County Archives
   Brooke County Archives
   James M. Burnside Papers
   Gideon D. Camden Papers
   Johnson Newlon Camden Papers
   Charles L. Campbell Typescripts
   Campbell Family Papers
   Chapin Family Papers
   John P. Clarke Papers
   Coal River and Kanawha Mining and Manufacturing Company Account Books
   Justus Collins Papers
   Courtney Family Papers
   James M. Crump Typescript
   Henry Gassaway Davis Papers
   John J. Davis Papers
   Ruth Woods Dayton Papers
   Deakins Family Papers
   Marmaduke Dent Papers
   J. Q. Dickinson and Company Papers
   Donnally and Steele Kanawha Salt Works Records, 1813–1815

William Henry Edwards Papers
Stephen B. Elkins Papers
William Ewin Papers
Ralph Fairfax Records
Fairmont General Store Records
Fleming Family Papers
Freeman Family Papers
M. J. Garrison and Company Records
A. C. L. Gatewood Papers
David Goff Papers
Great Kanawha Coal, Oil, and Metallurgic Company Papers
Jacob Guseman Records
Harrison Hagans Papers
William Hall Papers
Hamilton Family Typescript
Felix G. Hansford Papers
Harpers Ferry Typescript
Harrison County Tax Book
R. H. Hendershot Shipping Bills
Henderson-Tomlinson Families Papers
Adolphus P. Howard Papers
Alfred Hughes Stock Certificates
Ice's Ferry Typescript
Iron Furnaces Typescript
George W. Johnson Papers
Kanawha County Archives
John Pendleton Kennedy Papers
Peter T. Laisley Papers
Frederick B. Lambert Papers
Legislative Petitions of Kanawha County
Eugene Levassor Papers
Lewis Family Papers
Lightburn Family Papers
John R. Lynch Papers
John Williamson Marshall Papers
Marshall County Archives
John D. Martin Papers
Lewis Maxwell Papers
Maysville, Kentucky, Papers
John McClaugherty Papers
McCoy Family Papers
Isaac McNeel Papers
McNeill Family Papers
Edward E. Meredith Papers
H. E. Metheny Papers
Henry O. Middleton Correspondence
Charles C. Miller Farm Records
William D. Mintz Papers
R. Emmett Mockler Papers
Monongalia County Land and Legal Papers, 1783–1859
Monroe County Archives

Monroe County Road Records, 1812–1862
James Rogers Moreland Papers
William P. L. Neale Manuscript
Fred T. Newbaugh Papers
Bradford Noyes Recollections
Lawrence William Nuttall Papers
Parkersburg Town Council Journals, 1855–1862
Carleton Custer Pierce Papers
George McCandless Porter Papers
Preston County Papers, 1775–1918
William Price Papers
Raleigh County Archives
Rathbone Family Papers
Thomas P. Ray Diary, 1829–1852
Rector, C. R. "Westward down the Ohio" (typescript)
John Rogers Papers
William Starke Rosencrans Papers
Henry and William Henry Ruffner Papers
Ruffner-Donally and Company Records
"Salt Manufacturing in Mason County, West Virginia" (typescript)
Salt Sulphur Springs Records
James B. Shahan Letter
Sharp, W. H. "Oil Field of Wood and Ritchie" (typescript), Wood and Ritchie
    Counties Manuscript No. 1029
Samuel W. Shingleton Records
Sloan Brothers Papers
George W. Smith Papers
George Cookman Sturgiss Papers
Summers County Archives
Sweet Springs Records
Talbott-Tolbert Family Papers
Taverns Typescript
Harry F. Temple Typescripts
Roy Thistle Papers
Samuel D. Thorn Ledger
White Sulphur Springs Company Records
Luke Willcox Diary, 1843–1854
Wilson-Lewis Family Papers
Wilson and Stribling Families Papers
Winifrede Mining and Manufacturing Company Documents
Wood and Ritchie Counties Manuscript No. 271
Woodbridge-Blennerhassett Papers
William Gordon Worley Papers

Nashville, Tennessee
Tennessee Historical Society
  George Hale Journal, 1826–1827
Tennessee State Library and Archives
  Appalachian County Tax List Manuscripts
  William P. Grohse Typescripts
  Chris D. Livesay Papers

Pippa Passes, Kentucky
Appalachian Oral History Project, Alice Lloyd College
  Frank Harmon, interview by Carolyn Hunter and Vicki McCarty, 19 June 1973,
    interview 468AB (transcript)
  Melvin Proffitt, interview by Bill Weinberg, 11 August 1975, interview 1165 (tran-
    script)

Richmond, Virginia
Virginia Historical Society
  John E. Fletcher Papers
Virginia State Library and Archives
  Appalachian County Tax List Manuscripts

Salt Lake City, Utah
Family History Center, Church of Jesus Christ of the Latter Day Saints
  Appalachian County Tax List Manuscripts
  Bradley County, Tennessee, Poor Commission, 1880–1884
  Claiborne County, Tennessee, Stagecoach Book, 1846–1848
  Frederick County, Virginia, Court Papers
  Kentucky Land Office Records: Nonresident Land Owners, 1792–1843
  Staunton, Virginia, Poor Records, 1770–1872
  Washington County, Tennessee, Court Records

Troy, Alabama
Troy State University Library
  John Horry Dent Farm Journals and Account Books, 1840–1892

Washington, D.C.
Library of Congress
  Map of Frederick and Jefferson Counties, Virginia, 1809. Photocopy.
  Sophia S. Wilson Diary, 1831
National Archives
  Census Enumerator Manuscripts, 1860, for Appalachian Counties: Census of Pop-
    ulation, Slave Schedules, Census of Agriculture, and Census of Manufacturing
  Census Roll, 1835, of the Cherokee Indians East of the Mississippi
  Records of the Cherokee Indian Agency in Tennessee, 1801–1835

Published Primary Sources

Abdy, Edward S. *Journal of a Residence and Tour in the United States of America from
  April 1833 to October 1834*. 3 vols. London: John Murray, 1835.
"The A. S. Merrimon Journal." Edited by A. R. Newsome. *North Carolina Historical
  Review* 8 (1931): 300–330.
Adair's History of the American Indians, 1775. Edited by Samuel Williams. Johnson
  City, Tenn.: Watauga Press, 1930.
"Albermarle in 1815: Notes of Christopher Daniel Ebeling." Edited by John L. Rior-
  dan. *Papers of the Albermarle County Historical Society* 12 (1951–52).
Alden, John R., ed. "The Eighteenth-Century Cherokee Archives." *American Archiv-
  ist* 5 (1942): 240–44.
American State Papers. 38 vols. Washington, D.C.: Gales and Seaton, 1831–60.

Ansted, D. T. "On the Copper Lodes of Ducktown in East Tennessee." *Quarterly Journal of the Geological Society of London* 13 (1857): 245–54.

Ashe, Thomas. *Travels in America in 1806*. London: E. M. Blount, 1808.

Atkeson, Thomas C., and Mary M. Atkeson. *Pioneering in Agriculture: One Hundred Years of American Farming and Farm Leadership*. New York: Orange Judd Publishing Company, 1937.

"Autobiography of Gideon Lincecum." *Mississippi Historical Society Publications* 8 (1910): 443–519.

Ball, Charles. *Slavery in the United States: A Narrative of the Life and Adventures of Charles Ball, A Black Man*. 1837. Reprint, New York: Negro Universities Press, 1969.

Bartram, William. *Travels through North and South Carolina, Georgia, East and West Florida, the Cherokee Country*. Philadelphia: James and Johnson, 1792.

Beeman, Richard R., ed. "Trade and Travel in Post-revolutionary Virginia: A Diary of an Itinerant Peddler, 1807–1808." *Virginia Magazine of History and Biography* 84 (1976): 174–88.

Bernard, Duke of Saxe-Weimar. *Travels through North America during the Years 1825 and 1826*. Philadelphia: N.p., 1828.

Bridges, Steven A. *Virginians in 1800: Counties of West Virginia*. Trumbull, Conn.: By Author, 1987.

Bryan, T. Conn, ed. "Letters Concerning Georgia Gold Mines." *Collections of the Georgia Historical Society* 39 (1955): 401–9, and 44 (1960): 338–46.

Buckingham, James S. *The Slave States of America*. 2 vols. London: Fisher, 1842.

Buni, Andrew, ed. " 'Rambles among the Virginia Mountains': The Journal of Mary Jane Boggs, 1851." *Virginia Magazine of History and Biography* 77 (1969): 78–111.

Byrd, William, II. *Histories of the Dividing Line betwixt Virginia and North Carolina*. Edited by W. K. Boyd. Mineola, N.Y.: Dover Books, 1929.

Calendar of the Tennessee and King's Mountain Papers of the Draper Collection of Manuscripts. Madison, Wis.: State Historical Society of Wisconsin, 1929.

Calendar of Virginia State Papers and Other Manuscripts. 11 vols. Edited by W. P. Palmer et al. Richmond: State of Virginia, 1875–93.

Candler, Isaac. *A Summary View of America: Comprising a Description of the Face of the Country and of Several of the Principal Cities*. London, 1824.

Carey, Matthew. "Essays on the Public Charities of Philadelphia, 1828." Reprinted in *The Jacksonians on the Poor: Collected Pamphlets*. Edited by David J. Rothman. New York: Arno Press, 1971.

The Carolina Chronicles of Dr. Francis LeJau, 1707–1717. Edited by Frank J. Klingberg. Berkeley: University of California Press, 1956.

Carpenter, Charles, ed. "Henry Dana Ward: Early Diary Keeper of the Kanawha Valley." *West Virginia History* 37 (1976): 34–48.

Catesby, Mark. *The Natural History of Carolina, Florida, and Bahama Islands*. 1683–1749. Reprint, Spartanburg, S.C.: Beehive Press, 1974.

Chambers, William. *Things as They Are in America*. Philadelphia: Lippincott, Grambo and Co., 1854.

Charter of the Coal River and Kanawha Mining and Manufacturing Company, Virginia, Together with the Report of Joseph Gill, Esq., State Engineer. New York: n.p., 1855.

Clift, G. Glenn, comp. *"Second Census" of Kentucky*. Baltimore: Genealogical Publishing, 1966.

Code of 1883 of North Carolina. 2 vols. Raleigh: P. M. Hall, 1885.

The Code of the State of Georgia. Edited by R. H. Clark, T. R. R. Cobb, and D. Irwin. Atlanta: State of Georgia, 1861.

Coffey, David W., ed. "'Into the Valley of Virginia': The 1852 Travel Account of Curran Swain." *Virginia Cavalcade* 39 (Spring 1990): 14–27.

Cole, Arthur H. *Wholesale Commodity Prices in the United States, 1700–1861.* Cambridge: Harvard University Press, 1938.

Collins, Lewis. *Historical Sketches of Kentucky.* Maysville, Ky.: By Author, 1847.

Colonial Records of North Carolina. 10 vols. Edited by William L. Saunders. Raleigh: P. M. Hall, 1886.

Colonial Records of South Carolina: Documents Relating to Indian Affairs, 1750–1765. 2 vols. Edited by W. L. McDowell. Columbia: South Carolina Archives Department, 1958–72.

Colonial Records of South Carolina: Journals of the Commissioners of the Indian Trade, September 20, 1710–August 29, 1718. Edited by W. L. McDowell. Columbia: South Carolina Archives Department, 1955.

Colonial Records of the State of Georgia. 26 vols. Compiled by A. D. Chandler. Atlanta: State of Georgia, 1904–16.

Coombs, Edith I. *America Visited: Famous Travellers Report on the United States in the 18th and 19th Centuries.* New York: Book League of America, n.d.

Coxe, Tench. *A Statement of the Arts and Manufactures of the United States of America for the Year 1810.* Philadelphia: A. Cornman, 1814.

"David Stuart's Report to President Washington on Agricultural Conditions in Northern Virginia." Edited by G. R. B. Richards. *Virginia Magazine of History and Biography* 61 (1953): 283–92.

De Bow, J. D. B. *Industrial Resources of the Western and Southern States.* 4 vols. New Orleans, 1853.

De Brahm's Report of the General Survey in the Southern District of North America. Edited by Louis De Vorsey. Columbia: University of South Carolina Press, 1971.

"Diary of a Geological Tour by Dr. Elisha Mitchell in 1827 and 1828." *James Sprunt Historical Monographs* 6 (1905): 1–74.

A Documentary History of American Industrial Society. 11 vols. Edited by J. R. Commons et al. Cleveland: Arthur H. Clark Co., 1910.

Doddridge, Joseph. *Notes on the Settlement and Indian Wars of the Western Parts of Virginia and Pennsylvania from 1763 to 1783.* Wellsburg, Va.: By author, 1824.

Egypt, Ophelia, H. Masuoka, and C. S. Johnson, comps. "Unwritten History of Slavery: Autobiographical Account of Negro Ex-Slaves." Fisk University Social Science Document No. 1, Mimeographed Typescript, 1945.

Elliott and Nye. *Virginia Directory and Business Register for 1852.* Richmond, 1852.

Evans, E. Raymond, ed. "Jeddiah Morse's Report to the Secretary of War on Cherokee Indian Affairs in 1822." *Journal of Cherokee Studies* 6 (1981): 60–78.

Evans, Louis. *General Map of the Middle British Colonies and of the Country of the Confederate Indians.* 2d ed. Philadelphia, 1755.

Executive Journals of the Council of Colonial Virginia. 6 vols. Edited by H. R. McIlwaine and Wilmer Hall. Richmond: Virginia State Library, 1925–66.

Feastonhough, G. W. *Excursion through the Slave States, From Washington on the Potomac to the Frontier of Mexico, With Sketches of Popular Manners and Geological Notices.* 2 vols. 1844. Reprint, New York: Negro Universities, 1968.

———. *A Canoe Voyage up the Minnay Sotor.* 2 vols. London: Richard Bentley, 1847.

Ferry Hill Plantation Journal: Life on the Potomac River and Chesapeake and Ohio Canal: 4 January 1838–15 January 1839. Edited by Fletcher M. Green, Thomas F. Hahn, and Nathalie W. Hahn. Shepherdstown, W.Va.: American Canal and Transportation Center, 1975.

Folmsbee, Stanley J., and Madeline Lewis, eds. "Journals of the Juan Pardo Expeditions, 1566–1567." *East Tennessee Historical Society Publications* 37 (1965): 106–21.

Ford, Worthington, ed. *The Writings of George Washington.* 12 vols. New York, 1889.

"General Slade's Journal of a Trip to Tennessee." *Historical Society of Trinity College Papers* 6 (1906): 37–56.

Goodloe, D. R. *Inquiry into the Causes Which Have Retarded the Accumulation of Wealth and Increase of Population in the Southern States.* Washington, D.C.: By Author, 1846.

Gosse, Philip H. *Letters from Alabama, Chiefly Relating to Natural History.* London: Morgan and Chase, 1859.

Grund, Francis J. *The Americans in Their Moral, Social, and Political Relations.* Boston: Marsh, Capen, and Lyon, 1837.

Hagy, James W., and Stanley J. Folmsbee, eds. "The Lost Archives of the Cherokee Nation." *East Tennessee Historical Society Publications* 43–45 (1971–73).

Hall, James. *Notes on the Western States.* Philadelphia: Harrison Hall, 1838.

Hamilton, Kenneth G., ed. "Minutes of the Mission Conference Held in Spring Place." *Atlanta Historical Bulletin* 29 (Winter 1970): 1–72.

Hayne, Robert Y. "Address in Behalf of the Knoxville Convention, to the Citizens of the State Interested in the Proposed Louisville, Cincinnati, and Charleston Railroad." Charleston, S.C.: Louisville, Cincinnati, and Charleston Railroad Co., 1836. Pamphlet.

Hendrix, GeLee C., comp. *Pendleton County, South Carolina, Deed Book A and B.* Greenville, S.C.: By Author, 1980.

Hening, William W., ed. *The Statutes at Large of Virginia, 1619–1792.* 3 vols. Philadelphia: Bartow, 1809–23.

Hewatt, Alexander. *An Historical Account of the Rise and Progress of the Colonies of South Carolina and Georgia.* London: Alexander Donaldson, 1779.

Hill's Tennessee, Alabama, and Mississippi Almanac and State Register. Nashville, 1861.

Historical Collections of South Carolina. 2 vols. Edited by B. R. Carroll. New York: Harper and Bros., 1836.

Hopkins, James F., ed. *The Papers of Henry Clay.* 11 vols. Lexington: University of Kentucky Press, 1959.

Hunt, Gaillard, ed. *The Writings of James Madison.* New York: G. P. Putnam's Sons, 1901.

Huth, Hans, and W. J. Pugh, eds. *Talleyrand in America as a Financial Promoter, 1794–96: Unpublished Letters and Memoirs.* Washington, D.C.: Government Printing Office, 1942.

Jacobs, Wilbur R., ed. *Indians of the Southern Colonial Frontier: The Edmund Atkin Report and Plan of 1755.* Columbia: University of South Carolina Press, 1954.

Jennings, Ralph D. "Consumption of Feed by Livestock, 1909–1956." *United States Department of Agriculture Production Research Report,* no. 21 (1958).

Jillson, Willard R., comp. *The Kentucky Land Grants: A Systematic Index to All of the Land Grants Recorded in the State Land Office, 1782–1924.* Baltimore: Genealogical Publishing, 1971.

"John Brown's Journal of Travel in Western North Carolina in 1795." Edited by A. R. Newsome. *North Carolina Historical Review* 11 (1934): 284–313.

Johnston, James F. W. *Notes on North America, Agricultural, Economical, and Social.* Boston: Edinburgh and London, 1851.

Jones, Charles C., ed. *Antiquities of the Southern Indians, Particularly of the Georgia Tribes.* New York: Appleton and Co., 1873.

Journal of Colonel John Herbert, Commissioner of Indian Affairs for the Province of South

Carolina. Edited by A. S. Salley. Columbia: Historical Commission of South Carolina, 1936.

Journal of the Commons House of Assembly of South Carolina: November 1, 1725–April 30, 1726. Edited by A. S. Salley. Columbia: General Assembly of South Carolina, 1945.

Journals of the Continental Congress, 1774–1789. 34 vols. Washington, D.C.: Government Printing Office, 1904–37.

Journal of the Grand Council of South Carolina, 1721–1775. Edited by A. S. Salley. Columbia, S.C.: Archives Dept, 1908.

"Journal of John Sevier." *Tennessee Historical Magazine* 5 and 6 (1919–20): 156–94, 232–64, 18–68.

Journal of the Proceedings of the Honourable Governor and Council, May 29, 1721–June 10, 1721. Edited by A. S. Salley. Atlanta: Foote and Davies Co., 1930.

"Journal of the Surry County Agricultural Society." Edited by Nannie M. Tilley. *North Carolina Historical Review* 24 (1947): 494–531.

Kappler, Charles J. *Indian Affairs: Laws and Treaties.* 6 vols. Washington, D.C.: Government Printing Office, 1903–29.

Killebrew, J. B., and J. M. Safford. *Introduction to Resources of Tennessee.* Nashville: Tavel, Eastman, and Howell, 1874.

Killion, Ronald, and Charles Waller, comps. *Slavery Time When I Was Chillun down on Marster's Plantation.* Savannah: Beehive Press, 1973.

Kimsey, Herbert B., comp. *Early Genealogical and Historical Records: Habersham County, Georgia.* Athens, Ga.: By author, 1988.

Knowlton, Daniel C., ed. "The Journal of William H. Crawford." *Smith College Studies in History* 11 (1925): 5–64.

Lanman, Charles. *Letters from the Allegheny Mountains.* New York: G. B. Putnam, 1849.

———. *Adventures in the Wilds of the United States and British American Provinces.* Philadelphia, 1856.

Laws or Laws Relative to Lands and Intestate Estates. Knoxville: Roulstone and Wilson, 1800.

Lawson, John. *History of North Carolina.* London: W. Taylor and F. Baker, 1714.

Lesley, J. Peter. *The Iron Manufacturer's Guide to the Furnaces, Forges, and Rolling Mills of the United States.* New York: John Wiley, 1854.

"Letters of Benjamin Hawkins." *Georgia Historical Collections* 9 (1924).

"Letters of 1831–32 about Kentucky." *Filson Club Historical Quarterly* 16 (1942): 220–27.

"Letters to Jefferson from Archibald Cary and Robert Gamble." *William and Mary Quarterly* 6 (1926): 122–32.

"Life of a Wanderer: The Memoirs of Edward Stephenson III." *West Virginia History* 28 (1967): 73–100.

"The Lonaconing Journals: The Founding of a Coal and Iron Community, 1837–1840." Edited by Katherine A. Harvey. *Transactions of the American Philosophical Society* 67, no. 2 (1977).

Long, Alexander. "A Small Postscript of the Ways and Manners of the Indians Called Charikees, 1725." *Southern Indian Studies* 21 (1969): 3–49.

Lord, Clifford L., and Elizabeth S. Lord. *Historical Atlas of the United States.* New York: Johnson Reprint Corporation, 1969.

Lord, William G. *Blue Ridge Parkway Guide.* 2 vols. Washington, D.C.: Eastern Acorn Press, 1990.

Lossiah, Aggie R. "The Story of My Life as Far Back as I Can Remember." *Journal of Cherokee Studies* 9, no. 2 (1984): 89–99.

Louis-Phillipe. *Diary of My Travels in America, 1796–99.* Translated by Stephen Becker. New York: Delacorte Press, 1977.

McDonald, Cornelia P. *A Woman's Civil War: A Diary with Reminiscences of the War from March 1862.* Edited by Minrose C. Gwin. Madison: University of Wisconsin Press, 1992.

McDonald, John Y., ed. "Specifications for Planting Orchards in Early Leases: George Washington's Lease to Jacob Fry." *Magazine of the Jefferson County Historical Society* 36 (1970).

Mackay, Charles. *Life and Liberty in America, or Sketches of a Tour in the United States and Canada in 1857–8.* London, 1859.

McPherson, R. G., ed. *Journal of the Earl of Egmont: Abstract of the Trustees' Proceedings for Establishing the Colony of Georgia, 1732–1738.* Athens: University of Georgia Press, 1962.

Marryat, Frederick. *A Diary in America with Remarks on Its Institutions.* Philadelphia: Carey and Hart, 1839.

Martin, Joseph. *A New and Comprehensive Gazetteer of Virginia and the District of Columbia.* Charlottesville: By Author, 1836.

Mason, Frances N., ed. *John Norton and Sons, Merchants of London and Virginia: Being the Papers for Their Counting House for the Years 1750 to 1795.* Richmond: Dietz Press, 1937.

Melish, John. *The Traveler's Directory through the United States, Containing a Description of All the Principal Roads.* Philadelphia: By Author, 1822.

"Memorandum of M. Austin's Journey from the Lead Mines in the County of Wythe in the State of Virginia to the Lead Mines in the Province of Louisiana, 1796–1797." *American Historical Review* 5 (1899–1900): 518–41.

Mereness, N. D., ed. *Travels in the American Colonies.* New York: Macmillan, 1916.

Michaux, Francois A. *Travels to the Westward of the Allegheny Mountains.* London, 1805.

Mills, Robert. *Statistics of South Carolina.* 1826. Reprint, Spartanburg, S.C.: Reprint Co., 1972.

Mississippi Provincial Archives, 1729–1740. 4 vols. Edited by Dunbar Rowland and A. G. Sanders. Jackson, Miss.: Department of Archives and History, 1927–32.

Moore, Glover. *A Calhoun County, Alabama, Boy in the 1860s.* Jackson: University Press of Mississippi, 1978.

Moorman, John J. *The Virginia Springs: Comprising an Account of All the Principal Mineral Springs of Virginia.* Richmond: J. W. Randolph, 1854.

Morris, Eastin. *The Tennessee Gazetteer or Topographical Dictionary.* Nashville: W. H. Hunt and Co., 1834.

Mulkearn, Lois, ed. *George Mercer Papers Relating to the Ohio Company of Virginia.* Pittsburgh: University of Pittsburgh Press, 1954.

The Narrative of Bethany Veney: A Slave Woman. Worcester, Mass.: A. P. Bicknell, 1890.

Newsome, A. R., ed. "Simeon Colton's Railroad Report, 1840." *North Carolina Historical Review* 11 (1934): 215–24.

Norona, Delf, ed. "Joshua Fry's Report on the Back Settlements of Virginia (May 8, 1751)." *Virginia Magazine of History and Biography* 46 (1948): 22–41.

The Official Letters of Alexander Spotswood, Lieutenant-Governor of the Colony of Virginia, 1710–1722. 2 vols. Richmond: Virginia Historical Society, 1882–85.

Olmsted, Frederick L. *A Journey in the Back Country, 1853–1854.* New York: Burt Franklin, 1860.

——. *Journey in the Seaboard Slave States.* 1859. Reprint, New York: Negro Universities Press, 1968.

"100 Historic Sites and Structures in Rockbridge County." Lexington, Va.: Association for Preservation of Virginia Antiquities, 1979.

Owen, David D. *Third Report of the Geological Survey in Kentucky*. Frankfort, Ky.: A. G. Hodges, 1857.

Pencil, Mark. *The White Sulphur Papers or Life at the Springs of Western Virginia*. New York, 1839.

Peters, Margaret T. *A Guidebook to Virginia's Historical Markers*. Charlottesville: University Press of Virginia, 1985.

The Proceedings of the Agricultural Convention of the State Agricultural Society of South Carolina. Columbia, S.C.: Summer and Carroll, 1846.

Rawick, George P., comp. *The American Slave: A Composite Autobiography*. 19 vols. Westport, Conn.: Greenwood Press, 1972.

——. *The American Slave: A Composite Autobiography, Supplement I*. 12 vols. Westport, Conn.: Greenwood Publishing, 1977.

——. *The American Slave: A Composite Autobiography, Supplement II*. 10 vols. Westport, Conn.: Greenwood Publishing, 1979.

Rawlings, Mary, and W. E. Hemphill, eds. "Dr. Charles Brown's Reminiscences of Early Albermarle." *Papers of the Albermarle County Historical Society* 8 (1947–48): 55–68.

Records in the British Public Record Office Relating to South Carolina, 1663–1684. Edited by A. S. Salley. Columbia: Historical Commission of South Carolina, 1928–47.

Records of the Moravians in North Carolina. 11 vols. Edited by Adelaide L. Fries. Raleigh: Edwards and Broughton, 1922–30.

The Registers of Free Blacks, 1810–1864: Augusta County, Virginia, and Staunton, Virginia. Edited by Katherine G. Bushman. Verona, Va.: Midvalley Press, 1989.

Reid, Joseph D. "Antebellum Southern Rental Contracts." *Explorations in Economic History* 13 (1976).

Report of the Board of Internal Improvement for East Tennessee to the General Assembly of the State of Tennessee. Nashville: Southern Christian Advocate, 1837.

Report of the Commissioner of Patents: Agriculture, 1849. Washington, D.C.: U.S. House of Representatives, 1850.

Report of the Commissioner of Patents: Agriculture, 1850. Washington, D.C.: U.S. House of Representatives, 1851.

Report of the Commissioner of Patents: Agriculture, 1851. Washington, D.C.: U.S. House of Representatives, 1852.

Report of the Indian Commissioner, 1848. Washington, D.C.: Department of the Interior, 1850.

Report of the Indian Commissioner, 1884. Washington, D.C.: Department of the Interior, 1886.

The Revised Code of North Carolina. Raleigh: State of North Carolina, 1883.

Richardson, James D. *A Compilation of the Messages and Papers of the Presidents*. 20 vols. New York: Bureau of National Literature, 1897.

Robertson, James R., ed. *Petitions of the Early Inhabitants of Kentucky to the General Assembly of Virginia, 1769 to 1792*. Louisville: Filson Club Publications, 1914.

Rochefoucauld-Laincourt, Duc de la. *Travels through the United States of North America in the Years 1795, 1796, 1797*. London, 1799.

Royall, Anne. *Sketches of History, Life, and Manners in the United States by a Traveller*. New Haven, Conn.: By Author, 1826.

——. *Southern Tour, or Second Series of the Black Book*. 3 vols. Washington, D.C.: By Author, 1830–31.

Russell, Robert. *North America, Its Agriculture and Climate; Containing Observations on the Agriculture and Climate of Canada, the United States, and the Island of Cuba.* London, 1863.

Safford, James M. *A Geological Reconnaissance of the State of Tennessee.* Nashville: Tennessee Geological Survey, 1856.

Schoepf, Johann D. *Travels in the Confederation, 1783–1784.* 2 vols. Translated by A. J. Morrison. Philadelphia: William J. Campbell, 1911.

Shepard, E. Lee, ed. "Trip to the Virginia Springs: An Extract from the Diary of Blair Bollings, 1838." *Virginia Magazine of History and Biography* 96, no. 2 (1988): 193–212.

Siler, Tom. *Tennessee Towns: From Adams to Yorkville.* Knoxville: East Tennessee Historical Society, 1985.

Sims Index: Land Grants of West Virginia. Edited by Edgar B. Sims. Charleston, W.Va.: State Auditor's Office, 1952.

Smith, G. Hulbert, ed. "A Letter from Kentucky, 1785." *Mississippi Valley Historical Review* 19 (1932): 90–95.

Smith, J. Gray. *A Brief Historical, Statistical, and Descriptive Review of East Tennessee, United States of America: Developing Its Immense Agricultural, Mining, and Manufacturing Advantages, with Remarks to Emigrants.* London: J. Leath, 1842.

Smyth, John F. D. *A Tour of the U.S.A., Containing an Account of the Present Situation of that Country.* 2 vols. London: G. Robinson, 1784.

State Records of North Carolina. 26 vols. Edited by Walter Clark. Raleigh: Winston and Goldsboro, 1895–1906.

Statutes at Large of South Carolina. 10 vols. Edited by Thomas Cooper and Daniel McCord. Columbia, S.C.: Archives Department, 1836–40.

Sturtevant, William C., ed. "John Ridge on Cherokee Civilization in 1826." *Journal of Cherokee Studies* 6 (1981): 79–91.

Sutcliff, Robert. *Travels in Some Parts of North America in the Years 1804, 1805, and 1806.* York, Eng., 1815.

Tanner, H. S. *A Description of the Canals and Railroads of the United States Comprehending Notices of All Works of Internal Improvement throughout the Several States.* New York: Tanner and Disturnell, 1840.

Taylor, Richard C. *Statistics of Coal: The Geographical and Geological Distribution.* Philadelphia: J. W. Moore, 1848.

The Tennessee Civil War Veterans Questionnaires. Compiled by Gustavus W. Dyer and John T. Moore. Easley, S.C.: Southern Historical Press, 1985.

Tennessee Historical Markers. Nashville: Tennessee Historical Commission, 1980.

Thomas Jefferson's Farm Book with Commentary and Relevant Extracts from Other Writings. Edited by Edwin M. Betts. Princeton: American Philosophical Society, 1953.

Thomas Jefferson's Garden Book, 1766–1824, with Relevant Extracts from His Other Writings. Edited by Edwin M. Betts. Philadelphia: American Philosophical Society, 1944.

"Thomas Lenoir's Journey to Tennessee in 1806." Edited by James W. Patton. *Tennessee Historical Quarterly* 17 (1958): 156–66.

Thompson, Kathy, ed. *In Touch with the Past: A Guide to Historic Places and Homes in Fannin County, Georgia, and Polk County, Tennessee.* Blue Ridge, Ga.: By Author, 1982.

———. *Touching Home: A Collection of History and Folklore from the Copper Basin, Fannin County, Area.* Orlando, Fla.: Daniels Publishers, 1976.

Thorndale, William, and William Dollarhide. *Map Guide to the U.S. Federal Censuses, 1790–1920.* Baltimore: Genealogical Publishing, 1987.

Thwaites, Reuben G., ed. *Early Western Travels*. 32 vols. Cleveland: Arthur H. Clark Co., 1904–7.

Toulmin, Harry. *The Western Country in 1793: Reports on Kentucky and Virginia*. 1794. Reprint, San Marino, Calif.: Castle Press, 1948.

Townsend, Joseph. "Dissertation on the Poor Laws by a Well-Wisher to Mankind." In *A Select Collection of Scarce and Valuable Economical Tracts*, pp. 403–19. London: n.p., 1859.

Travels in Virginia in Revolutionary Times. Lynchburg, Va.: J. P. Bell Co., 1922.

Troost, Gerard. *Fifth Geological Report of the State of Tennessee*. Nashville: State of Tennessee, 1840.

U.S. Census Office. *Aggregate Amount of Persons within the United States in the Year 1810*. Washington, D.C.: Gales and Seaton, 1811.

———. *Agriculture of the United States in 1860*. Washington, D.C.: Government Printing Office, 1864.

———. *Census for 1820*. Washington, D.C.: Gales and Seaton, 1821.

———. *Compendium of the Enumeration of the Inhabitants and Statistics of the United States*. Washington, D.C.: Thomas Allen, 1841.

———. *Digest of Accounts of Manufacturing Establishments in the United States and Their Manufactures*. Washington, D.C.: Gales and Seaton, 1823.

———. *Fifth Census or Enumeration of the Inhabitants of the U.S., 1830*. Washington, D.C.: D. Green, 1832.

———. *Heads of Families at the First Census of the U.S. Taken in the Year 1790: South Carolina*. Washington, D.C.: Government Printing Office, 1908.

———. *Instructions to United States Marshals, 8th Census*. Washington, D.C.: Government Printing Office, 1860.

———. *Manufactures of the United States in 1860*. Washington, D.C.: Government Printing Office, 1865.

———. *Mortality Statistics of the Seventh Census of the United States, 1850*. Washington, D.C.: A. O. P. Nicholson, 1855.

———. *Population of the United States in 1860*. Washington, D.C.: Government Printing Office, 1864.

———. *Report on Indians Taxed and Indians Not Taxed in the United States*. Washington, D.C.: Government Printing Office, 1894.

———. *Special Reports: Mines and Quarries, 1902*. Washington, D.C.: Government Printing Office, 1905.

———. *Statistical View of the United States Being a Compendium of the Seventh Census*. Washington, D.C.: A. O. P. Nicholson, 1854.

———. *Statistics of the United States, Including Mortality and Property*. Washington, D.C.: Government Printing Office, 1866.

———. *Thirteenth Census of the United States Taken in the Year 1910: Agriculture, 1909–1910, Reports by States with Statistics for Counties*. Washington, D.C.: Government Printing Office, 1913.

United States Commissioner of Education Report, 1899–1900. Washington, D.C.: Government Printing Office, 1900.

U.S. Department of Agriculture. *Agricultural Statistics*. Washington, D.C.: Government Printing Office, 1942.

"Uria Brown's Journal of 1816." *Maryland Historical Magazine* 10 and 11 (1915–16).

Vandiver, Wellington, ed. "Pioneer Talladega, Its Minutes and Memories." *Alabama Historical Quarterly* 16 (1954): 1–210.

"Vineland in Tennessee, 1852: The Journal of Rosine Parmentier." Edited by Ben H.

McClary and Le Roy P. Graf. *East Tennessee Historical Society Publications* 31 (1959): 95–111.

Washington, Booker T. *Up from Slavery: An Autobiography*. New York: Association Press, 1901.

Weld, Isaac. *Travels through the States of North America and the Provinces of Upper and Lower Canada during the Years 1795, 1796, and 1797*. London: John Stockdale, 1800.

West Virginia: Centennial of Statehood, 1863–1963: An Exhibition in the Library of Congress. Washington, D.C.: Library of Congress, 1964.

White, George. *Statistics of the State of Georgia*. Savannah: W. Thorne Williams, 1849.

White, Robert H., ed. *Messages of the Governors of Tennessee*. Nashville: Tennessee Historical Commission, 1952.

Whitney, Henry D. *The Land Laws of Tennessee*. Chattanooga: J. J. Deardorr and Sons, 1891.

Williams, Samuel C., ed. *Lieutenant Henry Timberlake's Memoirs*. Johnson City, Tenn.: Watauga Press, 1927.

——. *Early Travels in the Tennessee Country, 1540–1800*. Johnson City, Tenn.: Watauga Press, 1928.

——. "Journal of Events of David Anderson Deaderick." *East Tennessee Historical Society Publications* 8 (1936): 121–37.

The WPA Guide to Tennessee. 1939. Reprint, Knoxville: University of Tennessee Press, 1986.

Writings of Colonel William Byrd of Westover in Virginia, Esquire. New York: Doubleday-Page, 1901.

Writings of George Washington from the Original Manuscript Sources, 1745–1799. 39 vols. Edited by John C. Fitzpatrick. Washington, D.C.: Government Printing Office, 1944.

Secondary Sources

Abbott, Phyllis R. "The Development and Operation of an American Land System to 1800." Ph.D. diss., University of Wisconsin, 1959.

Abernethy, Thomas P. "The Early Development of Commerce and Banking in Tennessee." *Mississippi Valley Historical Review* 14 (1927): 311–25.

——. *Three Virginia Frontiers*. Gloucester: Peter Smith, 1962.

——. *Western Lands and the American Revolution*. New York: Appleton-Century, 1937.

Agnew, John. *The United States in the World Economy: A Regional Geography*. Cambridge: Cambridge University Press, 1987.

Aguirre-Beltran, Gonzalo. *Regions of Refuge*. Washington, D.C.: Society for Applied Anthropology, 1979.

Ahern, L. R., and R. F. Hunt. "The Boatyard Store, 1814–1825." *Tennessee Historical Quarterly* 14 (1955): 257–77.

Alden, John R. *John Stuart and the Southern Colonial Frontier: A Study of Indian Relations, War Trade, and Land Problems in the Southern Wilderness, 1754–1775*. New York: Gordian Press, 1966.

Allen, Jay D. "The Mount Savage Iron Works, Mount Savage, Maryland: A Case Study in Pre–Civil War Industrial Development." Master's thesis, University of Maryland, 1970.

Allen, Michael. *Western Rivermen, 1763–1861: Ohio and Mississippi Boatmen and the Myth of the Alligator Horse*. Baton Rouge: Louisiana State University Press, 1990.

Allen, Turner W. "The Turnpike System in Kentucky: A Review of State Road Policy in the 19th Century." *Filson Club Historical Quarterly* 28 (1954): 239–59.

Allman, John M. "Yeoman Regions in the Antebellum Deep South: Settlement and Economy in Northern Alabama, 1815–1860." Ph.D. diss., University of Maryland, 1979.

Ambler, Charles H. *A History of Transportation in the Ohio Valley.* Glendale, Calif.: Arthur H. Clark, 1932.

———. *A History of West Virginia.* New York: Prentice-Hall, 1933.

———. *Sectionalism in Virginia from 1776 to 1861.* New York: Russell and Russell, 1964.

Amin, Samir. *Accumulation on a World Scale: A Critique of the Theory of Underdevelopment.* New York: Monthly Review Press, 1974.

———. *Class and Nation: Historically and in the Current Crisis.* New York: Monthly Review Press, 1980.

———. "Social Characteristics of Peripheral Formations: An Outline of an Historical Sociology." *Berkeley Journal of Sociology* 21 (1976): 27–50.

Anderson, Margo J. *The American Census: A Social History.* New Haven, Conn.: Yale University Press, 1988.

Anderson, William L. "Cherokee Clay, from Duche to Wedgewood: The Journal of Thomas Griffiths, 1767–1768." *North Carolina Historical Review* 63 (1986): 477–510.

Anderson-Green, Paula H. "The New River Frontier Settlement on the Virginia–North Carolina Border, 1760–1820." *Virginia Magazine of History and Biography* 86 (1978): 413–31.

Andrews, Charles M. *The Colonial Period of American History: England's Commercial and Colonial Policy.* 4 vols. New Haven: Yale University Press, 1938.

Anthony, J. D. "Cherokee County, Alabama: Reminiscences of Its Settlement." *Alabama Historical Quarterly* 8 (1946): 329–42.

Appalachia—A Reference Book. Washington, D.C.: Appalachian Regional Commission, 1979.

Appalachian Land Ownership Task Force. *Who Owns Appalachia? Land Ownership and Its Impact.* Lexington: University of Kentucky Press, 1981.

Appleby, Joyce. "Commercial Farming and the 'Agrarian Myth' in the Early Republic." *Journal of American History* 68 (1982): 833–49.

Applewhite, Joseph D. "Early Trade and Navigation on the Cumberland River." Master's thesis, Vanderbilt University, 1940.

Applewhite, Marjorie M. "Sharecropper and Tenant in the Courts of North Carolina." *North Carolina Historical Review* 31 (1954): 134–49.

Arbuckle, Robert D. "John Nicholson, 1757–1800: A Case Study of an Early American Land Speculator, Financier, and Entrepreneur." Ph.D. diss., Pennsylvania State University, 1972.

Armstrong, Thomas F. "Urban Vision in Virginia: A Comparative Study of Antebellum Fredericksburg, Lynchburg, and Staunton." Ph.D. diss., University of Virginia, 1974.

Armstrong, Zella. *The History of Hamilton County and Chattanooga, Tennessee.* Chattanooga: Lookout Publishing Co., 1931.

Arrighi, Giovanni. "Peripheralization of Southern Africa, I: Changes in Production Processes." *Review of the Fernand Braudel Center* 3 (1979): 161–92.

Arrighi, Giovanni, and John S. Saul. *Essays on the Political Economy of Africa.* New York: Monthly Review Press, 1973.

Arthur, John P. *Western North Carolina: A History from 1730–1913.* Raleigh: Edward and Broughton, 1914.

Ashe, Samuel A. *History of North Carolina*. Raleigh: Edward and Broughton, 1925.

Ashton, John. "History of Jack Stock and Mules in Missouri." *Missouri State Board of Agriculture Monthly Bulletin* 22 (1924).

Atack, Jeremy. "The Agricultural Ladder Revisited: A New Look at an Old Question with Some Data for 1860." *Agricultural History* 63 (1989): 1–25.

Atack, Jeremy, and Fred Bateman. "Land and the Development of Mid-Nineteenth Century American Agriculture in the Northern States." *Research in Economic History* 14 (1989): 279–312.

Atherton, Lewis E. "Itinerant Merchandising in the Antebellum South." *Bulletin of the Business Historical Society* 19 (1945).

———. "The Services of the Frontier Merchant." *Mississippi Valley Historical Review* 24 (1937): 153–70.

———. *The Southern Country Store, 1800–1860*. Baton Rouge: Louisiana State University Press, 1949.

Bacon, H. Phillip. "Nashville's Trade at the Beginning of the Nineteenth Century." *Tennessee Historical Quarterly* 15 (1956): 30–36.

Bacot, D. Huger. "The South Carolina Up Country at the End of the 18th Century." *American Historical Review* 28 (1923): 682–98.

Badham, Richard. "The Sociology of Industrial and Post-Industrial Societies." *Current Sociology* 32 (1984): 1–189.

Baker, Andrew H., and Holly V. Izard. "New England Farmers and the Marketplace, 1780–1865: A Case Study." *Agricultural History* 65 (1991): 29–52.

Ball, Richard A. "The Poverty Case: The Analgesic Subculture of the Southern Appalachians." *American Sociological Review* 33 (1968): 885–95.

Banks, Alan J. "Emergence of a Capitalistic Labor Market in Eastern Kentucky." *Appalachian Journal* 7 (1980): 188–99.

Banks, Enoch M. *The Economics of Land Tenure in Georgia*. New York: Columbia University Press, 1905.

Banta, R. E. *The Ohio*. New York: Rinehart and Co., 1949.

Barbosa, Luis C. "The World-System and the Destruction of the Brazilian Amazon Rain Forest." *Review of the Fernand Braudel Center* 16, no. 2 (1993): 215–40.

Bateman, Fred, and Thomas Weiss. "Comparative Regional Development in Antebellum Manufacturing." *Journal of Economic History* 35 (1975): 182–208.

Battalio, Raymond C., and John Kagel. "The Structure of Antebellum Agriculture: South Carolina, A Case Study." In *The Structure of the Cotton Economy of the Antebellum South*, edited by William N. Parker, pp. 25–43. Washington, D.C.: Agricultural History Society, 1970.

Batteau, Allen. "Appalachia and the Concept of Culture: A Theory of Shared Misunderstandings." *Appalachian Journal* 7 (1979–80): 9–32.

Battey, George M. *A History of Rome and Floyd County*. 2 vols. Atlanta: Webb and Vary Co., 1922.

Battis, J. Emery. *Saints and Sectaries: Anne Hutchinson and the Antinomian Controversy in the Massachusetts Bay Colony*. Chapel Hill: University of North Carolina Press, 1962.

Bays, Brad A. "The Historical Geography of Cattle Herding among the Cherokee Indians, 1761–1861." Master's thesis, University of Tennessee, 1991.

Beaver, Patricia. *Rural Community in the Appalachian South*. Lexington: University Press of Kentucky, 1986.

Belissary, Constantine S. "Industry and Industrial Philosophy in Tennessee, 1850–1860." *East Tennessee Historical Society Publications* 23 (1951): 46–57.

Bennett, William D. "Josiah Brandon's Burke County, North Carolina, 1777–1800." *North Carolina Genealogical Society Journal* 7, no. 1 (1981): 2–11.
———. "Early Settlement on the New River System." *North Carolina Genealogical Society Journal* 10, no. 1 (1984): 2–23.
Berdan, Marshall S. "The Spa Life: Taking the Cure in Antebellum Bath County." *Virginia Cavalcade* 40, no. 3 (1991): 110–19.
Bernard, James A. "An Analysis of British Mercantilism As It Related to Patterns of South Carolina Trade from 1717 to 1767." Ph.D. diss., Notre Dame University, 1973.
Bernstein, Harry. "African Peasantries: A Theoretical Framework." *Journal of Peasant Studies* 6 (1979): 421–43.
Bidwell, Percy W. "Rural Economy in New England at the Beginning of the Nineteenth Century." *Transactions of the Connecticut Academy of Arts and Sciences* 20 (1916): 241–399.
Bidwell, Percy W., and John I. Falconer. *History of Agriculture in the Northern United States, 1620–1860.* New York: Peter Smith, 1941.
Billings, Dwight, Kathleen Blee, and Louis Swanson. "Culture, Family, and Community in Preindustrial America." *Appalachian Journal* 13 (1986): 150–70.
Billington, Ray A. *Westward Expansion: A History of the American Frontier.* New York: Macmillan, 1967.
Bissell, Richard. *The Monongahela.* New York: Rinehart and Co., 1949.
Bizzell, William B. *Farm Tenancy in the United States.* Texas Agricultural Experiment Station Bulletin, no. 278. Austin: University of Texas, 1921.
Blackmun, Ora. *Western North Carolina: Its Mountains and Its People to 1880.* 2 vols. Boone, N.C.: Appalachian Consortium Press, 1977.
Blethen, Tyler, and Curtis Wood. "The Antebellum Iron Industry in Western North Carolina." Paper delivered to annual meeting of Appalachian Studies Association, Berea, Kentucky, March 1991.
Bliss, Willard F. "The Rise of Tenancy in Virginia." *Virginia Magazine of History and Biography* 58 (1950): 427–41.
Bloom, Leonard. "The Acculturation of the Eastern Cherokees." *North Carolina Historical Review* 19 (1942): 323–58.
Blunt, Ruth H. "Lynchburg's Tobacco Warehouses." *Virginia Cavalcade* 14, no. 3 (1964): 16–21.
Bode, Frederick A., and Donald E. Ginter. *Farm Tenancy and the Census in Antebellum Georgia.* Athens, Ga.: University of Georgia Press, 1987.
Bogue, Allan G. *From Prairie to Corn Belt: Farming on the Illinois and Iowa Prairies in the 19th Century.* Chicago: University of Chicago Press, 1963.
Bogue, Allan G., and Margaret Bogue. "Profits and the Frontier Land Speculator." *Journal of Economic History* 17 (1957): 1–24.
Bohm, David. *Wholeness and the Implicate Order.* London: Routledge and Kegan Paul, 1980.
Boozer, Jack D. "Jacksonville, Alabama: 1833–1846." Master's thesis, University of Alabama, 1951.
Boughter, Isaac F. "Internal Improvements in Northwestern Virginia: A Study of State Policy Prior to the Civil War." Ph.d. diss., University of Pittsburgh, 1931.
Bouwman, Robert E. "Native Americans and Georgia's Frontier Heritage." *Early Georgia* 10 (1982): 3–12.
———. *Traveler's Rest and the Tugaloo Crossroads.* N.p.: Georgia Department of Natural Resources, 1980.

Boydston, Jeanne. "To Earn Her Daily Bread: Housework and Antebellum Working-Class Subsistence." *Radical History Review* 35 (1986): 7–25.

Brantley, William H. *Banking in Alabama, 1816–1860*. Birmingham: By Author, 1961.

Braudel, Fernand. *Afterthoughts on Material Civilization and Capitalism*. Translated by Patricia Ranum. Baltimore: Johns Hopkins University Press, 1977.

———. *Civilization and Capitalism, 15th–18th Century*. 3 vols. Translated by Sian Reynolds. New York: Harper and Row, 1981.

Braudel Center Research Working Group. "Cyclical Rhythms and Secular Trends of the Capitalist World-Economy: Some Premises, Hypotheses, and Questions." *Review of the Fernand Braudel Center* 2 (1979): 483–500.

Brewer, George E. "History of Coosa County." *Alabama Historical Quarterly* 4 (1942): 33–49.

Brewster, Lawrence F. "The Summer Migrations and Resorts of South Carolina Low-Country Planters." Ph.D. diss., Duke University, 1942.

Brooks, Robert P. *The Agrarian Revolution in Georgia, 1865–1912*. Madison: University of Wisconsin Press, 1914.

Brown, Cecil K. *A State Movement in Railroad Development: The Story of North Carolina's First Effort to Establish an East and West Trunk Line Railroad*. Chapel Hill: University of North Carolina Press, 1928.

Brown, Philip M. "Early Indian Trade in the Development of South Carolina: Politics, Economic and Social Mobility during the Proprietary Period, 1670–1719." *South Carolina Historical Magazine* 76 (1975): 118–28.

Brown, Richard D. *Modernization: The Transformation of American Life, 1600–1865*. New York: Hill and Wang, 1976.

Browne, Gary L. *Baltimore in the Nation, 1789–1861*. Chapel Hill: University of North Carolina Press, 1980.

Bruce, Kathleen. *Virginia Iron Manufacture in the Slave Era*. New York: Century Co., 1939.

Bruchey, Stuart. "The Business Economy of Marketing Change, 1790–1840: A Study of Sources of Efficiency." *Agricultural History* 46 (1972): 216–30.

———. *The Roots of American Economic Growth, 1607–1861: An Essay in Social Causation*. New York: Harper and Row, 1965.

Bryan, Alfred C. "History of State Banking in Maryland." *Johns Hopkins University Studies in History and Political Science* 17, nos. 1–3 (1899).

Buchanan, David P. "The Relations of the Cherokee Indians with the English in America Prior to 1763." Master's thesis, University of Tennessee, 1923.

Burford, Herschel W. "Steam Packets on the Kanawha River." *West Virginia History* 27 (1966): 111–35.

Burnett, Edmund C. "Hog Raising and Hog Driving in the Region of the French Broad River." *Agricultural History* 20 (1946): 86–103.

Burns, Inez. "Settlement and Early History of the Coves of Blount County, Tennessee." *East Tennessee Historical Society Publications* 24 (1952): 44–67.

Bushman, Richard L. *From Puritan to Yankee: Character and the Social Order in Connecticut: 1690–1765*. Cambridge: Harvard University Press, 1967.

Buttel, Frederick H., and Howard Newby, eds. *The Rural Sociology of the Advanced Societies: Critical Perspectives*. London: Croom Helm, 1980.

Buttel, Frederick H., and Philip McMichael. "Sociology and Rural History: Summary and Critique." *Social Science History* 12, no. 2 (1988): 93–120.

Buzzell, L. H. "An Economic Picture of Randolph County, Virginia." *Randolph County Historical Society Magazine* 10 (1942): 62–74.

Byres, T. J. "Historical Perspectives on Sharecropping." *Journal of Peasant Studies* 10 (1983): 1–40.

Caldwell, Nancy A. *A History of Brooke County*. Wellsburg, W.Va.: Brooke County Historical Society, 1975.

Caldwell, Norman W. "The Southern Frontier during King George's War." *Journal of Southern History* 7 (1941): 37–54.

Camp, Henry R. *Sequatchie County*. Memphis: Memphis State University, 1984.

Campbell, Claude A. "Branch Banking in Tennessee Prior to the Civil War." *East Tennessee Historical Society Publications* 11 (1939): 34–46.

——. *The Development of Banking in Tennessee*. Nashville: Vanderbilt University, 1932.

Campbell, John C. *The Southern Highlander and His Homeland*. New York: Russell Sage Foundation, 1921.

Campbell, T. J. *The Upper Tennessee*. Chattanooga: By Author, 1932.

Cappon, Lester J. "Iron Making—A Forgotten Industry of North Carolina." *North Carolina Historical Review* 9 (1932): 331–48.

——. "Trend of Southern Iron Industry under the Plantation System." *Journal of Economic and Business History* 2 (1930): 353–81.

Capron, John D. "Virginia Iron Furnaces of the Confederacy." *Virginia Cavalcade* 17, no. 2 (1967): 10–18.

Carlson, Alvar W. "America's Botanical Drug Connection to the Orient." *Economic Botany* 40 (1986): 229–51.

Carr, Lucien. *Dress and Ornaments of Certain American Indians*. Worcester: Charles Hamilton Press, 1897.

Carson, W. Wallace. "Transportation and Traffic on the Ohio and the Mississippi before the Steamboat." *Mississippi Valley Historical Review* 7 (1920): 26–38.

Carter, Clarence E. "British Policy towards the American Indians in the South, 1763–1768." *English Historical Review* 33 (1918): 37–56.

Cathey, Cornelius O. "Agricultural Development in North Carolina, 1783–1860." *James Sprunt Historical Monographs* 38 (1956).

Catton, William B. "John W. Garrett of the Baltimore and Ohio: A Study in Seaport and Railroad Competition, 1820–1874." Ph.D. diss., Northwestern University, 1959.

Caudill, Harry M. *Night Comes to the Cumberlands: A Biography of a Depressed Area*. Boston: Little, Brown and Co., 1962.

Chalkey, Lyman. "Before the Gates of the Wilderness Road: The Settlement of Southwestern Virginia." *Virginia Historical Magazine* 30 (1922): 183–202.

Chandler, Alfred N. *Land Title Origins: A Tale of Force and Fraud*. New York: Robert Schalkenbach Foundation, 1945.

Chapman, Jefferson. *Tellico Archaeology: 12,000 Years of Native American History*. Knoxville: Tennessee Valley Authority, 1985.

Chappell, Gordon T. "The Life and Activities of John Coffee." Ph.D. diss., Vanderbilt University, 1941.

——. "Some Patterns of Land Speculation in the Old Southwest." *Journal of Southern History* 15 (1949): 463–77.

Chase-Dunn, Christopher. "The Development of Core Capitalism in the Antebellum United States: Tariff Policies and Class Struggle in an Upwardly Mobile Semi-periphery." In *Studies of the Modern World-System*, edited by A. Bergesen, pp. 189–230. New York: Academic Press, 1980.

——. *Global Formation: Structures of the World-Economy*. London: Basil Blackwell, 1989.

Chenault, William. "The Early History of Madison County." *Register of the Kentucky State Historical Society* 30 (1932): 119–61.

Chevalier, Jacques M. "There Is Nothing Simple about Simple Commodity Production." *Journal of Peasant Studies* 10 (1983): 153–86.

Chirot, Daniel, and Tom D. Hall. "World-System Theory." *Annual Review of Sociology* 81 (1982): 81–106.

Chitty, Arthur B. "A Brief History of Sewanee." *Franklin County Historical Review* 2 (1970): 39–44.

Clark, Christopher. "The Household Economy, Market Exchange, and the Rise of Capitalism in the Connecticut Valley, 1800–1860." *Journal of Social History* 13 (1979): 169–89.

——. *The Roots of Rural Capitalism: Western Massachusetts, 1780–1860*. Ithaca: Cornell University Press, 1990.

Clark, Colin, and Margaret Haswell. *The Economics of Subsistence Agriculture.* London: Macmillan, 1967.

Clark, John G. "The Antebellum Grain Trade of New Orleans: Changing Patterns in the Relations of New Orleans with the Old Northwest." *Agricultural History* 38 (1964): 131–42.

Clark, Thomas D. "Early Lumbering Activities in Kentucky." *Northern Logger* 13 (1965): 43–58.

——. *The Kentucky*. Lexington, Ky.: Henry Clay Press, 1969.

——. "Trade between Kentucky and the Cotton Kingdom in Livestock, Hemp, and Slaves from 1840 to 1860." Master's thesis, University of Kentucky, 1929.

Clarkson, Roy B. *Tumult on the Mountains: Lumbering in West Virginia, 1770–1920*. Parsons, W.Va.: McClain Printing Co., 1964.

Clayton, La Reine W. "The Irish Peddler-Boy and Old Deery Inn." *Tennessee Historical Quarterly* 36 (1977): 149–60.

Clemens, P. G. E. *The Atlantic Economy and Colonial Maryland's Eastern Shore*. Ithaca: Cornell University Press, 1980.

Clowse, Converse. "The Charleston Export Trade, 1717–1737." Ph.D. diss., Northwestern University, 1963.

Coclanis, Peter A. *The Shadow of a Dream: Economic Life and Death in the South Carolina Low Country, 1670–1920*. New York: Oxford University Press, 1989.

Cochran, Thomas C. *Frontiers of Change: Early Industrialism in America*. New York: Oxford University Press, 1981.

Cohen, Stan. *Historic Springs of the Virginias*. Charleston, W.Va.: Pictorial Histories Publishing, 1981.

——. *Kanawha County Images: A Bicentennial History, 1788–1988*. Charleston, W.Va.: Pictorial Histories Publishing, 1987.

Coleman, Elizabeth D. "Richmond's Flowering Second Market." *Virginia Cavalcade* 4, no. 4 (1955): 8–13.

Coleman, Elizabeth D., and W. Edwin Hemphill. "Boats beyond the Blue Ridge." *Virginia Cavalcade* 3, no. 4 (1954): 8–13.

Coleman, J. Winston. "Kentucky River Steamboats." *Register of the Kentucky State Historical Society* 63 (1965): 299–322.

——. "Old Kentucky Iron Furnaces." *Filson Club Historical Quarterly* 31 (1957): 227–42.

——. *The Springs of Kentucky: An Account of the Famed Watering-Places of the Bluegrass State, 1800–1935*. Lexington: Winburn Press, 1955.

Coleman, Kenneth, ed. *A History of Georgia*. Athens: University of Georgia Press, 1991.

Connelley, William E., and E. M. Coulter. *History of Kentucky*. 5 vols. Chicago: American Historical Society, 1922.

Cooke, Leonard C. "The Development of the Road System of Alabama." Master's thesis, University of Alabama, 1935.

Corkran, David. *The Cherokee Frontier: Conflict and Survival, 1740–1762.* Norman: University of Oklahoma Press, 1962.

Corry, John P. "Indian Affairs in Georgia, 1732–1756." Ph.D. diss., University of Pennsylvania, 1936.

Cotterill, R. S. *The Southern Indians: The Story of the Civilized Tribes before Removal.* Norman: University of Oklahoma Press, 1954.

Couper, William. *History of the Shenandoah Valley.* 2 vols. New York: Lewis Historical Publishing, 1952.

Cox, Oliver. *Capitalism as a System.* New York: Monthly Review Press, 1964.

Crane, Verner. *The Southern Frontier, 1670–1732.* Ann Arbor: University of Michigan Press, 1929.

——. "The Tennessee River as the Road to Carolina: The Beginnings of Exploration and Trade." *Mississippi Valley Historical Review* 3 (1916): 3–18.

Crapster, Basil L. "Hampton Furnace in Colonial Frederick County." *Maryland Historical Magazine* 80 (1985): 1–8.

Craven, Avery O. "Soil Exhaustion as a Factor in the Agricultural History of Virginia and Maryland, 1606–1860." *University of Illinois Studies in the Social Sciences* 13 (1926).

Crosby, Alfred W. "Biotic Change in Nineteenth-Century New Zealand." *Review of the Fernand Braudel Center* 9 (1986): 325–38.

Crowther, M. A. *The Workhouse System, 1834–1929.* Athens, Ga.: University of Georgia Press, 1981.

Cummings, Richard O. *The American Ice Harvests: A Historical Study in Technology, 1800–1918.* Berkeley: University of California Press, 1949.

Cunningham, Rodger. *Apples on the Flood: The Southern Mountain Experience.* Knoxville: University of Tennessee Press, 1987.

Curry, J. L. M. "Reminiscences of Talladega." *Alabama Historical Quarterly* 8 (1946): 349–64.

Dabney, Joseph E. *Mountain Spirits: A Chronicle of Corn Whiskey from King James' Ulster Plantation to America's Appalachians and the Moonshine Life.* New York: Charles Scribner's Sons, 1974.

Dabney, William A. "Jefferson's Albermarle: History of Albermarle County, Virginia, 1727–1819." Ph.D. diss., University of Virginia, 1951.

Danhof, Clarence C. "Farm Making Costs and the Safety Valve." *Journal of Political Economy* 49 (1941): 317–59.

Dater, Henry M. "Albert Gallatin—Land Speculator." *Mississippi Valley Historical Review* 26 (1938): 21–38.

David, Paul A., and Peter Solar. "A Bicentenary Contribution to the History of the Cost of Living in America." *Research in Economic History* 2 (1977): 1–80.

Davidson, Donald. *The Tennessee: The Old River, Frontier to Secession.* Knoxville: University of Tennessee Press, 1946.

Davis, Julia. *The Shenandoah.* New York: Farrar and Rinehart, 1945.

Deakin, Doris. "Appalachia—On the Way." *Appalachia* 12 (1979): 8–12.

Deane, Phyllis. "The Role of Capital in the Industrial Revolution." *Explorations in Economic History* 10 (1973): 349–64.

De Janvry, Alain. *The Agrarian Question and Reformism in Latin America.* Baltimore: Johns Hopkins University Press, 1981.

De Janvry, Alain, and Ann Vandeman. "Patterns of Proletarianization in Agriculture: An International Comparison." In *Household Economies and Their Transformations,* edited by Morgan D. Maclachlan, pp. 50–81. Lanham, Md.: University Press of America, 1987.

Delfino, Susanna. "Antebellum East Tennessee Elites and Industrialization: The Examples of the Iron Industry and Internal Improvements." *East Tennessee Historical Society Publications* 56–57 (1984–85): 102–19.

Depew, Chauncey M. *One Hundred Years of American Commerce, 1795–1895*. New York: D. O. Haynes, 1895.

Derthick, Lawrence. "The Indian Boundary Line in the Southern District of British North America, 1763–1779." Master's thesis, University of Tennessee, 1930.

Des Champs, Margaret B. "Early Days in the Cumberland Country." *Tennessee Historical Quarterly* 6 (1947): 195–229.

De Vorsey, Louis. *The Indian Boundary in the Southern Colonies, 1763–1775*. Chapel Hill: University of North Carolina Press, 1961.

Dewey, Davis R. *State Banking before the Civil War*. Washington, D.C.: Government Printing Office, 1910.

Deyton, Jason B. "The Toe River Valley to 1865." *North Carolina Historical Review* 24 (1947): 423–66.

Dickens, Roy. *Cherokee Prehistory: The Pisgah Phase in the Appalachian Summit Region*. Knoxville: University of Tennessee Press, 1976.

Dobyns, Henry F. *Their Number Become Thinned*. Knoxville: University of Tennessee Press, 1983.

Dodrill, Carlin F. "History of Cross Creek and Harmon Creek Country, Brooke and Hancock Counties, West Virginia." Master's thesis, West Virginia University, 1938.

Dolan, J. R. *The Yankee Peddlers of Early America*. New York: Clarkson and Potter, 1964.

Donnelly, Ralph W. "The Bartow County Confederate Saltpeter Works." *Georgia Historical Quarterly* 54 (1970): 305–19.

Douglas, Byrd. *Steamboatin' on the Cumberland*. Nashville: Tennessee Book Co., 1961.

Douglas, Elisha P. *The Coming of Age of American Business: Three Centuries of Enterprise, 1600–1900*. Chapel Hill: University of North Carolina Press, 1971.

Dowd, Douglas F. *The Twisted Dream: Capitalist Development in the United States since 1776*. Cambridge: Winthrop Publishers, 1974.

Druyvesteyn, Kent. "The James River and Kanawha Canal." *Virginia Cavalcade* 21, no. 3 (1972): 22–45.

Dublin, Thomas. "Rural Putting-out Work in Early Nineteenth-Century New England: Women and the Transition to Capitalism in the Countryside." *New England Quarterly* 64 (1991): 531–73.

Duboff, Richard B. "The Telegraph and the Structure of Markets in the United States, 1845–1890." *Research in Economic History* 8 (1983): 253–77.

Duffy, John. "Smallpox and the Indians in American Colonies." *Bulletin of the History of Medicine* 25 (1951): 324–41.

Dunaway, Wayland F. "History of the James River and Kanawha Company." *Columbia University Studies in History, Economics, and Public Law* 104, no. 2 (1922).

Dunaway, Wilma A. "The Incorporation of Southern Appalachia into the Capitalist World-Economy, 1700–1860." Ph.D. diss., University of Tennessee, 1994.

———. "The Southern Fur Trade and the Incorporation of Southern Appalachia into the World-Economy, 1690–1763." *Review of the Ferdinand Braudel Center* 17, no. 2 (1994): 215–42.

Duncan-Baretta, Silvio R., and John Markoff. "Civilization and Barbarism: Cattle Frontiers in Latin America." *Comparative Studies in Society and History* 20 (1978): 587–620.

Dunn, Durwood. *Cades Cove: The Life and Death of a Southern Appalachian Community, 1818–1937*. Knoxville: University of Tennessee, 1988.

Dupre, Daniel. "Ambivalent Capitalists on the Cotton Frontier: Settlement and Development in the Tennessee Valley of Alabama." *Journal of Southern History* 57 (1990): 215–40.

Durr, William A. *The Economic Problems of Forestry in the Appalachian Region.* Cambridge: Harvard University Press, 1949.

Durrenberger, Joseph A. *Turnpikes: A Study of the Toll Road Movement in the Middle Atlantic States and Maryland.* Cos Cob, Conn.: J. E. Edwards, 1931.

Dykeman, Wilma. *The French Broad.* New York: Holt, Rinehart and Winston, 1955.

——. "Appalachia in Context." In *An Appalachian Symposium: Essays Written in Honor of Cratis D. Williams*, edited by J. W. Williamson, pp. 28–42. Boone, N.C.: Appalachian Consortium Press, 1977.

Earle, Carville V. "Regional Economic Development West of the Appalachians, 1815–1860." In *North America: The Historical Geography of a Changing Continent*, edited by Robert D. Mitchell and Paul A. Groves, pp. 172–97. Totowa, N.J.: Rowman and Littlefield, 1987.

Earle, Carville V., and Ronald Hoffman. "Staple Crops and Urban Development in the Eighteenth-Century South." *Perspectives in American History* 10 (1976): 5–78.

Eisterhold, John A. "Charleston: Lumber and Trade in a Declining Southern Port." *South Carolina Historical Magazine* 74 (1973): 61–73.

——. "Lumber and Trade in the Lower Mississippi Valley and New Orleans, 1800–1860." *Louisiana History* 13 (1972): 71–91.

——. "Savannah: Lumber Center of the South Atlantic." *Georgia Historical Quarterly* 57 (1973): 526–45.

Eliades, David K. "The Indian Policy of Colonial South Carolina, 1670–1763." Ph.D. diss., University of South Carolina, 1981.

Eller, Ronald D. "Land and Family: An Historical View of Preindustrial Appalachia." *Appalachian Journal* 6 (1979): 83–110.

——. *Miners, Millhands, and Mountaineers: Industrialization of the Appalachian South, 1880–1930*. Knoxville: University of Tennessee Press, 1982.

Ellis, D. M., ed. *The Frontier in American Development: Essays in Honor of Paul Wallace Gates.* Ithaca: Cornell University Press, 1969.

Elrod, Frary. *Historical Notes of Jackson County, Georgia.* Jefferson, Ga.: By Author, 1967.

Ellwanger, Ella H. "Estill Springs: A Celebrated Summer Resort in Estill County." *Register of the Kentucky State Historical Society* 9 (1911): 45–53.

Elwert, George, and Diana Wong. "Subsistence Production and Commodity Production in the Third World." *Review of the Fernand Braudel Center* 3 (1980): 501–22.

Emmanuel, Arghiri. *Unequal Exchange: A Study of the Imperialism of Trade.* London: New Left Books, 1972.

Encyclopedia of Southern Culture. Edited by Charles R. Wilson and William Ferris. Chapel Hill: University of North Carolina Press, 1989.

Ethridge, Robbie F. "Flintlocks and Slave-Catchers: Economic Transformations of the Indians of Georgia." *Early Georgia* 10 (1982): 13–26.

"Etowah." *National Geographic* 180 (October 1991): 54–67.

Eubank, Sallie C. "The Iron Industry in Kentucky." Master's thesis, University of Kentucky, 1927.

Evans, E. Raymond. "Highways to Progress: 19th Century Roads in the Cherokee Nation." *Journal of Cherokee Studies* 2 (1977): 394–400.

Fairbanks, W. L., and W. S. Hamill. *The Coal Mining Industry of Maryland*. Baltimore: Maryland Development Bureau of the Baltimore Association of Commerce, 1932.

Fant, H. B. "The Indian Trade Policy of the Trustees for Establishing the Colony of Georgia in America." *Georgia Historical Quarterly* 15 (1931): 207–22.

Feder, Ernest. "The Odious Competition between Man and Animal over Agricultural Resources in the Underdeveloped Countries." *Review of the Fernand Braudel Center* 3 (1980): 463–500.

Finger, John R. *The Eastern Band of Cherokees, 1819–1900*. Knoxville: University of Tennessee Press, 1984.

Fink, Paul M. "The Bumpass Cove Mines and Embreeville." *East Tennessee Historical Society Publications* 16 (1944): 48–64.

Fischer, Charles E. "Internal Improvement Issues in Maryland, 1816–1826." Master's thesis, University of Maryland, 1972.

Fishlow, Albert. "Antebellum Interregional Trade Reconsidered." In *New Views on American Economic Development*, edited by A. L. Andreano, pp. 187–200. Cambridge: Schenkman Publishing, 1965.

Fitzhugh, William W. *Cultures in Contact: The Impact of European Contacts on Native Americans*. Washington, D.C.: Smithsonian Institution Press, 1985.

Fleming, John K. "Western Virginia as Seen by Foreign Travelers, 1789–1860." Master's thesis, West Virginia University, 1960.

Fogel, Robert W., and Stanley l. Engerman. *Time on the Cross: The Economics of American Negro Slavery*. 2 vols. Boston: Little, Brown and Co., 1974.

Fogelson, Raymond, and Paul Kutsche. "Cherokee Economic Cooperatives: The Gadugi." *Bureau of American Ethnology Bulletin* 180 (1961): 87–97.

Folmsbee, Stanley J. *Sectionalism and Internal Improvements in Tennessee, 1796–1845*. Knoxville: East Tennessee Historical Society, 1939.

——. "The Turnpike Phase of Tennessee's Internal Improvement System of 1836–1838." *Journal of Southern History* 3 (1937): 453–77.

Foner, Eric, ed. *The New American History*. Philadelphia, Temple University Press, 1990.

Ford, Amelia C. "Colonial Precedents of Our National Land System as It Existed in 1800." *Bulletin of the University of Wisconsin*, no. 352 (1910).

Ford, Lacy K. *Origins of Southern Radicalism: The South Carolina Upcountry, 1800–1860*. New York: Oxford University Press, 1988.

——. "Social Origins of a New South Carolina: The Upcountry in the Nineteenth Century." Ph.D. diss., University of South Carolina, 1983.

Ford, Thomas B. "An Analysis of Anglo-American-Cherokee Culture Contact during the Federal Period: The Hiwassee Tract, Eastern Tennessee." Master's thesis, University of Tennessee, 1982.

Foreman, Grant. *Indian Removal: The Emigration of the Five Civilized Tribes of Indians*. Norman: University of Oklahoma Press, 1953.

Fox, John, Jr. "The Southern Mountaineer." *Scribner's* 29 (1901): 387–92.

Fox-Genovese, Elizabeth. "Antebellum Southern Households: A New Perspective on a Familiar Question." *Review of the Fernand Braudel Center* 7 (1983): 215–54.

Frank, Andre Gundre. *Dependent Accumulation and Underdevelopment*. London: Macmillan Press, 1979.

——. *World Accumulation, 1491–1789*. New York: Monthly Review Press, 1978.

Franklin, W. Neil. "Virginia and the Cherokee Indian Trade, 1753–1775." *East Tennessee Historical Society Publications* 5 (1933): 22–38.

Friedenberg, Daniel M. *Life, Liberty, and the Pursuit of Land: The Plunder of Early America*. Buffalo: Prometheus Books, 1992.

Friedmann, Harriet. "Household Production and the National Economy: Concepts for the Analysis of Agrarian Formations." *Journal of Peasant Studies* 7 (1980): 158–84.

Friend, Craig. "Frontier Pendleton: A Town in Three Acts." *Proceedings of the South Carolina Historical Association* 58 (1988): 94–102.

"Furnaces and Forges." *Tennessee Historical Magazine* 9 (1925–26): 190–92.

Gallman, Robert E. "Self-Sufficiency in the Cotton Economy of the Antebellum South." In *The Structure of the Cotton Economy of the Antebellum South*, edited by William N. Parker, pp. 5–23. Washington, D.C.: Agricultural History Society, 1970.

Gamble, J. Mack. "Steamboats in West Virginia." *West Virginia History* 15 (1954): 124–38.

Gates, Paul W. *Frontier Landlords and Pioneer Tenants*. Ithaca: Cornell University Press, 1945.

———. "The Role of the Land Speculator in Western Development." *Pennsylvania Magazine of History* 66 (1942): 314–33.

———. "Tenants of the Log Cabin." *Mississippi Valley Historical Review* 49 (1962): 3–31.

Gauding, Harry H. "History of Water Transportation in East Tennessee Prior to the Civil War." Master's thesis, University of Tennessee, 1933.

Gaventa, John P. *Power and Powerlessness: Quiescence and Rebellion in an Appalachian Valley*. Urbana: University of Illinois Press, 1980.

Gazaway, Rena. *The Longest Mile*. Baltimore: Penguin Books, 1969.

Gearing, Frederick O. "Cherokee Political Organizations: 1730–1775." Ph.D. diss., University of Chicago, 1956.

Gereffi, Gary, and Miguel Korzeniewicz. "Commodity Chains and Footwear Exports in the Semiperiphery." In *Semiperipheral States in the World Economy*, edited by W. G. Martin, pp. 45–67. Westport, Conn.: Greenwood Press, 1990.

Giddens, Paul H. "Land Policies and Administration in Colonial Maryland, 1753–1769." *Maryland Historical Magazine* 28 (1933): 142–71.

Glickstein, Jonathan A. *Concepts of Free Labor in Antebellum America*. New Haven, Conn.: Yale University Press, 1991.

Goad, Sharon I. "Copper and the Southeastern Indians," *Early Georgia* 4 (1976): 61–76.

Gold, Thomas D. *History of Clarke County, Virginia*. Berryville, Va.: Chesapeake Book Co., 1962.

Goldin, Claudia, and High Rockoff, eds. *Strategic Factors in Nineteenth-Century American Economic History*. Chicago: University of Chicago, 1992.

Goodall, Elizabeth J. "The Manufacture of Salt—Kanawha's First Commercial Enterprise." *West Virginia History* 26 (1965): 234–50.

Goodspeed's History of Tennessee. Nashville: Goodspeed Publishing, 1887.

Goodwin, Gary C. *Cherokees in Transition: A Study of Changing Culture and Environment Prior to 1775*. Chicago: University of Chicago Press, 1977.

Gordon, David M., Richard Edwards, and Michael Reich. *Segmented Work, Divided Workers: The Historical Transformation of Labor in the United States*. Cambridge: Cambridge University Press, 1982.

Gouger, James B. "Agricultural Change in the Northern Neck of Virginia, 1700–1860: An Historical Geography." Ph.D. diss., University of Florida, 1976.

——. "The Northern Neck of Virginia: A Tidewater Grain-Farming Region in the Antebellum South." *West Georgia College Studies in the Social Sciences* 16 (1977): 73–90.

Gough, Kathleen. "Agrarian Relations in Southeast India, 1750–1976." *Review of the Fernand Braudel Center* 2, no. 1 (1978): 25–53.

Gould, Clarence P. "The Land System in Maryland, 1634–1820." *Johns Hopkins University Studies in History and Political Science* 31 (1913).

Govan, Gilbert E., and James W. Livingood. *The Chattanooga Country from Tomahawks to TVA*. 1952. Reprint, Knoxville: University of Tennessee, 1977.

Grant, Charles S. *Democracy in the Connecticut Frontier Town of Kent*. New York: Columbia University, 1961.

Gray, Lewis C. *History of Agriculture in the Southern United States to 1860*. 2 vols. Gloucester: Peter Smith, 1958.

Gray, Lewis C., Charles L. Stewart, and Howard A. Turner. "Farm Ownership and Tenancy." *Agriculture Yearbook 1923*. Washington, D.C.: U.S. Department of Agriculture, 1924.

Green, Fletcher M. "Georgia's Forgotten Industry: Gold Mining." *Georgia Historical Quarterly* 19 (1935): 93–111, 210–28.

——. "Gold Mining: A Forgotten Industry of Antebellum North Carolina." *North Carolina Historical Review* 14 (1937): 1–19; 135–55.

——. "Gold Mining in Antebellum Virginia." *Virginia Magazine of History and Biography* 45 (1937): 227–35, 357–66.

Gulick, John. *Cherokees at the Crossroads*. Chapel Hill: University of North Carolina Press, 1960.

Gusfield, Joseph R. *Symbolic Crusade: Status Politics and the American Temperance Movement*. Chicago: University of Illinois Press, 1963.

Gutheim, Frederick. *The Potomac*. New York: Rinehart and Co., 1949.

Gutkind, Peter C. W., ed. *Third World Workers: Comparative International Labour Studies*. Leiden: E. J. Brill, 1988.

Habib, Irfan. *The Agrarian System of Mughal India, 1556–1702*. New York: Asia Publishing House, 1963.

Hahn, Steven. *The Roots of Southern Populism: Yeoman Farmers and the Transformation of the Georgia Upcountry, 1850–1890*. New York: Oxford University Press, 1982.

Haites, Erik F., and James Mak. "Ohio and Mississippi River Transportation, 1810–1860." *Explorations in Economic History* 8 (1970): 153–80.

——. "Social Savings due to Western River Steamboats." *Research in Economic History* 3 (1978): 263–304.

Haites, Erik F., James Mak, and Gary M. Walton. *Western River Transportation*. Baltimore: Johns Hopkins University Press, 1975.

Hale, Will T. *Early History of Warren County*. McMinnville, Tenn.: Standard Printing, 1930.

Hall, Thomas D. *Social Change in the Southwest, 1350–1880*. Lawrence: University Press of Kansas, 1989.

Hamer, Philip M. "Anglo-French Rivalry in the Cherokee Country, 1754–1757." *North Carolina Historical Review* 2 (1925): 303–22.

——, ed. *Tennessee, A History, 1673–1932*. 4 vols. New York: American Historical Society, 1933.

Hammon, Neal O. "Land Acquisition on the Kentucky Frontier." *Register of the Kentucky State Historical Society* 78 (1980): 297–321.

——. "Settlers, Land Jobbers, and Outlyers: A Quantitative Analysis of Land Acquisition on the Kentucky Frontier." *Register of the Kentucky State Historical Society* 84 (1986): 241–62.

Haney, Lewis H. "A Congressional History of Railways in the United States to 1850." Ph.D. diss., University of Wisconsin, 1906.

Hardacre, Val. *Woodland Nuggets of Gold: The Story of American Ginseng Cultivation.* New York: Vantage Press, 1968.

Harlow, Alvin F. *Old Towpaths: The Story of the American Canal Era.* 1926. Reprint, Port Washington, N.Y.: Kennikat Press, 1954.

Harper, Roland M. "Development of Agriculture in Upper Georgia from 1850 to 1880." *Georgia Historical Quarterly* 6 (1922): 3–27.

Harris, Marshall. *Origin of the Land Tenure System in the United States.* Ames: Iowa State College Press, 1953.

Harrison, Lowell H. "Recollections of Kentucky's Roads." *Filson Club Historical Quarterly* 58, no. 3 (1984): 281–98.

Hartz, Louis. *The Liberal Tradition in America.* New York: Harcourt-Brace, 1955.

Harvey, Katherine A. *The Best-Dressed Miners: Life and Labor in the Maryland Coal Region, 1835–1910.* Ithaca: Cornell University Press, 1969.

——. "Building a Frontier Ironworks: Problems of Transport and Supply, 1837–1840." *Maryland Historical Magazine* 70, no. 1 (1975): 149–66.

——. "William Alexander: A Commission Merchant in a New Role, 1837–43." *Maryland Historical Magazine* 71, no. 1 (1976): 26–36.

Head, James W. *History and Comprehensive Description of Loudoun County, Virginia.* N.p.: Park View Press, 1908.

Head, Sylvia, and Elizabeth W. Etheridge. *The Neighborhood Mint: Dahlonega in the Age of Jackson.* Macon, Ga.: Mercer University Press, 1986.

Headlee, Sue. *The Political Economy of the Family Farm: The Agrarian Roots of American Capitalism.* New York: Praeger, 1991.

Heath, Milton S. *Constructive Liberalism: The Role of the State in Economic Development in Georgia to 1860.* Cambridge: Harvard University Press, 1954.

Hecht, Arthur. "Lead Production in Virginia during the Seventeenth and Eighteenth Centuries." *West Virginia History* 25 (1964): 173–83.

Hedley, Max J. "Rural Social Structure and the Ideology of the 'Family Farm.'" *Canadian Journal of Anthropology* 2 (1981): 85–89.

Henderson, Archibald. "A Pre-revolutionary Revolt in the Old Southwest." *Mississippi Valley Historical Review* 17 (1930): 191–212.

Henderson, William D. "A Great Deal of Enterprise: The Petersburg Cotton Mills in the Nineteenth Century." *Virginia Cavalcade* 30, no. 4 (1981): 176–85.

Henlein, Paul C. *Cattle Kingdom in the Ohio Valley, 1783–1860.* Lexington: University of Kentucky Press, 1959.

Henretta, James A. "Families and Farms: Mentalite in Pre-Industrial America." *William and Mary Quarterly* 35 (1978): 3–32.

——. *The Origins of American Capitalism.* Boston: Northeastern University Press, 1991.

Hersch, Alan. "The Development of the Iron Industry in East Tennessee." Master's thesis, University of Tennessee, 1958.

Hibbard, Benjamin H. *A History of the Public Land Policies.* New York: Peter Smith, 1939.

Hill, Carol A., and Duane DePaepe. "Saltpeter Mining in Kentucky Caves." *Register of the Kentucky State Historical Society* 77 (1979): 247–62.

Hill, Howard L. *The Herbert Walters Story.* Morristown, Tenn.: Morristown Printing Co., 1963.

Hilliard, Sam B. *Hog Meat and Hoecake: Food Supply in the Old South, 1840–1860.* Carbondale: Southern Illinois University Press, 1972.

Hillsman, Jack H. "The Bank of Tennessee, 1838–1866." Master's thesis, University of Tennessee, 1937.

Hinsdale, B. A. "The Western Land Policy of the British Government from 1763 to 1775." *Ohio Archaeological and Historical Publications* 1 (1987): 207–29.

Hirschman, Albert O. *The Strategy of Economic Development.* New Haven, Conn.: Yale University Press, 1963.

History of Etowah County, Alabama. Birmingham: Etowah County Centennial Committee, 1968.

Hoffman, Ronald, ed. *The Economy of Early America: The Revolutionary Period, 1763–1790.* Charlottesville: University Press of Virginia, 1988.

Hofstadter, Richard. *The Age of Reform: From Bryan to F.D.R.* New York: Knopf, 1955.

———. "The Myth of the Happy Yeoman." *American Heritage* 7 (1956): 43–53.

Hofstadter, Richard, and Seymour M. Lipset, eds. *Turner and the Sociology of the Frontier.* New York: Basic Books, 1968.

Hollander, Stanley C. "Nineteenth-Century Anti-Drummer Legislation in the United States." *Business History Review* 38 (1964): 479–500.

Holmes, George K. "Supply of Farm Labor." *United States Department of Agriculture Bureau of Statistics Bulletin* 94 (1912).

Holmes, Tony. "The Last Eight Ferry Boats in Tennessee." *Tennessee Historical Quarterly* 46 (1987): 65–78, 129–40.

Holt, Albert C. "Economic and Social Beginnings of Tennessee." Ph.D. diss., George Peabody College, 1923.

Holt, Edgar A. *Claiborne County.* Memphis: Memphis State University Press, 1981.

Holtfrerich, Carl-Ludwig. *Interactions in the World Economy.* London: Harvester-Wheatsheaf, 1989.

Hopkins, Terence K., and Immanuel Wallerstein. "Capitalism and the Incorporation of New Zones into the World-Economy." *Review of the Fernand Braudel Center* 10 (1987): 763–80.

———. "Commodity Chains in the World-Economy Prior to 1800." *Review of the Fernand Braudel Center* 10 (1987): 157–70.

———. "A Concluding Note." *Review of the Fernand Braudel Center* 10 (1987): 901–2.

———. "Patterns of Development of the Modern World-System." *Review of the Fernand Braudel Center* 10 (1986): 111–46.

———. "Structural Transformations of the World-Economy." In *World-System Analysis, Theory, and Methodology,* edited by Hopkins and Wallerstein et al., pp. 120–42. Beverly Hills, Calif.: Sage, 1982.

Hopkins, Terence K., and Immanuel Wallerstein, eds. *Processes of the World-System.* Beverly Hills, Calif.: Sage, 1980.

Hoskins, Katherine B. *Anderson County.* Memphis: Memphis State University Press, 1979.

Hsiung, David C. "Isolation and Integration in Upper East Tennessee, 1780–1860: The Historical Origins of Appalachian Characterizations." Ph.D. diss., University of Michigan, 1991.

Hudson, Charles. "The Cherokee Concept of Natural Balance." *Indian Historian* 3 (1970): 51–54.

Hulbert, Archer B. *Historic Highways of America.* 16 vols. Cleveland: Arthur H. Clark Co., 1901–11.

Hunt, Raymond F. "The Pactolus Ironworks." *Tennessee Historical Quarterly* 25 (1966): 176–96.

Hunter, Louis C. *Steamboats on the Western Rivers*. Cambridge: Harvard University Press, 1949.

——. "Studies in the Economic History of the Ohio Valley." *Smith College Studies in History* 19, nos. 1–2 (1934): 1–130.

Hunter, Robert F. "Turnpike Construction in Antebellum Virginia." *Technology and Culture* 4 (1963): 177–200.

——. "The Turnpike Movement in Virginia, 1815–1860." Ph.D. diss., Columbia University, 1957.

Hutchinson, William K., and Samuel H. Williamson. "The Self-Sufficiency of the Antebellum South: Estimates of the Food Supply." *Journal of Economic History* 31 (1971): 591–612.

Ierley, Merritt. *Traveling the National Road: Across the Centuries on America's First Highway*. Woodstock, N.Y.: Overlook Press, 1990.

Innes, Stephen Innes, ed. *Work and Labor in Early America*. Chapel Hill: University of North Carolina Press, 1988.

Inscoe, John C. *Mountain Masters, Slavery, and the Sectional Crisis in Western North Carolina*. Knoxville: University of Tennessee, 1989.

"Iron Industry in Jefferson County." *Magazine of the Jefferson County Historical Society* 30 (1964): 16–21.

Ivers, Larry E. *Colonial Forts of South Carolina, 1670–1775*. Columbia: University of South Carolina Press, 1970.

Jablow, Joseph. *The Cheyenne in Plains Indian Trade Relations, 1795–1840*. Seattle: University of Washington Press, 1950.

Jackson, Olin, ed. *A North Georgia Journal of History*. Woodstock, Ga.: Legacy Communications, 1989.

Jacobs, Wilbur R. *Diplomacy and Indian Gifts: Anglo-French Rivalry along the Ohio and Northwest Frontiers, 1748–1763*. London: Oxford University Press, 1950.

Jefferson, Josephine. *Wheeling Glass*. Columbus, Ohio: Heer Printing Co., 1947.

Jeffrey, Thomas E. "Internal Improvements and Political Parties in Antebellum North Carolina, 1836–1860." *North Carolina Historical Review* 55 (1978): 111–56.

Jenkins, Gary C. "The Mining of Alum Cave." *East Tennessee Historical Society Publications* 60 (1988): 78–87.

Jennings, Ralph D. "Consumption of Feed by Livestock, 1909–1956." *United States Department of Agriculture Production Research Report* 21 (1958).

Jillson, Willard R. "The Big Sandy Valley: A Regional History Prior to 1850." *Register of the Kentucky State Historical Society* 20 (1922).

——. "A History of the Coal Industry in Kentucky." Paper presented at a meeting of the Filson Club, Louisville, Kentucky, 7 November 1921.

Johnson, Emory R., T. W. Van Metre, G. G. Huebner, and D. S. Hanchett. *History of Domestic and Foreign Commerce of the United States*. Washington, D.C.: Carnegie Institute, 1915.

Johnson, Geraldine N. *Weaving Rag Rugs: A Women's Craft in Western Maryland*. Knoxville: University of Tennessee Press, 1985.

Johnson, Guion. *Antebellum North Carolina: A Social History*. Chapel Hill: University of North Carolina Press, 1937.

Johnson, Laurence A., and Marcia May. *Over the Counter and On the Shelf: Country Storekeeping in America, 1620–1920*. Rutland, Vt.: Charles E. Tuttle Co., 1961.

Jones, Fred M. "Middlemen in the Domestic Trade of the United States, 1800–1860." *University of Illinois Studies in the Social Sciences* 21, no. 3 (1937): 1–81.

Jones, Richard E. "A Study of the Economic Influence of the Chesapeake and Ohio Canal on Washington County." Master's thesis, Shippensburg State College, 1964.

Kahn, Charles. "A Linear-Programming Solution to the Slave Diet." In *Without Consent or Contract: The Rise and Fall of American Slavery: Technical Papers*, edited by Robert W. Fogel and Stanley L. Engerman, 2:522–36. New York: W. W. Norton and Co., 1992.

Kaplan, Berton H. *Blue Ridge: An Appalachian Community in Transition*. Morgantown: West Virginia University Press, 1971.

Kegley's Virginia Frontier, 1740–1783. Roanoke: Southwestern Virginia Historical Society, 1938.

Keith, Alice B. "Three North Carolina Blount Brothers in Business and Politics, 1783–1812." Ph.D. diss., University of North Carolina, 1940.

Kelly, Kevin D. "The Independent Mode of Production." *Review of Radical Political Economics* 11 (1979): 38–48.

Kemper, Charles E. "The Settlement of the Valley." *Virginia Historical Magazine* 30 (1922): 169–82.

Kenwood, A. G., and A. L. Lougheed. *The Growth of the International Economy, 1820–1980*. London: Allen and Unwin, 1983.

Kephart, Horace. *Our Southern Highlanders: A Narrative of Adventure in the Southern Appalachians and a Study of Life among the Mountains*. New York: Outing, 1933.

Kercheval, Samuel. *A History of the Valley of Virginia*. 1833. Reprint, Harrisonburg, Va.: C. J. Carrier Co., 1986.

Kessel, Elizabeth A. "Germans on the Maryland Frontier: A Social History of Frederick County, Maryland, 1730–1800." Ph.D. diss., Rice University, 1981.

Kincaid, Robert L. "The Wilderness Road in Tennessee." *East Tennessee Historical Society Publications* 20 (1948): 37–48.

King, Duane H., ed. *The Cherokee Indian Nation: A Troubled History*. Knoxville: University of Tennessee Press, 1962.

Kirby, David. "Canalization of New River." *West Virginia History* 15 (1954): 269–91.

Kirby, Jack T. *Rural Worlds Lost: The American South, 1920–1960*. Baton Rouge: Louisiana State University Press, 1987.

Klebaner, Benjamin. "Public Poor Relief in America, 1790–1860." Ph.D. diss., Columbia University, 1952.

Klein, Rachel N. "Ordering the Backcountry: The South Carolina Regulation." *William and Mary Quarterly* 38 (1981): 611–80.

——. *Unification of a Slave State: The Rise of the Planter Class in the South Carolina Backcountry, 1760–1808*. Chapel Hill: University of North Carolina Press, 1990.

Kondatrieff, N. D. "The Long Waves of Economic Life." *Review of the Fernand Braudel Center* 2, no. 4 (1979): 519–62.

Kriedte, Peter, Hans Medick, and Jurgen Schlumbohm. *Industrialization before Industrialization: Rural Industry in the Genesis of Capitalism*. Cambridge: Cambridge University Press, 1981.

Kulikoff, Allan. "The Transition to Capitalism in Rural America." *William and Mary Quarterly* 46 (1989): 120–44.

Kupperman, Karen O. *Settling with the Indians: The Meeting of English and Indian Cultures in America, 1580–1640*. Totowa, N.J.: Rowman and Littlefield, 1980.

Lacy, Eric R. *Vanquished Volunteers: East Tennessee Sectionalism from Statehood to Secession*. Johnson City, Tenn.: East Tennessee State University Press, 1965.

Laidley, W. S. "Large Land Owners." *West Virginia Historical Magazine* 3 (1903): 242–53.

Lamar, Howard, and Leonard Thompson. *The Frontier in History: North America and Southern Africa Compared*. New Haven: Yale University Press, 1981.

Lamb, Robert B. "The Mule in Southern Agriculture." *University of California Publications in Geography* 15 (1963): 1–89.

Lambert, Darwin. "The Oconaluftee Valley, 1800–1860: A Study of the Sources for Mountain History." *North Carolina Historical Review* 35 (1958): 415–26.

——. *The Undying Past of Shenandoah National Park.* Boulder, Colo.: Roberts-Rinehart, 1989.

Land, Aubrey C. "A Land Speculator in the Opening of Western Maryland." *Maryland Historical Magazine* 48 (1953): 191–203.

Lander, Ernest M. "Antebellum Milling in South Carolina." *South Carolina Historical and Genealogical Magazine* 52 (1951): 125–32.

Lauber, A. W. "Indian Slavery in Colonial Times within the Present Limits of the United States." *Columbia University Studies in History, Economics, and Public Law* 54 (1913).

Leavitt, Charles T. "The Meat and Dairy Livestock Industry, 1819–1860." Ph.D. diss., University of Chicago, 1931.

Lee, Susan P. "The Westward Movement of the Cotton Economy, 1840–1860." Ph.D. diss., Columbia University, 1975.

Lemon, James T. *The Best Poor Man's Country: A Geographical Study of Early Southeastern Pennsylvania.* Baltimore: Johns Hopkins University Press, 1972.

——. "Early Americans and Their Social Environment." *Journal of Historical Geography* 6 (1980): 115–31.

——. "Household Consumption in the Eighteenth Century and Its Relationship to Production and Trade: The Situation among Farmers in Southeastern Pennsylvania." *Agricultural History* 41 (1967): 59–70.

Lenin, V. I. *The Development of Capitalism in Russia.* Moscow: Progress, 1972.

Lesesne, J. Maulding. "The Nullification Controversy in an Upcountry District." *South Carolina Historical Association Proceedings* 8 (1939): 13–24.

Levine, Bruce. *Half Slave and Half Free: The Roots of Civil War.* New York: Hill and Wang, 1992.

Lewis, Eulalie M. "The Valley of the Conasauga." *Georgia Historical Quarterly* 42, no. 3 (1958): 313–22.

Lewis, Helen, Linda Johnson, and Donald Askins, eds. *Colonialism in Modern America: The Appalachian Case.* Boone, N.C.: Appalachian Consortium Press, 1978.

Lewis, Ronald L. *Coal, Iron, and Slaves: Industrial Slavery in Maryland and Virginia, 1715–1865.* Westport, Conn.: Greenwood Press, 1979.

Lewis, T. M. N., and Madeline Kneberg. "The First Tennesseeans: An Interpretation of Tennessee Prehistory." 1955. Mimeographed typescript.

Lillard, Roy G. *The History of Bradley County.* Cleveland, Tenn.: East Tennessee Historical Society, 1976.

Lindstrom, Diane. "Southern Dependence upon Interregional Grain Supplies: A Review of the Trade Flows, 1840–1860." In *The Structure of the Cotton Economy of the Antebellum South,* edited by W. N. Parker, pp. 101–13. Washington, D.C.: Agricultural History Society, 1970.

Lingeman, Richard. *Small-Town America: A Narrative History, 1620 to the Present.* Boston: Houghton-Mifflin, 1980.

Lipset, Seymour M. *The First New Nation: The United States in Historical and Comparative Perspectives.* New York: Basic Books, 1963.

Littlefield, Douglas R. "Maryland Sectionalism and the Development of the Potomac Route to the West." *Maryland Historian* 14 (1983): 31–52.

Livermore, Shaw. *Early American Land Companies: Their Influence on Corporate Development.* New York: Octagon Books, 1968.

Livingood, James W. "The Chattanooga Country in 1860." *Tennessee Historical Quarterly* 20 (1961): 159–66.

———. "The Tennessee Valley in American History: The Old Valley, Land of Challenge and Contention." *East Tennessee Historical Society Publications* 21 (1949): 19–32.

Lockridge, Kenneth A. *A New England Town, the First Hundred Years: Dedham, Massachusetts, 1636–1736*. New York: Norton, 1970.

Logan, John H. *A History of the Upper Country of South Carolina from the Earliest Periods to the Close of the War of Independence*. 2 vols. Charleston: S. G. Courtenay and Co., 1859.

Low, W. A. "Merchant and Planter Relations in Post-Revolutionary Virginia, 1783–1789." *Virginia Magazine of History and Biography* 61 (1953): 308–18.

Lowdermilk, Will H. *History of Cumberland, Maryland*. Washington, D.C.: James Anglum, 1878.

"Lucy Selina's Charcoal Era." *Virginia Cavalcade* 7, no. 2 (1957): 31–46.

Luxemburg, Rosa. *The Accumulation of Capital*. London: Routledge and Kegan Paul, 1913.

Mabry, William A. "Antebellum Cincinnati and Its Southern Trade." In *American Studies in Honor of William Kenneth Boyd*, edited by D. K. Jackson, pp. 60–85. Durham: Duke University Press, 1940.

MacArthur, William J. *Knoxville: Crossroads of the New South*. Knoxville: East Tennessee Historical Society, 1982.

McCormick, Allen. "Development of the Coal Industry of Grundy County, Tennessee." Master's thesis, George Peabody College, 1934.

McCusker, John J., and Russell R. Menard. *The Economy of British America, 1607–1789*. Chapel Hill: University of North Carolina Press, 1985.

McCrum, Summers. "The History of Aurora Community, 1787–1945." Master's thesis, West Virginia University, 1945.

McKee, James W. "Alfred E. Jackson: A Profile of an East Tennessee Entrepreneur, Railway Promoter, and Soldier." *East Tennessee Historical Society Publications* 49 (1977): 9–36.

McKenzie, Robert T. "From Old South to New South in the Volunteer State: The Economy and Society of Rural Tennessee, 1850–1880." Ph.D. diss., Vanderbilt University, 1988.

McKinney, Gordon B. "The Political Uses of Appalachian Identity after the Civil War." *Appalachian Journal* 7 (1980): 200–209.

McLoughlin, William G. "Thomas Jefferson and the Beginning of Cherokee Nationalism, 1806–1809." *William and Mary Quarterly* 32 (1975): 547–80.

McMichael, Philip. "Settlers and Primitive Accumulation: Foundations of Capitalism in Australia." *Review of the Fernand Braudel Center* 4 (1980): 307–34.

McNall, Neil A. *An Agricultural History of the Genesee Valley, 1790–1860*. Philadelphia: Temple University Press, 1952.

———. "John Greig, Land Agent and Speculator." *Business History Review* 33 (1959): 524–34.

Maizels, Alfred. *Commodities in Crisis: The Commodity Crisis of the 1980s and the Political Economy of International Commodity Policies*. New York: Clarendon Press, 1992.

Mak, James, and Gary M. Walton. "Steamboats and the Great Productivity Surge in River Transportation." *Journal of Economic History* 32 (1972): 619–40.

Malone, Henry T. *Cherokees of the Old South: A People in Transition*. Athens: University of Georgia Press, 1956.

——. "Cherokee-White Relations on the Southern Frontier in the Early Nineteenth Century." *North Carolina Historical Review* 34 (1957): 1–14.

Malone, Miles S. "Falmouth and the Shenandoah: Trade before the Revolution." *American Historical Review* 40 (1935): 693–703.

Mancall, Peter C. *Valley of Opportunity: Economic Culture along the Upper Susquehanna, 1700–1800.* Ithaca: Cornell University Press, 1991.

Mangum, Charles S. *The Legal Status of the Tenant Farmer in the Southeast.* Chapel Hill: University of North Carolina Press, 1952.

Mann, Susan A. *Agrarian Capitalism in Theory and Practice.* Chapel Hill: University of North Carolina Press, 1990.

Marlin, Lloyd G. *The History of Cherokee County, Georgia.* Atlanta: Walter W. Brown Publishing, 1932.

Marlowe, David. "Winchester Springs Hotel at Sleepy Hollow—1838." *Franklin County Historical Review* 7 (1976): 33–38.

Martin, William E. "Internal Improvements in Alabama." *Johns Hopkins University Studies in History and Political Science* 20, no. 4 (1902).

Martin, William G. "Incorporation of Southern Africa, 1870–1920." *Review of the Fernand Braudel Center* 10 (1987): 849–900.

Marx, Karl. *Capital.* 3 vols. New York: International Publishers, 1967.

Matvey, Joseph J. "Central Appalachia: Distortions in Development, 1750–1986." Ph.D. diss., University of Pittsburgh, 1987.

Maxwell, Hu. "The Use and Abuse of Forests by the Virginia Indians." *William and Mary Quarterly* 19 (1910): 73–103.

May, Earl C. *Principio to Wheeling, 1715–1945.* New York: Harper and Bros., 1945.

Meillassoux, Claude, ed. *The Development of Indigenous Trade and Markets in West Africa.* London: Oxford University Press, 1971.

Mendenhall, Marjorie S. "The Rise of Southern Tenancy." *Yale Review* 27 (1937): 110–29.

Meriwether, Robert L. *The Expansion of South Carolina, 1729–1765.* Kingsport, Tenn.: Southern Publications, 1940.

Merrill, Michael. "Cash Is Good to Eat: Self-Sufficiency and Exchange in the Rural Economy of the United States." *Radical History Review* 3 (1977): 42–71.

Mies, Maria, Veronika Bennholdt-Thomsen, and Claudia von Werhof, eds. *Women: The Last Colony.* London: Zed Books, 1988.

Milling, Chapman J. *Red Carolinians.* Chapel Hill: University of North Carolina Press, 1940.

Mintz, Sidney. "The Caribbean as a Socio-cultural Area." *Journal of World History* 9, no. 4 (1966).

Mitchell, Robert D. *Commercialism and Frontier: Perspectives on the Early Shenandoah Valley.* Charlottesville: University Press of Virginia, 1977.

——. "The Shenandoah Valley Frontier." *Annals of the Association of American Geographers* 62 (1972): 461–86.

——, ed. *Appalachian Frontiers: Settlement, Society, and Development in the Preindustrial Era.* Lexington: University Press of Kentucky, 1990.

Moler, Nellie H. "Traders Settle at Harper's Ferry in 1707." *Magazine of the Jefferson County Historical Society* 8 (1942): 24.

Monongalia Historical Society. *Morgantown: A Bicentennial History.* Morgantown, W.Va.: Pioneer Press, 1985.

Mood, Fulmer, ed. *The Early Writings of Frederick Jackson Turner.* Madison: University of Wisconsin Press, 1938.

Mooney, James. "Myths of the Cherokee." *Bureau of American Ethnology Annual Report* 19 (1900).

Moore, Tyrel G. "An Historical Geography of Economic Development in Appalachian Kentucky, 1800–1930." Ph.D. diss., University of Tennessee, 1984.

——. "The Role of Ferry Crossings in the Development of the Transportation Network in East Tennessee, 1790–1974." Master's thesis, University of Tennessee, 1975.

Morel, James R. "The Early Iron Industry in the Cheat Mountains." *West Virginia Review* 14 (1936): 16–19, 32.

Morgan, Lewis H. *League of the Ho-de-no-sau-nee or Iroquois.* New York: Dodd-Mead, 1904.

Morgan, Mike. "Old Salem and Falls Mill." *Franklin County Historical Review* 4, no. 1 (1973): 3–6.

Morris, Richard B. *Government and Labor in Early America.* New York: Columbia University Press, 1946.

Morrison, A. J. "The Virginia Indian Trade to 1763." *William and Mary Quarterly* 1 (1921): 217–36.

Morrison, Charles. "Frontier Forts in the South Branch Valley." *West Virginia History* 36 (1975): 131–39.

Morton, Oren F. *A History of Rockbridge County, Virginia.* Staunton, Va.: McClure Co., 1920.

Mosby, Maryida W. "Salt Industry in the Kanawha Valley." Master's thesis, University of Kentucky, 1950.

Mosley, Hugh. "The Founding Fathers and the Accumulation of Capital." *Politics and Society* 6 (1976): 105–16.

Munslow, B., and B. Finch, eds. *Proletarianisation in the Third World: Studies in the Creation of a Labour Force under Dependent Capitalism.* London: Croom Helm, 1984.

Murphy, James M. "Transportation on the Little Kanawha River in Gilmer County." Master's thesis, West Virginia University, 1950.

Mutch, Robert E. "Colonial America and the Debate about the Transition to Capitalism." *Theory and Society* 9 (1980): 847–64.

Nave, Robert T. "A History of the Iron Industry in Carter County to 1860." Master's thesis, East Tennessee State College, 1953.

Nesbitt, William A., and Anthony Netboy. "The History of Settlement and Land Use in the Bent Creek Forest." *Agricultural History* 20 (1946): 121–27.

Nicholson, James L. *Grundy County.* Memphis: Memphis State University Press, 1982.

Niemi, Albert W. "A Further Look at Interregional Canals and Economic Specialization, 1820–1840." *Explorations in Economic History* 7 (1970): 499–520.

Niles, Blair. *The James: From Iron Gate to the Sea.* New York: Rinehart and Co., 1939.

Nobles, Gregory. "Capitalism in the Countryside: The Transformation of Rural Society in the United States." *Radical History Review* 41 (1988): 163–76.

Norris, E. J. *History of the Lower Shenandoah Valley Counties of Frederick, Berkeley, Jefferson and Clarke.* Chicago: A. Warner and Co., 1890.

North, Douglass C. *The Economic Growth of the United States, 1790–1860.* New York: W. W. Norton, 1966.

——. "Location Theory and Regional Economic Growth." *Journal of Political Economy* 63 (1955): 243–58.

——. "Sources of Productivity Change in Ocean Shipping, 1600–1850." *Journal of Political Economy* 76 (1968): 953–70.

North, Douglass C., and Robert P. Thomas. "An Economic Theory of the Growth of the Western World." *Economic History Review* 23 (1970): 1–17.

Northrup, David. "The Compatibility of the Slave and Palm Oil Trades in the Bight of Biafra." *Journal of African History* 17, no. 3 (1976): 353–64.

Nusbaum, Arthur. *A History of the Dollar*. New York: Columbia University Press, 1967.

Nyden, Paul J. "An Internal Colony: Labor Conflict and Capitalism in Appalachian Coal." *Insurgent Sociologist* 8 (1979): 33–43.

O'Connor, James. "A Note on Independent Commodity Production and Petty Capitalism." *Monthly Review* 28 (1976): 60–63.

Oland, Dwight D. "New Bremen Glass Manufactory." *Maryland Historical Magazine* 68 (1973): 255–72.

Opie, John. "Where American History Began: Appalachia and the Small Independent Family Farm." In *Appalachia/America*, edited by W. Somerville, pp. 58–67. Boone, N.C.: Appalachian Consortium Press, 1981.

Orchard, W. C. *The Penn Wampum Belts*. New York: Museum of the American Indians, 1925.

Orren, Karren. *Belated Feudalism: Labor, the Law, and Liberal Development in the United States*. Cambridge: Cambridge University Press, 1991.

Orser, Charles E. *The Material Basis of the Postbellum Tenant Plantation: Historical Archaeology of the South Carolina Piedmont*. Athens: University of Georgia Press, 1988.

Osgood, Herbert L. *The American Colonies in the Seventeenth Century*. 3 vols. New York: Macmillan, 1904–7.

Otto, John S. *The Southern Frontiers, 1607–1860: The Agricultural Evolution of the Colonial and Antebellum South*. New York: Greenwood Press, 1989.

Owen, Marie B. *The Story of Alabama: A History of the State*. New York: Lewis Historical Publishing, 1949.

Owl, Henry. "The Eastern Band of Cherokees before and after Removal." Master's thesis: University of North Carolina, 1929.

Parker, William N. "Slavery and Southern Economic Development: An Hypothesis and Some Evidence." *Agricultural History* 44 (1970): 115–25.

Parr, Elizabeth L. "Kentucky's Overland Trade with the Antebellum South." Paper presented at a meeting of the Filson Club, Louisville, Kentucky, 7 November 1927.

Pawlett, Nathaniel M. *A Brief History of the Roads of Virginia, 1607–1840*. Charlottesville: Virginia Highway and Transportation Research Council, 1977.

Pearre, Nancy C. "Mining for Copper and Related Minerals in Maryland." *Maryland Historical Magazine* 59 (1964): 15–33.

Pearsall, Marion. *Little Smoky Ridge: The Natural History of a Southern Appalachian Neighborhood*. University: University of Alabama Press, 1959.

Pease, Louise M. "The Great Kanawha in the Old South, 1671–1861." Ph.D. diss., West Virginia University, 1959.

Perdue, Theda. *Slavery and the Evolution of Cherokee Society, 1540–1866*. Knoxville: University of Tennessee Press, 1979.

Perkins, Edwin J. "The Entrepreneurial Spirit in Colonial America: The Foundations of Modern Business History." *Business History Review* 63 (1989): 160–86.

Peterson, Arthur G. "Flour and Grist Milling in Virginia: A Brief History." *Virginia Magazine of History and Biography* 43 (1935): 97–108.

Petrusewicz, Marta. "Wage-Earners but Not Proletarians: Wage Labor and Social Relations in the Nineteenth-Century Calabrian Latifondo." *Review of the Fernand Braudel Center* 10 (1987): 471–506.

Phillips, Paul C. *The Fur Trade.* 2 vols. Norman: University of Oklahoma Press, 1961.

Phillips, Peter D. "Incorporation of the Caribbean, 1650–1700." *Review of the Fernand Braudel Center* 10 (1987): 781–804.

Phillips, Ulrich B. *A History of Transportation in the Eastern Cotton Belt to 1860.* 1908. Reprint, New York: Octagon Books, 1968.

——. *Life and Labor in the Old South.* New York: Grosset and Dunlap, 1929.

Pickel, Eugene M. "A History of Roane County, Tennessee, to 1860." Master's thesis, University of Tennessee, 1971.

Pickett, Albert J. *History of Alabama, and Incidentally of Georgia and Mississippi, from the Earliest Period.* 2 vols. Charleston: Walker and James, 1851.

Plater, David D. "Building the North Wales Mill of William Allason." *Virginia Magazine of History and Biography* 85 (1977): 45–50.

Porter, Frank W. "From Backcountry to County: The Delayed Settlement of Western Maryland." *Maryland Historical Magazine* 70 (1975): 329–49.

Post, Charles. "The American Road to Capitalism." *New Left Review,* no. 133 (1982): 30–51.

"Pottery in the 1800s: The Weiss Pottery, Shepherdstown, West Virginia." *Magazine of the Jefferson County Historical Society* 47 (1981): 23–29.

Poulantzas, Nicos. *Political Power and Social Classes.* Translated by T. O'Hagan. London: Verso, 1968.

Powell, George. "A Description and History of Blount County." *Alabama Historical Quarterly* 27 (1965): 95–132.

Prigogine, Ilya. "Time, Structure, and Fluctuations." *Science,* 1 September 1978, pp. 777–85.

Prude, Jonathan. *The Coming of Industrial Order: Town and Factory Life in Rural Massachusetts, 1810–1860.* Cambridge: Cambridge University Press, 1983.

Pruitt, Bettye H. "Self-Sufficiency and the Agricultural Economy of Eighteenth-century Massachusetts." *William and Mary Quarterly* 61 (1984): 333–64.

Pudup, Mary B. "The Limits of Subsistence: Agriculture and Industry in Central Appalachia." *Agricultural History* 64 (1990): 61–89.

Raine, James W. *The Land of Saddle Bags: A Study of the Mountain People of Appalachia.* New York: Council of Women for Home Missions, 1924.

Ramsey, John G. M. *Annals of Tennessee.* 1853. Reprint, Kingsport, Tenn.: Kingsport Press, 1926.

Rau, Charles. *Ancient Aboriginal Trade in North America.* Washington, D.C.: Smithsonian Institution, 1873.

Raulston, J. Leonard, and James W. Livingood. *Sequatchie: A Story of the Southern Cumberlands.* Knoxville: University of Tennessee Press, 1974.

Rawlings, Mary. *Albermarle of Other Days.* Charlottesville, Va.: Michie Co., 1925.

Reid, John P. *A Better Kind of Hatchet: Law, Trade, and Diplomacy in the Cherokee Nation during the Early Years of European Contact.* University Park: Pennsylvania State University Press, 1976.

——. *A Law of Blood: The Primitive Law of the Cherokee Nation.* New York: New York University Press, 1970.

Reizenstein, Milton. "The Economic History of the Baltimore and Ohio Railroad, 1827–1853." *Johns Hopkins University Studies in History and Political Science* 15, nos. 7–8 (1897).

Reniers, Perceval. *The Springs of Virginia: Life, Love, and Death at the Waters, 1775–1900.* Chapel Hill: University of North Carolina Press, 1941.

Research Working Group. "Cyclical Rhythms and Secular Trends of the Capitalist

World-Economy: Some Premises, Hypotheses, and Questions." *Review of the Fernand Braudel Center* 2, no. 4 (1979): 483–500.

Reynolds, Hughes. *The Coosa River Valley*. Cynthiana, Ky.: Hobson Book Press, 1944.

Rice, A. H., and John Stroudt. *The Shenandoah Pottery*. Strasburg, Va.: Shenandoah Publishing House, 1929.

Rice, Otis K. *The Allegheny Frontier*. Lexington: University Press of Kentucky: 1970.

———. "Coal Mining in the Kanawha Valley to 1861: A View of Industrialization in the Old South." *Journal of Southern History* 31 (1965): 393–416.

Rice, Philip M. "Internal Improvements in Virginia, 1775–1860." Ph.D. diss.: University of North Carolina, 1948.

Rich, E. E. "Trade Habits and Economic Motivation among the Indians of North America." *Canadian Journal of Economic and Political Science* 26 (1960): 35–63.

Ritchie, Andrew J. *Sketches of Rabun County History*. Clayton, Ga.: By Author, 1948.

Rivers, William J. *A Sketch of the History of South Carolina to the Close of the Proprietary Government by the Revolution of 1719*. Charleston: McCarter and Co., 1856.

Robert, Joseph C. "Rise of the Tobacco Warehouse Auction System in Virginia, 1800–1860." *Agricultural History* 7 (1933): 170–82.

———. *The Tobacco Kingdom: Plantation, Market, and Factory in Virginia and North Carolina, 1800–1860*. 1938. Reprint, Gloucester: Peter Smith, 1965.

Roberts, Bruce, and Nancy Roberts. *Where Time Stood Still: A Portrait of Appalachia*. New York: Crowell-Collier Press, 1970.

Roberts, Nancy. *The Gold Seekers: Gold, Ghosts, and Legends from Carolina to California*. Columbia: University of South Carolina Press, 1989.

Robertson, Roland. *Globalization: Social Theory and Global Culture*. Newbury Park, Calif.: Sage, 1992.

Robertson, Roland, and F. Lechner. "Modernization, Globalization, and the Problem of Culture in World-System Theory." *Theory, Culture, and Society* 2, no. 3 (1985): 103–18.

Robinson, W. Stitt. *The Southern Colonial Frontier, 1607–1763*. Albuquerque: University of New Mexico Press, 1979.

Rohrbough, Malcolm J. *The Land Office Business: The Settlement and Administration of American Public Lands, 1789–1837*. New York: Oxford University Press, 1968.

———. *The Trans-Appalachian Frontier: People, Societies, and Institutions, 1775–1850*. New York: Oxford University Press, 1978.

Rollins, Leonard H. "The Tennessee River as a Trade Route and Its Relation to the Economic Development of East Tennessee." Master's thesis, University of Tennessee, 1928.

Roosevelt, Theodore. *The Winning of the West*. New York: G. Putnam's Sons, 1900.

Roseberry, William. "From Peasant Studies to Proletarianization Studies." *Studies in Comparative International Development* 18 (1983): 69–89.

Rosengarten, Theodore. *All God's Dangers: The Life of Nate Shaw*. New York: Knopf, 1975.

Rothenberg, Winifred B. "The Emergence of a Capital Market in Rural Massachusetts, 1730–1838." *Journal of Economic History* 45 (1985): 781–808.

———. "The Emergence of Farm Labor Markets and the Transformation of the Rural Economy: Massachusetts, 1750–1855." *Journal of Economic History* 48 (1988): 537–66.

———. "The Market and Massachusetts Farmers, 1750–1855." *Journal of Economic History* 41 (1981): 283–314.

Rothrock, Mary U. "Carolina Traders among the Overhill Cherokees, 1690–1760." *East Tennessee Historical Society Publications* 1 (1929): 3–26.

Rothstein, Frances. "The New Proletarians: Third World Reality and First World Categories." *Comparative Studies in Society and History* 28 (1986): 217–38.

Round, Harold F. "The Wilderness." *Virginia Cavalcade* 14 (1964): 4–9.

Rouse, Parke. *The Great Wagon Road from Philadelphia to the South.* New York: McGraw-Hill, 1973.

Royce, Charles C. *Cherokee Nation of Indians.* Washington, D.C.: Bureau of American Ethnology, 1884.

Rutman, D. B., ed. *The Old Dominion: Essays for Thomas Perkins Abernethy.* Charlottesville: University Press of Virginia, 1964.

Rutter, Frank R. "South American Trade of Baltimore." *Johns Hopkins University Studies in History and Political Science* 15, no. 9 (1897).

Sahlins, Marshall D. *Stone-Age Economics.* Chicago: Aldine-Atherton, 1972.

Sakolski, A. M. *The Great American Land Bubble: The Amazing Story of Land-Grabbing, Speculations, and Booms from Colonial Days to the Present Time.* New York: Harper and Brothers, 1932.

Sakowski, Carolyn. *Touring Western North Carolina Backroads.* Winston-Salem, N.C.: John F. Blair Publishing, 1990.

Salmon, John S. *The Washington Iron Works of Franklin County, Virginia.* Richmond: Virginia State Library, 1986.

Samuel, Raphael. "Workshop of the World: Steam Power and Hand Technology in Mid-Victorian Britain." *History Workshop* 3 (Spring 1977): 6–72.

Sanderlin, Walter S. *The Great National Project: A History of the Chesapeake and Ohio Canal.* Baltimore: Johns Hopkins University Press, 1946.

Satz, Ronald N. *Tennessee's Indian Peoples from White Contact to Removal, 1540–1840.* Knoxville: University of Tennessee Press, 1979.

Saville, John. "Primitive Accumulation and Early Industrialization in Britain." In *Socialist Register*, pp. 247–71. London: Merlin Press, 1969.

Sayre, Greek. "History of Morgantown to 1853." Master's thesis, West Virginia University, 1920.

Scalf, Henry P. *Kentucky's Last Frontier.* Prestonburg, Ky.: By Author, 1966.

Scharf, J. Thomas. *History of Western Maryland.* 2 vols. Philadelphia: Louis H. Everts, 1882.

Schlotterbeck, John T. "Plantation and Farm: Social and Economic Change in Orange and Greene Counties, Virginia, 1716 to 1860." Ph.D. diss., Johns Hopkins University, 1980.

Schweikart, Larry. *Banking in the American South from the Age of Jackson to Reconstruction.* Baton Rouge: Louisiana State University Press, 1987.

Scruggs, Carroll P. *Northeast Georgia: A Brief History.* Helen, Ga.: Bay Tree Grove Publishing, 1987. Pamphlet.

Seals, Monroe. *History of White County, Tennessee.* Spartanburg: Reprint Co. Publishers, 1974.

Searight, Thomas B. *The Old Pike.* Uniontown, Pa.: By Author, 1894.

Sears, W. H. "The State in Certain Areas and Periods of the Prehistoric Southeastern United States." *Ethnohistory* 9 (1962): 109–25.

Seeber, R. Clifford. "A History of Anderson County, Tennessee." Master's thesis, University of Tennessee, 1928.

Sellers, Charles. *The Market Revolution: Jacksonian America, 1815–1846.* New York: Oxford University Press, 1991.

Sellers, Leila. *Charleston Business on the Eve of the American Revolution.* Chapel Hill: University of North Carolina Press, 1934.

Semes, Robert L. "200 Years at Rockbridge Alum Springs." *Proceedings of the Rockbridge Historical Society* 7 (1966–69): 46–54.

Shaffer, Lynda N. *Native Americans before 1492: The Moundbuilding Centers of the Eastern Woodlands.* Armonk, N.Y.: M. E. Sharpe, 1992.

Shammas, Carole. "How Self-Sufficient Was Early America?" *Journal of Interdisciplinary History* 13 (1982): 247–72.

Shapiro, Henry. *Appalachia on Our Mind: The Southern Mountains and Mountaineers in the American Consciousness, 1870–1920.* Chapel Hill: University of North Carolina Press, 1978.

Sharrer, G. Terry. "The Merchant Millers: Baltimore's Flour Milling Industry, 1783–1860." *Agricultural History* 56 (1982): 138–50.

Shaw, Helen L. "British Administration of the Southern Indians, 1756–1783." Ph.D. diss., Bryn Mawr College, 1929.

Shepherd, James F., and Gary M. Walton. *Shipping, Maritime Trade, and the Economic Development of Colonial North America.* Cambridge: Cambridge University Press, 1971.

Siener, William H. "Staples Rates, the Grain Trade, and Economic Development in Fredericksburg, Virginia, 1750–1810." *Virginia Magazine of History and Biography* 93, no. 4 (1985): 409–26.

Silver, Timothy. *A New Face on the Countryside: Indians, Colonists, and Slaves in South Atlantic Forests, 1500–1800.* New York: Cambridge University Press, 1990.

Simms, L. Moody. "John Jordan: Builder and Entrepreneur." *Virginia Cavalcade* 23, no. 1 (1973): 19–29.

Simon, Richard M. "Uneven Development and the Case of West Virginia: Going beyond the Colonialism Model." *Appalachian Journal* 8 (1981): 165–86.

"Simply the Stolen Continent." *New Internationalist* 226 (December 1991): 21–25.

Skaggs, David C. "John Semple and the Development of the Potomac Valley, 1750–1773." *Virginia Magazine of History and Biography* 92 (1984): 282–308.

Skidmore, Robert L. "A Social History of the Eastern Panhandle Counties of West Virginia to 1810." Master's thesis, West Virginia University, 1953.

Slaughter, Thomas P. *The Whiskey Rebellion: Frontier Epilogue to the American Revolution.* New York: Oxford University Press, 1986.

Slotkin, Richard. *The Fatal Environment: The Myth of the Frontier in the Age of Industrialization, 1800–1890.* New York: Atheneum, 1985.

Smathers, George H. *The History of Land Titles in Western North Carolina.* Asheville, N.C.: Miller Printing, 1938.

Smith, George W. "Antebellum Attempts of Northern Business Interests to 'Redeem' the Upper South." *Journal of Southern History* 11 (1945): 177–213.

Smith, James L. "Historical Geography of the Southern Charcoal Iron Industry, 1800–1860." Ph.D. diss., University of Tennessee, 1982.

Smith, James M. *Seventeenth-Century America: Essays in Colonial History.* Chapel Hill: University of North Carolina Press, 1976.

Smith, Joan, Immanuel Wallerstein, and Hans-Dieter Evers, eds. *Households and the World-Economy.* Beverly Hills, Calif.: Sage, 1984.

Smith, Marvin T. *Archaeology of Aboriginal Culture Change in the Interior South: Depopulation during the Early Historic Period.* Gainesville: University of Florida Press, 1987.

Smith, Marvin T., and J. Mark Williams. "European Trade Material from Tugalo, 9ST1." *Early Georgia* 6 (1978): 42–49.

Smith, Merritt R. *Harpers Ferry Armory and the New Technology.* Ithaca, N.Y.: Cornell University Press, 1977.

Smith, Philip R. "John H. Hall, Virginia Gunmaker." *Virginia Cavalcade* 11, no. 4 (1962): 28–32.

Snell, William R. "Indian Slavery in Colonial South Carolina, 1671–1795." Ph.D. diss., University of Alabama, 1972.

Soltow, J. H. "Scottish Traders in Virginia, 1750–1775." *Economic History Review* 12 (1959): 83–98.

Soltow, Lee. "Land Inequality on the Frontier: The Distribution of Land in East Tennessee at the Beginning of the 19th Century." *Social Science History* 5 (1981): 275–91.

——. "Land Speculation in West Virginia in the Early Federal Period: Randolph County as a Specific Case." *West Virginia History* 44 (1983): 111–34.

——. *Men and Wealth in the United States, 1850–1870.* New Haven: Yale University Press, 1975.

Spence, Robert Y. *The Land of the Guyandote: A History of Logan County.* Detroit: Harlo Press, 1976.

Spencer, Esther A. "Transportation in the Kanawha Valley, 1784–1890." Master's thesis, Marshall College, 1941.

Stampp, Kenneth. *The Peculiar Institution: Slavery in the Antebellum South.* New York: Alfred A. Knopf, 1956.

Starobin, Robert S. *Industrial Slavery in the Old South.* New York: Oxford University Press, 1970.

Stauth, George. "Capitalist Farming and Small Households in Egypt." *Review of the Fernand Braudel Center* 7 (1983): 285–331.

Stealey, John E. "The Salt Industry of the Great Kanawha Valley of Virginia: A Study in Antebellum Internal Commerce." Ph.D. diss., West Virginia University, 1970.

Stephenson, Wendell H. "Antebellum New Orleans as an Agricultural Focus." *Agricultural History* 15 (1941): 161–74.

Stevens, William O. *The Shenandoah and Its Byways.* New York: Dodd, Mead and Co., 1941.

Stewart, Charles L. "Land Tenure in the United States with Special Reference to Illinois." *University of Illinois Studies in the Social Sciences* 5, no. 3 (1916).

Stone, Richard G. "Captain Paul Demere at Fort Loudon, 1757–1760." *East Tennessee Historical Society Publications* 41 (1969): 17–32.

Stotik, Jeffrey P. "The Political Economy of Appalachia: A Critique and Synthesis of Radical Approaches to Underdevelopment." Master's thesis, University of Tennessee, 1990.

Strickland, Rennard. *Fire and the Spirits: Cherokee Law from Clan to Court.* Norman: University of Oklahoma Press, 1975.

Strohfeldt, Thomas A. "Warriors in Williamsburg: The Cherokee Presence in Virginia's Eighteenth-Century Capital." *Journal of Cherokee Studies* 11 (1986): 4–18.

Summers, George W. "James Swan's Western Lands." *West Virginia Review* 12 (1934–35): 13–15.

Sutch, Richard. "The Care and Feeding of Slaves." In *Reckoning with Slavery: A Critical Study in the Quantitative History of American Negro Slavery,* edited by P. A. David, H. G. Gutman, R. Sutch, P. Temin, and G. Wright, pp. 231–301. New York: Oxford University Press, 1976.

Swanton, John R. *The Indians of the Southeastern United States.* Washington, D.C.: Bureau of American Ethnology, 1946.

Swierenga, Robert P. *Pioneers and Profits: Land Speculation on the Iowa Frontier.* Ames: Iowa State College Press, 1968.

——. "The 'Western Land Business': The Story of Easley and Willingham, Speculators." *Business History Review* 41 (1967): 1–20.

Szymanski, Albert. *Class Structure: A Critical Perspective.* New York: Praeger, 1983.

Taff, Nollie O. *History of State Revenue and Taxation in Kentucky.* Nashville: George Peabody College, 1931.

Talley, William M. "Salt Lick Creek and Its Salt Works." *Register of the Kentucky State Historical Society* 64 (1966): 85–109.

Tarkington, Terry W. "Saltpeter Mining in the Tennessee Valley." *Tennessee Valley Historical Review* 2 (1973): 17–25.

Taylor, Rosser H. *Antebellum South Carolina: A Social and Cultural History.* Chapel Hill: University of North Carolina Press, 1942.

Templin, Eleanor. "Making a Road through the Wilderness." *Franklin County Historical Review* 6, no. 2 (1975): 80–87.

Tennessee Valley Authority. *A History of Navigation on the Tennessee River System.* Washington, D.C.: Government Printing Office, 1937.

ter Braake, Alex L. "Postal History of the James River and Kanawha Turnpike." *West Virginia History* 33 (1971): 27–54.

Terrell, Bruce G. "The James River Bateau." *Virginia Cavalcade* 38, no. 4 (1989): 180–91.

Terrell, John U. *Traders of the Western Morning: Aboriginal Commerce in Precolumbian North America.* Los Angeles: Southwest Museum, 1967.

Teute, Frederika J. "Land, Liberty, and Labor in the Post-Revolutionary Era: Kentucky as the Promised Land." Ph.D. diss., Johns Hopkins University, 1988.

Teuton, Frank L. "Steamboating on the Upper Tennessee." *Tennessee Valley Perspective* 7 (1976): 11–16.

Thorne, Charles B. "The Watering Spas of Middle Tennessee." *Tennessee Historical Quarterly* 29 (1970–71): 321–25.

Thornton, Russell. *The Cherokees: A Population History.* Lincoln: University of Nebraska Press, 1990.

Tilly, Charles. "Flows of Capital and Forms of Industry in Europe, 1500–1900." *Theory and Society* 12, no. 2 (1983): 123–42.

Tocqueville, Alexis de. *Democracy in America.* 2 vols. New York: J. and H. G. Langley, 1845.

Todd, George D. "How the Pioneers of the West Obtained Their Supplies Prior to 1800 and What They Paid for Them." Paper presented at a meeting of the Filson Club, Louisville, Kentucky, 19 May 1903.

Toothman, Fred R. *Great Coal Leaders of West Virginia.* Huntington, W.Va.: Vandalia Book Co., 1988.

Treat, Payson J. *The National Land System, 1785–1820.* New York: E. B. Treat, 1910.

Trout, W. E. "The Goose Creek and Little River Navigation." *Virginia Cavalcade* 16, no. 3 (1967): 31–34.

Turner, Charles W. "Early Virginia Railroad Entrepreneurs and Personnel." *Virginia Magazine of History and Biography* 58 (1958): 325–34.

——. "Railroad Service to Virginia Farmers, 1828–1860." *Agricultural History* 22 (1948): 239–47.

Ulshofer, Petra. "Household and Enterprise: Towards a New Model of the Plantation." *Review of the Fernand Braudel Center* 7 (1983): 181–214.

U.S. Department of Agriculture. *Agriculture in the Southern Appalachian and White Mountain Watersheds.* Washington, D.C.: Government Printing Office, 1908.

Uselding, Paul J. "A Note on the Interregional Trade in Manufactures in 1840." *Journal of Economic History* 36 (1976): 428–35.

Van Benthuysen, Robert N. "The Sequent Occupance of Tellico Plains, Tennessee." Master's thesis, University of Tennessee, 1951.

Vellenga, Dorothy D. "Women, Households, and Food Commodity Chains in Southern Ghana: Contradictions between the Search for Profits and the Struggle for Survival." *Review of the Fernand Braudel Center* 8 (1985): 293–318.

Verhoeff, Mary. *The Kentucky Mountains: Transportation and Commerce, 1750 to 1911.* Filson Club Publication No. 26. Louisville, Ky.: Filson Club, 1911.

———. *The Kentucky River Navigation.* Filson Club Publications No. 28. Louisville, Ky.: Filson Club, 1917.

Vickers, Daniel. "Competency and Competition: Economic Culture in Early America." *William and Mary Quarterly* 47 (1990): 3–29.

Vincent, George E. "A Retarded Frontier." *American Journal of Sociology* 4 (1898): 1–20.

Wallace, David D. *South Carolina: A Short History, 1520–1948.* Chapel Hill: University of North Carolina Press, 1961.

Wallerstein, Immanuel. *The Capitalist World-Economy.* Cambridge: Cambridge University Press, 1979.

———. "Crisis as Transition." In *Dynamics of Global Crisis*, edited by S. Amin, pp. 11–54. New York: Monthly Review Press, 1982.

———. *Geopolitics and Geoculture: Essays on the Changing World-System.* Cambridge: Cambridge University Press, 1991.

———. *Historical Capitalism.* London: Verso Editions, 1983.

———. "The Incorporation of the Indian Subcontinent into the Capitalist World-Economy." Paper presented at the Seminar on the Indian Ocean, New Delhi, 20 February 1985.

———. *The Modern World-System I: Capitalist Agriculture and the Origins of the European World-Economy in the Sixteenth Century.* New York: Academic Press, 1974.

———. *The Modern World-System II: Mercantilism and the Consolidation of the European World-Economy, 1600–1750.* New York: Academic Press, 1980.

———. *The Modern World-System III: The Second Era of Great Expansion of the Capitalist World-Economy, 1730–1840s.* New York: Academic Press, 1989.

———. *The Politics of the World-Economy.* Cambridge: Cambridge University Press, 1984.

———. *Unthinking Social Science: The Limits of Nineteenth-Century Paradigms.* Cambridge: Polity Press, 1991.

———. "World-System Analysis: The Second Phase." *Review of the Fernand Braudel Center* 13, no. 2 (1990): 287–93.

Wallerstein, Immanuel, and William G. Martin. "Peripheralization of Southern Africa, II: Changes in Household Structure and Labor-Force Formation." *Review of the Fernand Braudel Center* 3 (1979): 193–210.

Wallerstein, Immanuel, William G. Martin, and Torry Dickinson. "Household Structures and Production Processes: Preliminary Theses and Findings." *Review of the Fernand Braudel Center* 5 (1982): 437–59.

Walls, David S., and Dwight Billings. "The Sociology of Southern Appalachia." *Appalachian Journal* 5 (1977): 131–44.

Walsh, Margaret. "From Pork Merchant to Meat Packer: The Midwestern Meat Industry in the Mid-Nineteenth Century." *Agricultural History* 56 (1982): 127–37.

———. "The Spatial Evolution of the Midwestern Pork Industry, 1835–75." *Journal of Historical Geography* 4, no. 1 (1978): 1–22.

Walthall, John A. *Prehistoric Indians of the Southeast.* University: University of Alabama Press, 1980.

Waples, Eliot. "Farm Ownership Processes in a Low Tenancy Area." Ph.D. diss., University of Wisconsin, 1946.

Ward, Harry M. *"Unite or Die": Intercolony Relations, 1690–1763.* Port Washington, N.Y.: Kennikat Press, 1971.

Ward, Kathryn B. *Women Workers and Global Restructuring.* Ithaca, N.Y.: Cornell University Press, 1990.

Watson, Alan D. "The Ferry in Colonial North Carolina: A Vital Link in Transportation." *North Carolina Historical Review* 51 (1974): 247–60.

Wayland, John W. "The Germans of the Valley." *Virginia Magazine of History and Biography* 9 (1902): 337–52, and 10 (1902): 33–48, 113–30.

——. *A History of Shenandoah County, Virginia.* Strasburg, Va.: Shenandoah Publishing House, 1927.

——. *The Valley Turnpike: Winchester to Staunton.* Winchester, Va.: Winchester-Frederick County Historical Society, 1967.

Weaver, C. C. "Internal Improvements in North Carolina Previous to 1860." *Johns Hopkins University Studies in History and Political Science* 21, nos. 3–4 (1903).

Webb, Thomas G. "The Pottery Industry of DeKalb, White, and Putnam Counties." *Tennessee Historical Quarterly* 30 (1971): 100–112.

Weeden, William B. "Indian Money as a Factor in New England Civilization." *Johns Hopkins University Studies in History and Political Science* 8–9 (1884): 5–51.

Weiman, David F. "Farmers and the Market in Antebellum America: A View from the Georgia Up-country." *Journal of Economic History* 48 (1987): 627–48.

Weller, Jack E. *Yesterday's People: Life in Contemporary Appalachia.* Lexington: University of Kentucky Press, 1966.

Wellington, Raynor G. *The Political and Sectional Influence of the Public Lands, 1828–1842.* New York: Riverside Press, 1914.

Wellman, Manly W. *The Kingdom of Madison.* Chapel Hill: University of North Carolina Press, 1973.

Wentworth, Edward N. *America's Sheep Trails.* Ames: Iowa State College Press, 1948.

"West Virginia River Ferries." *West Virginia Review* 13 (1935): 172–73.

Westfall, Eugenia. "The Internal Improvements of the Great Kanawha River." Master's thesis, West Virginia University, 1943.

Whisnant, David E. *All That Is Native and Fine: The Politics of Culture in an American Region.* Chapel Hill: University of North Carolina Press, 1983.

Whitaker, A. P. "The Muscle Shoals Speculation, 1783–1789." *Mississippi Valley Historical Review* 13 (1927): 365–86.

White, Roy R. "The Salt Industry of Clay County." *Register of the Kentucky State Historical Society* 50, no. 172 (1952): 237–48.

Wilcox, David. "Skins, Rum, and Ruin: The Colonial Deerskin Trade." *Southern Exposure* 13 (1985): 57–61.

Wiley, Richard T. *Monongahela, The River and Its Region.* Butler, Pa.: Ziegler Co., 1937.

Wilhelm, Lewis D. "Local Institutions of Maryland." *Johns Hopkins University Studies in History and Political Science* 3 (1885).

Wilk, Richard R. *Household Ecology: Economic Change and Domestic Life among the Kekchi Maya in Belize.* Tucson: University of Arizona Press, 1991.

Williams, Eric. *Capitalism and Slavery.* London: Andre Deutsch, 1944.

Williams, John A. *West Virginia: A History.* New York: W. W. Norton and Co., 1984.

Williams, Mark. "Indians along the Oconee after De Soto: The Beginning of the End." *Early Georgia* 10 (1982): 30–41.

Williams, Michael. *Americans and Their Forests: A Historical Geography*. Cambridge: Cambridge University Press, 1989.

Williams, Samuel C. *Beginnings of West Tennessee*. Johnson City, Tenn.: Watauga Press, 1930.

———. *Dawn of Tennessee Valley and Tennessee History*. Johnson City, Tenn.: Watauga Press, 1937.

———. "Early Iron Works in the Tennessee Country." *Tennessee Historical Quarterly* 6 (1947): 39–46.

———. "Fort Robinson on the Holston." *East Tennessee Historical Society Publications* 4 (1932): 22–31.

Williams, Thomas J. C. *A History of Washington County, Maryland, from the Earliest Settlement to the Present Time, Including a History of Hagerstown*. Hagerstown: By Author, 1906.

———. "Washington County, Maryland." *Maryland Historical Magazine* 2 (1907): 345–58.

Williams, Thomas J. C., and Folger McKinsey. *History of Frederick County, Maryland*. 2 vols. Baltimore: L. R. Titsworth and Co., 1910.

Willis, William S. "Colonial Conflict and the Cherokee Indians: 1710–1760." Ph.D. diss., Columbia University, 1955.

Willoughby, Lynn. *Fair to Middlin': The Antebellum Cotton Trade of the Apalachicola/Chattahooche River Valley*. Tuscaloosa: University of Alabama Press, 1993.

Wilms, Douglas C. "Cherokee Indian Land Use in Georgia, 1800–1838." Ph.D. diss., University of Georgia, 1974.

———. "Cherokee Settlement Patterns in Nineteenth-Century Georgia." *Southeastern Geographer* 14 (1974): 46–53.

Winters, Donald L. "The Agricultural Ladder in Southern Agriculture: Tennessee, 1850–1870." *Agricultural History* 61 (1987): 36–52.

Wisner, Elizabeth. *Social Welfare in the South from Colonial Times to World War I*. Baton Rouge: Louisiana State University Press, 1970.

Wolf, Eric R. *Europe and the People without History*. Berkeley: University of California Press, 1982.

Wood, Curtis W. "Antebellum Mercantile Activity as Illustrated by the R. G. Dun Collection." Paper presented at the annual meeting of the Appalachian Studies Association, Johnson City, Tenn., March 1993.

Wood, Walter K. "The Alleghany Turnpike and Internal Improvements, 1800–1850." Master's thesis: Virginia Polytechnic Institute, 1969.

Woodlief, Ann. *In River Time: The Way of the James*. Chapel Hill: Algonquin Books, 1985.

Woodman, Harold D. *King Cotton and His Retainers: Financing and Marketing the Cotton Crop of the South, 1800–1925*. Lexington: University of Kentucky Press, 1968.

———. "Post–Civil War Southern Agriculture and the Law." *Agricultural History* 53 (1979): 195–212.

Woodward, Grace S. *The Cherokees*. Norman: University of Oklahoma Press, 1963.

Woofter, T. J. *Landlord and Tenant on the Cotton Plantation*. New York: Negro Universities Press, 1969.

Worsley, Peter. *The Three Worlds: Culture and World Development*. Chicago: University of Chicago Press, 1984.

Wright, Gavin. *Old South, New South: Revolutions in the Southern Economy since the Civil War*. New York: Basic Books, 1986.

Wright, J. Leitch. *The Only Land They Knew: The Tragic Story of the American Indians in the Old South*. New York: Free Press, 1981.

Wright, Nathalia. "Montvale Springs under the Proprietorship of Sterling Lanier, 1857–1863." *East Tennessee Historical Society Publications* 19 (1947): 48–63.

Wyatt, Edward A. "Rise of Industry in Antebellum Petersburg." *William and Mary Quarterly* 17, no. 1 (1937): 1–36.

Yang, Donghyu. "Farm Tenancy in the Antebellum North." In *Strategic Factors in Nineteenth-Century American Economic History*, edited by C. Goldin and H. Rockoff, pp. 135–58. Chicago: University of Chicago, 1992.

Yergin, Daniel. *The Prize: The Epic Quest for Oil, Money, and Power.* New York: Simon and Schuster, 1991.

Young, Otis E. "Origins of the American Copper Industry." *Journal of the Early Republic* 3 (1983): 117–38.

——. "The Southern Gold Rush, 1828–1836." *Journal of Southern History* 48 (1982): 373–92.

Yowell, Claude L. *A History of Madison County, Virginia.* Strasburg, Va.: Shenandoah Publishing, 1926.

Economy, 251, 294, 311, 312; preindustrial, 3–6, 7, 8, 9, 19, 88, 123, 128, 147–48, 152, 238, 249, 257, 298; national, 5, 7, 21, 76, 80, 136, 215, 237–39, 245, 293, 295, 297, 298, 302, 308, 309, 313–16, 320; world, 5, 10, 12, 17–20, 24, 28, 29, 31, 32, 34, 39, 44, 45, 46, 48, 49, 50–51, 53, 76, 81, 84, 85, 88, 90, 93, 108, 120, 127, 137, 154, 155, 157, 188, 191–94, 227, 229, 231, 233, 238, 242, 246–47, 250, 254, 255, 262, 269, 276, 277, 283, 284, 288, 291, 292, 295, 298, 299, 303, 308, 311–21 passim; Appalachian, 17, 18, 20, 85, 87, 119, 121, 136, 145, 152, 232, 288–89, 298, 299, 300–305, 311, 318, 320–22, 375 (n. 2); precapitalist, 18, 39, 123, 127, 136–37, 152, 231, 232, 254, 283, 296, 298, 358 (n. 24); informal, 121, 289–90, 292, 381 (n. 9); southern, 171, 195–97, 222–23, 283, 288, 292, 293, 303, 315, 318, 321–22

Education, 81, 108, 119, 253, 259–69, 270–75, 292, 293, 319, 381 (n. 10), 350 (n. 69), 378 (n. 44). *See also* Literacy

Elites: Appalachian, 2, 20, 57, 64, 65, 68, 73, 74, 83, 95, 96, 97, 98, 99, 102, 105, 108, 129, 130, 136, 145, 149, 152, 154, 174, 237, 251, 252, 254, 257–63, 266, 287, 289, 295, 345 (n. 15), 347 (n. 41), 348 (n. 52), 349 (nn. 57, 58, 60), 352 (n. 23), 355 (n. 64), 366 (n. 61), 376 (n. 24), 377 (n. 28), 378–79 (n. 53), 389 (n. 74); Cherokee, 30, 31, 42, 43, 341 (n. 63); southern, 53, 56–58, 63, 73, 82, 96, 98, 102, 345 (n. 24), 352 (n. 16), 383 (n. 43). *See also* Merchants, Appalachian; Plantations: Appalachian

England: exploration of Appalachia, 11–12, 47; relations with Cherokees, 16, 25–29, 32–39, 48, 336 (n. 7), 337 (nn. 13–17), 339 (n. 45), 340 (n. 50), 341 (n. 65), 342 (nn. 77–78); in North America, 25, 48. *See also* Hegemony: rivalry for global

Entrepôts, 20, 184, 206–8, 321, 343 (n. 83). *See also* Baltimore; Charles-

ton, S.C.; Mobile, Ala.; New Orleans, La.; New York; Philadelphia, Pa.; Savannah, Ga.

Environment: as theoretical element, 17, 19, 250, 276–78, 381 (n. 94); degradation of, 44–46, 50, 196, 278–83, 285, 319, 342 (n. 73), 380 (n. 79)

Epidemics, 1, 24, 44–45, 282

Exports: agricultural, 20, 136–45, 152, 196–98, 201–8, 212–15, 218–21, 225–26, 228–31, 235–43, 244–46, 358 (n. 26); Appalachian, 60, 85, 251, 252, 263, 269, 278, 283, 288, 292, 300, 318–21; manufactured, 146, 149–52, 165–66, 196–97, 199, 201–3, 206–8, 212–15, 217, 222, 228, 230–31, 235–36, 239, 241–47, 298–99; extractive, 146, 166–88, 195–99, 201, 202, 204–6, 208, 211, 212–15, 217, 222, 226–31, 235–36, 240–41, 246, 299; decline in, 287, 296–98, 308. *See also* Fur trade; Livestock: exports

External arena, 17–18, 23–24, 48, 136, 222, 250, 276, 283, 284, 285

Extraction, surplus, 13. *See also* Debt peonage; Slave laborers; Surplus: drains from region; Tenancy; Women

Extractive industries: Appalachian, 5, 20, 63, 131, 155, 164–88, 252, 253, 269–74, 275, 288, 291, 298–99, 309–13, 317, 319–20, 322; in the world system, 12, 13, 194. *See also* Coal; Copper; Gold; Iron; Lead; Manganese; Quarrying; Salt

Farm operators: landless, 91–106; landed, 125–36. *See also* Subsistence: producers; Tenancy

Farms: ownership of, 65, 70, 76–80, 81–83, 84, 86, 91–93, 120, 129, 258–59, 288–89, 328, 351 (n. 12); family, 76, 82, 123; capitalist, 87–88, 90–91, 93, 97, 98, 103–17 passim, 120, 124–25, 131–36, 173, 187, 188, 189, 190, 258, 266–68, 263–66, 290, 296; subsistent, 88, 125–28, 229; Cherokee, 130–31, 217, 255; crop production of, 131–34; Appalachian, 238; in industrial enclaves, 271–73,

20, 75–84, 106–8, 87–89, 120, 121,
123, 125, 127, 128, 189, 190, 227,
229, 230, 249, 258, 290–91, 316,
318–19, 321, 349 (n. 63); coerced,
12, 13, 15, 20, 90, 108–14, 117–19,
120, 125, 135, 150, 222, 255, 262,
284, 321, 351 (n. 6), 357 (n. 3);
agrarian, 13, 19, 20, 80–81, 86, 87–
114, 123, 124, 133, 229, 232, 249,
258, 262, 266–69, 288–90, 296, 298,
300, 309, 314, 318–19, 349 (n. 63),
351 (nn. 3, 5), 353 (n. 33), 354
(n. 51), 357 (n. 3); Cherokee, 31, 32,
37, 38, 49, 50, 108–9, 111, 120, 289,
338 (n. 46); indentured, 111–14,
251–52, 258, 351 (n. 5), 354 (n. 60),
355 (nn. 70, 71), 356 (nn. 72, 75);
industrial, 145, 147, 148, 149, 155,
157–58, 160, 162, 164–65, 171, 176–
77, 179, 188–91, 227, 229, 230, 245–
46, 258–59, 269–76, 284, 290–92,
318, 360–61 (n. 3), 367 (n. 78), 377
(n. 28); immigrant, 190–91, 227,
258, 269, 272–75, 291, 314, 377
(n. 28); commercial, 229, 291–92.
See also Free blacks; Slave laborers
Land: speculation, 13, 19, 20, 47,
53–61, 63, 66, 71–73, 85, 87, 90, 95,
101, 102, 106, 119, 179, 182, 192,
252–54, 262, 277, 293, 313, 316–17,
319, 343 (n. 3), 344 (nn. 8, 15), 345
(nn. 15, 18, 24, 27), 346 (n. 28),
346–47 (n. 37), 348 (nn. 48, 54), 349
(n. 59), 376 (n. 13); concentration,
13, 68, 77, 82–86, 117–19, 128–31,
253, 262, 271, 285, 288, 347 (n. 42);
ownership, 19, 20, 21, 56–57, 68–70,
73–75, 81–84, 86, 91–93, 119–20,
123, 129–30, 131, 189–90, 262, 327,
347 (n. 43); in capitalist expansion,
19, 51–53, 75–84, 276–78, 285, 360
(n. 54); scarcity, 19, 68, 74–81, 86,
119; Cherokee cessions of, 43, 46–48,
255; companies, 52, 55–56, 63, 343
(n. 5), 345 (n. 24), 346 (n. 31), 364
(n. 39), 376 (n. 13); granting, 54, 56,
58–59, 67–68, 73; clearing, 278–80
Laws: Cherokee, 30, 99–100, 114, 356
(n. 76); land, 51, 58, 64–65, 70,
256, 347 (n. 37), 354 (n. 58), 355

(n. 66); labor, 90, 93, 98–99, 106,
112, 251, 266–67, 268, 274–75, 291,
351 (n. 9), 353 (n. 33), 354 (n. 60),
355 (n. 70), 357 (n. 3), 377 (n. 40);
race, 113–14; trade, 241, 242. 374
(n. 37), 375 (n. 7)
Lead, 47, 63, 82, 166, 169, 185, 193,
236, 253, 265, 313
Leather, 12, 32, 33, 34, 49, 183, 184,
196, 242, 271, 299
Lexington, Ky., 60, 180, 198, 205, 235
Literacy, 21, 81, 260, 268, 287, 292, 321
Livestock, 81, 93–94, 97–107 passim,
108, 118, 263, 265, 267, 273, 292,
298; drives, 20, 141, 152, 202, 206,
218–21, 226, 236, 237–38, 280, 305,
307, 371 (n. 54); production, 131–33;
exports, 137–39, 141–43, 196, 201,
202, 203, 204, 205, 206, 214, 215,
218–21, 225, 236–46 passim, 295,
319–20; herd replacement, 139,
358 (nn. 17, 24); stands, 152, 226,
237–38; frontiers, 195–96; feeding,
236–37. *See also* Cattle; Hogs;
Horses; Meatpacking; Mules; Sheep:
Wool
Louisville, Ky., 141, 172, 177, 178, 182,
184, 186, 205, 207, 215, 218, 227,
234, 235, 240, 241, 247, 301
Lumber, 169, 177, 183–84, 202, 206,
214, 239, 241, 272, 313
Lynchburg, 173, 198, 204, 213, 235

McCormick, Cyrus, 217
Manganese, 63, 166, 169, 185, 193,
201
Manufacturing: in the United States,
6, 7, 13, 161–65, 362 (n. 7); in the
world system, 12–14, 190–94; Appalachian, 20, 60, 61, 71, 145–52,
157–66, 195, 197, 199, 222, 232, 245,
246, 252, 269, 272–73, 298–99, 317,
308–16, 319, 320, 321, 361 (nn. 4, 5,
6); linkage of to agriculture, 20, 145–
52, 155; southern, 157, 158, 161–65.
See also Distilleries; Meatpacking;
Milling
Marble, 169, 188, 193, 253, 366 (n. 70)
Market, 4, 5, 6, 7, 8, 13, 18, 52, 53, 59,
71, 76, 87, 90, 93, 95, 100, 103, 157,

Mining, 103, 104, 164, 170, 174, 175, 178, 180, 181, 182, 185, 190–92, 194, 269, 272, 273, 274, 275, 281, 282, 283, 292, 309, 313, 362 (n. 14). *See also* Extractive industries; Quarrying

Mobile, Ala., 33, 68, 81, 87, 140, 141, 181, 184, 202, 203, 205, 208, 209, 214, 239, 245, 247, 259, 276

Mode of production, 6, 7; precapitalist, 18, 23, 31–32, 39, 52–53, 123, 127, 136–37, 152, 231, 232, 254, 283, 296, 298, 358 (n. 24); capitalism as dominant, 18, 232, 296

Money. *See* Banking; Cherokees: wampum; Currency

Montgomery, Ala., 185, 203, 205, 209, 212

Mountain gaps, 226–27

Mules, 100, 102, 106, 137, 141, 196, 202, 206, 209, 212, 386 (n. 9)

Myths: agrarian, 1–5, 6, 117, 123, 130, 136, 242, 298, 333 (n. 6); development, 1–6, 20, 131, 147–48, 249, 334 (nn. 8, 10), 357 (n. 1), 377 (n. 31); frontier, 3, 4, 10, 19, 252; isolation, 3, 4, 20, 92, 95, 98, 104, 123, 125, 136, 187, 191, 209, 215, 225–27, 231, 234–35; folk society, 3, 7, 123, 257, 284, 334 (n. 10); subsistence, 3–4, 5, 6, 10, 20, 117, 123, 124, 152, 153; labor, 4, 20, 88, 108, 117, 145, 159, 259, 262, 351 (n. 4); trade, 4, 20, 136, 238; land, 4, 76, 81; cultural, 5, 19, 136, 231, 257; ethnic, 7, 134

Nashville, Tenn., 176, 180, 181, 197, 202, 205, 215, 217, 240, 293, 348 (n. 48), 364 (n. 31)

Native Americans, 7, 9, 16, 19; enslavement of, 12, 14, 19, 29, 32, 284, 338 (nn. 27, 28); displacement of, 13, 256–57, 277, 348 (n. 53); populations of, 24–25, 27–29, 32, 44–45, 256

Natural gas, 169, 177, 186, 193, 201, 227, 362 (n. 13)

New Orleans, La., 141, 143, 150, 172, 175, 177, 178, 180, 181, 184, 186, 197, 202, 203, 204, 206–7, 208, 214, 218, 221, 228–31, 234, 235, 236,

239, 240, 315, 348 (n. 48), 358 (n. 26)

Newspapers: Appalachian, 105, 253; other regional, 60, 212, 214, 236, 273, 282, 307

New York, 13, 14, 34, 64, 73, 104, 169, 170, 173, 175, 183–86, 235, 241, 274

North Carolina, 23, 24, 25, 48, 52, 53, 56, 57–58, 59, 60, 63, 66–79 passim, 80, 81, 82, 83, 84, 88, 90, 93, 95, 96, 97, 98, 99, 100, 102, 103, 105, 106, 107, 108, 109, 125, 127, 128, 130, 131, 132, 134, 135, 138, 139, 140, 141, 143, 147, 149, 150, 151, 160, 162, 164, 165, 166, 169, 170, 171, 173, 174, 175, 176, 182, 184, 186, 189–90, 204, 205, 206, 207, 209, 217, 218, 219, 225, 226, 235–46 passim, 252, 253, 261, 265, 268, 279, 280, 281, 282, 290, 292–94, 295, 296–98, 301, 309, 312, 316, 324, 327, 328, 344 (n. 15), 351 (n. 9), 353 (n. 38), 355 (n. 66), 358 (n. 26), 363–64 (n. 27), 367 (n. 4), 372 (n. 1), 375 (n. 2)

Occupations, 92, 258, 290; agricultural, 78, 89, 126; nonagricultural, 78, 164, 165, 189, 193, 249, 287, 289–92, 313, 315–16, 366 (n. 74), 375 (n. 2). *See also* Laborers: agrarian; Laborers, commercial; Laborers, industrial

Oil. *See* Petroleum

Orchard fruits, 105, 140, 153, 236

Peripheralization, 14, 87, 120, 121, 154, 193, 232, 250, 255, 261, 276, 284, 287–322, 360 (n. 54)

Periphery, 10, 11, 12, 14, 15, 16, 17, 21, 48, 88, 108, 117, 154–55, 188, 193, 194, 196, 222, 227–29, 231, 257, 262, 283, 288, 289, 291, 296, 298, 299, 300, 308, 314, 318, 320–22, 339 (nn. 44, 45), 360 (n. 54), 367 (n. 3). *See also* Capitalism: peripheral

Petersburg, Va., 204

Petroleum, 169, 186, 187, 193. *See also* Kerosene

Philadelphia, Pa., 56, 58, 64, 73, 74, 151, 170, 173, 178, 184, 185, 187,

149–50, 217, 236, 238, 240, 244, 280; drains from region, 277–78, 316–19; defined, 329–31. *See also* Exports: agricultural; Farms: capitalist; Plantations: Appalachian